American Constitutional Law

American Constitutional Law

An Overview, Analysis, and Integration

William A. Kaplin
Professor of Law
The Catholic University of America

CAROLINA ACADEMIC PRESS
Durham, North Carolina

Library of Congress Cataloging-in-Publication Data

Kaplin, William A.
American constitutional law : an overview, analysis, and integration / by William A. Kaplin.
p. cm.
Includes bibliographical references and index.
ISBN 0-89089-084-6
1. Constitutional law--United States. I. Title.
KF4749 .K36 2004
342.73--dc22   2003025520

Carolina Academic Press
700 Kent Street
Durham, NC 27701
Telephone (919) 489-7486
Fax (919) 493-5668
www.cap-press.com

Printed in the United States of America

I dedicate this book to my father, Albert W. Kaplin (1911–2001), who died in the midst of my work on the manuscript. He was, and always will be, a model for me of personal integrity, personal diligence, and good stewardship in all aspects of life; and his example provides a continuing reminder to respect the dignity of all persons and to extend a helping hand whenever needed.

"Justice is the end of government. It is the end of civil society. It ever has been, and ever will be, pursued, until it be obtained, or until liberty be lost in the pursuit."

James Madison
Federalist No. 51

Contents

Preface

A. The Content of This Book

As the title suggests, this is a book about American constitutional law in both its broad sweep and its particulars. While the book addresses the major doctrinal areas of constitutional law and the key United States Supreme Court cases, it is not primarily a book about doctrine. To move the discussion beyond the doctrine and the individual cases, I have identified and developed the foundational concepts and first principles that undergird the substantive law and give it deeper meaning and greater coherence. In doing so, I have also identified and developed the key conceptual distinctions in constitutional law that guide all analysis and that enable students and practitioners to observe the constituent parts of constitutional law that make up the whole. In addition, I have sorted out the various doctrinal areas and the analytical problems that they present, and I have interwoven them into a "big picture" of American constitutional law, the United States Constitution, and the American constitutional system of government. In developing this integrated view, I have relied on U.S. Supreme Court cases from the entire history of the Court's work; but I have also utilized sources and perspectives that range well beyond the individual cases. In particular, I have relied on legal commentators as well as the cases themselves; and I have used perspectives from legal theory and jurisprudence, history, and political science selectively throughout the book.

Further specifics on the content of this book are in the Table of Contents and in the General Introduction that precedes Chapter 1, as well as in the remainder of this Preface.

B. Premises and Goals of This Book

I have built this book upon three interlocking premises, each of which is explained below. These premises give the book its own particular identity and character, and serve to distinguish it from other books on this subject. These three premises also serve to establish the goals and unifying themes for the book.

My first premise is this: *to understand constitutional law fully and use it effectively, one must develop an integrated view of the subject matter.* As suggested in part A of this Preface, one must see the "big picture" as well as the pieces or, stated differently, one must see "the constitutional forest" as well as "the constitutional trees." One goal of this book is to develop such an integrated presentation of American constitutional law and to assist readers in developing their own integrated views. To achieve this goal, I have focused as much on process issues as on substantive issues. I have placed considerable emphasis, for instance, on the sources of, and approaches to, constitutional interpretation and on the components of the analytical process for constitutional law issues. Similarly, I have addressed state constitutions as well as the federal Constitution and have sought to elucidate relationships between them. I have also treated theory as well as practice and interrelated them so that each enriches the overall picture.

I have also developed a synthesis of each of the substantive areas that I have covered, set out primarily in sections called "Conceptual Overviews". In doing so, I have given careful attention to conceptual distinctions that frame each substantive area and provide a foundation for analysis and argumentation. Examples of the broader or more global distinctions include: constitutional powers versus constitutional rights, judicial limits on constitutional powers versus political limits, free speech versus free press, non-establishment versus free exercise, substantive due process versus procedural due process, equal protection (egalitarian rights) versus due process (libertarian rights), and federal constitutional rights versus state constitutional rights. I have emphasized such distinctions and the importance of synthesis because one must identify and sort out the pieces (the trees) before one can assemble them into the big picture (the forest); and because moving from the pieces to the big picture requires that one have a workable synthesis of each substantive area to use as stepping stones.

Chapters 2 and 15 of this book are especially important to my goal of integration, and Chapters 4 and 9 play a supporting role in helping to integrate, respectively, the Constitution's power clauses and its rights clauses. The first sections of Chapters 10 and 12 perform a similar function regarding rights by looking at the entire Fourteenth Amendment (Chap. 10, Sec. A) before considering its individual clauses in Chapters 10 and 11; and by looking at the entire First Amendment (Chap. 12, Sec. A) before considering its individual clauses in Chapters 12 and 13.

My second basic premise is that *classical constitutional law — the classic cases and the classic commentaries — is still vastly important to a full understanding of American constitutional law.* The classical cases, as I perceive them, are the cases that establish fundamental principles, or mark a focal point or turning point in the development of constitutional law, or otherwise provide a spotlight that illumines the way for future courts and interpreters; and that also retain their historical or legal importance over a long expanse of time. The classical commentators are those who, in addressing the U.S. Constitution or constitutional cases decided by the courts, have developed fundamental principles or the theory behind them, or precipitated a turning point in the development of constitutional law, or otherwise provided illumination for a critical future pathway for courts and interpreters; and whose commentary has also retained its importance over a long expanse of time. This classical constitutional law has too often been de-emphasized, ignored, or perhaps just innocently forgotten in modern constitutional law. Thus, a second goal of this book is to recapture classical constitutional law and demonstrate its continuing importance to the disposition of contemporary cases and the development of contemporary trends. To fulfill this goal, I have emphasized both the classical cases and the classical commentaries in this book, and related their teachings to more modern developments.

Examples of the classical cases that I have discussed include the "old" classics *Marbury v. Madison, McCulloch v. Maryland, Gibbons v. Ogden, Prigg v. Pennsylvania, Cooley v. Board of Port Wardens, The Civil Rights Cases, Yick Wo v. Hopkins,* and *Plessy v. Ferguson;* and the Twentieth Century classics *Schenck v. United States, United States v. Darby, Skinner v. Oklahoma, Youngstown Sheet & Tube v. Sawyer, Everson v. Board of Education, Brown v. Board of Education, Engel v. Vitale, Griswold v. Connecticut, Reynolds v. Sims, New York Times v. Sullivan, Goldberg v. Kelly,* and *New York Times v. United States (The Pentagon Papers Case).* Examples of the classical commentators that I have quoted or cited include James Madison, the author of many of *The Federalist Papers;* St. George Tucker, the author of the very first constitutional law textbook—published in 1803, the year *Marbury v. Madison* was decided; and Joseph Story, early Supreme Court Justice and author of the famous COMMENTARIES ON THE CONSTITUTION, published in 1833, with an abridged successor volume titled A FAMILIAR EXPOSITION OF THE CONSTITUTION OF THE UNITED STATES following in 1840.

In addition to individual discussions of classical cases, I have also collected excerpts of first principles from these cases and included them in two sections of Chapter 2, both under the heading "In the Words of the Great Justices;" and I have developed two timelines of classical (and likely to become classical) cases, one for power cases in Chapter 4 and one for rights cases in Chapter 9. In emphasizing the classical cases, I do not short-change other more contemporary cases. Late Twentieth Century cases that I believe are already becoming classics, for instance, are also covered. Examples include *United States v. O'Brien, Moose Lodge v. Irvis, San Antonio Independent School District v. Rodriguez, Roe v. Wade,* and *Clark v. Community for Creative Non-Violence.* Moreover, I have also given substantial treatment to more recent cutting edge cases. Examples include *Employment Division v. Smith, Planned Parenthood of Southeastern Pennsylvania v. Casey, United States v. Lopez, City of Boerne v. Flores, Boy Scouts of America v. Dale, Grutter v. Bollinger* and *Gratz v. Bollinger,* and *Lawrence v. Texas.*

The third premise undergirding this book is that *constitutional law is too important to be left solely to the lawyers.* Non-lawyers also have needs and interests that intersect with the U.S. Constitution and American constitutional law. Moreover, lawyers need the broader context provided by the contributions that scholars and practitioners in other disciplines have made to the understanding of constitutional law. Thus the third goal for this book is to present constitutional law in a manner that is accessible and useful not only to lawyers, but also to those in other academic disciplines (such as government, history, political science, public administration, and philosophy of law) and other professional pursuits (such as public policy analysts, public interest advocates, and government officials), without slighting any of the legal complexities of the subject matter. To further this goal, I have selectively borrowed from political science, history, and legal philosophy in the textual discussions in this book, as well as in the text and footnote citations; and I have sought to weave these supplementary perspectives together with the legal concepts and principles.

I wish to be especially clear about this third premise. Although constitutional law is too important to be left solely to the lawyers, the work of lawyers was nevertheless central to the historical process of creating and implementing the Constitution, and the work of lawyers continues to be a central aspect of the ongoing process of constitutional interpretation and decisionmaking. Thus this book *is* written for lawyers (and law students), even though it is not written *solely* for them. I have therefore presented the U.S. Constitution as "hard law" useable by lawyers and courts (see Chap. 2, Sec. A.3); and I have focused on the lawyering process as it relates to the application of constitutional law principles and precedents. I have also sought to elucidate the decisionmaking of the courts (filled with judges who are lawyers) and to confront and shed light on the major interpretive disputes and analytical difficulties that engage the attention of lawyers.

C. Use of This Book by Law Students, Graduate Students, and Independent Learners

This book contains substantial study guidance for students who are studying American constitutional law in law school courses, in law-related graduate school courses, or as independent learners. Chapter 1 contains a set of introductory perspectives (Sec. B) that will orient the student to the subject matter; it also contains a section on print and Internet-based sources for constitutional law research and for tracking recent developments (Sec. C) and a listing of recommended reference resources on constitutional law (Sec. D). Chapter 2 contains the first two of ten study Exercises with answers included (Secs. D and G) that are presented in the book. Chapter 3 contains a set of eight practical steps to use in reading and analyzing a constitutional law case (Sec. C) and two more study Exercises that provide guided practice in such reading and analysis (Secs. D and E). Chapters 5 through 8 and 10 through 14 each end with a section on "Study Suggestions" that provides suggestions for reviewing the chapter's materials as well as sources "for further reading" on the chapter's subject matter.[1] These chapters also contain six more study Exercises, each adapted to the subject matter of a particular chapter or two adjoining chapters. Chapter 15 contains a section setting out a model, with four components, for use in analyzing constitutional law problems (Sec. C). Appendix A to the book contains a copy of the U.S. Constitution with key provisions emphasized in bold face type; and Appendix B contains a set of Study and Learning Suggestions designed specifically for students in formal courses.[2]

---

1. Even though the Study Suggestions sections appear at the end of the chapters, it may be beneficial for some readers to study these sections at the beginning of the chapters and then review them at the end.

2. For instructors in formal courses, I am planning to prepare a *Teacher's Manual* for use in conjunction with this book. This *Manual* will provide not only tips for instructors on using the

In addition to these various sections that specifically support the study of constitutional law, most of the rest of the sections in this book also provide guidance useful to law students, graduate students, and independent learners. Two chapters, for example, develop the essential contexts for the study, respectively, of constitutional powers (Chap. 4) and constitutional rights (Chap. 9). Chapters 5 through 8 and 10 through 13 each contain "Conceptual Overviews" that will introduce students to the particular subject matter to be studied and help them to synthesize the material as they proceed through their study. And Chapter 15 provides various perspectives and aids (in addition to the analytical model noted above) for integrating the subject of constitutional law at the conclusion of a course.

D. Tips on Using This Book

1. The cut-off date for including materials in this book is the end of 2003. The book thus includes pertinent new U.S. Supreme Court cases through the end of the 2002–2003 Court term. For the 2003–2004 term, however, the book includes only pertinent petitions for certiorari that the Court granted before the end of 2003 for cases to be decided during 2004. To locate the opinions in these cases, as well as all other cases decided after the cut-off-date for this book, readers should consult the sources described in Chapter 1, Section C, of this book. Among these sources are various websites that provide assistance in staying current with the Court's docket and with contemporary trends in constitutional law, and that also provide access to valuable research materials.

2. The citation form used in this book generally follows "The Bluebook" (A UNIFORM SYSTEM OF CITATION (Harvard Law Review Ass'n, *et al.*, 17th ed., 2000), with some exceptions to promote clarity of the citations for non-lawyers. Cites to law reviews, for instance, often contain more expansive abbreviations of the law review's name than that prescribed by The Bluebook. U.S. Supreme Court cases are cited only by their official citation (*U.S. Reports*), except for recent cases for which the official cites were not yet available at press time. These recent cases are cited by their *Supreme Court Reporter* citation.

3. To assist the reader, this book has a fully developed organizational scheme that is displayed in the Table of Contents and in the text with numerous descriptive section and subsection headings. This organizational scheme is further explained in the General Introduction to this book that immediately precedes Chapter 1. There is also a comprehensive Subject Matter Index with over 500 entries that pinpoint specific topics and subjects covered in the book; a Table of Cases that lists, and gives page references for, every case cited in the book; and a Table of Authorities that lists, and gives page references for, every book and article cited in the book. In addition, there are cross-references in the text of every chapter to aid the reader's integration of the subject matter, and a judicious use of footnotes throughout the book to provide additional explanation or provide additional supportive authority. For the cross-references, I have used the form "Sec. _____ above" or "Sec. _____ below" when the reference is to another section in the

---

book but also additional study guidance that instructors may make available to students (see, e.g., footnote 3 below). Contact the publisher for further details.

same chapter, and the form "Chap. _____, Sec. _____" when the reference is to a section in a different chapter. The footnotes appear at the bottom of the text pages and are numbered consecutively by chapter, so that the numbering begins again at 1 for each chapter. I have also frequently used quotations throughout the book to target the most important language in U.S. Supreme Court opinions and in key commentaries.

4. Because the personal and historical dramas behind constitutional cases reveal the human dimensions of conflict and may enhance readers' understanding, I have occasionally included brief stories—or citations to a source that tells a story—within my presentation of cases and topics. The primary examples are the story behind *Brown v. Board of Education* (Chap. 3, Sec. E); the story of Daniel Ellsberg and his involvement in the Pentagon Papers controversy (Chap. 3, Sec. D); the story of Belva Lockwood, the first woman to be admitted to the United States Supreme Court bar (Chap. 10, Sec. D.1); the story of Richard and Mildred Loving, petitioners in *Loving v. Virginia* (Chap. 10, Sec. D.2); the story of Angela Velez, one of the plaintiff welfare recipients in *Goldberg v. Kelly* (Chap. 11, Sec. D.1); and the story of George Eldridge, the disability benefits recipient who was the plaintiff in *Mathews v. Eldridge* (Chap. 11, Sec. D.3). For other stories, *see* CONSTITUTIONAL LAW STORIES, a 2004 book described in the bibliography in Chapter 1, Section D of this book; and for discussion on using stories for teaching and learning constitutional law, *see* William Kaplin, "Problem Solving and Storytelling in Constitutional Law Courses," 21 SEATTLE L. REV. 885 (1998).

5. In addition to the various uses suggested in parts B and C of this Preface, this book can also serve as a successor edition of my 1992 volume, THE CONCEPTS AND METHODS OF CONSTITUTIONAL LAW (Carolina Academic Press). Users of this earlier book will find, in this new book, expanded and updated discussions of most of the topics addressed in CONCEPTS AND METHODS, as well as revised and enhanced versions of most of the Exercises in that volume. The Practice Problems, Review Guidelines, and Analytical Frameworks in CONCEPTS AND METHODS, however, do not appear in this new book.[3] Conversely, there are many topics and much material included in this new book that have no counterpart in the earlier volume.

William A. Kaplin
Washington, D.C.

April 2004

---

3. I am planning to include these Practice Problems, Review Guidelines, and Analytical Frameworks in a *Teachers' Manual* available to teachers adopting this book for use in a formal course. Consult the publisher for further details.

Acknowledgments

Many persons have assisted me in preparing this book. The book and I have both benefitted greatly from their contributions.

A number of colleagues at my university and other universities graciously reviewed one or more draft chapters of this book and made helpful suggestions: Robert Bennett, Phil Frickey, George Garvey, Mike Gerhardt, Roger Hartley, Doug Kmiec, Tom Marks, Wilson Parker, Ken Pennington, Ronna Schneider, Dan Underwood, Bill Wagner, and Harvey Zuckman.

My student research assistants—Marie Callan, Gene Hansen, Tracy Hartzler-Toon, and Michael Provost—all capably provided essential help. In addition to his research services, Michael Provost also performed important cite-checking and proofreading services over almost two full years of this book's development.

Sabrina Hilliard capably organized my word processing files for this project; typed and retyped most sections of the manuscript as well as numerous page proof inserts; and compiled the final, publisher-ready manuscript. Donna Snyder also capably helped with manuscript preparation at critical times when I needed extra assistance. Linda Perez, Assistant Director of Faculty Support Services, kept the entire process running smoothly.

Yvette Brown, reference librarian, provided unfailingly prompt assistance by locating research resources and providing bibliographical information; in addition, she reviewed Chapter 1, Section C of the manuscript. Pat Petit, Associate Director of the law library, provided extensive assistance with computer support for cite-checking and for preparation of the Table of Cases and Table of Authorities. Steve Margeton, Director of the law library, provided me with a research office in the law library and kept all the library services running smoothly.

Catholic University Law School provided research grants to support my work on this book in the summers of 2001 and 2002. Former Dean Doug Kmiec and current Dean Bill Fox encouraged my efforts, and various colleagues at the law school commiserated with me and boosted my spirits during the most arduous phases of my work.

For each and every one of these persons, I am deeply grateful.

American Constitutional Law

General Introduction

This book provides an integrated presentation of the United States Constitution and American constitutional law. The fifteen chapters that follow cover the major substantive areas of constitutional law and the concepts, conceptual distinctions, first principles, and processes that undergird the substantive law. For illustration, United States Supreme Court cases, especially the classical and foundational cases, are analyzed throughout the book. For authority, in addition to court precedents, leading commentators are quoted and cited throughout the book—especially classical commentators such as James Madison and Joseph Story. For context, extensive background is drawn from history, political science, and jurisprudence to enhance understanding of legal developments. In addition, practical guidance on case analysis and problem-solving methodology, suggested readings, research resources, and other pertinent matters are interspersed throughout the book to enhance the utility of the law that is presented.

Chapters 1 through 3 of this book are foundational chapters. Chapter 1 introduces the body of law called constitutional law, distinguishes between constitutional law and the U.S. Constitution, and outlines the role of the courts in developing constitutional law (Section A). Chapter 1 also prescribes some initial perspectives from which to approach the subject matter; provides specific research guidance on finding constitutional law cases, briefs, and related resources; and provides a selected bibliography of supplemental research resources (Sections B, C, and D).

Chapter 2 introduces the United States Constitution and the formative evolutionary developments preceding it, beginning with the early Greek political theorists (Section A). This chapter then presents an overview of the American constitutional system of government (Sections B, C, and D) and an overview of the process by which the U.S. Constitution is interpreted and applied to specific factual circumstances (Sections E, F, and G). Chapter 2 is also the first of various chapters that contains practical, guided exercises for testing and extending understanding (Sections D and G). Throughout the chapter, the critical distinction between constitutional powers and constitutional rights is emphasized, especially in Section C.

Chapter 3 introduces the basic practical tools of constitutional law. These tools are the judicial opinions that courts issue when deciding constitutional law cases. Chapter 3 describes the legal status and function of such opinions (Section A); introduces the distinction between "explanation" and "justification," as it applies to the analysis of opinions, and the distinction between descriptive and normative analysis (Section B); and provides a practical step-by-step method for reading and analyzing opinions (Section C). This chapter then presents two exercises (Sections D and E) for building skills by applying this step-by-step method.

Chapter 4 sets the context for an understanding of constitutional powers. In particular, this chapter provides an overview of federal constitutional powers compared with state constitutional powers (Section A); introduces the concepts of federalism and separation of powers (Section B); and continues the discussion from Chapter 2 concerning the interpretive process, focusing specifically on the approaches used to analyze power clauses (Section C). Chapter 4 also provides an historical timeline from 1776 to the present listing the major developments concerning legislative, executive, and judicial powers (Section D).

Chapters 5 through 8 are substantive chapters. They address, successively, federal judicial powers (Chapter 5), federal legislative powers (Chapters 6 and 7), and federal executive powers (Chapter 8). Chapter 7 ("Federalistic Limits on the Exercise of State Power") is an extension of Chapter 6 ("Congressional Powers and Federalism") that views Congress' powers from the perspective of the states and explores when and how an expansion of federal power serves to limit state power. Chapters 5 through 8 each contain "Conceptual Overviews" of the various constitutional power clauses and power issues pertinent to each branch of government, as well as a "Study Suggestions" section that helps guide study of that chapter's materials and recommends articles and books "For Further Reading."

Chapter 9 sets the context for an understanding of constitutional rights. This chapter begins with an overview of federal constitutional rights (Section A), with particular emphasis on those rights that are not covered in the four rights chapters that follow. (A comparison of federal constitutional rights and state constitutional rights is postponed until Chapter 14.) Chapter 9, like Chapter 4, continues the Chapter 2 discussion of the interpretive process and also includes an historical timeline. The discussion of interpretation focuses at length on the "values approach" that is a special concern under the rights clauses (Sections B and C); the historical timeline lists the major rights developments from 1776 to the present. In addition, Chapter 9 includes a discussion and synthesis of the state action doctrine (Section D), a key conceptual foundation for the understanding of federal constitutional rights.

Chapters 10 through 13, like Chapters 5 through 8, are substantive chapters, but they address constitutional rights rather than constitutional powers. Chapters 10 and 11 address two major categories of Fourteenth Amendment rights—equal protection rights and due process rights. Chapters 12 and 13 address two major categories of First Amendment rights—freedom of expression rights and freedom of religion rights. These Chapters, like Chapters 5 through 8, each contain "Conceptual Overviews" of the clauses and issues they address, and a "Study Suggestions" section to guide study of the materials and recommend further readings. Moreover, Chapters 10 through 13 address, successively, the conceptual distinctions between equal protection and due process (Chapter 10, Section E), between "substantive" due process and "procedural" due process (Chapter 11, Section B); between freedom of speech and freedom of the press (Chapter 12, Section B.2); and between non-establishment of religion and free exercise of religion (Chapter 13, Secs. A and D). Chapter 11 (in Section E) and Chapter 13 (in Section E) also contain exercises that help sharpen understanding of these critical distinctions.

Chapter 14 is in part a substantive chapter, continuing the discussion of rights in a broader context and also picking up on some of the more complex aspects of constitutional powers discussed in Chapters 5 and 6. But Chapter 14 is also a chapter that begins the task of integrating all of the constitutional law discussed in the prior thirteen Chapters. Chapter 14 begins this critical task by elucidating relationships between federal constitutional rights and federal statutory rights (Section B), between federal constitutional rights and federal constitutional powers (Sections B, C, and D), and between federal constitutional rights and state constitutional rights (Section E). This Chapter also includes an exercise designed to illustrate these relationships (Section F), as well as a "Study Suggestions" section (Section G).

Chapter 15, the last chapter, continues the work of integration begun in Chapter 14. Chapter 15 places heavy emphasis on the development of an integrated, "big picture" understanding of constitutional law. Many parts of the earlier substantive chapters (5 through 8 and 10 through 13) also provide assistance in synthesizing particular substantive areas of constitutional law; in addition, the two context chapters (4 and 9) develop a foundation for a big picture view of powers and rights respectively, and Chapter 2 provides the frame in which to place the big picture. Chapter 15 builds on all of these earlier discussions by offering three ways to integrate one's understanding of constitutional law: through an integrated view of the process of constitutional litigation (Section B), through an integrated model of constitutional analysis (Section C), and through an integrated view of the process of constitutional interpretation (Section D).[1]

As this survey of Chapters makes clear, there is much substantive law in this book. But just as clearly, there is much more to find in, and take from, this book than substantive law. The reader should also look for the concepts that undergird the substantive law; for the processes through which substantive law is made; for the political, historical, and jurisprudential perspectives that elucidate substantive developments; and for the structures that help merge the various parts of constitutional law into an integrated whole.

---

1. There are also two appendices at the end of the book; the first sets out the Constitution of the United States, with editorial enhancements, and the second provides a set of suggestions for studying and learning constitutional law.

Chapter 1

Getting Oriented to Constitutional Law: Introductory Perspectives and Suggestions

Sec. A. The Purposes and Functions of Constitutional Law

A.1. The Relationship Between the U.S. Constitution and U.S. Constitutional Law

The Constitution of the United States was designed to govern not only the founding generation but also, as the Constitution's preamble states, their "Posterity." Thus the Constitution "was to endure through a long lapse of ages, the events of which were locked up in the inscrutable purposes of Providence" (*Martin v. Hunter's Lessee*, 14 U.S. (1 Wheat.) 304, 326 (1816) (Justice Story for the Court)). And, indeed, it has been so; America's Constitution "is the oldest written national constitution in the world" (Michael Kammen, "Introduction," in Michael Kammen (ed.), THE ORIGINS OF THE AMERICAN CONSTITUTION: A DOCUMENTARY HISTORY, p. xviii (Penguin Books, 1986)).

To help insure that the Constitution would endure, the framers devised an arduous process for amending it (U.S. Const., Art. V). A difficulty thereby arose. For the Constitution to endure for ages to come, remaining mostly intact, its amendment procedures had to stringently limit the likelihood and frequency of amendments. But the arduousness of the amending procedures would in turn make it difficult for the Constitution to accommodate pertinent societal, political, macro-economic, or international relations developments that "were locked up in the inscrutable purposes of Providence" during the framers' time but would surely emerge in the ages to come. Similarly, the arduous amending procedures would make it difficult for the Constitution to accommodate the wise insights and inspirations, and noble aspirations, of later generations of Americans.

The framers also helped to ensure the longevity of the Constitution by drafting it in language that is often general and abstract, even vague, so that the document would not be time-bound to the specific circumstances and understandings of late eighteenth-century life in the American colonies. Thus a second difficulty arose. To endure for the ages to come, the Constitution had to include much open-ended language and to be short on specifics in many respects; but the open-ended and general language in many critical provisions would in turn make it difficult to draw specific guidance from the Constitution in the innumerable future contexts and situations to which it would apply.

Fortunately, both difficulties could be resolved by the same means: a *process* for *interpreting* the Constitution and its various clauses, with the centerpiece (but not the only piece) being the concept of judicial review.[1] The need for such a process was not lost on the framers. Many of them were students of the law, and they understood the difficulties of legal drafting and the inherent limitations of language. In one of the "Federalist Papers" written to urge ratification of the Constitution, James Madison asserted that:

> All new laws, though penned with the greatest technical skill, and passed on the fullest and most mature deliberation, are considered as more or less obscure and equivocal, until their meaning be liquidated and ascertained by a series of particular discussions and adjudications. Besides, the obscurity arising from the complexity of objects, and the imperfection of the human faculties, the medium through which the conceptions of men are conveyed to each other, adds a fresh embarrassment. The use of words is to express ideas. Perspicuity therefore requires, not only that the ideas should be distinctly formed, but that they should be expressed by words distinctly and exclusively appropriated to them. But no language is so copious as to supply words and phrases for every complex idea, or so correct as not to include many, equivocally denoting different ideas. Hence it must happen, that however accurately objects may be discriminated in themselves, and however accurately the discrimination may be conceived, the definition of them may be rendered inaccurate, by the inaccuracy of the terms in which it is delivered. And this unavoidable inaccuracy must be greater or less, according to the complexity and novelty of the objects defined. [James Madison, *Federalist No. 37*, in THE FEDERALIST: THE GIDEON EDITION, p. 183 (George Carey and James McClellan, eds., Liberty Fund, 2001).][2]

---

1. Chapter 2, Section F of this book provides an introduction to the process of constitutional interpretation. Chapter 5, Sections A and B provide an introduction to judicial review.

2. There are many collections of the Federalist Papers. The one cited here, and used throughout this book, is one of the newest editions. It includes an editor's introduction covering the history of the Constitution's drafting and ratification and "the significance of the Federalist"; a "Reader's Guide to *The Federalist*"; a glossary of related historical documents; a copy of the Constitution cross-referenced to the Federalist Papers; and an index to the Federalist Papers. U.S.

In short, "the existence of various ambiguities in the Constitution meant that explication would subsequently be required by various authorities...." (Kammen, *supra*, at xix–xx).

Despite the perceived need for "particular discussions and adjudications" to ascertain the Constitution's meaning (Madison, above), the Constitution itself makes no explicit reference to constitutional interpretation. It does not tell us *who* will do the interpretation, or whose interpretations will be most authoritative. Neither the federal courts' authority to declare acts unconstitutional, nor the U.S. Supreme Court's status as the ultimate constitutional interpreter, were expressly established in the constitutional text (see Chap. 5, Sec. A). Similarly, the Constitution does not tell us *how* the interpretive function is to be undertaken. It does not tell us, for example, whether the "framers' intent" should be important to interpretation or, if so, how it should be ascertained (see Chap. 4, Sec. C.2).

The fulfillment of the needs described in the preceding paragraphs has become the work of constitutional law. Constitutional law addresses and helps to resolve the two critical difficulties discussed above by providing a process for constitutional interpretation and constitutional decisionmaking. Constitutional law provides a focal point and repository for the "discussions and adjudications," and the "explications," that are the products of the process and that give momentum to the American constitutional system. Constitutional law provides essential guidance on *who* interprets the Constitution (see Chap. 5, Secs. A, B, and C) and on *how* it is to be interpreted (see Chap. 4, Sec. C; Chap. 9, Sec. B; Chap. 15, Sec. C). Constitutional law provides the "precedents" that are the building blocks for constitutional arguments and the guideposts for the resolution of constitutional disputes (see Chap. 2, Sec. F.1; Chap. 3, Sec. A; Chap. 15, Sec. C.2).

Thus there is a clear and necessary relationship between the U.S. Constitution and American constitutional law; but just as clearly they are not one and the same. The American system of government and American judicial system require a fundamental written document that establishes the frame of government, states first principles and core values, and embodies the original consent of the governed; these are the functions of the Constitution. The American system of government and American judicial system also require an accepted process for interpreting the document over time, resolving the myriad of constitutional disputes that arise in every generation, and systematizing the understanding thus gained; these are the functions of constitutional law. Ultimately, the U.S. Constitution and American constitutional law, along with the state constitutions and state constitutional law, merge into the American constitutional system (see Chap. 2, Sec. B) and the ideology called American constitutionalism or American democratic constitutionalism (see Chap. 2, Sec. A.2).

Supreme Court Justices frequently cite papers from The Federalist in their opinions, a practice that increased beginning in the 1960's and especially since the 1980's; *see* Buckner Melton, "The Supreme Court and the Federalist: A Citation List and Analysis, 1789–1996," 85 KENTUCKY L. J. 243 (1996–97); Buckner Melton & Jennifer Miller, "The Supreme Court and the Federalist: A Supplement, 1996–2001," 90 KENTUCKY L. J. 415 (2001–2002).

A.2. The Role of the Courts in Developing Constitutional Law

Constitutional law primarily addresses two types of issues: *power* issues concerning the allocation and scope of the federal government's powers; and *rights* issues concerning individual rights that limit the reach of federal and state government powers (see Chap. 2, Sec. C). Resolving these issues has become primarily the work of the courts, federal and state, with the United States Supreme Court's interpretations being supreme over those of all other courts.

The courts work on the basis of case-by-case decisions. Each decision is responsive to a particularized dispute litigated by contending parties, and is based on the factual record developed in that case. Especially in the appellate courts (the courts that hear appeals of cases decided by the trial courts), and most especially in the U.S. Supreme Court, most decisions are issued in the form of written and published opinions (see Chap. 3, Sec. A). The function of such opinions is to "justify" the result reached in the case as being consistent with legal norms, applicable prior "precedents," and the facts in the record of the case (see Chap. 3, Sec. B). In constitutional law cases, the court's opinion provides an interpretation of the Constitution, usually of some particular power clause or rights clause. Each such written opinion becomes a constitutional law precedent that becomes authoritative law within the geographical area over which the deciding court has jurisdiction, and which binds lower courts within that jurisdiction. The opinions and decisions of the U.S. Supreme Court bind all other courts and in effect become the "law of the land" (see Chap. 5, Sec. B).

The courts are not the only governmental bodies whose job it is to interpret the Constitution and thus contribute to the development of constitutional law. Congress and the President also have interpretive responsibilities, as do most other governmental bodies and officers (see Chap. 5, Sec. C). But the constitutional decisions and interpretations of the courts are more often announced in written opinions following the principles of justification than is the case for other interpreters. Court opinions also are more systematized and more widely published than the constitutional opinions issued by most other governmental bodies and officers. And court opinions—in particular federal court opinions, and especially U.S. Supreme Court opinions—are supreme over the opinions of other governmental bodies and officers. Court opinions, therefore, constitute the great bulk of the precedents that make up constitutional law and are usually considered to be the most important repository of constitutional law.

Sec. B. Initial Perspectives on Constitutional Law: Prescriptions for Study and Practice

This section sets out some initial perspectives on the subject matter of constitutional law. It also contains practical suggestions on how to study this subject, whether in a formal course or as an independent learner.[3] These perspectives and suggestions are

---

3. Other suggestions are included in Appendix B and the end of this book.

organized into a series of "prescriptions," or "do's and don'ts," for developing perspective on, or for studying, constitutional law.

1. Do not underestimate the complexities of constitutional law. The study and practice of constitutional law is likely to be a demanding challenge. Do not be frustrated when your understanding does not come either quickly or easily. Although there are ways to make the subject appear simple, they are illusions. As one commentator has warned: "Those who seek to simplify the law misunderstand it profoundly. The complexity of law is the complexity of life" (Walter Oberer, "On Law, Lawyering, and Law Professing: *The Golden Sand*," 39 J. LEGAL EDUC. 203, 205 (1989)). Viewed honestly and fully, constitutional law remains a complex mixture of theory and practice, of abstraction and concrete human circumstances, that is difficult to conceptualize and organize. To help manage such subject matter, the student or practitioner should begin immediately to create a foundation on which to build an understanding of the subject and a framework within which to integrate all the material to be studied. Chapter 2 of this book is designed to provide initial assistance in this endeavor.

2. Do not view constitutional law as merely a body of rules and doctrines. Rules and doctrines will appear to be merely mechanical—even arbitrary—devices if they are not understood in a broader perspective and as part of a "big picture." An uncritical knowledge of the rules themselves is also counterproductive; one must appreciate the reason for, and role of, the rule in order to put it to practical use. In this sense, rules and doctrines are like the tools and materials of law; to build with them, students and practitioners must have a vision of what they are trying to build and must know what tasks the rules and doctrines can (and cannot) perform.

Moreover, rules and doctrines evolve over time in response to new problems, new knowledge, and new value judgments. A view of constitutional law focused only on existing rules and doctrines would leave students and practitioners unprepared to advocate or assimilate change in the law and would result in a static body of knowledge that becomes increasingly outdated with each passing year. As Justice Felix Frankfurter remarked in a 1954 speech at a prominent U.S. law school:

> It is very important [for law schools] to make lawyers and judges who do not carry out of the law schools a body of dogma, on the assumption that what they imbibed at the date of leaving the law school is man's ultimate wisdom and enduring truth.... Lawyers should carry out of the law school not dogma, but an attitude toward the process of law-making, law-growing, and law-changing, and a critical questioning attitude. [Felix Frankfurter, SOME OBSERVATIONS ON SUPREME COURT LITIGATION AND LEGAL EDUCATION 15 (U. Of Chicago Press, 1954).]

3. Do not think of constitutional law as law made only by, or important only for, the U.S. Supreme Court. Many actors other than the U.S. Supreme Court are involved in the process of constitutional decisionmaking. Justice Frankfurter had words of wisdom on this point as well that he included in the same speech quoted in prescription 2 above:

I think it is a very short-sighted view to talk about the upper-court myth, as though the Supreme Court is merely deciding only some hundred cases each term. The cases which that Court is deciding influence the lowest court in the smallest state in the union. They create a frame within which the lower courts move, the frame within which all officialdom moves, the frame within which every [person] who signs a document, or drafts one, or suggests this or that course to clients, must take into account, if he is a true counselor. [Frankfurter, *supra*, at 18–19.]

Constitutional law may seem rarified and esoteric, and of marginal utility, if viewed only in terms of how to get a case to and present a case before the U.S. Supreme Court, or how to critique the Supreme Court's opinions and compare the views of the various Justices. Constitutional law has a much broader scope than that. It is also of great importance in lower federal courts and the state courts—even in city and county trial courts—although lawyers do not necessarily use constitutional law in the same way in these courts as they would in the U.S. Supreme Court. Constitutional law also encompasses the work of forums other than courts. Committees of the U.S. Congress and the state legislatures, for example, may encounter constitutional questions in the course of their work. Similarly, federal and state administrative agencies, and public entities such as hospitals and universities, can confront various types of constitutional issues. Constitutional law can also become a crucial part of a city's, town's, village's or school board's work on particular matters—for example, a city's consideration of a night-time curfew ordinance for juveniles, a village or town's consideration of an ordinance requiring a permit before protesters can hold a demonstration in the town square; or a local school board's decision to suspend a student or teacher, or to adopt an affirmative action program. There are thus innumerable situations in which constitutional issues may arise in legislatures, administrative agencies, local governments, and indeed, virtually all governmental bodies.

In sum, lawyers, government officials, and other persons involved in public policy making always should keep the Constitution well in mind in their work because the Constitution provides the framework within which, and the fundamental principles by which, all government operates. Lawyers, in addition, should be prepared to raise constitutional issues and make constitutional arguments in a wide range of government decision-making forums besides the courts.

4. Do not think of constitutional law as wholly different and apart from other branches of law. Such a view of constitutional law would shut out much of what is important and worthwhile about the subject matter. Since constitutional law is the "frame within which all officialdom moves," as Justice Frankfurter stated (see prescription 3 above), it is linked to and superimposed upon all other branches of law. It creates the foundation and outer walls for every field of American law. Thus one cannot fully study or effectively practice other fields of law without understanding the constitutional law backdrop for that field.

Moreover, constitutional law involves many analytical skills that are also useful in studying or practicing other fields of law. For instance, interpretation of legal language is a pervasive problem in constitutional law; studying this subject will therefore help with the development of sound interpretive skills. Constitutional law addresses problems that have substantial social policy or political policy ramifications as well as legal ramifications; studying constitutional law therefore helps one to differentiate legal questions from policy questions. Constitutional law opinions are often complex and dense, and may involve clashes among majority, concurring, and dissenting viewpoints; the study of constitutional law therefore helps develop the skill of reading opinions with great care and analyzing them in a disciplined way.

This is not to suggest, of course, that constitutional law has all the same characteristics as other bodies of law. While each field of law has some similarities to other fields, each field of law also has some unique characteristics. It is important to discern what those unique characteristics are. In constitutional law, for example, constitutional interpretation is in some ways like statutory interpretation and in some ways it is different. The differences are attributable to the conceptual distinction between a statute and a constitution. As Justice Cardozo stated: "Statutes are designed to meet the fugitive exigencies of the hour.... A *constitution* states or ought to state not rules for the passing hour, but principles for an expanding future" (Benjamin Cardozo, THE NATURE OF THE JUDICIAL PROCESS, p. 83 (Yale Univ. Press, 1921)). The identification of such differences helps one to understand the uniqueness of constitutional law; the identification of such similarities helps one to understand law in general and the process of interpretation in general.

5. Do not dismiss judicial opinions on constitutional issues as merely "political," as merely judges following their own personal or political predilections. There is an understandable tendency, especially in the early stages of one's exposure to constitutional law, to feel unsettled or cynical about the legal basis for the U.S. Supreme Court's constitutional law opinions. Initiates may state (or ponder) such thoughts as: "I don't understand how the Court reached this decision; the precedents it cited don't seem to substantiate the result in this case." Or, "the Court could have reached any decision it wanted to reach; there were different precedents available to support whatever reasoning the Court chose to adopt." Or, "the Court reached this result because that is what the President and the Congress wanted; we all know that the Justices are sensitive to the way the political winds are blowing." Pursuing such lines of thought, one might easily conclude that legal concepts and rules, and methods of interpretation, do not really matter in constitutional law; that precedents are there to be disregarded; and that judicial opinions are simply rationalizations for results reached on grounds having more to do with political considerations, philosophical predispositions, and personal biases than law. Indeed, well-read students and practitioners may be aware of commentators—both on the left and on the right—whose work could be read to support such propositions about constitutional law.

Case examples can also be found to support the proposition that constitutional adjudication is, or can be, political. The leading contemporary example is *Bush v. Gore*, 531 U.S. 98 (2000), the highly publicized case about vote counts in the 2000 election for President. Addressing a variety of rights and power issues raised by the two candidates, the Court majority reversed the Florida Supreme Court's judgment ordering a recount of the votes cast in Florida in the Presidential election. The

Court's ruling had the effect of dismissing Vice-President Gore's challenges to the Florida vote count, thus securing the Florida electoral vote — and the election — for Governor Bush. The majority insisted that it had respected "the vital limits on judicial authority" and "the Constitution's design to leave the selection of the President... to the political process" (*Id.* at 111), and that it had merely accepted an "unsought responsibility" to resolve the constitutional issues presented to it. But many commentators have suggested that the Court's decision reflected political considerations (*see, e.g.,* Stephen Holmes, "Afterword: Can a Coin-Toss Election Trigger a Constitutional Earthquake?" in Jack Rakove, (ed.), THE UNFINISHED ELECTION OF 2000, pp. 238–247 (2001)), or judicial arrogance (*see* Suzanna Sherry, "Judges of Character," 38 WAKE FOREST L. REV. 793, 802–803 (2003); Larry Kramer, "The Supreme Court in Politics," in Rakove, (ed.), *supra,* at 105–152), more than it did neutral application of legal principles. Justice Stevens struck a similar theme in his dissent in *Bush v. Gore*, claiming that the majority's ruling would encourage cynicism about the work of judges and weaken confidence in the rule of law. He concluded: "Although we may never know with complete certainty the identity of the winner of this year's Presidential election, the identity of the loser is perfectly clear. It is the Nation's confidence in the judge as impartial guardian of the rule of law" (531 U.S. at 128 (Stevens, J., dissenting)).

But one should be wary of being co-opted by a "political" or "politicized" view of constitutional law. It may lead to the conclusion that constitutional law is not worthy of sustained, disciplined study, or that its precedents cannot be applied and relied on as is the case in other fields of law. This would not be a constructive vantage point from which to begin the analysis of constitutional law cases. Moreover, attachment to a politicized view of constitutional law may inhibit the capacity to see a fuller and more nuanced picture that places the "political" aspects of constitutional law into an appropriate context.

There is a U.S. Court of Appeals judge who, some years ago, clerked at the U.S. Supreme Court for Justice Lewis Powell. When he finished his clerkship, he wrote a book about his experience in which he asserted:

> Among the ideas most in vogue about the Supreme Court is that Justices, as upholders of the Constitution, simply consult their own preferences and do whatever they want, free of any obligation to apply and follow principles of law. Life-tenured judges, so the theory goes, interpreting such a nebulously worded document as the Constitution and its Bill of Rights, freely follow their own instincts and issue judgments that are, in reality, more political than legal....

> This is a stubborn impression, perhaps because it is partly true....

> But to say that judges [are "political"] is... "not the end but only the beginning of sophistication." And to say the Court is "political" is only to confirm de Tocqueville's ancient perception that "scarcely any political question arises in the United States that is not resolved, sooner or later, into a judicial question." The essential point remains, however, that the Supreme Court is *not*

merely political, and those who see it as a "third political branch" voice a tempting cliche, but one that ignores everything about the Supreme Court which is truly unique. [J. Harvey Wilkinson, SERVING JUSTICE: A SUPREME COURT CLERK'S VIEW 93–95 (1974) (footnotes omitted).] [4]

Pursuing the fuller and more nuanced view of constitutional law, another commentator has depicted constitutional law as "both the 'legal' process of 'interpreting' law and the 'political' process of 'making' law." The "political" part of the process is not political in the sense that legislative committees or lobbying groups are political, but rather in the broader sense of deliberation on "fundamental issues of constitutional value and policy," where "the value judgments involved in the ordering of legal materials include judgments of moral and political value" (Michael Perry, THE CONSTITUTION IN THE COURTS, pp. 7, 193, 202 (Oxford U. Press, 1994)). Thus courts in constitutional cases may indeed be "political" in the sense that they make policy judgments of a sort, and may in a sense make law as well as interpret it, but this judicial function "differs from the legislative and executive functions;... is peculiarly suited to the capabilities of the courts;... [and] will not likely be performed elsewhere if the courts do not assume it...." Alexander Bickel, THE LEAST DANGEROUS BRANCH, p. 24 (Yale Univ. Press, 2nd ed. 1986).

Even if the politicized characterization were substantially accurate as applied to a particular constitutional case or line of cases, it would still be unwise to allow that view to short-circuit one's study of that law. Suppose one could persuasively demonstrate that a particular Supreme Court constitutional law opinion is politicized—not based at all upon principled legal reasoning. Could a lawyer or judge therefore ignore this opinion in the course of his or her work? Of course not—because such an opinion, like all constitutional law opinions, is still a governmental decision that has binding effect upon lower courts and upon other governmental agencies and officials. Such an opinion is still a public legal document containing guidelines by which future conduct may be judged. (See Chap. 3, Sec. A.) Such an opinion is still subject to critique and interpretation and must be taken into account by anyone seeking to apply the law or improve its quality. Thus, even if an opinion is politicized and can be convincingly demonstrated to be so, it is still a reality that comprises part of the legal system. Lawyers, judges, government officials, and others must be able to deal effectively with such opinions not only in courts but in other forums as well.

6. Do look for the "big picture" of constitutional law. Constitutional law is a unitary body of law undergirded by numerous key concepts and analytical methods. An understanding of these concepts and methods, and the process by which they are applied (see prescription 7), will allow students and practitioners to perceive the structure and

---

4. For a subsequent and more comprehensive development of the issues raised in this quotation, see Michael Perry, THE CONSTITUTION IN THE COURTS (Oxford U. Press, 1994). Perry focuses the entire book on the question "Constitutional Adjudication: Law or Politics?" and, in the process, identifies and critiques other scholars' views on this question. For a more practical, hands-on slant on these issues, by a sitting judge, see *Newdow v. U.S. Congress*, 328 F.3d 466, 471 (9th Cir. 2003) (Reinhardt, J., concurring in denial of petitions for rehearing).

unifying themes of constitutional law. The result will be an integrated "big picture" that is more than the sum of its parts and that will facilitate retention of, and sensitive and meaningful application of, the subject matter. Chapters 2, 4, 9, and 15 of this book, in particular, are designed to focus attention on this big picture.

Constitutional law's unity is not immediately apparent. The study of constitutional law builds on itself; each successive "piece" of the law relates to almost every piece previously studied. Many pieces must be studied, from many angles, before they will fit together into the big picture. Students need to have patience with the subject matter, a capacity to engage their minds actively over an extended period of time, and a tenacity to stick with the challenge. Though it will not be quick or easy, the understanding—an enriched understanding—will come.

7. Do consider constitutional law to be a "process" rather than just a body of rules and doctrines. A large part of the big picture and broad perspective of constitutional law is the "process" that the law establishes for constitutional decisionmaking. Justice Frankfurter said it well when he focused on "the process of law-making, law-growing, and law-changing," and emphasized the importance of having a "critical questioning attitude" about this process (see prescription 2 above). Another commentator, expanding on this theme, asserted that:

> The law is more than a body of rules; it is the historical, living process of people legislating, adjudicating, administering, and negotiating the allocation of rights and duties. . . . Its premise, from which it derives its perceived legitimacy and therefore its authority, is that it strives to anticipate and give expression to what a people believes to be its collective destiny or ultimate meaning within a moral universe. [R. Neuhaus, THE NAKED PUBLIC SQUARE: RELIGION AND DEMOCRACY IN AMERICA, p. 253 (Eerdmans, 2nd ed., 1995).]

A full, integrated, view of constitutional law must include this "historical, living process" as well as the rules and doctrines developed through this process. A full view must include attention both to *who* interprets the Constitution within this process, and to *how* the Constitution is interpreted (see Chap. 2, Sec. F.1). A full view also must include the legal concepts and analytical methods that underlie the process and shape the rules and doctrines. And a full view must focus on the *standards* of judicial review, the development and application of which is a major function of the process of constitutional decisionmaking (see Chap. 5, Sec. F.7). These *standards* that courts use to reason through and resolve particular issues are usually the most important and useful component of the rules and doctrines of constitutional law.

8. Do distinguish between a "rough and tumble" view of constitutional law and an aspirational view. A "rough and tumble" view focuses on constitutional law as it actually operates, including its politicized or debased features (see prescription 5 above). An aspirational view, on the other hand, addresses what constitutional law is or could be at its best. If the latter view remains in focus as a counterpoint to the former view, then standards of excellence for judges and lawyers in constitutional cases may remain an object of concern for students and practitioners alike. As one scholar has asserted, "[A]t its worst, constitutional adjudication is little more than politics in a debased sense of 'politics'. . . . But the serious issue, for normative constitutional theory, is not what constitutional adjudication is at its worst, its most debased, but what constitutional adjudication can be at its best" (Michael Perry, THE CONSTITUTION IN THE COURTS, p. 202, prescription 5 above).

* * * *

These are the eight prescriptions for an initial perspective on constitutional law. Taken together, they should assist students to develop, and practitioners to maintain, a balanced and open perspective on the subject. (Students—whether in a formal course or engaged in independent study—may profit from reviewing these prescriptions periodically throughout their study to help maintain perspective.)

Sec. C. Constitutional Law Research: Finding Judicial Opinions and Related Resources

Court opinions are published in official and unofficial hard copy reporters, in current law services (in particular U.S. Law Week), on proprietary electronic websites (such as Westlaw and LexisNexis), and on free Internet websites (such as the courts' own websites, certain university websites, and a site called FindLaw). *See* Robert C. Berring & Elizabeth A. Edinger, FINDING THE LAW 23–27 (11th ed., West Group, 1999).

The official reporter for United States Supreme Court opinions and orders is *U.S. Reports* (cited as U.S.) and its predecessors. There are also two commercial reporters: West's *Supreme Court Reporter* (cited as S.Ct.) and LexisNexis' *U.S. Supreme Court Reports, Lawyer's Edition* (cited as L.Ed.). The commercial reporters generally publish new decisions more promptly than *U.S. Reports*. They also provide supplementary information, such as case histories, case summaries, case notes, or links to related topics. Both provide proprietary computer access via the Internet. *See* Berring & Edinger, *supra*, at 35–37, 42. In addition, the *United States Law Week*, published by the Bureau of National Affairs, is a looseleaf service that provides prompt publication of full-text slip opinions in U.S. Supreme Court cases as well as a record of the Court's docket and proceedings.

There are also hard copy collections of the legal briefs filed in U.S. Supreme Court cases, published by the Court. These collections may be found in the following law libraries that are depository libraries for the Government Printing Office (GPO): the University of Chicago Law Library, the Library of Congress, the Cornell Law Library, the Connecticut State Library, Indiana University/Bloomington Law Library, the University of Louisville Law Library, the University of Minnesota Law Library, the University of Texas Law Library, the University of Washington Law Library, the library of the Editorial Counsel, West Group (Eagen, MN), and the Yale Law School Library.

The website of the U.S. Supreme Court (http://www.supremecourtus.gov) includes electronic versions of the bound volumes of *U.S. Reports* beginning with volume 502 (the Court's 1991 Term), as well as "slip opinions" (single, unbound opinions) for the current Term and the Court's two prior Terms. This website also includes the orders issued by the Court in the current Term and the two prior Terms; a searchable docket containing information on the status of pending and decided cases in the current Term and decided cases from the prior Term; and transcripts of the oral arguments in cases before the Court, beginning with the arguments in the 2000 Term.[5]

The Westlaw and the LexisNexis electronic services both have databases of U.S. Supreme Court opinions from 1790 to the present. The Westlaw and LexisNexis websites also contain previews of cases pending before the Court, transcripts of oral arguments in cases before the Court, and briefs (the briefs of the parties as well as amicus briefs) filed in cases heard by the Court. The transcripts and briefs databases for each service begin with late twentieth century cases. Both services also have additional databases with supplementary information about U.S. Supreme Court cases.

FindLaw (http://www.findlaw.com) is a free website that has a Supreme Court Center (http://supreme.lp.findlaw.com/supreme_court/resources.html) that includes the opinions of the U.S. Supreme Court beginning with cases from the 1893 Court Term (vol. 150 of *U.S. Reports*). This website also includes supplementary information on the Court's docket and calendar, Court orders, legal briefs filed with the Court, and current news about the Court, as well as a message board for on-line discussions of current Court cases.

Other websites with pertinent information on U.S. Supreme Court cases include: On the Docket (http://journalism.medill.northwestern.edu/docket/), which presents the Court's docket for the current term and the previous four terms, as well as summaries of pending cases, current news about the Court, and features on selected current topics; the Office of the Solicitor General website (http://www.usdoj.gov/osg/briefs/search.html), which contains briefs filed with the U.S. Supreme Court by the Solicitor General of the United States, beginning with the 1982 Court Term; the Legal Information Institute of Cornell Law School (http://www.law.cornell.edu), which includes U.S. Supreme Court decisions from 1990 and a variety of other information about the Court and its docket (http://supct.law.cornell.edu/supct/); and the Oyez Project website (http://oyez.itcs.northwestern.edu/oyez/ frontpage), which includes audio recordings of oral arguments in all cases from 1994 onward and selected landmark cases from earlier years, printed transcripts of oral arguments, summaries of selected U.S. Supreme Court cases, and descriptions of current Court cases in the news. *See generally* Diana Botluk, THE LEGAL LIST: RESEARCH ON THE INTERNET §§ 7.2–7.4 (West Group, 2002).

The U.S. Courts of Appeals, the U.S. District Courts, and the state courts also issue their own constitutional law opinions. Opinions from the thirteen U.S. Courts of Appeals are published in West's *Federal Reporter* series (cited as F., F.2d, or F.3d). West's

---

5. For the U.S. Supreme Court, each year's Term begins on the first Monday in October and ends the following year on the day before the first Monday in October. Thus the 2001 Term, or October Term 2001, began on October 1, 2001 and ended on October 7, 2002.

Federal Supplement series (cited as F. Supp. or F. Supp. 2d) publishes decisions from the U.S. District Courts and the U.S. Court of Claims. State court decisions are found in separate official reporters for each of the states, as well as in West's regional reporter system. The *United States Law Week* also publishes abridged versions of selected, current federal and state court opinions on constitutional law issues.

The opinions and dockets of many of these lower courts are also available electronically on the Internet. Some courts have their own websites that include their own opinions. The U.S. Court of Appeals for the Second Circuit's website, for example, is at <http://www.ca2.uscourts.gov>. The Federal Judicial Center website (http://www.uscourts.gov/links.html) provides links to the websites for the U.S. Courts of Appeals and the U.S. District Courts. The Westlaw and LexisNexis proprietary sites include searchable databases for the various lower court systems. FindLaw (http://findlaw.com/casecode/courts/index.html) includes opinions from the U.S. Courts of Appeals, some of the federal district courts, and the highest courts of the states. The Cornell Law School Legal Information Institute has a search engine that provides access to the opinions of all the U.S. Courts of Appeals (http://www.law.cornell.edu:9999/USCA-ALL/search.html). *See generally* Botluk, THE LEGAL LIST, *supra*, §§ 7.5–7.12.

The text of the United States Constitution can be found at various free sites on the Internet—often in searchable format and sometimes with annotations. Good places to look are: FindLaw (http://www.findlaw.com/casecode/); the Cornell Law School Legal Information Institute (http://www.law.cornell.edu/constitution/constitution.overview.html); Emory Law School's U.S. Founding Documents (http://www.law.emory.edu/erd/docs.html); and the GPO Access website's Core Documents of U.S. Democracy (http://www.access.gpo.gov/su_docs/locators/coredocs/index.html). FindLaw and GPO Access also have searchable versions of the extensively annotated Constitution prepared by the Congressional Research Service of the Library of Congress. The Emory site also includes the Declaration of Independence and the Articles of Confederation in searchable format. GPO Access also has the Declaration of Independence and the Articles of Confederation. *See generally* Botluk, *supra*, § 5.2.

Sec. D. Selected Supplementary Resources to Enrich the Study and Practice of Constitutional Law

In the study and practice of constitutional law, it is often important to consult basic reference or background resources to supplement the study and application of judicial opinions. The following list contains citations to and brief descriptions of selected resources that are particularly useful for supplementary reading as well as for research.

1. For analysis of particular U.S. Supreme Court opinions, see the annual review of the previous term's decisions published each year in the November issue of the HARVARD LAW REVIEW (*The Supreme Court, _____ Term*).

2. For a clause-by-clause analytical and historical commentary on the Constitution, see Congressional Research Service, Library of Congress, THE CONSTITUTION OF THE UNITED STATES OF AMERICA: ANALYSIS AND INTERPRETATION (U.S. Government Printing Office; 1996 plus periodic pocket parts).

3. For a comprehensive analytical text on the commerce clause, including both the scope of Congressional power and federalistic limitations on state power, see Boris Bittker & Brannon Denning, BITTKER ON THE REGULATION OF INTERSTATE AND FOREIGN COMMERCE (Aspen Publishing, 1999).

4. For treatments of freedom of expression, see Daniel Farber, THE FIRST AMENDMENT (Foundation Press, 2nd ed. 2003); Rodney Smolla, SMOLLA & NIMMER ON FREEDOM OF SPEECH: A TREATISE ON THE THEORY OF THE FIRST AMENDMENT (Clark Boardman Callaghan, 3rd ed. 1996); and Martin Redish, FREEDOM OF EXPRESSION: A CRITICAL ANALYSIS (Michie Co., 1984).

5. For a text that explains and analyzes issues in all the major substantive areas of constitutional law, see Erwin Chemerinsky, CONSTITUTIONAL LAW: PRINCIPLES AND POLICIES (Aspen Publishing, 2nd ed. 2002).

6. For a comprehensive hornbook on constitutional law doctrines and cases, see John Nowak & Ronald Rotunda, CONSTITUTIONAL LAW (West Group, 7th ed. 2004).

7. For a systematic treatise presenting in-depth critical analysis of constitutional law, see Laurence Tribe, AMERICAN CONSTITUTIONAL LAW, vol. 1 (Foundation Press, 3rd ed. 2000). (The third edition also has a vol. 2 that was not yet published when this book went to press.)

8. For a concise description of state constitutions and an overview of state constitutional law, see Thomas Marks & John Cooper, STATE CONSTITUTIONAL LAW IN A NUTSHELL (West Group, 2nd ed. 2003).

9. For collections of edited articles on leading topics in constitutional law, with commentary by the editors and bibliographies of related readings, see John Garvey, T. Alexander Aleinikoff, & Daniel Farber (eds.), MODERN CONSTITUTIONAL THEORY: A READER (Thomson/West, 5th ed. 2004); and Michael Glennon, *et al.* (eds.), A CONSTITUTIONAL LAW ANTHOLOGY (Anderson Pub. Co., 2nd ed. 1997).

10. For a collection of stories about famous U.S. Supreme Court cases (including *Marbury, McCulloch, Dred Scott, Plessy, Korematsu, Roe v. Wade*, and *Baker v. Carr*), and the people and events behind these cases, see Michael Dorf (ed.), CONSTITUTIONAL LAW STORIES (Foundation Press, 2004).

11. For a classic and highly readable study of the U.S. Supreme Court's role in the development of the nation and the historical development of constitutional law, see Robert G. McCloskey, THE AMERICAN SUPREME COURT (University of Chicago Press, 3rd ed. 2000) (Sanford Levinson, reviser).

12. For a concise analysis of the history of the drafting and ratification of the Constitution and its amendments, see Daniel Farber & Suzanna Sherry, A HISTORY OF THE AMERICAN CONSTITUTION (West Group, 1990).

13. For a collection of the key documents of the founding generation, from 1776 to 1791, see Michael Kammen (ed.), THE ORIGINS OF THE AMERICAN CON-

STITUTION: A DOCUMENTARY HISTORY (Penguin, 1986). The collection includes selected Federalist papers, Anti-Federalist papers, private correspondence of the founders, and plans and resolutions submitted by the states to the Constitutional Convention, as well as the Articles of Confederation and an introductory essay by the Editor. For another, broader collection of source documents, organized by principle (*e.g.*, the principle of equality), see Neil Cogan, CONTEXTS OF THE CONSTITUTION: A DOCUMENTARY COLLECTION ON PRINCIPLES OF AMERICAN CONSTITUTIONAL LAW (Foundation Press, 1999).

14. For an extensive, five-volume set of commentaries on the text of the Constitution (up through the Twelfth Amendment) and the major themes of constitutional law, see Philip Kurland & Ralph Lerner (eds.), THE FOUNDERS' CONSTITUTION (U. of Chicago Press, 1987), republished by the Liberty Fund (2000). The commentaries are drawn primarily from original source documents and the writings of classical authors. Essays by the editors are also included.

15. For a survey of constitutional theory (especially theories of constitutional interpretation), along with critique and scholarly commentary, see Michael Gerhardt, Thomas Rowe, Rebecca Brown, & Girardeau Spann, CONSTITUTIONAL THEORY: ARGUMENTS AND PERSPECTIVES (Lexis Pub., 2nd ed. 2000).

16. For a general text on the political theories underlying the Constitution and the various approaches to interpreting the document, see Walter Murphy, James Fleming, & Sotirios Barber, AMERICAN CONSTITUTIONAL INTERPRETATION (Foundation Press, 3rd ed., revised 2001).

17. For analysis and examples of constitutional decisionmaking by governmental bodies *other than the courts*, see Louis Fisher & Neal Devins, POLITICAL DYNAMICS OF CONSTITUTIONAL LAW (West Group, 3rd ed. 2001).

18. For a comprehensive, six-volume collection of several thousand short entries and articles on all aspects of constitutional law, see Leonard Levy & Kenneth Karst (eds.), ENCYCLOPEDIA OF THE AMERICAN CONSTITUTION (MacMillan Reference USA, 2nd ed. 2000). The entries and articles cover leading U.S. Supreme Court cases, major themes and topics of constitutional law, leading figures in the history of constitutional law, and the various historical periods of constitutional law's development. There are also appendices with original source documents, a chronology of the Constitution's drafting and ratification (covering 1786–1791), a timeline of "important events in the development of American constitutional law" (covering 1215 to the present), and a glossary of legal terms pertinent to constitutional law.

Chapter 2

The Constitution of the United States of America

Sec. A. The Concept of a Constitution

A.1. Constitutions in General

The concept of a constitution has ancient roots. As the concept evolved, additional meanings were attributed to it, and the functions or purposes of constitutions evolved as well. Acceptance of the political theory of constitutionalism,[1] and the actual use of constitutions by the nations of the world, has increased over time, especially in the twentieth century. The American experience with its Constitution has been central to these developments. *See generally* Donald Lutz, THE ORIGINS OF AMERICAN CONSTITUTIONALISM (La. State U. Press, 1988).

The concept of a constitution appears in the writings of Plato and Aristotle, in Roman law, in the early canon law of the Roman Catholic Church, and in English law of the later middle ages. In its most primitive usage, a constitution was simply a law or royal edict of a secular authority or a regulation of an ecclesiastical authority. The term was often used in the plural to refer to a set of laws, edicts, or regulations.

With the Greek political philosophers, the concept of a constitution (the "politeia") took on the broader meaning of a framework of government, comprised of the political, social, and economic characteristics that describe the state. Aristotle, for instance, used the word constitution to mean government, or a form for government, with the government or constitution being the "supreme authority" in a state (Aristotle, POLITICS, Book III, ch. 7, at p. 139 (Benjamin Jowett, tr.) (Random House, 1943)). The government need not be a democracy, or have any other particular form; a constitution could provide for rule by "the one, or the few, or the many" (Id). But some constitu-

---

1. For elaboration of the theory of constitutionalism, *see, e.g.*, Larry Alexander, ed., CONSTITUTIONALISM: PHILOSOPHICAL FOUNDATIONS (Cambridge Univ. Press, 1998).

tions were better or truer than others, according to Aristotle. The "best" constitution, or form of government, was one formed by the "middle class," when the middle class was larger and stronger than the upper and lower classes (Aristotle, POLITICS, Book IV, ch. 11, at pp. 191–192; and *see generally* chs. 11–13); and the "true" constitution, or form of government, is one in which the rulers "govern with a view to the common interest" (Aristotle, POLITICS, Book III, ch. 7, at p. 139).

In the Greek conception, a constitution was not a written document as such, but an understanding, based upon custom or "nature," of the composition of the state. The salient function of this understanding was to *limit* the authority of government, whatever its form. *See generally* Charles H. McIlwain, CONSTITUTIONALISM ANCIENT AND MODERN, chap. II (rev. ed., Cornell Univ. Press, 1947).

In the era of the Roman Republic, the developing Roman conception of a constitution ("constitutio") did not encompass rule by "the one, the few, or the many," but instead emphasized non-monarchial institutions of government and governmental structures that provided a rudimentary form of representation for the people (or certain classes of people). Consistent with these developments, Roman thought added an important new element to constitutionalism: "the *populus*, and none but the whole *populus*, can be the ultimate source of legal authority" (McIlwain, *supra*, at 57). A constitution, then, and a commitment to constitutionalism, depended upon the people, not their rulers; and whatever limitations were placed on government derived from the consent of the people.

These strains of Roman republican thought, and the earlier strains of Greek thought, survived through the Middle Ages. During the medieval era, further thinking on constitutionalism was developed both by canonists addressing matters of church law and by political theorists addressing matters of secular government. These medieval theorists focused on matters such as the consent of the governed as the basis of constitutionalism, the proper limits to be placed on ecclesiastical and secular authority, the concept of representation, and the relationship between central and local governments (an early version of federalism). *See* Brian Tierney, RELIGION, LAW, AND THE GROWTH OF CONSTITUTIONAL THOUGHT, 1150–1650 (Cambridge U. Press, 1982).

In the late 1600s and into the 1700s, the strains of thought from ancient Greece, the Roman Republic, and the medieval period were further developed by English and other European theorists. Moreover, in fits and starts, theories of constitutionalism were tested, especially in England, through various crises and experiments in government. The concept of a constitution as a higher fundamental law emerged from these developments. So did the concept of a constitution as a means of protecting the individual liberty of the people, and a means of assuring popular political accountability of the government. *See generally* McIlwain, *supra*, at 41–135. In the mid-1700s, Lord Bolingbroke distinguished the English government from the English constitution, and described the English constitution as "derived from certain fixed principles of reason, directed to certain fixed objects of public good, that compose the general system, according to which the community hath agreed to be governed" (Bolingbroke, "A Dissertation Upon Parties" (1733–1734), in THE WORKS OF LORD BOLINGBROKE, v. II, p. 88 (Henry G. Bohn, 1844; reprinted by Frank Cass and Co., 1967)). The government is subject to the constitution, according to Bolingbroke, to the end that "the liberties of Great Britain be immortal" (*Id.* at 6). Similarly, in 1765, Blackstone described the English constitution as a "frame of government" or "system of laws" whose good is the protection of "political or civil liberty" for the people. This "spirit of liberty," according to Blackstone, is "deeply implanted in [the English] constitution" and consists of "three principal or primary articles; the right of personal security, the right of personal liberty, and the right of private property..." (Blackstone, Commentaries on the Laws of England, vol. 1, Book I, chap. 1 ("Of the Absolute Rights of Individuals"), pp. 94–96 (Wayne Morrison, ed., Cavendish Publishing Limited, 2001)).

The English experience also provided the beginnings of another contribution to the modern concept of a constitution. This contribution involved the commitment to writtenness—to reducing at least some of the constitutional understandings to writing. The British constitution has evolved over a great span of years, encompassing many documents as well as various other precedents and conventions, but commitment to writing has been a key part of the evolution. This aspect of British constitutionalism began in 1215 with the Magna Carta ("Great Charter") that imposed certain limits on the power of the King, especially in relation to the nobility. Another critical step was the Bill of Rights of 1689, which subordinated the English monarch to the new Parliament and established various individual rights of the people. *See generally* Rett Ludwikowski and William Fox, The Beginning of the Constitutional Era: A Bicentennial Comparative Analysis of the First Modern Constitutions 7–18 (The Catholic Univ. of America Press, 1993).

The American movement toward constitutionalism in the late eighteenth century drew upon these earlier strains of thought and experience. But the movement also added new elements to the concept of a constitution, making the American constitutions (the U.S. Constitution and those of the original states) unique in the history of the world. *See generally* Michael Kammen, "Introduction," in Michael Kammen (ed.), The Origins of the American Constitution: A Documentary History, vii–xxiii (Penguin Books, 1986).

One major contribution of American constitutionalism is the commitment to a single written document adopted at a particular point in time.

> [B]y the time the states confronted the task of devising their own constitutions in the 1770s, Americans had ceased to think of them as Englishmen did. In the New World, the term, constitution, no longer referred to the actual organization of power developed through custom, prescription, and precedent. Instead it had come to mean a written frame of government.... [T]he written constitution became the instrument by which the people entrusted power to their agents. [Oscar Handlin and Mary Handlin, The Dimensions of Liberty, p. 55 (Belknap Press, 1961).]

Thus "[t]he American Revolution [had] given birth to this new political phenomenon: in every state a written constitution was framed..." (St. George Tucker, View of the Constitution of the United States (1803) (Liberty Fund Edition, p. 104; Clyde Wilson (ed.), 1999)).

A second American contribution to the modern concept of a constitution was best captured at the time by Thomas Paine:

> A constitution is a thing *antecedent* to a government, and a government is only the creature of a constitution. The constitution of a country is not the act of its government, but of the people constituting a government. [Thomas Paine, RIGHTS OF MAN, part I, p. 48, in THE COMPLETE POLITICAL WORKS OF THOMAS PAINE, vol. II (The Freethought Press Ass'n, 1954); and *see generally* RIGHTS OF MAN, part II, ch. IV.]

Three critically important points are combined here. First, a constitution and a government are not one and the same (in contrast to the Greek concept of a constitution); second, the constitution precedes (or is "antecedent to") the government and serves to create, or constitute, the government; and third, the people create the constitution and thus the government. For Paine, then, and in the American experience, a constitution is a conscious constituent act of the people that is undertaken at a particular point in time and memorialized in a single written document. (*See generally* McIlwain, CONSTITUTIONALISM ANCIENT AND MODERN, *supra*, at 2–3, 8–9, 14.)

A third American contribution to modern constitutionalism was the emphasis on the representation of the people within the councils of government. These developments drew, perhaps, on strands of the medievalists' focus on representation and the British focus on popular political accountability of government. Under the American constitutions, development of the structures of government went hand in hand with considerations of how the people's will would inform, and be represented within, the various parts of the structure (*See generally* Cynthia Farina, "The Consent of the Governed: Against Simple Rules for a Complex World," 72 CHICAGO-KENT L. REV. 987, 1007–1118 (1997)). The American answer was a "polyphonic" answer: multiple voices would speak the people's will through both legislative and executive structures rather than a single voice through a single structure (*Id.* at 1017–1018).

The new American conception of a constitution thus borrowed from, yet it stood in contrast to, the English conception; and stood in even starker contrast to earlier conceptions that did not depend on a written document, or did not distinguish between constitution and government, or did not provide workable structures for representation.[2] But the American conception had something else in common with earlier conceptions as far back as the Greek and Roman: the key purpose of limiting governmental power. As McIlwain emphasized:

> [I]n all its successive phases, constitutionalism has one essential quality: it is a legal limitation on government; it is the antithesis of arbitrary rule; its op-

---

2. This new American conception of a written constitution significantly influenced the development of the next two national constitutions that followed upon the American experience: a 1791 constitution for Poland, and a 1791 constitution for France. See Rett Ludwikowski and William Fox, THE BEGINNING OF THE CONSTITUTIONAL ERA: A BICENTENNIAL COMPARATIVE ANALYSIS OF THE FIRST MODERN CONSTITUTIONS, pp. 1–4 (The Catholic University of America Press, 1993).

posite is despotic government, the government of will instead of law.... [T]he most ancient, the most persistent, and the most lasting of the essentials of true constitutionalism still remains what it has been almost from the beginning, the limitation of government by law. [McIlwain, *supra*, at pp. 21–22.]

A.2. The American Constitutions, State and Federal

The first American constitutions were state constitutions. Eight of the original thirteen states adopted constitutions during the year of independence, 1776.[3] Two others adopted constitutions in 1777, and in 1780 Massachusetts adopted its well-regarded constitution.

The leading examples of early state constitutions were the Virginia constitution of 1776, which pioneered a declaration of rights emulated by drafters of other state constitutions; the Pennsylvania constitution of 1776; and the Massachusetts constitution of 1780 that was drafted by John Adams.[4] *See generally* Robert Williams, "The State Constitutions of the Founding Decade: Pennsylvania's Radical 1776 Constitution and Its Influence on American Constitutionalism," 62 TEMPLE L. REV. 541 (1989). The Massachusetts constitution "was the first to be drafted by a convention elected just for that purpose [and] was the first American constitution to be submitted to the electorate (thereby setting a precedent for 1787–1788)" (Michael Kammen, "Introduction," in Michael Kammen (ed.), THE ORIGINS OF THE AMERICAN CONSTITUTION: A DOCUMENTARY HISTORY, at xi; and *see generally* vii–xiii (Penguin Books, 1986)).

Meanwhile, in November 1777, the Continental Congress signed the Articles of Confederation, the first American attempt to create a *national* government. The Articles were not ratified by the states until 1781, by which time most of the states had adopted their own constitutions. The Articles were in the form of a compact or league among the states and were thus quite different in origin and purpose from the states' own constitutions and from the U.S. Constitution that was ratified in 1788.

The state constitutions were therefore more direct forerunners of the federal Constitution than the Articles of Confederation, and state constitutions became (and remain) and an essential component of American constitutionalism. Though state constitutions may have structures and rights that parallel those in the U.S. Constitution, they are also distinctive documents, differing from the U.S. Constitution and from one another, and playing a unique role in the American constitutional system. *See generally* G. Alan Tarr, UNDERSTANDING STATE CONSTITUTIONS, chaps. 1 and 2 (Princeton Univ. Press, 1998).

---

3. In May of 1776, prior to adopting the Declaration of Independence, the Continental Congress had "passed a resolution calling for new constitutions in each of the states." Joseph J. Ellis, FOUNDING BROTHERS, p. 242 (Alfred A. Knopf, 2000).

4. For an account of John Adams' work as drafter of "A Constitution or Form of Government for the Commonwealth of Massachusetts," see David McCulloch, JOHN ADAMS, pp. 220–225 (Simon & Schuster, 2001).

A key characteristic of American constitutions (state and federal) was that they were written (see Sec. A.1 above). They did not depend on an accumulation of unwritten customs or on a collection of loosely fitted documents from different historical periods—as, for instance, the British "unwritten" constitution did. The single document setting out the frame of government all at one time (but subject to later amendment) became the uniquely American vehicle by which *the people* spoke and gave their consent to be governed according to the terms of the document. In this sense, the American written constitutions were "social contracts" or "social compacts" among the people that laid a foundation for self-government and established legitimacy for that government. In one of the U.S. Supreme Court's earliest cases, *Chisholm v. Georgia*, 2 U.S. (3 Dall.) 419, 471 (1793), Chief Justice Jay described the American constitutions in this way: "[E]very State constitution is a compact made by and between the citizens of a State to govern themselves in a certain manner; and the Constitution of the United States is, likewise, a compact made by the people of the United States, to govern themselves as to general objects in a certain manner." Similarly, an early commentator described the U.S. Constitution as "an original, written, federal, and social compact, freely, voluntarily, and solemnly entered into…" (St. George Tucker, VIEW OF THE CONSTITUTION OF THE UNITED STATES (1803) (Liberty Fund edition, p. 91), and *see generally* Liberty Fund edition, pp. 91–107 (Clyde Wilson, ed., 1999)).

But the American constitutions are not merely contracts or compacts. Contracts typically bind only the parties, but the American constitutions are to be enduring; the original consent serves to legitimate their application to later generations as well as the founding generation.[5] Moreover, a contract or compact can sometimes be terminated in the normal course of events, or a party can rescind or withdraw, or the contract may end upon the death of a party or the completion of the stated obligations. An American constitution, in contrast, is designed to be perpetual, with no provision made for terminating, concluding, or withdrawing from the arrangement. Some further description and understanding of the American constitutions is therefore necessary.

In his COMMENTARIES ON THE CONSTITUTION, Justice Story fills this need. Regarding state constitutions, he explained:

> [Their] proper character is that of a fundamental law prescribed by the will of the majority of the people of the State (who are entitled to prescribe it), for the government and regulation of the whole people. It binds them as a supreme rule ordained by the sovereign power, and not merely as a voluntary contract entered into by parties capable of contracting, and binding themselves by such terms as they choose to select. [Joseph Story, COMMENTARIES

---

5. There is considerable discussion about the theory of original consent in the literature on American constitutionalism. Some commentators question whether and how the acts of one generation may be said to bind later generations whose "people" were not represented in the original decisionmaking process. Other commentators question whether and how the political act of the founding generation, in which only white male property owners could vote, could bind later generations in which racial and ethnic minorities, females, and persons without property make up a large proportion of the voters.

ON THE CONSTITUTION OF THE UNITED STATES, vol. 1, § 349, p. 251 (5th ed., Melville Bigelow (ed.)) (Wm. S. Hein and Co., 1994) (footnotes omitted).]

Similarly, regarding the U.S. Constitution, Justice Story explained:

> There is nowhere found upon the face of the Constitution any clause inti-mating it to be a compact.... On the contrary, the preamble emphatically speaks of it as a solemn ordinance and establishment of government.... *The people* do *ordain* and *establish*, not contract and stipulate with each other.... The people ordain and establish a "*constitution*," not a "*confederation*...." The former is a permanent form of government, where the powers, once given, are irrevocable, and cannot be resumed or withdrawn at pleasure. Whether formed by a single people, or by different societies of people, in their political capacity, a constitution, though originating in consent, becomes, when rati-fied, obligatory, as a fundamental ordinance or law. [Story, COMMENTARIES, *supra*, §§ 351–352, pp. 252–253 (footnotes omitted).]

A.3. The U.S. Constitution[6]

The origins of the U.S. Constitution are traced in Sections A.1. and A.2 above. The U.S. Constitution is best understood in the light of those origins and what they reveal about the nature and functions of the document. In particular, it is critical to note two basic points. First, the Constitution was adopted by the People, not by the states or any other pre-existing government (Story, COMMENTARIES, *supra*, § 362, pp. 261–262 (5th ed., Melville Bigelow (ed.)) (Wm. S. Hein and Co., 1994 (footnotes omitted)). As the Constitution's preamble itself makes clear, "the People of the United States...do or-dain and establish this Constitution...." Second, the Constitution was created for "our-selves *and our posterity*" (U.S. Const., preamble; emphasis added). The document was thus "designed to approach immortality as nearly as human institutions can approach it" (*Cohens v. Virginia*, 19 U.S. (6 Wheat.) 264, 387 (1821)). The U.S. Supreme Court has captured these two essential characteristics of the Constitution in this way: "Our Constitution is a covenant running from the first generation of Americans to us and then to future generations. It is a coherent succession. Each generation must learn anew that the Constitution's written terms embody ideas and aspirations that must survive more ages than one" (*Planned Parenthood of Southeastern Pennsylvania v. Casey*, 505 U.S. 833, 901 (1992)).

Viewed in this light, the U.S. Constitution is a "constituent act" of the People by which a new federal government is "called into life" (*Missouri v. Holland*, 252 U.S. 416, 433 (1920)). It is "the basic charter of our society, setting out...the principles of gov-ernment" (*Poe v. Ullman*, 367 U.S. 497, 540 (1961) (Harlan, J., dissenting). Among the foremost of these principles, implicit in the entire document, is "the principle that ours is a government of laws, not of men, and that we submit ourselves to rulers only if

---

6. The text of the U.S. Constitution is set out in Appendix A at the end of this book.

under rules" (*Youngstown Sheet & Tube Co. v. Sawyer*, 343 U.S. 579, 646 (1952) (Jackson, J., concurring)).

As the nation's "basic charter," the U.S. Constitution has three central functions. (1) It establishes the structures and mechanisms through which the federal government operates and by which it interfaces with the separate governments of the states. (2) It delineates the powers of the federal government or, more particularly, of its three branches, as juxtaposed against the powers of the states. (3) It imposes limits upon the powers of the federal government as well as upon the powers of the states. The first two of these functions predominate in the original Constitution of 1788; the third function predominates in the Bill of Rights and subsequent amendments, most especially the Fourteenth Amendment. The first function is carried out in the document primarily through the "housekeeping" clauses; the second function primarily through the "power" or "empowerment" clauses; and the third function primarily through the "rights" clauses (see Sec. C below).

The Constitution also serves a fourth function, less pervasive than the other three but still critically important: the function of ordering relationships among the states. Most of the pertinent provisions that serve this function are in Article IV, in particular sections 1 and 2 and section 3, paragraph 1. Section 1 is the full faith and credit clause, providing that each slate will give "Full faith and Credit...to the public Acts, Records, and judicial Proceedings of every other State." Section 2, paragraph 1, is the interstate privileges and immunities clause, which is discussed in Chapter 7, Section E. Another clause, outside Article IV, that is important to relations among the states is Article I, section 10, paragraph 3, which provides that a state may not "enter into any Agreement or Compact with another State" unless it obtains "the Consent of the Congress." Yet another pertinent clause is in Article III, section 2, paragraph 1, which makes the federal courts a forum for the resolution of "Controversies between two or more States...." A state cannot claim immunity from such a suit brought by another state, since "the States by adoption of the Constitution, acting in their highest sovereign capacity...waived their exemption from judicial power" (*Principality of Monoco v. State of Mississippi*, 292 U.S. 313, 328–329 (1934) (citations omitted); *see also Alden v. Maine*, 527 U.S. 706, 755 (1999)).

Beyond the theoretical characteristics of the Constitution emphasized in Sections A.1 and A.2 above, there are three other theoretical—but also very practical—characteristics that will usefully guide the study and application of constitutional law: (1) the Constitution is *fundamental* law; (2) the Constitution is *supreme* law; and (3) the Constitution is *hard* law.[7]

First, the U.S. Constitution is *fundamental* law because it is the original act of the sovereign power—the People—whose purpose was to establish a new political community and set forth the first principles by which it would be governed. The Constitution is the repository for the aspirations and core values that define the United States

---

7. The phrase "hard law" comes from William Van Alstyne, "The Idea of the Constitution as Hard Law," 37 J. Legal Educ. 174 (1987).

as a nation. As Chief Justice Marshall recognized in *Marbury v. Madison*, 5 U.S. (1 Cranch) 137 (1803), the Constitution contains the "principles...on which the whole American fabric has been erected" (*Id.* at 176). These principles derive from "the original right" and supreme authority of "the people" to establish a government; the "exercise of this right is a very great exertion" that cannot and ought not "to be frequently repeated"; thus the document is "designed to be permanent" (*Id.*). "The principles... so established [therefore] are deemed *fundamental*," and the Constitution that contains these principles forms "the *fundamental* and paramount law of the nation...." (*Id.* at 176–177; emphasis added).

Second, the U.S. Constitution is *supreme* law because it is the expressed will of the supreme sovereign, the People. "[T]heir will, thus promulgated, is to be obeyed as the supreme law." Joseph Story, A FAMILIAR EXPOSITION OF THE CONSTITUTION OF THE UNITED STATES, §42, p. 37 (American Book Co., 1840). The Constitution is therefore the highest and most authoritative law in the nation's legal system, taking precedence over any other law or legal act of the federal government or any state or local government, and taking precedence over all the state constitutions. In *Marbury* (above), Chief Justice Marshall emphasized that "the constitution is superior to any ordinary act of the legislature" (5 U.S. (1 Cranch) at 178) and that "an act of the legislature, repugnant to the constitution, is void" (*Id.* at 177). The whole structure and theory of the constitution supports this conclusion, said Marshall, as does the supremacy clause (Art. VI, ¶2) itself: "[I]n declaring what shall be the *supreme* law of the land, the *constitution* itself is first mentioned; and not the laws of the United States generally, but those only which shall be made in *pursuance* of the constitution, have that rank" (5 U.S. (1 Cranch) at 180; emphasis in original).

Third, the U.S. Constitution is "*hard law*" because, unlike the constitutions of some other nations, it is a *legal* and not merely a *political* instrument, and as such it may "be invoked in court [and] used by judges" in actual cases (William Van Alstyne, "The Idea of the Constitution as Hard Law," 37 J. LEGAL EDUC. 174, 180 (1987)). Chief Justice Marshall also made this point clear in *Marbury*. "The framers of the constitution contemplated that instrument as a rule for the government of *courts*" as well as the other departments of government, he asserted, and the "*courts*, as well as other departments, are bound by that instrument" (5 U.S. (1 Cranch) at 179–180 (emphasis in original)). "[B]oth [a] law and the constitution [may] apply to a particular case," and the court must then determine whether they are in conflict. "This is the very essence of judicial duty." If there is a conflict, "the constitution, and not such ordinary act, must govern the case to which they both apply" (*Id.* at 178).[8]

The Constitution is also hard law in the fuller sense of being "reliable law [that] is not easily altered..." (Van Alstyne, *supra*, at 179–180), and that may therefore provide stability and consistency of judicial rulings over time. To achieve this purpose, there must be a strong judiciary, with substantial independence from the political branches. Unlike the Constitutions of some other countries, the U.S. Constitution fits this char-

---

8. This result is dictated by the second principle above: the Constitution is supreme law.

acterization because it is "readily enforceable in accessible and professionally serious courts" (*Id.* at 181).[9]

Sec. B. The Constitutional System of Government: In the Words of the Great Justices

The U.S. Constitution, as described in Section A.3 above, establishes a system of government and a structure for implementing this system. Undergirding the system and structure are a number of basic concepts that have guided the development of constitutional law. These concepts began to take shape in the debates on the drafting and ratification of the Constitution[10] and the Bill of Rights.[11] The arguments for ratification in the *Federalist Papers*, for example, contained conceptual analyses of many aspects of the original Constitution. After ratification of the Constitution, and the Bill of Rights, these concepts were further developed in leading U.S. Supreme Court cases. The opinions in these cases—the words of the Justices themselves—are the most authoritative statements of basic constitutional concepts. Key passages are highlighted in this section. Among the concepts developed in these excerpts are: (1) the "People," as the original source of the Constitution; (2) sovereignty, as lodged in both the federal government and the states; (3) "enumerated" and "limited" powers; (4) separation of powers (*i.e.*, the allocation of constitutional powers among the three branches of the federal government); (5) federalism (*i.e.*, the role of the states and state constitutions in the federal constitutional system; (6) supremacy; and (7) individual rights, and the constitutional role of the Bill of Rights and the post-Civil War amendments (Amends. 13, 14, and 15). In addressing these concepts, or principles, the excerpts below provide fur-

---

9. In the newer constitutions of the world, ratified since the late 1980s, there does appear to be a trend toward building in more of the characteristics of hard law. In many of these newer constitutions, however, a single court—usually called the Constitutional Court—is assigned the function of adjudicating all constitutional issues. *See, e.g.*, Rett Ludwikowski, CONSTITUTION–MAKING IN THE REGION OF FORMER SOVIET DOMINANCE, pp. 210–215 (Duke University Press, 1996). This centralized system contrasts with the American decentralized system in which all federal and state courts may usually rule on federal constitutional issues. To check out texts of the constitutions of other countries, see *The Constitution Finder*, <http://confinder.richmond.edu>.

10. For the original debate on the Constitution, and original understandings of American government and the American constitutional system, the Federalist Papers and the Anti-Federalist Papers are the best resource. A good edition of the former to use is George Carey and James McClellan (eds.), THE FEDERALIST: THE GIDEON EDITION, Carey and McClellan, eds. (Liberty Fund, 2001). A good edition of the latter to use is Herbert Storing (ed.), THE COMPLETE ANTI-FEDERALIST (U. Chicago Press, 1981).

11. For an overview of the drafting and ratification of the Bill of Rights, including the debates that were part of the drafting and ratification of the original Constitution, see Daniel Farber & Suzanna Sherry, A HISTORY OF THE AMERICAN CONSTITUTION, ch. 8 (West Pub. Co., 1990).

ther support and explication of the Constitution's theoretical underpinnings developed in Section A above.

1. Chief Justice John Marshall in *Marbury v. Madison*, 5 U.S. (1 Cranch) 137, 176–177 (1803):

> That the people have an original right to establish, for their future government, such principles as, in their opinion, shall most conduce to their own happiness, is the basis, on which the whole American fabric has been erected. The exercise of this original right is a very great exertion; nor can it, nor ought it to be frequently repeated. The principles, therefore, so established, are deemed fundamental. And as the authority, from which they proceed, is supreme, and can seldom act, they are designed to be permanent.

> This original and supreme will organizes the government, and assigns, to different departments, their respective powers. It may either stop here; or establish certain limits not to be transcended by those departments.

> The government of the United States is of the latter description. The powers of the legislature are defined, and limited; and that those limits may not be mistaken, or forgotten, the constitution is written. To what purpose are powers limited, and to what purpose is that limitation committed to writing, if these limits may, at any time, be passed by those intended to be restrained? The distinction between a government with limited and unlimited powers is abolished, if those limits do not confine the persons on whom they are imposed, and if acts prohibited and acts allowed, are of equal obligation. It is a proposition too plain to be contested, that the constitution controls any legislative act repugnant to it; or, that the legislature may alter the constitution by an ordinary act.

> Between these alternatives there is no middle ground. The constitution is either a superior, paramount law, unchangeable by ordinary means, or it is on a level with ordinary legislative acts, and, like other acts, is alterable when the legislature shall please to alter it.

> If the former part of the alternative be true, then a legislative act contrary to the constitution is not law: if the latter part be true, then written constitutions are absurd attempts, on the part of the people, to limit a power in its own nature illimitable.

> Certainly all those who have framed written constitutions contemplate them as forming the fundamental and paramount law of the nation, and consequently, the theory of every such government must be, that an act of the legislature, repugnant to the constitution, is void.

> This theory is essentially attached to a written constitution, and is, consequently, to be considered, by this court, as one of the fundamental principles of our society.

2. Justice Joseph Story in *Martin v. Hunter's Lessee*, 14 U.S. (1 Wheat.) 304, 324–26 (1816):

The constitution of the United States was ordained and established, not by the states in their sovereign capacities, but emphatically, as the preamble of the constitution declares, by "the people of the United States." There can be no doubt that it was competent to the people to invest the general government with all the powers which they might deem proper and necessary; to extend or restrain these powers according to their own good pleasure, and to give them a paramount and supreme authority. As little doubt can there be, that the people had a right to prohibit to the states the exercise of any powers which were, in their judgment, incompatible with the objects of the general compact; to make the powers of the state governments, in given cases, subordinate to those of the nation, or to reserve to themselves those sovereign authorities which they might not choose to delegate to either. The constitution was not, therefore, necessarily carved out of existing state sovereignties, nor a surrender of powers already existing in state institutions, for the powers of the states depend upon their own constitutions; and the people of every state had the right to modify and restrain them, according to their own views of policy or principle. On the other hand, it is perfectly clear that the sovereign powers vested in the state governments, by their respective constitutions, remained unaltered and unimpaired, except so far as they were granted to the government of the United States.

These deductions do not rest upon general reasoning, plain and obvious as they seem to be. They have been positively recognized by one of the articles in amendment of the constitution [the 10th Amendment], which declares, that "the powers not delegated to the United States by the constitution, nor prohibited by it to the states, are reserved to the *states* respectively, or *to the people.*

3. Chief Justice John Marshall in *McCulloch v. Maryland*, 17 U.S. (4 Wheat.) 316, 403–406 (1819):

The government proceeds directly from the people; is "ordained and established" in the name of the people; and is declared to be ordained, "in order to form a more perfect union, establish justice, insure domestic tranquility, and secure the blessings of liberty to themselves and to their posterity." The assent of the States, in their sovereign capacity, is implied in calling a Convention and thus submitting that instrument to the people. But the people were at perfect liberty to accept or reject it; and their act was final. It required not the affirmance, and could not be negatived, by the State governments. The constitution, when thus adopted, was of complete obligation, and bound the State sovereignties.

It has been said, that the people had already surrendered all their powers to the State sovereignties, and had nothing more to give. But, surely, the question whether they may resume and modify the powers granted to government does not remain to be settled in this country. Much more might the legitimacy of the general government be doubted, had it been created by the States. The powers delegated to the State sovereignties were to be exercised by themselves, not by a distinct and independent sovereignty, created by themselves. To the formation of the league, such as was the confederation, the State sovereignties were certainly competent. But when, "in order to form a more perfect union," it was deemed necessary to change this alliance into an effective government, possessing great and sovereign powers, and acting directly on the people, the necessity of referring it to the people, and of deriving its powers directly from them, was felt and acknowledged by all.

The government of the Union, then…, is emphatically, and truly, a government of the people. In form and in substance it emanates from them. Its powers are granted by them, and are to be exercised directly on them, and for their benefit.

This government is acknowledged by all to be one of enumerated powers. The principle, that it can exercise only the powers granted to it, would seem too apparent to have required to be enforced by all those arguments which its enlightened friends, while it was depending before the people, found it necessary to urge. That principle is now universally admitted. But the question respecting the extent of the powers actually granted, is perpetually arising, and will probably continue to arise, as long as our system shall exist.

* * *

If any one proposition could command the universal assent of mankind, we might expect it would be this—that the government of the Union, though limited in its powers, is supreme within its sphere of action. This would seem to result necessarily from its nature. It is the government of all; its powers are delegated by all; it represents all, and acts for all. Though any one State may be willing to control its operations, no State is willing to allow others to control them. The nation, on those subjects on which it can act, must necessarily bind its component parts. But this question is not left to mere reason: the people have, in express terms, decided it, by saying, "this constitution, and the laws of the United States which shall be made in pursuance thereof," "shall be the supreme law of the land" [Art. VI, ¶2], and by requiring that the members of the State legislatures, and the officers of the executive and judicial departments of the States, shall take the oath of fidelity to it [Art. VI, ¶3].

The government of the United States, then, though limited in its powers, is supreme; and its laws, when made in pursuance of the constitution, form the supreme law of the land, "anything in the constitution or laws of any State to the contrary notwithstanding" [Art. VI, ¶2].

4. Chief Justice John Marshall in *Barron v. City of Baltimore*, 32 U.S. (7 Pet.) 243, 247, 250 (1833):

The constitution was ordained and established by the people of the United States for themselves, for their own government, and not for the government of the individual states. Each state established a constitution for itself, and, in that constitution, provided such limitations and restrictions on the powers of its particular government as its judgment dictated. The people of the United

States framed such a government for the United States as they supposed best adapted to their situation, and best calculated to promote their interests. The powers they conferred on this government were to be exercised by itself; and the limitations on power, if expressed in general terms, are naturally, and, we think, necessarily applicable to the government created by the instrument. They are limitations of power, granted in the instrument itself.

* * *

But it is universally understood, it is a part of the history of the day, that the great revolution which established the constitution of the United States, was not effected without immense opposition. Serious fears were extensively entertained that those powers which the patriot statesmen, who then watched over the interests of our country, deemed essential to union, and to the attainment of those invaluable objects for which union was sought, might be exercised in a manner dangerous to liberty. In almost every convention by which the constitution was adopted, amendments to guard against the abuse of power were recommended. These amendments demanded security against the apprehended encroachments of the general government.... In compliance with a sentiment thus generally expressed, to quiet fears thus extensively entertained, amendments were proposed by the required majority in congress, and adopted by the states.[12]

5. Justice William Strong in *Ex Parte Virginia*, 100 U.S. 339, 345–346 (1879):

[The post-Civil War amendments][13] were intended to be, what they really are, limitations of the power of the States and enlargements of the power of Congress. They are to some extent declaratory of rights, and though in form prohibitions, they imply immunities, such as may be protected by congressional legislation.

* * *

[E]nforcement [of these amendments] is no invasion of State sovereignty.... [I]n exercising her rights, a State cannot disregard the limitations which the Federal Constitution has applied to her power. Her rights do not reach to that extent. Nor can she deny to the general government the right to exercise all its granted powers, though they may interfere with the full enjoyment of rights she would have if those powers had not been thus granted. Indeed, every addition of power to the general government involves a corresponding diminution of the governmental powers of the States....

6. Justice Louis Brandeis in *Whitney v. California*, 274 U.S. 357, 375–377 (1927):

[A]ll fundamental rights comprised within the term liberty are protected by the federal Constitution from invasion by the states. The right of free speech, the right to teach and the right of assembly are, of course, fundamental

---

12. The reference here is to the Bill of Rights, that is, the first ten Amendments, and particularly Amendments 1–8.

13. The reference is to the 13th, 14th, and 15th Amendments.

rights.... These may not be denied or abridged. But, although the rights of free speech and assembly are fundamental, they are not in their nature absolute. Their exercise is subject to restriction, if the particular restriction proposed is required in order to protect the state from destruction or from serious injury, political, economic or moral....

* * *

[W]e must bear in mind why a state is, ordinarily, denied the power to prohibit dissemination of social, economic and political doctrine which a vast majority of its citizens believes to be false and fraught with evil consequence.

Those who won our independence believed that the final end of the state was to make men free to develop their faculties, and that in its government the deliberative forces should prevail over the arbitrary. They valued liberty both as an end and as a means. They believed liberty to be the secret of happiness and courage to be the secret of liberty.... They recognized the risks to which all human institutions are subject. But they knew that order cannot be secured merely through fear of punishment for its infraction; that it is hazardous to discourage thought, hope and imagination; that fear breeds repression; that repression breeds hate; that hate menaces stable government; that the path of safety lies in the opportunity to discuss freely supposed grievances and proposed remedies; and that the fitting remedy for evil counsels is good ones. Believing in the power of reason as applied through public discussion, they eschewed silence coerced by law—the argument of force in its worst form. Recognizing the occasional tyrannies of governing majorities, they amended the Constitution so that free speech and assembly should be guaranteed.

7. Justice Robert Jackson in *West Virginia St. Bd. of Education v. Barnette*, 319 U.S. 624, 638, 639–40 (1943):

The very purpose of a Bill of Rights was to withdraw certain subjects from the vicissitudes of political controversy, to place them beyond the reach of majorities and officials and to establish them as legal principles to be applied by the courts. One's right to life, liberty, and property, to free speech, a free press, freedom of worship and assembly, and other fundamental rights may not be submitted to vote; they depend on the outcome of no elections.

* * *

[T]he task of translating the majestic generalities of the Bill of Rights, conceived as part of the pattern of liberal government in the eighteenth century, into concrete restraints on officials dealing with the problems of the twentieth century, is one to disturb self-confidence. These principles grew in soil which also produced a philosophy that the individual was the center of society, that his liberty was attainable through mere absence of governmental restraints, and that government should be entrusted with few controls and only the mildest supervision over men's affairs. We must transplant these rights to a soil in which the *laissez-faire* concept or principle of non-interference has withered at least as to economic affairs, and social advancements are increasingly sought through closer integration of society and through expanded and strengthened governmental controls.

Sec. C. The Distinction Between Constitutional Powers and Constitutional Rights

As Section A.3 above indicates, two of the Constitution's basic functions are to *grant* power, and to *limit* power. Some provisions of the Constitution primarily serve the first function, and others primarily serve the second. Provisions of the first type may be called "empowerment" or "power" provisions; an example would be the commerce clause in Article I, section 8, paragraph 3. Provisions of the second type may be called "limitation" provisions, the most common form of which is the "rights" provision— for example the free speech clause in the First Amendment. These two basic types of constitutional clauses give rise to the two basic types of issues in constitutional law: power issues, which concern application of the first type of provision (see Chapters 5 through 8 of this book); and limitation issues, which concern application of the second type of provision. There are two types of limitation issues. First and foremost are the rights issues that arise from the Constitution's individual rights provisions (see Chapters 10 through 13 of this book). Second are the limitation issues that arise from the power provisions themselves; an example is the implicit limitation that the commerce clause places on state power to regulate commerce (see Chapter 7 of this book).

It is necessary to study "powers" and "rights" as constitutional law concepts whose meaning may differ from that which these terms may have in other fields of law, as well as from the meaning that these terms may have to a lay person. A "power," in constitutional law, means a power *of government*, not a power of private individuals or corporations. It may be a power that a particular branch or level of government has over some other branch or level of government, or a power that a particular branch or level of government has over private individuals or corporations. A "right," in contrast, means a right *of private individuals or corporations*; governments generally do not have constitutional rights. Individuals and corporations may assert their constitutional rights *against government* in order to protect themselves against invasive exercises of government power. But individuals and corporations may not assert constitutional rights against other private individuals or corporations,[14] since constitutional rights limit only government actions, and not the actions of private actors.

In the text of the Constitution, constitutional *powers* are occasionally phrased as constitutional *duties*. Congress has a duty, for example, to provide for a census (or

---

14. There is one exception: The Thirteenth Amendment creates "anti-slavery" rights that private individuals may assert against other private individuals or corporations.

"Enumeration") every ten years (Art. I, sec. 2, ¶ 3); the President has a duty to faithfully execute the laws (Art. II, sec. 3); and "the United States" has a duty to "guarantee…a Republican Form of Government" for each of the states (Art. IV, sec. 4). Even though the duty may not be accompanied by an express grant of power to fulfill the duty, such power is implicit in the duty itself. Congress, for instance, may enact laws which are "necessary and proper as means to carry into effect…duties expressly enjoined" upon it by the Constitution. "[T]he power flows as a necessary means to accomplish the end." (*Prigg v. Commonwealth of Pennsylvania*, 41 U.S. (16 Pet.) 539, 618-619 (1842).)[15] The general principle, then, is that when the Constitution assigns a "duty" to the federal government, "the ability to perform it is contemplated to exist, on the part of the functionaries to whom it is intrusted" (*Id.* at 615). Thus the difference between a constitutional power unaccompanied by a duty, and a constitutional power to fulfill a duty, is simply that the former is discretionary while the latter is mandatory. "The national government…*is bound*, through its own proper departments, legislative, judicial, or executive, as the case may require, to carry into effect all the…*duties* imposed upon it by the [C]onstitution" (*Id.* at 616; emphasis added).[16]

For the federal government, there is a necessary interrelationship between the Constitution's power clauses and its rights clauses. A branch or agency of the federal government may or may not have power, under one of the power clauses, to undertake a particular action. If it did not have such power, the action would be unconstitutional. If the government branch or agency did have power, the action could nevertheless be unconstitutional if the power were exercised in such a way as to violate a rights clause. Congress may have power under the commerce clause to regulate the sale of newspapers across state lines, for example, but if Congress exercised this power by regulating the content of newspapers, the regulation would be unconstitutional under the First Amendment's speech and press clauses.

Thus an act of the federal government may be challenged in two basic ways: (1) that it is beyond the scope of the federal government's constitutional powers (legislative, executive, or judicial, as the case may be); and (2) that it violates an individual rights

---

15. The same principle may apply to Congress' power to enforce individual rights granted by the federal Constitution (see *Prigg*, 41 U.S. at 615-620). In *Prigg*, Justice Story used the example of the habeas corpus clause (Art. I, sec. 9, ¶ 2) to make this point. "No express power is given to [C]ongress to secure this invaluable right," said Story, yet such power is "deemed, by necessary implication, within the scope of the legislative power of [C]ongress" (41 U.S. at 619-620). For some other constitutional rights, however, in particular those in the Thirteenth, Fourteenth, and Fifteenth Amendments, the constitutional text expressly grants Congress the power to enforce the right (see Chap. 6, Sec. E).

16. Constitutional duties—or what are sometimes called mandates—are more prominent in state constitutions and state constitutional law than in the federal Constitution and federal constitutional law. It is common, for instance, for state constitutions to assign to the legislature a duty to maintain a state-wide system of free public education. State constitutions may also authorize the legislature to impose duties or mandates on local governments.

guarantee or otherwise transgresses some limitation that the Constitution imposes upon the exercise of federal power. An act of a state or local government, however, may be challenged only in the second way: that it violates individual rights or otherwise transgresses some limitation (especially a federalistic limit as discussed in Chapter 7) that the Constitution imposes on the exercise of state and local power.

When the governmental act being challenged is a statute or other written law or policy, the challenge may be either a "facial" challenge or an "as applied" challenge. In the former situation, the law is challenged "on its face" and in its entirety; in the latter situation, it is challenged only as applied to particular persons and particular sets of circumstances. *See, e.g., Maryland v. Munson*, 467 U.S. 947, 965–968 (1984); *Members of City Council of Los Angeles v. Taxpayers for Vincent*, 466 U.S. 789, 796–797 (1984). *Bowen v. Kendrick*, 487 U.S. 589 (1988), illustrates the distinction. The case concerned the federal Adolescent Family Life Act, 42 U.S.C. § 300z *et. seq.*, which authorizes grants to public and private organizations, including religiously affiliated organizations, for counseling adolescents on sexual relations and pregnancy. The plaintiffs challenged the Act's coverage of religious organizations as a violation of the establishment clause (see Chap. 13, Sec. B). The U.S. Supreme Court, like the district court, considered both facial and as applied challenges to the Act. The Supreme Court held that the Act's provisions covering religious organizations were constitutional on their face. But it remanded the case for further proceedings on whether these provisions were unconstitutional as applied to particular grants that funded activities involving particular risks of promoting religion.

There are some provisions in the Constitution that do not fall neatly into either the powers category or the rights category. These are the "housekeeping provisions" (Alexander Bickel, THE LEAST DANGEROUS BRANCH, p. 36 (Yale Univ. Press, 2nd ed. 1986)) — those governing the internal operations of the respective branches and establishing the mechanisms through which the government operates. Examples would include Article I, section 2, paragraphs 1–3, which establish the electoral system for House members; Article I, section 2, paragraph 5; Article I, section 3, paragraphs 6 and 7; and Article III, section 2, paragraph 3, which govern impeachment; Article I, section 3, paragraph 4, which makes the Vice President the President of the Senate; Article I, section 5, paragraph 4, which establishes rules for the adjournment of Congress; Article II, section 1, paragraphs 2 and 3, and the Twelfth Amendment, which provide for the operation of the Electoral College; and Article II, section 1, paragraph 5, and the Twenty-second Amendment, which establish qualifications for eligibility for the Office of President. Although such clauses are as important as the power and rights clauses, they are seldom litigated and are discussed only infrequently in most constitutional law courses.

The Constitution's power and rights provisions do not simply empower and limit "the Government of the United States" as such. Thus, just as it is important to determine whether a particular provision is a power or a rights provision, it is equally important to determine what officials or entities (*e.g.,* Congress? the lower federal courts? federal administrative agencies? the states?) are empowered or limited by each such provision. These and other matters concerning power clauses and rights clauses are the subject of section D below.

Sec. D. Exercise No. 1: Who Is Empowered and Who is Limited by the Constitution?[17]

Read and study the text of the U.S. Constitution and its amendments, contained in Appendix A at the end of this book. Then, against the backdrop of the materials in Sections A through C above, complete the two tasks listed below as QUES. 1 and QUES. 2. Following these questions, there are answers to each one. When you have completed your work on the questions, the answers will help you test your understanding and will also fill in gaps or uncertainties in your understanding.

Questions

QUES. 1. Working through each provision of the Constitution, determine which provisions are empowerment or power provisions, which are rights or limitation provisions, and which are housekeeping or operational provisions. For each power or rights provision that you identify, determine who (what official or entity) is empowered or limited by that provision. Give particular attention, by way of illustration, to Article I, section 8, clause 3 (the commerce clause); Article I, section 10, paragraph 1; Article III, section 1, sentence 1; the Tenth Amendment; the Fourteenth Amendment, section 1, sentence 2; and the Fourteenth Amendment, section 5.

QUES. 2. Consider the following list:

a) Congress (both houses together);
b) the Senate and the House of Representatives (each house separate from the other);
c) the President;
d) the Vice-President;
e) the U.S. Supreme Court;
f) lower federal courts;
g) federal administrative agencies;
h) the states (including their legislative, executive, and judicial branches);
i) local governments (counties, cities, towns, school districts, etc.);
j) individuals, either persons in their private capacities or private corporations;
k) the "People."

Which of the officials or entities on this list are directly empowered by the Constitution, and how so? Which are directly limited (in particular by rights provisions), and how so? If an official or entity on the list is neither directly empowered nor directly limited by the Constitution, what status does that official or entity have under the Constitution?

---

17. This exercise was inspired by an exercise included in Paul Brest, PROCESSES OF CONSTITUTIONAL DECISIONMAKING, p. 10 (Little, Brown, 1st ed., 1975).

Answers

ANS. to QUES. 1. Article I, section 8, clause 3; Article III, section 1, sentence 1; and Amendment 14, section 5 are empowerment provisions. Article I, section 8, clause 3 empowers Congress by authorizing it to regulate three types of commerce: foreign commerce, interstate commerce, and commerce with "the Indian Tribes." Article III, section 1, sentence 1 empowers the U.S. Supreme Court by vesting it with "the judicial power"; this clause also empowers Congress to vest some of the judicial power in lower federal courts. Amendment 14, section 5 empowers Congress to enforce the preceding provisions of that amendment, in particular the rights provisions in section 1, sentence 2. Article I, section 10, paragraph 1 is a limitation provision that limits the states. Some of the limitations are stated in terms of individual rights—the bill of attainder clause, the ex post facto clause, and the contracts clause—which are among the few rights provisions in the original (1787) Constitution. The Tenth Amendment is a type of limitation provision; it affirms that the federal government is a government of delegated and limited powers, and it reserves power for (but does not grant power to) the states (*see* especially excerpt 2 in section B above, where Justice Story sets forth the propositions about state power that may be deduced from the Tenth Amendment.) The Fourteenth Amendment, section 1, sentence 2 is a rights provision ; it contains three rights clauses that form the core of the post-Civil War amendments. These rights clauses—the "privileges or immunities" clause, the "due process" clause, and the "equal protection" clause—limit the states by creating rights enforceable against them.

Other major power provisions are in other clauses of Article I, section 8; and in Article II, sections 2 & 3. Other major rights provisions are in the first eight amendments in the Bill of Rights and in the Thirteenth and Fifteenth Amendments. Examples of housekeeping clauses are in Section C above.

ANS. to QUES. 2. Regarding powers, all the following entities are directly empowered by the Constitution: Congress; the Senate and House individually, to a small extent (*e.g.*, the Senate's advise and consent power over treaties in Article II, section 2, paragraph 2); the President; and the U. S. Supreme Court. The lower federal courts are provided for in the Constitution (in Article I, section 8, paragraph 9, and Article III, section 1), but the Constitution does not itself directly create or empower these courts (as it does the U.S. Supreme Court). Rather, the constitutional provisions on lower federal courts authorize Congress to create these courts and, within the constraints of Article III, to determine their jurisdiction.

Administrative agencies are recognized by the Constitution, in particular through the references to "Departments" and "Officers" in Article II, section 2, paragraphs 1 and 2; but, like the lower federal courts, administrative agencies are not directly created or empowered by the Constitution. Instead, they may be created by both Congress and the President, acting pursuant to their own enumerated powers. Congress has used its commerce power, for instance, to create the Interstate Commerce Commission. In effect, either branch may delegate a slice of its enumerated power to an administrative agency, which in turn may implement or enforce that power within the guidelines established by the delegating branch.

The states and their local governments are not empowered by the federal Constitution.[18] State powers are granted under state law through the state constitutions. But the states' capacity to have constitutions, establish local governments, and otherwise exercise sovereignty is protected by the federal Constitution, especially the Tenth Amendment. As Justice Story stated in *Martin v. Hunter's Lessee* (excerpt 2 in section B above), "[T]he powers of the states depend upon their own Constitutions; and the people of every state had the right to modify and restrain them, according to their own views of policy or principle." At the same time, however, as Chief Justice Marshall points out in excerpt 3 in Section B above, when states exercise their powers in an area in which the federal Constitution has delegated authority to the federal government, the federal power is "supreme" over that of the states.

Regarding limitations on powers, all of the federal entities just discussed above are directly limited by various of the Constitution's rights provisions, in particular the first eight amendments of the Bill of Rights. The states are also directly limited by various of the Constitution's rights provisions, in particular the Fourteenth Amendment, even though the states are empowered by their own state constitutions rather than the federal Constitution. The federal Constitution, therefore, does *limit* power that it does not *grant*.

The local governments of the states are also directly limited by the federal Constitution, even though they are not mentioned in the Constitution's text. Local governments are created by the states, either directly by the state constitution or by the state legislature acting pursuant to powers granted to it by the state constitution. Local governments are therefore considered part of the state and are limited by the federal Constitution's rights clauses to the same extent as the state is limited.

Although the early case of *Barron v. Mayor and City Council of Baltimore* (excerpt 4 in Section B above) confirmed that the Bill of Rights limits only the federal government, in more recent years the Court has applied most of the Bill of Rights' first eight amendments to the states by incorporating these rights into the Fourteenth Amendment through a process called "selective incorporation." This matter is discussed in Chapter 11, Section A.2 of this book.

Private individuals, with one exception, are neither directly empowered nor directly limited by the Constitution. The exception is the Thirteenth Amendment, a rights provision that limits individuals as well as government. (The Eighteenth Amendment, on "Prohibition," was once also an exception, until repealed by the Twenty-First Amendment.) Individuals, of course, nevertheless play an extremely important role under the

---

18. There is one significant exception to this statement: States are granted certain authority over elections for federal offices, in particular, authority to regulate the times, places, and manner of federal elections (Art. I, sec. 4, cl. 1), to appoint the state's electors for election of the President (Art. II, sec. 1, cl. 2), and authority to fill vacancies in the state's House or Senate seats that occur between elections (Art. I, sec. 2, paragraph 4; Amend. 17, paragraph 2). In the first two situations, the authority is granted specifically to the state's "Legislature," and in the third situation, the authority is granted specifically to the state's "Executive Authority." See Chap. 4, Sec. A.1.

Constitution; they are the *beneficiaries* of the constraints that federalism and separation of powers place upon federal power and, more particularly, the *beneficiaries* of the rights provisions that limit federal and state power. It is individuals, in effect, who "possess" these rights and may assert them as shields against invasive exercises of government power.

The "People" is a theoretical concept referring to the cumulative body of individuals from which the Constitution emerged and through which it is perpetuated by each succeeding generation. In this sense, the "People" is not an entity empowered or limited by the Constitution but rather, as confirmed in the Constitution's Preamble, is the original source of constitutional powers and rights and the reason for their existence. In *Marbury v. Madison* (excerpt 1 in section B above), Chief Justice John Marshall declared the people to be the "original and supreme will." Later, in *McCulloch v. Maryland* (excerpt 3 in Section B above), he emphasized that the federal government established by the Constitution "proceeds directly from the people" and is "declared to be ordained" on their behalf. The federal government's "powers are granted by [the people], and are to be exercised directly on them, and "for their benefit." The *government* and the *People* are therefore not synonymous. The People created the government, and the government's representative branches speak for the People; but the People, conceptually, remain outside the government (*see* Cynthia Farina, "The Consent of the Governed: Against Simple Rules for a Complex World," 72 Chicago-Kent L. Rev. 987, 1007–1018 (1997)). Thus, there is a "just distinction between the sovereignty, and the government…; the former was found to reside in the *People*, and to be unalienable from them; the latter in their *servants* and *agents*… (St. George Tucker, View of the Constitution of the United States (1803) (Liberty Fund edition, p. 104) (Clyde Wilson, ed., 1999).

Sec. E. Interpreting the Constitution: In the Words of the Great Justices

To apply the Constitution's provisions to the myriad, ever-changing circumstances that fall within their domain, interpretation is required. The starting point for considering how to approach and interpret the Constitution as a legal document is the commentary of the U.S. Supreme Court Justices themselves, as highlighted in this section. As you study these excerpts, seek to identify the perspectives and attitudes that the Justices bring to the interpretation of the Constitution, and consider whether and how interpretation of the Constitution differs from interpretation of a statute or a commercial contract.

1. Justice Joseph Story in *Martin v. Hunter's Lessee*, 14 U.S.(1 Wheat.) 304, 326–27 (1816):

> The constitution unavoidably deals in general language. It did not suit the purposes of the people, in framing this great charter of our liberties, to provide for minute specifications of its powers, or to declare the means by which

those powers should be carried into execution. It was foreseen that this would be a perilous and difficult, if not an impracticable, task. The instrument was not intended to provide merely for the exigencies of a few years, but was to endure through a long lapse of ages, the events of which were locked up in the inscrutable purposes of Providence. It could not be foreseen what new changes and modifications of power might be indispensable to effectuate the general objects of the charter; and restrictions and specifications, which, at the present, might seem salutary, might, in the end, prove the overthrow of the system itself. Hence its powers are expressed in general terms, leaving to the legislature, from time to time, to adopt its own means to effectuate legitimate objects, and to mould and model the exercise of its powers, as its own wisdom, and the public interests, should require.

2. Chief Justice John Marshall in *McCulloch v. Maryland*, 17 U.S. (4 Wheat.) 316, 407 (1819):

A constitution, to contain an accurate detail of all the subdivisions of which its great powers will admit, and of all the means by which they may be carried into execution, would partake of the prolixity of a legal code, and could scarcely be embraced by the human mind. It would probably never be understood by the public. Its nature, therefore, requires, that only its great outlines should be marked, its important objects designated, and the minor ingredients which compose those objects be deduced from the nature of the objects themselves. That this idea was entertained by the framers of the American constitution, is not only to be inferred from the nature of the instrument, but from the language.

* * *

It is also, in some degree, warranted by their having omitted to use any restrictive term which might prevent its receiving a fair and just interpretation.... [W]e must never forget, that it is a constitution we are expounding.

3. Chief Justice John Marshall in *Cohens v. Virginia*, 19 U.S. (6 Wheat.) 264, 387 (1821):

But a constitution is framed for ages to come, and is designed to approach immortality as nearly as human institutions can approach it. Its course cannot always be tranquil. It is exposed to storms and tempests, and its framers must be unwise statesmen indeed, if they have not provided it, as far as its nature will permit, with the means of self-preservation from the perils it may be destined to encounter. No government ought to be so defective in its organization, as not to contain within itself the means of securing the execution of its own laws against other dangers than those which occur every day.

4. Justice Oliver Wendell Holmes, Jr. in *Gompers v. United States*, 233 U.S. 604, 610 (1914):

But the provisions of the Constitution are not mathematical formulas having their essence in their form; they are organic living institutions transplanted from English soil. Their significance is vital not formal; it is to be gathered not simply by taking the words and a dictionary, but by considering their origin and the line of their growth (citing *Robertson v. Baldwin*, 165 U.S. 275, 282, (1897)).

5. Justice Oliver Wendell Holmes, Jr. in *Missouri v. Holland*, 252 U.S. 416, 433 (1920):

[W]hen we are dealing with words that also are a constituent act, like the Constitution of the United States, we must realize that they have called into life a being the development of which could not have been foreseen completely by the most gifted of its begetters. It was enough for them to realize or to hope that they had created an organism; it has taken a century and has cost their successors much sweat and blood to prove that they created a nation. The case before us must be considered in the light of our whole experience and not merely in that of what was said a hundred years ago.

6. Justice Rufus Peckham in *Maxwell v. Dow*, 176 U.S. 581, 602 (1900):

The safe way [to construe a constitutional amendment] is to read its language in connection with the known condition of affairs out of which the occasion for its adoption may have arisen, and then to construe it, if there be therein any doubtful expressions, in a way so far as is reasonably possible, to forward the known purpose or object for which the amendment was adopted. This rule could not, of course, be so used as to limit the force and effect of an amendment in a manner which the plain and unambiguous language used therein would not justify or permit.

7. Justice Joseph McKenna in *Weems v. United States*, 217 U.S. 349, 373 (1910) (speaking primarily of rights provisions):

Time works changes, brings into existence new conditions and purposes. Therefore a principle to be vital must be capable of wider application than the mischief which gave it birth. This is peculiarly true of constitutions. They are not ephemeral enactments, designed to meet passing occasions. They are, to use the words of Chief Justice Marshall, "designed to approach immortality as nearly as human institutions can approach it." The future is their care and provision for events of good and bad tendencies of which no prophecy can be made. In the application of a constitution, therefore, our contemplation cannot be only of what has been, but of what may be.

8. Justice Felix Frankfurter in *Rochin v. California*, 342 U.S. 165, 169–170 (1952):

In dealing not with the machinery of government but with human rights, the absence of formal exactitude, or want of fixity of meaning, is not an unusual or even regrettable attribute of constitutional provisions. Words being symbols do not speak without a gloss. On the one hand, the gloss may be the deposit of history, whereby a term gains technical content.... On the other hand, the gloss of some of the verbal symbols of the Constitution does not give them a fixed technical content. It exacts a continuing process of application.

When the gloss has thus not been fixed but is a function of the process of judgment, the judgment is bound to fall differently at different times and differently at the same time through different judges.

9. Justice John M. Harlan (dissenting) in *Poe v. Ullman*, 367 U.S. 497, 539–540 (1961):

> But precisely because it is the Constitution alone which warrants judicial interference in sovereign operations of the State, the basis of judgment as to the Constitutionality of state action must be a rational one, approaching the text which is the only commission for our power not in a literalistic way, as if we had a tax statute before us, but as the basic charter of our society, setting out in spare but meaningful terms the principles of government (citing *McCulloch v. Maryland*, 17 U.S. (4 Wheat.) 316, 407 (1819)).

Sec. F. A First Look at the Process of Constitutional Interpretation

F.1. Overview

The process of constitutional interpretation is the process by which interpreters apply the Constitution to, and thereby resolve, particular problems regarding the scope and allocation of government power and the rights of individuals. There are two foundational questions to ask about this process: *who* are the "official" interpreters of the Constitution, and *how* do these interpreters undertake to interpret the Constitution? The two questions are interrelated, such that exploration of the "how" question will at points intersect exploration of the "who" question. The "who" question is addressed in Chapter 5, especially Section C; a first look at the "how" question is presented here.

Since the late 1950s, and especially since the 1980s, scholars and jurists have continually expanded the theoretical scholarship on how to interpret the Constitution. What in older times was a debate about strict versus liberal construction of the Constitution, or about judicial restraint versus judicial activism, has given way to a more helpful and sophisticated debate about sources for constitutional interpretation and the interpretive approaches that emerge from these sources. These sources and approaches are introduced in Sections F.2 and F.3 below.

F.2. Sources of Constitutional Interpretation

In law, as in other disciplines concerned with interpretation, the sources of interpretation may be classified as either primary or secondary. Primary sources in law are the root sources—the original raw materials from which all interpretation derives. Each such source must stake its own claim to legitimacy. Secondary sources in law are those derived from the primary sources. Their legitimacy depends on the legitimacy of the primary sources on which they are based.

There are four sources that plausibly qualify as primary sources for constitutional interpreters to consult. These four sources are (1) the constitutional text, (2) original constitutional history, (3) the overall structure of the Constitution and the inferences that may be drawn from this structure; and (4) the values that are embedded in or reflected in the

Constitution. Although most commentators would acknowledge the legitimacy of the first three interpretive sources (text, history, structure), and many would acknowledge the legitimacy of the fourth (values), there is no consensus on the appropriate use of these sources. Just as there are strict and liberal "textualists," for instance, there are strict and moderate "originalists" (users of original constitutional history); and there are values interpreters who would substantially confine their identification and use of values (sometimes called "supplementers") as well as those who would engage in wide-ranging explorations of moral goodness (sometimes called "noninterpretivists"). Nevertheless, each of these four sources is represented in opinions of the United States Supreme Court, and each is reflected in the evolutionary growth of constitutional law. Taken together, these four sources provide an appropriate basis for a model of constitutional interpretation.

The major secondary source for constitutional interpretation is precedent. Precedents are derived over time from the four primary sources. Precedents are more concrete than the primary sources and are more frequently utilized in modern interpretation. They are the lawyer's (and the student's) day-to-day tools of the trade. The most accessible and most utilized body of precedent, of course, is that which courts develop on a case-by-case basis and adhere to under the doctrine of "stare decisis."[19] Precedent, however, may also be developed by other constitutional interpreters. The Congress may create precedent, for example, when it accepts or rejects a bill provision partly on the basis of documented constitutional issues; a President may create precedent when vetoing a bill for constitutional reasons; or an attorney general of the United States or of a state may create precedent when releasing a legal opinion advising another government official about certain constitutional issues.

A type of precedent may also be created when the Congress or the Executive has, over a long period of time, implemented or applied a constitutional clause in a particular way, or consistently acquiesced in the other branch's implementation or application. (See, for example, the discussion of Justice Frankfurter's historical gloss theory in Chapter 7, Sections A and D.1.) The same principles may also apply to the consistent application of a particular clause by the state governors, or the consistent acquiescence of the state governors in a particular constitutional interpretation of the Congress or the Executive. In *Prigg v. Commonwealth of Pennsylvania*, 41 U.S. (16 Pet.) 539, 620-621 (1842), for instance, as the Court was interpreting the fugitive-from-justice clause (Art. IV, sec. 2, ¶ 2), it declared that "every executive in the Union has constantly acted upon and admitted [the] validity" of a federal law implementing the clause; and that [t]his very acquiescence...of the highest state functionaries, is a most decisive proof...that the act is founded in a just construction of the [C]onstitution."

F.3.   Approaches to Constitutional Interpretation

From the four primary sources of constitutional interpretation emerge four interpretive approaches or methodologies for deriving meaning from the Constitution: the

---

19. Latin for "to stand by things decided." See Chap. 3, Sec. A, and Chap. 15, Sec. B.2.

textual approach, the historical approach, the structural approach, and the values approach. These four approaches, in turn, provide the basis for four generic types of constitutional argument: arguments from text, arguments from history, arguments from structure, and arguments from values. The first approach, textual interpretation, is the starting point for most interpretive efforts. It is discussed immediately below. The other three approaches, which are subordinate to the text, are discussed in later chapters (Chap. 4, Sec. C, Chap. 9, Sec. B, and Chap. 15, Sec. D). No one of these other three approaches—historical interpretation, structural interpretation, and values interpretation—controls or has priority over the other two. Instead, these approaches are often used in combination with each other and with the textual approach. The applicability and utility of each approach will depend on the constitutional provision that is being interpreted and the particular problem being addressed.

In the world of modern law study and practice, of course, interpretation will usually begin with and proceed from judicial precedents, a secondary source, rather than the primary sources of history, structure, and values (see Section F.2 above). In other words, the "precedential approach" will usually be the predominant modern approach to constitutional interpretation and problem-solving. But even when this approach is followed, text, history, structure, and values can still be pertinent considerations. An argument drawn from precedent may be more forceful when couched as an argument based on the constitutional text, or on original history, structural inference, or constitutional values. Particular judicial precedents may be understood more completely when they are viewed from the perspective of the constitutional text that the court addresses, the original history that the court finds pertinent, the inferences that the court draws from the Constitution's structure, or the constitutional values that the court identifies and applies to the issue at hand. And particular precedents may be critiqued more persuasively by considering whether the court made appropriate use of text, history, structure, and values and had suitable support for any statements it made concerning these sources.[20] (Chapter 3 below includes further discussion on analyzing judicial precedents.)

F.4. The Starting Point: The Textual Approach

The textual approach has its source in the written text of the Constitution. The focus is on the language itself, not on the intentions of the drafters that may lurk behind the language, and the search is for the meaning that words convey to a reader unfamiliar with the drafters' intentions. *See, e.g.,* Randy Barnette, "An Originalism for Nonoriginalists," 45 LOYOLA L. REV. 611 (1999). Although other interpretive sources may be used along with the text, no other source may "supercede [the text's] natural and just inter-

---

20. Although the interpretation of state constitutions must be clearly distinguished from interpretation of the federal Constitution, the sources and approaches set out in this section may nevertheless have parallels in the process of state constitutional interpretation. *See generally,* G. Alan Tarr, UNDERSTANDING STATE CONSTITUTIONS, ch. 6 (Princeton Univ. Press, 1998).

pretation" or otherwise "abrogate the text...." (Joseph Story, COMMENTARIES ON THE CONSTITUTION OF THE UNITED STATES, vol. I, §§ 406–407 (5th ed., Melville Bigelow, ed.) (William S. Hein and Co., 1994)).

The promise of the textual approach lies in the common core of meaning that particular usages of particular words and phrases may convey. At least some words and phrases, it is argued, are sufficiently clear that almost everyone would agree on their meaning in at least some of their applications. Common examples include the numerical phrases in the Constitution, such as the clause specifying that a person must be at least 35 years of age to be eligible for the Presidency (Art. II, sec. 1, ¶ 5). Other words and phrases, although less clear, nevertheless convey sufficient sense to narrow the range of possible meanings that they could have in concrete situations; thus, to a lesser extent and in varying degrees, such language also constrains the interpreter. One prominent example is the word "person" in the Fourteenth Amendment, which the U.S. Supreme Court, using a textual approach, has construed to exclude the unborn. *Roe v. Wade*, 410 U.S. 113, 156–59 (1973).

Even with the text itself, however, numerous interpretive challenges arise. Some words, for example, may have technical as well as common sense meanings, or literal as well as figurative meanings. Ready examples of the former include the words "privileges" and "immunities" as used in Article IV, section 2, and in the Fourteenth Amendment, Section 1; the word "speech" as used in the First Amendment; and the word "Jury" as used in the Sixth Amendment. Ready examples of the latter include the word "necessary" in the necessary and proper clause (Art. I, sec. 8, cl. 18), the word "papers" in the Fourth Amendment, the phrase "life and limb" in the Fifth Amendment's double jeopardy clause, the word "writings" in the copyright clause (Art. I, sec. 8, cl. 8), and the word "coin" in the clause authorizing Congress to establish a monetary system (Art. I, sec. 8, cl. 5). Constitutional words that share such double meanings may create ambiguities, and the difficulty in determining which meaning to attribute to the word may in turn result in difficulties in interpreting the clause or provision in which the word appears.

Moreover, much language in legal documents, and certainly in the Constitution, is a product of compromise that may reflect or leave room for varying viewpoints. There may be no common viewpoint and no clear single meaning embodied in particular words or phrases chosen by the drafters. The drafters(and certainly the drafters of the Constitution) may also have worked with strongly contested concepts and highly complex ideas that could not be captured precisely in words—thus increasing the interpretive difficulties.

The case of *Department of Commerce v. House of Representatives*, 525 U.S. 316 (1999) provides a modern-day example of a textual interpretation problem. The issue was whether the U.S. Census Bureau (Bureau) could use statistical sampling in the 2000 Census to determine the population of congressional districts for apportionment purposes. The Bureau contended that statistical sampling would rectify chronic "undercounting" of certain identifiable groups, including inner city minorities. Several plaintiffs challenged this planned use of statistical sampling, alleging that it would violate the Census Act (13 U.S.C. § 1 *et seq.*) and would violate the census clause in the U.S.

Constitution: "The actual Enumeration shall be made within three Years after the first Meeting of the Congress of the United States, and within every subsequent Term of ten Years, in such Manner as they shall by Law direct." Justice O'Connor, writing for the majority, held that the Census Act prohibited the planned use of statistical sampling, and did not need to analyze the census clause. In concurring opinions, however, both Justice Scalia and Justice Stevens did examine the clause's text, reaching opposite conclusions concerning the clause's meaning.

For both Justices, the constitutional issue was whether the constitutional text prohibited the planned statistical sampling. Justice Scalia focused on the phrase "actual Enumeration" and concluded that it is "unquestionably doubtful whether the constitutional requirement of an "actual Enumeration," Art. I, § 2, cl. 3, is satisfied by statistical sampling" (*Id.* at 346). To bolster this argument, Scalia relied on the word usage in 18th and 19th century dictionaries. "Dictionaries roughly contemporaneous with the ratification of the Constitution demonstrate than an "enumeration" requires an actual counting, and not just an estimation of number.... The notion of counting "singly," "separately," "number by number," "distinctly," which runs through these definitions is incompatible...with gross statistical estimates" (*Id.* at 346–47). Thus relying on text (and also on early historical practices regarding the census), Justice Scalia concluded that "a strong case can be made that an apportionment census conducted with the use of "sampling techniques" is not the "actual Enumeration" that the Constitution requires" (*Id.* at 349).

Rather than focusing on the literal meaning of an "actual Enumeration," Justice Stevens relied on the full text of the census clause. He found that the text did provide a constitutional basis for the planned statistical sampling. For Justice Stevens, the authority of Congress to choose the "Manner" of the enumeration was dispositive. "The words 'actual Enumeration' require...apportionments to be based on actual population counts, rather than mere speculation or bare estimate, but they do not purport to limit the authority of Congress to direct the 'Manner' in which such counts should be made" (*Id.* at 363).

Then, reading the text in light of the purposes of the census clause, rather than sticking strictly to the words themselves, Justice Stevens reasoned that: "The census is intended to serve 'the constitutional goal of equal representation.' That goal is best served by the use of a 'Manner' that is most likely to be complete and accurate.... Since it is perfectly clear that the use of sampling will make the census more accurate than an admittedly futile attempt to count every individual by personal inspection, interview, or written interrogatory, the proposed method is a legitimate means of making the 'actual Enumeration' that the Constitution commands" (*Id.* at 364).

Three years after the *Department of Commerce* case, in *Utah v. Evans*, 536 U.S. 452 (2002), the Court faced another issue concerning the text of the census clause. For the 2000 census, the Census Bureau had used a methodology called "hot-deck imputation" to resolve certain gaps and conflicts in the information it had collected, and Utah challenged the Bureau's use of this methodology as violative of the Census Act and the Constitution's census clause. This time the Court held that the Census Bureau's practice did not violate the Census Act, and therefore had to address the text of the census clause. The majority, per Justice Breyer, relied on its own reading of the clause's language, and supported its reading with definitions of the word "enumeration" from late 18th century dictionaries, the history of drafting changes made to the clause in the Constitutional Convention, a contrasting use of the word "Enumeration" in another clause of the Constitution (Art. I, sec. 9, ¶ 4), and other usages of this word in other contemporaneous legal documents such as the First Census Act. The majority concluded that the census clause's "text uses a general word, 'enumeration,' that refers to a counting process without describing the count's methodological details," and that the phrase "'in such Manner as' Congress itself 'shall by Law direct,'" suggests "the breadth of congressional methodological authority, rather than its limitation" (536 U.S. at 455). The census clause's text, therefore, did not prohibit the Census Bureau from using its "hot-deck imputation" methodology.

Since constitutional phrases may share double meanings, may be the product of compromise, and may reflect the drafters' struggles with contested concepts and complex ideas that words cannot capture precisely, it would be unrealistic to expect that the Constitution's language can reveal—or that the drafters intended it to reveal—all the contours or content of the concepts and ideas being expressed. To the contrary, much of the Constitution's language may have varying degrees of "open texture" or vagueness within which meaning cannot be specifically determined or must be ascertained by resort to sources other than the language. *See* H.L.A. Hart, THE CONCEPT OF LAW 121–127 (1961). Indeed, the drafters may have made deliberate use of language's open texture, using vague words with no precise and fixed meaning, so as to allow future interpreters a range of discretion in attributing specific meanings to words in unforeseen circumstances.

Sec. G. Exercise No. 2: Textual Interpretation of the Constitution

Although the starting point for interpretation is the provision's express language, as indicated in Section F.4 above, even seemingly specific words may not have clear meaning in all their applications. Some words or phrases may have both technical and common-sense meanings; some words or phrases may have both literal and figurative meanings; some words or phrases may be ambiguous in other ways, conveying two or more definite meanings that are very different from one another. Other words and phrases, moreover, may be vague; they do not convey any definite meaning at all in many or most of their applications.

Because language usage varies from one constitutional provision to another, different provisions pose different problems of interpretation. Some provisions have more unclear applications than others. Some provisions apply to a broader range of situations than others. With the relatively unclear and broad type of provision, of course, it is unlikely that issues concerning its application can be resolved solely by resort to the provision's language. The interpreter may therefore have greater latitude to look elsewhere for meaning than is the case with the narrower and clearer type of provision.

With this information in mind, re–read the U.S. Constitution (in Appendix A at the end of this book) and complete the tasks set out as questions 1–3 below. Following these questions are answers to each one. When you have completed your work on the questions, the answers will help you test your understanding and will also fill in gaps or uncertainties in your understanding.

Questions

QUES. 1. Identify the constitutional provisions that you think have the clearest language, being neither ambiguous nor vague and conveying clear meaning in all or most of their applications.

QUES. 2. Identify the constitutional provisions that you think are the most ambiguous or vague, and therefore convey no definite meaning in many or most of their applications. Concentrate particularly on these provisions as major examples: (a) Article I, section 6, clause 2 (the "ineligibility clause"); (b) Article I, section 8, clause 3 (the commerce clause); (c) Article I, section 9, clause 3 (the bill of attainder clause); and (d) the jury trial clause of the Sixth Amendment. Try to determine what words in these clauses are ambiguous or vague, and describe the ambiguities or vagueness in these words or phrases.

QUES. 3. Speculate on where an interpreter might look (what sources an interpreter might consult) to resolve the ambiguities or vagueness in particular constitutional provisions that you have identified in QUES. 2. Use the same examples as in QUES. 2.

Remember that this is a *preliminary* inquiry into a very complex topic.

Answers

ANS. to QUES. 1. The numerical clauses—those using numbers to specify such matters as age requirements, time limits, and voting majorities—are usually considered to have the clearest meaning and application. Various other housekeeping provisions may also be quite clear in most of their applications. Most power clauses and rights clauses, however, will be vague, or ambiguous, or both, in the bulk of their applications. Generally speaking, vague language is more prevalent in these clauses than ambiguous language and poses greater interpretive problems.

ANS. to QUES. 2. Section F.4 above sets out some examples of ambiguous provisions. Many of the power clauses and rights clauses are vague. The commerce clause is a good example of a vague power provision, and the jury trial clause is a good example of a vague rights provision. The due process clause of the Fourteenth Amendment is probably the best example of all of a vague constitutional provision.

Regarding the examples in QUES. 2: the "ineligibility clause" (Art. I, sec. 6, cl. 2), although seemingly specific and clear on first reading, may be ambiguous in some of its applications. Consider the following sequence of events: (1) Senator X is elected to a six-year term in the United States Senate. (2) The President proposes, and the Senate (and House) approve, raises for all members of the President's cabinet. Senator X votes in favor. (3) After the pay raise becomes effective, the Attorney General of the United

States resigns. (4) The President nominates Senator X to be Attorney General, a cabinet position for which the salary had been raised. (5) To remedy the problem that otherwise would exist under the ineligibility clause, the President proposes legislation that would roll back the Attorney General's salary to what it was at the start of the Senator's term, prior to the recent raise.[21] In that situation, would the phrase "Emoluments (*e.g.*, salary) whereof shall have been increased" in Article I, section 6, clause 2 continue to apply and to prohibit the nomination? The answer would apparently depend on whether the language refers to (1) an historical fact—that the salary had in fact been increased during the Senator's term; or (2) the state of affairs existing at the time that the Attorney General's appointment becomes effective—that the salary at that time was no longer increased. The existence of two such plausible yet conflicting readings of the same language creates the ambiguity.[22]

The bill of attainder clause (Art. I, sec. 9, cl. 3) may also be ambiguous. It may have a technical meaning: the particular type of act that was considered a bill of attainder at the time the Constitution was drafted. It may also have a non-technical or perhaps figurative meaning: any legislative act that would have effects similar to and create evils similar to what were originally understood to be bills of attainder, regardless of whether such an act could fit the technical, historical definition of a bill of attainder.

The commerce clause (Art. I, sec. 8, cl. 3) is both vague and ambiguous. Does the term "commerce" cover transportation systems, *e.g.*, navigation by boat? Does it cover the movement of people as opposed to goods? Does the phrase "among the several states" mean commerce involving *all* the states, or *three or more* states, or *more than one* state? At what point does a transaction originating in one state become commerce "among the states," and at what point does it cease to be commerce "among the states"? Does "commerce" include only transactions having a commercial or profit-making objective, or do non-commercial transactions fit within this term as well? Must transactions have an economic purpose or have economic effects in order to be considered "commerce"?

The Sixth Amendment's jury trial clause is vague. What is a "jury"? For example, how many people must be in the group before it will be considered a jury: twelve? six? three? By what vote must such a group arrive at its decisions: unanimous? two-thirds? majority? In what kinds of cases must there be a jury: capital cases only? felony cases only? all criminal cases? *See, e.g.*, *Williams v. Florida*, 399 U.S. 78, 86–103 (White, J., for the majority) and 122–126 (Harlan, J., concurring), which analyzes the question concerning the size of a Sixth Amendment jury.

ANS. to QUES. 3. If the text is ambiguous or vague as applied to the particular problem at issue, resort may be made to one or a combination of the other three primary sources of interpretation: original history, structural inferences, and constitutional values (see Chap. 4, Sec. C and Chap. 9, Sec. B). In *Williams v. Florida* (above), for in-

---

21. These events parallel real life events that occurred between 1969 and 1973 when President Nixon nominated Senator William Saxbe of Ohio to be the Attorney General.

22. This example is discussed at length in Paul Brest, Processes of Constitutional Decisionmaking, pp. 15–31 (Little, Brown, 1st ed. 1975).

stance, the majority and concurring justices consulted historical practices concerning juries in English common law in an attempt to bring further meaning to the word "jury." A showing that the text is vague or ambiguous, as applied to the particular problem at hand, is a prerequisite to the use of history, structure, and values as interpretive sources.

Chapter 3

Judicial Opinions on Constitutional Law Issues

Sec. A. The Judicial Opinion As a Legal Document

A judicial opinion is a particular kind of legal document, drafted by a judge and is-sued by a court in order to resolve a lawsuit, to dispose of particular issues arising in on-going litigation, or to concur in or dissent from the resolution or disposition of other judges. The published opinion of a trial-level court, or of the majority of an ap-pellate court, becomes an authoritative precedent binding on that court and other lower courts in that jurisdiction. *See generally* Frederick Schauer, "Precedent," 39 STAN-FORD L. REV. 571 (1987). The published majority opinions of the U.S. Supreme Court become authoritative precedent binding on all courts within the United States (see Chap. 5, Sec. A).

Judicial opinions resolving constitutional law issues are the product or end-result of the process of constitutional interpretation (see Chap. 2, Sec. F above). Such opin-ions, when joined by a majority of the court, become precedents that are a key "sec-ondary source" for constitutional interpretation (see Chap. 2, Sec. F.2). Constitutional law opinions serve many purposes in constitutional analysis. For instance, they pro-vide case holdings that may be invoked by advocates and applied by courts in later cases; they articulate particular standards and tests to use in constitutional analysis; they provide information on what types of facts are relevant to the analysis of partic-ular constitutional issues; and they provide assistance in determining which interpre-tive sources and approaches (see Chap. 2, Sec. F) are most suitable for particular con-stitutional clauses. (Chapter 15, Section B.2 contains additional discussion on the uses of precedent.)

The drafter of a judicial opinion, like the drafter of other legal documents, "is try-ing to control…the future itself…, trying to stabilize a part of the future, set it on a course, make it more foreseeable and more reliable" (Charles Curtis, "A Better Theory of Legal Interpretation," 3 VANDERBILT L. REV. 407, 422 (1950)). The drafter seeks to accomplish this goal by establishing standards to guide interpreters or decision-makers who may in the future apply the precedent being created. Thus in a judicial opinion, as in other legal documents, the "words…are simply delegations to others of authority to give them meaning by applying them to particular things or occasions.… And the more imprecise the words are, the greater is the delegation, simply because then they can be applied or not to more particulars" (*Id.* at 426).

For the reader of a judicial opinion, as for the reader of other legal documents, the starting point for interpretation is the express language of the document. The reader's first task in analyzing a constitutional law opinion is thus to read it carefully, being attentive to each word, to *determine what the opinion says*. This task may be termed "descriptive" analysis. Using such analysis, the reader should develop a description of: (1) the result that the court reaches in its opinion and the court's holding on which the result is based; (2) the steps in the court's reasoning that lead to and support the result and holding; (3) the facts that are relevant to the reasoning and result; (4) the primary interpretive sources that the opinion relies on, if any; (5) the precedents (the secondary sources) that the court relies on in its opinion; and (6) the standards that the court identifies and applies in resolving the issues—and that may be used in resolving similar issues in the future.

The reader's second, more complex, task in analyzing a constitutional law opinion is to *evaluate* the opinion. This task may be called "normative" analysis. The goal, simply put, is to determine whether the opinion is "good law." One particularly helpful way to undertake this second task is to focus on the concept of "justification" (as opposed to "explanation") and to ask whether the opinion serves to "justify" the result reached by the court. The concept of justification is explored in the next section below.

Sec. B. The Difference Between Explaining Constitutional Law Decisions ("Explanation") and Justifying Constitutional Law Decisions ("Justification")

There is an important distinction between analysis that is used to *explain* judicial decisions and analysis that is used to *justify* judicial decisions. As Professor Paul Brest has noted, "there are at least two basically different ways of examining the work of a court." One way is to "*explain*—in historical, sociological, or psychological terms— why the court decided cases the way it did." The other way is to treat the court's "decisions critically and evaluat[e] them in terms of certain normative criteria" (Paul Brest, Processes of Constitutional Decisionmaking, pp. 2–3 (Little, Brown, 1975) (emphasis added). Under the latter approach:

> There are several viewpoints from which to criticize judicial decisions. For example, one can ask whether they tend to make our society more just, free, stable or prosperous, or whether the judiciary acts so as to strengthen its po-

sition with respect to other institutions. [Alternatively, one can focus on] criteria intrinsic to the processes of constitutional decision-making. [One can] inquir[e], for example, whether a court makes proper use of the sources for constitutional interpretation, and whether it acts within the bounds of its institutional authority and competence.

Central among these intrinsic criteria for evaluating a court's work is *how well its opinions justify its decisions....* [Brest, Processes of Constitutional Decisionmaking, at 2–3 (emphasis added).]

Professor Owen Fiss has further described this concept of justification:

The obligation to justify a decision has given rise to never-ending debates as to the proper sources of judicial decisions — text, intentions of the Framers, general structure of the Constitution, ethics, the good of the nation, etc. For the notion of justification, as opposed to explanation, implies that the reasons supporting a decision be "good" reasons, and this in turn requires norms or rules for determining what counts as a "good" reason. My intention is... to stress two facts that all seem to agree on as to what might count as a "good" reason. The first is that the reason cannot consist of a preference, be it a preference of the contestants, of the body politic, or of the judge. The statement, "I prefer" or "we prefer" in the context of a judicial, rather than a legislative decision, merely constitutes an explanation, not a justification. Second, the reason must somehow transcend beliefs of the judge or the body politic as to what is right or just or what should be done. Something more is required to transform these personal beliefs into values that are worthy of the status "constitutional" and all that it implies — binding on society as a whole, entitled to endure, not forever but long enough to give our public morality an inner coherence, and largely to be enforced by courts. [Owen Fiss, "Forward to the Supreme Court 1978 Term: The Forms of Justice," 93 Harv. L. Rev. 1, 13–14 (1979).]

How important is this goal of "justification," and is it possible for judges to achieve this goal in their opinions? According to Professor Henry Monaghan:

The tendency toward substitution of will — "I have five votes, that is how I distinguish the contrary decisions" — for reason is one which can be, if not eliminated, at least constrained. That at least is the faith of all those off the Court who place so much confidence in the Court's capacity to act in a principled fashion. This confidence is, indeed, the fundamental premise of constitutional theorizing in this country. If this premise of reasoned decisionmaking is systematically rejected, constitutional adjudication is thereby excommunicated from the legal system as lawyers deal with it. Our legal traditions reject as a working premise the view, variously framed, that the rational form of judicial opinions simply masks nonrational imperatives, the origins of which are explicable in terms of economic factors, motivational psychology, sociobiology, or other determinants. Whatever the *explanatory power* of these approaches in other contexts, the legal order posits as an article of faith that there are rational aspects to human decision-making which the adjudicatory process seeks to maximize through its systematic reliance upon devices such as pleadings, evidence, oral and written argument, appeals and—of central concern—written opinions publicly exposed for criticism as to the adequacy of their reasoning....

Of course, some opinions will be insufficiently principled in the sense that they will contain obscurities. At times this will result from the necessity for compromise if the opinion writer truly seeks to issue a collective product. On other occasions, the obscurity will appear in hard cases—situations in which an acceptable controlling principle cannot be adequately perceived until fleshed out by a series of cases. Seeking the goal of an adequately principled opinion reflecting shared agreement is, after all, not a demand for impossible perfection. The premises of our legal system do assume that in practice an adequately principled opinion is a generally achievable goal, and in any event, a necessary aspirational feature of the judicial process. [Henry Monaghan, "Taking Supreme Court Opinions Seriously," 39 MARYLAND L. REV. 1, 19–20, 24–25 (1979).]

This goal of principled opinions justifying judicial decisions is, according to Archibald Cox, a central facet of our legal system:

Ability to rationalize a constitutional judgment in terms of principles referable to accepted sources of law is an essential, major element of constitutional adjudication. It is one of the ultimate sources of the power of the Court.... Constitutional government must operate by consent of the governed. Court decrees draw no authority from the participation of the people. Their power to command consent comes to an important degree from the continuing force of the rule of law—from the belief that the major influence in judicial decisions is not fiat but principles which bind the judges as well as the litigants and apply consistently yesterday, today, and tomorrow....A chief function of the judicial opinion is to preserve this element in the Court's power to command the consent of the governed. [Archibald Cox, "Foreword to the Supreme Court 1965 Term: Constitutional Adjudication and the Promotion of Human Rights," 80 HARV. L. REV. 91, 98 (1966).]

When analyzing a constitutional law opinion, it is therefore necessary, as the authors above suggest, to focus on how well the opinion justifies the decision that the court has reached. The necessary predicate to this *normative analysis*, of course, is a careful *descriptive analysis* of the opinion to determine what it says. In light of the understanding gained from descriptive analysis, one can then consider the opinion's consistency with legal and constitutional norms. In doing so, one may weigh considerations such as:

1. Whether the opinion's reasoning and result are supported by applicable precedent.
2. Whether the opinion's reasoning and result are supported by the facts in the record.
3. Whether the opinion is grounded in legitimate sources of interpretation (see Chap. 2, Sec. F.2).

4. Whether the result or decision is consistent with relevant institutional or legal policy considerations—for example, considerations regarding the competence of the court or the maintenance of a stable and coherent rule of law (see Chap. 15, Sec. C.5).

This focus on justification does not mean that attempts to *explain* why the court decided the way it did are inappropriate or invalid. Thus, after analyzing an opinion and considering the extent to which it justifies the decision, one may then consider political, psychological, historical, or other *explanations* for why the court decided the case as it did. Such an inquiry may be particularly appropriate when it seems that sufficient justification is lacking, and one seeks an explanation for why the court would research a result that it could not satisfactorily justify. It is important to understand, however, that such attempts to explain would rely on types of analysis that are much different from those used for justifications, and would employ norms and materials from disciplines other than law.

Sec. C. A Practical Method for Reading and Analyzing Constitutional Law Opinions

The constitutional law opinions of the courts are the building blocks with which lawyers and judges, work, and the typical diet of students in constitutional law courses. Success in both study and practice depends in part on the capacity to analyze and apply these opinions effectively. It is thus critically important to develop techniques for careful reading and analysis of opinions. The following eight steps provide a starting point. Step 1 sets the stage for reading the opinion; steps 2 through 7 guide descriptive analysis; and step 8 shifts to normative analysis.

1. Think of the opinion as a legal document, with a judge or court as the drafter. As with other legal documents, begin with the *words* themselves and read them as scrupulously as possible.
2. Identify the constitutional provision(s) at issue and the officials or entities (from the list in Chap. 2, Sec. D) whose power or rights are at issue. Then frame each *issue* in the case as an empowerment issue or a rights issue, connecting each issue to the particular constitutional provision and to the particular officials or entities involved.
3. For each issue, identify the relevant facts, the result reached, the holding, and the rationale—as you would with judicial opinions in other fields of law. Check to see how the court uses precedent to support its rationale, how the Court uses the facts, and what other considerations (if any) the court takes into account. As you analyze the rationale, look particularly for the "analytical framework" or "analytical pathway" that the court uses to organize its reasoning. This framework or pathway should reveal a step-by-step logical progression in the court's reasoning.

4. Think of the opinion as a document controlling the future (as other legal documents do). Ask: how and to what extent does this opinion control governmental actions in the future? In particular, what legal standards does this opinion establish by which future actions may be judged, and who is bound by these standards?

5. Check to see how the court interprets the constitutional clause or clauses at issue. What interpretive *sources* does the court consult and what interpretive *approaches* does it use? (See Chap. 2, Sec. F.) What do these sources and approaches reveal (according to the court) about the constitutional text, original constitutional history, the constitutional structure, or constitutional values? Courts may consult both primary and secondary interpretive sources (Chap. 2, Sec. F.2). In relatively well-developed areas of law, however, the secondary sources—precedents established in earlier opinions—may be the only sources that courts consult.

6. When the opinion is an appellate court opinion, check to see if it commands a majority of the court. In some cases, especially in the U.S. Supreme Court, there is no majority opinion; instead there is only an opinion "announcing the judgment of the Court" or a *plurality* opinion, neither of which has the status of an authoritative precedent that controls the future. For an example, see *Mitchell v. Helms*, 530 U.S. 793 (2000) (plurality opinion of Justice Thomas); and *see generally* Novak, Note, "The Precedential Value of Supreme Court Plurality Decisions," 80 COLUM. L. REV. 756 (1980). In other cases, the main opinion will command a majority for some of its parts but not for others, and it becomes important to distinguish the parts that constitute a majority opinion from those that do not. For an example, see *Planned Parenthood of Southeastern Pennsylvania v. Casey*, 505 U.S. 833 (1992) ("joint opinion" of Justices O'-Connor, Kennedy, and Souter).

   Moreover, some majority opinions are joined by judges who write concurring opinions that limit the scope of their agreement with the majority. When the vote of the concurring judge is needed to constitute the majority, then the majority opinion must be read and applied in the light of whatever qualifications or narrower perspective the concurring opinion introduces into the analysis. In *Rosenberger v. Rector and Visitors of the University of Virginia*, 515 U.S. 819 (1995), for example, Justice O'Connor joined Justice Kennedy's majority opinion as the fifth vote but also wrote a concurring opinion employing narrower reasoning than the majority opinion. And in *United States v. Lopez*, 514 U.S. 549 (1995), Justices Kennedy and O'Connor joined Chief Justice Rehnquist's majority opinion as the fourth and fifth votes but also joined in a concurring opinion that employed narrower reasoning than the Rehnquist majority opinion.

7. Check to see if there are concurring or dissenting opinions.[1] For concurrences, distinguish between an opinion that concurs in the majority opinion's rea-

---

1. For a brief history of the origins of the dissent in the U.S. Supreme Court, see Meredith Kolsky, Note, "Justice William Johnson and the History of the Supreme Court Dissent," 83 GEORGETOWN L. J. 2069 (1995).

soning and result and an opinion that concurs "in the result" only. Read any concurring or dissenting opinions carefully for any additional light they may shed on the reasoning in the majority opinion. Look particularly for ways in which concurring or dissenting opinions may help the reader to discern the "analytical framework" of the majority opinion, to identify the legal standards established by the majority opinion, or to identify the interpretive sources and approaches that the majority uses (see points 3 through 5 above). Also check the analysis of each concurrence or dissent to see how its reasoning differs from that of the majority (or plurality) opinion.

Do not underestimate the importance of concurrences and dissents. They may shed important light on the majority opinion's holding and analysis. A concurring opinion by a judge who joined the majority, as indicated in point 6 above, may even limit the scope of the majority opinion. Moreover, concurrences and dissents frequently mount a challenge to, or provide a revisionist view of, existing law that may sow the seeds for future changes in later cases. As Chief Justice Charles Evans Hughes remarked: "A dissent in a court of last resort is an appeal to the brooding spirit of the law, to the intelligence of a future day, when a later decision may possibly correct the error into which the dissenting judge believes the court to have been betrayed" (Charles Evans Hughes, THE SUPREME COURT OF THE UNITED STATES: ITS FOUNDATION, METHODS, AND ACHIEVEMENTS, p. 68 (Garden City Pub. Co., 1936)). For further discussion of the role of dissents, see Edward Gaffney, Jr., "The Importance of Dissent and the Imperative of Judicial Civility," 28 VALPARAISO U. L. REV. 583 (1994).

8. On the basis of the understanding gained by working through points 1–7, ask whether the court's opinion in the case serves to justify the result the court reaches (see Sec. B above).

Sec. D. Exercise No. 3: Analyzing a U.S. Supreme Court Case: *New York Times v. United States* (the Tension Between Free Press and National Security)

The case of *New York Times v. United States*, 403 U.S. 713 (1971), arose from a pressing public controversy concerning national security during the Vietnam War and was decided during the presidency of Richard Nixon. The case is usually called "The Pentagon Papers Case" because it involved a 47-volume, 7,000 page set of top secret Department of Defense papers concerning the history of the United States' involvement in Vietnam. The *New York Times* obtained access to these "Pentagon Papers" through Daniel Ellsberg, a researcher and analyst with the RAND Corporation (a "think tank") and a former Defense Department official. The historical study that became the Pentagon Papers was commissioned by Robert McNamara when he was Secretary of Defense in the Johnson Administration. One of the copies of the final report had been stored in a classified storage safe at RAND Corporation offices in Santa Monica, California, where Ellsberg received permission to read the papers. *See* David Rudenstine, THE DAY THE PRESSES STOPPED, 15–65 (U. Calif. Press, 1996).

On June 13, 1971, the *New York Times* published the first article in a planned series of articles on the Pentagon Papers. Two days later, the Nixon Administration went to court seeking an injunction against further publication by the *Times*. On Friday, June 18, the *Washington Post*, having also gained access to some of the Pentagon Papers, began publishing its own series of articles. *See* Rudenstine, *supra*, at 125–138. The Nixon Administration then sought to enjoin the *Post*. The ensuing litigation occasioned what is probably the most significant clash between the federal government and the press in American history. The constitutional aspects of the controversy, as reflected in the various opinions of the Justices, encompass crucial issues concerning both government power and individual rights. *See* Rudenstine, *supra*, at 139–356.[2]

The *Pentagon Papers Case* also set the stage for an interesting later development involving litigation against Daniel Ellsberg. After the Nixon Administration lost the *Pentagon Papers Case*, it filed criminal charges against Mr. Ellsberg and a colleague, Anthony Russo, who allegedly assisted him with the copying of the Pentagon Papers (see Rudenstine at 42, 341-342). The indictment charged Ellsberg with stealing or converting government property (18 U.S.C. § 641) and with delivering or transmitting government documents regarding national defense to unauthorized persons (18 U.S.C. §§ 793(d) and (e)) and named Russo as a co-conspirator (*United States v. Russo*, No. 9373-(WMB)-CD Cal., Dec. 29, 1971). On May 11, 1973, the trial judge granted the defendant's motion to dismiss due to government misconduct in the preparation of the case. The dismissal left unanswered a number of First Amendment issues concerning the use of these federal statutes as *subsequent* restraints on speech. For a telling of this story and an analysis of the issues raised by the criminal prosecution, *see* Melville Nimmer, "National Security Secrets v. Free Speech: The Issues Left Undecided in the Ellsberg Case," 26 STANFORD L. REV. 311 (1974).

The U.S. Supreme Court's decision in the Pentagon Papers case is unusual in that it was issued in a brief *"per curiam"* opinion. A *"per curiam"* opinion is a majority opinion, sometimes a unanimous opinion, that is issued by the Court itself rather than by a particular Justice. No Justice wrote a majority opinion as such, and no majority view was expressed other than what is in the brief *per curiam* opinion. Instead,

---

2. In the U.S. Supreme Court, Alexander Bickel, a prominent Yale Law School professor, argued for the *New York Times*, and William R. Glendon, a litigator with the firm of Rogers and Wells, argued the case for the *Washington Post*. For Professor Bickel's commentary on the case, see Alexander Bickel, THE MORALITY OF CONSENT, pp. 60-62, 79–82 (Yale Univ. Press, 1975). For Mr. Glendon's personal reflections about the case, see William R. Glendon, "Fifteen Days in June that Shook the First Amendment: A First Person Account of the Pentagon Papers Case," 65 N.Y. STATE BAR J. 24 (1993). Erwin Griswold, the U.S. Solicitor General (and former Dean of the Harvard Law School) argued the case for the United States. For his personal reflections, see Erwin Griswold, OULD FIELDS, NEW CORNE: THE PERSONAL MEMOIRS OF A TWENTIETH CENTURY LAWYER, pp. 296–313 (West Pub. Co., 1992).

individual Justices issued their own concurring and dissenting opinions with reasoning much more extensive than that in the *per curiam* opinion. These various opinions provide an unusual opportunity for reading and analysis.

In light of the discussion in Sections A, B, and C above, study the *per curiam* opinion and the concurrences and dissents in *New York Times v. United States* which appear below. Based on your own careful reading of these opinions, answer the questions that are set out at the end of the case. You may wish to review these questions before you study the case. Following the questions are a set of brief answers that will test your understanding and provide feedback on analyzing this case and others. You should consult these answers only after you have considered the questions.

NEW YORK TIMES CO. v. UNITED STATES
and
UNITED STATES v. WASHINGTON POST CO.
Supreme Court of the United States
403 U.S. 713 (1971)**

PER CURIAM.

We granted certiorari in these cases in which the United States seeks to enjoin the New York Times and the Washington Post from publishing the contents of a classified study entitled "History of U.S. Decision-Making Process on Viet Nam Policy."

"Any system of prior restraints of expression comes to this Court bearing a heavy presumption against its constitutional validity." *Bantam Books, Inc. v. Sullivan*, 372 U.S. 58, 70 (1963); see also *Near v. Minnesota*, 283 U.S. 697 (1931). The Government "thus carries a heavy burden of showing justification for the imposition of such a restraint." *Organization for a Better Austin v. Keefe*, 402 U.S. 415, 419 (1971). The District Court for the Southern District of New York in the *New York Times* case and the District Court for the District of Columbia and the Court of Appeals for the District of Columbia Circuit in the *Washington Post* case held that the Government had not met that burden. We agree. The judgment of the Court of Appeals for the District of Columbia Circuit is therefore affirmed. The order of the Court of Appeals for the Second Circuit is reversed and the case is remanded with directions to enter a judgment affirming the judgment of the District Court for the Southern District of New York. The stays entered June 25, 1971, by the Court are vacated. The judgments shall issue forthwith.

So ordered.

Mr. Justice Black, with whom Mr. Justice Douglas joins, concurring.

** The opinion of Chief Justice Burger is omitted. In the other opinions, some of the Justices' citations and footnotes are omitted. The remaining footnotes retain their original numbering, and the name of the Justice writing the opinion is included in parentheses in the footnote for clarification.

I adhere to the view that the Government's case against the *Washington Post* should have been dismissed and that the injunction against the *New York Times* should have been vacated without oral argument when the cases were first presented to this Court. I believe that every moment's continuance of the injunctions against these newspapers amounts to a flagrant, indefensible, and continuing violation of the First Amendment. Furthermore, after oral argument, I agree completely that we must affirm the judgment of the Court of Appeals for the District of Columbia Circuit and reverse the judgment of the Court of Appeals for the Second Circuit for the reasons stated by my Brothers DOUGLAS and BRENNAN. In my view it is unfortunate that some of my Brethren are apparently willing to hold that the publication of news may sometimes be enjoined. Such a holding would make a shambles of the First Amendment.

* * * *

In the First Amendment the Founding Fathers gave the free press the protection it must have to fulfill its essential role in our democracy. The press was to serve the governed, not the governors. The Government's power to censor the press was abolished so that the press would remain forever free to censure the Government. The press was protected so that it could bare the secrets of government and inform the people. Only a free and unrestrained press can effectively expose deception in government. And paramount among the responsibilities of a free press is the duty to prevent any part of the government from deceiving the people and sending them off to distant lands to die of foreign fevers and foreign shot and shell. In my view, far from deserving condemnation for their courageous reporting, the New York Times, the Washington Post, and other newspapers should be commended for serving the purpose that the Founding Fathers saw so clearly. In revealing the workings of government that led to the Vietnam war, the newspapers nobly did precisely that which the Founders hoped and trusted they would do.

The Government's case here is based on premises entirely different from those that guided the Framers of the First Amendment. The Solicitor General has carefully and emphatically stated:

> "Now, MR. JUSTICE [BLACK], your construction of... [the First Amendment] is well known, and I certainly respect it. You say that no law means no law, and that should be obvious. I can only say, Mr. Justice, that to me it is equally obvious that 'no law' does not mean 'no law', and I would seek to persuade the Court that is true.... [T]here are other parts of the Constitution that grant powers and responsibilities to the Executive, and... the First Amendment was not intended to make it impossible for the Executive to function or to protect the security of the United States." [3]

And the Government argues in its brief that in spite of the First Amendment, "[t]he authority of the Executive Department to protect the nation against publication of information whose disclosure would endanger the national security stems from two in-

---

3. (Black fn.) Tr. of Oral Arg. 76.

terrelated sources: the constitutional power of the President over the conduct of foreign affairs and his authority as Commander-in-Chief."[4]

In other words, we are asked to hold that despite the First Amendment's emphatic command, the Executive Branch, the Congress, and the Judiciary can make laws enjoining publication of current news and abridging freedom of the press in the name of "national security." The Government does not even attempt to rely on any act of Congress. Instead it makes the bold and dangerously far-reaching contention that the courts should take it upon themselves to "make" a law abridging freedom of the press in the name of equity, presidential power and national security, even when the representatives of the people in Congress have adhered to the command of the First Amendment and refused to make such a law.[5] See concurring opinion of Mr. Justice Douglas, post. To find that the President has "inherent power" to halt the publication of news by resort to the courts would wipe out the First Amendment and destroy the fundamental liberty and security of the very people the Government hopes to make "secure." No one can read the history of the adoption of the First Amendment without being convinced beyond any doubt that it was injunctions like those sought here that Madison and his collaborators intended to outlaw in this Nation for all time.

* * * *

Mr. Justice Douglas, with whom Mr. Justice Black joins, concurring.

While I join the opinion of the Court I believe it necessary to express my views more fully.

It should be noted at the outset that the First Amendment provides that "Congress shall make no law...abridging the freedom of speech, or of the press." That leaves, in my view, no room for governmental restraint on the press.

There is, moreover, no statute barring the publication by the press of the material which the *Times* and the *Post* seek to use. Title 18 U.S.C. §793 (e) provides that "[w]hoever having unauthorized possession of, access to, or control over any document, writing...or information relating to the national defense which information the possessor has reason to believe could be used to the injury of the United States or to the advantage of any foreign nation, willfully communicates...the same to any person not entitled to receive it...[s]hall be fined not more than $ 10,000 or imprisoned not more than ten years, or both."

---

4. (Black fn.) Brief for the United States 13–14.

5. (Black fn.) Compare the views of the Solicitor General with those of James Madison, the author of the First Amendment. When speaking of the Bill of Rights in the House of Representatives, Madison said: "If they [the first ten amendments] are incorporated into the Constitution, independent tribunals of justice will consider themselves in a peculiar manner the guardians of those rights; they will be an impenetrable bulwark against every assumption of power in the Legislative or Executive; they will be naturally led to resist every encroachment upon rights expressly stipulated for in the Constitution by the declaration of rights." 1 Annals of Cong. 439.

The Government suggests that the word "communicates" is broad enough to encompass publication.

There are eight sections in the chapter on espionage and censorship, §§ 792–799. In three of those eight "publish" is specifically mentioned: § 794 (b) applies to "Whoever, in time of war, with intent that the same shall be communicated to the enemy, collects, records, *publishes*, or communicates... [the disposition of armed forces]."

Section 797 applies to whoever "reproduces, *publishes*, sells, or gives away" photographs of defense installations.

Section 798 relating to cryptography applies to whoever: "communicates, furnishes, transmits, or otherwise makes available... *or publishes*" the described material.[2] (Emphasis added.)

Thus it is apparent that Congress was capable of and did distinguish between publishing and communication in the various sections of the Espionage Act.

The other evidence that § 793 does not apply to the press is a rejected version of § 793. That version read: "During any national emergency resulting from a war to which the United States is a party, or from threat of such a war, the President may, by proclamation, declare the existence of such emergency and, by proclamation, prohibit the publishing or communicating of, or the attempting to publish or communicate any information relating to the national defense which, in his judgment, is of such character that it is or might be useful to the enemy." 55 Cong. Rec. 1763. During the debates in the Senate the First Amendment was specifically cited and that provision was defeated. 55 Cong. Rec. 2167.

Judge Gurfein's holding in the *Times* case that this Act does not apply to this case was therefore preeminently sound. Moreover, the Act of September 23, 1950, in amending 18 U.S.C. § 793 states in § 1 (b) that:

Nothing in this Act shall be construed to authorize, require, or establish military or civilian censorship or in any way to limit or infringe upon freedom of the press or of speech as guaranteed by the Constitution of the United States and no regulation shall be promulgated hereunder having that effect. 64 Stat. 987.

Thus Congress has been faithful to the command of the First Amendment in this area.

So any power that the Government possesses must come from its "inherent power."

The power to wage war is "the power to wage war successfully." See *Hirabayashi v. United States*, 320 U.S. 81, 93. But the war power stems from a declaration of war. The Constitution by Art. I, § 8, gives Congress, not the President, power "[t]o declare War." Nowhere are presidential wars authorized. We need not decide therefore what leveling effect the war power of Congress might have.

---

2. (Douglas fn.) These documents contain data concerning the communications system of the United States, the publication of which is made a crime. But the criminal sanction is not urged by the United States as the basis of equity power.

These disclosures[3] may have a serious impact. But that is no basis for sanctioning a previous restraint on the press. As stated by Chief Justice Hughes in *Near v. Minnesota*, 283 U.S. 697, 719–720:

> While reckless assaults upon public men, and efforts to bring obloquy upon those who are endeavoring faithfully to discharge official duties, exert a baleful influence and deserve the severest condemnation in public opinion, it cannot be said that this abuse is greater, and it is believed to be less, than that which characterized the period in which our institutions took shape. Meanwhile, the administration of government has become more complex, the opportunities for malfeasance and corruption have multiplied, crime has grown to most serious proportions, and the danger of its protection by unfaithful officials and of the impairment of the fundamental security of life and property by criminal alliances and official neglect, emphasizes the primary need of a vigilant and courageous press, especially in great cities. The fact that the liberty of the press may be abused by miscreant purveyors of scandal does not make any the less necessary the immunity of the press from previous restraint in dealing with official misconduct.

* * * *

I would affirm the judgment of the Court of Appeals in the *Post* case, vacate the stay of the Court of Appeals in the *Times* case and direct that it affirm the District Court.

The stays in these cases that have been in effect for more than a week constitute a flouting of the principles of the First Amendment as interpreted in *Near v. Minnesota*.

MR. JUSTICE BRENNAN, concurring.

I

I write separately in these cases only to emphasize what should be apparent: that our judgments in the present cases may not be taken to indicate the propriety, in the future, of issuing temporary stays and restraining orders to block the publication of material sought to be suppressed by the Government.

* * * *

II

The error that has pervaded these cases from the outset was the granting of any injunctive relief whatsoever, interim or otherwise. The entire thrust of the Government's claim throughout these cases has been that publication of the material sought to be enjoined "could," or "might," or "may" prejudice the national interest in various ways. But the First Amendment tolerates absolutely no prior judicial restraints of the press

---

3. (Douglas fn.) There are numerous sets of this material in existence and they apparently are not under any controlled custody. Moreover, the President has sent a set to the Congress. We start then with a case where there already is rather wide distribution of the material that is destined for publicity, not secrecy. I have gone over the material listed in the in camera brief of the United States. It is all history, not future events. None of it is more recent than 1968.

predicated upon surmise or conjecture that untoward consequences may result. Our cases, it is true, have indicated that there is a single, extremely narrow class of cases in which the First Amendment's ban on prior judicial restraint may be overridden. Our cases have thus far indicated that such cases may arise only when the Nation "is at war," *Schenck v. United States*, 249 U.S. 47, 52 (1919), during which times "[n]o one would question but that a government might prevent actual obstruction to its recruiting service or the publication of the sailing dates of transports or the number and location of troops." *Near v. Minnesota*, 283 U.S. 697, 716 (1931). Even if the present world situation were assumed to be tantamount to a time of war, or if the power of presently available armaments would justify even in peacetime the suppression of information that would set in motion a nuclear holocaust, in neither of these actions has the Government presented or even alleged that publication of items from or based upon the material at issue would cause the happening of an event of that nature. "[T]he chief purpose of [the First Amendment's] guaranty [is] to prevent previous restraints upon publication." *Near v. Minnesota*, supra, at 713. Thus, only governmental allegation and proof that publication must inevitably, directly, and immediately cause the occurrence of an event kindred to imperiling the safety of a transport already at sea can support even the issuance of an interim restraining order. In no event may mere conclusions be sufficient: for if the Executive Branch seeks judicial aid in preventing publication, it must inevitably submit the basis upon which that aid is sought to scrutiny by the judiciary. And therefore, every restraint issued in this case, whatever its form, has violated the First Amendment—and not less so because that restraint was justified as necessary to afford the courts an opportunity to examine the claim more thoroughly. Unless and until the Government has clearly made out its case, the First Amendment commands that no injunction may issue.

Mr. Justice Stewart, with whom Mr. Justice White joins, concurring.

In the governmental structure created by our Constitution, the Executive is endowed with enormous power in the two related areas of national defense and international relations. This power, largely unchecked by the Legislative[1] and Judicial branches, has been pressed to the very hilt since the advent of the nuclear missile age. For better or for worse, the simple fact is that a President of the United States possesses vastly greater constitutional independence in these two vital areas of power than does, say, a prime minister of a country with a parliamentary form of government.

* * * *

---

1. (Stewart fn.) The President's power to make treaties and to appoint ambassadors is, of course, limited by the requirement of Art. II, § 2, of the Constitution that he obtain the advice and consent of the Senate. Article I, § 8, empowers Congress to "raise and support Armies," and "provide and maintain a Navy." And, of course, Congress alone can declare war. This power was last exercised almost 30 years ago at the inception of World War II. Since the end of that war in 1945, the Armed Forces of the United States have suffered approximately half a million casualties in various parts of the world.

[I]t is clear to me that it is the constitutional duty of the Executive—as a matter of law as the courts know law—through the promulgation and enforcement of executive regulations, to protect...[t]he confidentiality necessary to carry out its responsibilities in the fields of international relations and national defense.

This is not to say that Congress and the courts have no role to play. Undoubtedly Congress has the power to enact specific and appropriate criminal laws to protect government property and preserve government secrets. Congress has passed such laws, and several of them are of very colorable relevance to the apparent circumstances of these cases. And if a criminal prosecution is instituted, it will be the responsibility of the courts to decide the applicability of the criminal law under which the charge is brought. Moreover, if Congress should pass a specific law authorizing civil proceedings in this field, the courts would likewise have the duty to decide the constitutionality of such a law as well as its applicability to the facts proved.

But in the cases before us we are asked neither to construe specific regulations nor to apply specific laws. We are asked, instead, to perform a function that the Constitution gave to the Executive, not the Judiciary. We are asked, quite simply, to prevent the publication by two newspapers of material that the Executive Branch insists should not, in the national interest, be published. I am convinced that the Executive is correct with respect to some of the documents involved. But I cannot say that disclosure of any of them will surely result in direct, immediate, and irreparable damage to our Nation or its people. That being so, there can under the First Amendment be but one judicial resolution of the issues before us. I join the judgments of the Court.

Mr. Justice White, with whom Mr. Justice Stewart joins, concurring.

I concur in today's judgments, but only because of the concededly extraordinary protection against prior restraints enjoyed by the press under our constitutional system. I do not say that in no circumstances would the First Amendment permit an injunction against publishing information about government plans or operations. Nor, after examining the materials the Government characterizes as the most sensitive and destructive, can I deny that revelation of these documents will do substantial damage to public interests. Indeed, I am confident that their disclosure will have that result. But I nevertheless agree that the United States has not satisfied the very heavy burden that it must meet to warrant an injunction against publication in these cases, at least in the absence of express and appropriately limited congressional authorization for prior restraints in circumstances such as these.

The Government's position is simply stated: The responsibility of the Executive for the conduct of the foreign affairs and for the security of the Nation is so basic that the President is entitled to an injunction against publication of a newspaper story whenever he can convince a court that the information to be revealed threatens "grave and irreparable" injury to the public interest;[2] and the injunction should issue whether or

---

2. (White fn.) "The grave and irreparable danger" standard is that asserted by the Government in this Court. In remanding to Judge Gurfein for further hearings in the *Times* litigation,

not the material to be published is classified, whether or not publication would be lawful under relevant criminal statutes enacted by Congress, and regardless of the circumstances by which the newspaper came into possession of the information.

At least in the absence of legislation by Congress, based on its own investigations and findings, I am quite unable to agree that the inherent powers of the Executive and the courts reach so far as to authorize remedies having such sweeping potential for inhibiting publications by the press. Much of the difficulty inheres in the "grave and irreparable danger" standard suggested by the United States. If the United States were to have judgment under such a standard in these cases, our decision would be of little guidance to other courts in other cases, for the material at issue here would not be available from the Court's opinion or from public records, nor would it be published by the press. Indeed, even today where we hold that the United States has not met its burden, the material remains sealed in court records and it is properly not discussed in today's opinions. Moreover, because the material poses substantial dangers to national interests and because of the hazards of criminal sanctions, a responsible press may choose never to publish the more sensitive materials. To sustain the Government in these cases would start the courts down a long and hazardous road that I am not willing to travel, at least without congressional guidance and direction.

* * * *

What is more, terminating the ban on publication of the relatively few sensitive documents the Government now seeks to suppress does not mean that the law either requires or invites newspapers or others to publish them or that they will be immune from criminal action if they do. Prior restraints require an unusually heavy justification under the First Amendment; but failure by the Government to justify prior restraints does not measure its constitutional entitlement to a conviction for criminal publication. That the Government mistakenly chose to proceed by injunction does not mean that it could not successfully proceed in another way.

The Criminal Code contains numerous provisions potentially relevant to these cases. Section 797 makes it a crime to publish certain photographs or drawings of military installations. Section 798, also in precise language, proscribes knowing and willful publication of any classified information concerning the cryptographic systems or communication intelligence activities of the United States as well as any information obtained from communication intelligence operations. If any of the material here at issue is of this nature, the newspapers are presumably now on full notice of the position of the United States and must face the consequences if they publish. I would have no difficulty in sustaining convictions under these sections on facts that would not justify the intervention of equity and the imposition of a prior restraint.

----

five members of the Court of Appeals for the Second Circuit directed him to determine whether disclosure of certain items specified with particularity by the Government would "pose such grave and immediate danger to the security of the United States as to warrant their publication being enjoined."

The same would be true under those sections of the Criminal Code casting a wider net to protect the national defense. Section 793 (e) makes it a criminal act for any unauthorized possessor of a document "relating to the national defense" either (1) willfully to communicate or cause to be communicated that document to any person not entitled to receive it or (2) willfully to retain the document and fail to deliver it to an officer of the United States entitled to receive it....

* * * *

It is thus clear that Congress has addressed itself to the problems of protecting the security of the country and the national defense from unauthorized disclosure of potentially damaging information. Cf. *Youngstown Sheet & Tube Co. v. Sawyer*, 343 U.S. 579, 585–586 (1952); see also id., at 593–628 (Frankfurter, J., concurring). It has not, however, authorized the injunctive remedy against threatened publication. It has apparently been satisfied to rely on criminal sanctions and their deterrent effect on the responsible as well as the irresponsible press. I am not, of course, saying that either of these newspapers has yet committed a crime or that either would commit a crime if it published all the material now in its possession. That matter must await resolution in the context of a criminal proceeding if one is instituted by the United States. In that event, the issue of guilt or innocence would be determined by procedures and standards quite different from those that have purported to govern these injunctive proceedings.

MR. JUSTICE MARSHALL, concurring.

The Government contends that the only issue in these cases is whether in a suit by the United States, "the First Amendment bars a court from prohibiting a newspaper from publishing material whose disclosure would pose a 'grave and immediate danger to the security of the United States.'" Brief for the United States 7. With all due respect, I believe the ultimate issue in these cases is even more basic than the one posed by the Solicitor General. The issue is whether this Court or the Congress has the power to make law.

In these cases there is no problem concerning the President's power to classify information as "secret" or "topsecret." Congress has specifically recognized Presidential authority, which has been formally exercised in Exec. Order 10501 (1953), to classify documents and information. See, *e.g.*, 18 U.S.C. § 798; 50 U.S.C. § 783. Nor is there any issue here regarding the President's power as Chief Executive and Commander-in-Chief to protect national security by disciplining employees who disclose information and by taking precautions to prevent leaks.

The problem here is whether in these particular cases the Executive Branch has authority to invoke the equity jurisdiction of the courts to protect what it believes to be the national interest. The Government argues that in addition to the inherent power of any government to protect itself, the President's power to conduct foreign affairs and his position as Commander in Chief give him authority to impose censorship on the press to protect his ability to deal effectively with foreign nations and to conduct the military affairs of the country. Of course, it is beyond cavil that the President has broad powers by virtue of his primary responsibility for the conduct of our foreign affairs and his position as Commander in Chief. *Chicago & Southern Air Lines v. Waterman S.S. Corp.*, 333 U.S. 103 (1948); *Hirabayashi v. United States*, 320 U.S. 81, 93 (1943); *United States v. Curtiss-Wright Corp.*, 299 U.S. 304 (1936)....[2]

It would, however, be utterly inconsistent with the concept of separation of powers for this Court to use its power of contempt to prevent behavior that Congress has specifically declined to prohibit. There would be a similar damage to the basic concept of these co-equal branches of Government if when the Executive Branch has adequate authority granted by Congress to protect "national security" it can choose instead to invoke the contempt power of a court to enjoin the threatened conduct. The Constitution provides that Congress shall make laws, the President execute laws, and courts interpret laws. *Youngstown Sheet & Tube Co. v. Sawyer*, 343 U.S. 579 (1952). It did not provide for government by injunction in which the courts and the Executive Branch can "make law" without regard to the action of Congress. It may be more convenient for the Executive Branch if it need only convince a judge to prohibit conduct rather than ask the Congress to pass a law, and it may be more convenient to enforce a contempt order than to seek a criminal conviction in a jury trial. Moreover, it may be considered politically wise to get a court to share the responsibility for arresting those who the Executive Branch has probable cause to believe are violating the law. But convenience and political considerations of the moment do not justify a basic departure from the principles of our system of government.

In these cases we are not faced with a situation where Congress has failed to provide the Executive with broad power to protect the Nation from disclosure of damaging state secrets. Congress has on several occasions given extensive consideration to the problem of protecting the military and strategic secrets of the United States. This consideration has resulted in the enactment of statutes making it a crime to receive, disclose, communicate, withhold, and publish certain documents, photographs, instruments, appliances, and information. The bulk of these statutes is found in chapter 37 of U.S.C., Title 18, entitled Espionage and Censorship. In that chapter, Congress has provided penalties ranging from a $ 10,000 fine to death for violating the various statutes.

* * * *

Even if it is determined that the Government could not in good faith bring criminal prosecutions against the New York Times and the Washington Post, it is clear that Congress has specifically rejected passing legislation that would have clearly given the President the power he seeks here and made the current activity of the newspapers unlawful. When Congress specifically declines to make conduct unlawful it is not for this Court to re-decide those issues — to overrule Congress. *See Youngstown Sheet & Tube Co. v. Sawyer*, 343 U.S. 579 (1952).

* * * *

---

2. (Marshall fn.) But see *Kent v. Dulles*, 357 U.S. 116 (1958); *Youngstown Sheet & Tube Co. v. Sawyer*, 343 U.S. 579 (1952).

Either the Government has the power under statutory grant to use traditional criminal law to protect the country or, if there is no basis for arguing that Congress has made the activity a crime, it is plain that Congress has specifically refused to grant the authority the Government seeks from this Court. In either case this Court does not have authority to grant the requested relief. It is not for this Court to fling itself into every breach perceived by some Government official nor is it for this Court to take on itself the burden of enacting law, especially a law that Congress has refused to pass.

I believe that the judgment of the United States Court of Appeals for the District of Columbia Circuit should be affirmed and the judgment of the United States Court of Appeals for the Second Circuit should be reversed insofar as it remands the case for further hearings.

Mr. Justice Harlan, with whom The Chief Justice and Mr. Justice Blackmun join, dissenting.

These cases forcefully call to mind the wise admonition of Mr. Justice Holmes, dissenting in *Northern Securities Co. v. United States*, 193 U.S. 197, 400–401 (1904):

> Great cases like hard cases make bad law. For great cases are called great, not by reason of their real importance in shaping the law of the future, but because of some accident of immediate overwhelming interest which appeals to the feelings and distorts the judgment. These immediate interests exercise a kind of hydraulic pressure which makes what previously was clear seem doubtful, and before which even well settled principles of law will bend.

With all respect, I consider that the Court has been almost irresponsibly feverish in dealing with these cases.

* * * *

Forced as I am to reach the merits of these cases, I dissent from the opinion and judgments of the Court. Within the severe limitations imposed by the time constraints under which I have been required to operate, I can only state my reasons in telescoped form....

* * * *

It is plain to me that the scope of the judicial function in passing upon the activities of the Executive Branch of the Government in the field of foreign affairs is very narrowly restricted. This view is, I think, dictated by the concept of separation of powers upon which our constitutional system rests.

* * * *

I agree that, in performance of its duty to protect the values of the First Amendment against political pressures, the judiciary must review the initial Executive determination to the point of satisfying itself that the subject matter of the dispute does lie within the proper compass of the President's foreign relations power. Constitutional considerations forbid "a complete abandonment of judicial control." Cf. *United States v. Reynolds*, 345 U.S. 1, 8 (1953). Moreover, the judiciary may properly insist that the determination that disclosure of the subject matter would irreparably impair the national security be made by the head of the Executive Department concerned—here the Secretary of State or the Secretary of Defense—after actual personal consideration by that officer. This safeguard is required in the analogous area of executive claims of privilege for secrets of state.

But in my judgment the judiciary may not properly go beyond these two inquiries and redetermine for itself the probable impact of disclosure on the national security.

* * * *

Even if there is some room for the judiciary to override the executive determination, it is plain that the scope of review must be exceedingly narrow. I can see no indication in the opinions of either the District Court or the Court of Appeals in the *Post* litigation that the conclusions of the Executive were given even the deference owing to an administrative agency, much less that owing to a co-equal branch of the Government operating within the field of its constitutional prerogative.

Accordingly, I would vacate the judgment of the Court of Appeals for the District of Columbia Circuit on this ground and remand the case for further proceedings in the District Court. Before the commencement of such further proceedings, due opportunity should be afforded the Government for procuring from the Secretary of State or the Secretary of Defense or both an expression of their views on the issue of national security. The ensuing review by the District Court should be in accordance with the views expressed in this opinion. And…I would affirm the judgment of the Court of Appeals for the Second Circuit.

Pending further hearings in each case conducted under the appropriate ground rules, I would continue the restraints on publication. I cannot believe that the doctrine prohibiting prior restraints reaches to the point of preventing courts from maintaining the status quo long enough to act responsibly in matters of such national importance as those involved here.

Mr. Justice Blackmun, dissenting.

I join Mr. Justice Harlan in his dissent. I also am in substantial accord with much that Mr. Justice White says, by way of admonition, in the latter part of his opinion.

* * * *

The First Amendment, after all, is only one part of an entire Constitution. Article II of the great document vests in the Executive Branch primary power over the conduct of foreign affairs and places in that branch the responsibility for the Nation's safety. Each provision of the Constitution is important, and I cannot subscribe to a doctrine of unlimited absolutism for the First Amendment at the cost of downgrading other provisions. First Amendment absolutism has never commanded a majority of this Court. See, for example, *Near v. Minnesota*, 283 U.S. 697, 708 (1931), and *Schenck v. United States*, 249 U.S. 47, 52 (1919). What is needed here is a weighing, upon properly developed standards, of the broad right of the press to print and of the very narrow right of the Government to prevent. Such standards are not yet developed. The parties here are in disagreement as to what those standards should be. But even the newspapers concede that there are situations where restraint is in order and is constitutional. . . .

I therefore would remand these cases....

Questions

QUES. 1. Does the case raise power issues, or rights issues, or both? What are these issues? What constitutional provisions give rise to these issues?

QUES. 2. Who or what are the entities (from the list in Chapter 2, Sec. D) whose powers or rights are at issue?

QUES. 3. What does the case *say* about the validity of the Executive's actions? About Congress' power to deal with the problem the Executive had dealt with? (Consult the *per curiam* opinion first; then consult the individual opinions of the Justices.)

QUES. 4. What *standards* does the case establish for resolving future problems regarding (a) injunctions, or (b) criminal penalties, against the press for publishing national security information? First consider the *per curiam* opinion; then see, especially, Justice Black's opinion, Justice Brennan's opinion, Justice Stewart's opinion, and Justice White's opinion.)

QUES. 5. Do the opinions in the case *justify* the result that the Court reaches (see Sec. B above)? This is a complex question that you should not expect to resolve fully. But do attempt to identify passages in the opinions that provide *good legal reasons* for, or provide *good legal authority* to support, their conclusions—or that fail to do so. Seek also to distinguish such evidence of justification from any possible *explanations* for the result that may occur to you.

Answers

ANS. to QUES. 1. The various opinions in this case raise both power issues and rights issues. These issues might be stated as follows:

a. Whether the Executive has *power* (under the Commander-in-Chief power and foreign affairs power) to seek, and the Judiciary has power (under Art. III) to issue, this injunction?

b. Whether Congress has *power* (under Art. I, sec. 8) to pass a law authorizing the Executive to seek, and the Judiciary to issue, such an injunction?

c. Whether Congress has *power* (under Art. I, sec. 8) to pass a criminal law punishing newspapers which publish information such as that in this case?

d. Whether the newspapers have a *right* under the free press clause that protects them against, and prohibits the court from issuing, the requested injunction?

e. Whether newspapers have a *right* under the free press clause that would prohibit the issuance of such an injunction even if Congress had passed a law authorizing the Executive to seek and the Judiciary to issue it?

f. Whether the newspapers have a *right* under the free press clause that would protect them against criminal prosecution and punishment for having published information such as that in this case?

Issues a and d are the ones most directly implicated in the case.

ANS. to QUES. 2. Note the constitutional provisions and the officials/entities specified in the issue statements in QUES. 1. The rights of the newspapers under the free press clause are at issue with the newspapers being the individuals (corporate persons) who are the beneficiaries of the free press clause. The powers of all three coordinate branches of government are also at issue, in a separation-of-powers context. Each branch is a constitutional "actor" that is both empowered and limited by the Constitution.

ANS. to QUES. 3. The *per curiam* opinion says that the Executive had not met its burden, under the free press clause, of justifying these prior restraints on the press. Beyond that, there is no majority opinion, and one can only determine what individual Justices or groups of Justices say, rather that what the Court as such says. Most Justices speak primarily to the issue of free press rights under the First Amendment, but two Justices (Marshall and Harlan) do give precedence to the power issues. Several Justices also speak to the interrelationships between the power issues and the rights issues; Justice Black is probably clearest on this point, as he recites and refutes the government's argument. While most Justices focus on the validity of the Executives actions, Justice White also addresses questions concerning Congress, and Justice Marshall also addresses questions concerning the Court itself.

ANS. to QUES. 4. Both Justice Brennan and Justice Stewart articulate First Amendment standards for measuring the validity of prior restraints imposed upon the press in the name of national security. Justice Brennan asserts that such a prior restraint would be valid only if publication of the material would "inevitably, directly, and immediately cause the occurrence of an event kindred to imperiling the safety of a transport already at sea. . . ." Justice Stewart asserts that a prior restraint would be valid only if publication "will surely result in direct, immediate, and irreparable damage to our Nation or its people." Justice White discusses the prior restraint standard suggested by the government in this litigation. In contrast, Justice Black sets forth an absolutist position on prior restraints, asserting that all such restrains are invalid. Justice White also discusses what First Amendment standards might apply to a *subsequent restraint*, that is, a criminal penalty enacted by Congress.

ANS. to QUES. 5. This question can be asked with respect to any one of the individual opinions in the case or collectively with respect to all the opinions invalidating the restraint. In considering this question, seek to understand the distinction between justification and explanation (Chap. 3, Sec. B). An *explanation* for the result in this case might be that (were it true) the majority of Justices sympathized with the anti-war movement or with the institutional press, or that they were Democrats unsympathetic to the claims of a Republican administration, or that they were under severe time pressures and just did what intuitively seemed best in the circumstances. In contrast, a *justification* for the result might be that (were it true) the Justices faithfully followed the framers' intent regarding prior restraints on newspapers (*see, e.g.*, Justice Black's opinion), or that the Justices uncovered and applied sound First Amendment precedents that controlled the outcome (*see, e.g.*, Justice Brennan's opinion), or that the Justices otherwise decided the case consistent with applicable legal norms.

Sec. E. Exercise No. 4: Analyzing A U.S. Supreme Court Case: *Brown v. Board of Education* (Desegregating the Public Schools)

Problems concerning governmentally imposed racial segregation have a long and checkered history in the United States and in the jurisprudence of the U.S. Supreme Court. Historically, the problem of racial segregation is inextricably tied to this nation's practices of African slavery, and to the Civil War, Reconstruction, and the passage of the Reconstruction-Era constitutional amendments, the Thirteenth, Fourteenth and Fifteenth Amendments. During and after Reconstruction, "Jim Crow" laws prompted and enforced the separation of the races, and governmental policies of separation were accorded a constitutional stamp of approval in *Plessy v. Ferguson*, 163 U.S. 537 (1896).

In the first half of the twentieth century, the NAACP (eventually led by Thurgood Marshall) and others fought against governmental policies of racial segregation. *Brown v. Board of Education*, 347 U.S. 483 (1954), was a culmination of these efforts. In *Brown*, the U.S. Supreme Court unanimously invalidated the racial segregation policies of the four public school districts before the Court. For an extensive account of the case and its origins, see Richard Kluger, SIMPLE JUSTICE: THE HISTORY OF BROWN V. BOARD OF EDUCATION AND BLACK AMERICA'S STRUGGLE FOR EQUALITY (Alfred A. Knopf, 1976). For a somewhat different telling of the story, which brings it more up to date and focuses more on the difficulties encountered in the aftermath of *Brown*, *see* James Patterson, BROWN V. BOARD OF EDUCATION: A CIVIL RIGHTS MILESTONE AND ITS TROUBLED LEGACY (Oxford U. Press, 2001).

The Court's opinion in *Brown*, written by Chief Justice Earl Warren, is one of the most famous and important Supreme Court opinions of all time. It is set out in Chapter 9, Section C. After reading this opinion, return to this Section and consider the questions that appear immediately below. Following the questions are a set of brief answers that will test your understanding, provide feedback on analyzing this case and others, and set out some additional information about racial segregation issues. You should consult these answers only after you have considered the questions.

Questions

QUES. 1. Does the *Brown* case raise power issues, or rights issues, or both? What are these issues? What constitutional provisions give rise to these issues?

QUES 2. Who or what are the entities (from the list in Chapter 2, Section D) whose powers or rights are at issue?

QUES. 3. What does this opinion *say* about the validity of the school districts' actions? What *standards* does the *Brown* opinion establish for resolving future cases regarding racial segregation of students in public schools?

QUES. 4. How does the Court deal with the earlier case of *Plessy v. Ferguson*, 163 U.S. 537 (1896), which upheld a Louisiana statute requiring that railway companies maintain racially segregated passenger coaches? Does the Court rely on this case? Distinguish this case? Overrule this case?

QUES. 5. What *standards* does the *Brown* opinion establish for resolving future cases regarding racial segregation in public facilities other than public schools? Racial segregation in *private* schools? Segregation of students in public schools on the basis of gender?

QUES. 6. Does the Court's opinion in *Brown* serve to *justify* the result that the Court reaches (see Sec. B above)?

Answers

ANS. to QUES. 1. The *Brown* case primarily raises rights issues. These issues arise under the Fourteenth Amendment's equal protection clause. The Court states the main issue in this way: "Does segregation of children in public schools solely on the basis of race, even though the physical facilities and other 'tangible' factors may be equal, deprive the children of the minority groups of equal educational opportunities?" This statement could be sharpened in two ways: (1) by adding an explicit reference to the equal protection clause; and (2) by specifying that the segregation being addressed is *state-mandated* or *state-sanctioned* segregation—what is now generally known as "de jure" (as opposed to "de facto") segregation.

Another rights issue in *Brown*, raised in the litigation but not addressed by the Court, concerns the steps that the school districts must take in order to cure or remedy the constitutional violations they have committed. The Court addressed this issue a year later in its second *Brown* opinion ("*Brown* II"), 349 U.S. 294 (1955).

Lurking behind the rights issues in *Brown* are some critical power issues. For instance, does the Court have power under Article III of the Constitution to override state law and state policy created by the state's elected representatives (the state legislature and the Governor)? This is a federalism issue. Or, does the Court have authority to intervene in and resolve school segregation problems that may fall within the scope of Congress' legislative authority to enforce the Fourteenth Amendment (U.S. Const., Amend. 14, sec. 5), in which case the problems would be capable of resolution by the elected, representative branches of the federal government? This is a separation-of-powers issue. Although the Court did not explicitly address these power issues, it did implicitly answer them in the affirmative by ruling in *Brown I* that the school districts' actions were unconstitutional, and by ruling in *Brown II* that the federal courts could order the districts to desegregate.

ANS. to QUES. 2. In *Brown*, equal protection rights were claimed by minority school children in racially segregated public schools. These children, in effect, assumed the status of *beneficiaries* (see Chap. 2, Sec. D) of the rights protected by the equal protection clause. The entities that had allegedly violated the claimed rights were public school districts, which are local governments created by the state. The equal protection clause applies to public school districts to the same extent that it applies to the states and thus limits the districts' powers to operate the schools.

ANS. to QUES. 3. The Court ruled that all the school district policies that mandated or encouraged racial segregation of students are inconsistent with the equal protection clause and therefore unconstitutional. In so ruling, the Court refused to apply the separate-but-equal standard that it had used in previous cases. In place of the separate-but-equal standard, the Court used a "separate is unequal" standard. This standard applies to racial segregation in public schools whenever the segregation is state-mandated or state-sanctioned. The Court's opinion says that all such segregation creates inequality for minority children and is unconstitutional.

ANS. to QUES. 4. The Court rejects "[a]ny language" in *Plessy* that is inconsistent with "modern authority" about the harms that racial segregation imposes upon minority school children. The Court then refuses to apply the *Plessy* separate-but-equal standard to cases of racial segregation of students in public schools. But the Court does not expressly overrule *Plessy*. It says only that "in the field of public education," the *Plessy* separate-but-equal standard "has no place." At least in theory, then, the *Plessy* case still stood as precedent for cases concerning racial segregation in public transportation systems and for other cases that did not involve students in public schools. Shortly after *Brown*, however, in a series of brief *per curiam* opinions, the Court struck down racial segregation in public facilities other than schools (*see, e.g., Mayor and City Council of Baltimore City v. Dawson*, 350 U.S. 877 (1955)), including public transportation systems (*Owen v. Browder*, 352 U.S. 903 (1956)). These decisions served effectively to overrule *Plessy*.

ANS. to QUES. 5. As the answer to QUES. 4 suggests, the Court did not establish any new standard for racial segregation in public facilities other than schools. In subsequent *per curiam* decisions, however, the Court quickly applied its new "separate is unequal" standard to other types of public facilities as well (see *Dawson* case and *Owen v. Browder* in the answer to QUES. 4 above). Regarding segregation in private schools, the Court was silent; and the *Brown* standard has no application to truly private schools. The Fourteenth Amendment provides that "[n]o State shall" deny a person equal protection; hence the equal protection clause—and the *Brown* separate-is-unequal standard—applies only to actions involving the state or its local governments. Regarding segregation by gender in public schools, the *Brown* standard, as such, does not apply. The Court in *Brown* speaks only of the harms of *racial* segregation and says only that *racial* segregation is inherently unequal. The general emphasis on equality in *Brown*, however, did eventually lead to U.S. Supreme Court decisions invalidating gender discrimination in public education, using standards somewhat different from that in *Brown*. See, e.g., *United States v. Virginia*, 518 U.S. 515 (1996), discussed in Chapter 10, Section D.4.

ANS. to QUES. 6. The legal justification for *Brown* was the subject of vigorous debate after the opinion was rendered, and it remains a subject of debate today. The focus of the debate has been on whether the Court was guided by a legitimate source or sources of constitutional interpretation (see Chap. 2, Sec. F.2) sufficient to support the result reached. For a sampling of the early debate, see, *e.g.*, Charles Black, "The Lawfulness of the Segregation Decisions," 69 YALE L. J. 421 (1960); Herbert Wechsler, "Toward Neutral Principles of Constitutional Law," 73 HARV. L. REV. 1 (1959); and Alexander Bickel, "The Original Understanding and the Segregation Decision," 69 HARV. L. REV. 1 (1955).

Chapter 4

The Context for Considering Constitutional Power Questions

Sec. A. An Overview of Federal Constitutional Powers

A.1. The Powers of the Three Branches

Through its power clauses, or empowerment clauses (Chap. 2, Sec. C), the U.S. Constitution grants power to three branches of the federal government—the legislative, executive, and judicial branches—thus enabling them to act within their established spheres of responsibility. This Chapter provides the foundation and backdrop for a study of these constitutional powers. Successive chapters address the respective powers of each of the three branches. Judicial powers are addressed first (Chap. 5), followed by Congressional powers (Chaps. 6 & 7) and executive powers (Chap. 8). These chapters also explore the essential concepts of federalism and separation of powers that shape the distribution of powers between the federal government and the states and among the branches of the federal government. Congressional powers are analyzed primarily in the context of federalism (see Chap. 6, Sec. A), and executive powers are discussed primarily in the context of separation of powers (see Chap. 8, Sec. A). Judicial powers are considered both in a separation-of-powers context and a federalism context.

The constitutional powers of each of the three branches are *delegated*, *enumerated*, and *limited* powers. These powers are *delegated* in that they come from a higher source, the "People," who delegate some of their sovereign power to each branch. These powers are *enumerated* in that they are set out, or enumerated, in the constitutional text, and each branch has only the powers enumerated for it; any powers not enumerated either have been allocated by the People (of each state) to the respective state governments, or have not been allocated at all and are therefore retained by the People. These powers are *limited* in multiple senses: *first*, they are limited in that they comprise only a portion of all possible governmental powers, encompassing only limited aspects of public and private affairs; *second*, they are limited in that they are dispersed among the three branches, each of which has constitutional means available to it for limiting or checking the powers of the other two branches (see Chap. 8, Sec. A); and *third*, they are limited in that they are subject to individual rights guarantees that individuals may assert to limit the ways in which the three branches may exercise their powers.

With one narrow exception, the U.S. Constitution empowers only the federal government and not the states. The states derive their powers from their own state constitutions (see Chap. 2, Sec. A.2, and Sec. A.2 below). The one exception concerns elections for federal offices. In Article I, section 4, paragraph 1, the U.S. Constitution authorizes the states, in particular the state legislatures, to prescribe (subject to Congressional alteration) the "Times, Places and Manner of holding Elections for Senators and Representatives." Article II, section 1, paragraph 2 also authorizes the states to "appoint, in such Manner as the Legislature thereof may direct, a Number of Electors" to cast votes in the election of the President and Vice-President. Article I, section 2, paragraph 4, and the Seventeenth Amendment, paragraph 2, authorize the "executive authority" of each state to "issue Writs of Election" to fill vacancies in the state's Congressional seats that occur between elections; and the Seventeenth Amendment authorizes the legislature of each state to arrange for "temporary appointments" of Senators pending such an election.

In *Cook v. Gralike*, 531 U.S. 510 (2001), the U.S. Supreme Court characterized Article I, section 4, paragraph 1 as a "delegation of power" to the states, but limited it to "a grant of authority to issue procedural regulations, and not…a source of power to dictate electoral outcomes [or] to favor or disfavor a class of candidates.…" (531 U.S. at 523, quoting *U.S. Term Limits, Inc. v. Thornton*, 514 U.S. 779, 833–834 (1995)). In *Bush v. Gore*, 531 U.S. 98 (2000), the Court addressed Article II, section 1 as the source of "the State legislature's power to select the manner of appointing electors" (*Id.* at 104, citing *McPherson v. Blacker*, 146 U.S. 1, 35 (1892)). But the Justices disagreed on whether, or the extent to which, a state legislature's exercise of this federal power was subject to the constraints of the state's own constitution (*see* 531 U.S. at 123–129 (Stevens, J. dissenting), and 531 U.S. at 142–143 and note 3 (Ginsburg, J., dissenting)).

A.2. Federal Constitutional Powers Compared With State Constitutional Powers

According to American constitutional theory, the original source of both federal government powers and state government powers is "the People." Prior to the ratification of the federal Constitution, most states, through "the people" of the state, had already ratified their own state constitutions that established their own state governments. In ratifying the federal Constitution, the People of the several states transferred some of their power to the federal government. But the states, by their state constitutions, retained all power that the People had not delegated to the federal government or reserved to themselves. As St. George Tucker explained in an early commentary: "In the United States of America the people have retained the sovereignty in their own hands: they have in each state distributed the government…into two distinct branches, internal and external; the former of these, they have confided…to the state government; the latter to the federal government" ("Of the Several Forms of Government,"

in St. George Tucker, VIEW OF THE CONSTITUTION OF THE UNITED STATES WITH SE-
LECTED WRITINGS (1803), Clyde N. Wilson, ed. (Liberty Fund, 1999), p. 24). And as
Mr. Justice Story explained in his COMMENTARIES:

> The true view to be taken of our State constitutions is, that they are forms
> of government ordained and established by the people in their original sov-
> ereign capacity to promote their own happiness, and permanently to secure
> their rights, property, independence, and common welfare. In general, the im-
> port is that the people "ordain and establish," that is, in their sovereign ca-
> pacity, meet and declare what shall be the fundamental Law for government
> of themselves and their posterity. [Joseph Story, COMMENTARIES ON THE CON-
> STITUTION OF THE UNITED STATES, vol. 1, p. 243 (5th ed., Melville Bigelow,
> ed.) (William S. Hein and Co., 1994).]

In contrast to the federal government's limited powers under the federal Constitution, state governments have general powers under their constitutions. Madison made
this point emphatically in *The Federalist Papers*. While the powers of "the federal government are few and defined...," he said, the powers of "the state governments are numerous and indefinite.... [They] will extend to all the objects which, in the ordinary
course of affairs, concern the lives, liberties, and properties of the people, and the internal order, improvement, and prosperity of the State" (James Madison, *Federalist
Paper No. 45*, in THE FEDERALIST: THE GIDEON EDITION, p. 241 (Carey & McClellan,
eds., Liberty Fund, 2001)).

Consistent with Madison's reasoning, state governments—in particular the state
legislatures—are generally considered to possess all power except that which is denied
to them by their state constitutions or by the federal constitution. In support of this
proposition, it is sometimes argued that the state legislatures' powers are so broad because they are inherent powers inherited from Great Britain at the time the colonies
declared their independence. At other times, it is argued that state legislative powers
are so broad because "the People" granted power in such general and broad terms that
the grant is assumed to include all governmental power not otherwise denied. The latter view seems more compatible with the views of early constitutional theorists, who
relied on social compact and original consent theories to legitimize state constitutions
as well as the federal constitution (see Chap. 2, Secs. A.2 & B), and who often perceived
the efficacy of written constitutions to depend "upon the nature and extent of those
powers which the people have reserved to themselves, as the Sovereign... [and] the extent of those [powers], which they have delegated to the government" (St. George
Tucker, *supra*, at 28; and *see generally* 22–34). But under either view, the result is the
same: the states have broad powers that stand in marked contrast to the limited powers of the federal government. *See generally* Walter F. Dodd, "The Function of a State
Constitution," 30 POL. SCI. Q. 201, 205 (1915).

Thus, rather than enumerating powers, as the federal Constitution does, the state
constitutions' power provisions allocate the general powers among the various
branches, agencies, and levels of government; and then impose order, as well as limitations, on the exercise of these powers. State constitutions also establish duties and
mandates in some areas, in lieu of discretionary powers. A key example is the state leg-

islature's or state board of education's duty to maintain a state-wide system of free public schooling. The federal Constitution, in contrast, prescribes relatively few duties or mandates. (The primary example of such a duty is the President's duty to "take care that the laws be faithfully executed" (U.S. Const., Art. II, sec. 3).)

The state's broad regulatory powers are usually called "police powers," a term that encompasses the state's regulatory authority over the health, safety, morals, and welfare of the people of the state. The police powers belong "to the states, in virtue of their general sovereignty," extend "over all subjects within territorial limits of the states," and have "never been conceded to the United States" (*Prigg v. Commonwealth of Pennsylvania*, 41 U.S. (16 Pet.) 539, 625 (1842)). Consistent with this early understanding, judges and commentators have often stated that the federal government has no general police power. In modern times, however, Congress has accomplished some police power objectives by regulating subjects that fall within the scope of its enumerated powers. Congress has, for instance, regulated health and safety in the workplace by using its commerce power (*see* Occupational Safety and Health Act of 1970, 29 U.S.C. § 651 *et seq.*).

All state constitutions provide for three branches of government, as the federal Constitution does. All state constitutions except one provide that the state's legislative power shall be vested in a two-house (or bicameral) legislature. The exception is Nebraska, which has a one-house (or unicameral) legislature. The state constitutions also generally provide that the executive power is vested in a governor, whose functions may appear similar to the domestic powers of the United States President. Unlike the federal Constitution, each state constitution also establishes various executive branch officers other than the governor. The most common examples mentioned in state constitutions are the Attorney General, the Secretary of State, and the State Treasurer. The state constitutions may not only establish these offices, but may also establish a structure for the operation of these offices. All state constitutions also provide, either partially or completely, for the organization of a judicial branch of government. While the structure varies among the states, it is common that there is one court of last resort, the highest court of the state; a level of intermediate appellate courts; and two or more levels of trial and special courts of original jurisdiction such as civil courts, criminal courts, family courts, juvenile courts, and probate courts.

The states' powers are exercised not only through the officers and agencies of the state government, but also through the officers and agencies of local governments. The state constitutions either establish or direct the state legislature to establish a variety of local governments such as counties, cities, towns, and school districts. State power is delegated to such local governments either directly by the state constitution or through enabling legislation enacted by the state legislature.

The relationship between the state government and its local governments under the state constitutions is not analogous to the relationship between the federal government and the states under the federal Constitution. Under the federal Constitution, the states are separate sovereigns that retain their sovereign power upon entering the Union; under state constitutions, the local governments are created by the states and are considered to be political subdivisions of the states. Moreover, under the federal constitution, the federal government (the larger government) is a government of limited powers, and the states (the smaller governments) are governments of general powers; under state constitutions, in contrast, the larger government (the state) is a government of general powers, and the smaller governments (local governments) are governments of limited powers. In addition, according to constitutional theory, the federal government did not create the states; they were created by the People, and the original states existed before the federal government. The states, however, do create their local governments and authorize them to act within the scope of power delegated to them by the state constitution or state statutes.

A.3. Federal Constitutional Restrictions on the Structure of State Government

Many provisions of the federal Constitution reveal the framers' assumptions that state governments would have legislative, executive, and judicial branches as does the federal government. Article I, section 4, paragraph 1, for example, assigns to "the Legislature" of each state the authority to organize the elections for U.S. Senators and Representatives; while Article I, section 2, paragraph 4, and paragraph 2 of the Seventeenth Amendment give the "Executive Authority" of the state responsibility for filling vacancies in the House and Senate that occur between elections. (These election provisions are discussed in Section A.1 above.) And Article VI, paragraph 2, provides that "the Judges in every State" must adhere to the federal Constitution and federal law as the supreme law. But there is nothing in the federal Constitution that requires the states to allocate their powers, or organize their governments, in the same way as the federal Constitution does for the federal government. The U.S. Supreme Court has affirmed this conclusion on numerous occasions. In *Dreyer v. Illinois*, 187 U.S. 71 (1902), for instance, in addressing a state statute that assigned judicial powers to persons not in the judicial department, the Court stated that "whether the legislative, executive, and judicial powers of a state shall be kept altogether distinct and separate...is a determination of the state..." and does not raise due process issues under the Fourteenth Amendment (*Id.* at 84). Subsequently, in *Sweezy v. New Hampshire*, 354 U.S. 234 (1957), Justice Frankfurter, concurring, summarized the state of the law on this point:

> It would make the deepest inroads upon our federal system for this Court now to hold that it can determine the appropriate distribution of powers and their delegation within the...States....Whether the state legislature should operate largely by committees, as does the Congress, or whether committees should be the exception, as is true for the [British] House of Commons, whether the legislature should have two chambers or only one, as in Nebraska, whether the State's Chief Executive should have the pardoning power, whether the State's judicial branch must provide trial by jury [in civil cases], are all matters beyond the reviewing powers of this Court. [354 U.S. at 256–257 (Frankfurter, J., concurring).]

And in *Mayor of Philadelphia v. Educational Equality League*, 415 U.S. 605 (1974), the Court quoted Justice Frankfurter's concurrence in *Sweezy* and concluded that "the Constitution does not impose on the states any particular plan for the distribution of governmental powers" (*Id.* at 615, note 13).

There is one clear exception to the principle enunciated in these U.S. Supreme Court cases. In *Baker v. Carr*, 369 U.S. 186 (1962) (see Chap. 5, Sec. D.6), the Court determined that the Fourteenth Amendment's equal protection clause imposes limits on the way states apportion their state legislatures in the process of drawing legislative districts.[1] Subsequently, in *Reynolds v. Sims*, 377 U.S. 533 (1964) (see Chap. 10, Sec. D.8), the Court required the states to follow a "one person, one vote" principle in apportioning their state legislatures. This exception, however, goes only to the organization of the legislative branch and does not affect the powers that the legislative branch claims or exercises.

At first blush, it might also seem that the guarantee clause of Article IV, section 4, is also an exception to the rule that the Constitution does not specify how the states shall allocate their powers or organize their governments. This clause provides that the "United States shall guarantee to every State in this Union a Republican Form of Government." But the guarantee clause has not turned out to be such an exception. The phrase "Republican Form of Government," although it suggests some type of representative government, has not been given any technical or specific meaning (*see Pacific States Tel. and Tel. Co. v. Oregon*, 223 U.S. 118 (1912)). Moreover, the United States Supreme Court has determined that the guarantee clause is non-justiciable, and the federal courts therefore will not entertain suits asserting violations of this clause (*Baker v. Carr*, above, 369 U.S. at 217–227).

Even though the federal Constitution, for the most part, leaves the organization and allocation of state powers to the respective states, it by no means follows that *particular exercises* of state powers are beyond constitutional attack. To the contrary, when an issue arises concerning a particular use of state power, by whatever body or official happens to hold that power under state law, the action may be subject to various federal constitutional challenges. In particular, it may be asserted that the action violates an individual's federal constitutional rights (Chaps. 10 through 13) or violates some federalistic limit that the Constitution imposes upon the exercise of state power (Chap. 7).

Sec. B. Introduction to Federalism and Separation of Powers

Every federal power issue comes with a context that gives it shape and import. For the purposes of this Chapter and Chapters 5 through 8, the primary context is either

---

1. This exception based on *Baker v. Carr* did not exist in 1957 at the time Justice Frankfurter penned his concurrence in *Sweezy* and is therefore not accounted for in the concurrence. When the malapportionment of state legislatures did come before the court in 1962 in *Baker*, Justice Frankfurter dissented, arguing that such issues presented "political questions" that courts should not hear.

federalism or separation of powers. This section provides an introduction to these contexts—their historical origin, the ways in which they may be distinguished from one another, and the ways in which they may intersect in some cases. Federalism is further explored in Chapter 6, Section A, and separation of powers is further explored in Chapter 8, Section A.

The first attempt to join the new states together into a national government—the Articles of Confederation—proved unworkable. The failure of the Articles may be attributed, in large part, to the weaknesses of the government that the document established. (*See, e.g.*, Joseph Story, COMMENTARIES ON THE CONSTITUTION OF THE UNITED STATES, vol. 1, secs. 243–271, pp. 173–193 (5th ed., Melville Bigelow, ed.) (William S. Hein & Co., 1994)). There was a Congress composed of delegates appointed by the state legislatures, but there was neither an executive branch nor a judiciary. The powers of the Congress were narrow (there was no power to tax, for instance, and no power to regulate interstate commerce), and the decisions of the Congress had to be approved by the states before they could become effective (Article IX). The Articles also made clear that "each state retains its sovereignty, freedom, and independence, and every Power, Jurisdiction, and right, which is not by this confederation expressly delegated to the United States, in Congress assembled" (Article II).

The delegates assembled at the Constitutional Convention in 1787 realized that, to solve the problems encountered under the Articles of Confederation, more power must be vested in the national government. Such a concentration of power in the national government, however, posed its own conundrum. Improvidently wielded, this enhanced power could undermine liberty and lead to tyranny. In his *Federalist Paper No. 51*, James Madison emphasized the need to check concentrations of governmental power:

> If men were angels, no government would be necessary. If angels were to govern men, neither external nor internal controuls on government would be necessary. In framing a government which is to be administered by men over men, the great difficulty lies in this: You must first enable the government to controul the governed; and in the next place, oblige it to controul itself. A dependence on the people is no doubt the primary controul on the government; but experience has taught mankind the necessity of auxiliary precautions. [James Madison, *Federalist No. 51*, in THE FEDERALIST: THE GIDEON EDITION, p. 269 (Carey and McClellan, eds., Liberty Fund, 2001).]

Thus the quandary for the founders was how to increase the power of the national government while at the same time ensuring that such power would not be abused. The "auxiliary precautions" that the framers devised, and set forth in the Constitution, included both a vertical division of power between the federal government and the states (federalism) and a horizontal division of power among the three branches of the federal government (separation of powers). The framers, according to Madison, intended that these divisions of power, taken together, would "not only ... guard the society against the suppression of its rulers, but [also] guard one part of the society against the injustice of the other part" (*Id.* at 264).

In crafting the Constitution's vertical division of power—federalism—the framers "split the atom of sovereignty" (*U.S. Term Limits v. Thornton*, 514 U.S. 779, 838 (1995) (Kennedy, J., concurring)). In crafting the horizontal division of power, the framers allocated the federal government's share of sovereignty among the legislative, executive, and judicial branches in order to protect "against a gradual concentration of the several powers in the same department" (James Madison, *Federalist No. 51, supra* at 268).

Not mutually exclusive, both federalism and separation of powers exist to secure individual liberty by diffusing governmental powers. Taken together, these two concepts provide what James Madison termed "a double security" against the tyrannical use of concentrated power:

> In the compound republic of America, the power surrendered by the people is first divided between two distinct governments, and then the portion allotted to each subdivided among distinct and separate departments. Hence a double security arises to the rights of the people. The different governments will controul each other, at the same time that each will be controuled by itself. [*Federalist No. 51* at 264.]

In contemporary times, the U.S. Supreme Court has made this same point concerning the mutually reinforcing roles of federalism and separation of powers: "Just as the separation and independence of the coordinate branches of the Federal Government serves to prevent the accumulation of excessive power in any one branch, a healthy balance of power between the States and the Federal Government will reduce the risk of tyranny and abuse from either front" (*Gregory v. Ashcroft*, 501 U.S. 452, 458 (1991)).

When addressing issues of constitutional power, it is always important to ascertain whether the issue arises in the context of federalism (the potential incursion of the federal government upon the powers of the states or vice-versa); or whether it arises in the context of separation of powers (the potential incursion of one branch of the federal government upon the powers of another branch). Sometimes *both* federalism and separation-of-powers issues may arise in the same case. The seminal case of *McCulloch v. Maryland*, 17 U.S. (4 Wheat.) 316 (1819), provides a classic example.

In *McCulloch*, the primary issue was whether Congress had power to create a national bank, or whether powers over banking were reserved to the states. This was a federalism issue. In siding with Congress, the Court expansively described Congress' powers: "The sword and the purse, all the external relations, and no inconsiderable portion of the industry of the nation, are entrusted to its government..."; and also recognized Congress' authority to choose the appropriate means for implementing its powers: "All means which are appropriate, which are plainly adapted to the end,... are constitutional" (*Id.* at 407, 421). This resolution of the federalism issue, however, gave rise to a separation-of-powers issue. Who would have authority to determine whether a particular "means" is "necessary and proper," that is, "appropriate" or "plainly adapted to an end within the scope of Congress' powers"? Will that authority reside in Congress alone, or will the U.S. Supreme Court and the lower courts have final authority over such issues through judicial review of Congress' legislation? The Court made clear that Congress had "discretion, with respect to the means...which will enable that body to perform [its duties] in the manner most beneficial to the people" (*Id.* at 421), and that the courts should defer to Congress' determinations. The Court then specifically tied this conclusion to separation-of-powers principles: "[T]o undertake here to inquire into the degree of [a law's] necessity, would be to pass the line which circumscribes the judicial department, and to tread on legislative ground. This court disclaims all pretensions to such a power" (*Id.* at 423).

A more recent example of how both federalism and separation-of-powers issues may arise in the same case comes from *Katzenbach v. Morgan*, 384 U.S. 641 (1966). At issue in this case was section 4(e) of the Voting Rights Act of 1965 (42 U.S.C. § 1973b(e)), which provides that no person who has attained a sixth grade education in Puerto Rico (where instruction is primarily in Spanish) could be denied the right to vote due to an inability to read or write English. The primary purpose of section 4(e) was to enfranchise New York City's Puerto Rican residents, who were being denied the right to vote because of a New York state literacy test. The federalism issue was whether section 4(e) was a valid exercise of Congress' enforcement power under the section 5 of the Fourteenth Amendment (see Chap. 6, Sec. E), such that section 4(e) would prevail over the New York literacy law. The Court determined that the Fourteenth Amendment, in section 5, granted Congress "the same broad powers expressed in the Necessary and Proper Clause.... Thus the *McCulloch v. Maryland* standard is the measure of what constitutes 'appropriate legislation' under § 5 of the Fourteenth Amendment" (*Id.* at 650–651). Using this broad construction of Congressional power, the Court held that Congress could validly prohibit New York from using its literacy test to deny the right to vote to a large proportion of its Puerto Rican community.

Dissenting in *Katzenbach v. Morgan*, Justice Harlan disagreed with the majority's construction of Congress' power under section 5 of the Fourteenth Amendment, and with its holding that section 4(e) of the Voting Rights Act was within the scope of Congress' power. For Justice Harlan, separation of powers was just as much at issue in the case as federalism. "I do not see how § 4(e) of the Voting Rights Act...can be sustained except at the sacrifice of fundamentals in the American constitutional system—the separation between the legislative and judicial function and the boundaries between federal and state political authority" (*Id.* at 659). No court had held that the New York literacy test violated the equal protection clause. Thus, by passing section 4(e), Justice Harlan reasoned, Congress had in effect determined for itself that New York's literacy test violated equal protection. Under separation-of-powers principles, according to Justice Harlan, Congress lacks the power to make such a determination because it is the province of the judiciary to rule on the constitutionality of laws:

> [I]t is a judicial question whether the condition with which Congress has thus sought to deal is in truth an infringement of the Constitution, something that is the necessary prerequisite to bringing the [Fourteenth Amendment, section 5] power into play at all....
>
> The question here is not whether the statute is appropriate remedial legislation to cure an established violation of a constitutional command, but whether there has in fact been an infringement of that constitutional com-

mand.... That question is one for the judicial branch ultimately to determine. [384 U.S. at 666–667 (Harlan, J., dissenting).]

Section 4(e) was therefore unconstitutional in Justice Harlan's view because, in passing it, Congress had overstepped its legislative bounds and intruded upon judicial functions.

Sec. C. Interpreting the Power Clauses

C.1. Overview

The early U.S. Supreme Court cases on federal powers provide excellent illustrations of how to interpret the Constitution's power clauses. Among the best examples are Chief Justice Marshall's opinions in *Marbury v. Madison*, 5 U.S. (1 Cranch) 137 (1803) (discussed in Chapter 5, Section A), *McCulloch v. Maryland*, 17 U.S. (4 Wheat.) 316 (1819) (discussed in Chapter 6, Section B.3), and *Gibbons v. Ogden*, 22 U.S. (9 Wheat.) 1 (1824) (discussed in Chapter 6, Section C.1 and Chapter 7, Section A). Since the Court had issued relatively few opinions at the time it decided these cases, and none of its earlier opinions addressed the issues raised in these cases, Chief Justice Marshall could not rely on precedent as the source of his interpretations. Instead he utilized the "primary sources" of interpretation (see Chap. 2, Sec. F.2), in particular the constitutional text, original history, and structural inferences.

In *McCulloch*, for example, Chief Justice Marshall used the constitutional text, focusing at length on the word "necessary" in the necessary and proper clause (Art. I, sec. 8, cl. 18). Interpreting that word flexibly, rather than strictly as the State of Maryland had contended, the Chief Justice first considered its "common usage," that is, "its use in the common affairs of the world, or in approved authors" (17 U.S. at 413). He then compared the word's usage in the necessary and proper clause with its usage in Article I, section 10 (17 U.S. at 414–415), and finally he considered the context in which the word was used: the context of the necessary and proper clause and, more broadly, the context of Article I, section 8's listing of Congressional powers. Even in these early cases, however, answers to the concrete issues raised could not be derived solely from the text. It was thus necessary for the Court to use historical interpretation and structural interpretation as well. In *McCulloch*, for example, as explained in Section C.3 below, Chief Justice Marshall also relied heavily on inferences he drew from the Constitution's structure. Modern bodies of judicial precedent regarding federal constitutional powers have their genesis in the historical and structural approaches just as much as they do in the textual approach.

C.2. The Historical Approach to Interpretation

The historical approach to interpretation uses "original" history as its source. This approach—sometimes called "originalism"—focuses on the concept of "framers' intent," the presumed key (along with text) to the "original understanding" of the Constitution's provisions. The historical interpreter searches for this original understanding and seeks to follow it in resolving contemporary problems. Under the narrower version of this approach, the interpreter's task is to resolve a particular dispute in the same way that the "framers" resolved it or would have resolved it had the dispute come before them during their debates. Under the broader version of historical interpretation, the task is to discover the general principles that the framers would have used to resolve a particular type of dispute, or the general purposes the framers would ascribe to a particular constitutional provision, and resolve the dispute consistent with these principles or purposes. As the U.S. Supreme Court explained in an early case:

> [P]erhaps the safest rule of interpretation after all will be found to be to look to the nature and objects of the particular powers, duties, and rights, with all the lights and aids of contemporary history,[2] and to give to the words of each just such operation and force, consistent with their legitimate meaning, as may fairly secure and attain the ends proposed. [*Prigg v. Commonwealth of Pennsylvania*, 41 U.S. (16 Pet.) 539, 610–611 (1842).]

There are three historical periods within which the interpreter searches for original understanding by consulting the "lights and aids" of contemporaneous history: the period of the framing of the original Constitution, the period of the framing of the Bill of Rights, and the period of the framing of the post-Civil War amendments (the Thirteenth, Fourteenth, and Fifteenth Amendments). The first of these periods is the most pertinent for the power clauses. The second two periods are more pertinent to the rights clauses than the power clauses (see Chap. 9, Sec. B.1). The focus is on what the framers did, said, and thought, during that historical period, gleaned not only from records of the drafting, adoption, and ratification processes, but also from relevant historical context.

One must distinguish the "original history" of these three historical periods from later history encompassing events subsequent to the original history, up to and including the modern history of the recent past. Interpreters may also use this "subsequent history," but they use it for purposes quite different from those for which they use original history. In a rights case, *Lawrence v. Texas*, 123 S.Ct. 2472 (2003), for example, the U.S. Supreme Court reviewed the history of sodomy laws from colonial times to the present, focusing especially on "the past half century," in determining whether Fourteenth Amendment liberty interests protect the sexual intimacies of homosexual persons (see Chap. 11, Sec. C.3). And in a powers case, *Youngstown Sheet & Tube Co. v. Sawyer*, 343 U.S. 579 (1952), several Justices used 20th century history of Congressional consideration of legislation for resolving labor disputes, and 20th century history of Presidential seizures of private property, in determining whether the President had power under Article II to seize the nation's steel mills to avert a strike

---

2. [author's footnote] In context, the Court's reference to "contemporary history" meant the history contemporaneous with the passage of the constitutional clause at issue — in particular the contemporaneous history concerning the object or purpose of the clause — supplemented by the subsequent history of the clause's actual operation and acceptance up to the time of the litigation in which the court is interpreting the clause (41 U.S. (16 Pet.) at 610–612, 620–621).

during the Korean War (see Chap. 8, Sec. D.1). In neither case was this history used to support an original history approach to interpretation. It served instead as a kind of precedent that supported, or failed to support, the interpretations being asserted by the parties and considered by the Court (see Chap. 2, Sec. F.2).

Contemplation of the original history approach reveals substantial theoretical problems and substantial limits on its usefulness. The threshold question is one of legitimacy: Why should the framers' intentions, apart from those embodied in the text itself, be authoritative in constitutional interpretation? If the framers had a narrow view of Presidential powers or a broad view of the states' reserved powers, for example, or if the framers accepted gender discrimination, why should twenty-first century Americans be bound by these views?

The People who adopted the Constitution adopted only the written text, not any separate intentions of the framers. The constitutional text does not tell us that later generations are to be bound by the framers' intent, nor is there even a "framers' intent" that later generations must follow the framers' intent. *See* H. Jefferson Powell, "The Original Understanding of Original Intent," 98 HARV. L. REV. 885 (1985); *compare* Charles Lofgren, "The Original Understanding of Original Intent?" 5 CONSTITUTIONAL COMMENTARY 77 (1988).

Nor should interpreters be naturally inclined to follow the framers' intent because the framers were a representative cross-section of American society. To the contrary, they were not a representative cross-section then, and they would be even farther from being so today. The framers, for instance, did not include African Americans, or other racial minorities, or women, or unpropertied persons.

Moreover, it is questionable whether the framers had a collective state of mind that is capable of ascertainment—a collective state of mind, that is, concerning either the general principles and purposes that underlie particular constitutional provisions or structures, or the specific rules that are to be used to resolve particular problems. If there is no such collective state of mind, or if it cannot be perceived from our twenty-first century perspective, then the framers' intent as a source for interpretation is elusive at best, misleading and fruitless at worst. It may be argued, in this regard, that the debates and decisions of deliberative bodies such as the Constitutional Convention and the ratifying conventions are so influenced by political compromise and inconsistent mixtures of principle and expedience, so subject to unexpressed intentions and purposive vagueness, that no collective state of mind can be discerned for many matters of enduring importance. Justice Story cautioned about this problem many years ago:

> The Constitution was adopted by the people of the United States, and it was submitted to the whole upon a just survey of its provisions as they stood in the text itself. In different States and in different conventions, different and very opposite objections are known to have prevailed, and might well be presumed to prevail. Opposite interpretations, and different explanations of different provisions, may well be presumed to have been presented in different bodies to remove local objections, or to win local favor. And there can be no certainty, either that the different State conventions in ratifying the Constitu-

tion gave the same uniform interpretation to its language, or that even in a single State convention the same reasoning prevailed with a majority, much less with the whole of the supporters of it....It is not to be presumed that, even in the convention which framed the Constitution, from the causes above mentioned and other causes, the clauses were always understood in the same sense, or had precisely the same extent of operation. Every member necessarily judged for himself; and the judgment of no one could be, or ought to be, conclusive upon that of others. [Joseph Story, COMMENTARIES ON THE CONSTITUTION OF THE UNITED STATES, vol. 1, § 406, pp. 309–310 (5th ed., Melville Bigelow, ed.) (Wm. Hein and Co., 1994).]

Despite these theoretical difficulties, the legitimacy of the historical approach has been at least partly conceded by most interpreters over time. *See, e.g.*, Jeb Rubenfeld, "The Moment and the Millennium," 66 GEO. WASH. L. REV. 1085 (1998). Other questions then arise about the use of this approach. For example, who were the framers? The question must be asked separately for each of the three historical periods noted above. For the original Constitution, for instance, are the framers those who actually drafted the language? Or all delegates to the Constitutional Convention who signed the document in Philadelphia? Or do the framers also include the delegates to the state ratifying conventions whose actions made the Constitution the law of the land? Most commentators now acknowledge that the framers include not only those who participated in the drafting and approval process but also those who participated in the ratifying conventions. The practical difficulties of searching for a framers' intent increase with this broadened definition of the group. One must explore not only the minds (or collective mind) of the delegates to the Convention in Philadelphia, but also the minds (or collective mind) of the delegates to the ratifying conventions in each of the states.

Another question concerns documentation. If there is a framers' intent that is theoretically ascertainable, then some credible historical record must be found or reliably reconstructed before the framers' intent can meaningfully guide interpretation. (*See generally* James H. Huston, "The Creation of the Constitution: The Integrity of the Documentary Record," 65 TEX. L. REV. 1 (1986)). The Constitutional Convention met in secrecy, however, and the sketchy official proceedings (recording only votes taken) were not transmitted to the state ratifying conventions. There thus was neither general public knowledge of Convention proceedings nor any official mechanism for informing the state conventions of these proceedings, let alone of the framers' "intentions" that undergirded these proceedings.[3] Records of some sort were

---

3. James Madison did record his own personal notes on the proceedings of the Constitutional Convention, and in 1840, after Madison's death, the Library of Congress published them in THE PAPERS OF JAMES MADISON, 3 vols., Henry D. Gilpin, ed. (1840). Seventy years later, Max Farrand pieced together and published a more extensive record of the Convention's proceedings, comprised primarily of Madison's notes supplemented by the surviving personal notes of various other delegates. *See* Max Farrand, THE RECORDS OF THE FEDERAL CONVENTION OF 1787, 3 vols. (Yale University Press, 1911), available online at <http://rs6.loc.gov/ammem/amlaw/ lwfr.html>. Farrand's

kept of the proceedings of most of the state ratifying conventions[4], but they are of limited utility in ascertaining the "intent" of a particular convention, let alone the overall framers' intent. Articles in newspapers and pamphlets of the era, recording the contemporaneous public debate, are also often consulted (*see* Maxwell Bloomfield, "Constitutional Values and the Literature of the Early Republic," 11:4 J. AM. CULTURE 53 (1988)). The Federalist Papers are, of course, a primary example.[5] These publications strike broad themes and portray the sides of the debate on broad issues, and they are valuable and fascinating historical documents. But they generally do not provide specific answers to concrete issues, nor do they document the weight of public opinion. Overall, many modern commentators have argued that the historical record is sparse and often less than enlightening—especially when the ratifiers are included among the framers. *See, e.g.*, Ronald Dworkin, "The Forum of Principle," 56 N.Y.U. L. REV., 469, 476–497 (1981). As Justice Jackson remarked, "[j]ust what our forefathers did envision, or would have envisioned had they foreseen modern conditions, must be divined from materials almost as enigmatic as the dreams Joseph was called upon to interpret for Pharaoh" (*Youngstown Sheet & Tube Co. v. Sawyer*, 343 U.S. 579, 634 (1952) (Jackson, J., concurring)).

Finally, with historical interpretation, there is also a problem of generality or abstraction. In situations where there is a framers' intent for which we have or can reconstruct a reliable historical account, the interpreter must determine the level of generality or abstraction on which to address and apply the historical data. Suppose that, for a given issue, the historical record reveals only the framers' general purposes regarding that subject, or only the general principles that the framers might apply in such a situation: Is that sufficient? Or should interpreters work with the framers' intent only if the historical record reveals a specific and concrete intent? Furthermore, suppose that the historical record supports two different versions of the framers' intent on a particular subject—one specific and concrete, grounded in the realities of the framers' own time period; the other more general and abstract, looking toward yet unknown future realities. Which intent should guide constitutional interpretation? For example, regarding the contract clause (U.S. Const., Art. I, sec. 10), is the framers' intent to protect creditors by prohibiting states from relieving debtors of their debts (a specific and concrete intent); or is the framers' intent a broader one of promoting economic stability (a general and abstract intent)? If interpreters follow the former intent, then the states may not interfere with the claims that creditors have against debtors, even in times of great fiscal distress. But if interpreters follow the latter intent, some relief of

introduction in this work reviews the lack of the official records of the Philadelphia convention and the extent and reliability of Madison's personal notes.

4. The best collection available is THE DEBATES IN THE SEVERAL STATE CONVENTIONS ON THE ADOPTION OF THE FEDERAL CONSTITUTION, 5 vols., Jonathan Elliot, ed. (J.B. Lippincott, 1891), available online at <http://rs6.loc.gov/ammem/amlaw/lwed.html>.

5. A good source of the Federalist Papers, and the one used in this book, is THE FEDERALIST: THE GIDEON EDITION, Carey & McClellan, eds. (Liberty Fund, 2001). The most cited source for the "anti-federalist papers" is Herbert Storing, ed., THE COMPLETE ANTI-FEDERALIST (7 vols.) (Univ. Of Chicago Press, 1981).

debtors in times of fiscal distress would be permissible when it promotes the stability of the state's economy. See *Home Building and Loan Association v. Blaisdell*, 290 U.S. 398 (1934), in which the Court majority took the latter approach, and four dissenting Justices took the former approach.

Even if an interpreter can determine a basis for choosing between a specific and a general framers' intent, either choice may present further problems. If one declines to generalize, using history only to find specific answers to specific problems that the framers resolved or envisioned, little or no guidance will be available for most contemporary constitutional issues. But if one generalizes, there must be some basis for determining a stopping point beyond which the generalization is too abstract to be useful or reliable. (This problem is further discussed, in the context of rights, in Chapter 9, Section B.3.)

Although the conceptual and practical difficulties of the historical approach do not undermine its role in interpretation, they do suggest that interpreters must be most circumspect in considering when and how to use history. "It is obvious," Justice Story remarked, that contemporaneous interpretations of the Constitution "must be resorted to with much qualification and reserve" (Joseph Story, *Commentaries on the Constitution, supra*, vol. 1 at p. 309. Thus original history may be helpful for some constitutional problems but not for others; and even for those problems where history is helpful, the role it should play may often be quite modest. *See generally* Richard B. Saphire, "Originalism and the Importance of Constitutional Aspirations," 24 HASTINGS CONST. L. Q. 599 (1997).

C.3. The Structural Approach to Interpretation

The structural approach has its source in the overall governmental structure that the Constitution establishes. As Justice Story explained this approach:

> In construing the Constitution of the United States, we are, in the first instance, to consider what are its nature and objects, its scope and design, as apparent from the structure of the instrument, viewed as a whole, and also viewed in its component parts.... Where the words admit of two senses each of which is comfortable to common usage, that sense is to be adopted which, without departing from the literal import of the words, best harmonizes with the nature and objects, the scope and design, of the instrument. [Joseph Story, COMMENTARIES ON THE CONSTITUTION OF THE UNITED STATES, vol. 1, pp. 307–308 (5th ed., Melville Bigelow, ed.) (Wm. Hein & Co., 1994).]

With the structural approach, therefore, the focus is on the document "as a whole" and its "component parts," rather than on any particular word or phrase. The key is to identify and understand constitutional mechanisms and relationships and the political principles that underlie them. The interpreter then draws inferences from that structure—inferences about how particular constitutional problems should be resolved in order to maintain the integrity of the structure or uphold the political principles upon which the structure is based. *See generally* Charles Black, STRUCTURE AND RELATIONSHIPS IN CONSTITUTIONAL LAW (Louisiana State Univ. Press, 1969). The structural approach thus requires the interpreter to work with the concepts of federalism and separation of powers (see Sec. B above) and with political principles regarding constitutionalism and representative democracy (see Chap. 2, Secs. A.2 and A.3).

The classic example of the structural approach is Chief Justice John Marshall's opinion in *McCulloch v. Maryland*, 17 U.S. (4 Wheat.) 316 (1819). In upholding Congress' power to incorporate the Bank of the United States, and also invalidating Maryland's tax on the bank, the Chief Justice relied on inferences that he drew from both the federal/state structure of the Constitution and from the structural relationship between Congress and the U.S. Supreme Court. *Marbury v. Madison* provides another example of structural interpretation. In recognizing the U.S. Supreme Court's power to declare acts of Congress unconstitutional, Chief Justice Marshall invoked the theory of written constitutions and limited powers, and emphasized the particular structure by which the U.S. Constitution limits the powers of the federal government's three branches.

Many twentieth century examples of structural interpretation come from the line of cases placing "federalistic" limits on the states' power to regulate trade (see Chap. 7, Sec. B). In *Baldwin v. G.A.F. Seelig, Inc.*, 294 U.S. 511, 523 (1935), for instance, the Supreme Court inferred that, under the Constitution, our nation is a single economic unit in which "the peoples of the several states must sink or swim together." Other leading examples of structural interpretation come from the cases on state autonomy and state immunity (see Chap. 6, Secs. C.3 to C.5). In *New York v. United States*, 505 U.S. 144 (1992), for instance, the Court invalidated a provision of a federal radioactive waste statute because the provision "infring[es] upon the core of state sovereignty reserved by the Tenth Amendment [and] is inconsistent with the federal structure of our Government established by the Constitution" (*Id.* at 177). And in *Alden v. Maine*, 527 U.S. 706 (1999), the Court granted the states immunity from certain suits in their own courts, holding that such protection is required by "our federalism" and is "preserved by constitutional design" (*Id.* at 748).

As with textual and historical interpretation, there are substantial limitations to the use of the structural approach. Different interpreters may have different understandings of the very same mechanism or relationship. Underlying principles may be unclear, or they may compete with other contrasting principles that speak to the same issue. For some problems, therefore, it may be possible to draw a range of differing inferences from structure, and there may be no reliable way to determine which one controls. For other problems there may be no sound inference to be drawn, since structural arrangements do not sufficiently address the matter. Thus, as with the textual and historical approaches, interpreters will often be unable to rely on the structural approach, standing alone, to solve constitutional power problems.

Sec. D. Historical Timeline for the Development of Federal Constitutional Powers

Before adopting the U.S. Constitution, the founders had already adopted state constitutions in most of the states and experimented with a minimal form of national government under the Articles of Confederation. The U.S. Constitution ratified in 1788 provided for a much stronger national government. This government's powers were expanded in the post-Civil War era due to ratification of the Thirteenth, Fourteenth, and Fifteenth Amendments, which enhanced Congressional and judicial power more than executive power. The time from the first experiments with state constitutions in 1776 to the Fifteenth Amendment's ratification in 1870 may be considered the first phase in the development of federal powers. The second phase may then be considered to be from 1870 to 1937. During this phase, the original powers and the newer powers evolved at an uneven pace. Regarding federalism, the balance of power at times continued to shift toward the federal government and at other times shifted back toward the states. Regarding separation of powers, there were many fewer constitutional developments and no clear trends. In general, the U.S. Supreme Court construed federal powers, especially Congressional powers, more expansively during the New Deal than it had previously, with the federalism pendulum clearly swinging toward the federal government beginning in 1937. The third phase in the development of federal powers begun in 1937, lasted until 1992, when the Court majority had its first success in a string of cases protecting state autonomy, and this pushing the federalism pendulum back toward the states.

The third phase then gave way to a fourth phase from 1992 to the present time. In the third and fourth phases, there have also been many more separation-of-powers cases than in the first two phases, but specific trends have not been nearly as evident as they have with federalism.

The following timeline traverses these four historical periods: 1776–1870, 1870–1937, 1937–1992, and 1992 to the present. Constitutional events that are milestones in the development of federal powers are identified and described, with respect to the most pertinent power clauses, and differentiations are made among the three branches of the federal government.

1776–1787: The newly independent "states" or "commonwealths" draft their own constitutions establishing their own governments. The new state constitutions generally provide for powers to be exercised through legislative, executive, and judicial branches of government, and many of the constitutions include some kind of separation-of-powers framework. The leading examples are Virginia (1776) and Massachusetts (1780).

1781: The Articles of Confederation go into effect. They provide for a confederation government of only one branch, the Congress, which has a narrow range of powers. The states retain their "sovereignty, freedom, and independence," and most decisions of Congress require the assent of the states before becoming effective.

1788: The original Constitution is ratified, containing substantial grants of enumerated powers for Congress (*e.g.*, the taxing and spending powers, the power to borrow money on the credit of the United States, the commerce power, and the power to declare war); for the President (*e.g.*, the power to execute the laws, the power to command the Armed Forces, the power to make treaties with foreign nations, and the power to "receive Ambassadors" and thus recognize foreign governments); and for the Judiciary (the power to hear and decide a broad range of federal question cases and certain other cases). The original Constitution also contains a supremacy clause that makes the federal Constitution, laws, and treaties the "supreme Law of the Land" and binds all state court systems to comply with this supreme law.

1791: The Bill of Rights is ratified, containing one amendment concerning power: the Tenth Amendment. This Amendment captures the original understanding of the balance of powers between the federal government and the states.

1798: The Eleventh Amendment reaffirms the understanding, implicit in Article III, that the states are immune from suits in federal court. This Amendment thus restricts the powers of the federal courts and protects the sovereignty of the states. It is the first amendment adopted for the purpose of overruling a U.S. Supreme Court decision (*Chisholm v. Georgia*, 2 U.S. (2 Dall.) 419 (1793)).

1803: In *Marbury v. Madison*, 5 U.S. (1 Cranch) 137 (1803), the U.S. Supreme Court asserts the power of judicial review of acts of Congress.

1816: In *Martin v. Hunter's Lessee*, 14 U.S. (1 Wheat.) 304 (1816), while reviewing and overturning a decision of Virginia's court of appeals, the U.S. Supreme Court affirms that it may review state court decisions in the exercise of its appellate jurisdiction, and that its interpretations of federal law prevail over the interpretations of the state courts. The Court's decision serves to extend the power of judicial review first set out in *Marbury* (1803).

1819: In *McCulloch v. Maryland*, 17 U.S. (4 Wheat.) 316 (1819), the Court recognizes that Congress has broad implied powers, under the necessary and proper clause, to enact laws that are appropriate means for effectuating ends within the scope of its express powers.

1824: The U.S. Supreme Court broadly defines Congress' power to regulate "commerce…among the several states" in *Gibbons v. Ogden*, 22 U.S. (9 Wheat.) 1 (1824).

1842: In *Prigg v. Commonwealth of Pennsylvania*, 41 U.S. (16 Pet.) 539 (1842), fifteen years before the *Dred Scott* case (see below under **1856**), the Court confronts the extraordinarily sensitive issue of slavery. The case concerns the interpretation of Article IV, section 2, paragraph 3 of the Constitution, the fugitive slave clause. The Court (per Justice Story) affirms "the power and duty of the national government" to enforce the property rights of slave owners under this clause; in addition, the Court declares this power and duty to be exclusive, leaving the states no room to regulate concerning fugitive slaves. In this sense, the ruling is favorable to southern slave states that sought protection for slave owners whose slaves escape to a northern state, and unfavorable to northern states that sought to provide protections for such slaves. More broadly, however, the opinion enhances federal constitutional power at the expense of state power — thus in the longer run presumably favoring the North. The Court does this by expounding important principles concerning constitutional interpretation, constitutional *duties* of the federal government, and exclusive versus concurrent powers — principles that are not confined to the facts and context of the dispute before the Court.

1851: In *Cooley v. Board of Wardens of the Port of Philadelphia*, 53 U.S. (12 How.) 299 (1851), the U.S. Supreme Court holds that, with respect to interstate commerce, the states are limited to regulating local matters that require different treatment in accord with local conditions. Regulation of matters of national concern that require uniform treatment is left exclusively to Congress.

1856: In *Dred Scott v. Sandford*, 60 U.S. (19 How.) 393 (1856), the Court utilizes its power of judicial review to invalidate an act of Congress for the first time since *Marbury* (see **1803**). The act was the Missouri Compromise Act of 1820 that prohibited slavery in part of the territory included in the Louisiana Purchase. (See also Chap. 9, Sec. E, under **1856**)

1863: In *The Prize Cases*, 67 U.S. (2 Black) 635 (1863), the Court upholds President Lincoln's blockade of the ports of states that had seceded from the Union. The Court recognizes that the President has power, as Commander-in-Chief, to repel attacks against the United States.

1865: The Thirteenth Amendment is ratified, prohibiting slavery and involuntary servitude. Under section 2, Congress is empowered to enforce the Amendment "by appropriate legislation."

1868: The Fourteenth Amendment is ratified, prohibiting the states from violating the privileges or immunities of national citizenship or denying any person due process or equal protection. Under section 5, Congress is authorized to enforce the Amendment "by appropriate legislation."

1870: The Fifteenth Amendment is ratified, prohibiting abridgment of the right to vote on grounds of race. Under section 2, Congress is authorized to enforce the amendment "by appropriate legislation."

1883: In *The Civil Rights Cases*, 109 U.S. 3 (1883), the Court narrowly construes the powers granted to Congress by section 5 of the Fourteenth Amendment and section 2 of the Thirteenth Amendment. In particular, the Court holds that Congress' section 5 enforcement power does not reach private actions and that Congress therefore may regulate only "state action" that violates the Fourteenth Amendment.

1895: In a highly controversial decision, *Pollock v. Farmers' Loan & Trust Co.*, 157 U.S. 429, *modified*, 158 U.S. 601 (1895), the Court holds unconstitutional a Congressional statute authorizing an income tax. This case marked the Court's second use of *Marbury* (see **1803**) to justify invalidation of an act of Congress. (For the first use, see **1857**.) Subsequently, the Court's *Pollock* decision was over-ridden by the Sixteenth Amendment (see **1913**).[6]

1905: Although *Lochner v. New York*, 198 U.S. 45 (1905), is a rights case, it authorizes courts to engage in expansive review of state legislative decisions for consistency with substantive due process principles. The case therefore greatly enhances the practical significance of the power of judicial review. The Court later relinquished its claim to such a broad authority to review state economic and business legislation (*see Nebbia v. New York*, 291 U.S. 502 (1934)), but then asserted broad authority to review other types of state decisions for consistency with substantive due process (*see Griswold v. Connecticut*, 381 U.S. 479 (1965)).

1913: The Sixteenth Amendment is ratified, granting Congress power to impose a tax on incomes. The Amendment serves to overrule the Court's controversial decision in *Pollock v. Farmers' Loan and Trust Co.* (see **1895**).

1918: In *Hammer v. Dagenhart (The Child Labor Case)*, 247 U.S. 251 (1918), by a 5 to 4 vote, the Court narrowly interprets Congress' commerce power and strikes down a Congressional statute prohibiting interstate transportation of goods made by child labor.

1935: The U.S. Supreme Court invalidates a centerpiece of New Deal legislation, the National Industrial Recovery Act, in A.L.A. *Schechter Poultry Corp. v. United States*, 295 U.S. 495 (1935). The Court asserts that the Act exceeded the scope of Congress' commerce power and also was an excessive delegation of legislative authority.

1936: In *Carter v. Carter Coal Co.*, 298 U.S. 238 (1936), the Court invalidates another major piece of New Deal legislation, the Coal Conservation Act, because it regulated local manufacturing rather than interstate commerce and was therefore beyond the scope of Congress' commerce power. In the same year, in *United States v. Butler*, 297 U.S. 1 (1936), the Court holds that Congress cannot use its spending power to regulate agricultural markets through agreements with farmers to curtail production, thus invalidating the Agriculture Adjustment Act of 1933.

1937: In a 5 to 4 decision in *National Labor Relations Board v. Jones & Laughlin Steel Corp.*, 301 U.S. 1 (1937), the Court majority becomes more receptive to Congress' use of its commerce power, upholding the labor/man-

---

6. For the fascinating history of *Pollock*, its use of *Marbury*, and the passage of the Sixteenth Amendment, *see* Davison Douglas, "The Rhetorical Uses of *Marbury v. Madison:* The Emergence of a Great Case," 38 WAKE FOREST L. REV. 375, 389–400 (2003).

agement relations provisions of the National Labor Relations Act. In the same year, the Court also expands Congress' taxing and spending powers in two cases. In *Steward Machine Company v. Davis*, 301 U.S. 548 (1937), the Court upholds the unemployment compensation provisions in the Social Security Act of 1935 because Congress had used its taxing and spending powers to "induce" rather than "coerce" the states to adopt federal unemployment compensation standards. In *Helvering v. Davis*, 301 U.S. 619 (1937), the Court upholds the Social Security Act's old age pension provisions because Congress had the discretion to respond to national needs by spending funds in pursuit of the "general welfare." Also in the same critical year, in *Sonzinsky v. United States*, 300 U.S. 506 (1937), the Court enhances Congress' tax power by declaring that federal courts would not investigate the "hidden motives" of Congress when reviewing tax legislation.

1941: In *United States v. Darby*, 312 U.S. 100 (1941), the Court expansively construes Congress' commerce power, upholding the Fair Labor Standards Act of 1938 which regulates the wages and hours of employment. In its opinion, the Court overrules *Hammer v. Dagenhart* (see **1918**).

1942: In *Wickard v. Filburn*, 317 U.S. 111 (1942), the Court again expansively construes the commerce power in upholding the Agricultural Adjustment Act of 1938.

1945: In *Southern Pacific Co. v. Arizona*, 325 U.S. 761 (1945), the Court uses a balancing of state and national interests to invalidate an Arizona statute regulating the length of interstate railroad trains operating within the state. The decision ushers in the modern era of "dormant commerce clause" analysis.

1952: In *Youngstown Sheet & Tube v. Sawyer (The Steel Seizure Case)*, 343 U.S. 579 (1952), the Court imposes limits on the President's power vis-à-vis that of Congress. The President cannot, without Congressional authorization, take control of a private enterprise in order to prevent jeopardy to national defense efforts. In seven opinions, the Justices set forth various approaches to interpreting Presidential powers and also initiate a debate on "formalist" versus "functionalist" approaches to separation-of-powers issues. (Justice Black for the majority takes a formalist approach; Justice Frankfurter and Justice Jackson, in concurrences, take functional approaches.)

1958: In *Cooper v. Aaron*, 358 U.S.1 (1958), a case concerning the southern states' resistance to school desegregation, the U.S. Supreme Court restates *Marbury v. Madison* to make it clear that the Court is supreme in the exposition of the law of the Constitution. The law that the Court pronounces is the supreme law of the land, binding on all state officials.

1964: In two cases, *Katzenbach v. McClung (The Ollie's Barbecue Case)*, 379 U.S. 294 (1964), and *Heart of Atlanta Motel v. United States*, 379 U.S. 241

(1964), the Court continues its expansive interpretation of Congress' commerce power by upholding a public accommodations law, Title II of the Civil Rights Act of 1964, as within the scope of the commerce clause. Congress thus accomplishes under the commerce clause in 1964 what the Court had prevented it from doing in 1883 under the Fourteenth Amendment enforcement power (*The Civil Rights Cases*): prohibit race discrimination in places of public accommodation.

1966:   In two cases under the Voting Rights Act of 1965, the Court broadly construes Congress' enforcement powers under the post-Civil War amendments. In *South Carolina v. Katzenbach*, 383 U.S. 301 (1966), the Court recognizes Congress' broad "remedial" power to remedy violations of the Amendments. In *Katzenbach v. Morgan*, 384 U.S. 641 (1966), the Court recognizes not only a broad "remedial" power but also a "substantive" power under which Congress may define for itself what state actions violate the Fourteenth Amendment. (The Court subsequently disavowed this "substantive" power; see particularly the *City of Boerne* case (under **1997**).)

1968:   In *Duncan v. Louisiana*, 391 U.S. 145 (1968), the Court "incorporates" the Sixth Amendment jury trial clause into the Fourteenth Amendment, thus reaching the apex of its ongoing process to "selectively incorporate" Bill of Rights provisions into that Amendment and apply them to the states. While all these cases were rights cases interpreting right clauses, the total effect was an alteration of the balance of power between the federal government and the states, and another enhancement of the federal courts' judicial review function.

1974:   In *United States v. Nixon*, 418 U.S. 683 (1974), the Court imposes limits on Presidential power vis-à-vis that of the federal courts. The President has an implied executive privilege based on the President's need for confidentiality, but it is a qualified privilege and does not prevail in this case over the Court's need for the information in order to ensure due process and the fair administration of criminal justice.

1983:   In *Immigration and Naturalization Service v. Chadha*, 462 U.S. 919 (1983), the Court uses separation-of-powers principles to invalidate a "legislative veto" provision in the federal Immigration and Nationality Act. The impact of the case is broad: the Court's reasoning apparently serves to invalidate "nearly 200" other legislative veto provisions in other statutes (462 U.S. at 968–1003 (White, J., dissenting)). The several opinions in the case also reinvigorate the "formalism" versus "functionalism" debate regarding separation-of-powers law. (Chief Justice Burger for the majority uses a formalist approach, while Justice Powell concurring and Justice White dissenting use functionalist approaches.) This case ushers in an era in which the Court is more frequently involved in the merits of separation-of-powers issues concerning Congress and the Executive.

1988: The Court decides *Morrison v. Olson*, 487 U.S. 654 (1988), rejecting a separation-of-powers challenge to a federal Independent Counsel statute. The decision is a primary example of the Court's willingness—charted in a line of decisions in the 1970s and 1980s—to review separation-of-powers issues on the merits. The Court's reasoning avoids and appears to reject the "unitary executive" thesis, and is more hospitable to Congress than most of the earlier 1970s and 1980s separation-of-powers cases.

1992: *New York v. United States*, 505 U.S. 144 (1992), in which the Court announces that Congress cannot "commandeer" the legislative processes of the states, begins a new federalism trend. Since this case, decided by a 6 to 3 vote, the Court has found various ways to protect the power and autonomy of the states.

1995: In *United States v. Lopez*, 514 U.S. 549 (1995), another 5 to 4 decision, the Court holds that Congress has exceeded the scope of its commerce power in passing a federal criminal statute prohibiting possession of firearms in local school zones. This case begins a trend toward a more stringent analysis of Congress' use of its commerce power to regulate local activities that affect interstate commerce.

1996: In *Seminole Tribe of Florida v. Florida*, 517 U.S. 44 (1996), the Court addresses whether Congress may "abrogate" the Eleventh Amendment sovereign immunity of the states. In a 5 to 4 decision, the Court rules that the commerce clause (the power at issue in this case) does not authorize Congress to abrogate. Distinguishing prior precedent authorizing Congress to abrogate state immunity using its power under section 5 of the Fourteenth Amendment, the Court majority indicates that the section 5 power (and presumably the Thirteenth and Fifteenth Amendment enforcement powers) provides the only basis for Congressional abrogation of state immunity.

1997: In *City of Boerne v. Flores*, 521 U.S. 507 (1997), the Court invalidates the Religious Freedom Restoration Act as beyond the scope of Congress' enforcement power under section 5 of the Fourteenth Amendment. This case explicitly rejects any concept of "substantive" power under section 5 (*see Katzenbach v. Morgan* under **1964**) and also begins a trend toward narrowing the scope of Congress' section 5 "remedial" power.

1999: *Alden v. Maine*, 527 U.S. 706 (1999), extends state immunity from suit to cover a private party's federal law claims filed against a state in *state* court. The Court again splits 5 to 4. The Court majority's reasoning makes clear that state immunity from suit is protected not only by the Eleventh Amendment, but also (and more broadly) by structural inferences drawn from the constitutional structure of federalism.

2000: In *United States v. Morrison*, 529 U.S. 598 (2000), the Court invalidates the federal Violence Against Women Act on both commerce clause and section 5 grounds. In both respects, the case contributes to the continued tightening of these two sources of Congressional power. In particular, regarding the section 5 remedial power, the Court affirms that it may only be used to remedy *state* action that violates the Fourteenth Amendment (see *The Civil Rights Cases* under the year **1883**).

2001: In *Board of Trustees of the University of Alabama v. Garrett*, 531 U.S. 356, (2001), by another 5 to 4 vote, the Court invalidates Title I of the Americans with Disabilities Act, insofar as it holds states monetarily liable for violating the Act in suits brought by private individuals. This case continues trends begun both in the *Seminole Tribe* case (see **1996**) and in the *City of Boerne* case (see **1997**), and serves both to further strengthen state claims to sovereign immunity from suit and to further narrow Congress' section 5 enforcement powers under the Fourteenth Amendment.

2002: In *Federal Maritime Commission v. South Carolina State Ports Authority*, 535 U.S. 743, 122 S. Ct. 1864 (2002), the Court extends state immunity beyond court suits to bar certain private party claims filed against a state in, and to be adjudicated by, a *federal administrative agency*. Once again, the decision is by a vote of 5 to 4.

Chapter 5

Judicial Power and Judicial Review

Sec. A. Conceptual Overview of Judicial Power

The judicial power is the focus of Article III of the Constitution. As its text reveals in section 1 and the first two paragraphs of section 2, Article III: (1) establishes the United States Supreme Court,[1] (2) provides for Congressional establishment of lower federal courts, (3) vests the Supreme Court and the lower federal courts with "[t]he judicial Power of the United States," (4) establishes the jurisdiction of the Supreme Court, and (5) draws the outer boundaries of the jurisdiction of the lower federal courts.

Just as the federal government is a government of limited powers, the federal courts are courts of limited jurisdiction. They may exercise only the jurisdiction that Article III prescribes in section 2, paragraph 1. This paragraph establishes nine categories of cases. The "judicial power" extends only to cases within one of these nine categories; all other types of cases must be left to the state courts or to non-judicial forums. The most important of the nine federal jurisdiction categories are (1) the "arising under" category, which is the basis for the statutory "federal question" jurisdiction in 28 U.S.C. § 1331; and (b) the "between citizens of different states" category, which is the basis for the statutory "diversity" jurisdiction in 28 U.S.C. § 1332.

---

1. For information on the U.S. Supreme Court, such as the Court's history, biographies of past and present Justices, and the court rules, see <http://www.supremecourtus.gov> (the Court's own website); <http://jurist.law.pitt.edu/supremecourt.htm>; and <http://supct.law.cornell.edu/supct>. The last of these sites also includes electronic versions of the constitutional provisions establishing the U.S. Supreme Court and the United States Code provisions setting out the Court's organization and jurisdiction. For a hard copy resource presenting historical and statistical information on the Court, and biographies and voting patterns of the Justices, see Lee Epstein, Jeffrey Segal, Harold Spaeth, and Thomas Walker, THE SUPREME COURT COMPENDIUM (CQ Press, 2002).

In section 2, paragraphs 1 and 2, Article III introduces the concept of "cases" or "controversies"—terms that are used specifically with reference to the Supreme Court but also have meaning for the lower federal courts. Within the nine jurisdictional categories, only disputes that take the form of a "case" or "controversy" may be decided by the federal courts (see Sec. D.3. below). In section 2, paragraph 2, Article III introduces the distinction between "original jurisdiction" and "appellate jurisdiction." The original jurisdiction covers the cases that come to the Supreme Court in the first instance, without having been considered by any lower federal or state courts. The appellate jurisdiction covers cases that reach the Supreme Court on appeal from the lower federal courts or the state courts. The Supreme Court has original jurisdiction over cases and controversies that fall within three of the nine jurisdictional categories in Article III and part of a fourth. For the remaining categories, the Supreme Court has appellate jurisdiction, and the original jurisdiction belongs to the federal district courts, the state trial courts, or both.

Not all jurisdictional issues under Article III are to be resolved by the courts themselves. By granting Congress power to establish lower federal courts, section 1 of Article III implicitly authorizes Congress to establish the jurisdiction of the lower courts that it establishes (*see Sheldon v. Sill*, 49 U.S. (8 How.) 441 (1850)). In addition, the "Exceptions" and "Regulations" clause in section 2, paragraph 2, grants Congress some authority over the Supreme Court's appellate jurisdiction (*Ex Parte McCardle*, 74 U.S. (7 Wall.) 506 (1869)). These provisions thus raise potentially sensitive issues concerning the scope of Congressional power to control the federal courts by limiting or changing their jurisdiction (see Sec. F.3 below).

The federal courts that operate under the authority of Article III are usually called "Article III courts" or "constitutional courts." This designation serves to distinguish them from other federal "courts" that Congress from time to time establishes pursuant to its Article I, section 8 powers. Examples of such other courts—usually called "Article I courts" or "legislative courts"—include the U.S. Tax Court, the local courts of the District of Columbia, the military courts (courts-martial), and The United States Court of Appeals for Veterans Claims. *See* Charles Alan Wright and Mary Kay Kane, LAW OF FEDERAL COURTS, sec. 11 (West, 6th ed. 2002).

The foundational case concerning Article III judicial power, of course, is *Marbury v. Madison*, 5 U.S. (1 Cranch) 137 (1803). In this separation-of-powers case, the U.S. Supreme Court, speaking through Chief Justice John Marshall, addressed both the relationship between the federal courts and Congress, and the relationship between the federal courts and the Executive branch. Chief Justice Marshall first upheld the Court's authority to review the Executive branch action being challenged, that is, the refusal by James Madison, Thomas Jefferson's Secretary of State, to deliver a judicial commission to Marbury, who had been appointed to the position by out-going President John Adams (see Chap. 8, Sec. D). Next, Marshall considered whether the Court had jurisdiction over the case. Reviewing Congress' authority over Supreme Court jurisdiction, the distinction between original and appellate jurisdiction, and the wording of the jurisdictional statute invoked by Marbury, Marshall determined that the statute gave the Court original jurisdiction over mandamus cases—cases that are not included within Article III's description of original jurisdiction. The jurisdictional statute was therefore in conflict with Article III of the Constitution. Marshall then addressed the issue that has become the heart of the *Marbury* case: whether "the judicial power" includes within it the power to review the constitutionality of acts of Congress. Chief Justice Marshall gave a direct and clear affirmative answer to this question, thus recognizing the concept of *judicial review* of Congressional acts. The breadth of this judicial review authority, however, is not entirely clear from Marshall's opinion. The opinion, for instance, does not address the question of how much deference the courts should give to Congress' own interpretations of the Constitution, or to Congress' own factual judgments, when they are at issue in litigation (see Sec. F.7 below). Most importantly, Marshall's opinion is not clear on whether and when the Court's rulings on constitutionality would be binding in the future on other officers and branches of government that were not parties to the case in which the Court made its ruling. In other words, although the Court clearly affirmed *judicial review* of Congressional action in *Marbury*, the Court was not clear whether the case also established *judicial supremacy*, that is, the supremacy of the Court's constitutional interpretations over those of the other two branches.

Through the years Chief Justice Marshall's reasoning in *Marbury* has been subject to frequent criticism. *See, e.g.,* Alexander Bickel, THE LEAST DANGEROUS BRANCH 1–14 (Yale Univ. Press, 2nd ed. 1986). The shortcomings in the *Marbury* reasoning are often a topic of discussion in the early weeks of constitutional law courses. (For a helpful review of these shortcomings, see William Van Alstyne, "A Critical Guide to Marbury v. Madison," 1969 DUKE L. J. 1.) But as students invariably learn, the judicial review principles in *Marbury* held firm despite the continuing criticism and eventually developed into a full-blown concept of judicial supremacy. The "modern meaning" of *Marbury*, in particular as stated in *Cooper v. Aaron*, 358 U.S. 1, 18 (1958) (discussed in Sec. B below, in Ans. to Ques. 4) entails a more expansive view of judicial power than the "original meaning" of *Marbury*.

The Article III concepts of judicial review and judicial supremacy, and their modern meaning, are the subject of the following section.

Sec. B. Exercise No. 5: Judicial Review and Judicial Supremacy (The Government's Use of Thermal Imaging Equipment for Surveillance Purposes[2])

The six questions below each present a situation concerning governmental use of thermal imaging equipment to conduct surveillance of private citizens. Each situation raises questions about judicial review and judicial supremacy in the federal courts. The settings of the questions are based on the U.S. Supreme Court case of *Kyllo v. United*

---

2. This problem was inspired by a related problem included in Paul Brest, PROCESSES OF CONSTITUTIONAL DECISIONMAKING 67–73 (Little, Brown, 1st ed. 1975).

States, which is summarized immediately below. Following the six questions is a suggested set of answers. You may wish to defer your review of the answers until you have studied the questions and formulated your own responses to them. Taken together, the questions and answers will test your understanding and also provide additional analysis of judicial review that will strengthen your grasp of both the original meaning and the modern meaning of the *Marbury* case and the modern concept of judicial supremacy.

In *Kyllo v. United States*, 533 U.S. 27 (2001), agents of the U.S. Department of the Interior had parked in a car across from Kyllo's home and used a "thermal imager" to scan the outside of the home. Thermal imagers detect infrared radiation emanating from a heat source and create images ("thermograms") indicating the relative warmth of an object or structure. The scan of Kyllo's home indicated hot areas on a roof and side wall that the federal agents suspected were caused by high-intensity lamps typically used to grow marijuana indoors. Subsequently, when Kyllo was indicted for violating federal drug laws, he argued that the thermal scan of his home was an unlawful search under the Fourth Amendment. The federal district court and U.S. Court of Appeals upheld the search, but the U.S. Supreme Court reversed, holding that the thermal imaging scan was a search within the meaning of the Fourth Amendment and that the search violated the Fourth Amendment.

Questions

QUES. 1. Was the U.S. Supreme Court acting within the scope of its judicial review power when it declared the search unconstitutional and prohibited the federal prosecutors from using the evidence?

QUES. 2. Suppose that, after the U.S. Supreme Court's ruling in *Kyllo*, the Department of the Interior agents resume thermal imaging scans at the home of Kyllo (hereinafter "K"). They do so pursuant to a new federal statute passed by Congress after the *Kyllo* decision. This statute authorizes federal Cabinet-level departments to obtain thermal imaging scans of private homes, without first obtaining a search warrant, in the course of their investigatory duties. The statute's legislative history makes clear that Congress disagrees with the U.S. Supreme Court's interpretation of the Constitution in K's case and has passed the statute in order to substitute its own interpretation for that of the Court. K's counsel seeks to have a federal district court declare the new statute unconstitutional. Must the court defer to Congress' interpretation, or may the court invalidate this statute, as applied to K, by relying on the authority of the Supreme Court's decision in *Kyllo*?

QUES. 3. Suppose that, after the U.S. Supreme Court's ruling in *Kyllo*, the Department of Interior agents resume thermal imaging scans at K's home. They do so at the order of the President of the United States, who has expressly disagreed with the U.S. Supreme Court's interpretation of the Constitution in K's case and has issued an Executive Order that expressly authorizes federal Departments to use thermal imaging equipment in criminal investigations without first obtaining a search warrant. (Assume that Congress has not passed any legislation concerning the use of thermal imaging.) K's counsel seeks to have a federal district court enjoin the Department from scanning K's home. Must the court defer to the President's interpretation, or may the court issue the injunction, relying on the authority of the Supreme Court's decision in *Kyllo*?

QUES. 4. Suppose that, after the U.S. Supreme Court's decision in *Kyllo*, another federal agency, the Drug Enforcement Administration (DEA) of the Department of Justice, uses thermal imaging equipment to scan the home of A without obtaining any search warrant. A is completely unrelated to K and lives in a different state. The DEA does the scanning in the same way and under the same circumstances as in the *Kyllo* case. A's counsel asks a federal district court to require the DEA to comply with the law as the U.S. Supreme Court expounded it in *Kyllo*, and to enjoin the DEA from scanning A's home. The DEA claims that it (and the Department of Justice) is not bound in its relations with A by a Court decision that deals with another separate person (K) and a different federal agency. Must the federal district court defer to the DEA's (and Department of Justice's) own interpretation of the Fourth Amendment's application to A, or may the court issue the injunction?

QUES. 5. Suppose that agents of a *state* Division of Narcotics suspects that B is violating *state* narcotics laws. They use thermal imaging equipment to scan B's home without obtaining any search warrant. The scanning is done in the same way and under the same circumstances as the scanning in the *Kyllo* case, except that the agents are state (not federal) agents. B's counsel goes into state court, claiming that the thermal imaging violates the Fourth Amendment of the U.S. Constitution, and asks the court to order the state Division of Narcotics to cease the scanning. Must the state trial and appellate courts apply *Kyllo* and prohibit the Division of Narcotics from engaging in the thermal imaging surveillance? If the state courts do not do so, and instead determine that the thermal imaging is *not* an unconstitutional search under the Fourth Amendment, may the U.S. Supreme Court take B's case on appeal and reject the state courts' constitutional interpretation?

QUES. 6. Suppose that the federal Drug Enforcement Administration develops an entirely new technology that allows its agents to position themselves up to 10 miles from a building or structure and closely observe the surrounding grounds. Congress passes a statute authorizing federal agencies to use this technology without a warrant, and the President issues an Executive Order implementing the statute. The constitutionality of this technology has never been tested in the federal courts. The DEA uses this technology, without obtaining a warrant, to conduct surveillance of the grounds surrounding the home of C. C discovers the surveillance. C's counsel claims that this surveillance is an unconstitutional search under the Fourth Amendment and asks a federal district court to enjoin the DEA from using this technology to conduct surveillance of C's property. The DEA argues that its actions are authorized by a Congressional statute and an Executive Order; that both Congress and the President have determined that warrantless use of this technology is permissible under the Fourth Amendment; and that the court must accept the constitutional interpretations of these two branches. Must the court do so? Or may the court interpret independently of Congress and the President, and if it determines the search to be unconstitutional, order the DEA to conform to its (the court's) interpretation?

Answers

ANS. to QUES. 1. Even under a narrow reading of *Marbury*, the U.S. Supreme Court may invalidate the search and exclude the evidence. The case came to the Court as a criminal prosecution under a federal statute. The defendant interjected the Fourth Amendment, making it part of the law to "be looked into" (*Marbury*, 5 U.S. (1 Cranch) at 179) to resolve the case. Although an executive branch department undertook the search, under *Marbury* the U.S. Supreme Court may review executive actions in the course of deciding a case. The Court was asked only to exclude the executive agency's evidence in the course of deciding the case. The court must do so if the search violates the Fourth Amendment, in order to avoid becoming an accomplice to the executive's unconstitutional action (the search). In this context, if there is any dispute about whether the search is unconstitutional under the Fourth Amendment, "[i]t is emphatically the province and duty of the judicial department to say what the law is" (*Marbury*, 5 U.S. (1 Cranch) at 177) for purposes of this litigation.

ANS. to QUES. 2. In this situation Congress has entered the fray on the side of the executive branch and the U.S. Department of the Interior. The federal district court is asked to reject Congress' (and an executive branch's) interpretation of the Constitution and hold that the U.S. Supreme Court's interpretation of the Fourth Amendment continues to control on the matter of scanning K's home. *Marbury* directly supports this result insofar as it holds that the Court may review Congressional statutes for constitutionality. But in another respect, this situation would extend judicial review of Congressional acts beyond what occurred in *Marbury*.

In *Marbury*, the U.S. Supreme Court addressed a Congressional statute that applied directly to the work of the courts (taking jurisdiction over cases), and the Court simply refused to apply that statute in the course of doing its own work. (In similar fashion, the Court in *Kyllo* had simply refused to consider the search evidence in the course of doing its own work; see Answer to Question 1, above.) In this Question, in contrast, the federal district court addresses a Congressional statute that governs the work of the executive branch (investigations and searches), not the work of the courts (taking and deciding cases). Moreover, since the statute is directed to the search itself, not the possible later use of the evidence in court, the statute does not directly interfere with the court's own work. By invalidating this statute as applied to K, then, the court would not simply be refusing to apply it in the course of doing its own work, as in *Marbury*, but would be directly interfering with the work of Congress and the Executive apart from the work of the courts.

Nevertheless, the modern meaning of *Marbury* clearly would extend judicial review to the situation described in this Question. Under the modern meaning, the federal courts' interpretations of the Constitution (and particularly the U.S. Supreme Court's interpretations) are superior to, or *supreme* over, any contrary interpretations of Congress, even if Congress has conscientiously considered and formally rejected a prior Court interpretation. Moreover, the federal courts' judicial review authority applies to all Congressional statutes, whether or not they address the work of the courts, and the courts may act affirmatively to prohibit the implementation of an unconstitutional statute, rather than just refusing to apply an unconstitutional statute in the course of their own work on a particular case.

It does not matter that a federal district court rather than the U.S. Supreme Court would invalidate the statute, since the "judicial power" and judicial review authority under Article III also vests in the lower federal courts.

ANS. to QUES. 3. In this situation, the President rather than Congress has intervened on the Department of Interior's side. The federal district court is asked to reject a Presidential interpretation of the Fourth Amendment, as applied to K, that is different from the U.S. Supreme Court's interpretation in *Kyllo*, which the President has expressly declined to follow. The Court is also asked to issue and enforce a court order directly against executive branch officials. In *Marbury*, although the Court did review executive action (the refusal to issue the commission), it did not reject any executive branch interpretation of the Constitution, nor did it subject executive officials to court orders to enforce the Court's ruling. The *Marbury* Court's ruling of unconstitutionality applied to Congress' jurisdictional statute, rather than to an executive action, and did not necessitate any injunctive relief. There was therefore no need to consider whether the executive branch could interpret the Constitution differently from the Court for purposes of its own executive branch business (*i.e.*, criminal investigations prior to or apart from any criminal prosecution).

Nevertheless, the modern meaning of *Marbury* clearly covers this type of review of executive branch action. Under the modern meaning, the Supreme Court's interpretation is superior to, or *supreme* over, the contrary interpretation of the Executive, even if the Executive has conscientiously considered and formally rejected a prior Court interpretation, and even if the Executive applies its interpretation only to its own executive functions outside the courts. Thus in the situation in this Question, if the executive branch persists in refusing to honor the U.S. Supreme Court's interpretation of the Fourth Amendment, the federal district court may order Executive compliance by enjoining the scanning of K's home.

It does not matter that a federal district court rather than the U.S. Supreme Court would issue the injunction in this case, since the "judicial power" and judicial review authority under Article III also vests in the lower federal courts.

ANS. to QUES. 4. In this situation, A's counsel seeks to apply the U.S. Supreme Court's constitutional ruling in the *Kyllo* case to persons and to government agencies that were not parties in that case. In effect, A's counsel is claiming that the Court's ruling in *Kyllo* protects all other persons in circumstances similar to K's and binds all other government agencies, even though they were not parties to the case. In other words, A's counsel is asserting that the U.S. Supreme Court's interpretation of the Constitution is the "*law of the land*" rather than just the "*law of the case.*" In *Marbury*, in contrast, it was sufficient for the Court's ruling to be the *law of the case*; the same jurisdictional issue would not arise again without there being another case, so the *law of the land* issue did not directly arise.[3]

---

3. One of the most famous statements about this dichotomy between *law of the case* and *law of the land* was made by Abraham Lincoln in his First Inaugural Address on March 4, 1861. Having in mind constitutional questions regarding slavery and secession, Lincoln conceded "that constitutional questions are to be decided by the Supreme Court" and "that such decisions must

Under the modern meaning of *Marbury*, however, the Court's pronouncements on constitutionality clearly are the supreme law of the land, binding on all government agencies in their relations with all persons. The leading case is *Cooper v. Aaron*, 358 U.S. 1 (1958), in which the U.S. Supreme Court addressed the desegregation of the Little Rock, Arkansas public schools in the wake of the U.S. Supreme Court's 1954 decision in *Brown v. Board of Education* (see Chap. 9, Sec. C, below). Neither the State of Arkansas nor any of its local school districts had been a party to the *Brown* litigation. Arkansas asserted that it was not bound, and its school districts were not bound, by the ruling in *Brown*. The U.S. Supreme Court sweepingly rejected this assertion, stating that "the federal judiciary is supreme in the exposition of the law of the Constitution," and therefore "the interpretation...enunciated...in the *Brown* case is the Supreme *law of the land*" (358 U.S. at 18).

The federal court in this Question may therefore apply the *Kyllo* ruling and enjoin the DEA from scanning A's property.

ANS. to QUES. 5. This situation differs from those in Questions 1-4 in that a state (rather than federal) agency is doing the surveillance and a state (rather than federal) court is doing the initial constitutional interpretation. Under the Supremacy Clause (U.S. Const., Art. VI, ¶ 2), however, it is clear that the state courts are bound by the federal Constitution and cannot issue judgments or orders that would be unconstitutional under the federal Constitution. It is also clear from early U.S. Supreme Court cases following *Marbury* that the state courts may interpret the federal Constitution for themselves but the U.S. Supreme Court may review their interpretations; in case of disagreement, the U.S. Supreme Court's interpretation is supreme. *Martin v. Hunter's Lessee*, 14 U.S. (1 Wheat.) 304 (1816); *Cohens v. Virginia*, 19 U.S. (6 Wheat.) 264 (1821).

Thus the state courts in this Question would be bound to apply the law as the U.S Supreme Court expounded it in *Kyllo*; and if they do not do so, the U.S. Supreme Court may review and reverse their contrary interpretations. The federal courts' judicial supremacy over the state courts, and over state agencies and officials, is just as broad as the federal courts' judicial supremacy over federal officials and agencies described in Questions 1–4, above.

ANS. to QUES. 6. This situation differs from Questions 1–5 in that there is no previous U.S. Supreme Court or federal court Fourth Amendment ruling on point, but there are already Congressional and Presidential determinations of constitutionality.

---

be binding in any case, upon the parties to a suit, as to the object of that suit...." But he forcefully denied that "vital questions" of public policy could be "irrevocably fixed by decisions of the Supreme Court, the instant they are made, in ordinary litigation between parties...." The most Lincoln would concede regarding such broader effects of Supreme Court decisions was that the Court's rulings are "entitled to a very high respect and consideration, in all parallel cases, by all other departments of the government." Roy Basler, ed., THE COLLECTED WORKS OF ABRAHAM LINCOLN, vol. IV, p. 268 (Rutgers Univ. Press, 1953). This would have been a fair and supportable description of judicial review at the time of the Civil War, but it would no longer be supportable after the U.S. Supreme Court's decision in *Cooper v. Aaron* (below) in 1957.

C's counsel brings the case to court specifically to obtain a constitutional ruling from the judicial branch. Nevertheless, the modern concept of judicial review, as developed in the answers to Questions 2, 3, and 4, would clearly extend to this situation. The federal district court should consider, and accord respect to, the interpretations of the President and Congress, but it need not defer to them (see Section C below). Taking as much guidance as it can from *Kyllo* and other Supreme Court cases on the Fourth Amendment, the federal district court may interpret the Constitution for itself, may reject the interpretations of the Congress and the President if contrary to its own, and may issue an injunction against the DEA if it determines that the DEA's surveillance activity violates the Fourth Amendment. The DEA could appeal a ruling against it to the U.S. Court of Appeals, and if it loses again could ask the U.S. Supreme Court to review the case by a writ of certiorari.

The result would be the same if a state agency were using the new surveillance technology, as authorized by its own state legislature and governor, and C's counsel had sued the state agency in federal court.

ANS. to QUES. 1–6 (SUMMARY). In sum, although it is not clear that the original understanding of *Marbury* would encompass all the applications of judicial power suggested in Questions 1–6, it is clear that the *modern* understanding of *Marbury*, confirmed by 20th century cases such as *Cooper v. Aaron*, does encompass all of these applications. Section F.1 below provides further elucidation of this modern understanding of judicial review and judicial supremacy.

Sec. C. Who Interprets the Constitution?

In illustrating the supremacy of federal court interpretations of the Constitution, Exercise No. 4 (Sec. B above) also raises questions about the roles that other governmental bodies and officers may play in the process of constitutional interpretation. These questions concern not only the role of state courts but also the roles of non-judicial bodies and officers at the federal, state, and local levels of government.

It is clear that state courts play an important interpretive role in our constitutional system that supplements the work of the federal courts. The Constitution expressly binds state court judges to the Constitution and requires them to take an oath to support the Constitution (Art. VI, ¶'s 2 & 3). In *Martin v. Hunter's Lessee*, 14 U.S. (1 Wheat.) 304 (1816), the U.S. Supreme Court confirmed an interpretive role for state courts in the course of upholding the U.S. Supreme Court's authority to review and reverse their constitutional interpretations.

Beyond the courts, non-judicial bodies and officers also have roles to play as constitutional interpreters. Consideration of these roles begins with *Marbury v. Madison*, 5 U.S. (1 Cranch) 137 (1803), in which the U.S. Supreme Court interpreted Article III differently than had the U.S. Congress and gave binding effect to its own interpretation. In so doing, however, the Court did not hold that Congress lacked authority to interpret the Constitution, or that it had no responsibility to do so. To the contrary, in declaring that the Constitution is "a rule for the government of *courts*," the Court simultaneously made clear that it is also a rule for the government "of the legislature" (*Id.* at 180); and in declaring that "the courts...are bound by" the Constitution, the Court simultaneously made clear that the "other departments" are also bound (*Id.*). It follows that Congress must have an interpretive role to play in assuring that it faithfully adheres to the Constitution as the binding rule governing all of its decision-making. The Court has clearly confirmed this understanding in the modern case of *City of Boerne v. Flores*, 521 U.S. 507 (1997). The majority, quoting James Madison, declared: "When Congress acts within its sphere of power and responsibilities, it has not just the right but the duty to make its own informed judgment on the meaning and force of the Constitution. This has been clear from the early days of the Republic" (*Id.* at 535). Justice O'Connor, in dissent, made the same point. She noted "Congress' obligation to draw its own conclusions regarding the Constitution's meaning" and declared that "Congress, no less than this Court, is called upon to consider the requirements of the Constitution and to act in accordance with its dictates" (*Id.* at 745–746 (O'Connor, J. dissenting)).[4]

Similar reasoning applies to the President and the Executive branch, and also to state and local legislative bodies and officials. The Constitution's empowerment provisions are addressed to the Executive just as much as they are to Congress and the federal courts. The Constitution's individual rights provisions are addressed to all policy-making agencies and officials of government — federal, state, and local — that are limited by these provisions. Moreover, the Constitution itself requires the President, the members of Congress, the members of the state legislatures, the state governors, and all other executive officials of the federal and state governments to take an oath to support the Constitution (Art. II, sec. 1, ¶ 8; Art. VI, ¶ 3). Since all are bound to uphold the Constitution, all are responsible for interpreting it insofar as constitutional questions arise in the course of their official duties. In this sense, the United States Congress may be said to be an official constitutional interpreter, as are the President, the heads of federal executive departments, the state legislatures, and the governors of the states. By extension, other officers or agencies that exercise delegated federal or state governmental power — such as a city council or the commissioners of a federal or state administrative agency — also may be considered official constitutional interpreters.

Thus, although it has become increasingly clear since *Marbury* that the United States Supreme Court is, for most purposes, the "ultimate interpreter of the Constitution" (*Powell v. McCormack*, 395 U.S. 486, 521, 549 (1969)), quoting *Baker v. Carr*, 369 U.S. 186, 211 (1962)), this judicial role does not obliterate the interpretive roles of non-judicial government officers and bodies. *See* Keith E. Whittington, "Extrajudicial Constitutional Interpretation: Three Objections and Responses," 80 N. CAROLINA L. REV. 773 (2002). They remain responsible for interpreting the Constitution, as applied to their

---

4. The majority opinion and Justice O'Connor's dissent in *Boerne* qualified these statements by indicating that Congress is not free to interpret the Constitution in ways that are inconsistent with the Court's own interpretations. The reasoning and result of the majority opinion in *Boerne* rely heavily on this qualification (see Chap. 6, Sec. E, and Chap. 14, Sec. C).

own activities and decisions, until such time as the courts have spoken definitively on the issues that arise. Such judicial pronouncements may not occur until years after an issue first arises, in large part because of the considerable financial costs and strategic difficulties of sustaining litigation. Occasionally such judicial pronouncements will not occur at all, due to judicial invocations of non-justiciability (see Sec. D.4 below) and the interpretation of the other government body will remain in effect.

When issues concerning the interpretations of other governmental officials and bodies do come before the courts, that official or body is responsible for presenting its constitutional interpretation to the court, and this interpretation is entitled to due respect—especially the interpretations of Congress and the Executive branch. The U.S. Supreme Court emphasized this point in *United States v. Nixon*, 418 U.S. 683, 703 (1974): "In the performance of assigned constitutional duties each branch of the government must initially interpret the Constitution, and the interpretation of its powers by any branch is due great respect from the others." When another branch's interpretation and related practices have been consistently applied over a long period of time, the courts may consider this interpretation to be of such "great weight" as to be "almost conclusive" (*Eldred v. Ashcroft*, 123 S.Ct. 769, 785 (2003), quoting *Burrow-Giles Lithographic Co. v. Sarony*, 111 U.S. 53, 57 (1884)). Such deference to a coordinate branch's interpretation is especially likely when it began as a "contemporary...exposition of the Constitution when the founders of our Government and framers of our Constitution were actively participating in public affairs," and has been "acquiesced in for a long term of years...." (*Eldred*, 123 S.Ct. at 785, quoting *Myers v. United States*, 272 U.S. 52, 175 (1926)). (Judicial deference to the interpretations and judgments of other branches of government is further developed in Chapter 15, Section C.5.)

Even when courts have previously ruled on matters that arise from the activities of government officers or bodies, the latter still have an interpretive role to play. The court's decision may establish guidelines that leave sensitive interpretive judgments to legislators or others whose activities were at issue. Additionally, if the officers or bodies disagree with the courts' interpretation, they may seek to raise the issue again, present the basis for their contrary interpretation, and urge judicial reconsideration. In all of these respects, non-judicial bodies and officers are important participants in the process of constitutional interpretation.

Sec. D. Jurisdiction and "Justiciability" in Federal Courts

D.1. Overview

There are several requirements that a prospective plaintiff must meet in order to invoke the Article III "judicial power" and thus litigate a claim in federal court. First, the claim must fall within one of Article III's nine jurisdictional categories, as implemented by Congress pursuant to its authority over federal court jurisdiction. Second, the underlying dispute must constitute a "case" or "controversy" within the meaning of Arti-

cle III, section 2, paragraphs 1 and 2. Third, the suit must conform to various "prudential" requirements intended to assure that the dispute is in a shape and form suitable for current judicial disposition on the merits. Thus not every legal dispute between
contending parties, nor every question of federal constitutional law, is subject to the
exercise of Article III "judicial power"; and not every party with an interest in a constitutional law question may litigate it in federal court.

The second and third requirements are governed by a variety of technical doctrines
concerning access to the federal courts. *See generally* Charles Alan Wright and Mary
Kay Kane, LAW OF FEDERAL COURTS, secs. 12, 13, 14, 52 and 52A (6th ed., 2002). The
doctrines, taken together, are often called doctrines of "justiciability."[5] A dispute that
is within the subject matter jurisdiction of the federal courts will be "justiciable" —
that is, litigable in the courts — only if it satisfies all the requirements of the justiciability doctrines. When courts consider whether a dispute qualifies as a "case or controversy," they are applying the "constitutional" components of justiciability. When
courts consider whether a case meets "prudential" requirements, they are applying the
"prudential" components of justiciability, that is, the components that are not mandated by the Constitution but that courts have created to channel their discretion in
the exercise of judicial self-restraint. (*See, e.g., Allen v. Wright,* 468 U.S. 737, 751 (1984).)

The law on justiciability encompasses three basic conditions that must be met before a federal court will hear and decide a legal claim on the merits: (1) there must be
proper parties (a "WHO" question); (2) there must be proper timing (a "WHEN" question); and (3) there must be a proper issue (a "WHAT" question). The courts have embodied these three generic conditions in six specific justiciability doctrines:

1. the advisory opinion doctrine (WHO, WHAT, and WHEN questions);
2. the standing doctrine (WHO questions);
3. the mootness doctrine (WHEN questions);
4. the ripeness doctrine (WHEN questions);
5. the political question doctrine (WHAT questions); and
6. the abstention doctrines (WHAT and WHEN questions).

When a dispute's characteristics (the "who," "what," and "when") are such as to meet
the constitutional and prudential requirements of these six doctrines, the federal court
will hear the dispute. When the dispute's characteristics fail to meet either the constitutional or the prudential aspects of one or more of these doctrines, the federal court
will not hear the dispute.

The justiciability doctrines are addressed seriatim in Sections D.2 through D.7 below,
followed by a discussion of the related doctrines of sovereign immunity in Section E.
Section F.4 below presents a critique of these doctrines. (In constitutional law courses,
full consideration of the justiciability doctrines is often left to the end of the course,
when the student is more able to manage their technicalities and can better appreciate
the relationship between these doctrines and the merits of particular constitutional

---

5. In this book, the term "justiciability" is used in its broader sense as described in *Flast v.
Cohen,* 392 U.S. 83, 94–97 (1968).

claims. For the same reasons, the reader may wish to defer further study of these doctrines until Chapter 15, the last chapter. Section B of Chapter 15 provides a suitable context for further study of these doctrines.)

D.2. The Advisory Opinion Doctrine

This is a classical doctrine that is one of the earliest manifestations of judicial concern about access to federal court. In effect, it combines elements of the more modern doctrines of standing, mootness, and ripeness. Arising directly from the "case" or "controversy" requirement, the advisory opinion doctrine serves to underscore that federal courts may not rule on hypothetical or abstract questions. In other words, this doctrine makes clear that no "what if" types of lawsuits, or suits without actual contending parties, are permissible in the federal courts. To be a case or controversy, the suit must involve real parties with concrete and adverse interests, one of whom has been harmed—or is currently threatened with harm—due to the action of the other party. If a suit does not have these characteristics, the court may consider it to be a request for an "advisory opinion" which, under the advisory opinion doctrine, the courts are prohibited from issuing.

Golden v. Zwickler, 394 U.S. 103 (1969), is an example of a lawsuit that fell within the advisory opinion doctrine. The complaint challenged a state statute that made it a crime to distribute anonymous literature in connection with an election campaign. The plaintiff, however, sought only to distribute literature regarding a Congressman who was no longer in office at the time of the lawsuit. Judging that the suit did not present an actual controversy, the U.S. Supreme Court recognized the general rule that:

> "[F]ederal courts...do not render advisory opinions. For adjudication of constitutional issues 'concrete legal issues, presented in actual cases, not abstractions' are requisite.... Basically, the question in each case is whether the facts alleged, under all the circumstances, show that there is a substantial controversy, between parties having adverse legal interests, of sufficient immediacy and reality..." [394 U.S. at 108, quoting *Maryland Casualty Co. v. Pacific Coal & Oil Co.*, 312 U.S. 270, 273 (1941).]

Golden also makes clear that the advisory opinion doctrine does not prohibit federal courts from issuing declaratory judgments. Unlike an advisory opinion, which is impermissible because it does not adjudicate an actual or immediate controversy, the declaratory judgment procedure allows adjudication of cases that present actual controversies but may not require the court to award damages or order any equitable relief. *See Aetna Life Ins. Co. v. Haworth*, 300 U.S. 227, 241 (1937).

D.3. The Standing Doctrine

The standing doctrine concerns the question of who is eligible to raise particular issues in federal court litigation. To apply the standing doctrine, one must separately consider each claim presented to the court, for a party may have standing to raise some claims but not others. Standing is primarily a plaintiff's problem. Occasionally, however, problems of "defensive standing" may arise when a defendant seeks to assert the rights of third parties as a defense to the lawsuit.

Standing law is based in part on Article III's case or controversy requirement. To comply with this constitutional component of standing, a plaintiff must allege and demonstrate (1) that he/she/it has sustained "injury in fact, economic or otherwise" (the "injury" requirement; *see Association of Data Processing Service Organizations, Inc. v. Camp*, 397 U.S. 150, 152 (1970)); (2) that this injury was caused by, and is thus traceable to, the action of the defendant (the "traceability" requirement); and (3) that the injury would likely be redressed by a court decision in the plaintiff's favor (the "redressability" requirement). As the U.S. Supreme Court has summarized these aspects of standing law:

> To establish an Article III case or controversy, a litigant first must clearly demonstrate that he has suffered an "injury in fact" [which is] concrete in both a qualitative and temporal sense. The complainant must allege an injury to himself that is "distinct and palpable," *Warth v. Seldin* 422 U.S. 490, 501 (1975), as opposed to merely "[a]bstract," *O'Shea v. Littleton*, 414 U.S. 488, 494 (1974), and the alleged harm must be actual or imminent, not "conjectural" or "hypothetical." *Los Angeles v. Lyons*, 461 U.S. 95, 101–102 (1983). Further, the litigant must satisfy the "causation" and "redressability" prongs of the Article III minima by showing that the injury "fairly can be traced to the challenged action," and "is likely to be redressed by a favorable decision." *Simon v. Eastern Kentucky Welfare Rights Org.*, 426 U.S. 26, 38, 41 (1976).... The litigant must clearly and specifically set forth facts sufficient to satisfy these Article III standing requirements. A federal court is powerless to create its own jurisdiction by embellishing otherwise deficient allegations of standing. *See Warth, supra,* at 508, 518. [*Whitmore v. Arkansas*, 495 U.S. 149, 155–156, (1990).]

Meeting these basic Article III requirements, however, does not guarantee standing; the plaintiff must also comply with the "prudential component" of the standing doctrine (*Allen v. Wright*, 468 U.S. 737, 751 (1984)). The requirements within this component are not mandated by Article III but rather arise from considerations of "prudence" that the courts impose upon themselves, in the exercise of judicial self-restraint, in order to husband judicial resources or promote separation of powers values (see Sec. D.1. above). The U.S. Supreme Court has provided these examples of prudential standing requirements: "the general prohibition on a litigant's raising another person's constitutional rights, the rule barring adjudication of generalized grievances more appropriately addressed in the representative branches, and the requirement that a plaintiff's complaint fall within the zone of interest protected by the law invoked" (*Allen v. Wright*, 468 U.S. at 751). Since such requirements are prudential rather than constitutionally required, federal courts will usually set them aside if a federal statute grants standing to litigants who do not meet the prudential requirements. Congress' authorization to sue alleviates the court's prudential concerns, thus allowing the plaintiffs to proceed with the particular type of suit authorized, so long as they are able to meet the constitutional (Article III) requirements. *See Lujan v. Defenders of Wildlife*, 504 U.S. 555, 571–578 (Scalia, J., for the majority) and 579–581 (Kennedy, J., concurring) (1992).

One type of standing problem that has received particular attention is the problem of "taxpayer" and "citizen" standing. Many of the standing cases typically covered in constitutional law casebooks concern this problem: *e.g.*, *Frothingham v. Mellon*, 262 U.S. 447 (1923); *Flast v. Cohen*, 392 U.S. 83 (1968); *United States v. Richardson*, 418 U.S. 166 (1974); *Schlesinger v. Reservists Committee to Stop the War*, 418 U.S. 208 (1974); and *Valley Forge Christian College v. Americans United for Separation of Church and State*, 454 U.S. 464 (1982). In cases such as these, plaintiffs have sought to obtain standing by alleging only their status as taxpayers or citizens, or both. In effect, such plaintiffs are suing as a representative of all other U.S. taxpayers or citizens in order to redress some alleged governmental action affecting the entire class. These actions are thus often called public actions or "private attorney general" actions. As the cases illustrate, the federal courts are most reluctant to accept such rationales as a basis for standing. *Flast v. Cohen*, in which a taxpayer sought to use the establishment clause to challenge expenditures of federal funds for educational services in religious schools, is the only U.S. Supreme Court case that grants federal taxpayer standing. The *Valley Forge* case later emphasized the narrowness of the *Flast* ruling; it applies only to situations where a plaintiff is using the establishment clause to challenge a federal statute (as opposed to a federal administrative agency decision), and the federal statute was passed pursuant to the spending power (as opposed to some other grant of Congressional power).

Most plaintiffs do not need to rely on taxpayer or citizen standing, of course, because they may assert standing based on personal involvement in a dispute that has exposed them to direct personal harm. In many of these situations, the personal injury attributable to governmental action is so obvious, and the likelihood that the injury will be redressed in the litigation is so clear, that standing will not be an issue. The school child who has been assigned on the basis of race to a segregated school or program; the applicant for employment who has been denied a job because of her sex; the individual whose driver's license (or other governmental license) has been revoked without any kind of hearing; the speaker who has been prohibited from speaking on a city's sidewalks because the city objects to her message: all are persons suffering personal types of harm who have a clear "personal stake" in the lawsuit they seek to bring. Such plaintiffs generally have no difficulty meeting the constitutional and prudential requirements of the standing doctrine.

D.4. The Mootness Doctrine

Mootness is a problem of timing. A defendant seeking to have the plaintiff's case dismissed on grounds of mootness would typically argue that the plaintiff has waited too long to bring the case or to file an appeal, that there is no longer any continuing injury to the plaintiff, and that the dispute between the parties has therefore ended. To avoid such a mootness problem, a plaintiff must generally demonstrate that there continues to be a "specific live grievance" (*Golden v. Zwickler*, 394 U.S. 103, 110 (1969)) such that his or her "concrete interest in the controversy has [not] terminated" (*Lewis v. Continental Bank Corp.*, 494 U.S. 472 (1990)).

In *DeFunis v. Odegaard*, 416 U.S. 312 (1974), for example, DeFunis challenged his denial of admission to law school on the ground that the school's affirmative action policy for admissions violated the equal protection clause. DeFunis had not brought his suit as a class action, and sought only an injunction mandating his admission to the law school. The trial court ordered the school to admit him, and he attended school while the case was being appealed; by the time the case was heard by the U.S. Supreme Court, DeFunis was in his last year of law school. The Court held that the case was moot, since all parties agreed that DeFunis was "entitled to complete his legal studies at the University of Washington and to receive his degree from that institution" (416 U.S. at 317). The Court saw no reason to depart from "[t]he usual rule in federal cases…that an actual controversy must exist at all stages of appellate or certiorari review, and not simply at the date the action is initiated" (416 U.S. at 319, quoting *Roe v. Wade*, 410 U.S. 113, 125 (1973)).

There is an important exception to the rule that a case will be dismissed when there is no longer a continuing, live controversy—the exception for issues that are "capable of repetition, yet evading review" (*Roe v. Wade, supra*, at 124–125). The courts will recognize this exception when two elements are present: "(1) the challenged action was in its duration too short to be fully litigated prior to its cessation or expiration, and (2) there was a reasonable expectation that the same complaining party would be subjected to the same action again" (*Weinstein v. Bradford*, 423 U.S. 147, 149 (1975)).[6] In *Roe v. Wade*, above (the landmark ruling on abortion), the Court applied this exception and refused to dismiss the case as moot, reasoning that the nine-month human gestation period made it unlikely that a plaintiff's claims would ever reach the stage of appellate review if mootness were invoked (410 U.S. at 124–125).

D.5. The Ripeness Doctrine

Ripeness is also a timing problem, but it is a timing problem on the opposite end of the spectrum from mootness. A defendant trying to have the plaintiff's case dismissed on grounds of ripeness would typically argue that the plaintiff has brought the claim too soon, since there is no concrete dispute yet and therefore no threat of harm yet. In order to avoid such a claim, the plaintiff must generally demonstrate that there is a realistic threat of immediate harm to his or her interests.

In *Hodel v. Virginia Surface Mining & Reclamation Ass'n.*, 452 U.S. 264 (1981), for example, the U.S. Supreme Court held that a due process challenge to certain provisions of

---

6. Another important exception to mootness rules applies to class action litigation. If the personal claim of the named plaintiff (the class representative) becomes moot, either before or after certification of the class, the suit may nevertheless proceed so long as one or more members of the class continue to have claims against the named defendant that are not moot. *See Sosna v. Iowa*, 419 U.S. 393, 402 (1975).

a federal mining statute was not ripe for decision. The Court reasoned that "in challenging the Act's civil penalty provisions appellees did not allege that they, or any one of them, have had civil penalties assessed against them. Moreover, the District Court did not find...that any of appellee coal mine operators have been affected or harmed by any of the statutory procedures for the assessment and collection of fines" (452 U.S. at 304).

D.6. The Political Question Doctrine

The political question doctrine protects separation-of-powers values. The doctrine has potential application only in federal court litigation that would require the court to interfere with the functions of a coordinate branch of government. Obviously not every such suit will present a political question that the courts should refuse to hear, for any suit challenging the constitutionality of Congressional or Executive action could result in judicial interference with a coordinate branch. The U.S. Supreme Court has made clear that "the presence of constitutional issues with significant political overtones does not automatically invoke the political question doctrine" (*INS v. Chadha*, 462 U.S. 919, 942–943 (1983)) and that "the mere fact that the suit seeks protection of a political right does not mean it presents a political question.... The doctrine...is one of 'political questions,' not one of 'political cases'" (*Baker v. Carr*, 369 U.S. 186, 209, 217 (1962)). Rather, the term "political question" is a term of art, referring only to challenges of Congressional or Executive action that display certain special characteristics.

Marbury v. Madison, 5 U.S. (1 Cranch) 137 (1803), provided the first indication of the characteristics of a political question. In determining whether it could review the Executive's refusal to deliver Marbury's commission, the U.S. Supreme Court reasoned:

> By the Constitution of the United States, the president is invested with certain important political powers, in the exercise of which he is to use his own discretion, and is accountable only to his country in his political character, and to his own conscience.... [W]here the heads of departments are the political or confidential agents of the executive...to act in cases in which the executive possesses a constitutional or legal discretion, nothing can be more perfectly clear than that their acts are only politically examinable.... Questions in their nature political, or which are, by the constitution and laws, submitted to the executive, can never be made in this court. [5 U.S. (1 Cranch), at 165–166, 170.]

The Court's description constitutes the classical formulation of the political question doctrine, and this formulation is considered to be a constitutional requirement that the Court must comply with, rather than merely a prudential aspect of the political question doctrine.

In more modern times, the Court has added other formulations to the classical formulation from *Marbury*. The Court summarized these formulations in the famous case of *Baker v. Carr*, 369 U.S. 186 (1962), in which it held that equal protection challenges to the malapportionment of state legislatures do not present political questions. Under *Baker's* formulations, a case may be considered to present a nonjusticiable political question if it involves:

(1) a textually demonstrable constitutional commitment of the issue to a co-ordinate political department; or (2) a lack of judicially discoverable and man-ageable standards for resolving [the issue]; or (3) the impossibility of decid-ing without an initial policy determination of a kind clearly for nonjudicial discretion; or (4) the impossibility of a court's undertaking independent res-olution without expressing lack of the respect due coordinate branches of gov-ernment; or (5) an unusual need for unquestioning adherence to a political decision already made; or (6) the potentiality of embarrassment from multi-farious pronouncements by various departments on one question. [369 U.S. at 217, numbering added.]

The first of these formulations is the modern rendition of the classical *Marbury* for-mulation; the other five formulations state prudential requirements that the Court has created to assure that the dispute is within its competency to decide and that deciding it would not unduly interfere with Congressional or Executive functions. If a dispute falls within any one of these six formulations, the federal court will refuse to hear the case. Of the six formulations, numbers 1 and 2 have the most current importance and provide the bases under which the federal courts are most likely to invoke the politi-cal question doctrine to dismiss a lawsuit. Suits challenging the foreign affairs powers of Congress or the Executive (see Chap. 6, Sec. F and Chap. 8, Sec. C.5) are the ones most likely to present political question issues.

D.7. The Abstention Doctrines

The abstention doctrines protect federalism values. Although there are a number of abstention doctrines, variously described and differentiated by courts and commenta-tors (*see, e.g.*, Charles Alan Wright and Mary Kay Kane, LAW OF FEDERAL COURTS, sec. 52, p. 325 (6th ed. 2002)), the two most important for constitutional law are: (1) the *Pullman* doctrine, named after *Railroad Comm'n v. Pullman Co.*, 312 U.S. 496 (1941); and (2) the *Younger* doctrine, named after *Younger v. Harris*, 401 U.S. 37 (1971). The latter is also often called the "comity" doctrine or the "noninterference" doctrine.

The *Pullman* doctrine applies to federal court litigation that raises constitutional is-sues as well as issues concerning the interpretation of state law, and resolution of state law issues could dispose of the lawsuit or re-cast the constitutional issues that are be-fore the federal court. In such situations the *Pullman* doctrine provides that a federal court should defer to the state courts by abstaining—that is, by postponing its con-sideration of the case—whenever there is substantial doubt about the meaning of state law. The state courts would then have the opportunity to resolve the disputed state law issues. In the *Pullman* case itself, the U.S. Supreme Court reasoned that:

[T]he last word on the statutory authority of the [state] Railroad Commission in this case, belongs neither to us nor to the [federal] district court but to the Supreme Court of Texas. In this situation a federal court of equity is asked to decide an issue by making a tentative answer which may be displaced tomor-row by a state adjudication.... The reign of law is hardly promoted if any un-necessary ruling of a federal court is thus supplanted by a controlling decision of a state court. The resources of equity are equal to an adjustment that will avoid the waste of a tentative decision as well as the friction of a premature constitutional adjudication. [312 U.S. at 500.]

The *Pullman* doctrine thus results in the federal court staying its hand pending the outcome of the state court proceedings on the disputed issues of state law. After the state courts have done their work, the federal court may proceed with the constitutional issues before it if the state court ruling has not resolved the controversy.

Application of the *Younger* doctrine, on the other hand, results in the actual dismissal of the federal court case. Conceptually distinct from the *Pullman* doctrine, the *Younger* doctrine applies to federal court litigation that presents a federal law challenge to (and thus would interfere with) an on-going or pending state proceeding such as a criminal trial. In such situations, the *Younger* doctrine provides that the federal court should (with some exceptions) defer to the state by abstaining — that is, by declining to hear the federal law issues in the case — because federal court action would interfere with the state's own proceeding and thus intrude upon federalism values. When there is no state proceeding that is on-going or pending at the time the federal action is filed, the *Younger* doctrine usually does not apply, at least not when the plaintiff seeks only a declaratory judgment. *See, e.g., Steffel v. Thompson*, 415 U.S. 452 (1974).

In *Younger*, the plaintiff in the federal court action was being prosecuted in a California state court for violation of that state's Criminal Syndicalism Act. He challenged the state law as facially invalid under the First Amendment's free speech and press clauses. The Supreme Court declined to grant the plaintiff injunctive relief from the state prosecution. The Court grounded this policy of noninterference on a:

vital consideration, the notion of "comity," that is, a proper respect for state functions, a recognition of the fact that the entire country is made up of a Union of separate state governments, and a continuance of the belief that the National Government will fare best if the States and their institutions are left free to perform their separate functions in their separate ways. This, perhaps for lack of a better and clearer way to describe it, is referred to by many as "Our Federalism." [401 U.S. at 44.]

Such considerations of "comity" led the Court to conclude that federal courts should not "stay or enjoin pending state court proceedings except under special circumstances," where the plaintiff can show that "he will, if the proceeding in the state court is not enjoined, suffer irreparable damage" (*Id.* at 41, 43). The situation most likely to result in such irreparable damage, according to *Younger*, is where the state proceeding was brought in bad faith to harass the defendant (the federal plaintiff).

Sec. E. Immunities from Suit

When a federal court suit is brought against a state, a state agency, or a state official, there is a threshold issue of whether the federal court may assert jurisdiction over such a defendant. The issue is a type of "WHO" question (see Sec. D.1 above) that focuses on the status of the defendant rather than the plaintiff. Similar questions arise when the suit is against the federal government or a federal agency or official.

The U.S. Supreme Court has developed various "immunity" doctrines to deal with questions concerning the suability of government defendants. The most frequently used doctrine is the "sovereign immunity" doctrine that protects states from certain suits in *federal* court and, under a new variation, in *state* courts as well. Other variations of immunity cover suits against the President, suits against federal executive officials, and suits against Senators or Representatives. In most of these circumstances, the immunity doctrines articulate *constitutional* rather than *prudential* requirements (see Sec. D.1 above). The immunity, in other words, is a limitation on the Article III judicial power, establishing a constitutional bar to certain suits against certain governmental defendants.[7] The constitutional bar is not based on the case or controversy requirement of Article III, as are doctrines such as standing (Sec. D.3 above); it is based instead on other constitutional provisions and concepts that are explained below. When the suit is against a state, constitutional values of federalism are implicated, since sovereign immunity provides the states a zone of protection against the authority of federal (and sometimes state) courts to enforce federal law. In contrast, when the suit is against the federal government or federal officials in federal court, separation of powers values are implicated.

Although the Eleventh Amendment is usually cited as the source of state sovereign immunity from federal court suit, a close reading of the Amendment's text suggests otherwise. By its terms, the Eleventh Amendment immunizes states only from suits brought "by Citizens of another State, or by Citizens or Subjects of any Foreign State." The language does not cover suits brought against a state by *its own* citizens. The better explanation of state immunity is that it existed before the Constitution's adoption, and that Article III implicitly recognized and continued this protection. The Eleventh Amendment amends Article III so as to remove doubts about whether sovereign immunity applied when a state was a defendant in a case falling within the Article III jurisdictional category for cases "between a State and citizens of another state" (Art. III, sec. 2, ¶ 1). In *Chisholm v. Georgia*, 2 U.S. (2 Dall.) 419 (1793), the U.S. Supreme Court had rejected the State of Georgia's claim of immunity in such a suit brought against

---

7. It is not entirely clear that the executive immunities covering the President, Presidential aides, and executive officers are constitutionally mandated. The alternative argument is that they are the result of judicial policy-making and thus a part of "constitutional common law." *See generally* Henry Monaghan, "Constitutional Common Law," 89 HARV. L. REV. 1 (1975). In the leading case, *Nixon v. Fitzgerald*, 457 U.S. 731 (1982) (Chap. 8, Sec. E), the Court majority alludes to the problem but does not resolve it (457 U.S. at 748, especially footnote 27); see also 457 U.S. at 798 (Blackmun, J., dissenting). The difference, as the Court suggests, is that a constitutional common law immunity could be modified or abolished by Congress; a constitutionally mandated immunity could not. Thus the Court in *Nixon v. Fitzgerald* noted that "our holding today need only be that the President is absolutely immune from civil damages liability for his official acts *in the absence of explicit affirmative action by Congress*" (457 U.S. at 748 n. 27 (emphasis added)).

the state by the executor of a South Carolina creditor seeking payment of a debt. The Eleventh Amendment was passed to override the *Chisholm* ruling.

Thus, as the U.S. Supreme Court explained in *Pennhurst State School and Hospital v. Halderman*, 465 U.S. 89, 98 (1984), the Eleventh Amendment affirms "that the fundamental principle of sovereign immunity limits the grant of judicial authority in Article III." The immunity from suit therefore extends to federal court suits brought against states by their own citizens (*Hans v. Louisiana*, 134 U.S. 1 (1890)), even though the Eleventh Amendment does not expressly so provide. The immunity does not extend to local governments such as cities, counties, and school districts, however, because they are considered to be "political subdivision(s)" of the state, rather than "arm(s) of the state," for Eleventh Amendment purposes (*Lake County Estates v. Tahoe Regional Planning Agency*, 440 U.S. 391, 401–402 (1979); *see also Lincoln County v. Luning*, 133 U.S. 529, 530 (1890)).

State sovereign immunity also does not extend to federal court suits brought against a state by the United States or by another state. In *United States v. Mississippi*, 380 U.S. 128 (1965), for example, the U.S. Supreme Court held that the United States could constitutionally bring suit against a State for race discrimination in voter registration (*Id.* at 140–141). And in *Employees of Department of Public Health and Welfare v. Department of Public Health*, 411 U.S. 279 (1973), the Court acknowledged that the U.S. Secretary of Labor could constitutionally sue a state for a violation of the Fair Labor Standards Act (29 U.S.C. §601 *et. seq.*) and seek unpaid minimum wages or overtime compensation on behalf of state employees (*Id.* at 285–286). The immunity doctrine does not apply to such suits because the states, by ratifying the Constitution or subsequently entering the Union, have consented to suits by the federal government (*Alden v. Maine*, 527 U.S. 706, 755–756 (1999)). The same principle of consent also applies to suits against a state by another state (*Id.* at 755).

There are three major exceptions to this doctrine of state sovereign immunity from private suits in federal court. First, a state may waive its immunity by consenting to suit, either in a particular case or in a category of cases (*see, e.g.*, *Gunter v. Atlantic Coastline Railway Co.*, 200 U.S. 273, 284 (1906)). Second, under the case of *Ex parte Young*, 209 U.S. 123 (1908), it is often permissible for private plaintiffs to sue state government *officials* (as opposed to the state itself) in federal court. The suit must contest some action that the official has taken or failed to take on behalf of the state, and the relief requested must be prospective relief (usually an injunction).[8] Third, Congress may use its enforcement powers (see Chap. 6, Sec. E, and Chap. 14, Sec. C) to expressly abrogate the states' immunity from federal court suit. Of these three major exceptions,

---

8. Alternatively, private suits for money damages may sometimes be brought against a state official in his/her "personal capacity" or "individual capacity" rather than his/her "official capacity." An "individual capacity" suit is one that is brought against the officer personally and seeks relief, in particular monetary damages, from the official personally. Most commonly, such suits allege that the official has violated the plaintiff's federal constitutional rights and are brought pursuant to 42 U.S.C. §1983 (see Chap. 14, Sec. B.2). This type of individual capacity suit is, in effect, another exception to (or end run around) the doctrine of state sovereign immunity.

the third—abrogation—has attracted the greatest controversy in recent times. This controversy is discussed in Chapter 6, Section C.4, and Chapter 14, Section D.

Although the Eleventh Amendment and Article III create a constitutional bar to private suits against states in *federal* court, private suits to enforce federal law against the states in *state* courts historically have been an alternative for plaintiffs shut out of federal court. In 1999, however, the U.S. Supreme Court drastically limited this option in *Alden v. Maine*, 527 U.S. 706 (1999). This case concerned the federal Fair Labor Standards Act (FLSA), in particular the provisions authorizing state employees to enforce their FLSA rights against the states in their own courts (29 U.S.C. §§ 216(b) & 203(x)). Claiming a violation of the FLSA overtime pay provisions, employees of the State of Maine originally filed suit against the state in federal court but re-filed the case in state court when the federal court held the state immune from federal court suit. The state court held that the state was immune from the suit in state court as well as federal court, and the U.S. Supreme Court affirmed by a 5 to 4 vote. Neither the Eleventh Amendment nor Article III applied to suits in state court, and they therefore could not provide the basis for the Court's decision. But the Court determined that, in a broader sense, sovereign immunity "derives not from the Eleventh Amendment but from the structure of the original Constitution itself" and that the "scope of the states' immunity from suit is demarcated not by the text of the Amendment alone, but by fundamental postulates implicit in the constitutional design" (527 U.S. at 728–729).[9]

When the *federal* government, or a *federal* agency or official, is the defendant in a federal court suit, the Eleventh Amendment does not apply; immunity protection is implicit in Article III itself. *See Larson v. Domestic and Foreign Commerce Corp.*, 337 U.S. 682 (1949). An exception applies for suits to which the federal government has consented. There is also an exception, comparable to that in *Ex parte Young*, for suits against federal officials for prospective relief. *See Dugan v. Rank*, 372 U.S. 609, 620–21 (1963). The "constitutional design," as in *Alden*, would also apparently protect the federal government from suit in the state courts.[10]

In addition to this sovereign immunity protection for the federal government, there is also an express legislative immunity in Article I, section 6 of the Constitution that protects members of Congress and their aides from suits concerning "any Speech or Debate in either House" (*see, e.g., Hutchinson v. Proxmire*, 443 U.S. 111 (1979)). The U.S. Supreme Court has also recognized an implied executive immunity (an *absolute* immunity) that protects the President from suits for money damages based on his official acts (*Nixon v. Fitzgerald*, 457 U.S. 731 (1982)). An implied immunity (a *qualified* immunity) also sometimes protects presidential aides (*Harlow v. Fitzgerald*, 457 U.S. 800 (1982)) and administrative agency officials (*Butz v. Economou*, 438 U.S. 478 (1978)) from suits for money damages. In the celebrated case of *Clinton v. Jones*, 520 U.S. 681

---

9. In another case three years later, the Court extended this structural version of state sovereign immunity to protect states against certain adjudicatory proceedings on private party claims filed with federal administrative agencies; see Chapter 14, Section D.

10. For more on federal and state sovereign immunity, and a comparison of the two, see Chapter 7, Section D.

(1997) (the Paula Jones sexual harassment case), however, the Court determined that the President is not immune from money damage suits based on his unofficial or private actions—in particular actions that had occurred before the President took office.

Sec. F. The Continuing Controversy Over Judicial Supremacy

F.1. Overview

Section B above (Exercise No. 5) illustrates the modern reach of judicial review and judicial supremacy. Under this modern understanding—which differs from the original understanding before and after *Marbury*—the Article III "judicial power" affords federal courts broad authority to interpret and enforce the Constitution. Specifically, under the modern understanding: (A) the federal courts may review the constitutionality of Congressional and Executive actions, as well as state and local government actions; (B) the federal courts' interpretations will prevail over contrary interpretations by Congress or the executive branch, or by states and local governments; (C) the U.S. Supreme Court's interpretations become the "law of the land," binding on all Congressional and Executive officials and agencies, and all state and local governments, current and future; and (D) U.S. Circuit Court and U.S. District Court interpretations become the "law of the land" for their respective circuits and districts, subject to further review (or later correction) by the U.S. Supreme Court. At the same time, under the modern understanding, other governmental decision-makers may participate— indeed have a duty to participate—in the interpretive process subject to the ultimate authority of the federal courts and the U.S. Supreme Court (see Sec. C above). Despite contemporary general agreement on these matters, judicial review historically has been a subject of controversy and remains so today. The modern controversy and its manifestations are more subtle than the historical controversies in the nation's early days. This continuing controversy exerts a pervasive influence on the development of constitutional law. The next section (F.2) considers why judicial review and judicial supremacy remain controversial. Sections F.3 through F.7 consider how that controversy manifests itself.

F.2. The Counter-Majoritarian Difficulty and Its Manifestations

Once it is understood that judicial review encompasses broad notions of judicial supremacy, it becomes apparent—as commentators often remark—that judicial review and judicial supremacy present what is called the "counter-majoritarian difficulty" (Alexander Bickel, THE LEAST DANGEROUS BRANCH, pp. 16–23 (Yale Univ. Press, 2nd ed. 1986)). According to Professor Bickel:

> The root difficulty is that judicial review is a counter-majoritarian force in our system.... [W]hen the Supreme Court declares unconstitutional a legislative act or the action of an elected executive, it thwarts the will of representatives

of the actual people of the here and now; it exercises control, not in behalf of the prevailing majority, but against it. [*Id.* at 16–17.]

Federal court rulings on constitutional issues create this counter-majoritarian difficulty because the courts are unelected bodies composed of judges with life tenure. Even though the federal courts have no electoral accountability, their rulings take precedence over the decisions of popularly elected officials and the representative branches of government. Thus what the Supreme Court says can in effect countermand the popular will, that is, the wishes of a popular majority either nationally or in a particular state or region. The early desegregation cases in the South (Chap. 3, Sec. E) provide a good illustration.

The real nub of the counter-majoritarian difficulty, then, is that the "judicial power" exists in tension with the concept of majority rule. That is why judicial review and judicial supremacy remain controversial today. On the one hand is the notion that federal courts are decision makers whose edicts are supreme over those of the representative branches; on the other hand is the notion that the representative branches of government are decision makers whose edicts represent the popular will and serve to implement majority rule in a representative democracy. How does this tension and the underlying controversy manifest itself in contemporary constitutional law? There are five primary ways; each is discussed in turn in Sections F.3 through F. 7 below. As these examples suggest, the debate is no longer simply about the validity and the reach of the *Marbury* opinion; it is a more subtle debate that underlies almost all analysis and argumentation in constitutional law. One cannot appreciate the subtleties of constitutional law or achieve any enriched understanding of the subject matter without an awareness of these modern manifestations of the controversy over judicial review and judicial supremacy.

F.3. Political Control of the Federal Courts

There is continuing controversy over the extent to which the federal courts, and particularly the U.S. Supreme Court, should be free of any "political control" by Congress or the Executive Branch. The President can assert such control—or at least influence—through the power to appoint judges; and the Senate can do so through its advice and consent power over Presidential judicial appointments (Art. II, sec. 2, ¶ 2). There are also various other political strategies that the Executive and Congress may employ; see William Ross, "The Resilience of *Marbury v. Madison*: Why Judicial Review Has Survived So Many Attacks," 38 WAKE FOREST L. REV. 733, 774–778 (2003).

Congress may also exert some control through legislation that limits the courts' Article III jurisdiction. Congress' authority over the lower federal courts arises from two constitutional clauses: Article III, section 1, which provides for such lower federal courts "as the Congress may from time to time ordain and establish"; and Article I, section 8, paragraph 9, which grants Congress power to "constitute Tribunals inferior to the Supreme Court." Congress' authority over the Supreme Court arises from a third clause: Article III, section 2, paragraph 2, which grants Congress power to make "exceptions" to and "regulations" for the Supreme Court's exercise of appellate jurisdiction.

The classic case of *Ex Parte McCardle*, 74 U.S. (7 Wall.) 506 (1869), provides an example of how Congress may wield its power over the Supreme Court's appellate jurisdiction. McCardle was a controversial newspaper editor in Reconstruction-era Mississippi who was arrested on charges of impeding reconstruction. He was held for trial by a military tribunal as authorized by the Reconstruction Act of March 2, 1867. To avoid this fate, McCardle brought suit in federal court in Mississippi, challenging the military trial provision in Congress' reconstruction plan and seeking to be freed by a writ of habeas corpus. He relied on an 1867 federal habeas corpus statute that authorized federal courts to order habeas corpus relief for persons being unconstitutionally restrained and also authorized appeals to the U.S. Supreme Court in such cases. After McCardle had lost in the lower federal court and appealed to the Supreme Court, Congress sought to rid itself of this politically charged case by repealing the provision of the 1867 habeas corpus statute that authorized the Court to hear the appeal. The Court held that Congress' repeal was an express "exception" to the Court's appellate jurisdiction that Congress could make under Article III, section 2, paragraph 2. The Court therefore dismissed McCardle's appeal; it could not "proceed to pronounce judgment in this case, for it…no longer [had] jurisdiction of the appeal" (*Id.* at 515).

Although the Court in *McCardle* thus clearly acknowledged and deferred to Congress' Article III "exceptions" power, its opinion did not clarify the scope of this power or its limits. At the end of the opinion, the Court noted that there was another pre-existing way for the Supreme Court to take jurisdiction over habeas petitions; and that Congress' partial repeal of the 1867 habeas corpus statute therefore had not revoked "the whole appellate power of the court, in cases of habeas corpus…." (*Id.*). *See Ex Parte Yerger*, 75 U.S. (8 Wall.) 85 (1868). It is arguable, then, that the Court did not yield complete authority to Congress to eliminate entire classes of cases from the Court's appellate jurisdiction, but only authorized Congress to eliminate some avenues of appeal if another avenue remains open. On the other hand, earlier passages in *McCardle* can be read more broadly. Since the Court has never clarified *McCardle*, the full extent of Congress' exceptions power remains unsettled to this day. *See, e.g.,* Leonard Ratner, "Majoritarian Constraints on Judicial Review: Congressional Control of Supreme Court Jurisdiction," 27 VILLANOVA L. REV. 929 (1981–82).

F.4. Justiciability

There is continuing controversy over the prerequisites for gaining access to the federal courts for purposes of airing particular issues on the merits. These prerequisites are found in the six justiciability doctrines discussed in Section D above. The technical requirements embodied in the justiciability doctrines have great practical import for litigants in particular types of cases and may exert considerable influence on the federal courts as they exercise their judicial review functions.

The history of litigation challenging the constitutionality of state regulation of contraceptives provides an outstanding example of the influence that justiciability doctrines may have upon the development of constitutional principles. The first such case reached the U.S. Supreme Court in 1943 (*Tileston v. Ullman,* 318 U.S. 44 (1943)). The plaintiff, a physician, challenged a Connecticut statute that prohibited the use, or provision of assistance in the use, of "drugs or instruments to prevent conception." This statute, the physician claimed, prevented him from giving advice on contraception to certain patients whose lives could be endangered by pregnancy, and thus violated the due process clause. The Court dismissed the case under the standing doctrine because the rights at stake were the patients', not the physician's, and the physician did not have standing to assert the due process rights of his patients. In 1961, contraception issues again reached the Court in *Poe v. Ullman*, 367 U.S. 497 (1961). This time the plaintiffs included married couples who clearly had standing to enforce their own right to use contraceptives. But the Court dismissed the case anyway under the ripeness doctrine, reasoning that the state was not prosecuting persons who may have violated its ban on contraceptives and that the case was therefore not ripe for consideration. Finally, in 1965, the Court reviewed another contraception case in which it addressed the issues on the merits. In *Griswold v. Connecticut*, 381 U.S. 479 (1965) (Chap. 11, Sec. C.2), the state had prosecuted the officers of birth control clinics, thus resolving the problem of ripeness; and the officers, as defendants in a criminal prosecution, had standing to raise the rights of the married couples whom the clinics served. On considering the merits, the Court held the Connecticut statute to be unconstitutional. Twenty-two years had passed from the Court's first exposure to these issues until the time it eventually ruled on them.

As the contraceptive cases illustrate, and as the "gatekeeper" role of the justiciability doctrines suggests, these doctrines serve to limit the federal courts' opportunities to issue rulings on the merits that may then become "the law of the land." From this perspective, the downside of the justiciability doctrines is that some constitutional questions may never be litigated, while others must wait many years for resolution. Constitutional rights of individuals may thus go without vindication or remedy, and governmental excesses of power may go unchecked. But from another perspective, on the upside, the justiciability doctrines allow the courts some control over their dockets and thus over the pace and vigor of constitutional developments. Such control in turn gives courts the flexibility and space to exercise their composite wisdom over time with due regard for the political branches' functions, thus alleviating the counter-majoritarian difficulty (Sec. F.2 above).

The ways in which the courts define and implement the doctrines of justiciability therefore affect the scope and operation of judicial review. The more flexible and lenient the doctrines of justiciability are, the more likely they are to funnel disputes into the federal courts and to result in judicial review of the merits of disputes. On the other hand, the tighter and stricter justiciability doctrines are, the more likely they are to keep disputes out of the federal courts, thus limiting the courts' opportunities to issue pronouncements that become the law of the land.

F.5. Immunities from Suit

There is continuing controversy about judicial review of suits against the states or the federal government, or against high level officers of either (*e.g.*, the President). In contemporary times, the controversy is particularly apparent with respect to suits against the states, either in federal or state court (see Sec. E above), and with respect to Congress' authority to abrogate this state immunity (see Chap. 6, Sec. C.4, and Chap. 14, Sec. D). As the scope of state sovereign immunity expands, and as Congress' abrogation authority is narrowed, more disputes involving states are removed from the reach of the judicial power. As a result, certain legal issues are insulated from judicial review on the merits and certain state governmental actions (including unconstitutional actions) may be insulated from judicial invalidation. The expansive protection of sovereign immunity therefore limits the range of cases subject to judicial review on the merits, while narrower protection for sovereign immunity expands the range of such cases.

F.6. Modes of Constitutional Interpretation

There is continuing controversy over the sources that a judge or other interpreter should consult, and the approaches an interpreter should use, in interpreting the Constitution (see Chap. 2, Secs. E and F). The available sources and approaches may be selected and used in ways that accord judges a broad range of discretion in applying the Constitution to new circumstances. On the other hand, the available sources and approaches may be selected and used in ways that accord judges a narrower range of discretion in making interpretive judgments. Judicial review in individual cases will tend to be more vigorous in the former circumstance than in the latter; and the range of questions that are resolved by the courts, rather than by the legislative or executive branches of government, will tend to be more expansive.

A textualist or originalist interpreter, for example, may emphasize the use of constitutional text and original history (see Chap. 2, Sec. F, and Chap. 4, Sec. C.2), and may adopt a strict or narrow account of how to use these sources. Such an interpreter may then find that text and history do not speak meaningfully to many contemporary issues and may thus leave such issues to the political branches of government. The result would be a restriction on the scope of judicial review and the operation of judicial supremacy principles. On the other hand, another interpreter may adopt a broader or more flexible account of how to use text and original history, and may also use constitutional structure (see Chap. 4, Sec. C.3) and constitutional values (see Chap. 9, Sec. B.2) to supplement text and history. Such an interpreter may find that these sources speak to a wide range of contemporary issues and may thus reserve the final judgment on such issues to the courts. The result would be an expansion of the scope of judicial review and of the operation of judicial supremacy principles.

F.7. Standards of Judicial Review

There is continuing controversy over the *standards* of judicial review, that is, the standards that courts create to guide their review and disposition of particular issues on the merits (see Chap. 3, Sec. C, point 4). In the opinions of the U.S. Supreme Court, there are many variations of standards of review. All these standards can be categorized in terms of the degree of scrutiny that they require courts to give to the challenged action. At one extreme is "strict scrutiny" of the government action being challenged. In cases of race discrimination under the equal protection clause, for example, courts will apply a strict scrutiny standard of review because they are highly suspicious of any governmental use of racial classifications and will presume such use to be unconstitutional unless and until the government proves otherwise. In many other discrimination cases, however—such as those where the government has used age, residency, or economic need in making decisions—courts will apply a "minimal scrutiny" standard because they are not suspicious about these factors and will presume their use to be constitutional unless and until the person alleging discrimination proves otherwise (see Chap. 10, Sec. C.4). Minimal scrutiny standards are at the opposite end of the spectrum from strict scrutiny standards.

If a court uses a strict scrutiny standard of review, it will look very closely at the government action and the justifications for it, and will assign the burden of proving constitutionality (the burden of proof) to the government. Under such a standard, the court would be relatively willing and likely to rule that the government's action is unconstitutional. On the other hand, if a court uses a minimal scrutiny standard of review, it will look very deferentially at the government action being challenged and the justifications for it, and will assign the burden of proving *un*constitutionality to the challenger. Under such a standard, the court would be relatively unwilling and unlikely to strike down the government's action. In between these strict and minimal scrutiny standards are a variety of other standards of review, generally called "intermediate scrutiny" standards. Courts may adapt these standards to the circumstances of particular types of issues that merit neither the suspicious treatment of strict scrutiny nor the deferential treatment of minimal scrutiny.

Thus, the stricter the standard of review a court uses, the less deferential the court will be to the political branches of government, and the more likely it will be to invalidate governmental decisions reached through majoritarian political processes. A key aspect of the standards-of-review controversy, then, is the concept of "deference" or "judicial deference"—phrases used to connote the extent to which the courts do and should defer to particular policy and factual determinations of the representative branches of government. This concept of deference, and its relation to standards of review, is endemic to all of constitutional law. (See Section C above for more on deference.) Much of the continuing debate on these matters reflects an abiding concern about judicial review and judicial supremacy, and thus about the role of courts in the American governmental structure.

Sec. G. Study Suggestions

Any study of judicial power should begin with a meticulous review of Article III of the United States Constitution. Unlike many other Constitutional provisions, Article III's text is sufficiently specific that a careful reading will yield answers to some important questions about judicial power and useful guidance for many others (Sec. A above). When the issues being addressed appear to implicate sovereign immunity (Sec. F.5 above), the text of the Eleventh Amendment must also be read in conjunction with the text of Article III.

As you read cases or do problems about judicial power, you should consider how each issue fits into or links up to Article III. The cases and problems will arise either in the context of separation of powers or the context of federalism (see Chap. 4, Sec. B). You should identify the particular context and the particular power relationships—between the courts and Congress, the courts and the Executive branch, or the courts and the states—that each situation presents. Always keep in mind the basic principles of judicial supremacy as you read cases about judicial power (see Sec. B above, under "Ans. to Ques. 1 through 6 (Summary)"). In addition, keep in mind that other branches of government may also interpret the Constitution and that questions may arise about the extent to which the courts do or should accord deference to such other interpretations (Sec. C above).

In contemporary constitutional law, questions about judicial power may lurk behind almost every federal court case implicating some constitutional issue, and such questions may arise at any stage of the litigation (see Chap. 15, Sec. D). In practical terms, however, judicial power issues will be most directly and sharply presented in cases concerning access to federal court, as discussed in Sections D and F.4 above. In reading the cases about court access, it is important to consider the role that each doctrine of justiciability plays and the differences between the various doctrines. You should also be attentive to the conceptual distinction between *constitutional* limits on judicial power and *prudential* limits on judicial power.

FOR FURTHER READING: (1) Davison Douglas, "The Rhetorical Uses of *Marbury v. Madison*: The Emergence of a 'Great Case,'" 38 WAKE FOREST L. REV. 375 (2003). (2) Daniel Farber, "Judicial Review and Its Alternatives: An American Tale," 38 WAKE FOREST L. REV. 415 (2003). (3) Daniel Farber, "The Supreme Court and the Rule of Law: *Cooper v. Aaron*, Revisited," 1982 U. ILL. L. REV. 387. (4) Roger Hartley, "The Alden Trilogy: Praise and Protest," 23 HARV. J. OF LAW AND PUB. POLICY 323 (2000). (5) Robert McCloskey, THE AMERICAN SUPREME COURT (Univ. of Chicago Press, 3d ed. 2000) (Sanford Levinson, revisor), chap. 1 ("The Genesis and Nature of Judicial Power") and Chap. 2 ("The Establishment of the Right to Decide"). (6) William Van Alstyne, "A Critical Guide to *Ex Parte McCardle*," 15 ARIZONA L. REV. 229 (1973). (7) William Van Alstyne, "A Critical Guide to *Marbury v. Madison*," 1969 DUKE L. J. 1.

Chapter 6

Congressional Powers and Federalism

Sec. A. The American Concept of Federalism

The United States Constitution creates a new federal government while at the same time acknowledging the separate existence of the state governments. The powers of sovereignty are divided between these two levels of government.[1] As Justice Anthony Kennedy has explained:

> Federalism was our Nation's own discovery. The Framers split the atom of sovereignty. It was the genius of their idea that our citizens would have two political capacities, one state and one federal, each protected from incursion by the other. The resulting Constitution created a legal system unprecedented in form and design, establishing two orders of government, each with its own direct relationship, its own privity, its own set of mutual rights and obligations to the people who sustain it and are governed by it. [*U.S. Term Limits, Inc. v. Thornton*, 514 U.S. 779, 838 (1995) (Kennedy, J., concurring).]

Within this federal system, "[t]he Federal and State Governments are in fact but different agents and trustees of the people, instituted with different powers, and designated for different purposes" (James Madison, *The Federalist No. 46*, in THE FEDERALIST: THE GIDEON EDITION, at 243 (Liberty Fund, 2001)). Moreover, "[T]he preservation of the States, and the maintenance of their governments, are as much within the design and care of the Constitution as the preservation of the Union and the maintenance of the National government. The Constitution, in all its provisions, looks to an indestructible Union, composed of indestructible States" (*Texas v. White*, 74 U.S. (7 Wall.) 700, 725 (1869), as quoted in *New York v. United States*, 505 U.S. 144, 162 (1992)).

---

1. Some sovereignty also remained with the indigenous Indian tribes. *See, e.g.*, U.S. Const., Art. I, Sec. 8, cl. 3, which distinguishes "the Indian Tribes" from the federal government, the states, and foreign nations; and *see also Talton v. Mayes*, 163 U.S. 376 (1896).

The Tenth Amendment elucidates the general relationship between federal and state powers: "The powers not delegated to the United States by the Constitution, nor prohibited by it to the States, are reserved to the States respectively, or to the people" (U.S. Const. Amend. 10). In addition to the Tenth Amendment, other constitutional provisions recognize the inherent sovereignty of the states and the important role the states play in constitutional governance. Article IV, Section 1, for example, requires that "Full Faith and Credit shall be given in each State to the public Acts, Records, and judicial Proceedings of every other State." Article IV, Section 4, provides that the United States will "guarantee to every state in this Union a Republican Form of Government" and protect them from invasion and domestic violence. The Constitution cannot be amended without the participation of the states; under Article V, all amendments must be "ratified by the Legislatures of three fourths of the several States, or by Conventions in three fourths thereof...." The territorial integrity of each state is also protected by the Constitution. Article IV, Section 3 provides that new states may be admitted to the Union "but no new State shall be formed or erected within the Jurisdiction of any other State; nor any State be formed by the Junction of two or more States, or Parts of States" unless the respective legislatures (and Congress) agree to such territorial alterations. Each state, regardless of population, is afforded two senators (Art. I, § 3, ¶ 1). Additionally, as strikingly illustrated in the election of 2000, the election of the President hinges on the states through the "Electoral College" to which each state appoints a number of electors equal to the sum of the state's Senators and Representatives (Art. II, Sec. 1, ¶'s 2 and 3; and Amend. 12). (George W. Bush in 2000, Rutherford B. Hayes in the election of 1876, and Benjamin Harrison in the election of 1888 can all thank this Electoral College system for their respective presidencies; each was elected into office without winning the popular vote.)

In sum, the states play a critical role in the constitutional framework. The Constitution created dual sovereigns, and understanding the interplay between them is critical to an understanding of Congressional powers and all of constitutional law.

Within the federalistic design, the federal government may exercise only those powers delegated to it by the Constitution. For Congress, the primary locus of these enumerated powers is Article I, section 8. Since federal powers are limited, the Constitution reserves substantial sovereign authority for the states. As James Madison explained in *Federalist No. 45*:

> The powers delegated by the proposed Constitution to the federal government are few and defined. Those which are to remain in the State governments are numerous and indefinite.... The powers reserved to the several States will extend to all the objects which, in the ordinary course of affairs, concern the lives, liberties, and properties of the people, and the internal order, improvement, and prosperity of the State. [James Madison, *Federalist No. 45*, in THE FEDERALIST, *supra*, at 241.]

Given the extensive powers that the states retain, it was inevitable that constitutional issues would arise concerning "the conflicting powers of the general [*i.e.*, federal] and state governments...and the supremacy of their respective laws, when they are in opposition" (*McCulloch v. Maryland*, 17 U.S. (4 Wheat.) 316, 405 (1819)). At first glance, it may seem that the states would hold the balance of power regarding such issues. The picture begins to change, however, when one takes account of the implied powers of the federal government, in particular the broad implied powers of Congress that Chief Justice Marshall recognized in the *McCulloch* case (see also Section B.3 below). In addition, the Supremacy Clause, which allows Congress to preempt state law whenever it is acting within the scope of its own powers, has given the federal government "a decided advantage in [the] delicate balance" between federal and state powers (*Gregory v. Ashcroft*, 501 U.S. 452, 460 (1990)). By providing that federal law and United States treaties "shall be the supreme Law of the Land," the Supremacy Clause lays the groundwork for the federal government's preeminence in the constitutional scheme. "As long as it is acting within the powers granted it under the Constitution, Congress may impose its will on the States. Congress may legislate in areas traditionally regulated by the States. This is an extraordinary power in a federalist system" (*Gregory*, 501 U.S. at 460).[2]

The constitutional design of federalism advances several important goals. "Perhaps the principal benefit of the federalist system is a check on the abuses of government power." *Gregory v. Ashcroft*, 501 U.S. 452, 458 (1990). "In the tension between federal and state power lies the promise of liberty" (*Gregory*, 501 U.S. at 459). Liberty, the Framers believed, was best achieved through the dispersal of power. By its recognition of dual sovereigns, federalism (like separation of powers) serves to disperse power. Each level of government therefore has power that it may use to check any abuses of power by the other. As Hamilton explained in *The Federalist Papers*:

> [I]n a confederacy the people, without exaggeration, may be said to be entirely the masters of their own fate. Power being almost always the rival of power, the general government will at all times stand ready to check the usurpations of the state governments, and these will have the same disposition towards the general government. The people, by throwing themselves into their scale, will infallibly make it preponderant. If their rights are invaded by either, they can make use of the other as the instrument of redress. [Hamilton, *Federalist No. 28* at 138–139, in THE FEDERALIST, *supra*.]

The framers thus maintained that strong state governments were necessary bulwarks of liberty. Madison argued that political forces would inherently protect state sovereignty from federal encroachment. Federal officials elected to office would have a predisposition "favorable to the States," and "[a] local spirit will infallibly prevail" over the federal government. The federal government will "be disinclined to invade the rights of the individual States, or the prerogatives of their governments" (James Madison, *The Federalist No. 46* at 245, 246, in THE FEDERALIST, *supra*.).

> Thus, the means of opposition to [unpopular Federal measures] are powerful and at hand. The disquietude of the people, their repugnance and perhaps refusal to co-operate with the officers of the Union, the frowns of the executive magistracy of the State, the embarrassments created by legislative devices, which would often be added on such occasions, would oppose in any State very serious impediments, and where the sentiments of several adjoining States

---

2. The subsequent case of *New York v. United States*, 505 U.S. 144 (1992), created a narrow exception to these principles. See Section C.5 of this Chapter.

happened to be in unison, would present obstructions which the Federal Government would hardly be willing to encounter. [*Id.* at 240–241.]

Federalism, then, disperses power and gives the people additional avenues of redress by which to limit tyranny and thus ensure liberty.

A second related goal of federalism is the promotion of democracy and democratic participation. Federalism certainly provides for greater participation in government than would a central government standing alone. Participation in local government provides training in the foundations of governance. As de Tocqueville noted in his observations of early American government:

> It is incontestably true that the love and the habits of republican government in the United States were engendered in the townships and in the provincial assemblies. [I]t is this same republican spirit, it is these manners and customs of a free people, which are engendered and nurtured in the different States, to be afterwards applied to the country at large. [1 A. de Tocqueville, DEMOCRACY IN AMERICA 181 (H. Reeve trans. 1961), as quoted in *FERC v. Mississippi*, 456 U.S. at 742, 789 (1982) (O'Connor, J., dissenting).]

Furthermore, federalism "assures a decentralized government that will be more sensitive to the diverse needs of a heterogeneous society" and "increases opportunity for citizen involvement in the political process…" (*Gregory*, 501 U.S. at 458). As one anti-federalist noted, "[o]ne government and general legislation alone, never can extend equal benefits to all parts of the United States: Different laws, customs, and opinion exist in the different sates, which by a uniform system of laws would be unreasonably invaded" ("Letter from The Federal Farmer" to The Republican, quoted in Herbert Storing (ed.), 2 THE COMPLETE ANTI-FEDERALIST 223, at 230 (2.8.13–14) (Univ. of Chicago Press, 1981)). Madison expanded on these points:

> Many considerations…seem to place it beyond doubt, that the first and most natural attachment of the people will be to the governments of their respective States. Into the administration of these, a greater number of individuals will expect to rise…. With the affairs of these, the people will be more familiarly and minutely conversant. And with the members of these, will a greater proportion of the people have the ties of personal acquaintance and friendship, and of family and party attachments; on the side of these therefore the popular bias, may well be expected most strongly to incline. [James Madison, *Federalist No. 46*, in THE FEDERALIST, *supra*, at 243.]

Thus, federalism advances democracy by bringing the government closer to the people, providing additional opportunities for government service and participation, and otherwise satisfying the diverse preferences and unique needs of the people of the various states.

A third important goal that federalism advances is efficiency. Certain subjects are "of such a nature" that they demand "a single uniform rule" by Congress. Where a concern is national in scope, then, it is most efficient for the federal government to act. Some subjects, however, are inherently local, "imperatively demanding that diversity which alone can meet the local necessities." *Cooley v. Board of Wardens of Port of*

Philadelphia, 53 U.S. (12 How.) 299, 319 (1851). State and local governments, then, may most efficiently attend to the "local peculiarities" of particular matters.

Finally, federalism promotes experimentation among the various state governments. Justice Louis D. Brandeis made this point well in *New State Ice Co. v. Liebmann*, 285 U.S. 262 (1932):

> There must be power in the States and the Nation to remould, through experimentation, our economic practices and institutions to meet changing social and economic needs....
>
> To stay experimentation in things social and economic is a grave responsibility. Denial of the right to experiment may be fraught with serious consequences to the Nation. It is one of the happy incidents of the federal system that a single courageous State may, if its citizens choose, serve as a laboratory; and try novel social and economic experiments without risk to the rest of the country. This Court has the power to prevent an experiment....But in the exercise of this high power, we must ever be on our guard, lest we erect our prejudices into legal principles. [285 U.S. at 311 (Brandeis, J., dissenting).]

In a later case, Justice Sandra Day O'Connor provided several specific examples of how state experimentation has benefitted the Nation:

> This state innovation is no judicial myth. When Wyoming became a State in 1890, it was the only State permitting women to vote. That novel idea did not bear national fruit for another 30 years. Wisconsin pioneered unemployment insurance, while Massachusetts initiated minimum wage laws for women and minors. After decades of academic debate, state experimentation finally provided an opportunity to observe no-fault automobile insurance in operation. Even in the field of environmental protection, an area subject to heavy federal regulation, the States have supplemented national standards with innovative and far-reaching statutes. [*FERC v. Mississippi*, 456 U.S. 742, 788–789 (1982) (O'Connor, J., dissenting).]

Disagreements over the balance of power between the federal government and the states have pervaded American history. The Constitutional Convention and ratifying conventions shaped but certainly did not quell the debate. Subsequent clashes of power were inevitable. As Chief Justice Marshall warned: "In our complex system, presenting the rare and difficult scheme of one general government, whose action extends over the whole, but which possesses only certain enumerated powers; and of numerous State governments, which retain and exercise all powers not delegated to the Union, contests respecting power must arise" (*Gibbons v. Ogden* 22 U.S. (9 Wheat.) 1, 204–205 (1824)).

In the early years of the new government, Alexander Hamilton, John Adams, and other founders advocating strong central government often clashed with Thomas Jefferson, James Madison, and others who put more emphasis on the limits of federal power and the role of the states. The Jefferson-Hamilton debate on the incorporation of a national bank is illustrative.

Congress' power to incorporate a national bank was not enumerated in the Constitution. The issue, then, was whether the Necessary and Proper Clause implicitly granted Congress the power to incorporate a bank. Jefferson argued in the negative:

> [T]he Constitution allows only the means which are "necessary," not those which are merely "convenient" for effecting the enumerated powers. If such a latitude of construction be allowed to this phrase as to give any non-enumerated power, it will go to every one, for there is not one which ingenuity may not torture into a *convenience* in some instance *or other*, to *some one* of so long a list of enumerated powers.... It would swallow up all the delegated powers.... [Thomas Jefferson, Opinion on the Constitutionality of the Bill for Establishing a National Bank, February 15, 1791, in Julian Boyd (ed.), 19 THE PAPERS OF THOMAS JEFFERSON, pp. 275, 278 (Princeton Univ. Press, 1974).]

Hamilton countered that the "bank has a natural relation to the power of collecting taxes; to that of borrowing money; to that of regulating trade; [and] to that of providing for the common defence...." (Alexander Hamilton, Opinion on the Constitutionality of an Act to Establish a Bank, February 23, 1791, in Harold Syrett (ed.), 8 THE PAPERS OF ALEXANDER HAMILTON, pp. 63, 129 (Columbia Univ. Press, 1965)). For Hamilton, a national bank was a means of realizing enumerated constitutional ends. Consequently, the creation of a national bank was "Necessary and Proper."

> [N]either the grammatical nor popular sense of the term ["necessary"] requires [Jefferson's] construction. According to both, necessary often means no more than *needful, requisite, incidental, useful or conducive to....* [Jefferson's] construction would beget endless uncertainty and embarrassment. The cases must be palpable and extreme, in which it could be pronounced, with certainty, that a measure was absolutely necessary, or one, without which the exercise of a given power would be nugatory. There are few measures of any government which would stand so severe a test. [*Id.* at 102–103.]

Hamilton's position eventually won the day. In the landmark decision of *McCulloch v. Maryland*, 17 U.S. (4 Wheat.) 316 (1819), discussed in Section B.3 below, the U.S. Supreme Court broadly construed Congress' implied powers to include the power to charter a national bank.

In the clashes between North and South that preceded the Civil War, disagreements over the balance of federalism intensified. Daniel Webster frequently spoke for the North, while John C. Calhoun became the chief spokesman for the "states' rights" interests of the South. In 1842, the U.S. Supreme Court decided an important federalism case concerning the federal fugitive slave law (*Prigg v. Commonwealth of Pennsylvania*, 41 U.S. (16 Pet.) 539 (1842); see Chap. 4, Sec. D, under **1842**), reaching a result favorable to the South but establishing constitutional principles that enhanced the power of the federal government. In the ensuing years, slavery increasingly became the focus of the tension-filled debate, especially during and after the U.S. Supreme Court's consideration of the infamous *Dred Scott* case, in which the Court invalidated the 1820 federal statute that prohibited slavery north and west of Missouri (*Dred Scott v. Sanford*, 60 U.S. (3 How.) 393 (1856); see Chap. 4, Sec. D, under **1856**). The Civil War that followed this case represented the ultimate schism over federalistic values.

The North's victory in the Civil War signified the indestructible nature of the Union and its preeminence over the states. President Lincoln's view that the federal government's legitimacy and power emanated from the people, and not from the states, prevailed. The Reconstruction Amendments, passed following the War, also marked a shift in federalism jurisprudence. The Fourteenth Amendment, in particular, shifted extensive power to the federal government. The Amendment emphasized the individual citizen's relationship with the *federal* government and prohibited the states from abridging the "privileges or immunities" of *national* citizenship. Moreover, by providing that "[n]o State shall...deprive any person" of due process of law or the equal protection of the laws, Section 1 of the Amendment limited state power and opened the door to wide-ranging federal judicial review of state actions. Concomitantly, Section 5 of the Amendment expanded the power of Congress by authorizing it to pass legislation enforcing the Amendment's provisions. The Fourteenth Amendment thus dramatically altered the federal/state balance of power.

The years following the Civil War witnessed a dramatic increase in the nation's population along with an expansion of industrialization and an integration of the economy into a national unit. In the process, more and more local problems and opportunities became national problems and opportunities. Congress increasingly responded to these developments with new legislation, and the courts were asked to evaluate the constitutionality of this legislation. The U.S. Supreme Court's handling of these disputes—which arose primarily under the commerce power and the taxing and spending powers—tended to be uneven and variable. In some cases, the Court struck down federal legislation as beyond the scope of Congress' powers; in other cases it upheld new legislative initiatives.

During the years of Franklin Delano Roosevelt's New Deal, the Court began to decide cases consistently in favor of expansive federal power. The "watershed" year is generally considered to be 1937, as marked by the cases of *NLRB v. Jones & Laughlin Steel Corp.*, 301 U.S. 1 (see Sec. C.1 below), *Steward Machine Co. v. Davis*, 301 U.S. 548 (see Sec. D below), and *Sonzinsky v. United States*, 300 U.S. 506 (a tax power case). From then on, the Court generally upheld Congressional legislation using principles that expanded the scope of Congress' powers. The Court also began imposing "federalistic" limits upon the states that restricted their exercise of state power as to subjects or objects that are within the scope of Congress' powers (see Chap. 7, Secs. B and C).

Near the end of the 20th century, however, the pendulum began to swing back in the direction of the states. The U.S. Supreme Court reemphasized the basic principle that the federal government is a government of limited powers and, in the process, created new protections against federal authority for the states and state agencies. In *New York v. United States*, 505 U.S. 144 (1992) and *Printz v. United States*, 521 U.S. 898 (1997), the Court recognized an "anti-commandeering" principle that protected state sovereignty (see Sec. G below). In *United States v. Lopez*, 514 U.S. 549 (1995), and again in *United States v. Morrison* 529 U.S. 598, 607–619 (2000), the Court reinvigorated limits on Congress' power to regulate private individuals and corporations, as well as the states, under the commerce power (see Sec. C below). In *Seminole Tribe v. Florida*, 517 U.S. 44 (1996), in several successor cases relying on *Seminole Tribe*, and in *Alden v. Maine*, 527 U.S. 706 (1999), the Court enhanced the states' immunity from suit in federal and state courts by restricting Congress' authority to abrogate state immunity (see Section G.2 below). In *City of Boerne v. Flores*, 521 U.S. 507 (1997), in several successor cases relying on *Boerne*, and in *United States v. Morrison* (above), 529 U.S. at 619–627, the Court narrowed Congress' authority to regulate the states under the civil rights enforcement powers (see Sec. E below). All of these cases presented controversial issues regarding federalism. The extent of the controversy, and the contested nature of the law in this arena, is illustrated by the votes in these cases; in every case, the Court reached its decision by a 5 to 4 vote.

Much of the contemporary debate about federalism, and much of the Court's recent change in direction, is fueled by the tension between judicial limits and political limits on Congressional power (see Sec. B.4 below). The tension becomes manifest in questions concerning the extent to which the Court should play an active role in protecting state sovereignty by creating "judicial limits" on Congress' powers. The New Deal and post-New Deal cases soft-pedaled judicial limits, instead taking the position that "[s]tate sovereign interests...are more properly protected by procedural safeguards inherent in the structure of the federal system than by judicially created limitations on federal power" (*Garcia v. San Antonio Metropolitan Transit Authority*, 469 U.S. 528, 552 (1985)). Under this approach, state sovereignty is protected, and the balance of federalism maintained, by Congress through its political processes, and ultimately by the people through the ballot box. In contrast, the Court has, since the 1990s, fostered more active judicial involvement in preserving state sovereignty, and in the process has held various federal statutes to be unconstitutional on their face or in particular applications. In taking this approach, the Court has asserted that the political (or structural) safeguards of federalism are insufficient protections for state sovereignty. As one Justice has stated the case: "Members of Congress are elected from the various States, but once in office they are Members of the Federal Government. Although the States participate in the Electoral College, this is hardly a reason to view the President as a representative of the States' interest against federal encroachment.... When the Congress exceeds the limits of its power, it is the duty of the federal judiciary 'to say what the law is' [*Marbury v. Madison*, 5 U.S. (1 Cranch) 137, 177 (1803)]. The States' role in our system of government is a matter of constitutional law, not of legislative grace" (*Garcia*, 469 U.S. at 564–565, 567 (Powell, J., dissenting)).

Sec. B. An Introduction to Congressional Powers

B.1. Congress' Powers in General

The focal point for a study of Congressional power is Article I, section 8, of the Constitution, which contains the primary listing of granted powers (¶'s 1–17) as well as the necessary and proper clause (¶ 18). The most important of these granted powers—as measured by the frequency of Congress' use of them and the frequency of their appearance in litigation—are the commerce power (Sec. C below), the taxing power (Sec. D below), the spending power (Sec. D below), and the foreign relations powers (Sec. F below). Other important powers in Article I, section 8 include the power to borrow money (Art. I, sec. 8, cl. 2); the power to establish uniform rules for bankruptcies (Art. I, sec. 8, cl. 4); the power to establish post offices (Art. I, sec. 8, cl. 7); and the power to protect intellectual property (Art. I, sec. 8, cl. 8). The Article I, section 8 powers are not the only ones granted to Congress; other grants are found elsewhere in the Constitution. The most important of these other grants are the "enforcement" powers in the Thirteenth, Fourteenth, and Fifteenth Amendments (Sec. E below), which empower Congress to "enforce" the civil rights and liberties that these amendments protect. Other important powers outside Article I include Article III, section 2, which grants Congress power to regulate the Supreme Court's appellate jurisdiction; Article IV, section 1, which grants Congress power to determine the manner in which the states are to give "Full Faith and Credit" to the "public Acts, Records, and judicial Proceedings" of other states; Article IV, section 3, which grants Congress power "to dispose of and make all needful Rules and Regulations respecting the Territory or other Property belonging to the United States"; and the Sixteenth Amendment which grants Congress power "to lay and collect taxes on incomes."

Congressional power issues may arise either in the context of federalism (see Sec. A above) or in the context of separation of powers (see Chap. 8, Sec. A). Sections C, D, and E of this chapter address Congressional powers in the federalism context. In contrast, Section F of this chapter addresses Congressional powers in the separation of powers context, as does Chapter 8, Section D.2.

The starting point for the analysis of Congressional power issues is the text of the provision that grants the power, read in conjunction with the necessary and proper clause (see Sec. B.3 below). The pertinent text should then be read and applied in the context of either federalism or separation of powers, as fits the situation in which the power issue arises. Sometimes both federalism and separation-of-powers concerns will be evident in a particular power problem, and both will therefore provide context for the reading and application of the pertinent constitutional text (see Chap. 4, Sec. B).

It is also often necessary to consider constitutional provisions other than those that grant the power at issue. Most of these other provisions give shape to the federalism or separation of powers context for the analysis. The supremacy clause in Article VI, paragraph 2, for example, establishes the supremacy of federal laws over state laws and state constitutions. The Tenth Amendment elucidates the general relationship between federal and state powers and gives added emphasis to the notion that Congress' powers are enumerated and limited. Article I, section 10 makes clear that certain federal powers are exclusive and cannot be exercised in any form by the states (*e.g.*, the power to enter into treaties and the power to coin money) or can be exercised by the states only with the consent of Congress (*e.g.*, the power to enter agreements with other states). The Article II and Article III provisions that delegate power to the Executive and the Judiciary may also suggest separation-of-powers limits on particular Congressional powers. The President's power as Commander-in-Chief (Art. II, sec. 2, para. 1), for instance, when compared with Congress' powers to declare war and "raise and support armies," (Art. I, sec. 8, ¶'s 11 and 12), may suggest limits on the latter powers. More broadly, the President's power (and duty) to faithfully execute the laws (Art. II, sec. 3), when compared with Congress' powers to make law, suggests that Congress cannot use its powers in ways that would spill over into the arena of executing law.

Sections B.2 through B.5 below examine various conceptual aspects concerning Congressional powers and the analysis of their scope and limits. It will be helpful to read these sections now because they provide essential background for an enriched understanding of the specific Congressional powers addressed in Sections C through F below. But some of the conceptual matters in Sections B.2 through B.5 are quite complex, and it will be helpful to refer back to them, and reconsider them, as you study the other sections of this Chapter.

B.2.   Exclusive Powers vs. Concurrent Powers

The concept of "exclusive powers" and the contrasting concept of "concurrent powers" are also important to an understanding of the relation between Congressional and state powers, as discussed in this chapter as well as in Chapter 7. Exclusive powers are based in part on Article I, section 10 (see Sec. B.1 above). The powers listed there are *express* exclusive powers of the federal government. For other enumerated powers of Congress that are not listed in Article I, section 10, the text does not make clear whether the powers are exclusive—that is, exercisable only by Congress, or exercisable by the states only with the consent of Congress, or whether they are concurrent—that is, exercisable either by Congress or the states, or by both together, subject to the supremacy of the federal power over state power in cases of conflict. *Gibbons v. Ogden*, 22 U.S. (9 Wheat.) 1 (1824), provides a classic example.

The *Gibbons* case concerned a New York State statute that granted a monopoly to Robert Fulton, inventor of the paddle-wheel steamboat, and his partner Robert Livingston, to operate steamboats in New York waters. Fulton and Livingston had, in turn, granted a license to Aaron Ogden to operate a steamboat ferry between New York City and Elizabethtown Point, New Jersey. Thomas Gibbons, a former partner of Ogden, operated a competing steamboat ferry between the same points. His steamboats were licensed as "vessels...in the coasting trade" under a federal statute passed in 1793. Ogden sued Gibbons in the New York courts, claiming that Gibbons was violating the New York monopoly law, and obtained an injunction prohibiting Gibbons from operating his steamboats in New York waters.

The case reached the U.S. Supreme Court because it involved not only state law issues concerning the New York statute but also federal law issues concerning the interstate commerce clause (Art. I, Sec. 8, cl. 3) and the supremacy clause (Art. VI, paragraph 2). The Court did an extensive analysis of the scope of the commerce clause, concluding that the word commerce "comprehends navigation" and that interstate navigation does not stop at the external boundary lines of the states. The commerce power thus may "pass the jurisdictional line of New York, and act upon the very waters to which [the New York statute] applies" (22 U.S. at 197). The question then was whether the commerce power is (a) an *exclusive* power, in which case only Congress could regulate the steamboating at issue, and the New York statute would therefore be invalid; or (b) a *concurrent* power, in which case New York could also regulate the steamboating at issue, and the New York statute would therefore be valid unless and until Congress had regulated navigation in a way inconsistent with the New York statute. (In the case of a conflict between state and federal law, the federal law would prevail under the supremacy clause).

Gibbons, of course, made the exclusive power argument, and the Court acknowledged that "there is great force in this argument, and the Court is not satisfied that it has been refuted [by Ogden]" (22 U.S. at 209). But the Court avoided a ruling on this point by refocusing its attention onto the federal statute (the 1793 coasting trade law) and asking "whether the laws of New York...have, in their application to this case, come into collision with an act of Congress" and therefore "must yield to the law of Congress..." (22 U.S. at 210). In other words, the Court switched its analysis from alternative (a) above to alternative (b). The Court then determined that the 1793 federal statute was a valid regulation of interstate commerce that applied to Gibbons and entitled him (via his coasting license) to operate his steamboats in New York waters. Since the New York monopoly law denied Gibbons this right, the New York law conflicted with the 1793 federal coasting law and was invalid under the federal Constitution's supremacy clause. In effect, the Court had reasoned that: (1) the commerce power may be an *exclusive* power; but (2) even if it is only a *concurrent* power, Gibbons would still win under the supremacy clause; and therefore (3) the Court would rule in Gibbons' favor under the *concurrent* power theory and leave for another day any definitive ruling on whether the commerce power is *exclusive*. (See Chapter 7, Sections A and B, to learn how the Court ultimately resolved this exclusivity issue under the commerce power.)

A subsequent case, *Prigg v. Commonwealth of Pennsylvania*, 41 U.S. (16 Pet.) 539 (1842), provides guidelines for determining whether a federal power is exclusive or concurrent in situations where the constitutional text does not specify. In those circumstances, the focus should be on "[t]he nature of the power, and the true objects to be attained by it" (*Id.* at 622, citing *Sturges v. Crowninshield*, 17 U.S. (4 Wheat.) 122, 193 (1819)). If the power's nature and objects "require that it should be controlled by one and the same will, and act uniformly by the same system of regulations throughout the Union," then the power is exclusive (*Prigg*, 41 U.S. at 623). The key is the need for "unity of purpose" and uniformity of "remedy and operation throughout the whole Union" (*Id.* at 624). If no such need is apparent, and it would be consistent with the nature and objects of the power for each state "to prescribe just such regulations as suit its own policy, local convenience and local feelings" (*Id.* at 623), then the power is concurrent.

B.3. Implied Powers

Since the federal government is a government of enumerated and limited powers (see Chap. 2, Sec. B), every exercise of power by Congress must be supported by some specific source of power granted in the Constitution.[3] It has been clear at least since *McCulloch v. Maryland*, 17 U.S. (4 Wheat.) 316 (1819), however, that the constitutional grants of power to Congress are construed broadly to include implied powers as well as those expressly granted. Under *McCulloch*, a Congressional statute will be a valid exercise of implied power if the statute is an "appropriate" MEANS for effectuating an END (or object) that is within the scope of one or more of Congress' express powers. In this means/ends framework, the Court's focus is primarily on the "ends" question: whether the end that the statute effectuates is within the scope of some power, or grouping of powers, granted to Congress. The "means" question—whether the statute is an "appropriate" means for effectuating the end—is a question concerning which courts will generally defer to Congress' judgment.

The *McCulloch* case provides the classical example of means/ends analysis. McCulloch was the cashier of the Baltimore branch of the second Bank of the United States, created by Congress in 1816. The State of Maryland sought to impose a tax upon the Baltimore branch, and to impose penalties for failure to pay the tax. In the ensuing litigation, Maryland challenged the constitutionality of the Second Bank of the United States. The U.S. Supreme Court posed the question whether Congress has "power to incorporate a bank" and answered it affirmatively. In so doing, the Court determined that Congress' enactment creating the bank (the MEANS) effectuated various ENDS or "objects" within the Article I, Section 8 grants of power to Congress: "Although, among the enumerated powers of government, we do not find the word 'bank' or 'incorporation,' we find the great powers, to lay and collect taxes; to borrow money; to regulate commerce; to declare and conduct a war; and to raise and support armies and navies" (*McCulloch*, 17 U.S. at 407). Congress could choose the means by which it executes these express powers, as the necessary and proper clause (Art. I, sec. 8, cl. 18) makes clear: "Congress shall have power... [t]o make all Laws which shall be necessary and proper for carrying into Execution the foregoing powers..." (that is, the powers in Art. I, section 8, clauses 1–17).

Maryland sought to severely limit Congress' choice of means by arguing for a narrow interpretation of the phrase "necessary and proper." The Court refused, deciding instead that the phrase included "all means which are appropriate, which are plainly adapted to [an] end" (17 U.S. at 421) within the Article I, section 8 grants of power. Since the bank served to effectuate the powers the Court had identified (*e.g.*, the power to lay and collect taxes), the Court upheld the legislation creating the bank as an appropriate means to a constitutional end. Questions about the "degree of... necessity" for the means (the Bank), according to the Court, were to be addressed by Congress, not by the courts; Congress has "discretion... with respect to the means by which [its]

---

3. A possible exception may exist in the realm of foreign affairs powers, which may, in part, be "inherent" powers that do not find their source directly in the Constitution. *United States v. Curtiss-Wright Export Corp.*, 299 U.S. 304, 315–18 (1936). The current viability and scope of this exception is unclear and, at any rate, is considered more often in the context of Executive power than in the context of Congressional power. See Chap. 8, Sec. C.4.

powers...are to be carried into execution...." (17 U.S. at 388, 421). The courts were to concern themselves with the ends, in particular with whether "Congress, under the *pretext* of executing its powers, pass[es] laws for the accomplishment of *objects not entrusted to the government...*" (17 U.S. at 423; emphasis added).

Congress also has implied power, under the necessary and proper clause, to pass laws "which shall be necessary and proper for carrying into Execution... *all other powers vested by this Constitution in the Government of the United States, or in any Department or Officer thereof*" (U.S. Const., Art. I, sec. 8, cl. 18; emphasis added). In short, Congress may legislate to implement not only its own powers but also those of the Executive and Judicial branches. The case of *Jinks v. Richland County*, 123 S.Ct. 1667 (2003), provides a contemporary example. This case was a challenge to a Congressional jurisdictional statute requiring the tolling of state statutes of limitation when a federal court has taken "supplemental" jurisdiction over a state claim. The Court upheld the statute, relying heavily on the necessary and proper clause and arguing, in part, that the statute "is necessary and proper for carrying into execution Congress's power...to assure that [the lower courts] may fairly and efficiently exercise '[t]he judicial Power of the United States,' [under] Art. III, § 1" (*Id.* at 1671). The unarticulated premise in such cases as *Jinks* is that Congress must use the necessary and proper clause to facilitate rather than to obstruct the execution of the other branch's independent powers.

B.4. Judicial Limits vs. Political Limits on Congress' Powers

It is clear from the Constitution's text that the powers of Congress (indeed of all three branches) are *limited* powers, and that other powers exist which are to be exercised by the states or retained by "the People" and not exercised by any government. But it is not entirely clear from the Constitution's text how the limits on Congress' powers (or those of the other branches) are to be ascertained and enforced. There are two basic approaches. First, the limits could be ascertained and enforced by the courts in cases properly before them. Second, the limits could be ascertained and enforced through the political processes and structures that the Constitution establishes. It has become well established over time that both approaches are part of the constitutional design.

Limits on Congress' powers that are ascertained by the courts are called "judicial limits" or "judicially enforceable limits." Both federal and state courts participate in this process but, under principles of judicial supremacy (Chap. 5, Sec. F), the U.S. Supreme Court plays the predominant role. Limits on Congress' powers attributable to the political processes and structures are called "political limits" or "politically enforceable limits." Regarding Congress' constitutional relationship with the states, political limits protecting the states arise from the constitutional structures for the representation of state interests in Congress. Regarding Congress' relationships with the Executive and Judicial branches, political limits arise from the various checks and balances built into the constitutional structure for a tripartite federal government (see Chap. 4, Sec. B, and Chap. 8, Sec. A).

There are two basic types of judicially enforceable limits on Congressional powers: *intrinsic* (or internal) limits and *extrinsic* (or external) limits. The intrinsic limits arise from the power clauses themselves and from "inferences" that the courts draw from the Constitution's structures (see Chap. 4, Sec. C.3 regarding structural inferences). The extrinsic limits arise from the rights clauses of the Constitution.

This Chapter focuses primarily on the intrinsic judicial limits on Congress' powers. (The extrinsic limits are addressed in Chapters 9–13.) This Chapter (as well as Chapter 7) also focuses primarily on intrinsic limits in the context of federalism. (Intrinsic limits regarding separation of powers are addressed in Chapters 5 and 8.)

There is a necessary connection between intrinsic judicial limits on Congressional powers and political limits on Congressional powers. Both types of limits work together to protect the "balance" of federalism. Thus, whenever a court is asked to impose a judicial limit on Congress, it must consider whether the particular federalism issue before it is amendable to judicial, as opposed to political, resolution. This dynamic between judicial and political limits is most clearly demonstrated in the state autonomy cases in Section C.3–C.5 and section G below. At the same time, the court must consider the extent to which it should defer to Congress' fact-finding and reasoning regarding the type of matter before the court. These matters of judicial deference are best illustrated by the commerce clause cases in Section C.1 below and the enforcement power cases in Section E.

B.5. The Role of the Tenth Amendment

It has already been established in Chapter 2, Section C, that the Tenth Amendment is not a power provision and does not itself *grant* any power to the states. Rather, it *reserves* power "to the States respectively, or to the people" (U.S. Const., Amend. 10). In this respect, the Tenth Amendment serves to recognize the sovereignty of the states and to affirm that the federal government is a government of limited powers. Is there any more specific role that the Tenth Amendment plays in the interpretation of the scope of Congress' powers? Many courts rely on it as a judicially enforceable limit—a type of extrinsic limit (see Sec. B.4 above)—on the scope of Congressional power; if it is so, then how are the courts to use the Amendment in this manner?

The U.S. Supreme Court has addressed these questions periodically throughout its history, but its answers have not always been clear and consistent. In *McCulloch v. Maryland*, 17 U.S. (4 Wheat.) 316 (1819) (Sec. B.3 above), Chief Justice Marshall deemphasized the role of the Tenth Amendment as a limit on Congress' power:

> Even the Tenth Amendment, which was framed for the purpose of quieting the excessive jealousies which had been excited, ... declares only, that the powers "not delegated to the United States, nor prohibited to the states, are reserved to the states or to the people;" thus leaving the question, whether the particular power which may become the subject of contest, has been delegated to the one government, or prohibited to the other, *to depend on a fair construction of the whole instrument.* [17 U.S. at 406 (emphasis added).]

In later cases, the Court sometimes adhered to this formulation of the Tenth Amendment's role (*see, e.g., Missouri v. Holland*, 252 U.S. 416, 432–434 (1920)); but other times the Court attributed more independent significance to the Amendment, as a limit on Congressional power, than what the Court in *McCulloch* had apparently intended. In a commerce clause case, *Hammer v. Dagenhart*, 247 U.S. 251 (1918), for example, the majority invalidated a federal statute prohibiting interstate shipment of goods made with child labor because it undermined the police powers of the states.

> The grant of power of Congress over the subject of interstate commerce was to enable it to regulate such commerce, and not to give it authority to control the states in their exercise of the police power over local trade and manufacture. The grant of authority over a purely federal matter was not intended to destroy the local power always existing and carefully reserved to the states in the Tenth Amendment to the Constitution. [247 U.S. at 273.]

And in *U.S. v. Butler*, 297 U.S. 1 (1936), a taxing and spending power case, the majority invalidated a federal statute designed to strengthen the market for agricultural commodities, by relying on "a stated principle of the Constitution." That principle was the principle of "reserved" powers embodied in the Tenth Amendment. As the Court explained:

> [A] principle embedded in our Constitution prohibits the enforcement of the Agricultural Adjustment Act. The act invades the reserved rights of the states.... From the accepted doctrine that the United States is a government of delegated powers, it follows that those not expressly granted, or reasonably to be implied from such as are conferred, are reserved to the states or to the people. To forestall any suggestion to the contrary, the Tenth Amendment was adopted. The same proposition, otherwise stated, is that powers not granted are prohibited. None to regulate agricultural production is given, and therefore legislation by Congress for that purpose is forbidden.
>
> "And we accept as established doctrine that any provision of an act of Congress ostensibly enacted under power granted by the Constitution, not naturally, and reasonably adapted to the effective exercise of such power, but solely to the achievement of something plainly within power reserved to the states, is invalid and cannot be enforced." *Linder v. United States*, 268 U.S. 5, 17 (1925). [297 U.S. at 68–69.]

Five years after *Butler*, and after the Court had begun to uphold New Deal legislation through more expansive interpretations of Congressional powers (see Sec. C.2 and Sec. C.3 below), the Court took pains to re-cast the Tenth Amendment into a mold closer to that originally struck by the Court in *McCulloch*. The key case was *United States v. Darby*, 312 U.S. 100 (1941). In upholding Congress' power, under the commerce clause, to pass the Fair Labor Standards Act, and overruling *Hammer v. Dagenhart* (above) in the process, the *Darby* court emphasized that "the Tenth Amendment... states but a truism that all is retained which has not been surrendered" (*Id.* at 123). (This aspect of *Darby* is further discussed in Sec. C.1 below.) Following *Darby*, the Court occasionally re-emphasized this diminished role for the Tenth Amendment and the reserved powers principle. In *Hodel v. Virginia Surface Mining and Reclamation*

Ass'n, 452 U.S. 264, 292 (1981), for instance, the Court declared: "It would...be a radical departure from long-established precedent for this Court to hold that the Tenth Amendment prohibits Congress from displacing state police power laws regulating private activity."

Beginning in the 1970's, primarily in cases concerning the states' immunities from Congressional regulation (Sections C.4 and C.5 below), various coalitions of Justices sought to establish a new, stronger role for the Tenth Amendment. In *National League of Cities v. Usery*, 426 U.S. 833 (1976) (Sec. C.4 below), the Tenth Amendment figured prominently in the majority's establishment of a state immunity that substantially limited Congress' authority to regulate the states directly. Nine years later, in *Garcia v. San Antonio Metro Transit Authority*, 469 U.S. 528 (1985), a different majority overruled *National League*, asserting that the Tenth Amendment was not an extrinsic, judicially enforceable limit on Congressional power and that the Tenth Amendment's implications for federalism were to be discerned more through the political process than the judicial process (see Sec C.4 below).

But the Tenth Amendment arose again in 1992 in a different kind of state immunity case that, according to the Court, was not controlled by *Garcia*. In *New York v. United States*, 505 U.S. 144 (1992) (Sec. C.5 below), the majority created a new state immunity that serves as a judicially enforceable limit on Congressional power. But the majority did not ground this immunity on the Tenth Amendment standing alone, nor did it treat the Amendment as a district extrinsic limit on Congress' powers. Rather, the majority treated the Tenth Amendment as a springboard to a *structural* interpretation of the limits on Congressional power over the states. These limits thus arise from the structure of the entire Constitution, as it relates to federalism, rather than from the text of the Tenth Amendment itself. In this analysis, the Tenth Amendment plays the role of (1) a sign or signal that there is a "core of state sovereignty" that the federal government may not infringe; and (2) an invitation to courts to use structural interpretation to determine the attributes of this core and the types of Congressional acts that would be considered infringements. Justice O'Connor, for the majority, provided this explanation of the Tenth Amendment's import and the Court's role in using the Amendment to ascertain limits on Congressional powers:

> If a power is delegated to Congress in the Constitution, the Tenth Amendment expressly disclaims any reservation of that power to the States; if a power is an attribute of state sovereignty reserved by the Tenth Amendment, it is necessarily a power the Constitution has not conferred on Congress.... It is in this sense that the Tenth Amendment "states but a truism that all is retained which has not been surrendered." *United States v. Darby*, 312 U.S. 100, 124 (1941).... The Tenth Amendment...restrains the power of Congress, but this limit is not derived from the text of the Tenth Amendment itself, which, as we have discussed, is essentially a tautology. Instead, the Tenth Amendment confirms that the power of the Federal Government is subject to limits that may, in a given instance, reserve power to the States. The Tenth Amendment thus directs us to determine, as in this case, whether an incident of state sovereignty is protected by a limitation on an Article I power.... Our task...consists not of de-

vising our preferred system of government, but of understanding and applying the framework set forth in the Constitution. [505 U.S. at 155–157.]

Sec. C. The Commerce Power

C.1. A Historical and Conceptual Overview

The commerce power is the most frequently invoked of Congress' domestic regulatory powers and the power that, historically, has been the most frequent subject of U.S. Supreme Court opinions. This power derives from the commerce clause in Article I, section 8, clause 3. The most pertinent language, for present purposes, provides that "The Congress shall have Power...To regulate commerce...among the several states...." This commerce power has a long and circuitous history. The regulation of commerce was a prominent topic of concern under the Articles of Confederation, during the Constitutional Convention in 1787, and in the early years under the Constitution. In 1824, the Supreme Court decided *Gibbons v. Ogden*, 22 U.S. (9 Wheat.) 1 (1824) (see Sec. B.2 above). The Court's lengthy opinion broadly defined the phrase "commerce...among the several states" to include any type of "commercial intercourse" that "concerns more states than one" (22 U.S. at 189–190, 194). The commerce clause thus covers not only traffic in "commodities" but also "navigation" such as the steamboating at issue in the case. The clause also covers all commerce except the "exclusively internal commerce of a state" which "does not extend to or affect other states" (22 U.S. at 195, 194). The *Gibbons* definitions established the foundation for a broad construction of Congress' power.

Many years passed, however, before the *Gibbons* concepts were consistently and expansively implemented by the Court. The commerce clause did not emerge as the premier source of Congress' domestic regulatory power until the end of the nineteenth century. By that time, the nation's economy was becoming national in scope and Congress had begun large-scale interventions into economic matters through enactments such as the Interstate Commerce Act of 1887 and the Sherman Antitrust Act of 1890. In cases arising under such federal regulatory statutes, the Supreme Court gave mixed signals concerning the scope of Congress' commerce power. The Court also experimented with various conceptual distinctions in determining what types of activities were within the commerce power: distinctions between commerce and manufacturing, between commerce and production, between activities directly affecting commerce and activities with only indirect effects on commerce, and between shipment of goods that are themselves evil or injurious and goods that are not.

Several leading cases from the "mixed signals era" broadly interpreted the commerce power. In *Champion v. Ames* (The Lottery Case), 188 U.S. 321 (1903), for instance, the Court upheld a federal act prohibiting interstate shipment of lottery tickets because such shipments are interstate commerce, and Congress may prohibit such shipments when they would "pollute" the commerce by facilitating an activity "injurious to public health or morality." In *Houston, E. & W. Texas R. R. Co. v. United States* (The Shreveport Rate Case), 234 U.S. 342 (1914), the Court upheld an Interstate Commerce Commission order on *intra*state railroad rates because these rates had an injurious effect on *inter*state rates, and there was a "close and substantial relation" between the intrastate and the interstate railroad traffic. And in *Stafford v. Wallace*, 258 U.S. 495 (1922),—a case that continues to have importance in contemporary commerce clause law—the Court upheld the Secretary of Agriculture's regulation of stockyard practices, pursuant to The Packers and Stockyards Act of 1921, because stockyards are part of a "current" or "stream" of interstate commerce in livestock and its products.

Other leading cases in the "mixed signals era" narrowly interpreted the commerce power. In *United States v. E.C. Knight Co.*, 156 U.S. 1 (1895), for instance, the Court held that the United States could not maintain a civil action under the Sherman Antitrust Act against a sugar refining monopoly because sugar refining involved "manufacture" rather than "commerce" and had only indirect effects on interstate commerce. In *Hammer v. Dagenhart* (*The Child Labor Case*), 247 U.S. 251 (1918), the Court invalidated a federal statute prohibiting the interstate shipment of goods produced with child labor because it actually regulated "production" rather than interstate commerce, and the goods involved were "ordinary commodities" that were "of themselves harmless." In A.L.A. *Schechter Poultry Corp. v. United States*, 295 U.S. 495 (1935), the Court invalidated the National Industrial Recovery Act of 1933 insofar as it regulated wages, hours, and trade practices that were part of the "internal commerce" of the states and had no "direct" effect on interstate commerce. And in *Carter v. Carter Coal Co.*, 298 U.S. 238 (1936), the Court invalidated the Bituminous Coal Conservation Act of 1935, regulating wages and hours of coal miners, because it applied to a "purely local activity" having only an "indirect effect" on interstate commerce.

The beginning of the end for the mixed signals era came in 1937 with the Court's decision in *NLRB v. Jones & Laughlin Steel Corp.*, 301 U.S. 1 (1937). In that case, the Court upheld the unfair labor practices provisions of the National Labor Relations Act (29 U.S.C. 151 *et. seq.*) as applied to a major steel corporation. The corporation, the Court reasoned, was a "completely integrated enterprise" with "far-flung activities" and whose labor practices had a "close and substantial" relationship to interstate commerce (301 U.S. at 26, 41, 37). After this case, the Court generally ceased drawing the distinctions used in earlier cases to limit the commerce power and—at least until 1995—typically construed the commerce power broadly to uphold a wide range of federal regulatory initiatives.

The leading cases that served to establish the modern commerce power include:

- *United States v. Darby*, 312 U.S. 100 (1941), in which the Court overruled *Hammer v. Dagenhart*, above, and upheld the minimum wage and maximum hours provisions of the Fair Labor Standards Act of 1938 (29 U.S.C. §§ 201 *et seq.*);
- *Wickard v. Filburn*, 317 U.S. 111 (1942), in which the Court upheld the marketing quotas in the Agricultural Adjustment Act of 1938;
- *Katzenbach v. McClung* (The Ollie's Barbecue Case), 379 U.S. 294 (1964), in which the Court upheld the nondiscrimination provisions of Title II of the Civil Rights Act of 1964 as applied to small local restaurants; and

- *Perez v. United States*, 402 U.S. 146 (1971), in which the Court upheld the prohibition on "extortionate credit transactions" in the Consumer Credit Protection Act of 1968.

These modern cases frequently relied on *Gibbons v. Ogden* as authority for upholding the legislation. In the *Wickard* case, for instance, the Court noted that "[a]t the beginning, Chief Justice Marshall described the federal commerce power with a breadth never yet exceeded" (317 U.S. at 120).

In the post-1937 era, the Court has used the definitions from *Gibbons*, combined with certain elements from the more expansive cases from the mixed signals era, to form the basis of various analytical techniques for determining the scope of Congress' commerce power. Using these techniques, the Court has upheld broad Congressional power when: (1) the objects or activities being regulated are *in* the "channels" or the "stream" of interstate commerce, or are part of the instrumentalities of interstate commerce; (2) the objects or articles being regulated are destined for shipment across state lines; and (3) the regulated activities, although local and intrastate, have a substantial adverse effect on interstate commerce.

Gibbons v. Ogden is an example of the first rationale, since the steamboats were "in" interstate commerce. Another good example is *Stafford v. Wallace*, above, in which the Court permitted Congress to regulate stockyards because they are "in the middle of [a] current of commerce" from the West to the East (*Id.* at 516). Regarding the "instrumentalities" aspect of the first rationale, an early example is *Houston, E. and W. Texas R.R. Co. v. United States* (the Shreveport Rate Case, above), in which intrastate railroad systems were instrumentalities of the interstate railroad system, thus allowing the ICC to regulate the intrastate railroad rates as well as the interstate rates. A more recent case that could serve as an instrumentalities example is *Heart of Atlanta Motel v. United States*, 379 U.S. 241 (1964), a companion case to *Katzenbach v. McClung* (above), in which motels serving interstate travelers could be considered instrumentalities of interstate commerce subject to regulation when their activities impede interstate travel.[4]

United States v. Darby exemplifies both the second and third rationales for regulating commerce. Using the second rationale, the Court in *Darby* upheld § 15(a)(1) of the Fair Labor Standards Act, which prohibits the shipment in interstate commerce of goods manufactured under substandard wage and hour conditions, because the goods at issue (lumber) were produced for interstate commerce (312 U.S. at 112–117).[5] Using the third rationale, *Darby* upheld § 15(a)(2) of the Fair Labor Standards Act, which regulates the wages and hours of employees engaged in the production of goods for interstate commerce, because production of the goods was "so related to [interstate] commerce and so affects it as to be within the reach of the commerce power" (*Id.* at

---

4. These instrumentality examples may suggest that there is no clear conceptual distinction between instrumentalities analysis on the one hand, and channel/stream analysis or substantial effects analysis on the other. It would then follow that most instrumentalities cases could also be argued as either channel/stream cases or substantial effects cases.

5. In the course of its reasoning on this point, the Court overruled the Court's 1918 decision in *Hammer v. Dagenhart* (above); *see* 312 U.S. at 115–117.

122–124). Other leading cases using the third rationale include *Wickard v. Filburn*, 317 U.S. 111 (1942), in which the Court upheld marketing quotas for wheat farmers because excess production adversely affected the interstate market in wheat; and *Katzenbach v. McClung*, 379 U.S. 294 (1964), in which the Court upheld Title II of the Civil Rights Act of 1964, as applied to race discrimination by small local restaurants, because such discrimination adversely affected the interstate flow of food products.

The reasoning utilized in cases such as *Wickard* and *McClung* derives from what is now called the "affect doctrine" or "affectation doctrine," which has become the predominant rationale that legislative drafters have used for devising modern commerce clause legislation and that courts have used to uphold such legislation. The "effect" on interstate commerce, for purposes of the affect doctrine, is not necessarily the effect of the *individual's* activities (the small farmer in *Wickard* or the small restaurant in *McClung*). Rather, using a process of "aggregation" or "cumulation," courts may consider the effect of the *entire class* that is regulated (for example, all small wheat farmers as in *Wickard*, or all small restaurants as in *McClung*). The relevant facts about effects on commerce may be found in the record compiled by Congress in the process of enacting the statute, as they were in the *McClung* case. Or such facts may be entered into the trial record of the case challenging Congress' statute, as they were in *Wickard*. In the former situation, when the evidence is in the legislative record, the Court will be deferential to Congress' judgment about the effects that the activity to be regulated has on interstate commerce. As indicated in *McClung*, the Court will use a "rational basis" standard of review, upholding the statute whenever Congress had "a rational basis for finding a chosen regulatory scheme necessary to the protection of [interstate] commerce" (379 U.S. at 304).

The *Darby* case (above) in 1941 also made two important conceptual points that were followed in later cases such as *McClung* (above). The first point addressed Darby's argument that Congress' regulation (§15(a)(1)), though "nominally a regulation of commerce," actually had a "motive or purpose" of regulating "wages and hours of persons engaged in" local manufacturing activities. Rejecting this argument, the Court emphasized that the "motive and purpose of a regulation of interstate commerce are matters for the legislative judgment upon the exercise of which the Constitution places no restriction and over which the courts are given no control" (312 U.S. at 115). This refusal to examine Congress' motives for passing a particular statutory provision is generally thought to minimize the possibility that plaintiffs could make successful "pretext" arguments of the type that Chief Justice Marshall had suggested in *McCulloch v. Maryland* (see Sec. B.3 above) and that the Court had sometimes utilized in later cases (*see, e.g., United States v. Butler*, 297 U.S. 1, 68–69 (1936)). To determine whether Congress was acting "under the pretext of executing its powers" (*McCulloch* at 423) but was actually seeking to regulate an activity beyond the scope of its powers, a court would presumably have to investigate Congress' motives. Since this avenue was apparently closed off by *Darby*, analysis of the scope of Congress' commerce power (and other powers as well) has become more objective than subjective, and thus more dependent upon factual data concerning the connection that the object or activity being regulated has with interstate commerce. The maturation of this development can clearly be seen in the most recent cases discussed in Section C.2 below.

The second conceptual point in *Darby* concerns the Tenth Amendment. In cases prior to 1937, the courts had sometimes looked to the Tenth Amendment as a kind of affirmative limit (extrinsic limit) on the exercise of Congressional powers (see Sec. B.5 above). The Court in *Darby* rejected this use of the Tenth Amendment:

> Our conclusion is unaffected by the Tenth Amendment which...states but a truism that all is retained which has not been surrendered. There is nothing in the history of its adoption to suggest that it was more than declaratory of the relationship between the national and state governments as it had been established by the Constitution before the amendment or that its purpose was other than to allay fears that the new national government might seek to exercise powers not granted, and that the states might not be able to exercise fully their reserved powers. [312 U.S. at 123–124][6]

C.2. The New Era of Commerce Clause Cases

In the mid 1990s, another new era in commerce clause law began as the U.S. Supreme Court attempted to re-establish meaningful limits on the commerce power. The effort has focused mainly on the affect or affectation doctrine that, at least in the view of the Court majority in these new cases, is subject to being used in ways that tread upon traditional areas of state sovereignty. The first key case was *United States v. Lopez*, 514 U.S. 549 (1995), in which the Court, by a 5-4 vote, invalidated a federal statute making it a crime to possess a firearm on or within 1000 feet of school grounds. The statute exceeded the scope of the commerce power, according to Chief Justice Rehnquist for the majority, because Congress had not required prosecutors to prove that the defendant or the firearm had some "nexus" to interstate commerce, nor had Congress made findings or produced evidence that gun possession on or near school grounds "substantially affects" interstate commerce. The Court was also concerned that gun possession was not an "economic enterprise" or "economic activity," and that any attempt to connect gun possession to interstate economic or commercial concerns would be too "attenuated" to meet the effect test. The Court emphasized that "criminal law enforcement" and "education" are areas "where States historically have been sovereign," thus making it especially important that Congress develop findings or evidence of a connection to interstate commerce that is not "tenuous." In sum, there are ascertainable limits on the commerce power, and this power does not extend to the regulation of all "activities that adversely affect the learning environment" or "include the authority to regulate each and every aspect of local schools" (514 U.S. at 565, 566).

Questions about the reach and significance of *United States v. Lopez* went before the U.S. Supreme Court again in *United States v. Morrison*, 529 U.S. 598 (2000). The issue

---

6. Although the Court has generally adhered to this dictum in later commerce clause cases, the Tenth Amendment has taken on new meaning in the line of state immunity cases beginning with *New York v. United States* in 1992; see Sec. B.5 above.

was whether the Violence Against Women Act (42 U.S.C. § 13981) was within the scope of Congress' commerce power. The U.S. Supreme Court decided that it was not and invalidated the Act. Relying heavily on *U.S. v. Lopez*, the Court majority held that Congress had not demonstrated that the violent acts targeted by the statute had a substantial adverse effect on interstate commerce. Unlike the *Lopez* case, in the *Morrison* case Congress had made numerous findings regarding adverse effects of gender violence on interstate commerce. But the Court rejected these findings as a basis for invoking the effect doctrine, considering them to be based on a "but-for causal chain" that was too "attenuated" and too focused on "noneconomic" conduct to justify the Act under the commerce clause.

Neither *Lopez* nor *Morrison* overruled any of the Court's prior cases from the era beginning in 1937. Thus, cases such as *Darby*, *Wickard*, and *McClung* are still good law. Nevertheless, it does seem clear that the Court is now being less deferential to Congress in commerce clause cases and that the Court is seeking to develop manageable limits on the commerce power beyond the minimal limits from the post-1937 cases. At the same time, the Court has sought to develop some kind of state immunity from certain Congressional commerce clause regulations; these developments are addressed in the next section.

C.3.   State Autonomy and the Commerce Power: An Overview

In commerce power cases such as those discussed in Section C above, the Supreme Court has considered, and has often upheld, Congressional regulation of *private* sector activities. In *U.S. v. Darby*, 312 U.S. 100 (1941), for example, the Court upheld use of the Fair Labor Standards Act, 29 U.S.C. sec. 201 et seq., to regulate wage and hour policies of lumber companies and other *private* employers. Suppose, however, that Congress sought to regulate the *public* sector under the commerce clause. For example, suppose Congress regulated the wage and hour policies of *public* employers, *i.e.*, state governments and local governments. Would Congress' commerce power support such regulation to the same extent as it supports regulation of the private sector? Or would the concept of *state autonomy*, or *state immunity*, interpose a limit on Congress' commerce power that would protect states and their local governments from some kinds of federal regulation that would be permissible in the private sector?

The state autonomy argument is based on notions of federalism (see Chap. 4, Sec. B). The existence and scope of state autonomy from federal regulation is ascertained through structural interpretation of the Constitution (see Chap. 4, Sec. C.3). The Tenth Amendment is also cited as textual support for the Constitution's protection of state autonomy. (See Section C.1 above for discussion of how the Court has explained the Tenth Amendment's role in state autonomy cases.)

There are two basic types of autonomy cases. The first type concerns "the authority of Congress to subject state governments to generally applicable laws"; these are the cases "in which Congress has subjected a State [or its local governments] to the same legislation applicable to private parties." *New York v. United States*, 505 U.S. 144, 160

(1992). The second type of case concerns Congressional legislation directed solely to the states or state officers (or to local governments or their officers); these are the cases in which Congress has "use[d] the States as implements of regulation" by "direct[ing] or otherwise motivat[ing] the States to regulate in a particular field or a particular way." *Id.* at 161. The U.S. Supreme Court has treated these two types of cases differently, being willing to invalidate legislation of the second type but not the first. The first type of case is discussed in Section C.4 below; the second type of case is discussed in Section C.5.

C.4. State Autonomy from General Congressional Regulation

The first type of immunity case is exemplified by two cases nine years apart—*National League of Cities v. Usery*, 426 U.S. 833 (1976), and *Garcia v. San Antonio Metro Transit Authority*, 469 U.S. 528 (1985). These cases strikingly illustrate the opposing views on whether and to what extent state autonomy limits Congress' power to apply generally applicable commerce clause regulations to state and local governments.

In *National League of Cities*, a 5-4 majority of the Supreme Court relied on the Tenth Amendment, and on inferences drawn from the federalistic structure of the Constitution, to invalidate the application of the Fair Labor Standards Acts' wage and hour provisions to state and local government employers. According to Justice Rehnquist for the Court:

> It is one thing to recognize the authority of Congress to enact laws regulating individual businesses necessarily subject to the dual sovereignty of the government of the Nation and of the State in which they reside. It is quite another to uphold a similar exercise of congressional authority directed, not to private citizens, but to the States as States. We have repeatedly recognized that there are attributes of sovereignty attaching to every state government which may not be impaired by Congress....

> * * * *

> [T]he dispositive factor is that Congress has attempted to exercise its Commerce Clause authority to prescribe minimum wages and maximum hours to be paid by the States in their capacities as sovereign governments....

> This exercise of congressional authority does not comport with the federal system of government embodied in the Constitution. We hold that insofar as the challenged amendments operate to directly displace the States' freedom to structure integral operations in areas of traditional government functions, they are not within the authority granted Congress by Article I, §8, cl. 3. [426 U.S. at 845, 852.]

Justice Brennan wrote the primary dissent, arguing that the Court should not interfere with Congress' use of the commerce power to regulate the states because "the political branches of our government are structured to protect the interests of the States, as well as the Nation as a whole, and...the States are fully able to protect their own interests...." [426 U.S. at 876 (Brennan, J., dissenting).]

In *Garcia*, another narrow 5-4 majority overruled *National League of Cities*. In upholding the application of the FLSA's overtime provisions to a metropolitan transit authority, the *Garcia* Court reasoned:

> Any rule of state immunity that looks to the "traditional," "integral," or "necessary" nature of governmental functions inevitably invites an unelected federal judiciary to make decisions about which state policies it favors and which ones it dislikes....
>
> We therefore now reject, as unsound in principle and unworkable in practice, a rule of state immunity from federal regulation that turns on a judicial appraisal of whether a particular governmental function is "integral" or "traditional."

* * * *

> ...Apart from the limitation on federal authority inherent in the delegated nature of Congress' Article I powers, the principal means chosen by the Framers to ensure the role of the States in the federal system lies in the structure of the Federal Government itself. It is no novelty to observe that the composition of the Federal Government was designed in large part to protect the States from overreaching by Congress.... State sovereign interests, then, are more properly protected by procedural safeguards inherent in the structure of the federal system than by judicially created limitations on federal power.

* * * *

> [T]he principal and basic limit on the federal commerce power is that inherent in all congressional action—the built-in restraints that our system provides through state participation in federal governmental action. The political process ensures that laws that unduly burden the states will not be promulgated.... [469 U.S. at 546–547, 550–552, 556.]

Justice Rehnquist, the author of the majority opinion in *National League*, was one of the four dissenters in *Garcia*. In his brief dissent he asserted that the then-overruled principles of *National League* "will, I am confident, in time again command the support of the majority of the Court." Although there have been numerous signs since the early 1990s that Justice Rehnquist's prediction may come to pass (see Section G below), the *Garcia* case remained intact as this book went to press.

Due to other developments, however, the *Garcia* case and its green light for direct Congressional regulation of the states now has less force than it originally did. In 1996, in the *Seminole Tribe* case (Section G.2 below), the Court held that Congress cannot use the commerce power to abrogate the states' immunity from private suits in federal court. Such suits, brought by individuals harmed by a state's noncompliance with Congressional regulations, had been a major means for enforcing commerce clause legislation such as that upheld in *Garcia*. Then, in *Alden v. Maine* (Section G.2 below), the Court held that Congress cannot use the commerce power to abrogate a state's immunity from private suits in the state's own courts.

The result is that, even though Congress may still regulate the states using the commerce power, it may not provide for the enforcement of commerce clause regulations against the states through private lawsuits by the individuals whom such regulations protect. If a state were to violate the FLSA wage and hour rights of certain state employees, for instance, these employees could no longer sue that state, either in federal or in state court, to enforce their rights. The result would be different, however, if Congress provides for private suits *against local governments* in federal court. Local governments do not share in the state's sovereign immunity from federal court suit (*Hans v. Louisiana*, 134 U.S. 1 (1890)).

C.5. State Autonomy from Congressional Regulations Uniquely Applicable to the States

The second type of state autonomy case is exemplified by *New York v. United States*, 505 U.S. 144 (1992). The legislation challenged in that case was the Low-Level Radioactive Waste Policy Amendments of 1985. It was clear that Congress could have directly regulated the interstate market in interstate waste disposal under its commerce power and preempted state regulation under the supremacy clause. Instead, in the 1985 Amendments, Congress required the states themselves to regulate radioactive waste in the ways that the Amendments prescribed. In particular, under the so-called "take title" provisions of the Amendments, Congress required states to either (a) regulate waste disposal in the manner directed by Congress, or (b) take title to the waste and be responsible for it themselves. The Court struck down this provision of the Amendments. Distinguishing *Garcia* as a case that applied only to situations "in which Congress has subjected a State to the same legislation applicable to private parties," the Court devised a new principle to govern cases in which Congress "use[d] the States as implements of regulation." Under this principle, which has come to be known as the "anti-commandeering" or "no commandeering" principle, the Court invalidated the take title provision because it "would 'commandeer' state governments into the service of federal regulatory purposes..." (505 U.S. at 175). Even though Congress could regulate the same subject matter itself, and even though the federal interest may be of the highest order, "Congress may not...'commandeer the legislative processes of the States by directly compelling them to enact and enforce a federal regulatory program....'" (*Id.* at 161, quoting *Hodel v. Virginia Surface Mining and Reclamation Ass'n*, 452 U.S. 264, 288 (1981)). In other words, Congress "may not conscript state governments as its agents" by "command[ing] a state government to enact *state* regulation...." (505 U.S. at 178). Because the take title provision crossed this line, said the Court, it was "inconsistent" with the Constitution's division of authority between federal and state governments." (*Id.* at 175).

In a later case, *Printz v. United States*, 521 U.S. 898 (1997), the Court used the same anti-commandeering principle to invalidate provisions of the Brady Handgun Violence Prevention Act that directed state and local law enforcement officers to conduct background checks on prospective handgun purchasers. The *Printz* opinion extends *New York v. United States* by prohibiting Congressional commandeering (or "conscripting") of state and local executive officials as well as of state legislatures: "The Federal Government may neither issue directives requiring the States to address particular problems, nor command the States' officers, or those of their political subdivisions, to administer or enforce a federal regulatory program" (521 U.S. at 935). The *Printz* opinion also further explains why commandeering statutes are unconstitutional: such a law "compromise[s] the structural framework of dual sovereignty.... It is the very *principle* of separate state sovereignty that such a law offends...." (521 U.S. at 932).[7]

This chain of events also provides a backdrop for further consideration of the distinction between *judicial* protection of state autonomy and state immunity provided through *judicially enforceable* limits on Congress' powers, and *political* protection provided through Congress and the federalistic structures of the political process (see Sec. B.4 above). The majority opinion in *Garcia* relies heavily on this distinction, as does the earlier dissent by Justice Brennan in *National League* (see Sec. C.4 above). Although *Garcia* tilts in the direction of political protections rather than judicial, the anti-commandeering cases (Sec. C.5 above) and the recent state immunity cases (Sec. G.2 below) clearly move the Court in the direction of judicial protections.

Sec. D. The Taxing and Spending Powers: A Conceptual Overview

The taxing power and the spending power both derive from Article I, section 8, clause 1. The taxing power arises from the words "To lay and collect Taxes, Duties, Imposts, and Excises." The spending power arises from the words "to pay the Debts and provide for the common Defense and general Welfare...." In *United States v. Butler*, 297 U.S. 1 (1936), the Court confirmed that the "general welfare" clause does not "[grant] power to provide for the general welfare, independently of the taxing power" (*Id.* at 64), but rather is qualifying language that limits the taxing and spending powers. What the clause grants, then, "is the power to tax for the purpose of providing funds for payment of the nation's debts and making provision for the general welfare [and common defense]" (*Id.* at 64). At the same time, adopting Alexander Hamilton's position on the taxing and spending powers (the "Hamiltonian" view) and rejecting James Madison's position (the "Madisonian" view), the *Butler* Court confirmed that these powers are separate from and not limited by the other enumerated powers that

---

7. In a case two years after *Printz*, *Alden v. Maine*, 527 U.S. 706 (1999) (Sec. G.2 below), the Court has apparently extended some of the *New York* and *Printz* reasoning to cases concerning the judicial branches of state governments. In upholding a state constitutional immunity from being sued in its own courts for violations of federal statutes, the Court majority argued that: "A power to press a State's own courts into federal service to coerce the other branches of the State...is the power...ultimately to *commandeer* the entire political machinery of the State against its will and at the behest of individuals (*Id.* at 749) (emphasis added). Thus, in *Alden*, the state autonomy cases on commandeering intersected with the state immunity cases on suits against states in their own courts.

are subsequently listed in Article I, section 8 (*Id.* at 66). Congress thus is not limited to taxing and spending in aid of its other powers such as the commerce power, but may tax and spend for any purposes that serve the common defense or general welfare.[8]

Although the taxing and spending powers are actually two separate powers, the power to tax on the one hand and the power to spend on the other, they are obviously related. Not only do they both derive from the same constitutional clauses, but they also may appear together in the same case. A plaintiff, for instance, could challenge an integrated program of taxing and spending (a specific tax whose proceeds are earmarked for a specific type of expenditure) by attacking the entire program as a violation of both the taxing and spending powers. The *Butler* case, above, is such an example. On the other hand, a plaintiff could attack a tax without reference to the expenditures that are made from the tax proceeds, or may challenge an expenditure of funds apart from the particular tax or other revenue source from which the expended funds are derived. An expenditure, for instance, may have been made from general appropriations and therefore not be traceable to any particular tax source.

Congress' taxing and spending powers have a historical development similar to that of the commerce power. Prior to and early in the New Deal, the U.S. Supreme Court sometimes narrowly construed the taxing and spending powers; later in the New Deal and subsequent to it, however, the Court issued opinions that more liberally construed these powers. The key year was 1937, the same year as the watershed decision regarding the commerce clause, *NLRB v. Jones & Laughlin Steel Corp.*, 301 U.S. 1 (1937).[9]

In February of 1937, President Roosevelt had proposed his controversial "Court-packing plan"—a plan to add up to six new Justices to the U.S. Supreme Court. The historical record is unclear as to whether this proposal—ultimately rejected by Congress—influenced the Court's change of direction. For the tax power the watershed case was *Sonzinsky v. United States*, 300 U.S. 506 (1937), which upheld a tax on firearms transactions even though the tax may have had the purpose and effect of restricting or regulating firearms. For the spending power, the watershed cases were *Steward Machine Co. v. Davis*, 301 U.S. 548 (1937), which upheld the federal unemployment compensation system created by Title XI of the Social Security Act of 1935, and *Helvering v. Davis*, 301 U.S. 619 (1937), which upheld the old age pension program in Titles II and VIII of the same Act. In both cases the Court indicated that it would uphold a Congressional exercise of the spending power so long as it serves to "induce" or "encourage" the states rather than "coerce" or "compel" them to act.

Since *Steward Machine v. Davis* and *Helvering v. Davis*, the Supreme Court has decided fewer taxing and spending power cases than commerce power cases. The decided cases have accorded Congress broad discretion to tax and spend, and to attach condi-

---

8. For a comprehensive historical, political science, and legal treatment of the spending power, *see* Theodore Sky, To Provide for the General Welfare: A History of the Federal Spending Power (U. Del. Press, 2003).

9. Coincidentally, 1937 was also the sesquicentennial of the Constitution's signing at the Constitutional Convention in Philadelphia.

tions to its spending, as it sees fit. In *South Dakota v. Dole*, 483 U.S. 203 (1987), the leading modern case, for instance, the Court considered Congressional legislation that conditioned the Secretary of Transportation's award of federal highway funds on the state's willingness to prohibit persons under 21 from purchasing or possessing alcoholic beverages in the state. States that did not comply with the condition lost 5% of their federal highway funds. The Court upheld the condition because it was "directly related to one of the main purposes for which highway funds are expended—safe interstate travel." Moreover, the 5% penalty was a "relatively mild encouragement" for the states to comply and did not constitute "coercion" or "compulsion."

In contrast to its actions in recent commerce clause cases (see Sec. C above), the Court has not cut back on its expansive interpretation of the taxing and spending powers. In effect, these powers have become even more important since the Court's 1995 decision in *U.S. v. Lopez* (Sec. C.2 above), because they may be used for new initiatives that Congress is now blocked from pursuing under the commerce power. Moreover, using the spending power, Congress apparently may condition the states' receipt of federal funds on their agreement to waive the sovereign immunity that otherwise would protect them from being sued for violating any of the conditions (including nondiscrimination conditions) attached to the federal spending program. By such means, Congress could lessen the impact of the Court's recent decisions expanding the sovereign immunity of the states from suit (see Chap. 14, Sec. D).

In the *Dole* case itself, however, the Court did sow seeds that could be used by future courts to impose new limits on the spending power. In his *Dole* majority opinion, Chief Justice Rehnquist discussed "the germaneness of the condition to federal purposes," thus suggesting a "germaneness" or "relatedness" requirement applicable to the relationship between a particular grant condition and the purposes for which the federal funds are expended (483 U.S. at 208 (text and accompanying note 3)). In addition, by indicating that the 5% penalty for noncompliance did not "pass the point at which 'pressure turns into compulsion'" (quoting *Steward Machine*) because it was "a relatively small percentage of certain federal highway funds" (483 U.S. at 211), Chief Justice Rehnquist implied that the loss of much larger percentages of the allocated funds or much larger total dollar amounts could be considered coercive and thus invalid. In a dissenting opinion in *Dole*, Justice O'Connor emphasized the first of these potential limits, arguing that the alcoholic beverages condition should be invalidated because it was "far too over-and under-inclusive" and thus not sufficiently related to safety on federal highways. Justice O'Connor asserted that she would apply the germaneness requirement more rigorously than the majority had done to assure that the relationship between the condition on spending and the purpose of the federal expenditures is not "attenuated or tangential."

There are also several other clauses of the Constitution that relate to the taxing and spending powers. Article I, section 2, clause 3, and Article I, section 9, clauses 4 and 5 establish express limitations on the power to tax. More importantly, the Sixteenth Amendment empowers Congress to lay and collect taxes on incomes, a power that the U.S. Supreme Court had found to be unavailable prior to that amendment because of the expressed restrictions in Article I, section 2, clause 3 and Article I, section 9, clause

4 (*Pollock v. Farmers' Loan & Trust Co.*, 157 U.S. 429 (1895)). There is also a related fiscal power in Article I, section 8, clause 2: Congress' power "to borrow Money on the credit of the United States."

Sec. E. The Enforcement Powers: A Conceptual Overview

Among the most important of Congress' other domestic powers are the "enforcement powers" authorizing Congress to enforce the guarantees of certain amendments, especially the Thirteenth, Fourteenth, and Fifteenth Amendments (*see* Amend. 13, sec. 2; Amend. 14, sec. 5; Amend. 15, sec. 2). Section 5 of the Fourteenth Amendment, for example, empowers Congress "to enforce, by appropriate legislation, the provisions of this article." In *Katzenbach v. Morgan*, 384 U.S. 641 (1966), the U.S. Supreme Court upheld Congress' use of this power to enact a provision of the Voting Rights Act of 1965 (42 U.S.C. §§ 1971 *et seq.*) that prohibited states from using English literacy tests in certain circumstances (42 U.S.C. § 1973b (e)). This provision, said the Court, was an appropriate exercise of Congressional discretion to secure the guarantee of equal protection. In determining whether the legislation was "appropriate" under Section 5, and thus in determining the scope of Congress' discretion, the Court relied on the necessary and proper clause in Article I, section 8:

> [T]he draftsmen sought to grant to Congress, by a specific provision applicable to the Fourteenth Amendment, the same broad powers expressed in the Necessary and Proper Clause.... Thus the *McCulloch v. Maryland* standard is the measure of what constitutes "appropriate legislation" under § 5 of the Fourteenth Amendment. Correctly viewed, § 5 is a positive grant of legislative power authorizing Congress to exercise its discretion in determining whether and what legislation is needed to secure the guarantees of the Fourteenth Amendment. [384 U.S. at 651.]

Similarly, in *South Carolina v. Katzenbach*, 383 U.S. 301 (1966), the Court upheld Congress' use of its Fifteenth Amendment enforcement power to enact various other provisions of the Voting Rights Act because these provisions were "appropriate means of combating the evil" of race discrimination in voting (383 U.S. at 328). "As against the reserved powers of the States," said the Court, "Congress may use any rational means to effectuate the constitutional prohibition of racial discrimination in voting" (*Id.* at 324). And in *Jones v. Alfred H. Mayer Co.*, 392 U.S. 409 (1968), the Court upheld Congress' use of its Thirteenth Amendment enforcement power to enact a statute prohibiting race discrimination in the sale of housing, recognizing the statute to be "rationally related" to the elimination of "badges and incidents of slavery" (*Id.* at 439, quoting the *Civil Rights Cases*, 109 U.S. 3, 20 (1883)).

In the *Katzenbach v. Morgan* case (above), the Court used two, alternative, rationales for broadly construing Congress' enforcement powers. The first was the "remedial" rationale, under which Congress could devise various means for alleviating conditions that courts have held, or predictably would hold, to violate a particular individual right protected by the Thirteenth, Fourteenth, or Fifteenth Amendment (*see* 384 U.S. at 652–53). The second rationale was the "substantive" rationale, under which Congress could define new violations of the Constitution's individual rights clauses that extend beyond any violations that the courts themselves had recognized (*see* 384 U.S. at 653–56). In later cases, the Court confirmed and relied upon the remedial rationale (*e.g., Rome v. United States*, 446 U.S. 156 (1980)) but questioned and did not rely on the substantive rationale (*e.g., Oregon v. Mitchell*, 400 U.S. 112 (1970)). In *City of Boerne v. Flores*, 521 U.S. 507 (1997), the Court capped these developments by firmly declaring the remedial rationale, and a related "preventive" or "prophylactic" rationale, to be the only bases for exerting the enforcement powers.

The *City of Boerne* case was a challenge to the Religious Freedom Restoration Act of 1993 (RFRA), 42 U.S.C.§§ 2000bb *et seq.* Congress had passed this statute to counteract the restriction that the Court had imposed on the First Amendment's free exercise clause (as incorporated into the Fourteenth Amendment) in the case of *Employment Division, Department of Human Resources v. Smith*, 494 U.S. 872 (1990) (Chap. 13, Sec. C.2). In *City of Boerne*, the Court invalidated RFRA because it was substantive rather than remedial legislation and was thus beyond the scope of Congress' enforcement power under Section 5 of the Fourteenth Amendment.

> Congress' power under §5...extends only to "enforcing" the provisions of the Fourteenth Amendment. The Court has described this power as "remedial," *South Carolina v. Katzenbach*, [383 U.S.] at 326. The design of the Amendment and the text of §5 are inconsistent with the suggestion that Congress has the power to decree the substance of the Fourteenth Amendment's restrictions on the States. Legislation which alters the meaning of the Free Exercise Clause cannot be said to be enforcing the Clause. Congress does not enforce a constitutional right by changing what the right is. It has been given the power "to enforce," not the power to determine what constitutes a constitutional violation. Were it not so, what Congress would be enforcing would no longer be, in any meaningful sense, the "provisions of [the Fourteenth Amendment]." [521 U.S. at 519.]

Further discussions of the enforcement powers, and the developments subsequent to the *City of Boerne* case, are deferred until Chapter 14, Sections C and D. The complexities may be better understood at that point, after consideration of the state action doctrine (Chap. 9, Sec. E) and the equal protection clause (Chap. 10, Secs. C and D), and in the context of federal civil rights legislation (Chap. 14, Sec. B).

Sec. F. Foreign Relations Powers

Article I, section 8 grants Congress seven major express powers over foreign relations: (1) the power to spend funds "for the common Defense...of the United States"; (2) the power to "regulate Commerce with foreign Nations"; (3) the power to "define...

Offenses against the Law of Nations"; (4) the power to "declare War"; (5) the power to "raise and support Armies"; (6) the power to "provide and maintain a Navy"; and (7) the power "to make Rules for the Government and Regulation of the land and naval Forces" (Art. I, sec. 8, ¶'s. 1, 3, 10, 11, 12, 13, and 14).[10] Under Article II, section 2, paragraph 2, the Senate also has an "Advice and Consent" power regarding Presidential treaty-making and the President's appointment of ambassadors.

In addition to these express powers, the necessary and proper clause (Art. I, sec. 8, ¶ 18) grants Congress implied powers for implementing not only its own express powers (see Section B.3 above) but also "all other Powers vested ... in the Government of the United States, or in any "Department or Officer thereof." This clause thus authorizes Congress to pass legislation that effectuates Presidential foreign relations initiatives. In *Missouri v. Holland*, 252 U.S. 416 (1920), for example, the Court upheld a Congressional statute (the Migratory Bird Treaty Act) that implemented a migratory bird treaty that the President had negotiated with Great Britain. The Court reasoned: "If the treaty is valid there can be no dispute about the validity of the statute under Article I, §8, as a necessary and proper means to execute the powers of the Government" (252 U.S. at 432). Similar reasoning was also used by Congress in 1973 to justify its passage of the War Powers Resolution, Pub. Law No. 93–148 (87 Stat. 555, 50 U.S.C. §§ 1541 *et seq.*), which establishes a framework for decision-making on the introduction of U.S. Armed Forces into hostilities. Section 1541(b) of the Resolution cites, as a constitutional basis for the Resolution, Congress' power "to make all laws necessary and proper for carrying into execution, not only its own powers but also all other powers vested by the Constitution" in other departments or officers.

Beyond these express and implied powers, it is sometimes suggested that Congress has "inherent" or extraconstitutional powers "to enact legislation for the effective regulation of foreign affairs" (*Perez v. Brownell*, 356 U.S. 44, 57 (1958)[11] citing *United States v. Curtiss-Wright Export Corp.*, 299 U.S. 304, 318 (1936)). If and to the extent Congress has such inherent powers, they are shared with the President, as discussed in Chapter 8, Section B.

In studying these foreign relations powers, it is critical to understand the distinctions between express powers, implied powers, and inherent powers, and to correctly categorize each source of power and each power argument that you confront. It is also critical, as shall be seen in Chapter 8, to consider these Congressional powers in a separation-of-powers framework, testing their scope and limits with reference to the competing foreign affairs powers vested in the President.

---

10. Congress also has the lesser used, and perhaps somewhat antiquated, powers to "define and punish Piracies and Felonies committed on the high seas," to "grant Letters of Marque and Reprisal," and to "make Rules concerning Captures on Land and Water" (Art. I, sec. 8, ¶s 10 and 11).

11. *Perez* was overruled, on grounds not implicating the validity of its statement about inherent powers, in *Afroyim v. Rusk*, 387 U.S. 253 (1967).

Sec. G. State Government Autonomy or Immunity from Congressional Legislation

G.1. Overview

In the commerce clause cases discussed in Section C above, state governments sought to impose state sovereignty limitations on Congress' enumerated powers. Such limitations, the states argued, arose from the Tenth Amendment or, more broadly, from the Constitution's federalistic structure of government. The U.S. Supreme Court struggled in these cases to determine its appropriate role in identifying and enforcing such implicit limits on Congressional power.

State immunity or autonomy arguments have also arisen in cases where Congress has taxed (rather than regulated) the states. In *New York v. United States*, 326 U.S. 572 (1946), for instance, the Court rejected a challenge to a federal tax on soft drinks as applied to New York State's sale of bottled mineral water from state-owned springs. Similarly, in *South Carolina v. Baker*, 485 U.S. 505 (1988), the Court rejected a challenge to a federal tax code provision that withdrew the tax exemption for unregistered state and local bonds, thus subjecting the interest on these bonds to federal income taxation.

The Court has also occasionally addressed state autonomy in the context of the spending powers. In *South Dakota v. Dole*, 483 U.S. 203 (1987), for example, the Court suggested that a "relatedness" or "germaneness" requirement may protect the states from Congressional overreaching in its imposition of grant conditions (see Sec. D above). More specifically, in *Pennhurst State School and Hospital v. Halderman*, 451 U.S.1 (1981), the Court emphasized Congress' obligation to assure that states may "voluntarily and knowingly" choose whether to accept a federal grant and comply with the federal conditions attached to the grant funds. Thus, said the Court, if Congress intends to impose such conditions, "it must do so unambiguously.... By insisting that Congress speak with a clear voice, we enable the States to exercise their choice knowingly, cognizant of the consequences of their participation" (451 U.S. at 17). Using these principles to protect Pennsylvania's autonomy, the Court refused to recognize or enforce an alleged condition that the plaintiffs claimed was attached to grants under the Developmentally Disabled Assistance and Bill of Rights Act. "Congress fell well short of providing clear notice to the States" that they would be obliged to comply with the alleged condition (regarding treatment conditions for disabled persons) if they accepted the funds. "Congress' power to legislate under the spending power... does not include surprising participating States with post acceptance or 'retroactive' conditions" (451 U.S. at 25).

These state autonomy protections under the spending power may differ from those under the commerce and taxing powers, however, where the protections are uniquely crafted for and available to the states and their local governments. Under the spending power, in contrast, similar protections may also apply to private organizations that receive federal grants.

The success of these "state autonomy" or "state immunity" arguments for limiting federal regulatory power has been quite modest. The second "commandeering" case, *Printz v. United States* (Section C.5 above) is the high water mark to date. Since 1996, however, when the Court decided *Seminole Tribe v. Florida*, 517 U.S. 44 (1996) (see Sec. G.2 below), the states have had remarkable success with another type of immunity argument—the argument for state sovereign immunity from being sued for money damages in court and in administrative agency proceedings. This type of immunity is discussed in the following section.

G.2. State Sovereign Immunity from Suits to Enforce Congressional Legislation

The state sovereign immunity doctrine is actually an old and well-worn doctrine (see Chap. 5, Sec. E), but the U.S. Supreme Court has expanded the doctrine's scope in a series of important cases beginning in 1996. This sovereign immunity doctrine addresses the scope of the Courts' judicial power rather than the scope of Congress' regulatory power, and sovereign immunity arguments are used to create limits on the authority of courts (and now also administrative agencies) to hear and decide private causes of action against the states. Often, however, Congress' effective assertion of its powers depends upon the federal government's capacity to enforce Congress' laws directly against the states, and state agencies and officials. Since the new sovereign immunity cases directly limit the federal government's options for doing so, these new cases have major implications for Congressional power as well as judicial power.

Although the states have traditionally argued that the Eleventh Amendment protects them from attempts of private persons to enforce federal law against them in federal courts (see Chap. 5, Sec. E), the U.S. Supreme Court in modern times had often permitted Congress to "abrogate" or override this state immunity if it chose to do so.[12] But Congress' authority to abrogate has been greatly restricted by the line of cases beginning with *Seminole Tribe v. Florida*, 517 U.S. 44 (1996). The *Seminole Tribe* case was a dispute concerning Congress' use of the commerce clause to regulate gambling businesses operated by Indian tribes. Congress' statute required the states to negotiate compacts with tribes seeking to conduct gambling activities on tribal lands, and authorized tribes to sue the states in federal court if they did not negotiate in good faith. By a 5 to 4 vote, the Court invalidated this Congressional attempt to abrogate state sovereign immunity because Congress had used the commerce power, a part of the original Constitution's Article I legislative powers, and these powers could not be used to remove a limit that a later amendment, the Eleventh Amendment, had placed on the original Constitution's Article III judicial power. As the Court stated:

---

12. For an example of Congressional abrogation, *see* the Civil Rights Remedies Equalization Amendment of 1986, 42 U.S.C. § 2000d-7.

"[e]ven when the Constitution vests in Congress complete lawmaking authority over a particular area [e.g., interstate commerce], the Eleventh Amendment prevents congressional authorization of suits by private parties against unconsenting States" (517 U.S. at 72).

The dissenters in *Seminole Tribe* complained that the majority's decision "prevents Congress from providing a federal [judicial] forum for a broad range of actions against States, from those sounding in copyright and patent law, to those concerning bankruptcy, environmental law, and the regulation of our vast national economy," (517 U.S. at 77 (Stevens, J., dissenting)).

The *Seminole Tribe* majority did acknowledge, however, that the no-abrogation principle does not apply to Congress' power to enforce the Fourteenth Amendment (see Sec. E above). That amendment was passed long after the Eleventh Amendment, and it expressly limits the states as such. Thus, in decisions both before and after *Seminole Tribe*, the Court has consistently held that the Fourteenth Amendment permits Congress to authorize private suits against unconsenting states that have allegedly violated the amendment (*see, e.g., Fitzpatrick v. Bitzer*, 427 U.S. 445 (1976)). But in a line of decisions following *Seminole Tribe*, the Court has substantially limited Congress' use of its Fourteenth Amendment authority to abrogate; discussion of these cases is deferred until Chapter 14, Section C, when the reader will be better prepared to confront their complexities.

The Court has also expanded state sovereign immunity in two other ways in cases after *Seminole Tribe*. First, in *Alden v. Maine*, 527 U.S. 706 (1999), the Court prohibited private plaintiffs from suing states in *state* courts (see Chap. 5, Sec. E). Second, in *Federal Maritime Commission v. South Carolina State Ports Authority*, 535 U.S. 743 (2002), the Court prohibited private plaintiffs from using federal administrative agency tribunals to bring federal claims against states and state agencies — at least when the administrative agency proceedings are adjudicative proceedings similar to civil litigation in the courts. In this case, a cruise ship operator had brought a claim against South Carolina's State Ports Authority, alleging a violation of a federal shipping act and seeking reparations as well as an order that the Ports Authority "cease and desist" from further violations of the shipping act. The Court, quoting the U.S. Court of Appeals, ruled that this proceeding "walks, talks, and squawks...like a lawsuit," and applied sovereign immunity. Both *Alden* and *State Ports Authority* were 5 to 4 decisions. In both cases, the majority emphasized that the Eleventh Amendment does not demarcate the full extent of state sovereign immunity, and used structural and historical arguments (see Chap. 4, Sec. C) to support the additional dimensions of immunity recognized in these cases.

When the *Alden* case and the *State Ports Authority* case are combined with the cases narrowing Congress' abrogation authority, the result is a historical shift in the federal-state balance of power. The effect of this shift is to limit severely the ability of Congress to enforce its laws by authorizing private parties to bring claims against states and state agencies that have allegedly violated these laws.

Sec. H. Exercise No. 6: The Fair Labor Standards Act, State Autonomy, and State Immunity

In light of the materials on state autonomy and state immunity in Sections C.3, G.1 and G.2 above, consider the implications of the following real-life chain of events:

1938: Congress passes the Fair Labor Standards Act (FLSA), 29 U.S.C. § 201 *et seq.*, regulating wage and hour policies of private employers.

1941: The U.S. Supreme Court upholds the FLSA as a constitutional exercise of the commerce power. *United States v. Darby*, 312 U.S. 100 (1941).

1966: Congress amends the FLSA to impose wage and hour regulations on state hospitals and schools (80 Stat. 831, September 23, 1966, codified as 29 U.S.C. § 203(r)).

1968: The U.S. Supreme Court, by a 7-2 vote, upholds the 1966 FLSA amendments as a constitutional exercise of the commerce power. *Maryland v. Wirtz*, 392 U.S. 183 (1968).

1973: In *Employees of the Department of Public Health and Welfare v. Department of Public Health and Welfare*, 411 U.S. 279 (1973), the U.S. Supreme Court holds that the plaintiffs, employees of Missouri state hospitals, could not sue the state for overtime pay allegedly due them under the FLSA as amended in 1966. Although acknowledging that the plaintiffs were protected by the 1966 amendments and that, under *Maryland v. Wirtz*, the state was constitutionally subject to the FLSA, the Court determines that the state's Eleventh Amendment immunity from suit in federal court nevertheless remains intact after passage of the 1966 amendments. Relief for employees such as the plaintiffs was to be obtained through suits brought on their behalf by the U.S. Secretary of Labor.

1974: Congress further amends the FLSA to impose wage and hour regulations on all state and local government employers (88 Stat. 58, April 8, 1974, codified as 29 U.S.C. § 203(d)).

1976: By a 5-4 vote, the U.S. Supreme Court invalidates the 1974 FLSA amendments as an unconstitutional exercise of the commerce power that invades state autonomy protected by the Tenth Amendment. *National League of Cities v. Usery*, 426 U.S. 833 (1976). In the process, the Court overrules *Maryland v. Wirtz* insofar as it had upheld the 1966 FLSA amendments.

1985: In *Garcia v. San Antonio Metropolitan Transit Authority*, 469 U.S. 528 (1985), the Court reconsiders and, by another 5-4 vote, overrules *National League of Cities*, thus upholding the constitutionality of the 1974 FLSA amendments.

1985: In the wake of *Garcia*, Congress again amends the FLSA. The amendments add new provisions that soften the regulatory impact on state and local government employers of the FLSA's wage and hour requirements (99

Stat. 787, 789, November 13, 1985, codified as 29 U.S.C. § 207(o) and (p)). One new provision, for example, allows state and local government employers to award "comp time" for certain overtime work rather than paying overtime wages.

1999: In *Alden v. Maine*, 527 U.S. 706 (1999), employees of the state of Maine, being barred by *Employees of the Department of Public Health and Welfare* from suing the state for FLSA violations in federal court (see also the *Seminole Tribe* case, 517 U.S. 44 (1996) (Sec. G.2 above)), seek instead to bring such a suit in state court. In a 5 to 4 decision, the U.S. Supreme Court rules that principles of sovereign immunity—"preserved by [the] constitutional design" of federalism, rather than by the Eleventh Amendment as such—prohibited the employees from bringing the suit in state court. Moreover, under *Seminole Tribe*, above, Congress could not "abrogate" this state court immunity (*Alden*, 527 U.S. at 754).

Questions

What does this chain of events regarding the FLSA illustrate about state autonomy/immunity as a limit on the commerce power? About the U.S. Supreme Court's role in protecting state autonomy/immunity? About Congress' role in protecting state autonomy? About Congress' role in limiting the state's immunity from suit? About the capacity of private parties to sue the states? About the constitutional plan for protecting state autonomy and preserving the state's immunity from suit?

Answers

The chain of events set out in this exercise suggests that the constitutional law on state autonomy and state immunity is still somewhat unsettled and that the Court continues to be sharply divided on such issues. The Court is thus also sharply divided concerning its role in maintaining the balance of federalism. The events depicted primarily emphasize the first of the two types of state autonomy problems (see Sec. G.1 above) and the sovereign immunity from suit problem (see G.2). The second type of autonomy problem (see Sec. G.2 above) is also implicated to the extent that the Court majority viewed its state immunity decision in *Alden* as a type of "anti-commandeering" principle (*Alden*, 527 U.S. at 748–749).

Regarding the *NLC/Garcia* autonomy, two overrulings occurred between 1976 and 1985, both by 5-4 votes, and the dissenters to the second overruling predicted that, in time, the Court would again overrule itself. It remains to be seen whether more recent changes in the Court's composition or more recent developments (concerning state immunity from suit (see Sec. G.2 above)) will occasion further shifts in the Court's view of this aspect of federalism.

Regarding Congress' 1985 legislation in the wake of *Garcia*, it is worth considering whether this event substantiates the *Garcia* majority's conclusion that the political process provides adequate protection for state autonomy. On one view, the rapid success of state and local governments in obtaining remedial legislation is proof of "the solicitude of the national political process for the continued vitality of the states" (*Garcia* at 557). On another view, the remedial legislation was only a narrow, short-range victory for the states, directed at immediate fiscal problems, that may detract attention from broader, longer-range problems regarding state autonomy. *See generally* Advisory Commission on Intergovernmental Relations, *Reflections on Garcia and Its Implications for Federalism* (Rpt. M-147, 1986).

This chain of events also provides a backdrop for consideration of the distinction between *judicial* protection of state autonomy and state immunity provided through *judicially enforceable* limits on Congress' powers, and *political* protection provided through Congress and the federalistic structures of the political process (see Chap. 4, Sec. B). The majority opinion in *Garcia* relies heavily on this distinction, as does the earlier dissent by Justice Brennan in *National League* (see Sec. C.4 above). Although *Garcia* tilts in the direction of political protections rather than judicial, the anti-commandeering cases (see Sec. C.5 above) and the recent state immunity cases clearly move the Court in the direction of judicial protections.

This chain of events also illustrates the existence of, and relationship between, two types of judicial protections for state autonomy/immunity. Under the first type, the courts prohibit Congress from regulating the states in certain ways (see the *National League* and *Garcia* cases above). Under the second type, the courts prohibit private parties from suing the states, thus removing the primary means by which Congress' legislation can be enforced against the states (see the *Employees of Department Health and Welfare* case and the *Alden* case, above). Even though *Garcia* eliminated the state autonomy protection (of the first type) created in *National League*, the expansion of the states' sovereign immunity from suit (the second type of protection) in cases such as *Alden* has provided a comparable protection for the states. In addition, the U.S. Supreme court has created a new state autonomy protection of the first type in *New York v. United States* (Sec. B.5 above) that co-exists with and supplements the protection (of the second type) available to the states under the sovereign immunity from suit cases. The continued force of these two parallel developments makes clear that the balance of federalism has been moving in the states' direction.

Sec. I. Study Suggestions

As you study the scope of Congress' grants of power, focus on the ends or "objects" that are entrusted to Congress under each of its powers. This focus will lead to questions such as: What is "interstate commerce" (the end of the commerce power)? What is a "tax" (the end of the taxing power)? What is "spending" (the end of the spending power)? When a statute is challenged as beyond Congress' power, the analytical task is to identify the grant of power that allegedly supports the statute, define the ends or "objects" that Congress may accomplish under this power, and then determine whether there is a demonstrable connection between the legislation being challenged and the particular power Congress is using.

In studying U.S. Supreme Court opinions on the scope of particular Congressional powers, you should also be attentive to uses of the implied powers concept and the means/ends analysis that derive from *McCulloch v. Maryland* (Sec. B.3 above). For each opinion, identify the grant of power (or power clause) that is at issue. Seek to identify any tests or standards that the Court uses to guide its application of that particular power clause. Consider the extent to which the test or standard used by the Court is deferential to the policy and factual judgments of Congress, and thus supports broad constructions of Congressional power. Also consider whether the Court inquired into Congress' motives for passing the particular statute that is being challenged (the Court has sometimes done so in the past) or whether the Court indicated that Congressional motives are not relevant to its analysis (they generally are not). In addition, consider whether the Tenth Amendment played any role in the Court's opinion.

The commerce clause cases provide a particularly fertile field for study. As you read these cases, seek to determine the particular analytical technique(s) (see Sec. C above) that the Court uses to ascertain whether Congress' legislation falls within the scope of the commerce power, and how these analytical techniques work. To do so, you will need to *synthesize* the relevant portions of the various precedents that are still good law today. (The modern commerce clause cases provide especially good opportunity to practice your powers of synthesis.) Then focus on the affect doctrine (the predominant analytical technique), and ask yourself whether the new, or reinvigorated, judicial limits on the commerce power that arise from *Lopez* and *Morrison* (Sec. C.2 above) will provide meaningful guidance for Congressional committees and committee counsel, and will be amenable to consistent application by the courts.

More broadly, as you study the cases on Congressional powers, consider how the concept of federalism has evolved over time. What role has the Tenth Amendment played in the Court's determinations, and what is its current role? Why has the federal/state "balance" of power seemingly shifted at critical points in the nation's history? Is such a shift occurring now through the federalism cases that began in 1992 with *New York v. United States* (Sec. C.5 above) and continued with *Lopez* in 1995 (Sec. C.2 above), *Seminole Tribe* in 1996 (Sec. G.2 above), *City of Boerne* in 1997 (Sec. E above), and later cases? In these cases, has the Court carved out a suitable institutional role for itself as a referee of the federal system? Does the Court defer sufficiently to the political processes and allow sufficient room for the "political limits" on Congressional power (Sec. B.4 above) that emerge from the Constitution's federalistic structures?

FOR FURTHER READING: (1) Lynn Baker, "Constitutional Federal Spending After *Lopez*," 95 Colum. L. Rev. 1911 (1995). (2) Jesse Choper and John Yoo, "The Scope of the Commerce Clause After *Morrison*," 25 Oklahoma City U. L. Rev. 843 (2000). (3) Roger Hartley, The New Federalism and the ADA: State Sovereign Immunity from Private Damage Suits after *Boerne*, 24 N.Y.U. Rev. L. and Soc. Change 481 (1998). (4) H. Jefferson Powell, "The Oldest Question of Constitutional Law," 79 Va. L. Rev. 633 (1993) (regarding federalism and *New York v. United States*).

Chapter 7

Federalistic Limits on the Exercise of State Power

Sec. A. A Conceptual Overview

Chapter 6 (Congressional Powers and Federalism) addresses the scope of Congress' powers by focusing on the constitutionality of legislation *passed by Congress*. In contrast, this chapter addresses the scope of Congress' powers by focusing on legislation *passed by the states and their local governments*. The basic premise of the chapter is that the power clauses of the federal constitution, sometimes combined with the supremacy clause (Article VI, paragraph 2), limit the scope of *state* power as well as *federal* power. These limits on state power are usually called "federalistic limits." This chapter explores the source and extent of these limits.

The pertinent constitutional provisions for this inquiry are Article I, section 10, which contains express limits on state power; Article I, section 8, which contains grants of power to Congress from which limitations on state power may be inferred; and Article VI, paragraph 2, which establishes the supremacy of federal law. The limits arising from these constitutional provisions are internal or "intrinsic" limits, deriving from the power clauses and power structures themselves, as opposed to the external or "extrinsic" limits on power arising from the individual rights clauses that are found elsewhere in the Constitution (see Chapter 6, Section B.4). State power is also limited by these rights clauses, of course, but with one exception (the interstate privileges and immunities clause) discussed in Section E below, individual rights clauses are not the concern of this Chapter.

The case of *Gibbons v. Ogden*, 22 U.S. (9 Wheat.) 1 (1824), discussed in Chapter 6, Sections A.1 and B.1, provides an early example of an intrinsic federalistic limits problem. The law being challenged was a state, not a federal, law—New York's steamboat monopoly law. The U.S. Supreme Court acknowledged that this state statute's regulation of steamboat navigation was a regulation of interstate commerce, a subject expressly within the regulatory authority of Congress (Art. I, sec. 8, cl. 3). The issue was whether the state could also regulate this subject (interstate steamboat navigation) or whether it was prevented from doing so by some federalistic limit on its power.

The Court broke this issue into two parts: (a) whether the state could regulate if Congress had not (that is, if Congress had been silent regarding the regulation of steamboating in interstate waterways); and (b) whether the state could regulate if Congress had already regulated this same subject. The Court suggested that the answer to part (a) depended on whether the commerce power was exclusive or concurrent but did not rule on this point. (Exclusive and concurrent powers are discussed in Chapter 6, Section A.2.) As to part (b), the Court determined that Congress had already used its commerce power to regulate via the 1793 coasting law, which applied to the steamboating in which Gibbons was engaged. The N.Y. steamboat monopoly law conflicted with this federal coasting law, said the Court, and the federal law prevailed in a case of conflict (Article VI, ¶ 2). The New York law was therefore unconstitutional because it ran afoul of a federalistic limit created by the commerce clause in conjunction with the supremacy clause. (This part of *Gibbons* provides an early example of federal law "preempting" state law. The "preemption" doctrine is discussed in Sections C.1. and C.2. below.)

Twenty seven years after *Gibbons*, the Court faced another interstate transportation problem in *Cooley v. Board of Wardens of the Port of Philadelphia*, 53 U.S. (12 How.) 299 (1851) — a case now considered a classic example of a federalistic limits problem and the originating source of modern doctrinal developments. The state statute at issue was an 1803 Pennsylvania pilotage law that required the masters of certain vessels entering or leaving the Port of Philadelphia to engage a local pilot to conduct the vessel to and from the port. Cooley, who had been assessed a penalty for violating this law, claimed that the law was an unconstitutional interference with Congress' commerce power. The Court quickly determined that the law regulated interstate and foreign navigation that was considered part of interstate and foreign commerce. The Court then considered and rejected the proposition, suggested in *Gibbons*, that the commerce power is exclusive and leaves no room for state regulation. To the contrary, "the mere grant to Congress of the power to regulate commerce did not deprive the states" of all power to legislate that subject (53 U.S. at 320).

This pronouncement did not mean, however, that the states had concurrent power to regulate commerce along with Congress. Rather, said the Court, the commerce power in toto was neither exclusive nor concurrent, and the nature of the power could be determined only with reference to the particular subjects to be regulated. When the subjects are "in their nature national, or admit[ting] only of one uniform system, or plan of regulation," Congress' power over these subjects is exclusive. When the subjects are "local and not national," and are best provided for through the legislative discretion of the states, taking into account "local peculiarities," Congress' power is concurrent (53 U.S. at 319). The Court determined that pilotage for local ports was the latter type of subject, and it therefore rejected *Cooley*'s challenge to the Pennsylvania statute.

Like *Gibbons*, the *Cooley* case also involved a federal statute, but the statute played a very different role from the one in *Gibbons*. The federal statute in *Cooley* was a 1789 law providing that pilots in the various ports of the United States would continue to be regulated by the laws of the states. While the state law in *Gibbons* was in conflict with the federal coasting law, the state law in *Cooley* was compatible with the federal pilotage law. Rather than overriding local regulation, like the federal coasting law in *Gibbons*, the federal pilotage law in *Cooley* in effect gave Congress' consent to state regulation. Thus, while the federal coasting law in *Gibbons* had supported the finding of a federalistic limit on state power, the federal pilotage law in *Cooley* supported the constitutionality of the Pennsylvania statute by rejecting any suggestion of a federalistic limit on state power.

As *Gibbons* and *Cooley* suggest, there are three conceptually distinct types of problems concerning intrinsic federalistic limits: (1) the "negative implication" or "dormant clause" problem; (2) the preemption problem; and (3) the Congressional consent problem. The first of these problems is discussed in Section B below; the second and third are discussed in Section C below. Each type of problem arises only in situations where the subject or object of state legislation is also a subject or object of federal concern, that is, a subject or object within the reach of Congress' constitutional powers. Thus the state's legislation must fall within a "field of federal concern"—a field covered by some grant of power to Congress—in order for an intrinsic federalistic limits problem to arise.

Sec. B. Negative Implication Cases: the Dormant Commerce Clause

B.1. Overview

The primary concern in the U.S. Supreme Court's cases on federalistic limits has been identification of the limits on state power that are implicit in the Article I, Section 8 grants of power to Congress and in the constitutional structure of federalism. The federal commerce power is the power most frequently implicated in these cases. The *Gibbons* case and the *Cooley* case, discussed in Section A above, are both examples of commerce clause cases presenting federalistic limits issues. In each of these cases, navigation was the subject or object of federal concern, and it fell within the field of interstate commerce, a field of federal concern under Article I, section 8, clause 3.

The first part of *Gibbons* (part (a)) illustrates the first type of problem listed above, specifically a negative implication problem concerning the "dormant" commerce clause. The issue was whether the state could regulate the interstate commerce (navigation by steamboat) if Congress had not regulated, that is, if Congress' commerce power lay "dormant." In this type of case, the Court considers whether the absence of Congressional regulation, considered against the backdrop of the framers' "vision" of a national economic unit free from burdensome state restrictions on commerce, raises a "negative implication" concerning the state's power to regulate. The *negative* implication would be an implication that the states were not to regulate the subject at issue. The Court's basic objective in this type of case, as indicated in its opinions in more modern cases, is to weed out state regulations that burden commerce to such an extent that they interfere with the constitutional vision of "national solidarity" based on the commitment to maintain a national economic unit. *See, e.g., Baldwin v. G.A.F. Seelig,* 294 U.S. 511, 523 (1935). The constitutional "vision" that is a touchstone of this analysis is the "vision of the framers" supported by inferences drawn from the Constitution's federalistic structure. Negative implication and dormant commerce clause analysis is thus based on historical and structural interpretation of the Constitution (see Chap. 4, Secs. C.2 and C.3).

Cooley, like the first part of *Gibbons,* also illustrates the dormant commerce clause problem. But the *Cooley* analysis—separating national subjects and interests from state subjects and interests—differs from *Gibbons. Cooley* is the forerunner of a balancing-of-interests methodology used in more modern dormant commerce clause cases such as *Southern Pacific Co. v. Arizona* and *Pike v. Bruce Church, Inc.,* discussed in Section B.3 below.

The modern dormant commerce clause cases divide conceptually into two sub-categories. The first contains the cases in which a plaintiff challenges a regulation or tax that discriminates against interstate commerce on its face or in its purpose and effect (see Sec. B.2 below). The second sub-category contains the cases in which a plaintiff challenges a non-discriminatory or "neutral" statute that "burdens" interstate commerce in the process of regulating all commerce, intrastate as well as interstate (see Sec. B.3 below). The courts are more suspicious of statutes in the first category, since they have greater potential to obstruct the free flow of interstate commerce. State statutes in the first sub-category are therefore subject to a stricter standard of judicial review, than statutes in the second sub-category.

B.2. Discriminatory State Laws

The first sub-category of dormant commerce clause cases originates from the case of *Welton v. Missouri,* 91 U.S. 275 (1875), where the Court invalidated a state law licensing peddlers because it applied only to peddlers selling goods from out-of-state. The law therefore discriminated on its face against out-of-state goods and thus against interstate commerce. In modern times, the best example of the Court's approach to discriminatory state laws is *Philadelphia v. New Jersey,* 437 U.S. 617 (1978). There the Court considered a state solid and liquid waste law that prohibited the importation of such waste into New Jersey from other states for disposal in New Jersey landfills. There was no comparable state control on disposal of waste generated within New Jersey. The Court characterized this law as "parochial legislation" that effected "economic isolation" or economic "protectionism." "On its face, [the New Jersey law] imposes on out-of-state commercial interests the full burden of conserving the State's remaining landfill space.... What is crucial is the attempt by one State to isolate itself from a problem common to many by erecting a barrier against the movement of interstate trade" (437 U.S. at 628). The Court therefore concluded that New Jersey's solid and liquid waste law was unconstitutional because it discriminated on its face against interstate commerce in order to accomplish economic isolationist or protectionist objective. Such statutes are subject to "a virtually *per se* rule of invalidity" (437 U.S. at 624). Even if a discriminatory law advances objectives *other than* economic isolationism, that is, if the law treats out-of-state interests differently for some legitimate reason "apart from their origin" (437 U.S. at 627), the law will still be subject to heightened judicial scrutiny. *Maine v. Taylor*, 477 U.S. 131 (1986).[1]

B.3. Neutral State Laws

The second sub-category of dormant commerce clause cases (cases on nondiscriminatory or neutral state laws) has its roots in *Cooley* (Sec. B.1 above). The modern period for these cases began in 1945 in *Southern Pacific Co. v. Arizona*, 325 U.S. 761 (1945), a case about state regulation of railroads. In invalidating an Arizona law limiting the length of passenger trains and freight trains, the Court adopted a balancing approach that weighed the state interests in regulating against the national interests at stake, including in particular the interest in the free flow of interstate commerce (*Id.* at 770–771, 775–776).

In *Pike v. Bruce Church, Inc.*, 397 U.S. 137 (1970), the Court synthesized the cases from *Southern Pacific* onward and provided a restatement of the balancing approach upon which later courts have built. *Pike* concerned an Arizona statute requiring that Arizona cantaloupes be processed in Arizona and labeled as Arizona grown. Church, an Arizona grower of high quality cantaloupes, had a practice of transporting the produce to a nearby California plant for processing. Pursuant to the statute, Arizona issued an order prohibiting Church from processing the cantaloupes in California and directing that the cantaloupes be processed in Arizona. Because of the perishable qualities of cantaloupes, compliance with the statute would have required Church to construct its own packing shed at a cost of $200,000, since no such facilities were located anywhere nearby in Arizona. Church argued that the order prohibiting it from processing the cantaloupes in California unconstitutionally burdened interstate commerce. Arizona countered that, even if its statute did burden interstate commerce, the state has the power to enact such legislation to promote and preserve the reputation of Arizona growers.

The Court quickly determined that "it is clear that [the State's] order does affect and burden interstate commerce...." Then the Court constructed and applied a balancing test for determining whether a particular burden on interstate commerce is unconstitutional:

> Where the statute regulates even-handedly to effectuate a legitimate local public interest, and its effects on interstate commerce are only incidental, it will be upheld unless the burden imposed on such commerce is clearly excessive in relation to the putative local benefits.... If a legitimate local purpose is

---

1. When the subject being regulated is intoxicating beverages, and the state regulation discriminates against out-of-state vendors or producers, the Twenty-first Amendment (acknowledging the states' authority to regulate the transportation and importation of liquor into their territory) provides a partial protection for the state against dormant commerce clause challenges to its regulation. *See, e.g., Bacchus Imports, Ltd. v. Dias*, 468 U.S. 263 (1984).

found, then the question becomes one of degree. And the extent of the burden that will be tolerated will of course depend on the nature of the local interest involved, and on whether it could be promoted as well with a lesser impact on interstate activities. [397 U.S. at 142 (citation omitted).]

Using this formulation, which came to be known as the "Pike test," the Court invalidated the statute's application to Church. The state's interests in promoting the reputation of Arizona growers were legitimate, but they were not strong enough to "constitutionally justify" the burden that would be placed on Church's interstate commerce by the requirement that the company build and operate an unneeded $200,000 packing plant in the State.

While balancing the pertinent interests as called for in cases like *Southern Pacific* and *Pike*, the Court has considered the extent to which the state statute creates burdens on commerce that fall disproportionately on out-of-state interests. In effect, the greater the disproportion is, the greater the doubts about the statute's constitutionality. In some cases, the disproportion may increase the weight of the burden on interstate commerce. In *Southern Pacific*, for example, the Court noted that almost 95% of the rail traffic regulated by the train length law was interstate and only 5% was intrastate. In other cases, the disproportion may cause the Court to discount the strength of the state's interests (safety or otherwise) that support the regulation. In *Kassel v. Consolidated Freightways Corp.*, 450 U.S. 662 (1981), for instance, Justice Powell noted that the Court should give less "deference" to the legislature's judgments about safety when the state's regulation "bears disproportionately on out-of-state residents and businesses" (450 U.S. at 675–676) (plurality opinion)). A disproportionate burden was evident in that case, and contributed to the invalidity of an Iowa statute regulating the length of trucks, because the legislature had provided various exceptions to the law that eased its burdens on in-state (but not out-of-state) interests.

In addition, the existence of disproportionate burdens may negate the Court's "assumption that where [state] regulations do not discriminate on their face against interstate commerce, their burden usually falls on local economic interests as well as other State's economic interests, thus insuring that a State's own political processes will serve as a check against unduly burdensome regulations" (*Raymond Motor Transportation v. Rice*, 434 U.S. 429, 444, n. 18 (1978); *see also Raymond* at 446–447). If the Court is satisfied that such a "political check" is working, it may accord a greater deference to the state legislature's judgments. But "to the extent that the burden of state regulation falls on interests outside the state, it is unlikely to be alleviated by the operation of these political restraints normally exerted when interests within the state are affected" (*Southern Pacific*, 325 U.S. at 768 n. 2). In such circumstances where a political check is not working, as in both *Southern Pacific* and *Kassel*, the Court will accord lesser deference to the state legislature's judgments. For this reason as well as those above, neutral statutes that cast substantially disproportionate burdens on out-of-state commerce are less likely to be constitutional than those whose burdens substantially affect in-state interests as well.

Despite the identification of analytical approaches such as those suggested in this section, the pertinent distinctions—*e.g.*, between protectionist and non-protectionist legislation, and between neutral and disproportionately burdensome legislation — remain difficult to draw, and the process for decisionmaking remains a subject of controversy. Thus contentious debate continues among both judges and scholars concerning the Court's appropriate role in this arena of federalism — in particular its appropriate role in reviewing neutral statutes that burden interstate commerce. Disagreements concern the appropriate tests to use; the appropriate facts to consult (those before the legislature or those later presented in court); the degree to which courts should defer to a state legislature's judgments, especially concerning safety; and even whether the courts should decline any role in these cases, leaving the issues to Congress and the political structures of federalism. The *Kassell* case provides the best review of the judicial debate; compare Justice Powell's plurality opinion (450 U.S. at 662–679) with Justice Brennan's concurrence (450 U.S. at 679–687) and Justice Rehnquist's dissent (450 U.S. at 687–706).

B.4. The Market Participant Exception

For both the cases on discrimination against interstate commerce (Sec. B.2 above) and the cases on burdening interstate commerce (Sec. B.3 above), there is an important exception that sometimes insulates discriminatory or burdensome state policies from constitutional attack. Called the "market participant exception," it protects a state when it is acting as a buyer or seller in the economic marketplace rather than as a regulator of the market or a taxing entity. In *Reeves, Inc. v. Stake*, 447 U.S. 429 (1980), for instance, South Dakota owned and operated a cement plant, and restricted the sale of cement to state residents. The Court held that the state was acting as a proprietor rather than a regulator, and its actions fell within the market participant exception. The state's residents-only sales policy thus did not violate the dormant commerce clause, despite its obvious discrimination against interstate commerce. In contrast, had the state regulated a private cement plant in the state, and restricted its sales to state residents, it seems clear that the regulation would have violated the commerce clause.

Based on the few cases the Court has decided under the market participant exception, it appears that a state as buyer or seller may accord pricing preferences, hiring preferences, or other economic preferences to its own residents if it wishes, or it may restrict sales and purchases of particular state property solely to its own residents. In effect, when a state functions like a private proprietor or entrepreneur, the Court will allow it the freedom that the private actor has in the economic marketplace — including the freedom to transact business in ways that disadvantage out-of-state buyers or sellers. Apparently, however, this freedom extends only to transactions "within the market in which [the state] is a participant" and does not protect a state's buying or selling policies that burden commerce "outside of that particular market" (*South-Central Timber Development, Inc. v. Wunnicke*, 467 U.S. 82, 97 (1984) (plurality opinion)). In the *Wunnicke* case, for instance, the Court reviewed a condition that Alaska had placed on sales of state-owned timber: that the purchaser must partially process the lumber in the state before shipping it out of state. In the plurality opinion that remanded the case to the lower court, Justice White concluded that this condition was outside the protection of the market participant exception because it imposed a burden on the timber *processing* market—a different market from the one (the timber *selling* market) in which the state was participating.

There are only a handful of U.S. Supreme Court cases on the market participant exception. The rationale for the exception remains elusive, and the particulars of its scope and application remain unclear. In selective situations, however, it can provide an important sanctuary for a state seeking creative ways to promote its own economy without running afoul of the commerce clause.

Sec. C. Preemption and Consent

C.1. Congressional Authority to Preempt or Consent

As the discussion in Section B demonstrates, courts may wield considerable power in federalistic limits disputes. The courts are not the only important decision-makers in this arena, however, nor even the primary decision-makers. That role falls to Congress, which may resolve federalistic limits problems itself if it so chooses, either before or after such problems have been litigated. Congress may do so either through the device of preemption or the device of consent. Using the former device, Congress may "preempt" state laws that burden interstate commerce or intrude upon any other "field of federal concern" (see Sec. A above). Using the latter device, Congress may consent to and thus permit state laws that burden interstate commerce or intrude upon some other "field of federal concern." In either case, Congress must of course be acting within the scope of its delegated powers. When it does so, Congress may effectuate its decisions either by legislation that itself serves to preempt or consent to particular types of state laws, or by legislation that authorizes federal administrative agencies to enact regulations preempting or consenting to particular types of state laws. Congress may preempt or consent to state statutes and state administrative regulations, as well as the ordinances and regulations of the states' local governments. As the U.S. Supreme Court noted in *Hillsborough County, Florida v. Automated Medical Laboratories*, 471 U.S. 707, 713 (1985): "We have held repeatedly that state laws can be preempted by federal regulations as well as by federal statutes.... Also, for the purposes of the Supremacy Clause, the constitutionality of local ordinances is analyzed in the same way as that of statewide laws."

Analysis of preemption and consent issues generally has three components. First, there is usually a considerable amount of statutory interpretation (of both federal and state law) to be done before the relationship between the federal and state law may be ascertained. Second, supremacy principles (Art. VI, ¶ 2) are applied to determine whether federal law serves either to supercede or authorize the state law. Third, to guide the statutory analysis and the application of supremacy principles—to a greater or lesser extent depending on the type of preemption or consent issue—federalism factors concerning the nature and strength of the federal and state interests at stake are considered. These factors are much the same as those the Court considers in negative implication cases concerning neutral state statutes that burden commerce (Sec. B.3. above).

C.2. Preemption

The second part of the *Gibbons* case (part b), discussed in Sec. A above, illustrates the preemption problem. This type of federalistic limits problem arises when the state has regulated a subject matter that Congress has also regulated. The issue is whether Congress' regulation "preempts" (or precludes) the state from regulating the same subject. The governing law is built on the "familiar and well-established principle that the Supremacy Clause...invalidates state laws that 'interfere with or are contrary to,' federal law" (*Hillsborough County, Florida v. Automated Medical Laboratories, Inc.* 471 U.S. 707, 712–713 (1985), quoting Chief Justice Marshall in *Gibbons v. Ogden*, 22 U.S. (9 Wheat.) 1, 211 (1824)). Thus, when a state law conflicts with a federal law, within the scope of Congress' powers, as in *Gibbons*, there is preemption; and the state law is invalid under the supremacy clause. Preemption will also occur, as demonstrated in other cases, when the federal statute contains a preemption clause expressly preempting particular state regulations, and when the federal law is so extensive that it has "occupied the field" of regulation that the state seeks to enter.

The Court has synthesized these three approaches to preemption as follows:

(1) It is well established that [when acting] within Constitutional limits Congress may preempt state authority by so stating in express terms. *Jones v. Rath Packing Co.*, 430 U.S. 519, 525 (1977).

(2) Absent explicit preemptive language, Congress' intent to supercede state law altogether may be found (a) from a "scheme of federal regulation...so pervasive as to make reasonable the inference that Congress left no room to supplement it," (b) because "the Act of Congress may touch a field in which the federal interest is so dominant that the federal system will be assumed to preclude enforcement of state laws on the same subject," or (c) because "the object sought to be obtained by federal law and the character of obligations imposed by it may reveal the same purpose." *Fidelity Federal Savings & Loan Ass'n v. de la Cuesta*, 458 U.S. 141, 153, (1982), quoting *Rice v. Santa Fe Elevator Corp.*, 331 U.S. 218, 230, (1947).

(3) Even where Congress has not entirely displaced state regulation in a specific area, state law is pre-empted to the extent that it actually conflicts with federal law. Such a conflict arises (a) when "compliance with both federal and state regulations is a physical impossibility," *Florida Lime & Avocado Growers, Inc. v. Paul*, 373 U.S. 132, 142–143 (1963), or (b) where state law "stands as an obstacle to the accomplishment and execution of the full purposes and objectives of Congress." *Hines v. Davidowitz*, 312 U.S. 52, 67 (1941). [*Pacific Gas and Electric Co. v. State Energy Resources Conservation and Development Commission*, 461 U.S. 190, 203–204 (1983) (numbering and lettering added).]

The first type of preemption is usually called "express preemption"; the second type is usually called "field preemption"; and the third type (the type illustrated by *Gibbons*) is usually called "conflict preemption."

Of the three approaches, field preemption generally is the most difficult to apply. This is because field preemption is an *implied* preemption that must be discerned through a careful study of an array of federal statutory provisions, and sometimes administrative regulations as well, combined with a sensitive consideration of federalism values (see Sec. C.1 above, and see generally Chap. 6, Sec. A). Because the analysis is so nuanced, and because Congress is able to have the last word if it chooses, the Supreme Court has created a kind of presumption against preemption: "the historic police powers of the States [are] not to be superceded by [federal law] unless that was the clear and manifest purpose of Congress" (*Rice v. Santa Fe Elevator Corp.*, 331 U.S. 218, 230 (1947)).

One particular difficulty with field preemption is that of defining the "field" that Congress has allegedly occupied and the "field" that the state has allegedly entered. In *Pacific Gas and Electric Co. v. State Energy Resources Conservation and Development Comm'n*, 461 U.S. 190 (1983), for example, the State of California had regulated the in-state disposal of nuclear waste. The petitioner argued that the federal Atomic Energy Act and its various amendments had occupied the field and preempted the state regulation, and that the federally occupied field was "all matters nuclear." The Court determined that the field was more limited, covering only "the radiological safety aspects" of nuclear energy or "nuclear safety concerns." Then the Court determined that the state regulation had a "non-safety rationale"; California's concern was the "economic" problems associated with nuclear waste, such as "unpredictably high costs" of disposal. Since the state thus had not entered the field of nuclear *safety*, the field occupied by the federal government, the state law was not preempted by the Atomic Energy Act. According to the Court, any further consideration of whether the state's regulatory purposes might be differently construed should be left to Congress. Moreover, "it is for Congress to rethink the division of regulatory authority in light of its possible exercise by the states to undercut a federal objective" (461 U.S. at 223).

Preemption is a highly practical area of law that is encountered frequently in practice. Given the huge expanse of federal and state regulation that now exists, there are innumerable possibilities for overlap between federal and state law. Thus, whenever federal or state statutes or administrative regulations are drafted, construed, or applied, there are potential preemption issues. Analysis of these issues may not look like typical constitutional power analysis. The focus may initially be more on statutory interpretation than on constitutional interpretation of Congress' delegated powers; and for express preemption and the first type of conflict preemption (see (1) and (3)(a) in the set-off quote above), the focus may remain primarily on statutory interpretation. Moreover, the contexts for preemption problems are wide-ranging and extend far beyond familiar commerce clause concerns such as regulation of trade and transportation. In *Cipollone v. Liggett Group, Inc.*, 505 U.S. 504 (1992), for instance, the issue was whether federal cigarette labeling requirements (15 U.S.C. §§ 1331 *et. seq.*, preempted traditional state tort law remedies as applied to personal harms caused by smoking. (The Court said no.) In *Lorillard Tobacco Co. v. Reilly*, 533 U.S. 525 (2001), the issue was whether federal cigarette advertising requirements (15 U.S.C. § 1331 *et seq.*) preempted state regulation of certain types of cigarette advertising. (The Court said yes.) In *California Federal Savings and Loan Association v. Guerra*, 479 U.S. 272 (1987), the issue was whether the federal Title VII employment discrimination statute (42 U.S.C. § 2000e *et seq.* preempted a state maternity leave statute. (The Court said no.) And in *Gade v. National Solid Wastes Management Association*, 505 U.S. 88 (1992), the issue was whether the federal Occupational Safety and Health Act (29 U.S.C. § 651 *et seq.*) regulations preempted state licensing provisions for workers who handle hazardous waste. (The Court said yes.)

C.3. Congressional Consent

Some questions about Congress' authority to consent to state laws are answered expressly in the Constitution. Article I, section 10, in particular, contains a list of actions that states may not undertake under any circumstances, and another list of actions that states may take only with the consent of Congress. The first list provides, *inter alia*, that states may not "enter into any Treaty, Alliance, or Confederation;... [or] coin Money..." (Art. I, sec. 10, ¶ 1). The second list provides, *inter alia*, that: "No State shall, without the consent of Congress...enter into any Agreement or Compact with another State, or with a foreign power..." (Art. I, sec. 10, ¶'s 2 and 3). It is clear that Congress is prohibited from consenting to state actions on the first list; and it is equally clear that Congress is authorized to consent to state actions on the second list.

But what of the great range of potential state actions that are beyond the confines of Article I, section 10? Here, the Constitution provides answers only by implication. Historically, the U.S. Supreme Court has struggled to discover these answers by examining the particular delegated power upon which Congress has grounded its consent, and any inferences that may be drawn from the structure of federalism (see Chap. 4, Sec. C.3). As with the negative implication cases (sec. B. above), the commerce power is the most likely power to be at issue in consent cases. The Court now adheres to the general rule "that Congress may 'redefine the distribution of power over interstate commerce' by '[permitting] the states to regulate the commerce in a manner which would otherwise not be permissible'" (*South-Central Timber Development, Inc. v. Wunnicke*, 467 U.S. 82, 87–88 (1984), quoting *Southern Pacific Co. v. Arizona*, 325 U.S. 761, 769 (1945)).

The Court's opinion in *Cooley v. Board of Wardens of the Port of Philadelphia*, 53 U.S. (12 How.) 299 (1851) (Secs. A and B.1 above), while composed primarily of dormant commerce clause (or negative implication) analysis, also includes a rudimentary example of the consent type of problem. In the 1789 federal statute on pilotage that was at issue in *Cooley*, Congress in effect consented to state regulation of pilots in lieu of federal regulation. The Court relied on this statute as an indication that pilotage in harbors (at that time in American history) was a state and local, rather than a national, concern and thus regulable by the states. Similarly, in more modern cases, a clear statutory expression of Congressional consent can convert a type 1 (dormant clause) problem into a type 3 (consent) problem, thus opening the door to some state regulations that the Court may have found unconstitutional absent the consent.

The theoretical justification for this Congressional authority to consent has not always been clear. In *Cooley*, the Court suggested that Congress could not delegate back to the states' power that the Constitution had delegated to Congress (*Cooley*, 53 U.S. at 302), and more modern cases tend to accept this conclusion. A sounder justification would be that Congress may, by consent legislation, express its judgments on what subjects of commerce are local (in *Cooley* terminology) or on what state regulations of commerce would not interfere with national interests or be unduly burdensome (in the terminology of more modern cases); and that the courts will defer to the judgments of Congress. Presumably the Court in *Wunnicke* had something like this rationale in mind when it affirmed that Congress may "redefine the distribution of power over interstate commerce" between Congress and the states (see above in this subsection).

The *Wunnicke* case, above, provides an illustrative modern example of a consent problem. Again, the context is the commerce power. Alaska had arranged to sell some timber that it owned. As a condition of sale, Alaska required the buyer to partially process the timber within the state before shipping it out of state. An interested buyer, the plaintiff, argued that the condition burdened interstate commerce and thus violated the dormant commerce clause. Alaska countered by arguing that Congress has authorized it to impose the processing condition. The evidence of consent, Alaska argued, could be found in U.S. Department of Agriculture regulations and federal statutes that for many years had imposed a similar condition on *federal* government sales of timber from *federal* lands within Alaska. The Court agreed that Congress could have consented to the state requirement (see the quote from this case earlier in this subsection) but disagreed that Congress had actually done so:

> The fact that the state policy in this case appears to be consistent with federal policy—or even that state policy furthers the goals we might believe that Congress had in mind—is an insufficient indicium of congressional intent. Congress acted only with respect to federal lands; we cannot infer from that fact that it intended to authorize a similar policy with respect to state lands. [467 U.S. at 92–93.]

In support of this result, the Court emphasized that "for a state regulation to be removed from the reach of the dormant Commerce Clause, congressional intent must be unmistakably clear" (467 U.S. at 91).

Thus, in a consent case, there are two basic questions: *could* Congress consent (that is, did it have the authority to consent), and *did* Congress consent. For the first question, the answer is usually affirmative if Congress has acted pursuant to the commerce clause and within the scope of its commerce power; under other clauses, the answer may not be clear. For the second question, *Wunnicke's* rule of unmistakable clarity (sometimes called the clear statement rule) will apply.

Sec. D. Intergovernmental Immunities

Just as questions arise concerning state immunity or state autonomy from federal legislation (Chap. 6, Secs. C.3 and C.4), questions also arise concerning federal government immunity or autonomy from state legislation. These federal immunities constitute additional federalistic limits on the states that may be invoked in situations where the state seeks to regulate or tax the federal government or its instrumentalities. The federal immunities cases, taken together with the state immunities cases, carve out a doctrinal area called intergovernmental immunities. This area covers immunities from regulation by the other sovereign, immunities from taxation by the other sovereign, and immunities from suit on claims based on the other sovereign laws. The variations that may arise on these issues, and the leading cases or constitutional provisions for each variation, are outlined below. The outline first reviews the state immunities that have already been addressed in earlier sections of this book and then briefly sets out the contrasting federal government immunities.

I.   State Immunities

A. *State immunity from federal regulation.* The key cases are *Garcia v. San Antonio Metropolitan Transit Authority*, 469 U.S. 528 (1985), which holds that states do not have any immunity from federal regulations that apply alike to state governments and the private sector (see Chap. 6, Sec. C.4); and *New York v. United States*, 505 U.S. 144 (1992), which grants states a limited immunity from federal regulations that apply uniquely to the states and "commandeer" their legislative or administrative processes (see Chap. 6, Sec. C.5).

B. *State immunity from federal taxation.* The key cases are *New York v. United States*, 326 U.S. 572 (1946), and *South Carolina v. Baker*, 485 U.S. 505 (1988) (see Chap. 6, Sec. G.1). Under such cases, any state immunities from federal taxation seem to be quite minimal.

C. *State immunity from suit on federal claims.*

1. *Suits in federal court.* The states are generally immune from lawsuits raising federal law claims that are brought against them by private parties in the federal courts (see Chap. 5, Sec. E). But Congress may use its Fourteenth Amendment enforcement power to "abrogate" this immunity in a narrow range of situations (see Chap. 6, Sec. C.4), and may also be able to use its spending power to condition a state's receipt of federal funding upon a limited waiver of sovereign immunity from private party suits (see Chap. 14, Sec. D).

2. *Suits in state court.* The states are also generally immune from lawsuits brought against them in their own courts by private parties alleging federal law claims. The key case is *Alden v. Maine*, 527 U.S. 706 (1999) (Chap. 6, Sec. G.2).

3. *Suits before federal administrative agencies.* The states are also generally immune from federal claims brought against them by private parties in adju-

dicatory proceedings of federal administrative agencies. The key case is *Federal Maritime Commission v. South Carolina State Ports Authority*, 535 U.S. 743 (2002), discussed in Chap. 6, Sec. G.2.

4. *Suits brought by the federal government.* The states are *not* immune from suits brought against them by the federal government itself (see Chap. 5, Sec. E and Chap. 14, Sec. D).

II. *Federal Immunities*

A. *Federal governmental immunity from state regulation.* The classic case is *Johnson v. Maryland*, 254 U.S. 51 (1920), which held that the state could not require a U.S. postal driver to obtain a state driver's license as a condition to driving within the state, since the license "requires qualifications in addition to those that the [federal] Government has pronounced sufficient." Such federal immunities may be established and applied using a reasoning process similar to that used for conflict preemption (Sec. C.2. above). In *Leslie Miller, Inc. v. Arkansas*, 352 U.S. 187 (1956), for instance, the Court held a federal contractor immune from a state contractor licensing statute because of "conflict" between the state requirements and the federal procurement policy.

B. *Federal governmental immunity from state taxation.* The classic case is *McCulloch v. Maryland*, 17 U.S. (4 Wheat.) 316, 425–437 (1819) (see Chap. 6, Sec. B.3). The second part of the *McCulloch* opinion posed the question "Whether the State of Maryland may, without violating the constitution, tax [the Baltimore branch of the Bank of the United States]?" (17 U.S. at 425). The Court answered in the negative, using the famous phrase, "the power to tax involves the power to destroy."

C. *Federal governmental immunity from suit on state law claims.*

1. *Suits in federal court.* The United States is generally immune from suits brought against it by private parties in its own courts. The applicable principles are similar to those for state immunity (see Chap. 5, Sec. E), but the constitutional basis for these principles is different because the Eleventh Amendment does not apply to the federal government. Instead, the federal immunity is implicit in Article III itself, which is said to preserve the common law sovereign immunity that existed prior to adoption of the Constitution. Article III does in fact establish federal court jurisdiction over "controversies in which the United States shall be a party" (U.S. Const., Art. III, sec. 2, ¶ 1), but the U.S. Supreme Court has interpreted that clause to include only suits to which the United States has consented (*see, e.g., Principality of Monoco v. State of Mississippi*, 292 U.S. 313, 321 (1934)). Moreover, since the federal courts are courts of limited jurisdiction (see Chap. 5, Sec. A), most state law claims would fall outside the scope of Article III jurisdiction and could not be brought in federal court even if there were no federal immunity from suit.

2. *Suits in state courts.* In *Alden v. Maine*, 527 U.S. 706, 749 (1999), in which the U.S. Supreme Court protected the state's immunity from certain suits

in state court, the Court also confirmed that "[i]t is unquestioned that the Federal Government retains its own immunity from suit...in state tribunals...."

3. *Suits before state administrative agencies.* From the sovereign immunity principles developed in *Federal Maritime Commission v. South Carolina State Ports Authority*, 535 U.S. 743 (2002) (part I.C.3 of this outline), it is clear that the United States would be immune from suit by private parties in an adjudicative proceeding before a state administrative agency.

4. *Suits brought by a state government.* The United States is immune from suits brought against it by a state in federal court. *State of Kansas v. United States*, 204 U.S. 331 (1907). The U.S. Supreme Court emphasized in this case that "[i]t does *not* follow that because a state may be sued by the United States without its consent [see part I.C.4 of this outline], therefore the United States may be sued by a state without its consent" (*Id.* at 324 (emphasis added)). Under this case's reasoning and that in *Alden v. Maine* (part I.C.2 of this outline), the United States *is* immune from suits by a state in the state's own courts.

D. *Federal governmental activities that are within an "enclave."* Article I, section 8, paragraph 17 of the U.S. Constitution, supplemented by Article IV, section 3, paragraph 2, authorizes Congress to establish federal "enclaves" within which federal law, not state law, will govern. The primary example is a federal military installation. Activities within a federal enclave may be immune from state regulation and taxation. Congress may establish a federal enclave only with the consent of the state legislature of the state where the land is situated.

Although the Constitution does provide for federal enclaves (part II.D. of the outline above), it does not otherwise expressly provide for governmental immunities, for either the federal government or the states, from regulation or taxation by the other. In *McCulloch v. Maryland* (part II. B. of the outline above), however, the U.S. Supreme Court determined that, at least for the federal government, such immunities are implicit in the supremacy clause and the Constitution's federalistic structure of government. Later, in the late twentieth century, the Court confirmed that some state government immunities from federal regulation are also implicit in the structure of federalism (see Chap. 6, Sec. C.5). Intergovernmental immunities are thus developed through structural interpretation of the Constitution (see Chap. 4, Sec. C.3).

McCulloch also made clear that federal immunities and state immunities are not symmetrical or reciprocal. Given the concept of federal supremacy and the nature of federalism, federal immunities may be more expansive than whatever immunities attach to the states. The differences, according to Chief Justice Marshall in *McCulloch*, arise because "[t]he people of all the States, and the States themselves, are represented in Congress, and, by their representatives, exercise...power." The reverse is not true, that is, the federal government is not represented in the state legislatures when the latter seek to exercise power over the former. "The difference is that which always exists, and always must exist, between the action of the whole on a part, and the action of a part on the whole—between the laws of a government declared to be supreme, and those of a government which, when in opposition to those laws, is not supreme" (17 U.S. at 435–436).

In addition to the immunities from regulation and taxation, as the above outline indicates, both the states and the federal government have certain immunities from suit in the courts of the other. This has been the immunity arena (of the three) that has generated the most judicial activity in recent times, specifically as to cases concerning state immunity from suit. These cases differ somewhat from other immunity cases in that there is some explicit constitutional text supporting immunity—the Eleventh Amendment. Moreover, in one of the state immunity cases, *Alden v. Maine* in 1999, the Court majority expressly stated that the states' immunity from suit is "reciprocal" with that of the federal government (*Alden*, 527 U.S. at 749–750)—thus apparently departing somewhat from the theory of governmental immunities developed by Chief Justice Marshall in *McCulloch* (above).

Sec. E. The Interstate Privileges and Immunities Clause (Article IV)

E.1. Comparison With Fourteenth Amendment Privileges and Immunities

In addition to the three types of "intrinsic" federalistic limits problems discussed in Sections A and B above, there is one other type of federalism problem that arises under the "privileges and immunities" clause in Article IV of the Constitution: "The Citizens of each State shall be entitled to all Privileges and Immunities of Citizens in the several States" (U.S. Const., Art. IV, sec. 2, ¶ 1). This clause is a rights provision rather than a power provision, and is thus an extrinsic rather than intrinsic limit on power, but it nevertheless plays a direct role in maintaining the federal system. The Article IV clause must be distinguished from the "privileges or immunities" clause in the Fourteenth Amendment (U.S. Const., Amend. 14, sec. 1, sentence 2), another extrinsic limit on state power. The former clause protects privileges and immunities of *state* citizenship; the latter protects privileges and immunities of *national* citizenship.

The Article IV clause, called the "interstate privileges and immunities clause," prohibits both states and local governments from unjustifiably discriminating against the residents of other states. *United Building and Construction Trades Council v. Mayor and Council of Camden*, 465 U.S. 208, 215–217 (1984). This clause thus promotes interstate harmony by guaranteeing certain rights of equal treatment to the "citizens" (residents) of each state when they enter other states in which they are not citizens. Corporations are not considered to be "citizens" for purposes of the clause and therefore are not protected by it. See *Bank of Augusta v. Earle*, 38 U.S. (13 Pet.) 519 (1839).

E.2.   Protection of Interstate (Personal) Mobility

The interstate privileges and immunities clause is often said to protect *interstate mobility* or *personal mobility*, that is, the free movement of people across state lines. In this respect, the clause complements the dormant commerce clause's role in protecting the free movement of goods and commodities, and of modes of transportation (trucks, trains, boats, *etc.*), across state lines. The Article IV clause, however, is not the exclusive constitutional means of protecting personal mobility. The courts have sometimes also used the dormant commerce clause to protect the movement of people across state lines. The classic example is *Edwards v. California*, 314 U.S. 160 (1941), a case arising during the Depression, in which the U.S. Supreme Court invalidated a California law making it a crime to bring a non-resident "indigent person" into the state. Concurring opinions in *Edwards* by Justices Douglas and Jackson emphasized yet another source of protection for interstate mobility — the Fourteenth Amendment's privileges or immunities clause (*See Id.* at 178 (Douglas, J., concurring); *Id.* at 182–183 (Jackson, J., concurring)). More recently, the Court apparently confirmed such a role for the Fourteenth Amendment clause in *Saenz v. Roe*, 526 U.S. 489 (1999), another case invalidating a California law; *Saenz* is discussed in Chapter 10, Section B. In addition, in other cases, the Court has recognized that the "right to travel" is a fundamental interest under the equal protection clause, which may therefore also be a source of protection for interstate mobility in situations where a state or local government's discrimination against non-residents burdens their freedom to travel.

E.3.   Analysis of Privileges and Immunities Issues

The analysis of rights issues arising under the interstate privileges and immunities clause differs considerably from the analysis of issues that arise in the other three types of federalistic limits problems discussed in Sections B and C above. The challenged state or local regulation need not intrude upon a field of federal concern, as defined in Section A above, in order to be subject to the interstate privileges and immunities clause. Instead, the initial focus is on whether the regulation discriminates against nonresidents.

Not all distinctions that a state or local government makes between residents and nonresidents fall within the purview of the privileges and immunities clause. The clause protects only privileges and immunities that are "fundamental to the promotion of interstate harmony" (*United Building and Construction Trades Council v. Mayor and Council of Camden*, 465 U.S. 208, 218).[2] A privilege or immunity will fall into this category

---

2. "Fundamental," as it applies to a privilege or immunity of state citizenship, means something different than "fundamental" as applied to an interest or right under the equal protection clause (Chap. 10, Sec. D.8) or under substantive due process (Chap. 11, Sec. C.4). Under the privileges and immunities clause, a privilege or immunity is "fundamental" if it protects the values of federalism; while under the equal protection and due process clauses, other values are implicated in the determination of whether an interest or right is fundamental.

if its recognition would help maintain the "vitality of the Nation as a single entity" and, conversely, its infringement would "hinder the formation, the purpose, or the development of a single Union of [the] [s]tates" (*Baldwin v. Fish and Game Commission of Montana*, 436 U.S. 371, 383 (1978)). The primary examples of such privileges and immunities are the "pursuit of common callings within the State,...the ownership and disposition of privately held property within the State,...and...access to the courts of the State..." (*Id.*). In the *Baldwin* case, for example, the Court upheld a Montana regulation that imposed a $225 fee on nonresidents for an elk-hunting license while charging residents only $30. Hunting, said the Court, is not a common calling or "means of a livelihood" but only "recreation," and thus is not a privilege or immunity protected by Article IV, section 2.

Even when a regulation discriminates against non-residents with respect to a "fundamental" privilege or immunity, the state or local government may sometimes justify its discrimination. To do so, it must demonstrate that "(i) there is a substantial reason for the difference in treatment; and (ii) the discrimination practiced against nonresidents bears a substantial relationship to the State's objective" (*Supreme Court of New Hampshire v. Piper*, 470 U.S. 274, 284 (1985)). In *Piper*, for instance, New Hampshire had a rule that restricted bar admissions to lawyers who were state residents. The Court held that the "privilege" of bar membership was fundamental and thus covered by the privileges and immunities clause. New Hampshire, however, had asserted various justifications for its rule. The Court rejected these justifications and invalidated the rule because "none of [the state's] reasons meet the test of 'substantiality,' and...the means chosen do not bear the necessary relationship to the state's objectives" (*Id.* at 285).

Sec. F. Study Suggestions

When you study the federalistic limits cases, you should initially ascertain which type of problem each case addresses: negative implication (*i.e.*, dormant clause), preemption, consent, interstate privileges and immunities, or the occasional special case concerning a federal government immunity from state law. More than one type of problem may be involved in a particular case. Next ascertain what constitutional clauses are pertinent to the case. For a privileges and immunities problem, the Article IV, section 2 clause will be at issue. For the other types of problems, a particular power clause from Article I, section 8 will be at issue; and for preemption cases (and federal immunity cases), the supremacy clause will be pertinent as well.

Once you have conceptualized the problem and issues, you will need to identify the particular tests or standards that the U.S. Supreme Court has used to resolve the problem. Also consider the extent to which the Court has deferred to state legislative judgments when applying the particular test or standard that you are considering.

More broadly, as you study the federalistic limits cases, attempt to discern the underlying federalism rationales for the legal principles that the Court has developed to govern each type of problem. Consider as well how the Court's role in applying federalistic limits to the states differs from its role in applying federalistic limits to Congress (see Chapter 6), and how well the Court is performing its role when reviewing state legislation.

FOR FURTHER READING: (1) Matthew Adler, "What States Owe Outsiders," 20 HASTINGS CONST. L. Q. 391 (1993). (2) Daniel Farber, "State Regulation and the Dormant Commerce Clause," 3 CONST. COMMENTARY 395 (1986). (3) Donald Regan, "The Supreme Court and State Protectionism: Making Sense of the Dormant Commerce Clause, 84 MICH. L. REV. 1091 (1986). (4) Jonathan Varat, "State 'Citizenship' and Interstate Equality," 48 U. CHI. L. REV. 487 (1981).

Chapter 8

Executive Powers and the Separation of Powers

Sec. A. The American Separation-of-Powers Concept

In crafting Articles I, II, and III of the federal Constitution, the framers created "the constitutional design for the separation of powers" (*Immigration and Naturalization Service v. Chadha*, 462 U.S. 919, 946 (1983)). Article I vests the Congress with "[a]ll legislative Powers herein granted." Article II vests the "executive Power" in the President. Article III vests the "judicial Power" in the Supreme Court and such "inferior courts" as Congress may establish. As the U.S. Supreme Court explained in an early case, there are "three great departments of government. The first was to pass laws, the second to approve and execute them, and the third to expound and enforce them" (*Martin v. Hunter's Lessee*, 14 U.S. (1 Wheat.) 304, 329 (1816)). Within this structure, the three branches are to be co-equal, each supreme within its own sphere of operations, and each held in equipoise by an intricate system of checks and balances.

The term "separation of powers" is somewhat of a misnomer. The Framers certainly did not intend a rigid separation that would allow each branch complete independence from the other two. Their separation of powers design was "not meant to affirm, that [the branches] must be kept wholly and entirely separate and distinct, and have no common link of connection or dependence, the one upon the other.... (Joseph Story, A FAMILIAR EXPOSITION OF THE CONSTITUTION OF THE UNITED STATES, p. 48 (American Book Co., 1840)). James Madison and others feared that an inflexible separation would provide insufficient checks on power and likely result in one branch, the legislature, usurping the power of the other two.

> Will it be sufficient to mark with precision the boundaries of these departments in the Constitution of the government, and to trust to these parchment barriers against the encroaching spirit of power? This is the security which appears to have been principally relied on by the compilers of most of the American Constitutions. But experience assures us, that the efficacy of [the separa-

tion of powers] has been greatly over-rated; and that some more adequate defense is indispensably necessary for the more feeble, against the more powerful, members of the government. The legislative department is everywhere extending the sphere of its activity, and drawing all power into its impetuous
vortex....

[A] mere demarcation on parchment of the constitutional limits of the several departments, is not a sufficient guard against those encroachments which
lead to a tyrannical concentration of all the powers of government in the same
hands. [James Madison, *Federalist No. 48*, in THE FEDERALIST: THE GIDEON
EDITION, pp. 256–257, 260 (Carey and McClellan, eds., Liberty Fund, 2001).]

To prevent the encroachment of one branch upon another and the concomitant
concentration of power, the Constitution establishes a system of checks and balances
as an essential part of the separation-of-powers design. This system allows each branch
to exert significant influence upon the functioning of the other branches. As Madison
explained:

"[T]he constant aim is to divide and arrange the several offices in such a manner as that each may be a check on the other.... [T]he great security against a
gradual concentration of the several powers in the same department, consists
in giving to those who administer each department, the necessary constitutional means, and personal motives, to resist encroachments of the others."
[James Madison, *Federalist No. 51*, in THE FEDERALIST, *supra*, at 269, 268.]

In modern times, the U.S. Supreme Court has made the same point:

We...have recognized Madison's teaching that the greatest security against...
the accumulation of excessive authority in a single branch...lies not in a her-
metic division between the Branches, but in a carefully crafted separation of
checked and balanced power within each Branch.... [The] concern of encroachment and aggrandizement...has animated our separation-of-powers
jurisprudence and aroused our vigilance against the 'hydraulic pressure inherent with each of the separate Branches to exceed the outer limits of its
power.' [*Mistretta v. United States*, 488 U.S. 361, 381–382 (1989), quoting *Immigration and Naturalization Services v. Chadha*, 462 U.S. 919, 951 (1983).]

Several examples concerning the President and Congress will illustrate how checks
and balances guard against the concentration and usurpation of power. Although
Congress is vested with the lawmaking power, the President also plays a critical role
in the lawmaking process. The President reports to Congress on "the State of the
Union" and recommends legislation to Congress (U.S. Const., Art. II, sec. 3). The
Vice-President presides over the Senate and may cast a vote in the case of a tie (U.S.
Const., Art. I, sec. 3, para. 4). Perhaps most significantly, the President has the power
to veto legislation (U.S. Const., Art. I, sec. 7). As James Madison asserted, "[a]n absolute negative, on the legislature, appears at first view to be the natural defense with
which the executive magistrate should be armed" (James Madison, *Federalist No. 51*,
in THE FEDERALIST, *supra*, at 269). This executive veto "establishes a salutary check
upon the legislative body, calculated to guard the community against the effects of

faction, precipitancy, or of any impulse unfriendly to the public good, which may happen to influence a majority of that body" (Alexander Hamilton, *Federalist No. 73*, in THE FEDERALIST, *supra*, at 381). *See also* James Kent, COMMENTARIES ON AMERICAN LAW, vol. 1, p. 225 (O. Halstead, 1826). In turn, "[t]he President's unilateral veto power . . . [is] limited by the power of two-thirds of both Houses of Congress to overrule a veto thereby precluding final arbitrary action of one person" (*Chadha*, 462 U.S. at 951). Similarly, although the President is vested with the executive power, Congress may check certain exercises of executive power. Congress, for example, must approve the fiscal appropriations for the operation of the executive branch. The Senate must give its advice and consent to treaties before they have the force and effect of law. The Senate must also approve the President's appointments of the primary executive branch officers. In addition, these officers as well as the President and Vice-President are subject to removal from office if impeached by the House of Representatives and convicted by the Senate.[1]

The primary goal of the separation of powers, as understood by the framers and as understood now, is to ensure liberty by preventing tyranny. "The accumulation of all powers legislative, executive and judiciary, in the same hands, whether of one, a few, or many, and whether hereditary, self-appointed, or elective, may justly be pronounced the very definition of tyranny" (James Madison, *Federalist No. 47*, in THE FEDERALIST, *supra*, at 249). Thus the "separate and distinct exercise of the different powers of government . . . [is] essential to the preservation of liberty. . . ." To guard "against a gradual concentration of the several powers in the same department," each branch must be accorded "the necessary constitutional means, and personal motives, to resist encroachments of the others. . . . Ambition must be made to counteract ambition" (James Madison, *Federalist No. 51*, in THE FEDERALIST, *supra*, at 268). In essence, each branch's hunger for power would check any usurpation of power by another branch.

Montesquieu, whose political theory was relied on by the framers, also linked the preservation of liberty to the separation of powers:

> When the legislative and executive powers are united in the same person, or in the same body of magistracy, there can be then no liberty; because apprehensions may arise, lest the same monarch or senate should enact tyrannical laws, to execute them in a tyrannical manner.
>
>   Again, there is no liberty, if the power of judging be not separated from the legislative and executive powers. Were it joined with the legislative, the life and liberty of the subject would be exposed to arbitrary control, for the judge

---

1. Similar examples of checks and balances apply to the U.S. Supreme Court and lower federal courts which, though vested with the judicial power, do not exercise it in isolation from the other branches. The President appoints federal judges and Supreme Court justices, for example, with the advice and consent of the Senate (U.S. Const. Art. II, sec. 2, ¶ 2); and Congress can establish the jurisdiction of the lower federal courts and regulate the appellate jurisdiction of the Supreme Court (see Chap. 5, Secs. A and F.3).

would then be the legislator. Were it joined to the executive power, the judge might behave with all the violence of an oppressor. [C. Montesquieu, THE SPIRIT OF LAWS, p. 202 (D. Carrithers ed. 1977).]

The modern Court agrees with this liberty goal for the separation of powers. In *Immigration and Naturalization Service v. Chadha*, for instance, the Court remarked that the basic purpose of separation of powers is "to divide and disperse power in order to protect liberty" (462 U.S. 919, 950 (1983)). And in *Bowsher v. Synar*, the Court noted: "The Framers recognized that, in the long term, structural protections against abuse of power were critical to preserving liberty" (478 U.S. 714, 730 (1986)).

In addition to promoting liberty, another goal or justification for separated powers was efficiency. The framers sought to design a government that would run more efficiently than that established by the Articles of Confederation. Under the Articles, there was only one branch of government. The Congress was charged not only with lawmaking but also with enforcement of its laws and the adjudication of legal disputes. It quickly became clear that this arrangement was highly inefficient and ineffective. By changing to a tripartite system, the framers allowed the federal government to effectuate a more complete set of functions, and also provided for the development of separate yet complementary competencies by each of the branches.

A system of separated powers, of course, is not the most efficient of all governmental structures. "[I]t is crystal clear... that the Framers ranked other values higher than efficiency" (*Chadha*, 462 U.S. at 958–959). They knew that the Constitution's tripartite design might "impose burdens on governmental processes that often seem clumsy, inefficient, even unworkable," but it was well worth this price to avoid living, as they once had, "under a form of government that permitted arbitrary governmental acts to go unchecked" (*Chadha*, 462 U.S. at 959).

Basic agreement about the separation of powers' primary goals has not resulted in agreement about the scope or application of separation-of-powers doctrine. As with federalism (Chap. 6, Sec. A), there has been continuing debate and dispute about the separation of powers since the Nation's founding. The debate began even earlier than the federalism debate, since it was a major consideration for the state constitutions drafted before the federal Constitution (*see* James Madison, *Federalist No. 47*, in THE FEDERALIST, *supra*, at 249–255). Part of this debate concerned which branch would or should be the strongest of the three, and which would or should be the weakest.

Most founders expected that the legislative branch would be the strongest. Madison, for example, asserted that "[i]n republican government, the legislative authority necessarily predominates" (James Madison, *Federalist No. 51*, in THE FEDERALIST, *supra*, at 269). After the Constitution was ratified and in effect for almost 40 years, noted scholar James Kent confirmed this understanding of legislative power:

> [It] is a transcendent power, and if [the legislative body] be a full and equal representation of the people, there is a danger of its pressing with destructive weight upon all the other parts of the machinery of government. It has therefore been thought necessary... that strong barriers should be erected for the protection and security of the other necessary [executive and judicial] powers

of the government. [James Kent, COMMENTARIES ON AMERICAN LAW, vol. 1, pp. 225–226 (O. Halstead, 1826).]

The judicial branch, on the other hand, was the one most founders expected to be the weakest. Alexander Hamilton's views on "the least dangerous branch" are the most often quoted:

> Whoever attentively considers the different departments of power must perceive, that in a government in which they are separated from each other, the judiciary, from the nature of its functions, will always be the least dangerous to the political rights of the constitution; because it will be least in a capacity to annoy or injure them. The executive not only dispenses honors, but holds the sword of the community. The legislature not only commands the purse, but prescribes the rules by which the duties and rights of every citizen are to be regulated. The judiciary on the contrary has no influence over either the sword or the purse, but direction either of the strength or of the wealth of the society, and can take no active resolution whatever. It may truly be said to have neither Force nor Will, but merely judgment; and must ultimately depend upon the aid of the executive arm for the efficacy of its judgments. [Alexander Hamilton, *Federalist No. 78*, in THE FEDERALIST, *supra*, at 402.]

These original expectations do not mesh particularly well with the contemporary picture of the three branches. Over time, their relative strengths, and the working relationships among them, have adjusted and readjusted to changes in the Nation and the world. The U.S. Supreme Court and lower federal courts have become stronger and more influential as the concept of judicial supremacy (Chap. 5, Sec. B) has matured. Even more striking is the evolution in the authority and influence of the President and the executive branch.

As the world has grown and the United States has become a major world power, the President's foreign affairs powers (see Sec. C.1 and C.5 below) have attained salutary importance. At the same time, the Nation's need for a single representative and unitary voice in foreign relations has enhanced the President's influence in comparison to that of Congress. World Wars I and II, and the "Cold War" era following World War II, are key historical points for these developments; and it appears that the early 21st century "War Against Terrorism" may become a key historical point as well. Moreover, as the Nation's economic and social life has grown in complexity, requiring more federal legislation and more concerted federal law enforcement, the President's role in assuring "that the Laws be faithfully executed" (U.S. Const., Art. II, sec. 3) has expanded exponentially. The growth and pervasiveness of federal administrative agencies are testament to the executive branch's expanded influence as executor of the laws. President Roosevelt's New Deal and President Johnson's Great Society are key historical points for these developments, and President George W. Bush's "Homeland Security" initiatives may become one as well.

In addition to this historical debate about "how much power" for each branch, there has been a parallel debate about "how much separateness." This debate has concerned the intermingling of, and interrelationships among, the three branches' powers. It is a debate, in other words, between independence on the one hand and interdependence on the other. As Justice Jackson has explained, "[T]he Constitution…contemplates that practice will integrate the dispersed powers into a workable government. It enjoins upon its branches separateness but interdependence, autonomy but reciprocity" (*Youngstown Sheet & Tube Co. v. Sawyer*, 343 U.S. 579, 635 (1952) (Jackson, J., concurring)).

Most of the framers agreed, as suggested above, that there should not be strict separation; the branches must have sufficient involvement in each others' business to protect their powers from encroachments by the others. The inclusion of the system of checks and balances in the Constitution settled the framers' debate for the moment. But periodically over time the debate has renewed with regard to the actual working of the separation of powers in practice. Should the three types of powers be strictly differentiated from each other and strictly reserved to the branch in which the power vests? Or should the powers be more flexibly delineated, acknowledging overlaps and uncertainties at the margins? Should the checks and balances be narrowly construed to preserve the independence of the three branches and keep them within their assigned spheres of power? Or should the checks and balances be more flexibly applied to foster interdependence and inter-branch cooperation when needed to achieve creative solutions to pressing governmental problems?

Historically, such questions have frequently arisen in war time — in particular questions about Congress' and the President's respective roles in waging war. How strictly, for instance, should Congress' power to declare war be construed as a limitation on the President's authority, as Commander-in-Chief, to engage in armed hostilities? *See generally* John Woo, "War and the Constitutional Text," 69 U. CHI. L. REV. 1639 (2002). Even in the United States' earlier years as a nation, but particularly since the Korean War in 1950–1953, Presidents have frequently engaged U.S. forces overseas without a Congressional declaration of war. The Vietnam War is still the primary example (*see generally* John Hart Ely, WAR AND RESPONSIBILITY: CONSTITUTIONAL LESSONS OF VIETNAM AND ITS AFTERMATH (Princeton Univ. Press, 1993)). After passing a resolution (the Gulf of Tonkin Resolution) approving of President Johnson's use of armed force, Congress stayed mainly on the sidelines (except for appropriating funds) as President Johnson, and then President Nixon, escalated the conflict in Southeast Asia.[2] Finally, as the War was winding down, Congress expressed its frustration over its diminished role in waging war by passing the War Powers Resolution of 1973, 50 U.S.C. §§ 1541 *et. seq.*, over President Nixon's veto. The War Powers Resolution substantially restricts the President's authority to introduce the Armed Forces into hostilities without express

---

2. For cases challenging the President's escalations of this conflict, *see, e.g.*, *Orlando v. Laird*, 443 F.2d 1039 (2nd Cir. 1971); *Mitchell v. Laird*, 488 F.2d 611 (D.C. Cir. 1973). *See also*, regarding U.S. bombing of Cambodia as an adjunct to Vietnam military operations, *Holtzman v. Schlesinger*, 361 F. Supp. 553 (E.D.N.Y. 1973) (enjoining President from conducting bombing operations in Cambodia), *sub. nom. Schlesinger v. Holtzman*, 414 U.S. 1321 (1973) (motion to vacate stay denied); *Holtzman v. Schlesinger*, 484 F.2d 1307 (2nd Cir. 1973) (complaint dismissed as presenting political question). For a case presenting similar issues regarding the Persian Gulf War, *see Dellums v. Bush*, 752 F. Supp 1141 (D.D.C. 1990).

Congressional authorization. Since its passage, Presidents have argued that these re-strictions unconstitutionally limit their powers as Commander-in-Chief and have continued to engage in military action without Congressional approval.

Another contemporary example of a "separateness" problem concerns Congress' and the President's respective roles in the budgeting and appropriations process. Should the checks and balances of the law-making process, for instance, preclude Congress and the President from cooperating in the creation of a "line-item veto"? *See Clinton v. New York*, Sec. D.2 below. Should the President have authority to "impound" (and thus refuse to spend) certain funds appropriated by Congress? *See* the Congressional Budget and Impoundment Control Act of 1974, 88 Stat. 297, codified at 2 U.S.C. 681–688; and *see generally* Abner J. Mikva & Michael F. Hertz, "Impoundment of Funds — The Courts, The Congress, and the President: A Constitutional Triangle," 69 NORTHWEST-ERN U. L. REV. 335 (1974). A third example concerns the executive privileges and executive immunities a President may assert to check Congress and the courts from obtaining confidential executive branch information (see Sec. E below). A fourth example concerns the roles that Congress and the courts might play in a process for prosecuting high-level executive officials alleged to have committed criminal acts. Since criminal prosecution is an executive branch function, and federal prosecutors are executive officials, are Congress and the courts therefore precluded from any involvement that would limit the executive branch's control over prosecutions of its own officials? *See Morrison v. Olson*, 487 U.S. 654 (1988), discussed in Section D.2 below.

In modern times, much of the debate on such issues, and on broader concerns about "how much separateness," have been encapsulated into two contrasting approaches: *formalism* and *functionalism. See generally* Peter Strauss, "Formal and Functional Approaches to Separation-of-Powers Questions: A Foolish Inconsistency? 72 CORNELL L. REV. 488 (1987). Formalist arguments tend to adhere more closely to constitutional text than do functionalist arguments, and tend to favor the creation and application of specific rules for resolving interbranch power disputes. This methodology facilitates ease or efficiency of decisionmaking and consistency in results — primary goals for formalists. Functionalist arguments tend to rely more on the purposes underlying the constitutional text, and on the use of standards or concepts to guide decisionmaking rather than specific rules. This methodology facilitates the crafting of just results that best fit the unique circumstances of the case, even if the outcome provides little predictability regarding future cases that may arise. *See generally* Laura Little, "Envy and Jealousy: A Study of Separation of Powers and Judicial Review," 52 HASTINGS L.J. 47, 107–114 (2000).

In general, the functional approach is the more fluid or flexible of the two approaches, being characterized by "common sense" and "flexibility and practicality" (*Mistretta v. United States*, 488 U.S. 361, 372 (1989)). It is the approach that is more likely to accommodate creative solutions to new governmental problems, including solutions that entail an intermingling of one branch's powers with another's. The formalist approach, on the other hand, is the more likely to yield predictability in future cases and clearer guidance for government officials engaged in separation-of-powers issues. Of the two approaches, functionalism seems more inclined toward permitting the branches to work out accommodations on their own — more inclined, that is, toward *political* rather than *judicial* resolution of separation-of-powers issues. In this sense, there is a rough similarity between the judicial versus political limits dichotomy apparent in federalism analysis (Chap. 6, Sec. B.4) and the formalism versus functionalism dichotomy in separation-of-powers analysis.

The historical sweep of the Court's work in separation of powers is not as extensive as its work with federalism (see Chap. 6, Sec. A). After the early, key case of *Marbury v. Madison*, presenting multiple separation-of-powers issues (see Chap. 5, Secs. A and B), the Court confronted such issues only sporadically. During the Civil War, for instance, the Court decided its first and only case addressing the scope of the President's Commander-in-Chief power (*The Prize Cases*, 67 U.S. (2 Black) 635 (1863)). In 1890 and 1895 (*Cunningham v. Neagle*, 135 U.S. 1 (1890); *In re Debs*, 158 U.S. 564 (1895)), the Court considered, and broadly construed, the President's authority to execute "the laws" even when he was not enforcing a specific Congressional statute. In 1926 and 1935 (*Myers v. United States*, 272 U.S. 52 (1926); *Humphrey's Executor v. United States*, 295 U.S. 602 (1935), the Court considered the scope of the President's authority to remove (rather than appoint) officers of government. Then in 1952, during the Korean War, the Court decided *The Steel Seizure Case* (*Youngstown Sheet and Tube Co. v. Sawyer*, 343 U.S. 579 (1952)); see Sec. D.1 below), ruling on whether the President, absent Congressional legislation authorizing the action, could seize the Nation's steel mills.

It was *The Steel Seizure Case* that became the precursor to the modern era of separation-of-powers law. The Court splintered badly, not only in the vote but also in the varied analyses of the Justices. Justice Black's majority opinion featured formalist reasoning, while the Frankfurter and Jackson concurrences were more inclined to functionalist reasoning — thus marking a tension in separation-of-powers analysis that has persisted in more recent cases. In the absence of any clear constitutional text or framers' intent to guide their analysis, different Justices in *Youngstown* sought guidance in different places. Frankfurter, for example, emphasized "the gloss which life has written upon" the constitutional text. "Deeply embedded traditional ways of conducting government cannot supplant the Constitution or legislation, but they give meaning to the words of a text or supply them" (343 U.S. at 610). Jackson, disavowing any analysis "dictated by a doctrinaire textualism" (343 U.S. at 640), sought evidence of governmental "practice" that would "integrate the dispersed powers into a workable government" (343 U.S. at 635). He also urged consideration of the exigencies of the time, what he called the "imperatives of events and contemporary imponderables" (343 U.S. at 637).

Given all the intricacies and tensions regarding the separation of powers, it is predictable that the U.S. Supreme Court would struggle in cases presenting these issues. The Court has indeed struggled, mightily, even before *Youngstown* but especially in the more modern cases following *Youngstown*. In his *Youngstown* concurrence, Justice Jackson predicted this state of affairs and provided a vivid description of the complexities of separation-of-powers cases:

> Just what our forefathers did envision, or would have envisioned had they foreseen modern conditions, must be divined from materials almost as enigmatic

as the dreams Joseph was called upon to interpret for Pharaoh. A century and a half of partisan debate and scholarly speculation yields no net result but only supplies more or less apt quotations from respected resources on each side of any question. They largely cancel each other. And court decisions are indecisive because of the judicial practice of dealing with the largest questions in the most narrow way. The actual art of governing under our Constitution does not and cannot conform to judicial definitions of the power of any of its branches based on isolated clauses or even single Articles torn from context.... [343 U.S. at 635.]

Sec. B. A Comparison of Presidential Powers and Congressional Powers

While issues of Congressional power have arisen most frequently in the context of federalism (Chap. 6, Sec. A), issues of Presidential power typically arise in the context of separation of powers (Sec. A above). Thus, just as one goal of studying Congress' powers is to better understand federalism, a goal of studying the Executive's powers is to better understand separation of powers. The separation-of-powers concept has already been encountered in Chapter 5 (Judicial Power and Judicial Review), particularly in the case of *Marbury v. Madison. Marbury's* contribution to understanding the Executive's position in the separation-of-powers framework is further discussed in Section E below.

When Congress exercises its powers, it usually does so by enacting a statute, and statutes are the targets of most challenges to Congressional powers.[3] The executive branch, in contrast, exercises its powers in a variety of ways providing a variety of targets for challenge. The President, for instance, may act:

- By issuing an *executive order*, for example, the order to seize the nation's steel mills (E.O. 10340) that President Truman issued during the Korean War (*see Youngstown Sheet & Tube Co. v. Sawyer*, 343 U.S. 579 (1952), discussed in Section D.1 below); or the order "to prescribe military areas" (E.O. 9066) that President Roosevelt issued during World War II and that was used to support the exclusion and detention of Japanese-American citizens on the West Coast (*see Korematsu v. United States*, 323 U.S. 214 (1944)).

---

3. Congress also sometimes issues Joint Resolutions that may be subject to challenge. Examples include the Joint Resolution at issue in *United States v. Curtiss-Wright Export Corp.*, 299 U.S. 304 (1936), by which Congress authorized President Roosevelt to prohibit arms sales to two South American countries then engaging in armed conflict; and the War Powers Resolution, 87 Stat. 555, 50 U.S.C. §§ 1541 *et. seq.*, passed in 1973 (at the end of the Vietnam War) to govern Congress' and the President's respective responsibilities regarding the initiation and continuation of armed hostilities.

- By entering an *executive agreement*, for example, the hostage release agreement executed by President Carter to end the Iranian Hostage Crisis)(see *Dames & Moore v. Regan*, 453 U.S. 654 (1981), discussed in Section C below).
- By issuing a *proclamation*, for example, President Roosevelt's proclamation prohibiting certain arms sales in *United States v. Curtiss-Wright Corp.*, 299 U.S. 304 (1936) (Sec. C below); President Roosevelt's Order of July 2, 1942 on military commissions, used to prosecute, convict, and hang the "German Saboteurs" during World War II (see *Ex Parte Quirin*, 317 U.S. 1 (1942));[4] or the "Emancipation Proclamation," 12 Stat. 1268 (1863), by which President Lincoln freed the slaves in the Southern states.
- By negotiating and signing a *treaty* (with the advice and consent of the Senate), for example, the Migratory Bird Treaty that President Wilson executed with Great Britain and that was at issue in *Missouri v. Holland* 252 U.S. 416 (1920).
- By issuing a *military order*, for example, the Military Order on Detention, Treatment, and Trial of Certain Non-Citizens in the War Against Terrorism, 66 Fed. Reg. 57833 (November 13, 2001), issued by President George W. Bush to provide for detention and trial — by military commission — of individuals considered to be terrorists or to harbor terrorists.
- By issuing *administrative rules* and *regulations* and similar directives — usually done through executive branch officials and agencies subordinate to the President, but some of which are approved directly by the President. Examples include the "Title IX" non-discrimination regulations of the federal agencies that grant funds for education programs (*e.g.*, 34 C.F.R. Part 106, the U.S. Department of Education's regulations implementing Title IX of the Education Amendments of 1972, 20 U.S.C. §§ 1681 *et seq.*, and signed by President Ford in May 1975); and the OMB Circulars issued by the Office of Management and Budget to guide cost accounting and other matters concerning federal agencies' administration of the grant-making process (*e.g.*, OMB Circular A-110, "Uniform Administrative Requirements for Grants and Other Agreements with Institutions of Higher Education, Hospitals, and Other Non-Profit Organizations" <http://www.whitehouse.gov/omb/circulars>).

Any of these listed actions, or other miscellaneous actions by the President or by subordinates exercising delegated Presidential power, may become the subject of a constitutional challenge.

A study of executive authority, like a study of Congressional authority, should focus on the sources and limits of power. There are far fewer judicial precedents on executive power to rely upon, however, than is the case with Congressional power. In turn, there are fewer specific tests and standards available for use in determining the sources and limits of executive power.

Moreover, the separation-of-powers context brings a set of constitutional considerations to bear upon problems of executive power that is different from that which the

---

4. For an interesting and enlightening retrospective on *Ex Parte Quirin*, *see* George Lardner, Jr., "Nazi Saboteurs Captured!", in The Washington Post Magazine (Jan. 13, 2002).

federalism context brings to bear on Congressional power. Regarding federalism, Congress is supreme over the states when acting within its own, broadly construed, sphere of operations. Regarding separation of powers, however, the three branches are co-equal, and the Executive is supreme only within its own sphere of operations. Even then it is subject to certain "checks and balances" by the other two branches. Thus the inferences that are drawn from the structure of separated powers and that serve to limit Executive power are quite different from the inferences that are drawn from the structure of federalism and that serve to limit Congressional power.

Occasionally, issues of Executive power do arise in a federalism context rather than a separation-of-powers context, in which case the analysis is more like that for Congressional powers. In *American Insurance Association v. Garamendi,* 123 S.Ct. 2374 (2003), for example, the President prevailed in a case of conflict between a state statute and the President's foreign policy initiatives. The state had passed a Holocaust Victim Insurance Relief Act that required state-based insurance companies to disclose information about insurance policies that they or their European subsidiaries sold during the time of the Third Reich. Applying principles of "conflict preemption" similar to those that it applies when a state regulation conflicts with Congressional legislation (see Chap. 7, Sec. C.2), the U.S. Supreme Court invalidated the California statute because it is inconsistent with the President's foreign policy on restitution for Holocaust victims, as expressed in executive agreements and official Presidential pronouncements, and "stands in the way of [his] diplomatic objectives" (*Id.* at 2393, quoting *Crosby v. National Foreign Trade Council*, 530 U.S. 363, 386 (2000)). By the same token, issues of Congressional power can and do sometimes arise in a separation-of-powers context rather than a federalism context, in which case the analysis is more like that for Presidential powers. Section D.2 below provides examples of this type of case.

These exceptions aside, considerable differences remain between Executive and Congressional power, both in practice and theory, and the sources and limits of executive power are thus ascertained in quite different ways than the sources and limits of Congressional power. In general, the law on executive power and separation of powers is less developed and more fluid, and offers less predictability, than the law on Congressional power and federalism. Due to the lack of specific tests and standards, there is a premium on identifying the various concepts and theories of executive power that have been articulated in majority, concurring, and dissenting opinions in the decided cases, and on using these concepts to guide analysis of executive power questions. The basic concepts of executive power, and the pertinent constitutional provisions, are discussed in the next section.

Sec. C. A Conceptual Overview of Presidential Powers

C.1. The Grants of Express Powers

Article II contains numerous grants of express power to the President, some applicable primarily to domestic affairs and others applicable primarily to foreign affairs.

Those powers most frequently addressed by the courts and commentators are: (1) the Commander-in-Chief power (Art. II, sec. 2, ¶ 1); (2) the treaty-making power (Art. II, sec. 2, ¶ 2); (3) the appointment power, that is, the power to appoint (and in some cases to remove) "Officers of the United States" (Art. II, sec. 2, ¶ 2); (4) the "recognition power," that is, the power to "receive Ambassadors and other public Ministers" and thus (by implication) to recognize foreign governments (Art. II, sec. 3; *see also* Art. II, sec. 2, on appointment of ambassadors); and (5) the "take care" power—and duty—under which the President must "take care that the Laws be faithfully executed" (Art. II, sec. 3). The appointment power and the take care power are usually considered to be, and usually used as, domestic powers; the Commander-in-Chief power, the treaty-making power, and the recognition power are considered to be, and are used as, foreign affairs powers. It is especially important to compare the President's foreign affairs powers with those of the Congress (Chap. 6, Sec. F). The President's war powers, in conjunction with those of Congress, are also discussed in Section A above.

Periodically, ever since the founding, the "vesting clause"—providing that "[t]he executive Power shall be vested in a President of the United States" (Art. II, sec. 1, ¶ 1)—has also been an object of attention. It has sometimes been argued that this clause grants *all* "executive" power to the President, leaving none to be exercised by Congress or the courts. Under this theory, usually called the "unitary executive" theory, Congress may not exert any control over officials who "execute" the laws, nor may Congress authorize anyone else to exert such control, except as specifically prescribed by the Constitution's system of checks and balances. *See generally* Steven Calabresi and Saikrishna Prakash, "The President's Power to Execute the Laws," 104 YALE L. J. 541 (1994); and *compare* Cass Sunstein, "The Myth of the Unitary Executive", 7 ADMIN. L. J. AMER. UNIV. 299 (1993). This argument, which is generally considered to be a "formalist" argument (see Sec. A above), has occasionally appeared in U.S. Supreme Court opinions, more often in dissenting and concurring opinions than in majority opinions.[5] In *Morrison v. Olson*, 487 U.S. 654 (1988) (Sec. D.2 below), for example, the Court considered the "independent counsel" statute that permitted Congress and the courts to exercise some control over the independent counsels who were executive branch officials. Chief Justice Rehnquist's majority opinion avoided the unitary executive thesis and upheld the statute because its provisions "[gave] the Executive Branch sufficient control over the independent counsel to ensure that the President is able to perform his constitutionally assigned duties" (*Id.* at 696). In dissent, however, Justice Scalia argued that the independent counsel statute was unconstitutional because it "deprive[d] the President of exclusive control over the exercise of [the executive] power" (*Id.* at 706). The nub of his argument was that: "Art. II, § 1, cl. 1 of the Constitution provides: 'the executive Power shall be vested in a President of the United States.' [T]his does not mean *some of* the executive power, but *all of* the executive power" (*Id.* at 705). Justice Scalia's opinion did not draw any other support from the Court; all other Justices (except Justice Kennedy who did not participate) concurred in the Rehnquist opinion.

---

5. *Myers v. United States*, 272 U.S. 52 (1926), is an early case (and the prime example of a case) in which the Court does employ unitary executive reasoning. See Section D.2 below.

Article II also includes several clauses presupposing and acknowledging the existence of executive departments and officers subordinate to the President. (See Article II, section 2, paragraph 1, regarding "the principal Officer in each of the executive Departments;" Article II, section 2, paragraph 2, regarding "Officers of the United States," and "the Heads of Departments;" and Article II, section 3 regarding "Officers of the United States.") These clauses, in conjunction with the execute-the-laws or "take care" clause, lay a foundation for the development of administrative agencies and set the stage for numerous issues concerning the President's authority over administrative agencies and officials in comparison with that of Congress. Such issues are a contemporary growth area in constitutional law, as exemplified by cases discussed in Section D.2 below.

Supplementing these Article II powers, the presentment clauses in Article I, section 7, paragraphs 2 and 3, delegate to the President the power to sign or to veto Congressional bills and Congressional resolutions. These clauses were at issue in *Immigration and Naturalization Service v. Chadha*, 462 U.S. 919 (1983), where the U.S. Supreme Court invalidated a statutory provision under which Congress could exercise a "legislative veto" of certain executive branch actions. Such a veto, said the Court, is inconsistent with the "finely wrought...procedure" by which the Constitution provides for the President's participation in lawmaking.

C.2. Presidential Implied Powers

In addition to these express powers, the President has implied powers that are inferred from either a particular express grant, the aggregate of Article II powers, or the structure of separation of powers. In *United States. v. Nixon*, 418 U.S. 683 (1974), for instance, the Court considered whether President Nixon had to surrender the "Watergate Tapes" pursuant to a subpoena issued by a federal district court. Although President Nixon ultimately lost the case, the court did agree that the President has power to maintain the confidentiality of Presidential communications by asserting executive privilege. Such a privilege is not expressly stated in Article II but, according to the Court, it "flow[s] from the nature of enumerated [Article II] powers" and "derive[s] from the supremacy of each branch within its own assigned area of constitutional duties" (418 U.S. at 705).

It is not clear from the constitutional text that the President's implied powers are subject to the same broad construction as Congress' implied powers under Article I (see Chap. 6, Sec. B.3). Article II conspicuously lacks any "necessary and proper" clause like that contained in Article I, section 8. It is sometimes argued that the vesting clause (see above), which vests "the executive Power" in the President, is akin to a broad grant of implied powers. That argument has not been accepted by the courts (*see, e.g., Youngstown Sheet & Tube Co. v. Sawyer*, 343 U.S. 579, 640–641 (1952) (Jackson, J. concurring)). But in a conclusory footnote in *United States v. Nixon*, the Court did apply to Presidential powers "the rule of constitutional interpretation announced in *McCulloch v. Maryland*, that that which was reasonably appropriate and relevant to the exercise of a granted power was to be considered as accompanying the grant...." (418 U.S. at 706 n.16).

C.3. Delegations of Authority From Congress

In addition to its express and implied powers, the executive branch also frequently acts pursuant to delegations of power from Congress. In *United States v. Curtiss-Wright Export Corp.*, 299 U.S. 304 (1936), for instance, the Court upheld a Presidential arms embargo in part because Congress had expressly authorized the President to take such actions. Delegations of authority from Congress are thus another source of power that the Executive may constitutionally invoke to support particular actions.

In two early New Deal cases, the U.S. Supreme Court applied a "nondelegation doctrine" to limit the extent to which Congress could delegate its powers (especially its domestic powers) to the Executive. A.L.A. *Schechter Poultry Corp. v. United States*, 295 U.S. 495, 529–530 (1935); *Panama Refining v. Ryan*, 293 U.S. 388 (1935). This doctrine was narrowed and de-emphasized in later cases, and apparently no longer has practical significance in constitutional law. In *Mistretta v. United States*, 488 U.S. 361 (1989), for example, the Court unanimously rejected an argument that the Sentencing Reform Act of 1984 (18 U.S.C. § 3551 *et seq.*) violated the nondelegation doctrine. The Court noted that it had invalidated statutes only twice using the nondelegation doctrine (the *Schechter* and *Panama Refining* cases in 1935), and since then has consistently rejected nondelegation challenges to federal statutes. Instead, the Court has been guided by "a practical understanding that in our increasingly complex society, replete with ever changing and more technical problems, Congress simply cannot do its job absent an ability to delegate power under broad general directives" (*Id.* at 371–374; *see also* 415–416 (Scalia, J., dissenting)). In contemporary usage, said the Court, "our application of the nondelegation doctrine principally has been limited... to giving narrow constructions to statutory delegations that might otherwise be thought to be unconstitutional" (*Id.* at 374 n. 7).

In the later case of *Whitman v. American Trucking Associations*, 531 U.S. 457 (2001)—a case concerning provisions of the Clean Air Act (42 U.S.C. §§ 7401 *et. seq.*) that delegated authority to the Environmental Protection Agency to set certain air quality standards—the Court again affirmed its deferential approach to delegation issues. The lower court, the U.S. Court of Appeals for the D.C. Circuit, had used reasoning calculated to put new teeth into the nondelegation doctrine, and had held that the statutory provisions at issue were an unconstitutional delegation of power (*American Trucking Associations v. EPA*, 175 F.3d 1027, *panel opinion modified*, 195 F.3d 4 (D.C. Cir. 1999)). The U.S. Supreme Court rejected both the D.C. Circuit's reasoning and its result, and upheld the Clean Air act provisions as "well within the outer limits of nondelegation precedents" (531 U.S. at 474; *see also* 531 U.S. at 472–476 (Scalia, J., for the Court) and 531 U.S. at 487–490 (Stevens, J., concurring in part and concurring in the judgment)).

Even an implied delegation from Congress may count as a source of executive power. In *Dames & Moore v. Regan*, 453 U.S. 654 (1981), for example, the Court considered the validity of President Carter's executive agreement with Iran providing for the release of 53 Americans who were taken hostage in Iran during the 1979 take-over of the U.S. Embassy in Tehran. The agreement created a process for the settlement of claims against Iran. Finding no express Congressional authorization for this claims settlement process, the Court went on to consider a lengthy history of Congressional and Presidential practices concerning the settlement of U.S. nationals' claims against foreign governments. To the Court, this history demonstrated a longstanding "congressional acquiescence in conduct of the sort engaged in by the President" which allowed the Court to conclude that "Congress has implicitly approved the practice of claim settlement by executive agreement" (453 U.S. at 678–79, 680).

C.4. The Possibility of Inherent Powers

Beyond all the power sources discussed in Sections C.1 to C.4 above, there is one other potential source of Presidential power that pertains specifically to foreign affairs. The executive branch frequently asserts, and the Court has occasionally accepted, a claim to "inherent" powers that arise not from the Constitution itself but from extra-constitutional understandings of nationhood and external sovereignty. The key case on this murky inherent powers concept is *United States v. Curtiss-Wright Export Corp.*, above. In considering the validity of the President's arms embargo, the Court emphasized that "the investment of the Federal government with the powers of external sovereignty did not depend upon the affirmative grants of the Constitution.... [I]f they had never been mentioned in the Constitution, [these powers] would have vested in the federal government as necessary concomitants of nationality." The Court then recognized that "[i]n this vast, external realm, with its important, complicated, delicate, and manifold problems, the President alone has the power to speak or listen as a representative of the nation." The arms embargo was supported, then, not only by a Congressional delegation of authority (see earlier discussion of *Curtiss-Wright*, above) but also by "the very delicate, plenary and exclusive power of the President as the sole organ of the federal government in the field of international relations..." (299 U.S. at 318–320).

C.5. Domestic Affairs Powers Versus Foreign Affairs Powers

Since *Curtiss-Wright* (Sec C.4, above), the Court has seldom returned to the matter of inherent powers. In part, the silence may be due to the controversial nature of inherent power claims, which seem to have no discernible limits. But the silence may also be due to the feasibility of re-packaging the Presidential power described in *Curtiss-Wright* as a broad Article II implied power—derived from the express powers to receive Ambassadors, to make treaties, and to execute the laws—thus eliminating (or at least minimizing) the need to rely on the inherent power rationale.

As *Curtiss-Wright* indicates, it is important to distinguish the Executive's domestic affairs powers from the Executive's foreign or external affairs powers. Presidential authority tends to be more expansive in the foreign affairs area than in domestic affairs, and courts tend to be more deferential to Presidential authority in foreign affairs and thus more reluctant to intervene in Presidential decisionmaking. In *United States v. Nixon*, above, for example, the Court rejected the President's "undifferentiated" and "general" claim of executive privilege, but suggested that it might have upheld a Presidential privilege claim based on a "need to protect military, diplomatic, or sensitive national security secrets" (418 U.S. at 706). "As to these areas of Article II duties the courts have traditionally shown the utmost deference to presidential responsibilities" (418 U.S. at 710). Sometimes this deference and reluctance in foreign affairs cases will lead a court to invoke justiciability doctrines (Chap. 5, Sec. D), especially the political question doctrine (Chap. 5, Sec. D.6), and refuse to review the merits of the case at all.

At the same time, in the foreign affairs arena, the division between executive and legislative powers tends to be even more indeterminate than it is in the domestic arena. Arguments concerning concurrent or overlapping powers, such as Justice Jackson's "twilight zone" argument in the *Youngstown* case (Sec. D.1 below), are thus more likely to be considered in the foreign affairs arena. And arguments concerning undefined "inherent" powers, which may be claimed by both Congress and the President, may still sometimes arise in the foreign affairs arena even though such arguments are not tolerated in the domestic realm.

Sec. D. Executive Branch Clashes with Congress

D.1. The *Youngstown* Case and Variations on Analysis

Classical separation-of-powers issues arise when the President or other executive branch officials take actions that allegedly conflict with actions of Congress or otherwise usurp Congress' constitutional authority.[6] The key foundational case is *Youngstown Sheet and Tube Co. v. Sawyer* (*The Steel Seizure Case*), 343 U.S. 579 (1952). This famous case arose during the Korean War (an undeclared war) when President Truman directed the U.S. Secretary of Commerce to take possession of, and operate, most of the country's steel mills. In 1951, a collective bargaining dispute had arisen between the management of the steel companies and the companies' employees who were represented by the United Steelworkers of America, C.I.O. On April 4, 1952, after lengthy and numerous attempts to resolve the dispute had failed, the union announced a nationwide strike to begin on April 9. Only hours before the strike was to begin, President Truman issued an executive order (E.O. 10340 (April 8, 1952)) directing the seizure of the steel mills. The next day, and again on April 21, the President officially reported his action to Congress. To justify his action, the President asserted that the strike would have resulted in a critical lack of steel, that steel was needed for weapons

---

6. Comparable issues may arise, of course, when *Congress* takes an action that conflicts with an *executive* branch action or usurps *executive* powers. *See, e.g.*, the cases in Section D.2 below.

and war materials to fight the war, and that the lack of steel would thus jeopardize our national defense. Congress took no action of its own. The steel companies thereupon filed suit challenging the validity of the President's executive order.[7]

By a 6-3 vote, the U.S. Supreme Court invalidated the President's executive order because it was essentially a legislative act that invaded Congress' prerogatives as the nation's lawmaker. Justice Black wrote the majority opinion that four other Justices joined; all four of these Justices (Jackson, Frankfurter, Burton, and Douglas) wrote their own concurring opinions; and the sixth Justice (Clark) wrote an opinion concurring in the majority opinion's result but not in its reasoning. There was considerable disagreement among the Justices, resulting in the numerous opinions. Few prior judicial precedents were available for the Justices to rely on in their opinions. Nor were there specific tests and standards to guide analysis like those sometimes available in federalism cases. Instead, the Justices relied on various concepts or theories of power in their opinions. In the majority opinion, for example, Justice Black drew a conceptual line between executive and legislative powers, which he considered to be mutually exclusive (343 U.S. at 587–588). Justice Jackson, in contrast, argued that some powers could fall within a "zone of twilight," or zone of "concurrent authority," in which powers were neither clearly legislative nor clearly executive (343 U.S. at 637 (Jackson, J., concurring)). Justice Frankfurter, in his concurrence, developed a historical "gloss" theory under which the reach of executive power is determined not only from the text of Article II but also from the "gloss" that history (that is, the history of Executive and Congressional practices concerning the type of matter before the Court) has placed upon the written words (343 U.S. at 601–611). And Justices Clark and Burton used a "Congressional check" theory under which the President would be prohibited from acting on his own if Congress had already "laid down specific procedures to deal with the type of crisis" at hand (343 U.S. at 662 (Clark, J., concurring in the result); *see also Id.* at 659–60 (Burton, J., concurring)).

By these various routes, a majority of the Court determined that the President's action was unconstitutional. Justice Black reasoned that the President's seizure of the steel mills was a legislative action falling on the legislative side of the conceptual line he had drawn, a realm that the President could not enter. Justice Jackson determined that the President's seizure did not fall within the twilight zone of concurrent authority, was inconsistent with congressional policy on labor disputes and on seizures of private property, and therefore was beyond the scope of Presidential power. Justice Frankfurter determined that the record of pertinent historical practice had not put a "gloss" on executive power that would support the President's seizure. Justices Clark and Burton determined that Congress, by various legislative actions, had already checked the President from undertaking the seizure. Though the reasoning differed, the conclusion was

---

7. For a full account of the case and the events preceding and following it, see Maeva Marcus, Truman and the Steel Seizure Case: The Limits of Presidential Power (Colum. Univ. Press, 1977); or Alan Westin, The Anatomy of a Constitutional Law Case (Macmillan, 1958, Columbia U. Press, 1990).

the same: President Truman had acted outside the scope of his powers and violated separation-of-powers principles when he seized the steel mills.

Over time since the *Youngstown* decision, Justice Jackson's concurring opinion has apparently become the most influential with the Court. In *Nixon v. Administrator of General Services*, 433 U.S. 425 (1977), for example, seven Justices joined an opinion endorsing a "pragmatic, flexible approach" that "essentially embraced Mr. Justice Jackson's" concurrence in *Youngstown* (*Id.* at 443); in *Dames & Moore v. Regan*, 453 U.S. 654 (1981), eight Justices joined an opinion that explicitly adopted and relied on the analytical framework of Justice Jackson's *Youngstown* concurrence and used it to resolve that case; and in *Mistretta v. United States*, 488 U.S. 361 (1989), eight Justices joined another opinion relying on Justice Jackson's analysis and calling it "the pragmatic, flexible view of differentiated governmental power to which we are heir...." (488 U.S. at 381).

Justice Jackson's framework entails three categories or types of executive power cases. In the first Jackson category, "the President acts pursuant to an express or implied authorization of Congress." In this circumstance, the President's "authority is at its maximum, for it includes all that he possesses in his own right plus all that Congress can delegate." In the second Jackson category, "the President acts in absence of either a congressional grant or denial of authority." This is the category in which the "twilight zone" becomes pertinent. The President "can only rely upon his own independent powers," and not on any delegated power from Congress. But the President's powers may be extended into the "zone of twilight" in which he may have "concurrent authority" with Congress. (In the later case of *Mistretta v. United States*, above, the Court expressly endorsed this twilight zone theory in an opinion joined by eight Justices: "[W]e have recognized...a 'twilight area' in which the activities of the separate Branches merge. (488 U.S. at 386).

In the third Jackson category, "the President takes measures incompatible with the expressed or implied will of Congress." In these cases, the President's "power is at its lowest ebb, for then he can rely only upon his own constitutional powers minus any constitutional powers of Congress over the matter." Thus the President is most likely to prevail in a category one case and most likely to lose in a category three case; category two is the flexible middle ground where "any actual test of power is likely to depend on the imperatives of events and contemporary imponderables rather than abstract theories of law" (343 U.S. at 635–637, Jackson, J., concurring).

D.2. Federal Administrative Agencies

Many of the recent separation-of-powers cases concern the President's and the Congress's respective authority over the actions of federal administrative agencies. In the 20th century, especially during and after Franklin D. Roosevelt's New Deal, the federal government experienced a tremendous growth of administrative agencies and administrative decisionmaking. The presence of administrative agencies is now so pervasive that it is tempting to consider them as a "fourth branch" of government. But, of course, they are not; they are created by action of one of the three constitutional branches (usually Congress), and their actions are controlled by one of the three branches (usually the Executive). Sometimes two branches (the Executive and Congress, or Congress and the Judiciary) cooperate in the creation or the control of administrative agency action. The opportunities are legion for conflicts between two branches (usually the Executive and Congress) or for alleged overreaching or usurpation by one of the branches (usually Congress).

Both Congress and the President have constitutional authority regarding administrative agencies. Congress has implied power under the necessary and proper clause to establish administrative agencies as a means of executing its express powers; thus Congress may delegate authority to administrative agencies or the heads of agencies to effectuate legislation that falls within the scope of Congress' constitutional powers (see Chap. 6, Sec. B). The President, in contrast, has express power under the appointments clause (Art. II, sec. 2, para. 2) to appoint "Officers of the United States," which would apparently include the heads of the administrative agencies within the executive branch. In addition, under the "take care" clause, the President has authority over administrative agencies that are executing laws passed by Congress. Where Congress' lawmaking power ends and the President's law-executing power begins is often unclear.

Issues may arise either when one branch has assumed "too much" control over an administrative agency or official or when one branch has granted or ceded "too much" authority over an administrative agency or official to the other branch. Most of the cases are in the former category and involve Congressional actions that allegedly intrude upon executive branch functions. Two of the earliest cases concern Congress' attempts to limit the President's authority to remove (or dismiss) administrative agency officials. The first of these cases, *Myers v. United States*, 272 U.S. 52 (1926), concerned a statute that required the consent of the U.S. Senate before the President could remove a postmaster (an official of what was then an executive department, the U.S. Post Office). Based on its reading of the framers' intent, and using "unitary executive" reasoning (see Sec. C above), the Court by a 6-3 vote invalidated the statute because it unduly interfered with the President's exclusive authority to remove officers of the executive branch. In the second case, *Humphrey's Executor v. United States*, 295 U.S. 602 (1935), Congress had provided that the President could remove a commissioner of the Federal Trade Commission only for "inefficiency, neglect of duty, or malfeasance in office." The Court upheld this statutory provision because the FTC exercises "quasi-legislative or quasi-judicial powers" rather than executive powers, and an FTC commissioner therefore "occupies no place in the executive department and...exercises no part of the executive power vested...in the President" (295 U.S. at 625, 628). The *Myers* case was distinguishable because the U.S. Post Office (as then constituted) was part of the executive branch—what is now called an "executive agency"—while the FTC is associated with the legislative or judicial branches—what is now called an "independent agency."[8]

---

8. Other examples of "independent" agencies include the Federal Communications Commission, the Federal Energy Regulation Commission, the National Labor Relations Board, and

Later cases address other situations in which Congress has allegedly intruded upon executive branch functions. In *Buckley v. Valeo*, 424 U.S. 1 (1976), for example, Congress had provided in the Federal Election Campaign Act of 1971 that the President pro tempore of the Senate and the Speaker of the House (legislative officials) could appoint some of the members of the Federal Election Commission. The Court held that this provision violated the appointments clause (Art. II, sec. 2) because the FEC performed sufficient executive functions to be considered part of the executive branch, and the FEC members had sufficient authority to be considered "principal" officers appointable only by the President.[9] In *Immigration and Naturalization Service v. Chadha*, 462 U.S. 919 (1983), the House of Representatives had reviewed and "vetoed" a deportation decision of the Immigration and Naturalization Service, as provided in a "legislative veto" provision in the federal immigration legislation. The Court invalidated Congress' action because it intruded upon the President's powers under the Presentment Clause (Art. I, sec. 7) to sign or veto bills. And in *Bowsher v. Synar*, 478 U.S. 714 (1986), as part of a major deficit-reduction statute, Congress had assigned budget-cutting power to the Comptroller General of the United States. The Court invalidated this legislation as well because it intruded upon Article II executive powers by assigning executive functions to an official (the Comptroller General) who was under the authority of Congress.

Although Congress lost in *Buckley*, *Chadha*, and *Bowsher*, having exercised "too much" control in each case, Congress did emerge victorious in a subsequent major case because the control it had exercised over administrative agency action was not "too much." The statute at issue provided for the appointment of "independent counsel" (special prosecutors) to investigate and prosecute criminal misconduct by high-level executive branch officials, including the President. Prosecutions for violation of federal laws is an executive branch function lodged in the Department of Justice under the control of the Attorney General, a presidential appointee. Under the statute, however, the independent counsels were appointed by a special court (called the "Special Division") established by the Act, were subject to some oversight by the Special Division and by Congress, and could be removed by the Attorney General only upon a showing of "good cause." This arrangement was broadly challenged in *Morrison v. Olson*, 487 U.S. 654 (1988), as an intrusion on the President's power to appoint executive officers (under the appointments clause), to remove executive officers, and to control executive agency functions. In an opinion that is considered to be a prime example of functionalist (versus formalist) reasoning (see Sec. A above), as well as a prime example of a refusal to follow the unitary executive thesis (see Sec. C.1 above), an eight-Justice majority in *Morrison* rejected all the challenges and upheld the independent

---

the Securities and Exchange Commission. *See generally* Marshall Breger and Gary Edlees, *Established by Practice: The Theory and Operation of Independent Agencies*, 52 Admin. L. Rev. 1111 (2000).

9. The Court in *Buckley* distinguished between "principal" officers and "inferior" officers, a distinction drawn from the text of the appointments clause. Congress may vest the appointment of "inferior" officers "in the Courts of Law, or in the Heads of Departments" rather than in the President (Art. II, sec. 2, para. 2).

counsel provisions of the Act. Independent counsels are "inferior" officers for purposes of the appointments clause, said the Court, and Congress may vest their appointment "in the Courts of Law or in the Heads of Departments" (Art. II, sec. 2, cl. 2). Appointment by a special court therefore did not infringe upon the President's appointment power. The "good cause" restriction on the Attorney General's authority to remove an independent counsel was "essential to establish the necessary independence" of the independent counsels (487 U.S. at 692–693), and does not "unduly tramme[l] on executive authority" (487 U.S. at 691) under the vesting clause or the take care clause. Nor did the oversight by the Special Division and the Congress unduly intrude upon the executive authority; the executive branch retains "sufficient control over the independent counsel to ensure that the President is able to perform his constitutionally assigned duties" (487 U.S. at 696). The Court therefore upheld the Act as consistent with the separation of powers, even though independent counsels are executive branch officials and the Act did authorize Congress and the courts to exercise some authority over executive branch functions. Had the Court followed the unitary executive thesis, as the dissent by Justice Scalia said it should have done, or had the Court used formalist (versus functional) reasoning, it presumably would have reached a different result.

All the cases above involved situations where one branch (Congress) allegedly exercised "too much" control over an administrative agency or official. There are far fewer cases in the second category, where one branch has granted or ceded "too much" authority to another branch. *Clinton v. New York*, 524 U.S. 417 (1998), which also involved a Congressional action, is the primary example. In the Line Item Veto Act, Congress had authorized the President to "cancel" or veto particular provisions in appropriations and tax bills after having signed them into law. The Court determined that the President's "line item" veto was the functional equivalent of a partial repeal or amendment of an act of Congress. The Constitution does not grant such authority to the President, said the Court; any partial repeal or amendment must be effectuated consistent with the procedures in Article I, in particular the presentment clause which requires that the President sign or return the *entire* bill *before* it becomes law. Congress therefore had unconstitutionally granted the President authority that the Constitution denied to him.

The administrative agency cases discussed in this section do not yield a clear or cohesive set of separation-of-powers principles. The reasoning and result of some cases is difficult to reconcile with that of others. (Compare *Myers* and *Buckley*, for instance, with *Morrison*.) Some, perhaps most, of the difficulty is due to the Court's vacillation over time between what commentators call the formalist and the functionalist understandings of separation of powers (see Sec. A above). The differences between formalist and functionalist reasoning also explain much of the disagreement between majority and dissenting Justices in particular cases.

From a *formalist* perspective, whenever the challenge concerns the procedures for lawmaking (that is, procedures for the passage, amendment, or repeal of a law, or their functional equivalents), it is important to ask whether Congress and the President have followed all the formalities in Article I, section 7 of the Constitution. If not, the action being challenged will probably be unconstitutional (see *Chadha*, above, and *Clinton v.*

New York, above). It is also important to ask whether the officer or agency at issue, and the officer's or agency's decision that is being challenged, are characterizable as executive on the one hand, or "quasi-legislative" or "quasi judicial" on the other. If the officer, agency, or decision is "executive" in character, it would probably be unconstitutional to vest any control in Congress (see *Myers, Buckley*, and *Bowsher*, all above). (There would be an exception for "inferior" executive officers, since the constitutional text expressly authorizes Congress to vest their appointment "in the Courts of Law, or in the Heads of Departments" rather than in the President; see footnote 9 above and *Morrison*, above, 487 U.S. at 670–677.)

From a *functionalist* perspective, in contrast, the forms and formalities of lawmaking are construed less literally and more flexibly (*see, e.g.*, Justice White's dissent in *Chadha*, 462 U.S. at 967–1013). The characterization of an officer, agency, or decision as "executive" (versus quasi-legislative or quasi-judicial) is not necessarily controlling (*see especially Morrison*). Instead, the Court focuses on factors that are more fluid and are matters of degree: Whether Congress has usurped the President's executive power by claiming for itself certain authority over the execution of the laws; and whether the Congress has interfered with the President's executive powers by delegating to others (e.g., the courts, as in *Morrison*) certain authority over the execution of the laws. In the *Morrison* case, for example, the Court asked whether the independent counsel statute "involve[s] an attempt by Congress to increase its own powers at the expense of the Executive Branch" (487 U.S. at 694), and then asked whether the statute "'impermissibly undermine[s]' the powers of the Executive Branch, or 'disrupts the proper balance between the coordinate branches [by] prevent[ing] the Executive Branch from accomplishing its constitutionally assigned functions'" (487 U.S. at 695). Answering both questions in the negative, the Court upheld the independent counsel statute, even though (from a formalist perspective) it permitted Congress and the courts (the Special Division) to exercise significant authority over an executive officer performing executive functions within the executive branch.

Sec. E. Executive Branch Clashes with the Courts

The study of executive power is not confined, of course, to Executive/Congressional power relationships. An exertion of executive power may also clash with the judicial power either because there is an actual conflict between the Executive's actions and the court's actions or because the Executive's action tends to usurp the judicial branch's constitutional prerogatives. *Marbury v. Madison*, 5 U.S. (1 Cranch) 137 (1803), provides a classic illustration. Although *Marbury* is known as a case concerning a judicial branch clash with Congress (see Chap. 5, Sec. A above), Chief Justice Marshall also gave important consideration to the relationship between the executive branch and the judicial branch. The basic issue was whether the Court could entertain a lawsuit against James Madison, President Jefferson's Secretary of State, and issue a judicial order requiring Madison to deliver a justice-of-the-peace commission to Marbury. Marbury had been appointed to this position by outgoing President John Adams at the close of his administration; but Adams' Secretary of State, who ironically was John Marshall,[10] had failed to deliver the commission. The Court inquired "whether the legality of an act of the head of a department be examinable in a court of justice or not" and determined that the answer "must always depend on the nature of that act" (5 U.S. at 165). For some executive acts, which are "political" in character or concern "political" subjects, the Constitution grants the Executive "a constitutional or legal discretion"; such acts "can never be examinable by the courts" (5 U.S. at 166). But for other executive acts, not of that character, an executive officer "is amenable to the laws for his conduct"; the courts can examine such acts and afford an appropriate remedy to an injured party whose rights have been violated. The act of denying the commission, said the Court, was of the latter type; the Court could therefore review the act and order Madison to deliver the commission. The Court did not do so, however, as explained in Chapter 5, Section A, because it determined that the statute granting jurisdiction over the case was unconstitutional.

The *Marbury* distinction between judicially reviewable and nonreviewable executive acts was difficult when drawn and remains troublesome today. Problems concerning the imposition of judicial orders and remedies upon executive officials also remain troublesome. Modern manifestations of these problems can be seen in the "political question" cases discussed in Chapter 5, Section D.6. Other examples are provided by the cases on executive privilege and executive immunities from judicial process, especially *United States v. Nixon*, 418 U.S. 683 (1974), the "Watergate Tapes Case."

In *United States v. Nixon*, the Court rejected a claim of privilege and affirmed the issuance of a judicial subpoena to President Nixon, ordering him to produce the secret "Watergate Tapes." In separation-of-powers terms, President Nixon's assertion of executive privilege to protect the Tapes was in conflict with the federal district court's issuance of the subpoena to the President. To resolve this conflict, the Court employed what could be called a "balance of competing constitutional interests" test. The goal was to "resolve [the] competing interests in a manner that preserves the essential functions of each branch" (*Id.* at 707). To do so, the Court focused on the "balance" between the President's interest (an interest in confidentiality of high-level communications) and the Judiciary's interest (an interest in obtaining relevant evidence for criminal trials). After identifying and balancing these respective interests, the Court determined that the judicial branch should prevail because, in the particular circumstances of the case, its interest in obtaining the Tapes was stronger than the President's interest in keeping them confidential.

But in a 5-4 decision in *Nixon v. Fitzgerald*, 457 U.S. 731 (1982), the Court held that courts could not impose monetary damage remedies upon the President in civil suits

---

10. John Marshall, who wrote the Court's opinion in *Marbury*, had served briefly as Secretary of State at the end of the Adams administration. President Adams appointed Marshall as Chief Justice in 1800, and Marshall took the oath of office on February 4, 1801. But he continued as well to serve as Secretary of State (a separation-of-powers violation?) until the Adams administration ended a month later.

challenging an "official" Presidential act. The President has an "absolute immunity" from such remedies in such cases. The result would differ, however, if the President were sued for money damages in a civil suit challenging an "unofficial" or private act, especially one taken before the President took office. In such a case, according to *Clinton v. Jones*, 520 U.S. 681 (1997), the President has no immunity from suit or from the imposition of money damages.

Sec. F. Study Suggestions

As you read the executive power cases, be sure to identify the inter-branch power relationship that is involved in each case, and the particular conflict or clash between the branches that gave rise to each case (see Secs. C and D above). Then seek to identify: (1) the particular source or sources of power that may support each executive action that is at issue in each case (see Sec. B above); (2) the source or sources of power of the other branch (Congress or the courts) that may be implicated in the dispute; and (3) the limits that the Court applies (or refuses to apply) to each source of executive power asserted in each case.

Then look more deeply at each case. Determine what consideration, if any, the Court gave to the historical practices of the branches involved in the case. Look for underlying concepts and theories of executive power that assist understanding and application of the law. Consult Justice Jackson's three analytical categories from his *Youngstown* concurrence (Sec. D.1 above), which provide a particularly helpful framework for identifying concepts and theories, and for ascertaining limits on powers. Also, consider whether the Court's reasoning is more formalist than functional, or vice-versa (see Secs. A and D.2 above). Remember also to distinguish foreign affairs cases or issues from domestic affairs cases or issues (see Sec. C above), and seek to understand why and how the courts may accord greater deference to the President's foreign affairs activities.

More broadly, as you read and compare the cases, consider the role that the federal courts play in separation-of-powers disputes, and why the U.S. Supreme Court has not always been consistent and clear in its performance of this role. Also consider the vision of separation of powers that emerges from the cases, including the values that are promoted and impeded by this tripartite system of government.

FOR FURTHER READING: (1) Kenneth Karst & Harold Horowitz, "Presidential Prerogatives and Judicial Review," 22 UCLA L. REV. 47 (1974) (on *United States v. Nixon*). (2) Paul Kauper, "The Steel Seizure Case: Congress, the President, and the Supreme Court," 51 MICH. L. REV. 141 (1952). (3) H. Jefferson Powell, THE PRESIDENT'S AUTHORITY OVER FOREIGN AFFAIRS: AN ESSAY IN CONSTITUTIONAL INTERPRETATION (Carolina Academic Press, 2002). (4) Peter Strauss, "The Place of Agencies in Government: Separation of Powers and the Fourth Branch," 84 COLUMBIA L. REV. 573 (1984). (5) Keith Werhan, "Toward an Eclectic Approach to Separation of Powers: *Morrison v. Olsen* Examined," 16 HASTINGS CONST. L. Q. 393 (1989).

Chapter 9

The Context for Considering Constitutional Rights Questions

Sec. A. An Overview of Federal Constitutional Rights

A.1. In General

This Chapter and Chapters 10–13 explore the terrain of constitutional rights. The distinction between constitutional power clauses and constitutional rights clauses (Chap. 2, Sec. C) is the starting point for a study of the materials in these chapters. The power clauses provide only one measure, an incomplete measure, of the constitutionality of federal government action; the individual rights clauses are also a necessary part of the picture. Moreover, even though the states are empowered by their own state constitutions rather than the federal Constitution, the actions of state and local governments are nevertheless subject to the federal Constitution's individual rights clauses.

Shifting the focus from powers issues to rights issues does not mean that federalism and separation of powers considerations (see Chap. 4, Sec. B) drop out of the picture. These considerations are less pervasive and prominent in rights analysis than in power analysis, but they are nevertheless an important part of the mix that one must take account of in order to do comprehensive and creative analysis. Federalism and separation-of-powers considerations, for example, were an essential aspect of the debate on incorporation of the Bill of Rights into the Fourteenth Amendment (see Chap. 11, Sec. A.2). These considerations are also a critical backdrop for the "state action" issues that are a threshold concern in some rights cases (see Sec. E below). In addition, federalism or separation-of-powers considerations sometimes lead courts to accord more deference to legislative and executive actions than they otherwise would in rights cases. In *San Antonio Independent School District v. Rodriguez*, 411 U.S. 1 (1973), for example, in rejecting an equal protection challenge to the Texas system for funding public education (see Chap. 10, Sec. D.8), the Court emphasized that "the Texas system is affirmative and reformatory and, therefore, should be scrutinized under judicial principles sensitive to the nature of the State's efforts and to the rights reserved to the States under the Constitution" (*Id.* at 39). Similarly, expanding its reasoning for denying the rights claim, the Court asserted: "[I]t would be difficult to imagine a case having greater potential impact on our federal system than the one now before us, in which we are urged to abrogate systems of financing public education presently in existence in virtually every State" (*Id.* at 44).

The individual rights clauses that typically receive the most attention from the courts and commentators, and also from instructors in constitutional law courses, are: the equal protection clause of the Fourteenth Amendment (Chap. 10), which binds the states and whose guarantees are also implicit in the Fifth Amendment due process clause, thus binding the federal government as well; the due process clauses of the Fourteenth and Fifth Amendments (Chap. 11), the former binding on the states and the latter on the federal government; the free speech and press clauses of the First Amendment (Chap. 12), directly applicable to the federal government and applicable to the states through "incorporation" (see Chap. 11, Sec. A.2) into the Fourteenth Amendment; and the First Amendment's religion clauses (Chap. 13), applicable to the federal government and the states in the same way as the free speech and press clauses.

The Fourth, Fifth, Sixth, and Eighth Amendment clauses concerning the criminal process also receive substantial attention from courts and commentators, and in criminal procedure and criminal justice courses. Of particular importance are the search and seizure provisions of the Fourth Amendment, the privilege against self-incrimination in the Fifth Amendment, the jury trial and right-to-counsel provisions of the Sixth Amendment, and the cruel-and-unusual punishment clause of the Eighth Amendment. Cruel-and-unusual punishments and Fourth Amendment searches and seizures are addressed in Sections A.2 and A.3 below. These and other criminal process provisions are also briefly discussed in various other sections (see Chap. 2, Sec. G (jury trial), Chap. 5, Sec. B (Fourth Amendment) and Chap. 11, Sec. A.2 (jury trial)), and in sections B and E below. Otherwise, however, the criminal process provisions are not a focus of this book.[1]

A.2. The Cruel and Unusual Punishment Clause

The cruel-and-unusual punishment clause applies only to punishments for *crimes* and thus does not apply to civil penalties or informal punishments such as corporal punishment of a student in a public school (*Ingraham v. Wright*, 430 U.S. 651, 664–671 (1977)). In the criminal context, the constitutionality of the death penalty has been the key issue under the cruel-and-unusual punishment clause. In *Furman v. Georgia*, 408 U.S. 238 (1972), the U.S. Supreme Court invalidated Georgia's capital punishment law,

---

1. For further discussion of the constitutional aspects of the criminal process, see Robert Bloom & Mark Brodin, CRIMINAL PROCEDURE: EXAMPLES AND EXPLANATIONS (Aspen, 3rd ed., 2000); Joshua Dressler, UNDERSTANDING CRIMINAL PROCEDURE (Lexis/Nexis, 3rd ed., 2002).

and those of 38 other states, because the death penalty, as administered in those states, was a "cruel and unusual punishment" under the Eighth Amendment. When the states amended their laws, however, and new cases came to the Court, the Court upheld most of the new laws; the death penalty, administered under these laws, was not "cruel and unusual." *Gregg v. Georgia*, 428 U.S. 153 (1976); *Proffitt v. Florida*, 428 U.S. 242 (1976); and *Jurek v. Texas*, 428 U.S. 262 (1976) (*see* Charles Black, "Due Process for Death: *Jurek v. Texas* and Companion Cases," 26 CATHOLIC UNIV. L. REV. 1 (1976)). The new laws that were not upheld were the ones that provided for a mandatory imposition of death, rather than leaving the decision to the carefully circumscribed discretion of juries. *Woodson v. North Carolina*, 428 U.S. 280 (1976). Since the 1976 cases, the Court has occasionally reviewed, and sometimes invalidated, particular aspects or applications of the states' capital punishment laws. In *Atkins v. Virginia*, 536 U.S. 304 (2002), for example, the Court held that it is cruel and unusual punishment to impose the death penalty on a mentally retarded person.

A.3. The Fourth Amendment

In addition to their role in the criminal law context, the Fourth Amendment's search and seizure provisions have important applications outside of criminal law and protect privacy interests in situations that do not involve criminal investigations. In *Vernonia School District, 47 J. v. Acton*, 515 U.S. 646 115 S. Ct. 2386 (1995), for example, the U.S. Supreme Court reviewed a public school board's policy that student-athletes must submit to *random*, suspicionless drug testing. The Court determined that the collection of urine samples from student-athletes is a search that is subject to the strictures of the Fourteenth Amendment. By a 6 to 3 vote, however, the Court majority upheld the policy. Applying a "reasonableness" test, the majority determined *inter alia*, that the school district has an "important, indeed perhaps compelling," interest in deterring school children from drug use as well as a more particular interest in protecting student-athletes from physical harm that could result from competing in events under the influence of drugs; that there was evidence of a disciplinary crisis in the school system "being fueled by alcohol and drug abuse," which underscored the immediacy of the district's concerns; and that the drug testing policy "effectively addressed" these concerns (*Id.* at 663). Subsequently, in *Board of Education of Independent School District No. 92 v. Earls*, 536 U.S. 822 (2002), the Court extended *Vernonia* to cover a school board policy that students participating in non-athletic extracurricular activities such as band, choir, and Future Farmers of America, must submit to random, suspicionless drug tests undertaken by collecting and screening urine samples. By a 5 to 4 vote, again using a "reasonableness" test, the Court determined that the testing was not an unconstitutional search and seizure and upheld the school board's policy.

A.4. The Second Amendment

Since the late 20th Century, the Second Amendment's "right...to keep and bear arms" has received considerable attention from politicians, the gun lobby and the gun-control lobby, academics, and the lower courts (especially U.S. Courts of Appeals). The basic questions concerning the Second Amendment are whether this "right" is a personal right, enforceable by private individuals like other rights in the Bill of Rights; and if so, whether this right has a narrowed scope of application because it is limited by the "well-regulated Militia" language at the beginning of the Amendment.

The U.S. Supreme Court has decided (as of the time this book went to press) only one Second Amendment case on the merits: *United States v. Miller*, 307 U.S. 174 (1939), in which the Court upheld an indictment charging the defendant with transporting in interstate commerce a certain unregistered shotgun "with a barrel less than 18 inches in length." *Miller's* reasoning is somewhat cryptic and is inconclusive regarding the scope of Second Amendment rights. Thus lower courts in more recent cases have struggled with the substantial interpretive challenges posed by the Second Amendment. Commentators have weighed in as well, and both the case law and the scholarship on the Second Amendment have burgeoned since the early 1990s. Absent any definitive Supreme Court precedent, courts and commentators have done extensive textual, historical, and structural interpretation (see Chap. 2, Sec. F of this book) of the Second Amendment. Contending positions have emerged, but no consensus. *See, e.g.*, Symposium, "The Second Amendment: Fresh Looks," 76 CHI-KENT L. REV. 3-715 (2000).

Two recent U.S. Court of Appeals rulings highlight the contending poles in the debate over whether the Second Amendment protects an individual's right to possess firearms. In *United States v. Emerson*, 270 F.3d 203 (5th Cir. 2001), the defendant had been indicted for possession of a firearm (a Beretta pistol) while subject to a restraining order in divorce proceedings (18 U.S.C. §922(g)(8)). He argued that the statute violated the Second Amendment. The Fifth Circuit held that the Second Amendment "protects the right of individuals, including those not then actually a member of any militia or engaged in active military service or training, to privately possess and bear their own firearms...that are suitable as personal, individual weapons" (*Id.* at 260). In so ruling, the court adopted what is called the "individual rights model" of the Second Amendment. Following this model, the court determined that the defendant had a constitutional right to possess a pistol but that his right was overridden in this case by the governmental interest in the effectiveness of the restraining order to which the defendant was subject.

In *Silveira v. Lockyer*, 312 F.3d 1052 (9th Cir. 2002), the plaintiffs were California residents who owned or sought to acquire "assault weapons." They asserted that the state's gun control laws that restricted possession, use and transfer of such weapons were unconstitutional under the Second Amendment. The Ninth Circuit held that the amendment "guarantees the right of the people to maintain effective state militias, but does not provide any individual right to own or possess weapons" (*Id.* at 1060). This court thus adopted what is called the "collective rights model" of the Second Amendment. Under this model, which rejects the notion that the amendment is a source of individual rights, the federal government and the states "have the full authority to enact prohibitions and restrictions on the use and possession of firearms...." (*Id.*).

Each court recognized (but did not endorse) a third model of the Second Amendment that would fit between the two poles of the individual rights model and the collective rights model. The Fifth Circuit described a "sophisticated collective rights" model based on the view that Second Amendment rights "can only be exercised by members of a functioning state militia who bear the arms while and as a part of actively participating in the organized militia's activities" (270 F.3d at 219). The Ninth Circuit described a "limited individual right model" based on the view that "individuals maintain a constitutional right to possess firearms insofar as such possession bears a reasonable relationship to militia service" (312 F.3d at 1060).

Both courts gave extensive attention to the Second Amendment's text. The court in *Emerson*, however, focused particularly on the second clause, or "substantive guarantee," of the Amendment: "the right of the people to keep and bear Arms, shall not be infringed"; while the court in *Silveira* focused particularly on the first clause or preamble: "A well regulated Militia, being necessary to the security of a free State…" (U.S. Const., Amend. 2). To the *Emerson* court, the second clause supported the individual rights interpretation of the Amendment, and the first clause did not refute this interpretation. To the *Silveira* court, the first clause supported the collective rights interpretation, and the second clause did not refute it.

Both courts also gave extensive consideration to the original history of the Amendment. Looking at the same historical materials, the two courts reached opposite conclusions regarding their import. The *Emerson* court found:

> no historical evidence that the Second Amendment was intended to convey militia power to the states, limit the federal government's power to maintain a standing army, or applies only to members of a select militia while on active duty. All of the evidence indicates that the Second Amendment, like other parts of the Bill of Rights, applies to and protects individual Americans. [270 F.3d at 260.]

The court in *Silveira*, in contrast, concluded that:

> Our review of the debates during the Constitutional Convention, the state ratifying conventions, and the First Congress, as well as the other historical materials we have discussed, confirmed what the text strongly suggested: that the amendment was adopted in order to protect the people from the threat of federal tyranny by preserving the right of the states to arm their militias. [312 F.3d at 1086–1087.]

A.5. Economic Rights (the Takings Clause and the Contract Clause)

In the realm of economic rights, the Fifth Amendment's eminent domain (or "takings") clause has been the subject of renewed attention from the U.S. Supreme Court. This clause — "nor shall private property be taken for public use, without just compensation" — is made applicable to the states by virtue of incorporation into the Fourteenth Amendment (see Chap. 11, Sec. A.2). In a line of cases beginning in the 1980s, for instance, the Court sharpened its distinction between "physical takings" of private property and "regulatory takings" and made a further distinction between complete or permanent regulatory takings on the one hand and partial or temporary regulatory takings on the other. *See, e.g., Tahoe-Sierra Preservation Council v. Tahoe Regional Planning Agency*, 535 U.S. 302, 321–323 (2002). In *Lucas v. South Carolina Coastal Council*, 505 U.S. 1003 (1992), for instance, Lucas had purchased two residential building lots that he could not develop because, two years after his purchase, the state legislature had enacted a beachfront anti-erosion law that precluded the building of permanent structures on the property. Lucas claimed that the state law, as applied to him, was a regulatory taking requiring just compensation. The state defended its law as a regulation of property use that served important public interests and required no compensation to the affected owners. The Court, by a 6 to 3 vote, ruled that, when "*no* productive or economically beneficial use of land is permitted," and the state has therefore deprived the owner of "*all* economically beneficial uses" of the land, a compensable regulatory taking has occurred (505 U.S. at 1017, 1019 (emphasis in original)).

Also in the economic realm, the obligation-of-contract clause (or contract clause) in Article I, section 10, clause 1 still occasionally makes an important appearance in the courts. This clause provides that: "No State shall…pass any…Law impairing the Obligation of Contracts…." (*See, e.g., Energy Resources Group v. Kansas Power and Light*, 459 U.S. 400 (1983).) Although the clause limits only the states, similar limitations applicable to the federal government would apparently arise from the Fifth Amendment due process clause's protections against deprivations of property.

A.6. The Thirteenth and Fifteenth Amendments

The Thirteenth and Fifteenth Amendments, together with the Fourteenth (see Chap. 10, Sec. A), are America's constitutional response to the Civil War and the slavery practices that helped precipitate the War. Both Amendments—the Thirteenth prohibiting slavery and involuntary servitude and the Fifteenth prohibiting race discrimination in voting)[2]—continue to play important roles in race relations matters. Specifically, both amendments add to the general prohibition on race discrimination that the courts have developed under the Fourteenth Amendment's equal protection clause (see Chap. 10, Sec. C). The Thirteenth Amendment's prohibition, for instance, applies not only to state action (see Sec. D below), but to private action as well: "As its text reveals, the Thirteenth Amendment 'is not a mere prohibition of state laws establishing or upholding slavery, but an absolute declaration that slavery or involuntary servitude shall not exist in any part of the United States'" (*Jones v. Alfred H. Mayer Co.*, 392 U.S. 409, 438 (1968), quoting the *Civil Rights Cases*, 109 U.S. 3, 20 (1883)). Moreover, the Thirteenth Amendment is not limited to African slavery as it existed in America before the Amendment was drafted, nor even to slavery or servitude based on race. Rather, the Amendment is "a charter of universal civil freedom for all persons, of whatever race,

---

2. Later amendments play vital roles in protecting individuals from other forms of discrimination in the voting process: the Nineteenth Amendment prohibiting sex discrimination in voting, the Twenty-Fourth Amendment outlawing poll taxes, and the Twenty-Sixth Amendment protecting persons who are 18 or older from age discrimination in voting.

color or estate, under the flag" (*Bailey v. State of Alabama*, 219 U.S. 219, 241 (1911); *compare United States v. Kozminski*, 487 U.S. 931 (1988)).

The Fifteenth Amendment provides special protection against race discrimination in voting. Since voting is the focus, the Amendment protects only "citizens," compared to the Fourteenth Amendment which protects" persons," including certain aliens as well as corporations. The Fifteenth Amendment limits both the federal government and the states (unlike the Fourteenth Amendment which limits only the states) and applies to both federal and state elections. The Court has emphasized that section 1 of the Fifteenth Amendment "has repeatedly been construed, without further legislative specification, to invalidate state voting qualifications or procedures which are discriminatory on their face or in practice" (*South Carolina v. Katzenbach*, 383 U.S. 301, 817 (1966)). Using section 1 (Amend. 15, sec. 1), for instance, the Court has invalidated grandfather clauses (*Guinn v. United States*, 238 U.S. 347 (1915)), white primaries (*Terry v. Adams*, 345 U.S. 461 (1953)), racial gerrymandering (*Gomillion v. Lightfoot*, 364 U.S. 339 (1960)), and racially discriminatory voter qualification tests (*Louisiana v. United States*, 380 U.S. 145 (1965)). As with the Fourteenth Amendment's equal protection clause, such actions are unconstitutional under the Fifteenth Amendment only if the government acted with a racially discriminatory intention or motivation (*see, e.g.*, *City of Mobile v. Bolden*, 446 U.S. 55, 61–65 (1980); and compare Chap. 10, Sec. C discussion of equal protection).

Even though the Thirteenth and Fifteenth Amendments are self-explanatory and need no "further legislative specification," Congress has nevertheless implemented, and extended the force of, these Amendments through legislation based on the enforcement power (Chap. 6, Sec. E) that is granted to Congress in section 2 of each of these Amendments. "Section 1981" (42 U.S.C. § 1981) and "Section 1982" (42 U.S. C. § 1982), for example, enforce the Thirteenth Amendment by eradicating certain "badges and incidents of slavery" such as racial discrimination in contracting (Section 1981) and racial discrimination in sale of real estate (Section 1982). Similarly, the Voting Rights Act of 1965 (42 U.S.C. Secs. 1973, 1973b, 1973, and 1973i) enforces the Fifteenth Amendment by prohibiting a wide range of practices that would perpetuate or foster racial discrimination in voting. Since such statutory rights are often broader and more specific than the constitutional rights protected by section 1 of each of these Amendments, the statutory rights have generally taken precedence over the constitutional rights in modern litigation (*see, e.g.*, *Jones v. Alfred H. Mayer Co.*, above, 392 U.S. at 437–443). (Chapter 14, Section B, includes further discussion of these statutory civil rights.)

A.7. Privileges and Immunities Clauses

The privileges and immunities clause in Article IV, section 2, clause 1, covering *interstate* privileges and immunities, and the privileges and immunities clause of the Fourteenth Amendment, covering *national* privileges and immunities, both received increased attention in the late 20th Century. The Fourteenth Amendment clause is addressed in Chapter 10, Section B. The Article IV clause, because of its close relationship to issues of federalism, is addressed in Chapter 7, Section E.

Sec. B. Interpreting the Individual Rights Clauses

B.1. Interpretive Approaches

Interpretation of individual rights clauses, like interpretation of power clauses, usually begins with the constitutional text. But for the key individual rights clauses, even more than for the power clauses, the language is particularly sparse and open-ended. Does a school board violate the equal protection clause if it maintains racially "separate-but-equal" schools? Does a state violate the due process clause if it restricts the freedom of women to obtain abortions? Does the federal government violate the free speech clause if it criminally punishes the act of flag burning? While the texts of the cited clauses may guide analysis of these issues in critically important ways, the text alone does not provide answers to these questions.

Lacking an answer from the text, an interpreter addressing a rights issue may seek to use the historical and structural approaches to interpretation, as is done with power clauses (see Chap. 4, Sec. C). Occasionally such attempts will be successful. In *Carrol v. United States*, 267 U.S. 132, 149 (1925), for example, the U.S. Supreme Court interpreted the Fourth Amendment in light of its original history, that is, "in light of what was deemed an unreasonable search and seizure when [the Amendment] was adopted." And in *Marsh v. Chambers*, 463 U.S. 783 (1983), the Court used historical arguments to analyze the validity of the Nebraska legislature's practice of opening each session with a prayer. Rejecting a challenge to this practice based on the establishment clause, the Court gave great weight to the historical record of legislative prayer "[f]rom colonial times through the founding of the Republic and ever since . . .," making clear that this practice "is deeply imbedded in the history and tradition of this country" (463 U.S. at 786).

Similarly, the Court has occasionally used structural arguments in exploring individual rights questions. The best example concerns the right to interstate travel, which the Court has described as "fundamental to the concept of our Federal Union" and a right that "finds no explicit mention in the Constitution" but is "so elementary [that it] was conceived from the beginning to be a necessary concomitant of the stranger Union the Constitution created" (*United States v. Guest*, 383 U.S. 745, 757–758 (1966)). The right to interstate travel, in other words, is inferred from the constitutional structure of federalism.

Another example, where the Court used structural analysis in rejecting rather than accepting an individual rights claim, comes from *San Antonio Independent School District v. Rodriguez*, 411 U.S. 1 (1973). The case concerned an equal protection challenge to Texas' system for financing public schools. In rejecting the challenge, the Court invoked the structure of federalism:

> It must be remembered also that every claim arising under the Equal Protection clause has implications for the relationship between national and state power under our federal system. [I]t would be difficult to imagine a case having a greater potential impact on our federal system than the one now before

us, in which we are urged to abrogate systems of financing public education presently in existence in virtually every state. [411 U.S. at 44.]

More often, however, interpreters will find that neither history nor structural inference will provide an answer to the individual rights issue being addressed. There may have been no original historical practices that are analogous to the contemporary practice at issue. If there were analogous original practices, the historical evidence of them may be unavailable or unclear, or the framers may not have considered these original practices, or their consideration may have been inconclusive. The historical approach would thus not yield a specific answer to the issue being addressed. Similarly, the rights issue being addressed may not have sufficient structural ramifications to allow the interpreter to identify and apply relevant structural inferences. Thus the structural approach also would not provide a specific answer. What then should an interpreter do? Are there other interpretive approaches to take under the individual rights clauses?

The answer is an affirmative one. In addition to the textual, historical, and structural approaches to constitutional interpretation, there is a fourth approach which might be called the "values" approach. It is addressed in subsections B.2 through B.4 below.

B.2. The Values Approach

The source for this approach to interpretation is constitutional values, and the approach may therefore be called the "constitutional values" approach. Other commentators have called such an approach the fundamental values approach, the ethics approach, the morality approach, or the policy approach. However labeled, this constitutional values approach has been used primarily for individual rights problems; it has been in its ascendancy since the 1954 decision in *Brown v. Board of Education*, 347 U.S. 483 (1954) (Chap. 3, Sec. E, and Sec. C below); and it reached a zenith in 1973 in the abortion rights case, *Roe v. Wade*, 410 U.S. 113 (1973) (see Chap. 11, Sec. C.2).

The values approach entails a search for the Constitution's elemental principles and the values they serve. Once identified, such basic values can be used as guides, or reference points, for interpretation. The interpreter seeks to resolve the problem at hand in a manner that will uphold the identified value as against other lesser values or interests that may be at stake. In *United States v. United States District Court*, 407 U.S. 297 (1972), for example, the President had claimed authority to conduct warrantless electronic surveillance in order to protect national security. The Court determined that such surveillance was an unconstitutional search under the Fourth Amendment. In a concurrence that relied on an earlier decision of the Court, Justice Douglas used these words to support the majority's invalidation of the warrantless surveillance:

> To defeat so terrifying a claim of inherent power [by the President], we need only stand by the enduring *values* served by the Fourth Amendment. As we stated last Term in *Coolidge v. New Hampshire*, 403 U.S. 443, 455: "In terms of unrest, whether caused by crime or racial conflict or fear of internal subversion, this basic law and the *values* that it represents may appear unrealistic or

'extravagant' to some. But the *values* were those of the authors of our fundamental constitutional concepts. In times not altogether unlike our own they won...a right of personal security against arbitrary intrusions....If times have changed, reducing everyman's scope to do as he pleases in an urban and industrial world, the changes have made the *values* served by the Fourth Amendment more, not less, important." [407 U.S. at 332–333; emphasis added (Douglas, J., concurring).]

The values approach is premised on a candid acknowledgment that the Constitution is a product of value judgments and that constitutional interpretation consequently requires resort to values. As one commentator has concluded, "[j]ust as the Constitution cannot be value-free, so our understanding of it must be informed by reflection on the principles it serves" (David Lyons, "Constitutional Interpretation and Original Meaning," 4 Soc. Phil. & Pol'y 75, 101 (1986)). The Constitution's preamble itself provides strong support for this notion. It sets out goals that embody values—for example, to "secure the Blessings of Liberty"—and makes clear that fulfillment of these goals and promotion of these values is the Constitution's task. Likewise, numerous constitutional provisions following the preamble are express invocations of values—for example, the Eighth Amendment's prohibition on "cruel and unusual punishments" and the Fourteenth Amendment's requirement of "equal" protection.

In considering the values approach, two threshold questions arise: (1) What kind of values qualify for use as reference points? and (2) Where may the interpreter search for these values? How one views the legitimacy and utility of this approach will depend in large part on the answers to these questions, discussed in Sections B.3 and B.4 below.

B.3.   What Kind of Values Count?

This much seems clear about the values eligible for consideration under the values approach. *First*, the eligible values must be public values; personal or other private values do not count. *Second*, they must be national values; regional or state or interest group values do not count. *Third*, they must be real values based on the shared cultural and political experience of the American people; artificial constructs or abstractions do not count. *Fourth*, they must be enduring values; mere transitory or popular values do not count. And *fifth*, they must be traceable historically to the time period preceding or contemporaneous with the adoption of the Constitution and Bill of Rights, or the adoption of a later amendment that is at issue; modern or contemporary values with no such historical roots do not count. The values meeting these criteria may be either "substantive values," that is, values concerning the particular benefits or detriments that individuals receive from government; or "process values," that is, values concerning the processes or procedures by which government dispenses benefits and detriments to individuals.

Regarding the first four of these specifications for constitutional values, there is probably general agreement—at least among those who accept the legitimacy of the values approach to interpretation. Regarding the fifth specification, however, there is some controversy. "Noninterpretivists" and some "supplementers" (as described in Section B.4 below) would likely not agree with this specification, thinking it too restrictive. The extent of the U.S. Supreme Court's agreement may now also be questionable, at least for substantive due process analysis, in light of *Lawrence v. Texas*, 123 S. Ct. 2472 (2003). As discussed below in this Section, the *Lawrence* majority did affirm that "history and tradition are the starting point" for analysis of due process liberty interests. But it also added that "history and tradition... [are] not in all cases the ending point..." (*Id.* at 2480). What is unclear is whether the values that are ascertained at "the ending point" must still be somehow rooted in or traceable to the original values discovered in the "original" history and tradition.

Like the historical approach (Chap. 4, Sec. C.2), the values approach raises problems concerning levels of generality, that is, the level of generality or abstraction with which a value may be stated. *See generally* Laurence H. Tribe & Michael C. Dorf, "Levels of Generality in the Definition of Rights," 57 U. OF CHI. L. REV. 1057 (1990). This is one of the most difficult aspects of the values approach, and a key concern to watch for when the Justices are divided on a sensitive individual rights issue, especially a substantive due process issue (see Chap. 11, Sec. C). In *Michael H. v. Gerald D.*, 491 U.S. 110 (1989), for example, the Court considered the constitutionality of a California paternity statute as applied to a man claiming to be the natural father of a child born while the mother was married to another man. Justice Scalia, for a plurality, stated that the privacy interest at stake encompassed only a natural father's "parental rights over a child born into a woman's existing marriage with another man" (491 U.S. at 125). Justice Brennan, in dissent, rejected this narrow view and argued that the value at stake concerned "a parent and child in their relationship with each other" (491 U.S. at 141–142). The Justices differed on the level of generality at which the value at stake could be stated; and the more specific (and narrower) statement won the day. As this case suggests, when the Court narrowly states a value, and thus refuses to generalize, it is likely to reject the constitutional right being claimed. But when the Court is willing to generalize, and thus state the value at stake more broadly—as, for instance, in the contraception cases and the abortion cases (Chap. 11, Sec. C.2)—it will likely recognize and protect the constitutional right being claimed. (For more on levels of generality, see Chapter 11, Section C.6.)

B.4. Where May an Interpreter Search for Values?

The second question—where may the interpreter search for the values to be used with the values approach—occasions a variety of answers. Certainly the text, original history, and structure of the Constitution are an appropriate and useful focus of the search. The text of the First Amendment, for example, expressly recognizes the value of free expression and the value of freedom of religion, and by implication a value of freedom of association; the text of the Fourteenth Amendment expressly recognizes a value of equality under law. In such situations, however, the text only establishes a guidepost; it does not map out the contours of the terrain. In some circumstances, original history may enhance our understanding of these textual values. The Fourteenth

Amendment's history, for example, helps us understand the equality value in the context of racial subjugation. Further, structure may provide insight into values apart from text. Structural inferences, for instance, are the source of a personal mobility value (freedom of travel), and a value of participation in representative government. In effect, the interpreter gathers evidence from all these sources and weaves it together to develop a value assessment in each particular case.

In other circumstances, the reliance on text, original history, and structure as the source of values may be less direct, or the reliance may be on a source external to the Constitution. Some commentators, for instance, have argued that the Declaration of Independence is a source of values that inform constitutional interpretation. It has also been argued that constitutional values emerge from a "set of philosophic presuppositions" held by the framers (Gary J. Jacobsohn, THE SUPREME COURT AND THE DECLINE OF CONSTITUTIONAL ASPIRATION, p. 75 (Rowman & Littlefield, 1986)); from "implicit background assumptions against which the Constitution was drafted" (Richard Epstein, Foreword to Stephen Macedo, THE NEW RIGHT V. THE CONSTITUTION, p. xiv (Cato Institute, 1986); or from "essential postulate(s)" that may lie [b]ehind the words of the constitutional provisions" and may "limit and control" these provisions (*Principality of Monaco v. State of Mississippi*, 292 U.S. 313, 322 (1934)). Probably the best example of such a presupposition, background assumption, or postulate is the institution of marriage and the privacy of the marital relationship. In *Griswold v. Connecticut*, 381 U.S. 479 (1965) (see Chap. 11, Sec. C.2), for example, Justice Douglas concluded his majority opinion by stating: "We deal with a right of privacy older than the Bill of Rights.... Marriage is... intimate to the degree of being sacred" (*Id.* at 486).

Similarly, it has often been argued that American, or Anglo-American, history and traditions are the source of constitutional values. Among judges, the second Justice Harlan is probably the most-often quoted on this point; he identified tradition as the source of values, specifically "the traditions from which [this country] developed as well as the traditions from which it broke." (*Poe v. Ullman*, 367 U.S. 497, 542 (1961) (Harlan J., dissenting)). A broader version of this argument is that values may be derived from "the entirety of our history," as it reveals "ideas in motion" and from which we extract "elements of experience and strains of thought that appear most relevant to our own time" (Terrance Sandalow, "Constitutional Interpretation," 79 MICH. L. REV. 1033, 1070–71 (1981)). The U.S. Supreme Court has apparently endorsed this broader version of values (at least for substantive due process purposes) in *Lawrence v. Texas*, 123 S.Ct. 2472 (2003) (see Chap. 11, Sec. C.3). There, in striking down a Texas sodomy statute, the Court majority focused on "our laws and traditions in the past half century" and the "emerging awareness" of liberty protections that these recent laws and traditions demonstrate (123 S.Ct. at 2480). Moreover, in a development of potentially great significance, the Court majority relied not only on this nation's recent laws and traditions but also those of other Western nations — specifically citing the European Convention on Human Rights, decisions of the European Court of Human Rights construing the Convention, and a report on homosexual offenses prepared for the British Parliament. *See generally* Charlene Smith & James Wilets, "Lessons from the Past and Strategies for the Future: Using Domestic,

International, and Comparative Law to Overturn Sodomy Laws," 24 Seattle U. L. Rev. 49, 51–52, 73–76 (2000).

When the evidence of a link between the value and the Constitution is weak, and especially when the claim is that the value source is unconnected to or external to the Constitution, the values approach generates controversy of major proportions. The crux of the controversy is whether, or to what extent, an interpreter may rely on "extraconstitutional values" that do not have roots in the Constitution's text, history, or structure, but instead are derived from external sources such as principles of morality. Commentators or judges who would rely on such extraconstitutional values have been (sometimes pejoratively) called "noninterpretivists" and their approach has been labeled "noninterpretivism." *See generally* Boris Bitker, "Interpreting the Constitution: Is the Intent of the Framers Controlling? If Not, What is?" 19 Harv. J. of Law and Pub. Policy 9, 41–51 (1995).

In the 1990's, noninterpretivism became a disfavored label, and this approach to values interpretation has been mostly replaced by a more restrained version called "supplementation." This version of values analysis is considered to be an interpretivist (rather than a noninterpretivist) approach. Under supplementation, interpreters may consult various high-order extraconstitutional values, but only to supplement values rooted in the Constitution and not to contradict or circumvent them. *See generally* David Crump, "How Do Courts *Really* Discover Unenumerated Fundamental Rights? Cataloguing the Methods of Judicial Alchemy," 19 Harv. J. of Law and Pub. Policy, 795, 829–837 (1996).

Competing arguments about the legitimate sources of values surround this interpretive concept of supplementation. The argument for rejecting this approach follows these lines: The only values that courts may uphold are those that the framers constitutionalized themselves. Courts cannot expand the framers' values or add new values never conceived by them. Thus any approach relying on values that are not rooted in the Constitution's text, original history, or structure is illegitimate. On the other hand, those supporting supplementation argue that the text of the Constitution itself anticipates the later development and refinement of values reflected in constitutional text, history, and structure, and perhaps even the identification of new values consistent with those reflected. The Ninth Amendment, for example, states that "the enumeration in the Constitution, of certain rights, shall not be construed to deny or disparage others retained by the people"—thus suggesting the existence of rights beyond those stated in the text. The Fourteenth Amendment provides that "[n]o state shall make or enforce any law which shall abridge the privileges or immunities of citizens of the United States," but does not state what those "privileges" and "immunities" are—thus suggesting that they are to be identified from sources beyond the Constitution. The Constitution's preamble lists the establishment of "justice" and the securing of "blessings of liberty" among the Constitution's goals—both appeals, it might be said, to broad enduring values to be developed by later interpreters.

Moreover, the language of many individual rights clauses—especially the clauses protecting freedom of speech and press, free exercise of religion, due process of law, equal protection of the laws, and freedom from cruel and unusual punishments—can be read to leave much developmental work to future generations. These so-called "open-textured" or "open-ended" clauses document values and *invite* later interpreters to develop them by making more refined value judgments over time in particular circumstances. (Thus these clauses might be termed "invitational clauses.") As one commentator has put the matter, the "Constitution is not stuffed but pregnant with meaning" (Charles P. Curtis, Lions Under the Throne (Houghton Mifflin Co. 1947)). It is thus left to interpreters to give birth to this meaning and to nurture it conscientiously over time.

The U.S. Supreme Court, from time to time, has also forthrightly acknowledged that the meaning of open-ended rights clauses is developed over time. Speaking of equal protection and due process, for example, the Court emphasized that:

> In determining what lines are unconstitutionally discriminatory we have never been confined to historic notions of equality, any more than we have restricted due process to a fixed catalogue of what was at a given time deemed to be the limits of fundamental rights. [*Harper v. Virginia Bd. of Elections*, 383 U.S. 663, 669 (1966), citing *Malloy v. Hogan*, 378 U.S. 1, 5–6 (1964).]

Addressing the cruel-and-unusual punishment clause, the Court remarked:

> [T]he Eighth Amendment's proscriptions are not limited to those practices condemned by the common law in 1789.... Not bound by the sparing humanitarian concessions of our forebears, the Amendment also recognizes the "evolving standards of decency that mark the progress of a maturing society." In addition to considering the barbarous methods generally outlawed in the 18th century, therefore, this Court takes into account objective evidence of contemporary values before determining whether a particular punishment comports with the fundamental human dignity that the Amendment protects. [*Ford v. Wainwright*, 477 U.S. 399, 406 (1986), quoting *Trop v. Dulles*, 356 U.S. 86, 101 (1958) (plurality opinion)); other citations omitted.]

Speaking of procedural due process, the Court has said:

> "Liberty" and "property" are broad and majestic terms. They are among the "[g]reat [constitutional] concepts... purposely left to gather meaning from experience.... [T]hey relate to the whole domain of social and economic fact, and the statesmen who founded this Nation knew too well that only a stagnant society remains unchanged. [*Board of Regents v. Roth*, 408 U.S. 564, 571 (1972), quoting *National Mutual Ins. Co. v. Tidewater Co.*, 337 U.S. 582, 646 (1949) (Frankfurter, J., dissenting).]

And speaking of substantive due process, in the *Lawrence v. Texas* case discussed above, the Court explained:

> In all events we think that our laws and traditions in the past half century are of most relevance here. These references show an emerging awareness that liberty gives substantial protection to adult persons in deciding how to conduct their private lives in matters pertaining to sex. "[H]istory and tradition are the starting point but not in all cases the ending point of the substantive due

process inquiry." *County of Sacramento v. Lewis*, 523 U.S. 833, 857 (1998) (Kennedy, J., concurring).

* * * *

Had those who drew and ratified the Due Process Clauses of the Fifth Amendment or the Fourteenth Amendment known the components of liberty in its manifold possibilities, they might have been more specific. They did not presume to have this insight. They knew times can blind us to certain truths and later generations can see that laws once thought necessary and proper in fact serve only to oppress. As the Constitution endures, persons in every generation can invoke its principles in their own search for greater freedom. [*Lawrence v. Texas*, 123 S.Ct. 2472, 2484 (2003).]

Aside from such theoretical arguments pro and con, there is also a very practical question about the values approach and its use in individual rights cases: Can individual rights under the Constitution, as we know them, be further supported and developed without resort to a values approach? The case of *Brown v. Board of Education*, above, is often used as the classic illustration. The result in this case, it is argued, is not evident from the text of the equal protection clause, the history of the clause's adoption, or the constitutional structure; instead, the Court developed the equality value by making a value judgment about racial segregation in public education—a judgment that did not depend upon the Fourteenth Amendment framers' intent about the Amendment's application to racially segregated schools. Similar arguments have been made to explain many of the Supreme Court's opinions on rights to privacy, gender discrimination, and freedom of speech and press. If these arguments are correct, then the absence of a values approach would make our future constitutional law much different from what it is today.

Sec. C. Exercise No. 7: Interpreting the Equal Protection Clause: *Brown v. Board of Education* (Racial Segregation in Public Schools)

In order to rule on the constitutionality of government policies sanctioning racial segregation in public schools and other public facilities, the U.S. Supreme Court has had to address complex issues concerning the interpretation of the Fourteenth Amendment's equal protection clause: "No state shall...deny to any person within its jurisdiction the equal protection of the laws." Two of the key cases are *Plessy v. Ferguson*, 163 U.S. 537 (1896), and *Brown v. Board of Education*, 347 U.S. 483 (1954), set out below. Although these cases focus specifically on equal protection, the insights to be drawn from them should apply as well to the interpretation of other individual rights clauses.

In examining the constitutionality of racial segregation in public facilities, *Plessy* and *Brown* employ quite different reasoning and reach quite different results. (For a basic analysis of the Court's opinion in *Brown*, see Chapter 3, Section E.) Paying particular attention to the *Brown* case, against the backdrop of *Plessy*, consider the questions that appear immediately after the cases. In considering the questions, it would be helpful to review Chapter 2, Section F. Following the questions are brief answers that will provide feedback for you on your analysis. You should consult these answers only after you have considered the questions.

PLESSY v. FERGUSON

Supreme Court of the United States
163 U.S. 537 (1896)

MR. JUSTICE BROWN, after stating the case, delivered the opinion of the court.

This case turns upon the constitutionality of an act of the General Assembly of the State of Louisiana, passed in 1890, providing for separate railway carriages for the white and colored races. Acts 1890, No. 111, p. 152.

The first section of the statute enacts "that all railway companies carrying passengers in their coaches in this State, shall provide equal but separate accommodations for the white, and colored races, by providing two or more passenger coaches for each passenger train, or by dividing the passenger coaches by a partition so as to secure separate accommodations. . . .

By the second section it was enacted "that the officers of such passenger trains shall have power and are hereby required to assign each passenger to the coach or compartment used for the race to which such passenger belongs; any passenger insisting on going into a coach or compartment to which by race he does not belong, shall be liable to a fine of twenty-five dollars, or in lieu thereof to imprisonment for a period of not more than twenty days in the parish prison. . . .

* * * *

The information filed in the criminal District Court charged in substance that Plessy, being a passenger between two stations within the State of Louisiana, was assigned by officers of the company to the coach used for the race to which he belonged, but he insisted upon going into a coach used by the race to which he did not belong. Neither in the information nor plea was his particular race or color averred.

The petition for the writ of prohibition averred that petitioner was seven-eighths Caucasian and one-eighth African blood; that the mixture of colored blood was not discernible in him, and that he was entitled to every right, privilege and immunity secured to citizens of the United States of the white race; and that, upon such theory, he took possession of a vacant seat in a coach where passengers of the white race were accommodated, and was ordered by the conductor to vacate said coach and take a seat in another assigned to persons of the colored race, and having refused to comply with such demand he was forcibly ejected with the aid of a police officer, and imprisoned in the parish jail to answer a charge of having violated the above act.

The constitutionality of this act is attacked upon the ground that it conflicts both with the Thirteenth Amendment of the Constitution, abolishing slavery, and the Fourteenth Amendment, which prohibits certain restrictive legislation on the part of the States. [Discussion of the Thirteenth Amendment is omitted.]

The object of the [fourteenth] amendment was undoubtedly to enforce the absolute equality of the two races before the law, but in the nature of things it could not have been intended to abolish distinctions based upon color, or to enforce social, as distinguished from political equality, or a commingling of the two races upon terms unsatisfactory to either. Laws permitting, and even requiring, their separation in places where they are liable to be brought into contact do not necessarily imply the inferiority of either race to the other, and have been generally, if not universally, recognized as within the competency of the state legislatures in the exercise of their police power. The most common instance of this is connected with the establishment of separate schools for white and colored children, which has been held to be a valid exercise of the legislative power even by courts of States where the political rights of the colored race have been longest and most earnestly enforced.

* * * *

The distinction between laws interfering with the political equality of the negro and those requiring the separation of the two races in schools, theaters and railway carriages has been frequently drawn by this court. Thus in *Strauder v. West Virginia*, 100 U.S. 303 (1879), it was held that a law of West Virginia limiting to white male persons, 21 years of age and citizens of the State, the right to sit upon juries, was a discrimination which implied a legal inferiority in civil society, which lessened the security of the right of the colored race, and was a step toward reducing them to a condition of servility.

* * * *

[I]t is . . . suggested by the learned counsel for the plaintiff in error that the same argument that will justify the state legislature in requiring railways to provide separate accommodations for the two races will also authorize them to require separate cars to be provided for people whose hair is of a certain color, or who are aliens, or who belong to certain nationalities, or to enact laws requiring colored people to walk upon one side of the street, and white people upon the other, or requiring white men's houses to be painted white, and colored men's black, or their vehicles or business signs to be of different colors, upon the theory that one side of the street is as good as the other, or that a house or vehicle of one color is as good as one of another color. The reply to all this is that every exercise of the police power must be reasonable, and extend only to such laws as are enacted in good faith for the promotion for the public good, and not for the annoyance or oppression of a particular class. Thus in *Yick Wo v. Hopkins*, 118 U.S. 356 (1886), it was held by this court that a municipal ordinance of the city of San Francisco, to regulate the carrying on the public laundries within the limits of the municipality, violated the provisions of the Constitution of the United States, if it conferred upon the municipal authorities arbitrary power, at their own will, and without regard to discretion, in the legal sense, of the term, to give or withhold consent as to persons or places, without regard to the competency of the persons applying, or the propriety of the places selected for the carrying on the business. It was held to be a covert attempt on the part of the municipality to make an arbitrary and unjust discrimination against the Chinese race....

So far, then, as a conflict with the Fourteenth Amendment is concerned, the case reduces itself to the question whether the statute of Louisiana is a reasonable regulation, and with respect to this there must necessarily be a large discretion on the part of the legislature. In determining the question of reasonableness it is at liberty to act with reference to the established usages, customs and traditions of the people, and with a view to the promotion of their comfort, and the preservation of the public peace and good order. Gauged by this standard, we cannot say that a law which authorizes or even requires the separation of the two races in public conveyances is unreasonable, or more obnoxious to the Fourteenth Amendment than the acts of Congress requiring separate schools for colored children in the District of Columbia, the constitutionality of which does not seem to have been questioned, or the corresponding acts of state legislatures.

We consider the underlying fallacy of the plaintiff's argument to consist in the assumption that the enforced separation of the two races stamps the colored race with a badge of inferiority. If this be so, it is not by reason of anything found in the act, but solely because the colored race chooses to put that construction upon it. The argument necessarily assumes that if, as has been more than once the case, and is not unlikely to be so again, the colored race should become the dominant power in the state legislature, and should enact a law in precisely similar terms, it would thereby relegate the white race to an inferior position. We imagine that the white race, at least, would not acquiesce in this assumption. The argument also assumes that social prejudices may be overcome by legislation, and that equal rights cannot be secured to the negro except by an enforced commingling of the two races. We cannot accept this proposition. If the two races are to meet upon terms of social equality, it must be the result of natural affinities, a mutual appreciation of each other's merits and a voluntary consent of individuals...." Legislation is powerless to eradicate racial instincts or to abolish distinctions based upon physical differences, and the attempt to do so can only result in accentuating the difficulties of the present situation. If the civil and political rights of both races be equal one cannot be inferior to the other civilly or politically. If one race be inferior to the other socially, the Constitution of the United States cannot put them upon the same plane.

* * * *

The judgment of the court below is, therefore,

Affirmed.

Mr. Justice Harlan dissenting.

* * * *

[The Thirteenth, Fourteenth, and Fifteenth Amendments] removed the race line from our governmental systems. They had, as this court has said, a common purpose, namely, to secure "to a race recently emancipated, a race that through many generations have been held in slavery, all the civil rights that the superior race enjoy." They declared, in legal effect, this court has further said, "that the law in the States shall be the same for the black as for the white; that all persons, whether colored or white, shall stand equal before the laws of the States, and, in regard to the colored race, for whose protection the amendment was primarily designed, that no discrimination shall be made against them by law because of their color." We also said: "The words of the amendment, it is true, are prohibitory, but they contain a necessary implication of a positive immunity, or right, most valuable to the colored race — the right to exemption from unfriendly legislation against them distinctively as colored — exemption from legal discriminations, implying inferiority in civil society, lessening the security of their enjoyment of the rights which others enjoy, and discriminations which are steps towards reducing them to the condition of a subject race." It was, consequently, adjudged that a state law that excluded citizens of the colored race from juries, because of their race and however well qualified in other respects to discharge the duties of jurymen, was repugnant to the Fourteenth Amendment. *Strauder v. West Virginia*, 100 U.S. 303, 306, 307 (1879)....

* * * *

It was said in argument that the statute of Louisiana does not discriminate against either race, but prescribes a rule applicable alike to white and colored citizens. But this argument does not meet the difficulty. Every one knows that the statute in question had its origin in the purpose, not so much to exclude white persons from railroad cars occupied by blacks, as to exclude colored people from coaches occupied by or assigned to white persons. Railroad corporations of Louisiana did not make discrimination among whites in the matter of accommodation for travellers. The thing to accomplish was, under the guise of giving equal accommodation for whites and blacks, to compel the latter to keep to themselves while traveling in railroad passenger coaches. No one would be so wanting in candor as to assert the contrary....

* * * *

The white race deems itself to be the dominant race in this country. And so it is, in prestige, in achievements, in education, in wealth and in power. So, I doubt not, it will continue to be for all time, if it remains true to its great heritage and holds fast to the principles of constitutional liberty. But in view of the Constitution, in the eye of the law, there is in this country no superior, dominant, ruling class of citizens. There is no caste here. Our Constitution is color-blind, and neither knows nor tolerates classes among citizens. In respect of civil rights, all citizens are equal before the law. The humblest is the peer of the most powerful. The law regards man as man, and takes no account of his surroundings or of his color when his civil rights as guaranteed by the supreme law of the land are involved. It is, therefore, to be regretted that this high tribunal, the final expositor of the fundamental law of the land, has reached the conclusion that it is competent for a State to regulate the enjoyment by citizens of their civil rights solely upon the basis of race.

In my opinion, the judgment this day rendered will, in time, prove to be quite as pernicious as the decision made by this tribunal in the *Dred Scott* case [60 U.S. (19

How.) 393 (1857)]. It was adjudged in that case that the descendants of Africans who were imported into this country and sold as slaves were not included nor intended to be included under the word "citizens" in the Constitution, and could not claim any of the rights and privileges which that instrument provided for and secured to citizens of the United States....

The destinies of the two races, in this country, are indissolubly linked together, and the interests of both require that the common government of all shall not permit the seeds of race hate to be planted under the sanction of law. What can more certainly arouse race hate, what more certainly create and perpetuate a feeling of distrust between these races, than state enactments, which, in fact, proceed on the ground that colored citizens are so inferior and degraded that they cannot be allowed to sit in public coaches occupied by white citizens? That, as all will admit, is the real meaning of such legislation as was enacted in Louisiana.

* * * *

If evils will result from the commingling of the two races upon public highways established for the benefit of all, they will be infinitely less than those that will surely come from state legislation regulating the enjoyment of civil rights upon the basis of race. We boast of the freedom enjoyed by our people above all other peoples. But it is difficult to reconcile that boast with a state of the law which, practically, puts the brand of servitude and degradation upon a large class of our fellow-citizens, our equals before the law. The thin disguise of "equal" accommodations for passengers in railroad coaches will not mislead any one, nor atone for the wrong this day done.

* * * *

For the reasons stated, I am constrained to withhold my assent from the opinion and judgment of the majority.

BROWN v. BOARD OF EDUCATION OF TOPEKA
Supreme Court of the United States
347 U.S. 483 (1954) *

MR. CHIEF JUSTICE WARREN delivered the opinion of the Court.

These cases come to us from the States of Kansas, South Carolina, Virginia, and Delaware. They are premised on different facts and different local conditions, but a common legal question justifies their consideration together in this consolidated opinion.

In each of the cases, minors of the Negro race, through their legal representatives, seek the aid of the courts in obtaining admission to the public schools of their community on a nonsegregated basis. In each instance, they had been denied admission to

---

* Some of the Court's footnotes are omitted. The footnotes that remain retain their original numbering.

schools attended by white children under laws requiring or permitting segregation according to race. This segregation was alleged to deprive the plaintiffs of the equal protection of the laws under the Fourteenth Amendment. In each of the cases other than the Delaware case, a three-judge federal district court denied relief to the plaintiffs on the so-called "separate but equal" doctrine announced by this Court in *Plessy v. Ferguson*, 163 U.S. 537. Under that doctrine, equality of treatment is accorded when the races are provided substantially equal facilities, even though these facilities be separate. In the Delaware case, the Supreme Court of Delaware adhered to that doctrine, but ordered that the plaintiffs be admitted to the white schools because of their superiority to the Negro schools.

The plaintiffs contend that segregated public schools are not "equal" and cannot be made "equal," and that hence they are deprived of the equal protection of the laws. Because of the obvious importance of the question presented, the Court took jurisdiction. Argument was heard in the 1952 Term, and reargument was heard this Term on certain questions propounded by the Court.

Reargument was largely devoted to the circumstances surrounding the adoption of the Fourteenth Amendment in 1868. It covered exhaustively consideration of the Amendment in Congress, ratification by the states, then existing practices in racial segregation, and the views of proponents and opponents of the Amendment. This discussion and our own investigation convince us that, although these sources cast some light, it is not enough to resolve the problem with which we are faced. At best, they are inconclusive. The most avid proponents of the post-War Amendments undoubtedly intended them to remove all legal distinctions among "all persons born or naturalized in the United States." Their opponents, just as certainly, were antagonistic to both the letter and the spirit of the Amendments and wished them to have the most limited effect. What others in Congress and the state legislatures had in mind cannot be determined with any degree of certainty.

An additional reason for the inconclusive nature of the Amendment's history, with respect to segregated schools, is the status of public education at that time.[4] In the

---

4. For a general study of the development of public education prior to the Amendment, see Butts and Cremin, A History of Education in American Culture (1953), Pts. I, II; Cubberley, Public Education in the United States (1934 ed.), cc. II–XII. School practices current at the time of the adoption of the Fourteenth Amendment are described in Butts and Cremin, supra, at 269–275; Cubberley, supra, at 288–339, 408–431; Knight, Public Education in the South (1922), cc. VIII, IX. See also H. Ex. Doc. No. 315, 41st Cong., 2d Sess. (1871). Although the demand for free public schools followed substantially the same pattern in both the North and the South, the development in the South did not begin to gain momentum until about 1850, some twenty years after that in the North. The reasons for the somewhat slower development in the South (e.g., the rural character of the South and the different regional attitudes toward state assistance) are well explained in Cubberley, supra, at 408–423. In the country as a whole, but particularly in the South, the War virtually stopped all progress in public education. Id., at 427–428. The low status of Negro education in all sections of the country, both before and immediately after the War, is described in Beale, A History of Freedom of Teaching in American Schools (1941), 112–132, 175–195. Compulsory school attendance laws were not generally adopted until after

South, the movement toward free common schools, supported by general taxation, had not yet taken hold. Education of white children was largely in the hands of private groups. Education of Negroes was almost nonexistent, and practically all of the race were illiterate. In fact, any education of Negroes was forbidden by law in some states. Today, in contrast, many Negroes have achieved outstanding success in the arts and sciences as well as in the business and professional world. It is true that public school education at the time of the Amendment had advanced further in the North, but the effect of the Amendment on Northern States was generally ignored in the congressional debates. Even in the North, the conditions of public education did not approximate those existing today. The curriculum was usually rudimentary; ungraded schools were common in rural areas; the school term was but three months a year in many states; and compulsory school attendance was virtually unknown. As a consequence, it is not surprising that there should be so little in the history of the Fourteenth Amendment relating to its intended effect on public education.

In the first cases in this Court construing the Fourteenth Amendment, decided shortly after its adoption, the Court interpreted it as proscribing all state-imposed discriminations against the Negro race.[5] The doctrine of "separate but equal" did not make its appearance in this Court until 1896 in the case of *Plessy v. Ferguson*, supra, involving not education but transportation. American courts have since labored with the doctrine for over half a century. In this Court, there have been six cases involving the "separate but equal" doctrine in the field of public education. In *Cumming v. County Board of Education*, 175 U.S. 528 (1899), and *Gong Lum v. Rice*, 275 U.S. 78 (1927), the validity of the doctrine itself was not challenged. In more recent cases, all on the graduate school level, inequality was found in that specific benefits enjoyed by white students were denied to Negro students of the same educational qualifications. *Missouri ex rel. Gaines v. Canada*, 305 U.S. 337 (1938); *Sipuel v. Oklahoma*, 332 U.S. 631(1948); *Sweatt v. Painter*, 339 U.S. 629 (1950); *McLaurin v. Oklahoma State Regents*, 339 U.S. 637 (1950). In none of these cases was it necessary to re-examine the doctrine to grant relief to the Negro plaintiff. And in *Sweatt v. Painter*, supra, the Court expressly reserved decision on the question whether *Plessy v. Ferguson* should be held inapplicable to public education.

In approaching this problem, we cannot turn the clock back to 1868 when the Amendment was adopted, or even to 1896 when *Plessy v. Ferguson* was written. We must consider public education in the light of its full development and its present place in American life throughout the Nation. Only in this way can it be determined if segregation in public schools deprives these plaintiffs of the equal protection of the laws.

Today, education is perhaps the most important function of state and local governments. Compulsory school attendance laws and the great expenditures for education both demonstrate our recognition of the importance of education to our democratic society. It is required in the performance of our most basic public responsibilities, even

---

the ratification of the Fourteenth Amendment, and it was not until 1918 that such laws were in force in all the states. Cubberley, supra, at 563–565.

5. *Slaughter-House Cases*, 83 U.S. (16 Wall.) 36, 67–72 (1872); *Strauder v. West Virginia*, 100 U.S. 303, 307–308 (1879).

service in the armed forces. It is the very foundation of good citizenship. Today it is a principal instrument in awakening the child to cultural values, in preparing him for later professional training, and in helping him to adjust normally to his environment. In these days, it is doubtful that any child may reasonably be expected to succeed in life if he is denied the opportunity of an education. Such an opportunity, where the state has undertaken to provide it, is a right which must be made available to all on equal terms.

We come then to the question presented: Does segregation of children in public schools solely on the basis of race, even though the physical facilities and other "tangible" factors may be equal, deprive the children of the minority group of equal educational opportunities? We believe that it does.

In *Sweatt v. Painter*, supra, in finding that a segregated law school for Negroes could not provide them equal educational opportunities, this Court relied in large part on "those qualities which are incapable of objective measurement but which make for greatness in a law school." In *McLaurin v. Oklahoma State Regents*, supra, the Court, in requiring that a Negro admitted to a white graduate school be treated like all other students, again resorted to intangible considerations: "...his ability to study, to engage in discussions and exchange views with other students, and, in general, to learn his profession." Such considerations apply with added force to children in grade and high schools. To separate them from others of similar age and qualifications solely because of their race generates a feeling of inferiority as to their status in the community that may affect their hearts and minds in a way unlikely ever to be undone. The effect of this separation on their educational opportunities was well stated by a finding in the Kansas case by a court which nevertheless felt compelled to rule against the Negro plaintiffs:

> Segregation of white and colored children in public schools has a detrimental effect upon the colored children. The impact is greater when it has the sanction of the law; for the policy of separating the races is usually interpreted as denoting the inferiority of the negro group. A sense of inferiority affects the motivation of a child to learn. Segregation with the sanction of law, therefore, has a tendency to [retard] the educational and mental development of negro children and to deprive them of some of the benefits they would receive in a [racially] integrated school system.[10]

Whatever may have been the extent of psychological knowledge at the time of *Plessy v. Ferguson*, this finding is amply supported by modern authority.[11] Any language in *Plessy v. Ferguson* [163 U.S. 537 (1896)] contrary to this finding is rejected.

---

10. A similar finding was made in the Delaware case: "I conclude from the testimony that in our Delaware society, State-imposed segregation in education itself results in the Negro children, as a class, receiving educational opportunities which are substantially inferior to those available to white children otherwise similarly situated." 87 A. 2d 862, 865.

11. K.B. Clark, Effect of Prejudice and Discrimination on Personality Development (Midcentury White House Conference on Children and Youth, 1950); Witmer and Kotinsky, Personality in the Making (1952), c. VI; Deutscher and Chein, The Psychological Effects of Enforced

We conclude that in the field of public education the doctrine of "separate but equal" has no place. Separate educational facilities are inherently unequal. Therefore, we hold that the plaintiffs and others similarly situated for whom the actions have been brought are, by reason of the segregation complained of, deprived of the equal protection of the laws guaranteed by the Fourteenth Amendment....

It is so ordered.

Questions

QUES. 1. The Court in *Brown* crafted this statement of the question before it: "Does segregation of children in public schools solely on the basis of race, even though the physical facilities and other 'tangible' factors may be equal, deprive the children of the minority groups of equal educational opportunities?" At the end of its opinion, the Court answered its question: "We conclude that in the field of public education the doctrine of 'separate but equal' has no place. Separate educational facilities are inherently unequal. Therefore, we hold that the plaintiffs... are, by reason of the segregation complained of, deprived of... equal protection of the laws." What "analytical pathway" did the Court take in moving from the question to the answer, and what legal support did it have for each step on this pathway? To what extent did the Court rely on precedent? To what extent did the Court rely on the text of the equal protection clause (textual interpretation; see Chap. 2, Sec. F.4)? To what extent did the Court rely on the original history of the equal protection clause and the Fourteenth Amendment (historical interpretation; see Chap. 4, Sec. C.2)? To what extent did the Court rely on structural inferences (structural interpretation; see Chap. 4, Sec. C.3)? To what extent did the Court rely on the constitutional values (values interpretation; see Sec. B.2 above)?

QUES. 2. According to the Court, what is the basis for the constitutional principle or norm that it developed in *Brown* (that is, the "separate is unequal" principle)? Is this principle or norm derivable from prior judicial precedents, the text of the equal protection clause, the original history of the Fourteenth Amendment, structural inferences, or values embedded in the Constitution? Or does the principle derive from current sociological knowledge, from public policy analysis, from popular political or social consensus, or from the personal predictions of the Justices?

QUES. 3. Suppose the original history of the equal protection clause had been clear and that this history indicated that the framers accepted the practice of racially segregated public education and did not intend to affect that practice by passage of the Fourteenth Amendment. In light of such historical evidence, would there have been any principled basis upon which the Court could nevertheless have reached the same result in *Brown*?

Segregation: A Survey of Social Science Opinion, 26 J. Psychol. 259 (1948); Chein, What are the Psychological Effects of Segregation Under Conditions of Equal Facilities?, 3 Int. J. Opinion and Attitude Res. 229 (1949); Brameld, Educational Costs, in Discrimination and National Welfare (MacIver, ed., 1949), 44–48; Frazier, The Negro in the United States (1949), 674–681. And see generally Myrdal, An American Dilemma (1944).

QUES. 4. Suppose the social science evidence submitted in the *Brown* case (see especially the Court's famous footnote 11) had been unavailable, or the available evidence had been inconclusive concerning the educational harms to minority school children that resulted from state-mandated segregation. Without sociological evidence such as that in footnote 11, is there any principled way in which the Court could nevertheless have reached the same result in *Brown*? Would the reasoning in Justice Harlan's dissent in *Plessy* have been of help?

Answers

ANS. to QUES. 1. In getting from the question to the answer, the Court used reasoning that is very different from the majority's reasoning in *Plessy* and even different from Justice Harlan's dissent in *Plessy*. The Court in *Brown* focused on the differences between white children's and minority children's educational experiences, the inequality that arose from these differences, and the educational harm that minority children suffered as a result of these differences. It is not clear, however, what legal support the Court had for some of the steps in its reasoning, particularly its points that racially separate schools are always unequal and that such "inherent" inequalities violate the equal protection clause.

Clearly the Court relied on precedent, its two recent rulings involving racial segregation in higher education (*Sweatt v. Painter*, 339 U.S. 629 (1950), and *McLaurin v. Oklahoma State Regents*, 339 U.S. 637 (1950)) being the most important. But neither case held that all racially separate facilities are unconstitutional, and neither case rejected the separate-but-equal doctrine. The Court also relied to some extent on the text of the equal protection clause, since that clause provided the focus on equality that was central to the case. But the text itself clearly did not provide an answer to the specific question posed. As for the original history of the Fourteenth Amendment, the Court expressly declined to rely on it, saying that this history is "inconclusive." There is thus a concern—actively debated in the aftermath of *Brown* and still debated today—about the adequacy of the Court's legal support for its reasoning and conclusion. Commentators over time have suggested that "values" derived from the Constitution provided the legal support for the decision (see Sec. B.2 above). As one commentator has reasoned:

> In *Brown*, the Court was dealing with state laws imposed by a dominant white majority on a politically powerless racial minority. The issue was whether such laws, explicitly classifying people by their race, could be squared with the fundamental values embodied in the Constitution. [William L. Taylor, "A Lawyer Looks at Social Science in the Courts," *Clearinghouse for Civil Rights Research*, p.3 (v. VII, nos. 3–4, Autumn/Winter 1979) (available at the Library of Congress in the Center for Nat'l Policy Review collection).]

Mr. Justice Harlan's dissent in *Plessy* also provides some interesting perspective on the values at stake in racial segregation cases and their constitutional basis.

ANS. to QUES. 2. If the separate-is-unequal principle of *Brown* had been based on current sociological knowledge, wouldn't the principle have to be reconsidered and perhaps revised whenever there was a change in sociological knowledge? If the principle had been based on public policy analysis or popular political or social consensus, wouldn't the Court be acting as a pure policymaker or a legislature rather than as an expounder of law? If the principle had been based on the Justices' personal predilections, wouldn't the opinion lack any basis in law and therefore have no legitimacy? If none of these sources could legitimize the *Brown* principle, then we are led back to a consideration of precedent, text, history, structure, and values, as in Ques. 1 above. And if precedent, text, history, and structure do not suitably support the Court's reasoning, as suggested in the answer to Question 1, then we are left with the suggestion that values, perhaps moral values (see Ans. to Ques. 4) may be the basis of the *Brown* principle. But then the question would be whether these are *constitutional* values that emerge from the Constitution, or instead are extra-constitutional values that arise from some other source (see Sec. B.3 above). For a justification of the *Brown* decision based on a revisionist view of original history, see Michael McConnell, "Originalsim and the Desegregation Decisions," 81 VA. L. REV. 947 (1995). For a justification of the *Brown* decision based on an equality value (a "quest for equality") written into the text of the Fourteenth Amendment and reflected in its original history, see Robert Bork, THE TEMPTING OF AMERICA: THE POLITICAL SEDUCTION OF THE LAW, 82–83 (The Free Press, 1990). For a justification of *Brown* based on a broader development of constitutional values or norms, see Michael Perry, WE THE PEOPLE: THE FOURTEENTH AMENDMENT AND THE SUPREME COURT 91–94 (Oxford Univ. Press, 1999).

Another possible interpretive approach would be a structural type of justification based on the "representation-reinforcing" theory of John Hart Ely; *see* Ely, DEMOCRACY AND DISTRUST: A THEORY OF JUDICIAL REVIEW (Harvard U. Press, 1980). Ely asserts that, in a representative democracy, the courts should intervene to invalidate certain decisions of the elected representatives when "the *process* is undeserving of trust" because, *inter alia*, "representatives beholden to an effective majority are systematically disadvantaging some minority out of simple hostility or a prejudiced refusal to recognize commonalities of interest, and thereby denying that minority the protection afforded other groups by a representative system" (*Id.* at 103; *see generally Id.* at 145–170).

This argument, if applied to *Brown*, would suggest that judicial intervention in *Brown* was justified because the representative process was being perverted in the states and local school districts before the Court; since the minority parents and children therefore could not protect their interests in the political process, they deserved judicial protection that would counter-act the political system's flaws. The conditions of racial segregation in education in the defendant school districts, in other words, violated the representation-reinforcing principle—a principle implicit in the constitutional structure and thus providing the basis for a structural approach to the *Brown* problem. (Alternatively, one might also characterize representation reinforcement as a constitutional *value*—a "process value"—that supports another type of *values* approach to the *Brown* problem; *see generally* Ely at 75 (asterisk footnote).)

ANS. to QUES. 3: One basic argument for departing from the original historical understanding would be that the framers did not intend for later generations to be bound for all time by the framers' specific original intentions. The purposefully vague and general, or open-ended, language of the equal protection clause could itself be evidence to support this proposition. Thus, later interpreters could depart from the specifics of the original history if contemporary facts and circumstances regarding segregation were very different from those prevailing at the time of the Fourteenth Amendment's adoption. (Note that the *Brown* Court does rely in part on such a changed circumstances argument.)

ANS. to QUES. 4: The basic consideration here is whether the social science data on educational harms is necessary to the reasoning and result in *Brown*. If it is — that is, if the *Brown* holding is dependent upon the existence of this particular type of "constitutional" or "legislative" fact (see Chap. 15, Sec. C.3) — then *Brown* presumably could be challenged or distinguished whenever different social science data were introduced in evidence or different fact findings about the effects of segregation were made by a court. That does not appear to be what the *Brown* Court intended, nor is it the way that *Brown* has been understood and applied. *See Stell v. Savannah-Chatham Board of Education*, 333 F.2d 55, 61 (5th Cir. 1964). Many commentators argue that the social science data were not central to the *Brown* holding itself but rather added weight and persuasiveness to the opinion that presumably would promote public acceptance. For example, one civil rights attorney stated the argument this way:

> Most civil rights lawyers (this one included) contend...that the *Brown* decision did not rest on the social science authority cited in footnote 11. Rather, we believe that the basis of *Brown* was the fundamental moral judgment made in the Fourteenth Amendment — that black people had a right "to exemption from unfriendly legislation" (*Strauder v. West Virginia*, 100 U.S. 303, 307–308 (1879)) directed against them because of their race, that racial classifications in this society can be upheld only if they meet the heaviest burden of justification. Social science authority was cited by the Court only to add weight to the decision — to persuade people that it was important for the Court to take this difficult step because the lives of children were being damaged by segregation laws. [William Taylor, "A Lawyer Looks at Social Science in the Courts," *supra* (Ans. to Ques. 1).]

Under this view, the same result could have been reached in *Brown*, even without the social science data cited by the Court, by relying on an infringement of an equality value embodied in the Constitution. The Court in 1954 understood this value very differently than did the Court majority in 1896 in *Plessy* — but not very differently than the first Justice Harlan did in his *Plessy* dissent.

Sec. D. The State Action Doctrine

D.1. Origins of the State Action Doctrine

It has long been accepted that the provisions of the Bill of Rights limit only the federal government and do not reach private (non-governmental) action. (See, *e.g., Barron v. Baltimore*, Section B above, under **1833**.) The provisions of the Fourteenth Amendment, and other rights amendments, are subject to a comparable understanding: they limit only state governments and their local governments, and do not limit private actors. This understanding arises from the text of the amendments themselves.[3] The Fourteenth Amendment, for example, provides that "No State shall" abridge privileges and immunities, "nor shall any State" deprive persons of due process or deny equal protection.

The U.S. Supreme Court confirmed this construction of the Fourteenth Amendment in the *Civil Rights Cases*, 109 U.S. 3 (1883). In the Reconstruction era, Congress had enacted a public accommodations law, the Civil Rights Act of 1875, providing that all "inns, public conveyances on land and water, theatres, and other places of public amusement" must be open "alike to citizens of every race and color, regardless of any previous condition of servitude." The Act's constitutionality was challenged on grounds that the Fourteenth Amendment limits only the states; that Congress could therefore enforce the Amendment only against the states; and that inns and other such places of public accommodation were private, not public or state, entities. The Court agreed with this argument and invalidated the Act because it regulated private activity rather than "State action." The Fourteenth Amendment prohibits the states from violating certain individual rights, said the Court; but "[i]ndividual invasion of individual rights is not the subject matter of the amendment," "[I]t is *State action* of a particular character" that is prohibited; Thus, "civil rights, such as are guaranteed by the Constitution against State aggression, cannot be impaired by the wrongful acts of individuals, *unsupported by State authority in the shape of laws, customs, or judicial or executive proceedings*" (109 U.S. at 11,17 (emphasis added)). The *Civil Rights Cases* continue to be cited as the source of the modern "state action" doctrine.

D.2. Purpose and Role of the State Action Doctrine

Often the presence of state action (or "federal action," in the case of the Bill of Rights' application to the federal government) will be obvious. When the state implements and enforces a criminal statute, for instance, it is clear that the state is the source of any resulting restriction on the rights of convicted persons, and that such persons may raise constitutional rights in their defense. On the other hand, it is often clear that state action does not exist. When a four-man card club that meets in the private home of a member declines to accept a woman into the club, the refusal is not itself state action, and the woman cannot claim that the club's refusal violates her constitutional rights. But between these two poles, there is a murky and shifting middle ground where the presence or absence of state action is often debatable. The courts then must play a difficult but critical role of separating "state" or "government" from private entities, thus drawing conceptual lines that differentiate the "public" sector from the "private" sector in American life. In these middle-ground cases, state action becomes a kind of threshold issue; one cannot confidently proceed to determine whether constitutional

---

3. The exception is the Thirteenth Amendment, which is stated as a general prohibition on slavery and thus limits private actors as well as the federal and state governments. *See The Civil Rights Cases*, 109 U.S. 3, 20–22 (1883).

rights have been violated until one has determined that state action requirements have been met.

Conceptually, therefore, state action issues (when they arise) can be related to the merits of individual rights issues by this two-step inquiry: (1) Does the challenged activity constitute state action? (2) If so, does this state action violate some particular individual rights clause of the Constitution? In *Edmonson v. Leesville Concrete Co.*, 500 U.S. 614 (1991), for example, the petitioner challenged the respondent's use of peremptory challenges to strike black persons from a prospective civil jury. The Supreme Court first considered whether use of peremptory strikes by a private litigant in civil litigation constituted state action; answering this question in the affirmative, the Court then considered (and remanded to the lower court) the question whether the litigant's strikes constituted race-based exclusions violative of equal protection. In other cases, however, the state action inquiry and the merits inquiry sometimes overlap or may not be clearly differentiated from one another by the court. In *Shelley v. Kraemer*, 334 U.S. (1948), for example, the Court merged its analysis of whether judicial enforcement of racially restrictive covenants constitutes state action with its analysis of whether these covenants, as enforced, violate the equal protection clause.

When courts address the state action inquiry, as the first step of a two-step inquiry, they focus on whether ostensibly private action is so related to or intertwined with the activities of government that the private action, or the government's particular involvement in it, will be subject to the constraints of the Constitution's individual rights guarantees. *Moose Lodge No. 107 v. Irvis*, 407 U.S. 163 (1972), provides an instructive example.

The Supreme Moose Lodge, a national fraternal organization, had a constitution which provided that: "The membership of the lodges shall be composed of male persons of the Caucasian or White race above the age of twenty-one years, and not married to someone of other than the Caucasian or White race, who are of good moral character, physically and mentally normal, who shall profess a belief in a Supreme Being" (from *Irvis v. Scott*, 318 F. Supp. 1246, 1247 (M.D. Pa. 1970). Acting pursuant to this provision, the Harrisburg, Pennsylvania lodge restricted membership to Caucasians and forbade members from bringing non-white guests onto the lodge premises. A member of the lodge nevertheless invited Mr. Irvis, an African-American, to the lodge for food and drink. After Mr. Irvis was denied service, he sued the Lodge for race discrimination violating the Fourteenth Amendment's equal protection clause.

Moose Lodge argued that the Fourteenth Amendment had no application to its discriminatory practices because it was a private entity. Irvis countered that the requisite state action was triggered by Pennsylvania's application of its pervasive liquor regulations to the lodge. As the holder of a liquor license, Irvis noted, the lodge acquiesced to many intrusions of the state. For example, "an applicant for a club license must make such physical alterations in its premises as the board may require, must file a list of the names and addressees of its members and employees, and must keep extensive financial records. The board is granted the right to inspect the licensed premises at any time when patrons, guests, or members are present" (*Moose Lodge, supra*, 407 U.S. at 176). In addition, the state limited the number of licenses that any municipality may have;

and since the Harrisburg quota had been filled for many years, the Lodge's license was a substantial state benefit. In a 6 to 3 decision, however, the U.S. Supreme Court held that the Pennsylvania regulatory scheme for liquor licensing did not involve the lodge in state action. The Court acknowledged the difficult and fact dependent nature of the analysis: "While the principle is easily stated, the question of whether particular discriminatory conduct is private, on the one hand, or amounts to 'state action,' on the other hand, frequently admits of no easy answer. 'Only by sifting facts and weighing circumstances can the non-obvious involvement of the State in private conduct be attributed its true significance" (*Id.* at 172, quoting *Burton v. Wilmington Parking Authority*, 365 U.S. 715, 722 (1961)). Examining the relationship between the lodge and the state, the Court determined that the state had not involved itself in the lodge's discriminatory practices: "Our holdings indicate that where the impetus for the discrimination is private, the State must have 'significantly involved itself with invidious discriminations'" (*Id.* at 173, quoting *Reitman v. Mulkey*, 387 U.S. 369, 380 (1967)).

Regarding the Pennsylvania liquor control regulations, the Court did not find any nexus or connection between these regulations and the race discrimination. "[T]he Pennsylvania Liquor Control Board plays absolutely no part in establishing or enforcing the membership or guest policies of the clubs that it licenses to serve liquor...." "However detailed this type of regulation may be in some particulars, it cannot be said to in any way foster or encourage racial discrimination" (*Id.* at 175–76). Although the liquor license undoubtedly benefited the lodge, the mere receipt of benefits or services from the State does not give rise to state action. "Since state-furnished services include such necessities of life as electricity, water, and police and fire protection, such a holding would utterly emasculate the distinction between private as distinguished from state conduct...." (*Id.* at 173). The Court contrasted Moose Lodge's situation to the situation of restaurants in the South that had been prosecuted under trespass laws after they had refused service to African-Americans "sitting-in" at the restaurant to protest segregation. (*See Peterson v. City of Greenville*, 373 U.S. 244 (1963).) In those cases, said the Court, there was a nexus between discrimination and the State: "[A]lthough the ostensible initiative for the trespass prosecution came from the proprietor, the existence of a local ordinance requiring segregation of races in such places was tantamount to the State having 'commanded a particular result'" (*Moose Lodge, supra*, 407 U.S. at 173).

The Court in *Moose Lodge* also looked at the overall relationship between the lodge and the state, asking whether they were sufficiently involved with one another — aside from the race discrimination itself — that state action would exist for that reason. In this inquiry, the Court was guided by *Burton v. Wilmington Parking Authority*, above, a case in which the Court determined that the racial discrimination of a restaurant located in a state-owned parking facility did constitute state action. The "symbiotic" qualities of the relationship between the restaurant and the state were manifest: the land and building where the restaurant was located were publicly owned; the building was dedicated to public uses; upkeep and maintenance of the building were the responsibilities of the State; the convenient state-provided parking facilitated the restaurant's business, while the restaurant business provided customers for the state's parking facility; and the restaurant rent payments helped the state to cover its operating expenses for the parking facility. Thus the restaurant's situation was different from Moose Lodge's situation:

> Here there is nothing approaching the symbiotic relationship between lessor and lessee that was present in *Burton*.... Unlike Burton, the Moose Lodge building is located on land owned by it, not by any public authority. Far from apparently holding itself out as a place of public accommodation, Moose Lodge quite ostentatiously proclaims the fact that it is not open to the public at large. Nor is it located and operated in such surroundings that although private in name, it discharges a function or performs a service that would otherwise in all likelihood be performed by the State. In short, while [the restaurant in *Burton*] was a public restaurant in a public building, Moose Lodge is a private social club in a private building. [407 U.S. at 175.]

D.3. Techniques for Analyzing State Action Problems

As the *Moose Lodge* case (Sec. D.2 above) suggests, the courts have developed various techniques, or approaches, for resolving state action questions. Commentators, and the courts themselves, have organized and labelled these approaches, and their underlying concepts, in various ways. The following outline organizes the approaches to state action in a way that parallels the language and distinctions usually employed by the courts and is consistent with the usages of most commentators:

I.   *The "State Involvement" or "Governmental Contacts" Approach*

    A.   *The "nexus" approach*

    B.   *The "symbiotic relationship" or "joint venturer" approach*

    C.   *The "entwinement" approach*

II. *The "Public Function" Approach*

The nexus approach (I.A.) focuses on the state's involvement in the particular action that is said to violate constitutional rights. The relevant inquiry, explicitly set forth in *Jackson v. Metropolitan Edison Co.*, 419 U.S. 345, 351 (1974), is "whether there is a sufficiently close nexus between the State and the challenged action of the regulated entity so that the action of the later may be fairly treated as that of the State itself." In *Moose Lodge*, the challenged action was the racial discrimination against guests, and the Court therefore focused on the state's involvement in that particular action of the lodge. The Court in *Moose Lodge* made clear that a nexus would exist, and state action would be found, if the state had "fostered or encouraged" the allegedly unconstitutional action. Other cases make clear that state action would also be found if the state has coerced or compelled the challenged action. *See, e.g.*, *Blum v. Yaretsky*, 457 U.S. 991, 1004 (1982).

The symbiotic relationship approach (I.B.) has a broader focus than the nexus approach; it looks to the full range of the relationships between the State and the private entity, rather than only the State's involvement in the particular private action being challenged. *Burton v. Wilmington Parking Authority*, discussed above, is the foundational case for the symbiotic relationship approach. The *Moose Lodge* case also utilized this approach when it distinguished Moose Lodge from the restaurant in the *Burton* case. With symbiotic relationship analysis, the focus is on the interdependency between the State and the private entity. The court looks for "benefits mutually conferred" between the State and the private entity. More broadly, a court will ask whether the state has "place[d] its power, property, and prestige" behind the unconstitutional action; and whether "[t]he State has so far insinuated itself into a position of interdependence with [the private entity] that it must be recognized as a joint participant in the challenged activity...." (*Burton*, 365 U.S. at 725). It is not sufficient for purposes of this approach that the private entity is "extensively regulated" by the state (*Blum v. Yaretsky*, 457 U.S. 991, 1011 (1982)), nor is it sufficient that the private entity is funded predominantly with governmental funds (*Rendell-Baker v. Kohn*, 457 U.S. 830, 840 (1982)). If the overall relationship between the State and the private entity involves more than either regulation or funding, and is symbiotic or interdependent within the meaning of *Burton*, state action will be found; it does not matter whether the state was involved in the particular action that is alleged to be unconstitutional.

The entwinement approach (I.C.) is the newest strand of the state action doctrine. It focuses, like the symbiotic relationship approach, on the overall relationship between the State and the private entity. Particular emphasis is apparently given, however, to the state's involvement in the *management* of the private entity. This approach arises from the case of *Brentwood Academy v. Tennessee Secondary School Athletic Association*, 531 U.S. 288 (2001), where the Court considered whether an interscholastic athletic association that regulated high school sports statewide was engaged in state action when it enforced its rules against its member schools. The plaintiff was a private parochial school and Association member that had been put on probation for violating Association rules on student-athlete recruitment. The defendant Association regulated both public school and private school athletic competitions, and both public and private schools were Association members. The public schools comprised 84% of the voting membership. State Board of Education members also sat ex officio on the Association's governing boards. The Court indicated that: "We have treated a nominally private entity as a state actor...when it is 'entwined with governmental policies' or when government is 'entwined in [its] management or control'" (531 U.S. at 296, quoting *Evans v. Newton*, 382 U.S. 296, 299, 301 (1966)). Following this approach, the Court majority, by a 5 to 4 vote, found state action because "[t]he nominally private character of the Association is overborne by the pervasive entwinement of public institutions and public officials in its composition and workings...." (531 U.S. at 298).

The entwinement identified by the Court was of two types: "entwinement...from the bottom up" and "entwinement from the top down" (531 U.S. at 300). The former concerned the relationship between the public school members of the Association (the bottom) and the Association itself; the latter concerned the relationship between the State Board of Education (the top) and the Association. Regarding "entwinement... up," said the Court, the Association is "overwhelmingly composed of public school officials who select representatives..., who in turn adopt and enforce the rules that make the system work" (531 U.S. at 299). As for "entwinement…down," State Board of Education members "are assigned ex officio to serve as members" of the Association's two governing boards; and in addition, the Association's paid employees "are treated as state employees to the extent of being eligible for membership in the state retirement system" (531 U.S. at 300). Based on these considerations, the Court majority concluded that entwinement "to the degree shown here" requires that the Association be "charged with a public character" as a state actor, and that its adoption and enforcement of athletics rules be "judged by constitutional standards" (531 U.S. at 302).

It is not clear whether the entwinement theory is a substitute for the symbiotic relationship approach, which has been seldom used in recent years, or whether there is some principled distinction between these two approaches. It is possible that the entwinement approach is limited to a focus on the governing structure and membership of the private entity, and the participation of state officials in that structure or the effectuation of state policies through that structure, rather than focusing on all facets of the relationship between state and private entity as the symbiotic relationship approach does. But the court in *Brentwood Academy* does not address the applicability of the *Burton* case, so the relationship between the symbiotic relationship approach and the new entwinement approach remains unclear. Rather than referencing *Burton*, the Court in *Brentwood Academy* argued that its entwinement approach came from the earlier case of *Evans v. Newton* (above); the four dissenters, however (and some commentators), doubt this assessment and consider entwinement to be a new and unfounded approach.

The public function approach (II in the outline above) is different from the other three approaches in that it focuses as much on the particular function performed by the private entity as on the relationship between the private entity and the state. If the function is sufficiently public and governmental, then the performance of that function will be considered to be state action. The Court used this approach to find state action in two cases from the 1940s. In *Marsh v. Alabama*, 326 U.S. 501 (1946), the Court held that a private ship building corporation was engaged in state action when it operated a "company town" where its employees lived. Since the company town was indistinguishable in its functions from public towns operated by local governments, the operation of the town was a public function. In *Smith v. Allwright*, 321 U.S. 649 (1944), the Court held that a private political party was engaged in a "state function" delegated to it by the state when it held its own primary election and excluded black candidates from the process. Since these early cases, the U.S. Supreme Court has seldom relied upon the public function doctrine as the basis for a state action finding, and the approach is thus less used in the lower courts than the other approaches listed above. This diminished use and significance has occurred because the Court has narrowed the definition of public function so much that it is extremely difficult to find any activity of a private entity that would meet the test. It is not enough that the private entity provides services to the public, even if the services are essential. In *Jackson v. Metropolitan Edison Co.*, above, the Court refused to find that a public utility company providing essential electric services was performing a public function. Under *Jackson*, only a function that is "traditionally exclusively reserved to the State [and] traditionally associated with sovereignty" (419 U.S. at 352–353) can be considered a public function.

Often courts will apply more than one of the state action approaches in their discussions of a particular case, and often more than one approach will be implicated in the analysis of a particular problem. If state action (or federal action in the case of the federal government) is found under any approach, this state action will be analyzed using the requirements of whatever individual rights guarantee (*e.g.*, equal protection, due process, free speech) is applicable to the problem.

In the U.S. Supreme Court, state action cases almost always result in a divided Court, the vote usually being 5 to 4 (as in the recent *Brentwood Academy* case) or 6 to 3 (as in *Moose Lodge*). The Justices often differ in their readings of the doctrine established in prior cases. More particularly, however, state action analysis is heavily fact-dependent, and the Justices, as well as lower courts, disagree on how the facts are to be marshaled in a particular case and on what facts are weighed most heavily. Moreover, there is a subtle consideration of competing constitutional values in most state action cases. On the one hand, the challenger's claim on the merits will involve some important public value, for example, racial equality under law, that will depend on the rights clause the challenger invokes. On the other hand, the private entity's claim to be free from constitutional constraints will involve some competing value, for example, freedom of association or sanctity of private property. The courts do not always articulate, or even acknowledge, these underlying values clashes, but in the *Brentwood Academy* case the Court made one of its most direct statements ever about this aspect of state action analysis: "Even facts that suffice to show public action (or, standing alone, would require such a finding) may be outweighed in the name of some value at odds with finding public accountability in the circumstances" (531 U.S. at 303). Arguments about such "countervailing values" did not work in *Brentwood*, but the Court clearly left some room for them to work in other cases.

In addition, federalism values (see Chap. 6, Sec. A) are at work in state action cases. If the courts *broaden* concepts of state action, more activity is covered by the individual rights guarantees and can thus be restrained by the federal judicial power and (since Congress has authority to enforce the individual rights clauses) by federal legislative power as well; to that extent the authority of the states is diminished. If the courts *narrow* concepts of state action, however, less activity is subject to such federal government oversight, and to that extent the authority of the states is enhanced. Either way, the courts' state action determinations affect the balance of federalism.

Thus, in state action cases, the Justices may, and usually do, disagree on doctrine and on the pertinence of the facts, but underlying these disagreements, and sometimes unarticulated, are deeper disagreements concerning values. Justices may disagree on whether and how such a consideration of values should be accommodated in state action analysis, on how to resolve such conflicts in values when they appear, or on which values should prevail over others in particular cases. These considerations that divide the Justices, of course, also affect the work of the litigants and the lower courts, and strongly influence the result, in state action cases.

Sec. E. Historical Timeline for the Development of Federal Constitutional Rights

Prior to the drafting of the U.S. Constitution, the Declaration of Independence (1776) paved the way for the development of "unalienable rights" in our nation and ascribed to government the role of "secur[ing] these rights." The original Constitution ratified in 1788, however, contained few rights clauses. To fill this gap, the Bill of Rights was ratified in 1791. Later, the post-Civil War amendments, adopted respectively in 1865, 1868, and 1870, added other important rights. Thus rights were added to the Constitution in three steps: the original Constitution in 1788, the Bill of Rights in 1791, and the Post-Civil War Amendments in 1865, 1868, and 1870. These dates in turn bracket three historical stages of constitutional rights development: the first stage from 1788–1791, the second from 1791–1870, and the third beginning in 1870. The third stage eventually led to the famous case of *Brown v. Board of Education* in 1954 (see Sec. C above), which changed the meaning and thrust of the Post-Civil War Amendments and marked what could be considered the end of stage three. Stage three thus covers from 1870 to 1954, and another, fourth stage covers from 1954 to the present.

The following timeline traverses these four historical phases, listing the Constitution's pertinent individual rights clauses, differentiating between clauses binding the federal government and those binding the states, and noting some of the dates and U.S. Supreme Court cases that were milestones in the interpretation and development of the individual rights guarantees. Most of the development, it will be seen, has taken place in the fourth phase that began in 1954, and most especially in the years from the mid-1960s onward.

1776: The Declaration of Independence is signed, declaring, *inter alia*, "that all men are created equal"; and that they have "certain unalienable rights," including the rights to "life, liberty, and the pursuit of happiness."

1776–1787: The newly independent "states" or "commonwealths" draft their own constitutions, many of which included a bill or declaration of rights. The leading example is the Virginia constitution (1776). The rights listed were usually described as inherent in the nature of personhood and were often stated as aspirations rather than specific and legally enforceable protections.

1788: The Original Constitution is ratified, containing these individual rights provisions:
Provisions limiting the federal government:
1) habeas corpus clause (Art. I, sec. 9);
2) bills of attainder clause (Art. I, sec. 9);
3) ex post facto laws (Art. I, sec. 9);
4) jury trial in federal criminal cases (Art. III, sec. 2, ¶ 3).
Provisions limiting the state governments:
1) bills of attainder clause (Art. I, sec. 10);

    2)   ex post facto clause (Art. I, sec. 10);

    3)   obligation of contract clause (Art. I, sec. 10);

    4)   interstate privileges and immunities clause (privileges and immunities of *state* citizenship) (Art. IV, sec. 2, ¶1).

1791: The Bill of Rights is ratified. *See generally* Leonard Levy, ORIGINS OF THE BILL OF RIGHTS (Yale Univ. Press, 1999). The first eight amendments contain various rights clauses, including the free speech and press clauses, and the establishment and free exercise of religion clauses, of the First Amendment.

1798: The Eleventh Amendment is ratified, limiting federal court jurisdiction over suits against the states, including suits to enforce federal constitutional rights.

1798: The Court decides *Calder v. Bull*, 3 U.S. (3 Dall.) 386 (1798), ruling that the ex post facto clause (Art. I, sec. 10) applies only to criminal statutes, and providing the earliest glimpse into how the U.S. Supreme Court might approach individual rights questions.

1819: The U.S. Supreme Court decides *Dartmouth College v. Woodward*, 17 U.S. (4 Wheat.) 518 (1819), another early individual rights case. The rights provision at issue was the contracts clause (Art. I, sec. 10, ¶1), and it served to invalidate New Hampshire's attempt unilaterally to amend the charter of Dartmouth College, a private institution. The case is famous in part because it was argued by Daniel Webster (an alumnus of Dartmouth) and decided in an opinion written by Chief Justice John Marshall.

1833: The Court decides *Barron v. Baltimore*, 32 U.S. (7 Pet.) 243 (1833), ruling that the federal Bill of Rights limits only the federal government and does not limit state governments or private actors. States are limited by their own constitutions, which may include guarantees similar to those in the federal Bill of Rights.

1856: The Court decides *Dred Scott v. Sandford*, 60 U.S. (19 How.) 393 (1856), ruling that neither slaves nor freed Blacks may become citizens under the federal Constitution and thus may not bring suit in the federal courts. The decision is generally considered to be one of the precipitating events for the Civil War, which in turn resulted in passage of the Fourteenth Amendment (see **1868**). For the history of the case and an analysis of its significance, *see* Don Fehrenbacher, THE DRED SCOTT CASE: ITS SIGNIFICANCE IN AMERICAN LAW AND POLITICS (Oxford Univ. Press, 1978).

1865: The Thirteenth Amendment is ratified, prohibiting slavery and involuntary servitude. The Amendment binds and limits private persons as well as the states and the federal government.

1868: The Fourteenth Amendment is ratified. It establishes state and national citizenship for "[a]ll persons born or naturalized in the United States." It also contains three rights clauses that limit the states:

1) the "privileges or immunities" clause, establishing the privileges and immunities of *national* citizenship;
2) the due process clause; and
3) the equal protection clause.

The Fourteenth Amendment, among other things, served to overrule the U.S. Supreme Court's decision in *Dred Scott* (see **1857**).

1870: The Fifteenth Amendment is ratified, prohibiting the abridgment of the right to vote on grounds of race. The Amendment expressly applies to the federal government as well as the states.

1872: The Fourteenth Amendment's privileges and immunities clause is very narrowly interpreted in the *Slaughter-House Cases*, 83 U.S. (16 Wall.) 36 (1872) and relegated to a position of marginal significance in constitutional law. The *Slaughter-House Cases* also suggest that the equal protection clause has little meaning outside the context of race discrimination.

1883: In the *Civil Rights Cases*, 109 U.S. 3 (1883), the Court begins the development of the "state action" doctrine. In invalidating a federal law prohibiting race discrimination in places of public accommodation, the Court determines that the Fourteenth Amendment prohibits only "state action" that violates the Amendment's rights clauses; the private actions of individuals are not covered. The Court also determines that, when Congress legislates to enforce the Fourteenth Amendment, it may regulate only "state action" and not the private actions of individuals.

1886: In *Santa Clara County v. Southern Pacific Railway*, 118 U.S. 394 (1886), the Court rules that the Fourteenth Amendment's rights clauses protect corporations as well as natural "persons."

1887: With *Mugler v. Kansas*, 123 U.S. 623 (1887), the heyday begins for substantive "economic" rights under the Fourteenth Amendment due process clause.

1896: In *Plessy v. Ferguson*, 163 U.S. 537 (1896), "separate but equal" becomes the reigning principle for applying the Fourteenth Amendment's equal protection clause to problems of racial segregation. The Court upholds a state statute mandating racial segregation in railway cars. (But see **1954**.)

1905: *Lochner v. New York*, 198 U.S. 45 (1905) marks the high point of protection for economic rights under substantive due process and ushers in the "*Lochner* era." (For the end of this era, see **1934**.)

1919: The U.S. Supreme Court has its first major encounter with free speech rights in four cases challenging convictions under the federal Espionage Act: *Schenck v. United States*, 249 U.S. 47 (1919); *Frohwerk v. United States*, 249 U.S. 204 (1919); *Debs v. United States*, 249 U.S. 211 (1919); *Abrams v. United States*, 250 U.S. 616 (1919). Justice Holmes articulates the "clear-and-present danger" test in *Schenck* and applies it in *Frohwerk* and *Debs*, but each time upholds the convictions. In *Abrams*, however, Justice

Holmes dissents from the majority's affirmance of the convictions and writes an influential opinion, joined by Justice Brandeis, that develops a strengthened version of the clear-and-present danger test.

1920: The Nineteenth Amendment is ratified, prohibiting the denial of the vote on grounds of sex and thus, in effect, guaranteeing women the right to vote.

1923: *Meyer v. Nebraska*, 262 U.S. 390 (1923), provides the first sign that the Court would extend substantive due process protections to non-economic personal or intimate matters. By overturning the conviction of a private school teacher who had violated a state law prohibiting the teaching of foreign languages, the Court in *Meyer* fostered the "liberty" of parents to direct the upbringing of their children.

1925: *Gitlow v. New York*, 268 U.S. 652 (1925) is the first case in which the Court suggests that it will apply provisions of the Bill of Rights against the states by incorporating them into the Fourteenth Amendment. (See also **1833**, **1937**, and **1968**.) The provisions at issue in *Gitlow* were the First Amendment's speech and press clauses.

1934: The "*Lochner* era"—the era in which the Court actively protected substantive economic rights under the due process clause—comes to an end in *Nebbia v. New York*, 291 U.S. 502 (1934).

1937: In *Palko v. Connecticut*, 302 U.S. 319 (1937), Justice Cardozo, for the Court, develops the first extensive statement of the "selective incorporation" approach to applying particular Bill of Rights guarantees to the states by "incorporating" them into the Fourteenth Amendment.

1938: *United States v. Carolene Products*, 304 U.S. 144 (1938) contains the famous footnote 4 (304 U.S. at 152 fn.4) in which Justice Stone, for the Court, suggests that "more exacting judicial scrutiny" under the Fourteenth Amendment may be appropriate for state legislation that "restricts those political processes which can ordinarily be expected to bring about repeal of undesirable legislation" or that discriminates against "particular religious,... [national origin], or racial minorities...."

1942: The Court decides *Chaplinsky v. New Hampshire*, 315 U.S. 568 (1942), a case that confirms and institutionalizes the "categorical exclusion" approach to free speech law, by which the Court justifies certain governmental restraints on speech because the speech has no or slight communicative value.

1942: In *Skinner v. Oklahoma*, 316 U.S. 535 (1942), the Court expands the reach of the equal protection clause by opening an important new avenue to heightened scrutiny of classifications that inpinge upon "fundamental" interests.

1944: In *Korematsu v. United States*, 323 U.S. 214 (1944), the Court first articulates the strict scrutiny approach for reviewing racial classifications under the equal protection clause. In this controversial case, however, the Court holds that the federal government's World War II program for detaining and relocating Japanese Americans on the West Coast actually does meet the strict scrutiny standard.

1947: The Court enters the thicket of church-state relations in *Everson v. Board of Education of Ewing Township*, 330 U.S. 1 (1947). In a 5 to 4 decision, the Court determines that governmental reimbursement of parents' costs of using public bus transportation to send their children to public and private schools, including religiously affiliated schools, did not violate the establishment clause.

1948: In *Toomer v. Witsell*, 334 U.S. 385 (1948), invalidating a South Carolina law imposing a much higher license fee on non-residents than residents harvesting shrimp in state waters, the Court provides the foundation for modern "privileges and immunities" analysis under Article IV, section 2.

1954: In *Brown v. Board of Education*, 347 U.S. 483 (1954), the Court holds that state sanctioned racial segregation in public education violates the equal protection clause. Although *Brown* did not directly overrule *Plessy v. Ferguson*, it struck the death knell for the separate-but-equal doctrine (see **1896**) and ushered in a growth era for the protection and expansion of constitutional rights.

1961: In *Mapp v. Ohio*, 367 U.S. 643 (1961), the Court applies the Fourth Amendment search and seizure clause, and particularly its "exclusionary rule," to the states, thus protecting criminal defendants against the admission of evidence that was the product of an unconstitutional search. This case, along with *Gideon v. Wainwright* (see **1963**) and *Miranda v. Arizona* (see **1966**), established the foundation and impetus for the modern development of the constitutional rights of the accused in criminal cases.

1962: In *Engel v. Vitale*, 370 U.S. 421 (1962), the Court tangles with the sensitive issue of religious exercises on public school premises and applies the establishment clause to invalidate the use of a state-composed prayer in New York State's public schools. An earlier case invalidating "released time" religious classes on public school premises, *McCollum v. Board of Education*, 333 U.S. 203 (1948), was the forerunner of the *Engel* type of case; *School District v. Schempp*, 374 U.S. 203 (1963), invalidating morning Bible reading in public schools, was the immediate successor of *Engel* and is a case often paired with *Engel*.)

1963: The Court decides *Gideon v. Wainwright*, 372 U.S. 335 (1963), declaring that the Sixth Amendment guarantees a right to appointed counsel for defendants in criminal cases.

1964: *New York Times v. Sullivan*, 376 U.S. 254 (1964), extends free speech and press protection to defamatory statements about public officials. This case begins a trend toward bringing within the First Amendment types of statements that previously were "categorically excluded" from the Amendment's protection. Justice Brennan's opinion for the Court also emphasizes the free speech and press clauses' central role of protecting "debate on public issues."

1964: In *Reynolds v. Sims*, 377 U.S. 533 (1964), the "fundamental interest" approach to heightened scrutiny under the equal protection clause (see **1944**) receives new impetus and is extended to classifications that deny or dilute the right to vote.

1965: In *Griswold v. Connecticut*, 381 U.S.479 (1965), substantive due process is resurrected to protect personal and intimate (rather than economic) rights. (See also **1887, 1905,** and **1923.**) The opinions in *Griswold* pave the way for strict scrutiny review of laws that impinge upon "fundamental" personal rights.

1966: In *Miranda v. Arizona*, 384 U.S. 436 (1966), the Court holds that, under the Fifth Amendment's privilege against self-incrimination and the Sixth Amendment's right to counsel, criminal suspects in police custody must be given "*Miranda* warnings" and cannot be interrogated without their counsel present unless they voluntarily waive their "*Miranda* rights."

1968: The "selective incorporation" process by which the Court applies provisions of the Bill of Rights through the Fourteenth Amendment to the states becomes fully matured in *Duncan v. Louisiana*, 391 U.S. 145 (1968). *Duncan* applied the Sixth Amendment jury trial clause to the states.

1969: In *Red Lion Broadcasting Co. v. FCC*, 395 U.S. 367 (1969), the Court accords less First Amendment protection to the broadcast media than it traditionally had accorded (and does accord) to the print media. The Court's reasoning opens the way for a "medium-specific analysis" of governmental restraints on the press—that is, an analysis that is shaped by the particular characteristics of the medium at issue and may therefore result in lower levels of protection for some media compared with others.

1970: *Goldberg v. Kelly*, 397 U.S. 254 (1970), in which the Court recognized the Fourteenth Amendment procedural due process rights of welfare recipients whose benefits were terminated, gives strong support to a due process revolution that had begun in the 1960s and projects that revolution forward through the 1970s. *Goldberg* is the high-water mark for procedural due process protections.

1971: The Twenty-Sixth Amendment is ratified, prohibiting the states and the federal government from denying the right to vote on the grounds of age.

1972: Congress proposes the Equal Rights Amendment (ERA), prohibiting sex discrimination by the United States or any state, and submits the Amendment to the states for ratification. (*See generally* Barbara Brown, Thomas Emerson, Gail Falk, and Ann Freedman, "The Equal Rights Amendment: A Constitutional Basis for Equal Rights For Women," 80 YALE L.J. 871

(1971).) The time period for ratifications, as later extended by Congress, was June 30, 1982. As of that date, 35 states had ratified the ERA, 3 short of the constitutionally required 38; the ERA was therefore not adopted. By that time, however, the U.S. Supreme Court had itself provided for heightened scrutiny of sex classifications under the equal protection clause (see **1976**).

1972: In *Moose Lodge v. Irvis*, 407 U.S. 163 (1972), a "state action" case, the Court rejects an equal protection, race discrimination claim against Moose Lodge because the Lodge was not engaged in state action. The Court applies both the "nexus" approach and the "symbiotic relationship" approach to state action issues, clarifying each approach but also limiting the reach of each approach. The *Moose Lodge* opinion thus signals the beginning of new trend in state action law in which it would become more difficult to apply individual rights clauses to ostensibly private entities.

1973: In *Roe v. Wade*, 410 U.S. 113 (1973), the Court upholds a woman's right to choose whether or not to terminate a pregnancy, thus highlighting and expanding the use of substantive due process concepts to protect personal liberties. The *Roe* decision became what was probably the most controversial decision of the 20th century. For a history of the case, the controversies about birth control that preceded it, and subsequent litigation up to *Planned Parenthood of Southeastern Pennsylvania v. Casey*, 505 U.S. 833 (1992), *see* David Garrow, LIBERTY AND SEXUALITY: THE RIGHT TO PRIVACY AND THE MAKING OF ROE V. WADE (U. Calif. Press, 1998).

1976: In *Craig v. Boren*, 429 U.S. 190 (1976), the Court, for the first time, articulates an intermediate scrutiny standard of review for equal protection cases involving gender discrimination. The Court's reasoning confirmed hints in earlier cases that equal protection analysis was not limited to the two review standards of strict scrutiny and minimal scrutiny.

1978: In *Regents of the University of California v. Bakke*, 438 U.S. 265 (1978), the Court decides its first "affirmative action" case under the equal protection clause—a case concerning the use of race in university admissions decisions. The decision ushers in an era of continuing controversy, concerning racial preferences in education, employment, government contracting, and government licensing.

1986: The Court decides *Bowers v. Hardwick*, 478 U.S. 186 (1986), a substantive due process case in which the majority, by a 5 to 4 vote, declares that homosexual persons do not have any constitutional privacy right to engage in consensual homosexual sodomy in their own homes. The majority opinion's reasoning signals not only the Court's disinclination to protect homosexual conduct but also, more broadly, the Court's inclination toward a narrower, more limited construction of substantive due process rights concerning personal intimacies as well as the sanctity of the home. (But see **2003**, *Lawrence v. Texas*.)

1996: In *Romer v. Evans*, 517 U.S. 620 (1996), the Court for the first time recognizes constitutional rights protecting the status and conduct of homosexual persons. Using equal protection principles, and implicitly confirming the viability of the "rational-basis-with-bite" review first applied in *Cleburne v. Cleburne Living Center*, 473 U.S. 432 (1985), the Court invalidates a Colorado constitutional amendment prohibiting state and local governments from according legal protections to homosexual persons on the basis of their sexual orientation.

1999: In *Saenz v. Roe*, 526 U.S. 489 (1999), the Court relies in part on the privileges or immunities clause of the Fourteenth Amendment to invalidate a state statute limiting the welfare benefits available to new state residents. The Court's opinion seems to breathe new life into this clause of the Fourteenth Amendment. (See **1873**.)

2002: In *Zelman v. Simmons-Harris*, 536 U.S. 639 (2002), a case upholding Ohio's school voucher plan for city of Cleveland, the Court caps a line of establishment clause cases providing increasing discretion for governments to provide extensive governmental aid to parents whose children will attend religiously affiliated schools and to higher education students who will enroll in programs of religious instruction or training. The roots of this trend are traceable to the 1983 case of *Mueller v. Allen*, 463 U.S. 388 (1983), and especially to the 1997 case of *Agostini v. Felton*, 521 U.S. 203 (1997).

2003: Just 25 years after *Regents of University of California v. Bakke* (**1978**), the Court decides two more cases on affirmative action in university admissions: *Grutter v. Bollinger*, 123 S.Ct. 2325 (2003), and *Gratz v. Bollinger*, 123 S.Ct. 2411 (2003), companion cases from the University of Michigan decided on the same day. The Court's opinions identify narrow circumstances in which race-conscious admissions plans would be constitutional under the equal protection clause, thus resolving some of the uncertainty that had existed since *Bakke* and setting the stage for the next generation of debate on affirmative action.

2003: In *Lawrence v. Texas*, 123 S.Ct. 2472 (2003), the Court overrules its prior decision in *Bowers v. Hardwick* (**1986**) and invalidates a Texas statute that criminalized same-sex sodomy but not heterosexual sodomy. In its majority opinion, the Court borrows from and approves of the reasoning in Justice Stevens' dissenting opinion in *Bowers*. The *Lawrence* majority opinion expresses an expansive view of liberty under the Fourteenth Amendment, which has both "spatial and more transcendent dimensions," but the majority opinion does not use a strict scrutiny standard of review.

Chapter 10

Equal Protection and Privileges or Immunities

Sec. A. Introduction to the Fourteenth Amendment

The Fourteenth Amendment is one of the three Reconstruction-Era amendments (the Thirteenth, Fourteenth, and Fifteenth Amendments) that abolished slavery[1] and resolved other slavery and Civil War-related issues. The Fourteenth Amendment: (1) established national and state citizenship for the former slaves and all other "persons born or naturalized in the United States" (sec. 1); (2) resolved issues concerning apportionment of representatives, office-holding, and the public debt (secs. 2–4); (3) established several new rights for individuals (sec. 1); and (4) granted Congress new powers to enforce these new rights (sec. 5). The citizenship clause (sec. 1, sentence 1) served to overturn the U.S. Supreme Court's *Dred Scott* decision (*Dred Scott v. Sanford*, 60 U.S. (19 How.) 393 (1856)), which had barred black persons, free or slave, from state and national citizenship. *See Slaughter-House Cases*, 83 U.S. (16 Wall.) 36, 73 (1872). (The Thirteenth and Fifteenth Amendments are briefly discussed in Chapter 9, Section A.6 and Chapter 14, Section C.)

One striking feature of the Fourteenth Amendment is that it both *grants* and *limits* power; it contains, in other words, both a power clause (the enforcement power clause in section 5) and several rights clauses (the privileges or immunities clause, the due process clause, and the equal protection clause in section 1). A second striking feature

---

1. President Lincoln's Emancipation Proclamation (Proclamation of January 1, 1863, 12 Stat. 1268) had abolished slavery only in the states that were in armed rebellion against the United States. *See generally* Derrick Bell, RACE, RACISM, AND AMERICAN LAW, pp. 28-32 (4th ed., 2000). The Thirteenth Amendment went beyond the Proclamation by abolishing slavery (and involuntary servitude) in all states and territories. It also provided a firm constitutional base for the abolition, in contrast to President Lincoln's Proclamation, which was an executive action whose constitutionality under Article II could have been questioned, at least after the Civil War had ended. *See Slaughter-House Cases*, 83 U.S. (16 Wall) 36, 68–70 (1872).

is that the Amendment *increases* the power of *Congress* but *limits* the power of *the states*. Moreover, since the rights clauses that limit the states ("No State shall…") are judicially enforceable, the Amendment also implicitly increases the power of the federal courts vis à vis the states. When these features of the Fourteenth Amendment are considered together, along with the Amendment's elevation of *national*, compared to state, citizenship, the potential effect on the balance of federalism is pronounced. The effect is even more dramatic and pronounced when the Fourteenth Amendment is considered in conjunction with the Thirteenth and Fifteenth Amendments. And indeed, the passage of the Reconstruction-Era amendments marks a key point in the history of federalism (see Chap. 6, Sec. A).

Historically, the Fourteenth Amendment has a clear racial context. The Amendment arose from the Civil War; it followed on the heels of the Thirteenth Amendment which abolished slavery; and it emphasized the concept of national citizenship in order to anchor the legal status of the former slaves. In the U.S. Supreme Court's first case concerning this Amendment, the court emphasized this racial context when it identified "the one pervading purpose" of the Reconstruction-Era amendments to be "the freedom of the slave race, the security and firm establishment of that freedom, and the protection of the newly-made freeman and citizen from the oppressions of those who had formerly exercised unlimited dominion over him" (*Slaughter-House Cases*, 83 U.S. (16 Wall) 36, 71 (1873); *see also Strauder v. West Virginia*, 100 U.S. 303 (1879)). Yet, the text of the Fourteenth Amendment does not itself address race or slavery; the rights are stated in general terms. And, as the Fourteenth Amendment has been developed over time in the courts, it has been extended far beyond its original racial context. The racial context remains critically important, however, with respect to the equal protection clause (see Sec. D.2 below).

As the Fourteenth Amendment grew beyond its immediate racial context, its impact on federalism grew as well. In the *Slaughter-House Cases*, above, the Court majority had insisted that every "section or phrase" of the Reconstruction-Era amendments should be construed in light of "the evil which they were designed to remedy" (83 U.S. at 72), and that the Amendment's framers did not intend to "radically change…the whole theory of the relations of the State and Federal governments to each other and of both these governments to the people…." (83 U.S. at 78). But over time the Fourteenth Amendment has extended far beyond the *Slaughter-House* majority's perception and expectation. This vastly enhanced role came in part from the development of the concept of substantive due process, first as applied to economic matters and then as applied to intimate personal matters (see Chap. 11, Sec. C below); in part from incorporation of the Bill of Rights into the Fourteenth Amendment (see Chap. 11, Sec. A.2 below); in part from the extension of equal protection clause protections to many types of discrimination beyond race discrimination (see this Chap., Secs. D.3, D.4, D.5, and D.8 below); and in part from the procedural due process revolution (see Chap. 11, Sec. D below). The key U.S. Supreme Court cases fueling these developments are noted in the historical timeline in Chapter 9, Section E.

Section 5 of the Fourteenth Amendment, the power clause, is addressed briefly in Chapter 6, Section E of this book and is developed in more depth in Chapter 14, Section B.3 below. Section 1 of the Amendment, with its three rights clauses, is the focus of this Chapter and Chapter 11.

Sec. B. A Conceptual Overview of Privileges or Immunities

The "privileges or immunities" clause, first in order in section 1 of the Fourteenth Amendment, was also the first to receive extensive consideration from the U.S. Supreme Court. This clause should be read in conjunction with the sentence on national citizenship that precedes it. The rights that the clause protects are associated with national citizenship, in contrast to the *state* privileges and immunities protected by Article IV, section 2 of the Constitution (see Chap. 7, Sec. E). Thus, rights under the Fourteenth Amendment privileges or immunities clause may be claimed only by "citizens of the United States." In contrast, the other rights that the Fourteenth Amendment protects— due process and equal protection—may be claimed by "any person," citizen and non-citizen alike (*see Strauder v. West Virginia*, 100 U.S. 303, 307–308 (1879)).[2]

In the *Slaughter-House Cases*, Sec. A above, a 5 to 4 majority of the Court rejected Fourteenth Amendment challenges to a state monopoly law that severely impinged upon the economic and property interests of butchers and slaughter-house owners who were not part of the one company granted the monopoly. The Court sharply distinguished between the privileges and immunities of *state* citizenship (see Chap. 7, Sec. E) and those of *national* citizenship, very narrowly construing the latter category. From that time on, the Fourteenth Amendment's privileges or immunities clause has had little significance as a source of individual rights.

Some movement toward revitalizing the clause may be evident, however, in the 1999 case of *Saenz v. Roe*, 526 U.S. 489 (1999), in which the Court invalidated a California law that provided a lower level of welfare benefits to newly arrived residents than to longer-term residents. The Court majority quoted the Fourteenth Amendment's citizenship clause and privileges or immunities clause as the source of "the new arrival's . . . status as a citizen of the United States" (526 U.S. at 502), and approvingly quoted language from the dissent in the *Slaughter-House Cases* that "[a] citizen of the United States has a perfect constitutional right to go to and reside in any state he chooses, and to claim citizenship therein, and an equality of rights with every other citizen. . . ." (526 U.S. at 503–504, quoting the *Slaughter-House Cases*, 83 U.S. at 112–113 (Bradley, J., dissenting)). The two dissenters in *Saenz*, Justice Thomas and Chief Justice Rehnquist, observed that "the majority appears to breathe new life into the [Privileges or Immunities] Clause" and called for a re-evaluation of the clause's meaning and possible enhancement of its role (526 U.S. at 527–528 (Thomas, J., dis-

---

2. Corporations are not considered to be citizens for purposes of the privileges or immunities clause (*Cf. Paul v. Virginia*, 75 U.S. (8 Wall.) 168, 177 (1868). For purposes of due process and equal protection, however, corporations are considered to be "persons." *See Santa Clara County v. Southern Pacific Railroad*, 118 U.S. 394 (1886).

senting)). *See generally* Laurence Tribe, *Comment,* "Saenz Prophecy: Does the Privileges or Immunities Revival Portend the Future—or Reveal the Structure of the Present?," 113 HARV. L. REV. 110 (1999).

While the ramifications of *Saenz* are as yet unclear, the case at least seems to make clear that the Fourteenth Amendment guarantees the status of *state* citizenship as well as *national* citizenship, and that the right to choose a state of residency and receive the full and equal benefit of citizenship there is itself a privilege or immunity of national citizenship. These conclusions result not from the privileges or immunities clause alone, but from that clause read together with the citizenship clause that precedes it. Moreover, and in contradistinction to the rest of section 1 of the Fourteenth Amendment, the citizenship clause "is a limitation on the powers of the National Government as well as the States" (526 U.S. at 508). Thus, both the states and the federal government are bound to respect each citizen's guarantee of state citizenship.

Sec. C. A Conceptual Overview of Equal Protection

C.1. Basic Equal Protection Theory

Equal protection law deals with governmental classifications that deprive a certain class of persons of benefits that persons in other classes are entitled to receive, or that subject a certain class of persons to burdens that are not imposed on persons in other classes. Statutes and other governmental regulations frequently create such classifications; they are an inevitable product of the line-drawing that is inherent in regulation. Since persons or classes of persons are not all alike in terms of their personal traits and life circumstances, government regulators typically must determine which class or classes should be covered in order to serve the regulation's purposes. If the purpose of a statute is to provide medical services for low-income persons, for example, the statute must define who is to be considered "low income" and thus eligible for the statutory benefits. If the purpose of a statute is to provide for the licensing of drivers, the statute must establish who is eligible to hold a driver's license and who is not. Or if the purpose of a statute is to impose safety requirements on certain retail businesses, the statute must identify which businesses pose safety risks of the type being regulated.

Most governmental classifications pose no serious problems under the equal protection clause. Courts recognize the necessity of such line-drawing and generally accord deference to the judgments of the legislatures and government agencies that create the classifications. On the other hand, courts have also recognized that certain types of classifications—a relatively small portion of the almost innumerable types of classifications used in government regulations—do raise equal protection problems. The essential task of equal protection analysis is to identify the classifications that do pose problems and then to distinguish classifications that are constitutionally justifiable from those that are not.

The law that has been developed to deal with these problems focuses on the equality concept, or equality value, in the U.S. Constitution. In regard to the states, this equality concept arises from the express wording of the equal protection clause. In regard to the federal government, this concept arises by implication from the Fifth Amendment's due process clause.[3] The U.S. Supreme Court has determined that the implied equality concept in the Fifth Amendment, as applied to the federal government, is the same as the express equality concept in the Fourteenth Amendment, as applied to the states. The Fourteenth Amendment's equal protection clause, therefore, is the primary focus of concern.

In the equal protection clause, the equality value is stated in general terms at a high level of abstraction, thus assuring that application of the clause will require some kind of values interpretation (see Chap. 9, Sec. B.2). The interpreter's job is to give meaning to the equality value, in concrete circumstances. When is it that government will have treated two classes of persons unequally under the Constitution? Under what conditions will government be found to have impinged unjustifiably upon the equality value and thus violated equal protection?

Over time the U.S. Supreme Court has developed a methodology for addressing questions such as these under the equal protection clause. The methodology reflects the numerous value judgments about equality that the Court has made over time in its interpretive enterprise. There are two methodological stages. The first (stage one) is outlined in Section C.2 below, and the second (stage two) is outlined in Section C.3. More specificity on the methodology is added by Sections C.4 and C.5.

C.2.   Differential Treatment of Similarly Situated Classes

At stage one of equal protection methodology, the inquiry is whether there is a discrimination. Not every governmental classification is necessarily discriminatory, and there is no equal protection issue unless there is a discrimination. A suggested shorthand definition of discrimination, consistent with the case law, is *differential treatment of similarly situated classes of persons*. The definition, in turn, as applied to a particular law or other governmental action, requires consideration of three other concepts: (1) a *class of persons*, which is determined by identifying the classifying factor or trait that the law uses to define a class; (2) *differential treatment*, which is determined by comparing the law's effect on the identified class with its effect on some other class of persons; and (3) *similarly situated* classes, which is determined by comparing each class's

---

3. The foundational case establishing this role for the Fifth Amendment due process clause is *Bolling v. Sharpe*, 347 U.S. 497 (1954), a case invalidating racial segregation in the District of Columbia public schools. *Bolling* was a companion case to *Brown v. Board of Education*, 347 U.S. 483 (1954) (see Chap. 9, Sec. C), but could not be decided under the Fourteenth Amendment, as *Brown* was, because the District of Columbia was considered to be an arm of the federal government. Nevertheless, relying on the Fifth Amendment, the Court reached the same decision in *Bolling* as it had in *Brown*, declaring that "it would be unthinkable that the same Constitution would impose a lesser duty on the Federal Government" (347 U.S. at 500). As part of its reasoning, the Court emphasized that "the concepts of equal protection and due process, both stemming from our American ideal of fairness, are not mutually exclusive" (*Id.* at 499).

relevant characteristics (traits) with the purposes of the law and asking whether the classes are similarly situated with respect to the law's purposes.[4] *See generally* Joseph Tussman & Jacobus ten Broek, "The Equal Protection of the Laws," 37 CALIFORNIA L. REV. 341, 343–353 (1949).

If the law (or other governmental action) does not treat one class of persons differently from some other identifiable class, or if the classes of persons that are treated differently do not have similarly relevant characteristics (that is, are not similarly situated), then there is no discrimination. If, for example, a state driver's license statute covered both (a) current residents who have never had a driver's license, and (b) new residents who have a valid driver's license from another state, but imposed the same licensing requirements (*e.g.*, the same driving test) on each class and extended the same driving privileges to each, there is no differential treatment and thus no discrimination. On the other hand, if the statute required that persons in the first class (class (a)) must pass a driving test but did not require persons in the second class (class (b)) to pass a driving test, there is differential treatment but the two classes are not similarly situated with respect to the law's purpose (highway safety). The first groups has no driving credential certifying that they have driving skills; the second group does have such a credential. Thus again, there is no discrimination. If there is no discrimination, the equal protection analysis is at an end.

A "class" is usually composed of numerous, perhaps innumerable, persons. However, in *Village of Willowbrook v. Olech*, 528 U.S. 562 (2000), a challenge to a local zoning decision, the Court confirmed that "successful equal protection claims [may be] brought by a 'class of one,' where the plaintiff alleges that she has been intentionally treated differently from others similarly situated...." (*Id.* at 564). This conclusion follows from the text of the equal protection clause, which protects every "*person* within [the State's] jurisdiction" (Amend. 14, sec. 1 (emphasis added)). Thus, even though equal protection analysis is class-based, this clause ultimately protects individual persons, not classes or groups as such.

The "similarly situated" concept is particularly slippery. To engage in equal protection analysis, one must identify at least two classes, one of which is treated differently than the other with respect to the purpose of the law at issue. But not all identifiable classes that are treated differently by a law are similarly situated. To be so, each class — or a significant number of members from each class — must either contribute in similar ways to the existence of or solution to the problem at which the law is directed; or benefit in similar ways from the opportunity or assistance that the law provides. Consider, for example, a juvenile curfew ordinance that prohibits minors from being on public streets after midnight and subjects parents or custodians of offending minors to misdemeanor charges. The purposes of the law are to protect minors from nighttime

---

4. In situations where the law being challenged is neutral on its face, and thus contains no facial classification, the law itself will not provide evidence of differential treatment. The courts then look for a *differential* (or *disproportionate*) *effect* of the law on one group compared to another similarly situated group, rather than differential treatment as such. This special problem is discussed in Section D.6 below.

drug-related violence and to inhibit minors from involvement in the drug trade. The law may treat parents of minors, as a class, differently from parents of adult children; the law may treat parents without custody, as a class, differently from custodial parents; and the law may treat parents, as a class, differently from non-parents. But it is doubtful that any of these differential treatments would be considered to be discrimination, because the groups paired together are apparently not similarly situated with respect to the law's two purposes. The two classes, in other words, do not contribute in similar ways to the creation or to the solution of the problem that the law addresses.

C.3. Tiers of Review and Levels of Scrutiny

If there is an affirmative answer to the stage one inquiry about discrimination (see Sec. C.2 above), the stage two inquiry is whether the identified discrimination is justifiable. Just as it is clear that not every differential treatment is discriminatory, it is also clear that not every discriminatory action is unconstitutional. In terms of methodology, how does one determine whether a particular discrimination is justifiable? In particular, it is necessary to identify the particular level of scrutiny that a court would give to the specific type of discrimination at issue and to focus on the standard of review used at that level. Different types of discrimination receive different levels of scrutiny. The standard of review at each level of scrutiny embodies a type of means and ends analysis. The level of scrutiny, in other words, is expressed in terms of a standard of review that will have both a means component and an ends component. The methodology at this point is similar to that for substantive due process (Chap. 11, Sec. C below), except that the *means* for equal protection purposes is the *classification* that the law employs.

There are three levels, or tiers, of scrutiny applicable to equal protection cases. The higher the tier, the stricter (or more "heightened") is the scrutiny of the classification. The upper tier, called "strict scrutiny," has two alternative bases for attaining this level of review: the "suspect class" alternative, a primary example of which is the racial classification (see Sec. D.2 below); and the fundamental interest alternative, a primary example of which is the fundamental interest in voting in elections for government representatives (see Sec. D.8 below). The middle tier, called "intermediate scrutiny," is used primarily for gender discrimination (see the *VMI* case in Sec. D.4 below). The lower tier, called "minimal scrutiny," has two sub-tiers. The higher sub-tier provides a newer, less deferential, "rational-basis-with-bite" type of review for cases in which personal prejudices of animosities may have affected governmental decisionmaking. The best elucidation of this approach appears in the debate between Justice White and Justice Marshall in *Cleburne v. Cleburne Living Center*, 473 U.S. 432, 446–450 (White, J., for maj.) & 458–460 (Marshall, J., concurring)); for a more recent example, see the *Romer* case (Sec. D.5 below).

The lowest tier (the lower of the two sub-tiers of the bottom tier) is the traditional, highly deferential "minimal rational basis" review that applies by default to all classifications that do not have characteristics justifying review on a higher tier. In *New Orleans v. Dukes*, for example, the Court upheld a city ordinance that discriminated against certain street vendors who had not continuously sold their wares for a period of eight years prior to the ordinance's adoption. The Court emphasized that the ordinance was "solely an economic regulation" that did not employ any suspect classification, and that the Court would therefore would "presume the constitutionality" of the classification and defer heavily to the city's legislative judgment, according the city "wide latitude" in regulating economic matters (*Id.* at 303). The classification need only be "rationally related to a legitimate state interest" to be valid; it is only "the wholly arbitrary act" that would violate equal protection" (*Id.* at 303–304). In such bottom tier cases, courts usually keep the burden of proof on the plaintiff and allow defendants to rely on "any reasonably conceivable state of facts that could provide a rational basis for the classification" (*Federal Communications Comm'n v. Beach Communications*, 508 U.S. 307, 313 (1993)). Thus challengers "attacking the rationality of the legislative classification have the burden 'to negative every conceivable basis which might support it'.... [I]t is entirely irrelevant for constitutional purposes whether the conceived reason for the challenged distinction actually motivated the legislature.... [A] legislative choice... may be based on national speculation unsupported by evidence or empirical data. (*Id.* at 315, quoting *Lehnhausen v. Lake Shore Auto Parts Co.*, 410 U.S. 356, 364 (1973)).

C.4. "Suspectness" and Heightened Scrutiny

To work with the tiers of review and levels of scrutiny (Sec. C.3 above), it will be necessary to focus, in each case, on the particular classification that government has used to differentiate one class of persons from another. Most laws classify persons in one way or another, and the vast majority of classifications that government uses raise no serious equal protection issues (Sec. C.1 above). These "run-of-the-mill" or "garden-variety" classifications are presumed constitutional and receive only minimal rational basis (bottom tier) scrutiny if challenged. But some classifications, a relative few of the many types of classifications, may be scrutinized more closely by the courts because there is some reason to be suspicious of them. The courts have developed various reasons for being suspicious of certain classifications; these reasons may be called the *indicia of suspectness*.[5] The more indicia of suspectness a classification has, the higher the level of scrutiny it will receive. Racial discrimination has more indicia of suspectness than any other type of discrimination; it is therefore the paradigm case of suspectness (see Sec. D.2 below). Other classifications are often compared with race; the more "race-like" another classification is, the more indicia of suspectness it will have, and the greater is the likelihood that it will receive heightened scrutiny (see Sec. D.3 below).[6]

There are two basic approaches for analyzing the relative suspectness of a particular classification. The first way is to focus on the *classifying factor* (or *classifying trait*)

---

5. The Court used this phrase in *San Antonio School District v. Rodriguez*, 411 U.S. 1, 28 (1973); see Sec. D.3 below.

6. This analysis does not apply to the fundamental interest strand of strict scrutiny that is part of upper tier review (see above). Fundamental interest analysis is discussed separately in Section D.8 below.

that is the basis for the classification and thus the differential treatment—the classifying factor, in other words, that government has used to differentiate between classes of persons, treating one class more favorably than the other. Examples of classifying factors include race, national origin, gender, sexual orientation, residence, and personal income. The second approach is to focus on the particular *class of persons* that is disadvantaged by the classification government has used—the class of persons, in other words, that is targeted by the classification for different, and disadvantageous, treatment. Examples of disadvantaged classes could include African-Americans, white persons, persons of Middle-Eastern European descent, females, gays and lesbians, nonresidents, and low-income persons. The first approach may be called *the classifying factor approach* (or sometimes just the classification approach); the second approach may be called the *class approach*, or *class-based approach*.

Under the classifying factor approach, one considers whether the classifying factor has sufficient indicia of suspectness to override the presumption of constitutionality that usually attaches to government classifications. If so, then all uses of that classifying factor will receive some type of heightened scrutiny. If race were the classifying factor, for example, it would receive strict scrutiny regardless of whether that factor is used to discriminate against a racial minority or against white persons. Similarly, if gender were the classifying factor, it would receive intermediate scrutiny regardless of whether that factor is used to discriminate against a female or a male.

Under the class approach, one considers whether the disadvantaged class—the class being discriminated against—has sufficient indicia of suspectness to override the presumption of constitutionality that usually attaches to government uses of classifications. If so, then all discriminations *against that class* will receive some type of heightened scrutiny. If African-Americans were the disadvantaged class, for instance, all discriminations against that class would receive strict scrutiny (but not necessarily discriminations against other racial groups, especially whites). Similarly, if women were the disadvantaged class, all discriminations against that class would receive intermediate scrutiny (but not necessarily discriminations against males).

The classifying factor approach and the class approach thus may reach different results, and it is important to determine which approach the courts have used for particular discriminations and which approach litigants should argue for in presenting their claims to a court. It now seems settled that, in race cases and gender cases, the U.S. Supreme Court will use the classifying factor approach. Any governmental use of race, whether used to discriminate against blacks or against whites (as in the case of affirmative action programs) will thus receive the same strict scrutiny. (See *Palmore v. Sidoti*, Sec. D.2 below; and *City of Richmond v. J.A. Croson, Co.*, Sec. D.7 below.) Similarly, any governmental use of gender, whether used to discriminate against females or males, will receive the same intermediate scrutiny. (See *Mississippi University for Women v. Hogan*, 458 U.S. 718 (1982); and the *VMI Case*, Sec. D.4 below.)[7] For

---

7. For an explanation and criticism of the shift from a class approach to a classifying factor approach, *see* Jeb Rubenfeld, "The New Unwritten Constitution," 51 DUKE L. J. 289, 301–303 (2001).

certain other classifications, the Court appears to use the class approach. For example, in a foundational case regarding alienage discrimination, *Graham v. Richardson*, 403 U.S. 365 (1971), the Court indicated that it would give strict scrutiny to some discriminations against aliens because "[a]liens as a class are a prime example of a 'discrete and insular' minority for whom such heightened judicial solicitude is appropriate" (403 U.S. at 372, quoting *United States v. Carolene Products Co.*, 304 U.S. 144, 152–153, n. 4 (1938)).

C.5. Standards of Review and Means/Ends Analysis

To work with the tiers of review and levels of scrutiny (Sec. C.3 above), it is also necessary to identify the particular standard applicable to each tier (or level) and then to sort the standard into its two operative components: the "means" component, which requires a "means-focused scrutiny" of the discrimination; and the "ends" component, which requires an "ends-focused scrutiny" of the discrimination. The ends component focuses on the end or objective that government seeks to achieve, or the interest that it seeks to serve, by using the particular classification at issue. The question is whether the end, qualitatively, is "compelling" (for strict scrutiny), or "important" (for intermediate scrutiny), or "legitimate" and "permissible" (for minimal scrutiny), and thus meets the ends test of the applicable standard. The means component focuses on the classification that the government has used (the means) and its relation or connection to the end that the government is pursuing. The question is whether the relationship between the means and the end is sufficient to meet the ends test of the applicable standard: a means "necessary" or "narrowly tailored" to the end (for strict scrutiny), a means "substantially related" to the end (for intermediate scrutiny), or a means "rationally related" to the end (for minimal scrutiny).

To apply the means test, and thus evaluate the connection between means and ends, it is necessary to understand the twin concepts of overinclusiveness and underinclusiveness. A law is overinclusive when it applies to some situations that *do not* serve its objectives. A law is underinclusive when it *does not* apply to some situations that *do* serve its objectives. In equal protection analysis, these two concepts address the relationship between the means and the end, that is, the relationship between the classification that government has utilized (the means) and the objective that government seeks to achieve or interest it seeks to serve (the end). If, for example, the U.S. Army had a policy of excluding women soldiers from ground combat,[8] one could test the relationship between the means (the gender-based combat exclusion) and

---

8. This is not a hypothetical situation. Historically, and at least up to the press deadline for this book, the Army has had such a policy. Regarding its constitutionality under the equal protection clause, *see, e.g.*, G. Sidney Buchanan, "Women in Combat: An Essay on Ultimate Rights and Responsibilities," 28 Houston L. Rev. 503, 506–541 (1991). This equal protection analysis would be better understood after reading Section D.4 of this book, below.

the ends (presumably, promoting the efficiency and effectiveness of the Army's combat forces) by asking if the Army's classification (men only for combat forces) is either overinclusive or underinclusive. Regarding overinclusive, an argument could be that the classification (men only) is overinclusiveness because it includes many men who *do not* have, or *may not* have, the capabilities to be effective combat soldiers. Regarding underinclusiveness, an argument could be that the classification is underinclusive because it excludes many women who *do* have the capabilities to be effective combat soldiers.

The overinclusiveness/underinclusiveness inquiry thus addresses the validity of a particular classification by focusing on the closeness of the fit between the classification (the means) and the government objective or interest (the ends) or, as some commentators have put it, focusing on the degree of congruence between the means and the ends. The more overinclusive or underinclusive a classification is, the looser is the fit, and the less congruence there is between means and ends. The degree of fit or congruence required in a particular case will depend on the tier of review; strict scrutiny tolerates very little under- or over-inclusiveness, while minimal scrutiny tolerates a great deal. In general, however, the looser the fit and the less the congruence between means and ends, the less likely it is that the classification will meet the applicable means test.

Sec. D. Equal Protection and Heightened Scrutiny

D.1. Historical Overview

As Sections D.2 through D.4 below make clear, a number of classifications now merit heightened scrutiny under the equal protection clause. This scrutiny, as applied by the courts, can be very strong indeed and highly favorable to the plaintiffs who fit within these classifications. Such high levels of scrutiny, however, are a relatively new development in the history of the equal protection clause. Even for race discrimination, the paradigm suspect class (Sec. D.2 below), the progress after passage of the Fourteenth Amendment was slow. Promising early cases such as *Strauder v. West Virginia*, 100 U.S. 303 (1879), in which the U.S. Supreme Court invalidated a state law prohibiting black persons from serving on juries, soon gave way to the separate-but-equal doctrine that the Court pronounced in *Plessy v. Ferguson*, 163 U.S. 537 (1896) (see Chap. 9, Sec. C). It was not until *Brown v. Board of Education*, 347 U.S. 483 (1954) (see Chap. 9, Sec. C) and *Loving v. Virginia*, 388 U.S. 1 (1967) (striking down statutes prohibiting inter-racial marriage) that American constitutional law discarded the separate-but-equal legacy and courts began regularly applying strict scrutiny to racial classifications.[9]

---

9. The U.S. Supreme Court had previously articulated a strict scrutiny standard of review for race and national origin classifications in *Korematsu v. United States*, 323 U.S. 214 (1944) — the World War II case in which the Court upheld the exclusion of Japanese-Americans from cer-

Similarly, for gender discrimination, the courts and government officials tolerated the legal subjugation of women for many years after the Fourteenth Amendment's passage before any semblance of heightened scrutiny appeared. In 1873, for instance, in *Bradwell v. Illinois*, 83 U.S. (16 Wall.) 130 (1872), the U.S. Supreme Court upheld the Illinois Supreme Court's decision barring Myra Bradwell from the practice of law because she was a married woman. In a concurrence, Justice Bradley explained that: "The natural and proper timidity and delicacy which belongs to the female sex evidently unfits it for many of the occupations of civil life" (*Id.* at 141). In the same year as *Bradwell*, in Washington, D.C., Belva Lockwood was also fighting for the right to practice law. In 1874, the U.S. Court of Claims rejected her application for admission; in 1876 the U.S. Supreme Court also ruled that she was ineligible for admission to that Court. Finally, after Lockwood's intense and sustained lobbying effort with Congress, it passed a resolution permitting Lockwood to apply for admission; and in 1879 she became the first woman to be admitted to practice before the U.S. Supreme Court. *See* Tom Schroeder, "Out of the Mud," in *The Washington Post Magazine*, pp. 45–46 (Dec. 8, 2002), citing Jill Norgren, "Before It Was Merely Difficult: Belva Lockwood's Life in Law and Politics," 23 J. OF SUP. CT. HISTORY 16 (1999).

Despite Belva Lockwood's victory, matters did not improve much for women's constitutional rights until 1971 when the Court decided *Reed v. Reed*, 404 U.S. 71 (1971). In unanimously invalidating a state statute preferring men over women for appointments to administer estates, the Court for the first time applied something more than minimalist rational basis, substituting instead what appeared to be a "rational basis with bite" review. Legal developments moved fairly quickly after that. A Court plurality pushed for strict scrutiny of discrimination against women in *Frontiero v. Richardson*, 411 U.S. 677 (1973), failing by one vote; and then the Court fixed on an intermediate scrutiny standard of review for all gender classifications in *Craig v. Boren*, 429 U.S. 190 (1976), a case striking down a statute prohibiting males from drinking beer until age 21, but permitting females to drink at 18.

On other fronts, the Court did not provide clear strict scrutiny review for some (but not all) alienage classifications until 1971 in *Graham v. Richardson*, 403 U.S. 365 (1971); *cf. Foley v. Connelie*, 435 U.S. 291 (1978) (rational basis review for state classifications involving participation in state governance and policy making), and *Mathews v. Diaz*, 426 U.S. 67 (1976) (rational basis review for the *federal* government's use of alienage classifications). Regarding classifications based on a disability, the Court did not provide heightened scrutiny—rational basis with bite—until 1985 in *City of Cleburne v. Cleburne Living Center*, 473 U.S. 432 (1985) (see especially pp. 446–450 (White, J., for the majority) and pp. 458–460 (Marshall, J., concurring)). Regarding sexual orientation, the Court did not provide heightened scrutiny—again rational basis with bite—until 1996 in *Romer v. Evans*, 517 U.S. 620 (1996), a case discussed at length in Section D.5 below.

---

tain areas on the West Coast. The Court majority applied strict scrutiny with so much deference to executive and military judgments, however, that the true meaning and impact of the standard could not be clearly ascertained.

D.2. Race Discrimination: The Paradigm Suspect Classification

The courts will look suspiciously at any governmental classification based on race. This suspicion applies even when the classification is allegedly used for a benign or ameliorative purpose, as in an affirmative action program (see Sec. D.7 below). Because courts look suspiciously at racial classifications, race is considered to be a "suspect classification" and a racial minority group is considered to be a "suspect class." Courts and commentators have articulated various reasons why race is accorded this treatment under the equal protection clause. The primary, and most authoritative, reasons are that: (1) the history of the adoption of the Reconstruction-Era Amendments, of which equal protection is a part, underscores the illegitimacy of race as a basis for treating some persons less favorably than others; and (2) a person's race is irrelevant to personal ability or personal worth and thus has no legitimate role in governmental decisionmaking.

Since, for these reasons, any governmental use of race is suspect, courts will scrutinize such uses with extreme care; they will, in other words, apply "strict scrutiny." The case of *Palmore v. Sidoti*, 466 U.S. 429 (1984), is a telling example.

When Linda Sidoti Palmore and Anthony Sidoti, a white couple, divorced in 1980, a Florida court awarded custody of the couples' three-year-old daughter to Palmore. A little over a year later, the father, Sidoti, filed a petition to transfer custody to him due to "changed circumstances." The change in circumstances was that the mother was now cohabiting with an African-American man (whom she married two months later). The trial court found that "there is no issue as to either party's devotion to the child, adequacy of housing facilities, or respectability of the new spouse of either parent" (*Id.* at 430, quoting the trial court). Addressing the father's changed circumstances argument, however, the court ruled that custody should be awarded to the father. The court reasoned that "despite the strides that have been made in bettering relations between the races in this country, it is inevitable that Melanie [the daughter] will, if allowed to remain in her present situation and attains school age and thus more vulnerable to peer pressures, suffer from the social stigmatization that is sure to come" (*Id.* at 431, quoting the trial court). The supposed social stigma from growing up in an interracial home, then, was the court's sole basis for wresting custody from the mother. A Florida appeals court affirmed the ruling, and the Supreme Court granted certiorari.

Although agreeing that "the child's welfare was the controlling factor," the U.S. Supreme Court emphasized that the Florida court had "made no effort to place its holding on any ground other than race.... [T]he outcome would have been different had [the mother] married a Caucasian male of similar respectability" (*Id.* at 432). Such a race-based classification demanded the strictest judicial scrutiny:

> A core purpose of the Fourteenth Amendment was to do away with all governmentally imposed discrimination based on race. See *Strauder v. West Virginia*, 100 U.S. 303, 307–308, 310 (1880). Classifying persons according to their race is more likely to reflect racial prejudice than legitimate public concerns;

the race, not the person, dictates the category. See *Personal Administrator of Mass. v. Feeney*, 442 U.S. 256, 272 (1979). Such classifications are subject to the most exacting scrutiny; to pass constitutional muster, they must be justified by a compelling governmental interest and must be 'necessary... to the accomplishment' of their legitimate purpose, *McLaughlin v. Florida*, 379 U.S. 184, 196 (1964). [466 U.S. at 432–33.][10]

As additional support for this analysis, the Court cited *Loving v. Virginia*, 388 U.S. 1 (1967), the famous case in which the Court invalidated a Virginia statute that made it a crime for Richard and Mildred Loving, and other interracial couples, to marry. (For the story of the Lovings, see Robert Pratt, "Crossing the Color Line: A Historical Assessment and Personal Narrative of *Loving v. Virginia*," 41 HOWARD L. J. 229 (1998).)

Having set forth the test in *Palmore*, the Court turned to examine whether Florida had a compelling interest in removing a child from an interracial home to protect the child from social stigma. The Court conceded that "[i]t would ignore reality to suggest that racial and ethnic prejudices do not exist or that all manifestations of those prejudices have been eliminated" (*Id.* at 433). But the Fourteenth Amendment forbids the State from acting on such considerations:

> There is a risk that a child living with a stepparent of a different race may be subject to a variety of pressures and stresses not present if the child were living with parents of the same racial or ethnic origin.
>
> The question, however, is whether the reality of private biases and the possible injury they might inflict are permissible considerations for removal of an infant child from the custody of its natural mother. We have little difficulty concluding that they are not. The Constitution cannot control such prejudices but neither can it tolerate them. Private biases may be outside the reach of the law, but the law cannot, directly or indirectly, give them effect. [466 U.S. at 433.]

In other words, since accommodation to private racial bias is not a legitimate governmental purpose under the equal protection clause, a state can never have a compelling interest in denying parental rights based on such considerations. The trial court's decision, based on a racial classification, could therefore not meet strict scrutiny. "The effects of racial prejudice, however real, cannot justify a racial classification removing an infant child from custody of its natural mother found to be an appropriate person to have such custody" (*Id.* at 434).

Palmore thus illustrates how to identify a racial classification; why race is a suspect classification; how strict scrutiny review is applied to race classifications; and why gov-

---

10. The Court has also, and increasingly, used an alternative formulation of the means component of strict scrutiny based on "narrow tailoring" or "narrow framing." In *Shaw v. Hunt*, 517 U.S. 899, 908 (1996), for example, the Court asserted that the "'means chosen to accomplish the state's asserted [compelling] purpose must be specifically and narrowly framed to accomplish that purpose'" (quoting *Wygant v. Jackson Board of Education*, 476 U.S. 267, 280 (opinion of Powell, J.), and that the defendant must therefore show that its means "'is narrowly tailored to achieve [its] compelling interest'" (quoting *Miller v. Johnson*, 515 U.S. 900, 920 (1995)).

ernment is unlikely to have any legitimate, let alone compelling, interest in using race as a basis for decisionmaking. Indeed, the only contemporary line of cases in which the U.S. Supreme Court has clearly held that government may have compelling interests in considering race in government decisionmaking is the affirmative action line of cases (see Sec. D.7 below).[11]

D.3. Other Classifications Meriting Heightened Scrutiny

As Section D.2 illustrates, race provides the paradigm for a suspect classification. Racial classifications are more closely tied than any other classification to the original history and purposes of the Fourteenth Amendment, and race provides the clearest example of a classification that is irrelevant to any legitimate governmental decisionmaking purpose. For other classifications to receive heightened scrutiny, they must share some of the characteristics of a race classification. If a particular classification does not share any of these characteristics or "indicia," it will receive only minimal rational basis scrutiny. In *San Antonio Independent School District v. Rodriguez*, 411 U.S. 1 (1973), for example, the Court held that a classification based on the school district in which a family lived, which created a class of families living in "property poor" school districts, merited only rational basis scrutiny because it had "none of the traditional indicia of suspectness." The Court described these indicia as whether "the class is…saddled with such disabilities, or subjected to such a history of purposeful unequal treatment, or relegated to such a position of political powerlessness as to command extraordinary protection from the majoritarian political process" (*Id.* at 28).[12]

When a classification does share one or more characteristics of a race classification, the level of scrutiny depends, in general, on how "race-like" the particular classification is; the more "race-like" it is, the higher the scrutiny should be. The primary char-

---

11. There may, however, be other narrow circumstances in which government could have a compelling interest in considering race when making a particular decision. In a prison desegregation case, *Lee v. Washington*, 390 U.S. 333 (1968), for example, three concurring Justices asserted that "prison authorities…acting in good faith and in particularized circumstances, [may] take into account racial tensions in maintaining security, discipline, and good order in prisons…." (*Id.* at 334; Black, J., Harlan, J., and Stewart, J., concurring). One lower court has also upheld the consideration of race in the hiring of a black supervisor for a prison "bootcamp" program in which almost 70% of the inmates were black; see *Wittmer v. Peters*, 87 F.3d 916 (7th Cir. 1996). And one might conceive of other carefully confined circumstances in which government might justify consideration of race. For instance, if a national park were casting the role of Frederick Douglass or Sojourner Truth in a historical drama, perhaps it could justify preferring an African-American or other person of color to fill the role. If a law enforcement agency were selecting an undercover agent to infiltrate the Ku Klux Klan, perhaps it could justify limiting its selection to white persons.

12. As *Rodriguez* also illustrated, however, classifications that have none of the indicia of suspectness may nevertheless receive heightened (strict) scrutiny if they impinge upon a "fundamental interest" of persons in the affected class (*Rodriguez*, 411 U.S. at 29). This aspect of equal protection is discussed in Section D.8 below.

acteristics or "indicia of suspectness" that courts address (or should address) in making this determination are: (1) whether there is a link between the classification and the Fourteenth Amendment's purposes as revealed in its original history; (2) whether there is a historical record of subjugation or marginalization of the class of persons being discriminated against; (3) whether the classification being used is largely unrelated to personal ability or personal worth; (4) whether the classification being used is largely unrelated to personal choice—that is, whether the classification focuses on an "unalterable trait" or "immutable characteristic" that individuals cannot change; and (5) whether the classification can otherwise be associated with personal bias or animosity. Which factors a court emphasizes will in turn depend on whether the court is applying the class approach or the classification approach to heightened scrutiny analysis, on whether original history is available concerning the class or classification at issue, and on what constitutional (legislative) facts (see Chap. 15, Sec. C.3) are available concerning the class or classification.

On the basis of such considerations, the U.S. Supreme Court has determined that national origin classifications, ethnicity classifications, and some (but not all) alienage classifications, like race, are suspect and thus accorded strict scrutiny. In *Hernandez v. Texas* 347 U.S. 475 (1954), for example, the Court ruled that the systematic exclusion of "persons of Mexican descent" from jury service is treated the same as exclusion on grounds of "race or color;" the exclusion of persons of Mexican descent was a classification based on "ancestry or national origin" (*Id.* at 479) that violated the equal protection clause. In *Keyes v. School District No. 1, Denver* 413 U.S. 189 (1973), a school segregation case, the Court focused on discrimination against "Hispanos" or "Chicanos"—a discrimination based on ethnicity—and treated it the same as race discrimination (*Id.* at 195–198). And in *Graham v. Richardson*, 403 U.S. 365 (1971), the Court invalidated state laws that discriminated against aliens (non-citizens) with respect to eligibility for welfare benefits. Reasoning that "[a]liens as a class are a prime example of a 'discrete and insular' minority (see *United States v. Carolene Products Co.* 304 U.S. 144, 152–153, n. 4 (1938))" deserving "heightened judicial solicitude," Justice Blackmun determined that "classifications based on alienage, like those based on nationality or race, are inherently suspect and subject to close judicial scrutiny" (403 U.S. at 372).[13]

Courts and commentators often do not clearly distinguish national origin and ethnicity classifications from race classifications, or national origin classifications from ethnicity classifications. To be sure, such distinctions may be difficult to draw, and there

---

13. In later cases, the Court created a very large exception for the states' use of alienage classifications to protect prerogatives of citizenship such as participating in the political process and exercising discretionary governmental powers. Such classifications receive only a minimal rational basis review. *See, e.g., Foley v. Connelie*, 435 U.S. 291 (1978). In addition, the Court has made clear that alienage classifications used by the *federal government*, as opposed to a *state* or *local government*, receive only minimal rational basis review. This is because the federal government is the sovereign charged with constitutional authority over foreign relations and immigration, and its judgments regarding alienage and United States citizenship are therefore given deference by the courts. *See, e.g., Mathews v. Diaz*, 426 U.S. 67 (1976).

may be disagreement about how such classifications should be drawn or whether they should be drawn at all, especially for race. *See generally* Ian F. Haney Lopez, WHITE BY LAW: THE LEGAL CONSTRUCTION OF RACE (Critical America Series) (New York Univ. Press, 1996). In *Saint Francis College v. Al-Khazraji*, 481 U.S. 604 (1987), Justice Brennan provided a specific example of the difficulty of drawing lines for national origin and ethnicity:

> [T]he line between discrimination based on "ancestry or ethnic characteristics," *ante*, and discrimination based on "place or nation of...origin," *ibid*, is not a bright one. It is true that one's ancestry—the ethnic group from which an individual and his or her ancestors are descended—is not necessarily the same as one's national origin—the country "where a person was *born*, or, more broadly, the country from which his or her ancestors *came*" [quoting *Espinoza v. Farah Manufacturing Co.*, 414 U.S. 86, 88 (1973) (emphasis added)]. Often, however, the two are identical as a factual matter: one as born in the nation whose primary stock is one's own ethnic group. [481 U.S. at 614 (Brennan, J., concurring).]

Understandings of the distinctions among race, ethnicity, and national origin have also changed over time. For instance, in the *Saint Francis College* case, above, Justice White's majority opinion explains that distinctions now thought to be based on ethnicity or national origin were considered in the Nineteenth Century to be racial distinctions (481 U.S. at 610–612). Moreover, with continual immigration of various ethnic groups into the United States and increases in intermarriages, the variety of ethnic classifications is growing, and understandings of race and ethnicity continue to evolve.

Fortunately, for purposes of the federal Constitution's equal protection clause, most of these difficulties of drawing distinctions may be avoided. Since it is clear that race, national origin, and ethnicity classifications all receive strict scrutiny, fine-grained distinctions among the three classifications are generally unnecessary to the analysis.[14] It does remain important, however, to distinguish race, national origin, and ethnic classifications from alienage classifications, since the latter do not always receive strict scrutiny.

In other cases, courts have determined that classifications, which are not as "race like" as national origin or ethnicity, are nevertheless sufficiently suspicious to receive "intermediate scrutiny" (between strict scrutiny and minimal scrutiny). Gender classifications (see Sec. D.4 below) and are the primary example of this type. Classifications based on illegitimacy (that is, based on a child's parents being unmarried at the time of the child's birth) are another example; *see Clark v. Jeter*, 486 U.S. 456 (1988). In yet other cases, courts have determined that certain classifications, while not as "race-

---

14. The distinctions may continue to have some importance, however, under *statutes* that prohibit certain types of discrimination (see Chap. 14, Sec. B.2). The *Saint Francis College* case, discussed in the text above, was a case arising under a federal non-discrimination statute (42 U.S.C. § 1981). For an illustration of how the distinctions may be sorted out under a federal statute, see 29 C.F.R. § 1606.1, a regulation implementing the federal "Title VII" statute on employment discrimination (42 U.S.C. § 2000e *et seq.*).

like" as gender, have some indicia of suspectness that entitle them to "rational-basis-with-bite" scrutiny (a step above minimal scrutiny), also known as "rational-basis-with-teeth" or "heightened rational basis" scrutiny. The primary examples of this type of classification are sexual orientation (*see* the *Romer* case in Sec. D.5 below) and mental disability (*see Cleburne v. Cleburne Living Center*, 473 U.S. 432 (1985)).

D.4. Gender Discrimination and Intermediate Scrutiny

The *VMI Case, United States v. Virginia*, 518 U.S. 515 (1996), is a leading case illustrating intermediate scrutiny review and a leading case illustrating the Court's analysis of gender classifications. From its founding in 1839, the Virginia Military Institute (VMI) had operated as an all-male bastion of citizen-soldiers. In 1990, the United States sued Virginia alleging that VMI's gender-based admissions policy violated the equal protection clause. The U.S. Court of Appeals for the Fourth Circuit agreed with the United States and ordered Virginia to adopt one of three options: (1) admit women to VMI; (2) establish a parallel institution or program for women; or (3) forego state-support, leaving VMI free to pursue its policies as a private institution. Virginia chose the second option, proposing to create the Virginia Women's Institute for Leadership (VWIL) at another Virginia college. On appeal, the U.S. Supreme Court considered two issues. First, does the exclusion of women from VMI violate equal protection? Second, if VMI's all-male policy does violate equal protection, is the creation of the VWIL an appropriate remedy for this constitutional violation? The Court answered the first question in the affirmative and the second in the negative, thus invalidating VMI's all-male admissions policy and its proposed solution for this discrimination. One Justice concurred in the result only (Rehnquist); one Justice did not participate in the decision (Thomas), and one Justice filed a lengthy and adamant dissent (Scalia).

The Court noted that VMI pursued its mission to create "citizen soldiers" through an "adversative method." This method, unique to VMI, "features 'physical rigor, mental stress, absolute equality of treatment, absence of privacy, minute regulation of behavior, and indoctrination in desirable values.'" The "'cadets live in spartan barracks where surveillance is constant and privacy nonexistent;'" and new cadets "are incessantly exposed to the rat line, 'an extreme form of the adversative model,' comparable in intensity to Marine Corps boot camp" (518 U.S. 522, quoting from 766 F. Supp. 1407, 1421–1424 (W.D. Va 1991)). Virginia provided no comparable experience for females.

The Court subjected VMI's male-only admissions policy to heightened judicial scrutiny:

> Parties who seek to defend gender-based government action must demonstrate an 'exceedingly persuasive justification' for that action.

* * * *

> The Court...has carefully inspected official action that closes a door or denies an opportunity to women (or to men).... Focusing on the differential

treatment or denial of opportunity for which relief is sought, the reviewing court must determine whether the proffered justification is "exceedingly persuasive." The burden of justification is demanding and it rests entirely on the State... The State must show "at least that the [challenged] classification serves 'important governmental objectives and that the discriminatory means employed' are 'substantially related to the achievement of those objectives.'"... The justification must be genuine, not hypothesized or invented *post hoc* in response to litigation. And it must not rely on overbroad generalizations about the different talents, capacities, or preferences of males and females. [518 U.S. at 531, 533, citing, *inter alia*, *Mississippi University for Women v. Hogan*, 458 U.S. 718, 724 (1982).]

To satisfy its burden under this intermediate judicial scrutiny, Virginia proffered two justifications for its male-only policy. First, it sought to maintain single-sex education because it provides "important educational benefits" and contributes to "diversity in educational approaches." Second, it sought to preserve VMI's unique "adversative method" of instruction, which "would have to be modified were VMI to admit women" (518 U.S. at 535).

As to Virginia's first argument about the pedagogical benefits of same-sex education, the Court retorted that the State had failed to show that the VMI case established or has been maintained to further this objective:

[W]e find no persuasive evidence in this record that VMI's male-only admission policy "is in furtherance of a state policy of diversity." [A] purpose genuinely to advance an array of educational options... is not served by VMI's historic and constant plan—a plan to "afford a unique educational benefit only to males." However "liberally" this plan serves the Commonwealth's sons, it makes no provision whatever for her daughters. [518 U.S. at 539–540.]

Thus, while educational diversity may be an "important governmental objective," it was not the "actual state purpose" for which Virginia established the male-only policy, but rather a "rationalization[ ] for actions in fact differently grounded" (518 U.S. at 535–536).

The Court similarly dismissed Virginia's second justification for justifying the male-only policy: preserving the adversative method. In pressing this argument, Virginia had improperly relied on overbroad generalizations about the interests and capabilities of the sexes:

It may be assumed... that most women would not choose VMI's adversative method.... [However,] it is also probable that "many men would not want to be educated in such an environment".... The issue... is... whether the Commonwealth can constitutionally deny to women who have the will and capacity, the training and attendant opportunities that VMI uniquely affords.

The notion that admission of women would downgrade VMI's stature, destroy the adversative system and, with it, even the school, is a judgment hardly proved, a prediction hardly different from other "self-fulfilling prophec[ies]"... once routinely used to deny rights or opportunities. [518 U.S. at 542–543.]

Virginia's male-only policy therefore was not "substantially related" to the state's objective of maintaining the adversative method, and Virginia's objective of educating "citizen-soldiers" was "not substantially advanced by women's categorical exclusion, in total disregard of their individual merit...." (518 U.S. at 545–546).

Since Virginia's arguments fell "far short of...the 'exceedingly persuasive justification'" necessary to sustain gender-based classifications, the Court held that the VMI all-male policy violated the equal protection clause. The Court then faced the remedy question—whether Virginia's establishment of the VWIL was a constitutionally sufficient remedy.

The leadership institute (VWIL) proposed by Virginia, the Court found, was plainly inadequate because the education it provided was not equal to a VMI education. In particular, the VMIL did not provide the adversative method approach to education. "VWIL affords women no opportunity to experience the rigorous military training for which VMI is famed.... Instead, the VWIL program 'de-emphasizes' military education...and uses a 'cooperative method' of education 'which reinforces self-esteem.'" In addition, "VWIL's student body, faculty, course offerings, and facilities hardly match VMI's." Nor can the VWIL graduate anticipate the benefits associated with VMI's 157-year history, the school's prestige, and its influential alumni network" (518 U.S. at 551). Virginia therefore had "failed to provide [a] 'comparable single-gender women's institution,'" and "had not shown substantial equality in the separate educational opportunities" at VWIL and VMI (518 U.S. at 554).

Presumably, had Virginia created a "comparable" women's institution substantially equal to VMI, that would have been a suitable remedy even though the arrangement would still provide gender-segregated education. Thus, the Court in *VMI* has pointed toward an important distinction in the Court's equal protection jurisprudence as applied to race and gender. While state-sponsored racial segregation is never permissible, the state may apparently separate persons by gender in some circumstances, at least in education programs, provided that both sexes are treated equally. Of course, as the Court's treatment of the proposed VWIL remedy demonstrates, the standard of equality will be rigorous, and it will therefore be difficult in most cases to justify such a separation of the sexes.

D.5. Sexual Orientation Discrimination and Rational-Basis-With-Bite Scrutiny

A leading example of rational-basis-with-bite scrutiny, and the primary example of the Court's analysis of sexual orientation classifications, is *Romer v. Evans*, 517 U.S. 620 (1996). The case involved a 1992 statewide referendum in which the State of Colorado adopted a constitutional amendment prohibiting the state, its state agencies, and its local governments from acting to protect gays and lesbians from discrimination. Amendment 2 read, in pertinent part:

> No Protected Status Based on Homosexuality, Lesbian or Bisexual Orientation. Neither the State of Colorado, through any of its branches or depart-

ments, nor any of its agencies, political subdivisions, municipalities or school districts, shall enact, adopt, or enforce any statute, regulation, ordinance, or policy whereby homosexual, lesbian, or bisexual orientation, conduct, practices, or relationships shall constitute or otherwise be the basis of or entitle any person or class of persons to have or claim any minority status, quota preferences, protected status or claim of discrimination.

In large part, Amendment 2 was a response to the ordinances of several liberal Colorado municipalities, such as Aspen and Boulder, that had enacted laws forbidding discrimination based on sexual orientation. The Amendment effectively repealed these ordinances and prohibited the municipalities from reenacting them; it also prohibited other state and local agencies from taking similar steps. Various plaintiffs, including homosexual persons and three municipalities, challenged Amendment 2 as a violation of the equal protection clause. The Colorado Supreme Court agreed with the plaintiffs, ruling that the Amendment "was subject to strict scrutiny under the Fourteenth Amendment because it infringed the fundamental right of gays and lesbians to participate in the political process" — a fundamental interest, rather than suspect class, argument for strict scrutiny (see Sec. D.8 below). By a 6-3 vote, the United States Supreme Court affirmed the Colorado Supreme Court's judgment that the amendment violated equal protection, but it did so on other grounds than those invoked by the Colorado court.

The U.S. Supreme Court, per Justice Kennedy, settled on rational basis review, under which the Court "will uphold the legislative classification so long as it bears a rational relation to some legitimate end" (517 U.S. at 631). The Court did not need to consider a higher level of review, since "Amendment 2 fails, indeed defies, even this conventional inquiry" (*Id.* at 632). According to the Court:

> First, the amendment has the peculiar property of imposing a broad and undifferentiated disability on a single named group, an exceptional and...invalid form of legislation. Second, its sheer breadth is so discontinuous with the reasons offered for it that the amendment seems inexplicable by anything but animus toward the class it affects; it lacks a rational relationship to legitimate state interests. [517 U.S. at 632.]

Amendment 2, noted Justice Kennedy, disqualified homosexuals from seeking any specific protection under the law. Colorado's argument that the measure merely denied homosexuals special rights was therefore "implausible." Rather than simply denying preferential treatment to homosexuals, Amendment 2:

> imposes a special disability upon those persons alone. Homosexuals are forbidden the safeguards that others enjoy or may seek without constraint. They can obtain specific protection against discrimination only by enlisting the citizenry of Colorado to amend the State Constitution or perhaps, on the State's view, by trying to pass helpful laws of general applicability. This is so no matter how local or discrete the harm, no matter how public and widespread the injury. [517 U.S. at 631.]

Consequently, Amendment 2:

is at once too narrow and too broad. It identifies persons by a single trait and then denies them protection across the board....It is not within our constitutional tradition to enact laws of this sort. Central both to the idea of the rule of law and to our own Constitution's guarantee of equal protection is the principle that government and each of its parts remain open on impartial terms to all who seek its assistance. [517 U.S. at 633.]

Perhaps most significantly, the Court believed animus toward homosexuals underpinned the measure. Colorado had offered two justifications for its treatment of homosexuals and lesbians: first, that Amendment 2 advanced "other citizens' freedom of association, and in particular the liberties of landlords or employers who have personal or religious objections to homosexuality"; and second, that the Amendment would conserve state resources to fight discrimination against other groups. The Court rejected both of Colorado's arguments: "[I]n making a general announcement that gays and lesbians shall not have any particular protections from the law, [Amendment 2] inflicts on them immediate, continuing, and real injuries that outrun and belie any legitimate justifications that may be claimed for it" (517 U.S. at 635). Further, "the breadth of the amendment is so far removed from these particular justifications that we find it impossible to credit them" (*Id.*). Amendment 2, the Court concluded, "classifies homosexuals not to further a proper legislative end but to make them unequal to everyone else. This Colorado cannot do. A State cannot so deem a class of persons a stranger to its laws" (*Id.*).

Amendment 2 therefore failed the rational basis test. Its actual ends were not those alleged by the state; the actual ends achieved by the Amendment were illegitimate and thus failed the ends scrutiny that the Court applied to the classification. Moreover, even if the state's alleged objectives were accepted as the real objectives of the classification, the Amendment was so under-and over-inclusive (as to these ends) that it was not rationally related to them. In this respect, the classification in the Amendment failed the means scrutiny applied by the Court. In its analysis—although the Court does not say so—it clearly applies the rational basis standard of review more assertively, and with less deference to the state, than is the case with traditional minimal scrutiny review. Hence this case provides a good example of the "bite" or "teeth" that courts will sometimes impart into the rational basis standard.

D.6. The Problem of Discriminatory Intent

In determining which classes or classifications receive heightened scrutiny, it is sometimes necessary to examine the concept of discriminatory intent. Only government actions that are *intentionally* discriminatory on the basis of some suspect (tier I) or quasi-suspect (tier II) trait are subject to heightened scrutiny. To understand when and how intent may become an issue in equal protection analysis, it is necessary to distinguish between "facially discriminatory" regulations and "facially neutral" regulations. A facially discriminatory regulation is one that employs an explicit classification based on some suspect or quasi-suspect trait; such a classification, in other words, appears "on the face" of the regulation. A facially neutral regulation, on the other hand, does not employ any such classification "on its face." The former type of law is subject to heightened scrutiny, since courts assume that lawmakers who adopt such an explicit classification do so intentionally in order to discriminate on the basis of the characteristic identified in the classification. If the regulation classifies by gender, for instance, courts will assume that the lawmakers have intentionally adopted the regulation to discriminate on the basis of gender, and the gender classification will receive intermediate scrutiny. The latter type of law (the facially neutral law) is treated quite differently. Courts will not assume that such a law is intentionally discriminatory. One must look beyond the face of the statute, therefore, for evidence of discrimination.

The U.S. Supreme Court has identified two circumstances in which a facially neutral law will be considered discriminatory and subject to heightened scrutiny: (1) when there is discrimination in the *administration* of the law; and (2) when there is discrimination in the *purpose and effect* of the law. To fit the first circumstance, a plaintiff must prove that (a) administrators have administered the law in a way that discriminates against a suspect or quasi-suspect class; and (b) these administrators have intentionally administered the law in this way in order to discriminate. To fit the second circumstance, a plaintiff must prove that (a) the law in its operation has a "discriminatory effect" or "disproportionate impact" on a suspect or quasi-suspect class; and (b) the lawmakers who enacted the law or maintained it after enactment did so intentionally in order to create such a discriminatory effect (or impact).

The relevant purpose and effect in this second circumstance may be found either in the initial enactment of the law (*see, e.g., Gomillion v. Lightfoot*, 364 U.S. 339 (1960)), the maintenance of the law over time (*see, e.g., Rogers v. Lodge*, 458 U.S. 613 (1982)), or a combination of the two (*cf. Personnel Administrator of Massachusetts v. Feeney*, 442 U.S. 256 (1979), discussed below in this Section). The same purpose and effect analysis that applies to the enactment and maintenance of allegedly discriminatory laws may also apply to other governmental decisions that are allegedly discriminatory. In *Village of Arlington Heights v. Metropolitan Housing Development Corp.*, 429 U.S. 252 (1977), for instance, the Court applied purpose and effect analysis to the village's denial of a request to re-zone a parcel of land, ultimately rejecting the respondent's equal protection challenge because they had not submitted sufficient proof of any discriminatory purpose or intent, that motivated the village's decision.

The classic case of *Yick Wo v. Hopkins*, 118 U.S. 356 (1886), illustrates the circumstance of discrimination in the administration of a law. The City of San Francisco had enacted ordinances requiring that any person operating a laundry in a building constructed of wood (versus brick or stone) had to receive a permit from the Board of Supervisors. Evidence showed that approximately 310 of 320 laundries in San Francisco were in buildings made of wood; that about 240 of the 320 laundries were operated by Chinese persons; that about 200 Chinese operators had applied for permits, and all had been denied; and that about 80 non-Chinese operators had applied for permits, and all but one had been granted. Yick Wo had operated a laundry for 22 years in the same wooden building before being denied a permit under the new ordinances, and he was convicted and imprisoned for continuing to do so after the permit denial.

The Court made clear that, even if a law "be fair on its face and impartial in its appearance," it will still violate equal protection "if it is applied and administered by public authority with an evil eye and an unequal hand...." (118 U.S. at 373–374). The administration of the laundry ordinances fit this description, the Court said, and constituted unconstitutional discrimination by race and nationality:

> [T]he cases present the ordinances in actual operation, and the facts shown establish an administration directed so exclusively against a particular class of persons as to warrant and require the conclusion that, whatever may have been the intent of the ordinances as adopted, they are applied by the public authorities charged with their administration, and thus representing the State itself, with a mind so unequal and oppressive as to amount to a practical denial by the State of that equal protection of the laws which is secured to the petitioners, as to all other persons, by the broad and benign provisions of the Fourteenth Amendment to the Constitution of the United States....
>
> The fact of this discrimination [against Chinese subjects] is admitted. No reason for it is shown, and the conclusion cannot be resisted, that no reason for it exists except hostility to the race and nationality to which the petitioners belong, and which in the eye of the law is not justified. The discrimination is, therefore, illegal, and the public administration which enforces it is a denial of the equal protection of the laws and a violation of the Fourteenth Amendment of the Constitution. [118 U.S. at 373–374.]

The circumstance of discrimination in the purpose and effect of the law arises more frequently in the modern cases than does discrimination in the administration of a law. The most contentious questions have concerned how to prove the requisite discriminatory intent (or purpose) on the part of the lawmakers. For many years there was an ongoing debate, in the courts and in the legal literature, about whether proof of discriminatory effect alone should be sufficient for the plaintiff's case against a facially neutral statute or, alternatively, whether discriminatory intent should be inferable from evidence of a disproportionate impact on a suspect or quasi-suspect class. *See, e.g.*, Gayle Binion, "'Intent' and Equal Protection: A Reconsideration," 1983 Sup. Ct. Rev. 397. But the U.S. Supreme Court has insisted on proof of discriminatory intent, in addition to proof of discriminatory effect, and has been unwilling to infer such intent from the effect itself, except in the most egregious (and unusual) case where there is a clear and stark statistical pattern of disproportionate impact (like that in *Yick Wo*). The following two cases illustrate current law concerning discriminatory intent and effect.

In *Washington v. Davis*, 426 U.S. 229 (1976), the Supreme Court considered whether the requirement of a written, personnel test for prospective members of the Washington, D.C. police force was constitutional if the test had a discriminatory impact on the black test-takers. The petitioners alleged that the test—designed to test "verbal ability, vocabulary, reading and comprehension" and used throughout the federal government's civil service program—"excluded a disproportionately high number" of minority applicants, and that its use therefore constituted race discrimination. Approximately four times as many blacks as whites failed the test.

Reviewing its prior cases, the Court emphasized that they "have not embraced the proposition that a law or other official act, without regard to whether it reflects a racially discriminatory purpose, is unconstitutional *solely* because it has a racially disproportionate impact" (426 U.S. at 239; italics in original). The Court acknowledged that "an invidious discriminatory purpose may often be inferred from the totality of the relevant facts, including the fact, if it is true, that the law bears more heavily on one race than another" (426 U.S. at 242). Nevertheless, said the Court:

> we have not held that a law, neutral on its face and serving ends otherwise within the power of government to pursue, is invalid under the Equal Protection Clause simply because it may affect a greater proportion of one race than of another. Disproportionate impact is not irrelevant, but it is not the sole touchstone of an invidious racial discrimination forbidden by the Constitution. Standing alone, it does not trigger the rule . . . that racial classifications are to be subjected to the strictest scrutiny and are justifiable only be the weightiest of considerations. [426 U.S. at 242.]

While a greater proportion of blacks failed the test, the petitioners were unable to prove that government officials intended to discriminate by race when they adopted and used the test. Since there was no discriminatory purpose, and thus no racial classification, the Court applied only rational basis scrutiny. Under this scrutiny, the Court easily found the test to be constitutional. "The test is neutral on its face and rationally may be said to serve a purpose the Government is constitutionally empowered to pursue"—the goal of a police force with a demonstrated basic level of literacy and reading comprehension.

A second case, *Personnel Administrator of Massachusetts v. Feeney*, 442 U.S. 256 (1979), dealt with discriminatory intent issues in the context of gender discrimination, confirming and extending the principles that *Washington v. Davis* applied to race discrimination. In Massachusetts, since the Revolutionary War, veterans had enjoyed an absolute lifetime preference over non-veterans in the Massachusetts civil service program. Feeney, a professional secretary, non-veteran, and twelve-year civil service employee, had in one year received "the second highest score on an examination for a job with the Board of Dental Examiners" and two years later had received "the third highest [score] on a test for an Administrative Assistant position with a mental health center." While her scores would have placed her near the top of an "eligible list" for available jobs, the state's veterans' preference placed tested veterans on the "eligible list" ahead of all non-veterans; the result was that Feeney was not considered for positions she was qualified for and that lower-scoring veterans were hired for these posts. The veterans' preference statute on its face was gender-neutral; it discriminated against non-veterans, not women, and discrimination against non-veterans would receive only minimal scrutiny. But Feeney claimed the veterans' preference statute nevertheless violated her equal protection rights under the Fourteenth Amendment because an overwhelming majority of veterans are males who seek the best civil service positions, therefore guaranteeing that women, a very small percentage of whom are veterans, will remain in the lower-level positions or not be hired. The data showed that, at the time of the litigation, over 98% of veterans in Massachusetts were male, and that more than a quarter of the Massachusetts population were veterans.

Citing *Washington v. Davis*, the Court asserted that "the Fourteenth Amendment guarantees equal laws, not equal results." Proof of discriminatory "impact provides 'an important starting point,' but purposeful discrimination is the condition that offends the Constitution" (442 U.S. at 274). The record did not contain sufficient proof of such purposeful discrimination by gender: "When the totality of legislative actions establishing and extending the Massachusetts veterans' preference are considered, the law remains what it purports to be: a preference for veterans of either sex over non-veterans of either sex, not for men over women" (442 U.S. at 280).

It was true, the Court admitted, that Massachusetts legislators must have known that the preference statute would adversely affect women.

> "Discriminatory purpose," however, implies more than intent as volition or intent as awareness of consequences.... It implies that the decisionmaker, in this case a state legislature, selected or reaffirmed a particular course of action [benefitting veterans] at least in part *"because of"* and not merely *"in spite of,"* of its adverse effects upon an identifiable group. Nothing in the record demonstrates that this preference for veterans was originally devised or subsequently re-enacted because it would accomplish the collateral goal of keeping women in a stereotypic and predefined place in the Massachusetts Civil Service. [442 U.S. at 279; emphasis in original.]

Since Feeney had failed to prove that the Massachusetts legislators passed and maintained the veterans' preference law "because of" its discriminatory effects on women, there was no gender discrimination and no basis for heightened scrutiny of the law.

D.7. Affirmative Action Programs

Affirmative action issues may arise under the equal protection clause when government uses a racial or gender preference in hiring employees, selecting students for an academic program, or allocating government contracts or licenses. Plaintiffs challenging such plans argue that the advantage or preferential treatment for members of racial minority groups or for women constitutes "reverse discrimination"; that is, discrimination against a group (whites or men) traditionally considered to be the more advantaged or politically powerful. Courts generally consider such discrimination to be intentional because it appears on the face of the affirmative action policy (see Sec. D.5 above). The issues usually focus on the standard of review and its application to the particular affirmative action plan at issue.

Affirmative action programs and the litigation concerning them have been the subject of intense controversy since the early 1970s. The U.S. Supreme Court's first decision on the merits in an affirmative action case was *Regents of the University of California v. Bakke*, 438 U.S. 265 (1978). The plaintiff, a white male twice rejected from the medical school of the University of California at Davis, challenged the affirmative action program that the school had used to select a portion of its entering class in each year that he was rejected. The particular facts concerning this program's operation were critical to its legality and were carefully analyzed in the court proceedings.

The medical school's "faculty had devised a special admissions program to increase the representation of 'disadvantaged' students in each medical school class. The special program consisted of a separate admissions system operating in coordination with the regular admissions process...." (438 U.S. at 272). The school used this program to give special consideration to applicants who were members of minority groups, "which the medical school apparently viewed as 'blacks,' 'Chicanos,' 'Asians,' and 'American Indians'" (438 U.S. at 272). Applicants seeking consideration through this special program were reviewed by a separate committee that did not compare these applicants to the other applicants being reviewed by the regular admissions committee. Sixteen places in the class of 100 were reserved for applicants in the special program (*see generally* 438 U.S. at 272–276 (opinion of Powell, J.)). The university sought to justify this program by citing four needs or state interests that supported it: providing doctors to work in underserved minority communities, compensating for the effects of societal discrimination against minorities, reducing the historical deficit of minorities in the medical profession, and diversifying the student body.

By a 5 to 4 vote, the U.S. Supreme Court held that this affirmative action program unlawfully discriminated against white applicants.[15] A different majority, however, again by a 5 to 4 vote, held that the medical school was not constitutionally prohibited from considering race as a factor in its admissions process; it could do so by other means that did not insulate minority applicants from competition with the regular applicants and did not utilize a quota or set-aside to reserve places for minority applicants. Justice Powell was the "swing voter" who joined both majorities.

The Justices wrote six opinions in the *Bakke* case, none of which commanded a majority of the Court. The various opinions debated the issues of what equal protection standards should apply, what the appropriate justifications for affirmative action programs are, and to what extent such programs can be race conscious. Justice Powell wrote the lead opinion announcing the Court's judgment, but the other members of the Court did not join the critical parts of his opinion regarding the standard of review to apply to affirmative action plans and the permissible justifications for affirmative action admission plans. Justice Powell applied a strict scrutiny standard— whether the University of California had a "compelling state interest" in giving a preference to minority applicants and whether the medical school's plan was "precisely tailored" to the effectuation of any such compelling interest (438 U.S. at 299). In contrast, four other Justices, led by Justice Brennan, applied an intermediate scrutiny standard, arguing that strict scrutiny was unnecessary because the discrimination was "benign," (that is, serving a worthy purpose that was not based on racial prejudice against, and

---

15. Four of these five Justices avoided the constitutional questions by relying on Title VI of the Civil Rights Act of 1964, 42 U.S.C. § 2000d, rather than the equal protection clause, as the basis for their decision. Title VI prohibits race discrimination by recipients of federal funding, and these four Justices ruled that the plaintiffs' rejection based in part on race was race discrimination within the meaning of Title VI.

did not stigmatize, the disadvantaged class) and "remedial" (that is, remedying or compensating for past discrimination) (438 U.S. at 358–359 (Brennan, J., concurring in part and dissenting)).

The standard-of-review issue concerning race-conscious affirmative action plans was finally resolved in *City of Richmond v. J.A. Croson Co.*, 488 U.S. 469 (1989), where the Court ruled 6 to 3 that a program to set aside public construction contract funds for award to minority subcontractors violated the equal protection clause. The City required that prime contractors who were awarded city construction contracts must subcontract at least thirty percent of the amount of each contract to minority-owned businesses. A majority of the Justices applied a strict scrutiny standard (*see* 488 U.S. at 494 (O'Connor, J.) and 488 U.S. at 520 (Scalia, J.)), requiring that the set-asides must be justified by a compelling governmental interest and narrowly tailored to accomplish their intended purpose of remedying past racial discrimination. Although recognizing the historical fact of race discrimination in government contracting programs, the Court majority characterized as "sheer speculation" the city's claim that its generalized findings of prior race discrimination justified the imposition of what the Court considered "a rigid racial quota":

> While there is no doubt that the sorry history of both private and public discrimination in this country has contributed to a lack of opportunities for black entrepreneurs, this observation, standing alone, cannot justify a rigid racial quota in the awarding of public contracts in Richmond, Virginia....
>
> * * * *
>
> While the States and their subdivisions may take remedial action when they possess evidence that their own spending practices are exacerbating a pattern of prior discrimination, they must identify that discrimination, public or private, with some specificity before they may use race-conscious relief. [488 U.S. at 498–499, 508.]

A successor case concerning federal government contracting programs, *Adarand Constructors v. Pena*, 515 U.S. 200 (1995), confirmed this strict scrutiny approach for reviewing race-conscious affirmative action programs.

The *Croson* and *Adarand* cases, like other U.S. Supreme Court affirmative action cases arising after the *Bakke* case, recognized only one justification for the use of racial preferences: remedying the present effects of past racial discrimination perpetrated or supported by the government or government agency that implements the affirmative action plan. In *Bakke*, however, Justice Powell (speaking only for himself) had endorsed a second justification applicable to higher education admissions plans: attainment of a racially and ethnically diverse student body. For Powell, such diversity must be "only one element in a range of factors" that the university considers to attain "the goal of a heterogeneous study body" (438 U.S. at 314 (opinion of Powell, J.)). Twenty-five years after *Bakke*, the Court returned to this contentious issue in two companion cases from the University of Michigan: *Grutter v. Bollinger*, 123 S.Ct. 2325 (2003), concerning the law school's admissions plan; and *Gratz v. Bollinger*, 123 S.Ct. 2411 (2003), concerning the undergraduate college's admissions plan.

In *Grutter*, by a 5 to 4 vote, the Court upheld the law school's race-conscious affirmative action plan. In *Gratz*, by a 6 to 3 vote, a different majority struck down the undergraduate college's plan.[16] Justice O'Connor, author of the majority opinion in *Grutter*, was the sole Justice to join the majority opinion in both cases. Both majority opinions utilized strict scrutiny review. There was considerable debate in the opinions, however, about the strictness of the review for affirmative action plans, and the majority in *Gratz* appears to have applied a stricter version than the majority in *Grutter*. Both majority opinions also utilized the principles of "narrow tailoring" (see below) developed in Justice Powell's opinion in *Bakke*.

In *Grutter*, the law school case, the Court held that "student body diversity is a compelling state interest that can justify the use of race in University admissions" (123 S.Ct. at 2338–2339)—thus expressly adopting Justice Powell's view in *Bakke*. Six Justices took this position—the majority plus Justice Kennedy (123 S.Ct. at 2370, 2373 (Kennedy, J., dissenting))—and a seventh Justice, the Chief Justice, did not dispute it (123 S.Ct. at 2365–2370 (Rehnquist, C.J., dissenting)). Diversity, said the majority, "promotes 'cross-racial understanding,'" helps students "to break down racial stereotypes…" (quoting from the district court's opinion in *Grutter*), and produces positive learning outcomes in the classroom. Moreover:

> [U]niversities, and in particular, law schools, represent the training ground for a large number of our Nation's leaders….
>
> In order to cultivate a set of leaders with legitimacy in the eyes of the citizenry, it is necessary that the path to leadership be visibly open to talented and qualified individuals of every race and ethnicity. All members of our heterogeneous society must have confidence in the openness and integrity of the educational institutions that provide…the training and education necessary to succeed in America. [123 S.Ct. at 2341.]

Having determined that the law school's affirmative action plan was supported by a compelling interest, the *Grutter* majority then held that the plan was "narrowly tailored" to achieve this compelling interest (student body diversity). The plaintiff, and the United States as *amicus curiae*, had argued that the Law School's plan did not meet the narrow tailoring requirement of strict scrutiny "because race-neutral means exist to obtain the educational benefits of student body diversity." In rejecting this argument, the majority reasoned that:

> Narrow tailoring does not require exhaustion of every conceivable race-neutral alternative.…Narrow tailoring does, however, require serious, good faith consideration of workable race-neutral alternatives.…
>
> * * * *
>
> We are satisfied that the Law School adequately considered race-neutral alternatives currently capable of producing a critical mass [of minority students]

---

16. Only five of the six Justices in the *Gratz* majority joined the majority opinion. The sixth Justice, Justice Breyer, wrote a separate concurring opinion agreeing with the result the majority reached but not with its reasoning.

without forcing the Law School to abandon the academic selectivity that is the cornerstone of its educational mission. [123 S.Ct. at 2344–2345.]

In the second case, *Gratz*, the Court focused on the narrow-tailoring requirement as applied to the undergraduate college's admissions plan, which was considerably different from the law school plan. Relying on Justice Powell's guidelines in his *Bakke* opinion, the *Gratz* majority determined that the undergraduate college plan was not sufficiently "flexible," since it did not provide for an "individualized consideration" of each applicant's potential contribution to diversity without the race factor being "decisive." According to the Court:

> The [undergraduate] policy automatically distributes 20 points to every single applicant from an "under-represented minority" group, as defined by the University.... [This] automatic distribution of 20 points has the effect of making "the factor of race...decisive" for virtually every minimally qualified under-represented minority applicant. [123 S.Ct. at 2478, quoting 438 U.S. at 317 (opinion of Powell, J.).]

Thus "the University's use of race in its current freshmen admissions policy is not narrowly tailored to achieve [its] asserted compelling interest in diversity;" and having failed this part of strict scrutiny review, "the admissions policy violates the Equal Protection Clause of the Fourteenth Amendment" (123 S. Ct. at 2430).

It is clear from *Croson*, *Adarand*, *Grutter*, and *Gratz* that all governmental affirmative action programs using race preferences are subject to strict scrutiny review. This review is triggered by any intentional use of race as a classifying factor; strict scrutiny "is not dependent on the race of those burdened or benefitted by a particular classification" (*Gratz*, 123 S.Ct. at 2427, quoting *Croson*, 488 U.S. at 494). The affirmative action cases are thus the leading examples of the Court's use of the "classifying factor approach" rather than the "class approach" to suspectness in race discrimination cases (see Sec. C.4 above). This approach to strict scrutiny is necessary, the Court has said, for determining "what classifications are 'benign' or 'remedial' and what classifications are in fact motivated by illegitimate notions of racial inferiority or simple racial politics." The Court thus applies strict scrutiny to all racial classifications "to 'smoke out' illegitimate uses of race by assuring that [government] is pursuing a goal important enough to warrant use of a highly suspect tool" (*Croson*, 488 U.S. at 493, quoted in *Grutter*, 123 S.Ct. at 2338).[17] In the *Gratz* case (above), however, Justices Ginsberg, Breyer, and Souter dissented from the Corut's application of the classifying factor approach, and the strict scrutiny standard, to genuine affirmative action plans:

> In implementing [the Fourteenth Amendment's] equality instruction,...government decisionmakers may properly distinguish between policies of exclusion and inclusion....Actions designed to burden groups long denied full citizenship stature are not sensibly ranked with measures taken to hasten the day when entrenched discrimination and its after effects have been extirpated.

---

17. If the affirmative action plan provided for gender preferences rather than race preferences, the Court would still follow the classifying factor approach; but intermediate scrutiny, rather than strict scrutiny, would apply.

[*Gratz*, 123 S.Ct. at 2444 (Ginsburg, J., dissenting; *cf. Bakke*, 438 U.S. at 357–362 (Brennan, J, concurring and dissenting).]

D.8.   Strict Scrutiny for Classifications Infringing Fundamental Interests

In equal protection analysis, as Section C suggests, there are two pathways to strict scrutiny. The first, the suspect classification pathway, is addressed in Sections D.2 and D.3 above. The alternative, the fundamental interest pathway, is discussed here. The genesis of this alternative approach is *Skinner v. Oklahoma*, 316 U.S. 535 (1942), set out and discussed in Chapter 11, Section E. The fundamental interest approach focuses on the personal interests of the class that is disadvantaged by the government's use of the classification at issue. If the interest infringed is one that the courts consider to be "fundamental," the classification receives strict scrutiny. The classification itself need not have any characteristics of suspectness (see Secs. D.2 and D.3 above); it is the interest infringed, not the classification used, that justifies the strict scrutiny. The strict scrutiny standard for fundamental interests is the same as that for suspect classifications: whether the classification is necessary to the accomplishment of (or is narrowly drawn to effectuate) a compelling government interest.

So-called "fundamental" interests are also a focus of concern in substantive due process analysis (see Chap. 11, Sec. C.4). There is some interrelation between the equal protection and substantive due process aspects of fundamental interests, in that fundamental interests recognized under substantive due process may also be considered fundamental interests for equal protection purposes (see point 1 below in this section, after the discussion of the *Rodriguez* case). But it is nevertheless important to distinguish conceptually between fundamental interest analysis under equal protection and that under substantive due process. The equal protection analysis in this Section considers fundamental interests as an aspect of *equality*—and the focus is on identifying situations where it is important for the courts to protect persons against identified inequalities even though the classification used is not suspect or quasi-suspect. In contrast, the substantive due process analysis in Chapter 11, Section C, considers fundamental interests as an aspect of *liberty*, and the focus is on identifying situations where it is important to protect persons against deprivations of liberty because the interest infringed is a "fundamental *liberty* interest." In short, under equal protection the concern about fundamental interests is an *egalitarian* concern, while under substantive due process it is a *libertarian* concern. Equal protection protects classes of persons from being treated differently than other classes with respect to governmental benefits or burdens that implicate fundamental interests; substantive due process protects individuals from deprivations of their fundamental liberty interests by creating substantive rights—"fundamental rights" – that they may assert against the government which created the deprivation.

A classic example of a fundamental interest under equal protection is the interest in *voting* for public officials. The key case is *Reynolds v. Sims*, 377 U.S. 533 (1964). In *Reynolds*, voters living in three densely populated, urban counties in Alabama sued various state executives and legislators for violating their right to vote protected by the equal protection clause. The Alabama legislature had not reapportioned state voting districts for statewide elections since the 1900 census. The plaintiff voters from the urban counties claimed that they were the victims of discrimination because they were under-represented in the state's 106-member House of Representatives and 35-member Senate, while voters in sparsely populated rural counties were over-represented. In the state House of Representatives, for instance, Bullock County with a population of 13,462 was allotted two seats, while Mobile County with a population of 314,301 was allotted only 3 seats; and in the state Senate, Lowndes County with a population of 15,417 was allotted one seat, while Jefferson County with a population of approximately 600,000 was also allotted one seat. The weight of a person's vote, and the strength of representation per person, thus depended on where the voter lived. This classification was based on residence, which is a classification that does not have characteristics of suspectness and does not receive heightened scrutiny.[18]

The Court in *Reynolds*, however, focused on the interest infringed, not the classification itself:

> It has been repeatedly recognized [by this Court] that all qualified voters have a constitutionally protected right to vote.... The right to vote freely for the candidate of one's choice is of the essence of a democratic society, and any restrictions on that right strike at the heart of representative government.... [377 U.S. at 555.]

Chief Justice Warren for the majority also emphasized that "the right to exercise the franchise in a free and unimpaired manner is preservative of other basic civil and political rights..." (377 U.S. at 562). Because voting plays such a critical role in the American democracy, a person's interest in voting is "fundamental": "Undoubtedly, the right of suffrage is a *fundamental* matter in a free and democratic society.... '[T]he political franchise of voting [is] a *fundamental* political right, because preservative of all rights'" (377 U.S. at 561–562, quoting *Yick Wo v. Hopkins*, 118 U.S. 356, 370 (1886) (emphasis added)). Alabama was infringing upon this fundamental interest by maintaining a malapportioned state legislature. "[T]he right of suffrage can be denied by a debasement or dilution of the weight of a citizen's vote just as effectively as by wholly prohibiting the free exercise of the franchise" (377 U.S. at 555). Since the interest at stake is fundamental, "any alleged infringement of the right of citizens to vote must be carefully and meticulously scrutinized" (377 U.S. at 562). Alabama's treatment of some voters differently than others, according to residence, was therefore subject to a strict scrutiny standard of review.

Applying strict scrutiny, the Court determined that "[t]he Equal Protection Clause guarantees the opportunity for equal participation by all voters in the election of state legislators" (377 U.S. at 566), and that population must be the "starting point for con-

---

18. For confirmation of this point, see *San Antonio Independent School District v. Rodriguez*, 411 U.S. 1 (1973), discussed in Section D.3 above, in which the Court accorded minimal rational basis scrutiny to a classification based on geography or residency—specifically a classification based on the school district in which a family lived.

sideration and the controlling criterion" in a state's reapportionment of its legislative districts. Both houses of the state legislature, therefore, "must be apportioned on a population basis," so that "an individual's right to vote ... [is not] diluted when compared with votes of citizens living in other parts of the State" (377 U.S. at 568) — a requirement that has come to be known as the "one-person, one-vote" standard.[19] Since Alabama's apportionment scheme did not meet this requirement, the Court held that it must reapportion its legislative districts under the guidance of the federal district court. In subsequent years, almost all the states had to reapportion their legislatures in accordance with the one-person, one-vote standard, and apportionments regularly reoccur after each federal decennial census.[20]

To move beyond *Reynolds v. Sims*, one must ask what interests, other than voting, has the Court recognized as fundamental for purposes of the equal protection clause, and what methodology does the Court use to make these determinations? These matters are controversial, much as they are when the Court identifies "fundamental" rights under substantive due process (see Chap. 11, Sec. C). In *San Antonio Independent School District v. Rodriguez*, 411 U.S. 1 (1973), while holding that access to adequate public education is not a fundamental interest, the Court tightened its methodology for making such determinations:

[It] is not the province of this Court to create substantive constitutional rights in the name of guaranteeing equal protection of the laws.... [T]he key to discovering whether education is "fundamental" is not to be found in comparisons of the relative societal significance of education as opposed to [other governmental services or functions, or] by weighing whether education is as important as [other personal interests]. Rather, the answer lies in assessing whether there is a right to education explicitly or implicitly guaranteed by the Constitution. [411 U.S. at 33.]

Since *Rodriguez*, the Court has adhered to three circumstances in which an interest will be considered to be "explicitly or implicitly guaranteed by the Constitution" and thus to be a fundamental interest for purposes of the equal protection clause. An interest will be fundamental if:

(1) it is protected as an implied (unenumerated) fundamental right under substantive due process (*see, e.g., Skinner v. Oklahoma*, 316 U.S. 535 (1942) (the

---

19. The phrase "one-person, one-vote" was originally used in an earlier voting case, *Gray v. Sanders*, 372 U.S. 368, 381 (1963), and was picked up in *Reynolds v. Sims* by Chief Justice Warren (377 U.S. at 558) as well as by Justice Clark in his concurrence (377 U.S. at 587–88) and by Justice Harlan in his dissent (377 U.S. at 593).

20. Beginning with reapportionments after the 1990 census, the courts began deciding cases in which states had allegedly taken race into account in drawing new voting district lines. In this "second generation" of reapportionment cases, the courts relied just as heavily on race discrimination principles emerging from modern race discrimination cases (see Secs. D.2, D.6, and D.7 above) as they did on reapportionment principles arising from the *Reynolds v. Sims* line of cases. The issues became especially complex. *See, e.g., Shaw v. Reno*, 509 U.S. 630 (1993); *Bush v. Vera*, 517 U.S. 952 (1996).

right to procreate and the right to marry); and see generally Chap. 11, Secs. C.2 and C.3.

(2) it is protected by an express constitutional right, e.g., freedom of speech (*see Chicago Police Department v. Mosley*, 408 U.S. 92 (1972) (the right to picket)); and

(3) it is protected as an implied constitutional right that is derived from the structure of the Constitution (*see Shapiro v. Thompson*, 394 U.S. 618 (1969) (the right to travel)).

In addition to these three approaches, the Court continues to recognize citizen voting as a fundamental interest, as in *Reynolds v. Sims*. But the Court no longer uses its particular methodology from *Reynolds*—whereby it apparently recognized voting as a substantive interest protected directly by the equal protection clause itself, without reference to substantive due process, express constitutional rights, or constitutional structure.

Sec. E. A Comparison of Equal Protection and Due Process

It is important to make a conceptual distinction between equal protection (the subject of this Chapter) on the one hand and due process (the subject of the next Chapter) on the other. Both clauses may be implicated in the same problem, and judges may rely on both by making alternative arguments to justify a particular decision. In *Loving v. Virginia*, 388 U.S. 1 (1967), for instance, the Court first held that Virginia's law prohibiting inter-racial marriage was race discrimination that violated the equal protection clause (*Id.* at 2-12); and then held, in the alternative, that the law was an infringement of the fundamental right to marry and thus violated substantive due process (*Id.* at 12). (See Chapter 11, Section. C, for discussion of substantive due process.) Judges may also disagree on which clause or type of analysis is more appropriate for a particular case. In *Boddie v. Connecticut*, 401 U.S. 371 (1971), for instance, the Court invalidated a state's charge of costs and fees to indigent persons seeking a divorce. Justice Harlan, for the majority, held that this state requirement violated due process; two concurring Justices reasoned that the requirement violated equal protection. Similarly, in *Lawrence v. Texas*, 123 S.Ct. 2472 (2003) (Chap. 11, Sec. C.3), the Court invalidated a state law prohibiting acts of sodomy between persons of the same sex. The five Justices joining the majority opinion held that the statute violated substantive due process; a sixth Justice concurring separately (Justice O'Connor) reasoned that the statute discriminated against homosexual persons and violated equal protection.

Despite such uncertainties at the margins, the Court has made clear that equal protection and due process are analytically distinct:

[E]ach [clause depends] on a different inquiry which emphasizes different factors. "Due Process" emphasizes fairness between the State and the individual dealing with the State, regardless of how other individuals in the same situation may be treated. "Equal Protection," on the other hand, emphasizes disparity in treatment by a State between classes of individuals whose situations are arguably indistinguishable. [*Ross v. Moffitt*, 417 U.S. 600, 609 (1974).]

At the same time, "[e]quality of treatment and...the substantive guarantee of liberty are linked in important respects,", and a decision upholding one of these principles may advance the other principle as well (*Lawrence*, above, 123 S.Ct. at 2482 (majority opinion)). In *Lawrence*, for example, the Court's invalidation of the sodomy statute as an infringement on "the substantive guarantee of liberty" may also further "equality of treatment" by removing the "stigma" associated with homosexuality and undercutting the sodomy law's "invitation to subject homosexual persons to discrimination both in the public and in the private spheres" (*Id.*).[21]

Analytically, the initial focus of equal protection is on the *classification* that government has employed (see Sec. C.2 above), while the initial focus for due process is on the particular procedure that government has provided or the particular substantive standard that it has created (see Chap. 11, Sec. B). The thrust of equal protection law is therefore not to prohibit government from using particular procedures or standards but rather to promote evenhandedness by requiring that government apply its standards and procedures to sufficiently broad (or narrow) classes of persons. According to Justice Jackson:

> Invocation of the equal protection clause...does not disable any governmental body from dealing with the subject at hand. It merely means that the prohibition or regulation must have a broader impact. I regard it as a salutary doctrine that cities, states and the Federal Government must exercise their powers so as not to discriminate between their inhabitants except upon some reasonable differentiation fairly related to the object of regulation. This equality is not merely abstract justice. The framers of the Constitution knew, and we should not forget today, that there is no more effective practical guaranty against arbitrary and unreasonable government than to require that the principles of law such officials would impose upon a minority must be imposed generally. Conversely, nothing opens the door to arbitrary action so effectively as to allow those officials to pick and choose only a few to whom they will apply legislation and thus to escape the political retribution that might be visited upon them if larger numbers were affected. Courts can take no better measure to assure that laws will be just than to require that laws be equal in operation. [*Railway Express Agency v. New York*, 336 U.S. 106, 112-113 (1949) (Jackson, J., concurring).]

To consider a concrete example, suppose a public school board has a rule that requires principals to suspend any student who becomes an unwed mother. Such a rule would potentially raise equal protection issues concerning discrimination against unwed mothers (vs. unwed fathers) or unwed mothers (vs. married mothers), or—

---

21. For an example in the opposite direction, when an equal protection decision also furthered substantive liberty interests, *see Skinner v. Oklahoma*, 316 U.S. 535 (1942), set out and discussed in Chap. 11, Sec. E; and see generally Sec. D.8. above.

more broadly—discrimination against females (vs. males). But independently of these claims, the rule would raise procedural due process issues concerning the adequacy of procedural protections available to the student charged with a rule violation, as well as substantive due process issues concerning intrusion upon the fundamental liberty interests of procreation and child rearing. If the school board rule were invalid under equal protection, it could presumably be redrawn to apply to both unwed mothers and unwed fathers (and perhaps to both unwed and wedded mothers and fathers), and the school board could again enforce its rule. If the rule were invalid under procedural due process, presumably procedural protections could be added to the rule, and the school board could again enforce it. But if the rule were invalid under substantive due process, that would be the end of the rule; the school board could no longer enforce it, no matter how broadly or narrowly it defined the class subject to the rule and no matter how many procedures it added to the law.

The ability to make such conceptual distinctions will enhance one's understanding of equal protection law as well as due process law. In addition, it will substantially sharpen one's abilities to analyze and resolve real-life constitutional law problems.

Sec. F. Study Suggestions for Equal Protection

Equal protection analysis begins with the identification of a "differential treatment of similarly situated classes of persons" (Sec. C.2 above). Even though court opinions may sometimes skip over or de-emphasize this stage one inquiry, be sure that you do not do so. Your reading of a case or analysis of a problem will be sharpened if you take time to carefully identify the class of persons that is subject to the disadvantageous treatment and the "similarly situated" class that is receiving favorable treatment. By identifying and comparing these classes, you will reveal the particular classification that government has used to differentiate one class from the other, and the particulars of government's different treatment of these classes.

At the second stage of equal protection analysis, you will need to work effectively with the tiers of review. To do so, you should address these questions as you read and synthesize the cases: (A) What types of cases (or classifications) belong in each tier? (B) What are the common characteristics of the types of cases (classifications) that belong in each tier (e.g., what are the indicia of "suspectness" that would merit placing a case in tier I)? (C) What are the underlying rationales for recognizing particular indicia of suspectness and for placing each type of case (classification) into the particular tier in which it belongs? (D) What standards of review are used for each tier to determine, for a particular case on that tier, whether the classification used is justifiable and thus constitutional?

When you identify and work with the standards of review (question D above), it will be critically important to differentiate between the specific means test and the specific ends test that is used for each standard. You should also determine, for each standard, whether the end used in the analysis must be the actual or articulated objective that led government to use the classification, or whether it is permissible instead to use an objective that is hypothesized or invented (by the government or by the court) in order to defend the classification against challenge. Whenever you read an opinion in which the court holds that a particular classification fails to meet the applicable standard of review (or whenever you reach that conclusion in your own analysis of a problem), be sure to determine whether the classification fails the means test, or the ends test, or both; and be sure to identify the reasons for the failure.

FOR FURTHER READING: (1) Paul Brest, "Foreword: In Defense of the Anti-discrimination Principle," 90 Harv. L. Rev. 1 (1976). (2) Russell Galloway, "Basic Equal Protection Analysis," 29 Santa Clara L. Rev. 121 (1989). (3) Gerald Gunther, "In Search of Evolving Doctrine on a Changing Court: A Model for a Newer Equal Protection," 86 Harv. L. Rev. 1 (1972). (4) Richard Kluger, Simple Justice, The History of Brown v. Board of Education and Black America's Struggle for Equality, (Alfred A. Knopf, 1976).

Chapter 11

Due Process

Sec. A. The Content of the Due Process Clauses

A.1. The Various Types of Due Process

The Fourteenth's Amendment's due process clause is brief in its language but extensive in its coverage. An overview of the content of this clause — of the ground it covers — will provide a useful perspective from which to study its particular applications. There are several key distinctions that separate one type of content from another. First, the due process clause is divisible into its "incorporated" content, derivable from particular provisions of the Bill of Rights, and its "non-incorporated" content derivable directly from the clause itself, independent of the Bill of Rights. Thus the "non-incorporated" content of the due process clause is clearly different from, and additional to, the incorporated content. "[L]iberty encompasses . . . more than those rights already guaranteed to the individual against federal interference by the express provisions of the first eight amendments" (*Planned Parenthood of Southeastern Pennsylvania v. Casey*, 505 U.S. 833, 847 (1992)). Non-incorporated due process "is a discrete concept which subsists as an independent guarantee of liberty and procedural fairness, more general and inclusive than the specific prohibitions [of the Bill of Rights]" (*Poe v. Ullman*, 367 U.S. 497, 542 (1961) (Harlan, J., dissenting from dismissal on jurisdictional grounds)).

Besides the division between incorporated and non-incorporated due process, the non-incorporated part of due process is further divisible into its "substantive" content and its "procedural" content. The result is three sectors or types of due process: (1) the incorporated sector, or incorporated due process; (2) the non-incorporated substantive sector, or substantive due process; and (3) the non-incorporated procedural sector, or procedural due process. Finally, the second sector, substantive due process, is in turn subdivided into a component covering economic rights and another component covering intimate personal rights. Every due process issue and every due process argument can be placed within a particular sector or component of the due process clause. Since the applicable law differs from one sector and component to another, it is critically important to understand these conceptual distinctions concerning due process law.

The incorporated content of due process is addressed in Section A.2 below. The conceptual distinction between substantive due process and procedural due process is addressed in Section B. Substantive due process is addressed in Section C, with the distinction between economic rights and intimate personal rights being addressed in Section C.1. Procedural due process is addressed in Section D.

The Fifth Amendment also has a due process clause that binds the federal government. It has no incorporated content, as such, since it is already part of the Bill of Rights. But the Fifth Amendment due process clause does have substantive and procedural (non-incorporated) components that parallel those of the Fourteenth Amendment clause. *Mathews v. Eldridge*, 424 U.S. 319 (1976), for example, was a Fifth Amendment procedural due process challenge to the procedures used to effectuate a termination of disability benefits under a federal disability program; and *Harris v. McRae*, 448 U.S. 297 (1980), was a Fifth Amendment substantive due process challenge to a federal government prohibition on using federal Medicaid funds to pay for abortions.

The Fifth Amendment due process clause also has an equal protection component that the U.S. Supreme Court has found to be implicit in the clause. Some commentators call this a type of "reverse incorporation," by which a part of the Fourteenth Amendment is incorporated into the Fifth Amendment's due process clause. In *Weinberger v. Wiesenfeld*, 420 U.S. 636 (1975), for example, the Court used equal protection principles from the Fifth Amendment to invalidate a federal Social Security requirement that provided fewer family benefits upon the death of a wife and mother than on the death of a husband and father. The equal protection principles that limit the federal government through the Fifth Amendment are the same, and are applied in the same way, as those that limit the states under the Fourteenth Amendment (*see, e.g., Adarand Constructors, Inc. v. Pena*, 515 U.S. 200 (1995)).

A.2. The "Incorporated" Content of Fourteenth Amendment Due Process

The "incorporated" sector of due process draws its name from the process of "selective incorporation" by which the U.S. Supreme Court has incorporated Bill of Rights' protections into the Fourteenth Amendment, thus making them applicable to the states. The line of incorporation cases, beginning with *Gitlow v. New York*, 268 U.S. 652 (1925) (see Chap. 9, Sec. E, under **1925**), had the effect of overturning the early nineteenth century case of *Barron v. City of Baltimore*, 32 U.S. (7 Pet.) 243 (1833), in which the Court had held that the Bill of Rights applied only to the federal government (see Chap. 9, Sec. E, under **1833**). Proceeding one clause at a time and one case at a time, the Court has held most of the clauses in the first eight amendments to be encompassed within the meaning of due process under the Fourteenth Amendment. Specifically, by this selective incorporation process, the Court has applied to the states the First Amendment's free speech and press clauses, the First Amendment's establishment and free exercise clauses, the Fourth Amendment's search and seizure clause, and the Fifth, Sixth, and Eighth Amendment clauses protecting criminal defendants.

Duncan v. Louisiana, 391 U.S. 145 (1968), is a primary example of selective incorporation and represents the culmination of this approach to due process. The Court incorporated the Sixth Amendment's jury trial clause into the Fourteenth Amendment and indicated that the clause, once incorporated, binds the states in the same way and to the same extent that it binds the federal government. To determine whether the jury trial clause qualified for incorporation, the Court asked whether guarantee of a jury was "fundamental to the American scheme of justice" (391 U.S. at 149). Clarifying this test, the Court explained that it does not focus on whether the procedure at issue is "fundamental to fairness in every [civilized] criminal system that might be imagined," but rather on whether it is "fundamental in the context of the criminal processes maintained by the American States" (391 U.S. at 149, n. 14). Thus the "question…is whether given this kind of system a particular procedure is fundamental—whether, that is, a procedure is necessary to an Anglo-American regime of ordered liberty" (*Id.*).

In the 1930s through the 1970s, a great debate had raged within the Court concerning this matter of incorporation. There were many facets to the debate: the approaches to interpreting the due process clause; whether the due process clause has substantive content; (many of the Bill of Rights guarantees—free speech and press, for example—are substantive rights); the concept of "fundamental" rights and how it applies to the Bill of Rights; the values of federalism and whether applying the Bill of Rights to the states would undercut these values; the institutional importance (for the courts) of having uniform standards for constitutional rights, applicable to the federal government and states alike. Three positions on incorporation were eventually staked out by the various Justices participating in the debate: (1) the total incorporation position, espoused most strenuously by Justice Black, which posited that *all* of the Bill of Rights' first eight amendments were applicable to the states (*see* especially, *Adamson v. California*, 332 U.S. 46, 68–92 (1947) (Black, J., dissenting)); (2) the non-incorporation position, espoused most forcefully by Justice Frankfurter (*see* especially, *Id.* at 62–68 (Frankfurter, J., concurring)), and then Justice Harlan (*see* especially, *Duncan v. Louisiana*, 391 U.S. 145, 174–183 (Harlan, J., dissenting)), which posited that *none* of the Bill of Rights applies as such to the states; and (3) the selective incorporation position, espoused especially by Justice Cardozo (see especially, *Palko v. Connecticut*, 302 U.S. 319 (1937)), and then Justice Brennan (*see* especially, *Malloy v. Hogan*, 378 U.S. 1 (1964)), which posited that the Court must decide on a right-by-right and clause-by-clause basis whether a particular right or clause is sufficiently "fundamental" to be considered a necessary part of due process of law. Selective incorporation eventually won the day.

In applying the incorporated clauses to the states, the Court has generally followed the rule that each clause is "to be enforced against the States under the Fourteenth Amendment according to the same standards that protect those personal rights against federal encroachment" (*Malloy v. Hogan*, 378 U.S. at 10). This is the stronger version of selective incorporation espoused by Justice Brennan and other Justices in the 1960s and 1970s, in comparison to the weaker and earlier version espoused by Justice Cardozo in *Palko* (above). The weaker version would bind the states to the core meaning of the incorporated clause but would afford states discretion at the margins to deviate from particular aspects of the clause's application to the federal government. Even after selective incorporation became the Court's accepted approach, Justice Harlan and occasionally other Justices argued strenuously in dissents for the weaker version (*see, e.g., Duncan v. Louisiana*, 391 U.S. at 181 (Harlan, J., dissenting)). The last clear example of this minority approach to selective incorporation seems to be Justice Powell's concurrence in *Apodaca v. Oregon*, 406 U.S. 404, 369–376 (1972), in which he argued that the jury unanimity (unanimous verdict) feature of the Sixth Amendment jury trial clause applied to the federal government but not the states. The other eight Justices in that case all followed the stronger version of selective incorporation.[1]

Sec. B. The Distinction Between Substantive Due Process and Procedural Due Process

A study of due process will be enhanced by early attention to the conceptual distinction between *substantive* due process and *procedural* due process (see Sec. A.1 above). This Section provides a starting point for drawing this distinction. It is also important to distinguish these two concepts of due process from the concept of equal protection; Section E of Chapter 10 elucidates that distinction. An exercise near the end of this Chapter (Chap. 11, Sec. E) provides further assistance in differentiating and interrelating these three areas of law.

To understand the difference between substantive and procedural due process, one must first understand the difference between substantive and procedural *decisions* or *actions*:

> A distinction is commonly taken in constitutional law between procedural and substantive decisions, as they are called; and it is generally valid, because procedural decisions for the most part point to infirmities that are curable. They deal with the 'how' of governmental action, whereas substantive decisions go to ends, dealing with the "what." [Alexander Bickel, THE LEAST DANGEROUS BRANCH, p. 233 (Yale Univ. Press, 2nd ed. 1986).]

The validity of substantive governmental decisions is the province of substantive due process, and the validity of government's procedures for enforcing its substantive decisions is the province of procedural due process:

---

1. These eight Justices split 4 to 4, however, on whether jury unanimity is a feature of the Sixth Amendment jury trial clause. Four Justices concluded that the clause required jury unanimity both for the federal government and the states; the other four concluded that the clause did not require jury unanimity for either the federal government or the states. Justice Powell's vote for *not* applying jury unanimity to the states was thus the deciding vote. Notice the irony: eight of the nine Justices agreed that the Sixth Amendment meant the same for the states as the federal government; yet the *result* of the case was that jury unanimity applied to the federal government but not the states (see *Apodaca*, 406 U.S. at 395 (Brennan, J., dissenting)).

[S]ubstantive due process comprises whatever norms the Supreme Court has invoked, formally in the name of the due process clauses, to limit the sorts of policy choices governmental officials, in particular legislators, may make. *Procedural due process*, by contrast, comprises the norms the Court has invoked, in the name of due process, to limit the ways in which, the procedures through which, officials, in particular those charged with administering law, may enforce policy choices once made. [Michael Perry, THE CONSTITUTION, THE COURTS, AND HUMAN RIGHTS, p. 117, fn. (1982).]

The U.S. Supreme Court has recognized this dichotomy between substantive and procedural due process at least since the 1880's. As the Court majority explained in *Planned Parenthood of Southeastern Pennsylvania v. Casey*, 505 U.S. 833 (1992):

Although a literal reading of the [Due Process] Clause might suggest that it governs only the procedures by which a State may deprive persons of liberty, for at least 105 years, since *Mugler v. Kansas*, 123 U.S. 623, 660–661 (1887), the Clause has been understood to contain a substantive component as well, one "barring certain government actions regardless of the fairness of the procedures used to implement them." *Daniels v. Williams*, 474 U.S. 327, 331 (1986). As Justice Brandeis (joined by Justice Holmes) observed, "[d]espite arguments to the contrary which had seemed to me persuasive, it is settled that the due process clause of the Fourteenth Amendment applies to matters of substantive law as well as to matters of procedure." *Whitney v. California*, 274 U.S. 357, 373 (1927) (concurring opinion). "[T]he guaranties of due process, though having their roots in Magna Carta's '*per legem terrae*' and considered as procedural safeguards 'against executive usurpation and tyranny,' have in this country 'become bulwarks also against arbitrary legislation.'" *Poe v. Ullman*, 367 U.S. 497, 541 (1961) (Harlan, J., dissenting from dismissal on jurisdictional grounds) (quoting *Hurtado v. California*, 110 U.S. 516, 532 (1884)). [505 U.S. at 846–847.]

Substantive and procedural due process thus differ markedly in their application and import. Substantive due process limits the legal standards or requirements that government may establish in its laws, and the substantive results or objectives that government may achieve through its laws. The goal is "to prevent governmental power from being 'used for purposes of oppression'" (*Daniels v. Williams*, 474 U.S. 327, 332 (1986) (quoting *Murray's Lessee v. Hoboken Land and Improvement Co.*, 59 U.S. (18 How.) 272, 277 (1856)). Procedural due process limits the types of procedures that government may use when applying its legal standards or requirements to particular persons. The goal is to establish "appropriate procedures" that promote "fairness" to individuals whom government agents may deprive of their life, liberty, or property (*Id.* at 331). Substantive due process limits apply regardless of how much procedural protection government may provide for individuals subjected to the law at issue. Thus, "identifying the contours of the substantive right remains a task distinct from deciding what procedural protections are necessary to protect that right" (*Washington v. Harper*, 494 U.S. 210, 220 (1990)).

Consider, for example, a public school board rule providing that any student who has a child out of wedlock (as a mother or as a father) will be suspended from school. If the board provides no procedural protections for students charged with a violation of this rule, the rule's application could be challenged on procedural grounds. But even if the board were to provide a full-blown hearing to accused students, the rule itself may nevertheless be challenged on substantive grounds. The predominant problem, in other words, may be the standard the board has set and the objective it seeks to achieve rather than the procedure it uses to enforce the rule.

Sec. C. Substantive Due Process: A Conceptual Overview

C.1. The Two Eras of Substantive Due Process

Substantive due process comprises the non-incorporated, substantive content of the due process clause (see Sec. A above). There is an "older" and a "newer" substantive due process, the former covering the economic rights component of substantive due process and the latter covering the intimate personal rights component. The era of the older substantive due process was from the 1880s to the 1930s. The U.S. Supreme Court was then concerned with government regulation of business and industry. It used the due process clause as a source of substantive "economic" rights that protected business owners and businesses from state interference with their "liberty of contract."[2] The era of the newer substantive due process began in the 1960s and is still ongoing. In this era, the Court has been concerned with government regulation of personal and private matters such as marriage, procreation, family relationships, sexual practices, and the dying process. The Court has used the due process clause as a source of substantive "personal" rights that protect individuals from state interference with core aspects of their personal autonomy, in particular with respect to various rights to "privacy."

The first clear U.S. Supreme Court statement of the older substantive due process concept comes from *Mugler v. Kansas*, 123 U.S. 623 (1887), where the Court explained:

---

2. In this earlier era, the Court did also decide three cases in which it protected the personal rights of parents to direct the upbringing of their children: *Meyer v. Nebraska*, 262 U.S. 390 (1923); *Pierce v. Society of Sisters*, 268 U.S. 510 (1925); and *Farrington v. Tokushige*, 273 U.S. 284 (1927). These cases survived into the newer era of substantive due process and provided initial support for the Court's protection of intimate personal rights under the due process clause. In 1927, Justice Brandeis laid a foundation for these later developments in a concurring opinion that cited *Meyer*, *Pierce*, and *Farrington* for the proposition that the Fourteenth Amendment's due process clause "applies to matters of substantive law as well as to matters of procedure. Thus all *fundamental rights* comprised within the term *liberty* are protected by the federal Constitution from invasion by the states" (*Whitney v. California*, 274 U.S. 357, 373 (1927) (Brandeis, J., concurring).

It does not at all follow that every statute enacted ostensibly for the... [protection of the public morals, the public health, or the public safety] is to be accepted as a legitimate exertion of the police powers of the State. ... The courts are not bound by mere forms nor are they to be misled by mere pretenses. They are at liberty — indeed, are under a solemn duty — *to look at the substance of things*, whenever they enter upon the inquiry whether the legislature has transcended the limits of its authority. If, therefore, a statute purporting to have been enacted to protect the public health, the public morals, or the public safety, *has no real or substantial relation to those objects*... it is duty of the courts to so adjudge.... [123 U.S. at 661 (emphasis added).]

The high-water mark for this judicial role was *Lochner v. New York*, 198 U.S. 45 (1905), where the Court struck down a New York State statute prescribing maximum work hours for employees of bakeries. The substantive due process argument had been made by a bakery owner who had been convicted and fined for violating the law. The Court declined to accord any deference to the state's policy judgments concerning the benefits of the law: "There is no reasonable ground for interfering with the liberty of person or the right of free contract, by determining the hours of labor, in the occupation of a baker" (198 U.S. at 57).

The Court's withdrawal from this "Lochnerizing" brand of substantive due process came almost thirty years later in *Nebbia v. New York*, 291 U.S. 502 (1934), another case challenging a New York State law. This time the Court upheld the law, which established minimum and maximum retail prices for the sale of milk. Although the Court stated the standard of review in language similar to what it used in *Mugler* and *Lochner*, the Court applied the standard with far more deference to legislative judgments:

[N]either property rights nor contract rights are absolute; for government cannot exist if the citizen may at will use his property to the detriment of his fellows, or exercise his freedom of contract to work them harm. Equally fundamental with the private right is that of the public to regulate it in the common interest.... So far as the requirement of due process is concerned... a state is free to adopt whatever economic policy may reasonably be deemed to promote public welfare, and to enforce that policy by legislation adopted to its purpose. [291 U.S. at 523, 537.]

The newer, contemporary era of substantive due process was ushered in by the famous case of *Griswold v. Connecticut*, 381 U.S. 479 (1965), in which the Court invalidated a Connecticut birth control law. The statute prohibited individuals, including married couples, from using contraceptive drugs or devices, and also prohibited doctors and others from aiding and abetting the use of contraceptives. In 1961, the Planned Parenthood League of Connecticut had established a clinic in New Haven that provided medical information and consultation on contraception to married individuals. The executive director, medical director, and staff distributed materials, devices, and medication to the clientele as aids in preventing conception. Open less than two weeks, the clinic was closed by state officials, who charged the executive director and medical director with violating the aiding and abetting provisions of the Connecticut statute. Specifically, the state claimed the directors had violated the law when they assisted three married women who had visited the clinic for counseling and services. The women testified that they had used the preventive information and/or devices within the confines of their material relationships.

Emphasizing the destructive impact of the law on the privacy interests of married couples, the Court declared the Connecticut statute unconstitutional by a 7 to 2 vote. The seven Justices in the majority did not all agree on a rationale for the decision; indeed not all agreed on substantive due process as the basis for the decision. In the majority opinion, Justice Douglas determined that a married couple's right to privacy came from "penumbras, formed by emanations from" the specific guarantees in the Bill of Rights, which "create zones of privacy" (381 U.S. at 484). The right of married couples to use contraceptives, said Justice Douglas, fell "within the zone of privacy created by several fundamental [Bill of Rights] guarantees" (381 U.S. 485). Thus, Justice Douglas' majority opinion in *Griswold* is based on the *incorporated* content of the due process clause, drawn from the Bill of Rights (see Sec. A.2 above). By this reasoning, the marital privacy infringed by the Connecticut law had existed before the Bill of Rights—"[w]e deal with a right of privacy older than the Bill of Rights"—and was implicitly included within it.

Justice Goldberg, in contrast, relied on the unincorporated content of the due process clause. He grounded marital privacy in "the concept of liberty [in the Fourteenth Amendment] that protects those personal rights that are fundamental, and [that is] not confined to the specific terms of the Bill of Rights" (381 U.S. at 486) (Goldberg, J., concurring). Justice Goldberg also found support for his reasoning in the Ninth Amendment (U.S. Const., Amend. 9). But he did not claim that the Ninth Amendment is an independent source of law providing an alternative ground for his decision. Rather, his argument is that "the Ninth Amendment simply lends strong support to the view that the 'liberty' protected by the Fifth and 14th Amendments... is not restricted to rights specifically mentioned in the first eight amendments" (381 U.S. at 493).

Justice Harlan, in contrast to both Douglas and Goldberg, found the marital right to privacy squarely with the Fourteenth Amendment, without the need for any additional boost from the Bill of Rights or from the Ninth Amendment. For him, marital privacy arises from "basic values 'implicit in the concept of ordered liberty'" that embrace "fundamental" rights belonging to "the citizens of all free governments" (381 U.S. at 500) (Harlan, J. concurring in the judgment and referencing *Poe v. Ullman*, 367 U.S. 497, 541–542 (1961) (Harlan, J., dissenting), and quoting *Corfield v. Coryell*, 6 F. Cas. 546 (No. 3,230), 4 Wash. C.C. 371, 380 (1825)). Justice White also wrote a separate opinion that paralleled and extended part of Justice Harlan's reasoning. Thus the Goldberg, Harlan, and White concurring opinions—rather the Douglas majority opinion—are the "true" substantive due process opinions that usher in the modern era of substantive due process. Since Chief Justice Warren and Justice Brennan concurred in Justice Goldberg's decision, a total of five Justices in *Griswold*, a majority, supported the substantive due process approach.

C.2. The Newer Era Cases: Contraception and Abortion

In 1972, building upon *Griswold v. Connecticut* (Sec. C.1 above), the U.S. Supreme Court expanded the right to use contraceptives from married couples to unmarried individuals and also extended protection beyond the use of contraceptives to their distribution and receipt. The case was *Eisenstadt v. Baird*, 405 U.S. 438 (1972), invalidating a Massachusetts law banning the distribution of contraceptives. Although it decided this case on equal protection grounds, the Court addressed the individual's right to privacy in the course of explaining why an unmarried person could not be treated differently from a married person. In contrast to *Griswold's* emphasis on marital privacy, Justice Brennan in *Eisenstadt* wrote that:

> [T]he marital couple is not an independent entity with a heart and mind of its own, but an association of two individuals, each with a separate intellectual and emotional makeup. If the right of privacy means anything, it is the right of the *individual*, married or single, to be free from unwarranted governmental intrusion into matters so fundamentally affecting a person as the decision whether to bear or begat a child. [405 U.S. at 453; Court's emphasis.]

Thus Justice Brennan's analysis suggested that the marital privacy in *Griswold* was evolving into an individual privacy right concerning contraception—and, more broadly, reproductive freedom—that applies irrespective of whether the individual is married. This evolution was confirmed in *Carey v. Population Services International*, 431 U.S. 678 (1977) (discussed in Section C.6 below).

Like the right to conceive or not, the Court has stated that the right to bear a child, or not (as noted in *Eisenstadt*), is also protected by substantive due process. In the landmark case of *Roe v. Wade*, 410 U.S. 113 (1973), the Court decided that a Texas criminal statute prohibiting women from choosing to terminate a pregnancy infringed on women's liberty interests and was unconstitutional. At the time of *Roe*, Texas' century-old criminal statute governing abortion was similar to others still in effect in the majority of states—prohibiting all abortions except those necessary to save the pregnant woman's life. The law prevented Jane Roe,[3] an unmarried, pregnant woman, from obtaining an abortion performed by a medical professional in a clinical setting. Due to the cost, traveling to another jurisdiction for such a procedure was not feasible for Roe. A physician, who had been charged in two criminal prosecutions for allegedly performing prohibited abortions, joined Roe in challenging the Texas law.

Justice Blackmun, writing for the majority in *Roe*, acknowledged Justice Goldberg's opinion in *Griswold* and Justice Brennan's opinion in *Eisenstadt*, and the right to privacy that these cases recognized. He then stated: "This right of privacy, whether it be

---

3. This was not the plaintiff's real name. "Jane Roe" and "John Doe" are the usual substitute names given to persons who are suing or being sued under cover of anonymity or whose identities are otherwise unknown. The plaintiff in *Roe v. Wade* revealed her true identity a short time after the Supreme Court's decision. *See* Norma McCorvey & Andy Meisler, I Am Roe: My Life, Roe v. Wade, and Freedom of Choice (Harper Collins, 1994).

founded in the Fourteenth Amendment's concept of personal liberty...as we feel it is, or as the District Court determined, in the [Ninth Amendment], is broad enough to encompass a woman's decision whether or not to terminate her pregnancy" (410 U.S. at 153; emphasis added). Since the woman's right was a "fundamental right" under the due process clause, the Court determined that the Texas statute infringing this right was subject to strict scrutiny review. A state "regulation limiting [fundamental] rights," said the Court, "may be justified only by a 'compelling state interest,'" and such "legislative enactments must be narrowly drawn to express only the legitimate state interests at stake" (410 U.S. at 155, citing *inter alia, Shapiro v. Thompson,* 394 U.S. 618, 634 (1969)). Since the Texas statute could not meet either aspect of this standard, the Court held that it violated substantive due process.

In a dissenting opinion, Justice Rehnquist (not yet Chief Justice) disagreed with the majority's reliance on a broad concept of "liberty." He argued that "the asserted right to an abortion is not 'so rooted in the traditions and conscience of our people as to be ranked as fundamental,' and that the history of the adoption of the Fourteenth Amendment indicated that "the drafters did not intend to have the Fourteenth Amendment withdraw from the States the power to legislate" regarding abortion (410 U.S. at 174–177). According to Rehnquist, the Court should have applied a rational basis standard of review to the Texas statute, rather than strict scrutiny review, and the state met this test because it had a legitimate interest in protecting fetal life.

By selecting "the 14th Amendment's concept of personal liberty" as the source of the right to choose, the Court clearly grounded its decision in the non-incorporated substantive sector of due process. There was no split on this point, as there had been in *Griswold*; no Justice invoked the incorporated sector of due process by using a Bill of Rights' penumbras argument.

Although the Court reasoned that the woman's right to choose falls within one of the "zones of privacy" and is therefore a "fundamental" right for due process purposes, the Court did not define the particular zone of privacy that covers abortion or explain specifically why the right-to-choose is a "fundamental" aspect of privacy. It said only that the right to personal privacy "has some extension to activities relating to marriage, procreation, contraception, family relationships, and child rearing and education"; and that the right of privacy is therefore "broad enough to encompass" the abortion decision (410 U.S. at 152–153). Presumably, the Court meant that the right to choose is supported by a fundamental liberty interest or value falling within the Fourteenth Amendment's concept of personal liberty, but the Court did not specifically identify this interest or value.

For many years after the Court's decision in *Roe v. Wade*, other cases came to the Court challenging new abortion regulations that states had enacted after *Roe* in an attempt to comply with the decision while at the same time regulating the abortion decision as fully as *Roe* would permit. The Court tended to distinguish between *prohibitory regulations*, that is, regulations preventing meaningful choice and therefore treatable like the prohibition in *Roe*; and *non-prohibitory regulations* that imposed conditions on the abortion decision but nevertheless preserved a genuine choice for the woman. The Court continued to develop its substantive due process principles in this line of cases. In *Maher v. Roe*, 432 U.S. 464 (1977), for example, the Court considered a Connecticut law that granted medical benefits to poor women for childbirth but denied benefits to those who chose medically unnecessary abortions. The Court upheld the statute as a non-prohibitory regulation: "[The] right [in *Roe v. Wade* and its progeny] protects the woman from unduly burdensome interference with her freedom to decide whether to terminate her pregnancy.... The Connecticut regulation places no obstacles — absolute or otherwise — in the pregnant woman's path to an abortion.... The state may have made childbirth a more attractive alternative [by offering Medicaid benefits], but it has imposed no restriction on access to abortions that was not already there" (432 U.S. at 473–474).

This line of cases culminated in *Planned Parenthood of Southeastern Pennsylvania v. Casey*, 505 U.S. 833 (1992). In multiple opinions, most notably the "joint opinion" of Justices Kennedy, O'Connor, and Souter, the Court reviewed five provisions of a Pennsylvania abortion statute. A 5 to 4 majority of the Court specifically rejected arguments to overrule *Roe* and instead confirmed and adhered to "*Roe*'s essential holding" and "the essence of" the *Roe* decision (505 U.S. at 846, 869). The "essence" did not include every aspect of the original *Roe* decision; for instance, a majority rejected Roe's "trimester" approach that defined how a state may regulate and when a state may prohibit a woman's right to choose. In place of the trimester approach, the Court in *Casey* substituted a viability approach. "The woman's liberty is not so unlimited, however, that from the outset the State cannot show its concern for the life of the unborn, and at a later point in fetal development the State's interest in life has sufficient force so that the right of the woman to terminate the pregnancy can be restricted. We conclude the line should be drawn at viability, so that before that time the woman has a right to choose to terminate her pregnancy" (505 U.S. at 869–870).

The joint opinion in *Casey* does a better job than the original *Roe* opinion in explaining the "liberty" concept under the due process clause and what interests are central to this concept. "Personal decisions relating to marriage, procreation, contraception, family relationships, child rearing, and education," said the joint opinion, "'involv[e] the most intimate and personal choices a person may make in a lifetime, choices central to personal dignity and autonomy [and thus] central to the liberty protected by the Fourteenth Amendment. At the heart of liberty is the right to define one's own concept of existence, of meaning, of the universe, and of the mystery of human life. Beliefs about these matters could not define the attributes of personhood were they formed under compulsion of the State" (505 U.S. at 851).

The joint opinion also does a better job explaining why the woman's right to choose falls within these central aspects of liberty.

> In some critical respects the abortion decision is of the same character as the decision to use contraception, to which *Griswold v. Connecticut*, *Eisenstadt v. Baird*, and *Carey v. Population Services International* afford constitutional protection. We have no doubt as to the correctness of those decisions. They support the reasoning in *Roe* relating to the woman's liberty because they involve personal decisions concerning not only the meaning of procreation but also human responsibility and respect for it. As with abortion, reasonable people

will have differences of opinion about these matters. One view is based on such reverence for the wonder of creation that any pregnancy ought to be welcomed and carried to full term no matter how difficult it will be to provide for the child and ensure its well-being. Another is that the inability to provide for the nurture and care of the infant is a cruelty to the child and an anguish to the parent. These are intimate views with infinite variations, and their deep, personal character underlay our decisions in *Griswold, Eisenstadt,* and *Carey.* The same concerns are present when the woman confronts the reality that, perhaps despite her attempts to avoid it, she has become pregnant. [505 U.S. at 852–853.]

Thus *procreative choice,* or reproductive freedom, is the value that supports the right to choose and is the focal point of the joint opinion. This value—or this central aspect of liberty—may be considered to be the basis for both *Roe* and *Casey.*

In addition, the *Casey* joint opinion focuses on *bodily integrity*—the freedom from physical restraint of the body and governmental intrusions into the body—as an additional value or central aspect of liberty that underlies the right to choose. "It is settled now," the joint opinion remarks, that the Constitution places limits on a State's right to interfere with a person's most basic decisions about family and parenthood, *as well as bodily integrity*" (505 U.S. at 849; emphasis added). Similarly, in his separate opinion, Justice Blackmun emphasized that "[t]he Court re-affirms today the long recognized rights of privacy *and bodily integrity.*... [Our] cases embody the principle that personal decisions that profoundly affect *bodily integrity,* identity, and destiny should be largely beyond the reach of government.... In *Roe v. Wade,* this Court correctly applied these principles to a woman's right to choose abortion" (505 U.S. at 926–27; emphasis added).[4]

In addition to changing the point in time when the state's interest may permit substantial regulation of a woman's choice to terminate her pregnancy, the joint opinion in *Casey* applies a different standard of review than what the Court had used in Roe. "To protect the central right recognized by *Roe v. Wade* while at the same time accommodating the State's profound interest in potential life," the joint opinion employed an "undue burden analysis" rather than strict scrutiny. "An undue burden exists, and therefore a provision of law is invalid, if its purpose or effect is to place a substantial obstacle in the path of a woman seeking an abortion before the fetus attains viability" (505 U.S. at 878). "[A]n undue burden is an unconstitutional burden" (505 U.S. at 877). A majority of the Court, however, did not join this part of the joint opinion.

---

4. The source of this bodily integrity value is *Rochin v. California,* 342 U.S. 165 (1952), as the Court later noted in *Washington v. Glucksberg,* 521 U.S. 702, 720 (1997). In *Rochin,* police had forcibly taken Rochin to a hospital and directed a doctor to "pump" his stomach in order to recover two swallowed capsules that the police suspected to contain narcotics. The Court held that "[t]his is conduct that shocks the conscience" and violates the Fourteenth Amendment's due process clause.

C.3. The Newer-Era Cases: Other Rights to Privacy

Building on the groundwork established in the *Griswold* concurrences and the majority opinions in the abortion cases, the Court has decided a variety of other substantive due process cases regarding personal rights. In some cases the Court has recognized liberty interests and rights beyond those in *Griswold* and *Roe*; and in other cases the Court has refused to do so. In most but not all of these cases, the Court has used fundamental rights analysis.

In *Roberts v. United States Jaycees*, 468 U.S. 609 (1984), for example, the Court recognized the "freedom of intimate association" to be "a fundamental element of personal liberty" (468 U.S. at 618). The Court explained that "choices to enter into and maintain certain intimate human relationships," including but not limited to marital and family relationships, play "a critical role" in "cultivating and transmitting shared ideals and beliefs;" and that "individuals draw much of their emotional enrichment" and sense of identity from such relationships (468 U.S. at 617–619). The Court again recognized this freedom in *Board of Directors of Rotary International v. Rotary Club*, 481 U.S. 537 (1987). (For a distinction between freedom of *intimate* association and freedom of *expressive* association, see Chapter 12, Section G; and *see generally* Douglas Lindner, "Freedom of Association After Roberts v. United States Jaycees," 82 Mich. L. Rev. 1878 (1984).)

In *Cruzan v. Director, Missouri Dept. of Health*, 497 U.S. 261 (1990), its first "right-to-die" case, the Court acknowledged that "a competent person has a constitutionally protected liberty interest in refusing unwanted medical treatment" (*Id.* at 278 (Rehnquist, C.J., for majority); *see also Id.* at 287–288 (O'Connor, J., concurring)). This right, for which the Court did not use the label "fundamental," is apparently based on a value of bodily integrity much like the Court later developed in the *Casey* abortion decision (Sec. C.2 above). As Justice O'Connor explained in her important concurring opinion in *Cruzan*:

> [T]he liberty interest in refusing medical treatment flows from decisions involving the State's invasions into the body. Because our notions of liberty are inextricably entwined with our idea of physical freedom and self-determination, the Court has often deemed state incursions into the body repugnant to the interests protected by the Due Process Clause. [497 U.S. at 287 (O'Connor, J., concurring).]

This liberty interest did not serve to protect the plaintiff Nancy Cruzan, however, whose parents had sought to terminate the artificial nutrition and hydration systems that were sustaining her in a persistent vegetative state. Because she was then unconscious and had not previously expressed her wishes on the subject of artificial life support, the plaintiff was not a "competent person" and could not make a conscious choice to "refus[e] unwanted medical treatment."

In contrast, in *Washington v. Glucksberg*, 521 U.S. 702 (1997), the Court refused to recognize any new liberty interest that would protect competent, terminally ill patients in severe pain who seek the assistance of a physician in choosing when and how to die.

Expressly utilizing fundamental rights analysis, the Court determined that "the asserted 'right' to assistance in committing suicide is not a fundamental liberty interest protected by the Due Process Clause" (*Id.* at 728). Strict scrutiny therefore did not apply, and the Court rejected the plaintiff's claim using a rational basis standard of review.

The recent case of *Lawrence v. Texas*, 123 S. Ct. 2472 (2003), juxtaposed against the earlier case of *Bowers v. Hardwick*, 478 U.S. 186 (1986), is a telling illustration of the ferment that still surrounds cases concerning substantive due process claims. In *Bowers*, the Court determined that the constitutional right to privacy does not extend to sexual intimacies between two consenting adult males. The Court stated the question as "whether the Federal Constitution confers a fundamental right upon homosexuals to engage in [consensual] sodomy…" (478 U.S. at 190). In answering no to this question, the five-Justice majority emphasized that "[p]roscriptions against [consensual sodomy] have ancient roots" (478 U.S. at 192). Relying on the *Griswold* and *Roe* line of cases, the Court reasoned that "none of the rights announced in those cases bears any resemblance to the claimed constitutional right of homosexuals to engage in acts of sodomy," and that there is "[n]o connection between family, marriage, or procreation on the one hand and homosexual activity on the other…" (478 U.S. at 191). The Court also rejected any reliance on "the privacy of the home" as support for the claimed right. Having determined that no fundamental right was at stake, the Court applied rational basis review and—over strong dissents by Justice Blackmun (see Chap. 9, Sec. B.3) and Justice Stevens—upheld Georgia's sodomy law because it represented the legitimate "moral choice[ ]" of the people Georgia.

Seventeen years later in *Lawrence v. Texas*, the Court determined, contrary to *Bowers*, that the due process clause *does* extend to and protect the sexual intimacies between consenting adults of the same sex. The Court therefore invalidated the Texas sodomy statute under which Lawrence and his partner had been convicted.[5] In an opinion by Justice Kennedy, the five-Justice majority in *Lawrence* argued that the *Bowers* majority had failed "to appreciate the extent of the liberty at stake" and had therefore "misapprehended the claim of liberty there presented to it" (123 S.Ct. at 2478). The *Lawrence* majority also disagreed with the *Bowers* majority's reading of the history of sodomy laws: "[T]he historical grounds relied upon in *Bowers* are more complex than the majority opinion…indicate[s]. Their historical premises are not without doubt and, at the very least, are overstated" (*Id.* at 2480). Moreover, said the *Lawrence* majority, "our laws and traditions in the past half century … show an emerging awareness that liberty gives substantial protection to adult persons in deciding how to conduct their private lives in matters pertaining to sex," and "[t]his emerging recognition should have been apparent when *Bowers* was decided" (*Id.* at 2480). In addition, the *Lawrence* majority pointed to "[t]wo principal cases decided after *Bowers* [that] cast its holding into

---

5. The statute at issue in *Lawrence,* unlike the Georgia statute at issue in *Bowers*, applied only to same-sex sodomy. While that distinction is important to Justice O'Connor's concurrence, relying on equal protection analysis (see Chap. 10, Sec. E), it does not seem to be significant to the majority's analysis using substantive due process.

even more doubt"—the *Casey* abortion case (see Sec. C.2 above) and the *Romer* case invalidating a Colorado constitutional amendment disadvantaging homosexual persons (see Chap. 10, Sec. D.5). Based on this reasoning, the Court expressly overruled *Bowers* because it "was not correct when it was decided [and] is not correct today" (123 S.Ct. at 2484), and "[i]ts continuance as precedent demeans the lives of homosexual persons" (*Id.* at 2482).

In overruling *Bowers*, however, the Court in *Lawrence* did *not* declare that the right to engage in consensual homosexual sodomy is a *fundamental* right. Instead, the Court analyzed the issues only in terms of liberty interests and "the substantive reach of liberty under the Due Process Clause" (123 S.Ct. at 2476). The liberty interest at stake deserved protection because it involved "the most private human conduct, sexual behavior,... in the most private of places, the home" and because it involved not only "intimate conduct" but also a personal relationship and "personal bond" that two persons enter into by choice (*Id.* at 2478). Thus, unlike the *Bowers* majority, the *Lawrence* majority recognized both the intimacy of personal relationships and the privacy of the home as important constitutional interests. These interests serve to support a substantive due process right of adult persons, "with full and mutual consent," to engage in private "sexual practices common to a homosexual lifestyle" (*Id.* at 2484). This right takes precedence over Texas' interest in using "the power of the State to enforce [its moral] views on the whole society" (*Id.* at 2480) which, according to the *Lawrence* majority, is not a "legitimate state interest" (*Id.* at 2484).

C.4. Fundamental Rights Analysis: An Introduction

Since *Griswold* and *Roe*, as Sections C.1 to C.3 above suggest, the courts have engaged in a process of recognizing "fundamental" personal rights and according them special protection under the due process clause. These rights are "implied" or "unenumerated" rights, in contrast to the express substantive rights, such as free speech, that are in the Bill of Rights and the incorporated sector of Fourteenth Amendment due process (Sec. A.2 above). The concept of implied fundamental rights—as opposed to non-fundamental rights—is one of the most elusive concepts in all of constitutional law, and the court decisions recognizing such rights are among the most controversial in all of constitutional law. The elusiveness is due to the difficulties of determining the legitimate source or sources of such rights (if they are not in the text, then where do they come from?) and constructing any concrete guidelines by which courts and lawyers can distinguish fundamental from non-fundamental rights. The controversy is due to the potential for subjectivity in fundamental rights analysis and the concern about limiting subjectivity "lest the liberty protected by the Due Process Clause be subtly transformed into the policy preferences" of U.S. Supreme Court Justices and other judges (*Washington v. Glucksberg*, 521 U.S. 702, 720 (1997)).

The courts have long struggled with this problem of subjectivity in due process analysis, and U.S. Supreme Court Justices have often debated this problem in their opinions. The potential for subjective decisionmaking was a central aspect of the debate on whether to incorporate the Bill of Rights into the Fourteenth Amendment (see

Sec. A.2 above; and *see, e.g.*, Justice Frankfurter's concurrence and Justice Black's dissent in *Adamson v. California*, 332 U.S. 46, 65–66 (Frankfurter, J.) and 89–92 (Black, J.)). It was also a central aspect of the debate concerning the 1905 *Lochner* case and the "*Lochner* era" (see Sec. C.1 above; and *see, e.g.*, Justice Harlan's and Holmes' dissents in *Lochner*, 198 U.S. at 68–72 (Harlan) and 75–76 (Holmes)). In 1952, in *Rochin v. California*, 342 U.S. 165 (1952), the Court's opinion included this particularly pointed commentary on subjectivity and substantive due process:

> The vague contours of the Due Process Clause do not leave judges at large. We may not draw on our merely personal and private notions and disregard the limits that bind judges in their judicial function. Even though the concept of due process of law is not final and fixed, these limits are derived from considerations that are fused in the whole nature of our judicial process. See Cardozo, The Nature of the Judicial Process; The Growth of the Law; The Paradoxes of Legal Science. These are considerations deeply rooted in reason and in the compelling traditions of the legal profession....
>
> Due process of law thus conceived is not to be derided as resort to a revival of 'natural law'.... To practice the requisite detachment and to achieve sufficient objectivity no doubt demands of judges the habit of self-discipline and self-criticism, incertitude that one's own views are incontestable and alert tolerance toward views not shared. [342 U.S. at 170–172 (footnotes omitted).]

(For more on the exercise of judicial judgment, see Chapter 15, Section D.3.)

In addition to the inconsistencies and uncertainties about the law's application that subjective decisionmaking can create, it can also raise issues concerning the judiciary's functions compared to those of the representative branches of government. As the Court emphasized in *Washington v. Glucksberg*: "We must exercise the utmost care" when deciding substantive due process cases because "[b]y extending constitutional protection to an asserted right or liberty interest, we, to a great extent, place the matter outside the arena of public debate and legislative action" (521 U.S. at 720). Thus subtle considerations of federalism (see Chap. 6, Sec. A) and separation of powers (see Chap. 8, Sec. A) lurk just beneath the surface of the fundamental rights controversy, insofar as the cases necessarily test the relative authority and competence of the courts and legislatures (state and federal) to make decisions on matters of personal privacy and intimacy.

The presumption of constitutionality that attaches to economic and business legislation does not attach to legislation burdening personal rights that the courts deem to be fundamental. Such legislation thus invokes a high level of judicial scrutiny that disavows any deference to legislative judgments. (This phenomenon—a reversing of the presumption of constitutionality that usually attaches to state and federal legislation—is also evident in equal protection analysis when the courts apply heightened scrutiny to a classification (see Chap. 10, Secs. C.3 and C.4) and in the analysis under various other individual rights clauses.) Rights deemed to be fundamental thus become "super-protected" because government may not infringe upon them unless it can meet the rigorous standards of strict scrutiny review (see discussion of *Roe v. Wade* in Sec. C.2 above).

The key threshold question in substantive due process analysis, therefore, is whether the right infringed is a "fundamental" right. As suggested above, answering this question is an elusive undertaking, and clear answers are unlikely unless the right being asserted falls squarely within existing U.S. Supreme Court precedents. In general, a right (or a liberty interest) is fundamental only if a study of American history and traditions or, more broadly, a study of Anglo-American legal traditions, reveals that governments have recognized the right (or liberty interest) over a long time period to be of central importance to society. As the Court has summarized the approaches it has taken to the identification of fundamental rights:

> [W]e have regularly observed that the Due Process Clause specifically protects those fundamental rights and liberties which are, objectively, "deeply rooted in this Nation's history and tradition," and "implicit in the concept of ordered liberty," such that "neither liberty nor justice would exist if they were sacrificed." [*Washington v. Glucksberg*, 521 U.S. at 720–721, quoting *inter alia, Moore v. East Cleveland*, 431 U.S. 494, 503 (1977) (plurality opinion); *Palko v. Connecticut* 302 U.S. 319, 325, 326 (1937).]

C.5. Fundamental "Rights" vs. Fundamental "Liberty Interests" vs. Fundamental "Values"

In order to anchor fundamental rights analysis to the due process clause, and to apply this analysis in concrete cases, it is necessary to consider the relationship between "liberty interests" and "rights." These two concepts are distinguishable from one another, and the distinction is at least implicit in the U.S. Supreme Court's substantive due process work. But the courts often have not explained the distinction between liberty interests and rights in their opinions and have often used the two terms interchangeably. The discussion below defines and differentiates the two terms and shows how sorting them out would promote the clarity and coherency of substantive due process analysis.

"Liberty interests," for purposes of due process, are the interests that (along with life and property interests) are expressly protected by the due process clause. "Rights" are the specific substantive rights that courts have recognized in order to protect some particular aspect or component of "liberty" and to allow particular individuals to claim this protection in court. Liberty interests and rights may be further distinguished and interrelated as follows:

1. Liberty interests are explicit, at least to the extent that they are expressly referenced in the "deprivation of...liberty" language in the due process clause. Rights are implied, or "unenumerated," rather than explicit. They are implied from a liberty interest or, more precisely, from the pertinent history and tradition that is linked to a particular liberty interest. Rights thus arise from or are grounded in liberty interests. Procreative choice is a liberty interest, for example; and the right to use contraceptives is a substantive right arising from that liberty interest.

2. Liberty interests are more general and abstract than rights. Rights are more specific and concrete than liberty interests. In *Meyer v. Nebraska*, 262 U.S. 390 (1923), while making one of its earliest and strongest statements about liberty interests, the Court defined "liberty" with a fairly high degree of abstraction:

> [T]his court has not attempted to define with exactness the liberty [protected by the Fourteenth Amendment].... Without doubt, it denotes not merely freedom from bodily restraint but also the right of the individual to contract, to engage in any of the common occupations of life, to acquire useful knowledge, to marry, establish a home and bring up children, to worship God according to the dictates of his own conscience, and generally to enjoy those privileges long recognized at common law as essential to the orderly pursuit of happiness by free men. [262 U.S. at 399.]

Similarly, in a more recent case, the Court has said that liberty has "both...spatial and more transcendent dimensions;" and "presumes an autonomy of self that includes freedom of thought, belief, expression, and certain intimate conduct" (*Lawrence v. Texas*, 123 S.Ct. 2472, 2475 (2003)).

In other cases, the Court has emphasized that liberty "is not a series of isolated points" but "a rational continuum...." (*Planned Parenthood of Southeastern Pennsylvania v. Casey*, 505 U.S. at 848, quoting *Poe v. Ullman*, 367 U.S. at 543 (Harlan, J., dissenting)); and that liberty is a "broad and majestic term [ ]...among the 'great [constitutional] concepts...purposely left to gather meaning from experience'" (*Board of Regents v. Roth*, 408 U.S. 564, 571, quoting *National Mutual Ins. Co. v. Tidewater Co.*, 337 U.S. 582, 646 (Frankfurter, J., dissenting)). The Court has also emphasized that "[i]n a Constitution for a free people, there can be no doubt that the meaning of 'liberty' must be broad indeed" (*Roth*, 408 U.S. at 572). In order to particularize this "broad" and "majestic" concept of *liberty interests*, and to confirm the "meaning" it has gathered "from experience," the Court has recognized various specific *rights* on a case-by-case basis.

3. Of the various liberty interests that fall within the broad definitions above, only a small number are ranked as "fundamental." A right to choose what job to hold is a liberty interest, for instance, but has not been held to be a *fundamental* liberty interest. When a right arises from or is grounded in a liberty interest that is fundamental, then the right becomes fundamental as well. Just as liberty interests are more general and abstract than rights, fundamental liberty interests are more general and abstract than fundamental rights.

4. Fundamental liberty interests receive special protection or are "super-protected"; non-fundamental liberty interests are not. Fundamental rights, which arise from fundamental liberty interests, also receive special protection and become "super-protected"; non-fundamental rights do not. In *Washington v. Glucksberg*, 521 U.S. 702 (1997) (Secs. C.3 and C.4 above), after being less than clear in some earlier opinions, the Court apparently settled on "fundamental liberty interests" and "fundamental rights" as the operative substantive due process terminology and distinguished between the two. "Fundamental rights" are the "concrete examples," according to *Glucksberg*, by which the

Court has "carefully refined" the "outlines of the 'liberty' specially protected by the Fourteenth Amendment" (521 U.S. at 720).

5. Because due process rights arise from liberty interests, and because liberty interests are more abstract than rights, the same fundamental liberty interest may support many "concrete examples" of fundamental rights. For example, the fundamental liberty interest of procreative choice or reproductive freedom may support the fundamental right to use contraceptives, the fundamental right to distribute or receive contraceptives, and the fundamental right to terminate a pregnancy.

6. To apply these distinctions to the right to privacy, one would speak of *liberty interests* in privacy on the one hand, and privacy *rights* on the other. Not every liberty interest in privacy is fundamental, and therefore not every claimed right to personal privacy will be considered fundamental. The liberty interests in privacy that are ranked as fundamental create "zones of privacy" (*see, e.g.*, the *Roe* majority opinion, Sec. C.2 above) that are specially protected. Privacy rights that fall within these zones are considered fundamental as well and therefore receive special protection.

If these various conceptual distinctions were consistently recognized and relied on in substantive due process analysis, the analysis would become clearer because its various components would have been separately identified and considered. There would also be a clearer analytical methodology for identifying and sorting out the relatively few liberty interests and rights that are fundamental and super-protected, and a better understanding of why it is important to work with "concrete" and carefully confined definitions of rights at the rights stage of the analysis. Moreover, adhering to the conceptual distinctions above would help alleviate the "levels of generality" problem in substantive due process analysis, as suggested in Section C.6 below.

In addition, it would be helpful to understand the role of "values" in substantive due process analysis. Both courts and commentators sometimes use values terminology in substantive due process discussions. In his *Griswold* concurrence, for example, Justice Harlan spoke of "*basic values* 'implicit in the concept of ordered liberty'" (381 U.S. at 500; emphasis added). Similarly, Justice Douglas, in his concurrence in *Roe v. Wade*, spoke of certain rights that "are basic to Fourteenth Amendment *values*" (410 U.S. at 219–220, emphasis added); Justice Blackmun, in his dissent in *Bowers* (see Sec. C.6 below), spoke of "the *values* that underlie the constitutional right to privacy" (478 U.S. at 199; emphasis added), and Justice Souter, in his concurrence in *Glucksberg* (see Secs. C.3 and C.4 above), spoke of "*values* . . . truly deserving constitutional stature" and "the history of our *values* as a people" (521 U.S. at 764; emphasis added).[6] Among commentators, the values terminology is more common than it is among courts. *See, e.g.*,

---

6. The U.S. Supreme Court has also used values terminology with respect to constitutional rights other than substantive due process. *See, e.g., Alderman v. United States*, 394 U.S. 165, 175 (1969) (security of persons and property under Fourth Amendment as a "fundamental value"); *Epperson v. Arkansas*, 393 U.S. 97, 104 (1968) (freedom of speech "and inquiry and of belief" as "fundamental values"); *Murphy v. Waterfront Comm'n of New York Harbor*, 378 U.S. 52, 55 (1964) (Fifth Amendment privilege against self-incrimination as reflecting "fundamental values").

John Hart Ely, "The Supreme Court, 1977 Term—Forward: On Discovering Fundamental Values," 92 HARV. L. REV. 5 (1978); and *compare* Ira Lupu, "Untangling the
Strands of the Fourteenth Amendment," 77 U. MICH. L. REV. 981, 1030–1050 (1979)
(discussing "fundamental value discovery"). Generally speaking, a value in the sense
used by these courts and commentators is much the same as a liberty interest for purposes of substantive due process, and a fundamental value is much the same as a fundamental liberty interest.

To understand the "values" terminology used in substantive due process analysis,
and to harmonize it with liberty interest terminology, one should think of liberty interests as being supported by, and definable by, some value or set of values reflected in
the nation's history and traditions. A liberty interest may then be considered fundamental when it is undergirded by some value (the "underlying value") that has been
held in such consistently high regard, in our history and traditions, that it may be considered a fundamental value. Procreative choice, for instance, may be considered a fundamental *liberty interest* because it is undergirded by the fundamental *value* of procreative choice; and marital intimacy or marital autonomy may be considered a
fundamental *liberty interest* because it is undergirded by the fundamental *value* of marital intimacy or autonomy. Courts give special protection to such liberty interests because it is necessary to do so in order to uphold values deemed to be fundamental; and
in protecting the liberty interest, courts recognize whatever specific substantive rights
are needed to safeguard the fundamental liberty interest and thus uphold the fundamental value on which it rests. This approach has the advantage of frankly acknowledging that substantive due process necessitates value judgments—judgments about
values that are anchored to the Constitution through the Fourteenth Amendment's
concept of liberty and are deeply rooted in American history and traditions. This approach also has the advantage of associating substantive due process analysis with the
values approach to constitutional interpretation (see Chap. 9, Secs. B.2 to B.4), thus
placing the analysis within a methodological framework that helps guide its application.

C.6. Levels of Generality (or Abstraction) in Fundamental Rights Analysis

Much of the confusion in substantive due process law, and much of the disagreement among Justices, is attributable to the lack of well-developed conceptual distinctions between rights and liberty interests and between rights and values. Some Justices
and lower courts have focused on *the specific right* being claimed, searching history and
tradition for evidence of the recognition accorded *to this specific right*. If the *specific
right* is sufficiently recognized and prized, then it is fundamental and super-protected.
Other Justices and lower courts have focused on the broader *liberty interest* (or value)
at stake, searching history and tradition for evidence of the recognition accorded *to this
liberty interest* (or the value that underlies the liberty interest). If the *liberty interest* is
sufficiently recognized and prized, then it is fundamental, and any specific right that
must be safeguarded to preserve that liberty interest will be fundamental and super-

protected. The result one reaches about the fundamentality of the right at issue may often differ depending on which of these two analytical approaches is taken.

If one seeks to determine whether the right to distribute or receive contraceptives is fundamental, for example, one may search history and tradition for evidence of the recognition accorded *this specific right*, or one may search for evidence of the recognition accorded the broader *liberty interest* of reproductive freedom. One may reach a different conclusion under the second approach than under the first, since the evidence for reproductive freedom—a more general concept embracing a greater range of circumstances—is likely to be stronger than the evidence for the right to distribute or receive contraceptives. The right to distribute or receive is therefore more likely to be recognized as a fundamental right under the second approach than under the first. In *Carey v. Population Services International*, 431 U.S. 678 (1977), for example, the Court invalidated a state law restricting the sale of contraceptives to adults because such restrictions implicate "a decision as fundamental as that of whether to bear or beget a child" (*Id.* at 686). The Court emphasized that, read "in light of its progeny, the teaching of *Griswold* [Sec. C.1 above] is that the Constitution protects individual decisions in matters of childbearing from unjustified intrusion by the State" (*Id.* at 687).

Similarly, if one were to search history and tradition for evidence that the right to engage in homosexual sodomy is fundamental, one may reach a different result than if one were to search history and tradition for evidence that the broader privacy of intimate associations is fundamental. These differing perspectives were vividly illustrated by *Bowers v. Hardwick*, 478 U.S. 186 (1986), a case subsequently overruled by *Lawrence v. Texas*, 123 S.Ct. 2472 (2003) (see Sec. C.3 above). In *Bowers*, Justice White, for a majority of five, focused narrowly on history regarding homosexual sodomy and found no evidence to support a claim that the right to engage in consensual homosexual sodomy is fundamental. In contrast, Justice Blackmun, writing for the four dissenting Justices, focused more broadly on "the freedom [of] an individual...to choose the form and nature of...intensely personal [relationships]" (478 U.S. at 205). Taking this broader approach that emphasized the need to consider "the values that underlie the constitutional right to privacy," the dissenters found sufficient grounds for declaring the plaintiff's claimed right to be fundamental.

When *Lawrence* later overruled *Bowers*, the Court majority not only criticized the *Bowers* majority's reading of history but also its "failure to appreciate the extent of the liberty interest at stake" (123 S.Ct. at 2478). In so doing, the *Lawrence* court was moving the analysis to a higher level of generality. At this higher level, rather than focusing merely on a particular type of sexual act, the Court emphasized sexual conduct in general as "the most private human conduct" and as "intimate conduct;" and also emphasized that "sexuality" is "but one element in a personal bond" of intimacy that may be "enduring" (123 S.Ct. at 2478). The weighty importance of these liberty interests convinced the majority in *Lawrence*, unlike that in *Bowers*, to protect the right to engage in consensual homosexual sodomy, which was necessarily subsumed within these broader liberty interests.

The problem illustrated by *Bowers* and *Lawrence*, and by the two contrasting approaches to fundamental rights described above, is often called the "levels of generality" or "levels of abstraction" problem. Under the first approach, focusing on *the spe-cific right* claimed, the search into history and tradition takes place at a very low level of generality or abstraction. Under the second approach, focusing on *the liberty inter-est* or value at stake, the search takes place at a higher level of generality or abstraction, since liberty interests (or values) are considered to be more general or abstract than the specific rights that they encompass. There is no agreement among the Justices or among the lower courts on the appropriate level of generality for substantive due process analysis or on how to make such determinations. *See generally* David Crump, "How Do Courts Really Discover Unenumerated Fundamental Rights? Cataloguing the Methods of Judicial Alchemy," 19 Harv. J. of Law and Pub. Policy 795, 863-871 (1996). Similar problems may also arise concerning values interpretation generally (see Chap. 9, Sec. B.3, re: "levels of generality") and historical interpretation generally (see Chap. 4, Sec. C.2, re: "generality or abstraction").

C.7. Standards of Review for Substantive Due Process

The standards of review applicable to substantive due process cases, like those for equal protection, always embody some kind of means-ends analysis, thus providing both a "means" test and an "ends" test that will apply to the challenged legislation. Also as with equal protection, substantive due process standards of review typically require an analysis of the governmental interests at stake. *Government interests*—that is, the ends or objectives that government seeks to achieve through the legislation at issue— are very different from the *liberty interests* that individuals may assert. In fundamental rights cases, when strict scrutiny applies (see, e.g., *Roe v. Wade*, Sec. C.2 above), the gov-ernment interest must be a "compelling" interest. Although this concept plays a criti-cal role in modern substantive due process analysis—as well as in equal protection, free speech and press, and free exercise of religion analysis—the Supreme Court has provided little guidance on how to differentiate compelling interests from the range of other legitimate interests possessed by government. Given the paucity of definitions and guidelines, analysis must often proceed by analogy; the more analogous a partic-ular interest is to one already deemed compelling by the courts, the more likely it is that this interest will also be characterized as compelling.

When a court determines that the right claimed by the individual is not a funda-mental right, the court will then usually apply rational basis review rather than strict scrutiny. This standard of review parallels that for rational basis review under the equal protection clause (Chap. 10, Sec. C.3). The court asks whether the government's in-fringement of a liberty interest is "rationally related to legitimate government interests" (*Washington v. Glucksberg*, 521 U.S. 702, 728 (1997)). In effect, under this standard, the challenger has the burden of showing that the government's decision is irrational, or as courts sometimes say, "arbitrary and capricious" (*see Board of Curators of the University of Missouri v. Horowitz*, 435 U.S. 78, 91–92 (1978)). Since this is a minimalist standard of review, the courts will usually reject claims that are not based on fundamental rights. The Court reached this result in *Glucksberg*, for instance, as well as in *Bowers v. Hard-wick*, 478 U.S. 186 (1986), using rational basis review in each case (see Sec. C.3 above).

In some cases there is no plausible claim that an infringed right is fundamental, and the case would therefore originate and proceed (if it proceeds at all) as a rational basis review case. The defendant generally prevails in such suits, often on a motion for summary judgment. This result is especially likely if the interest infringed is an alleged property interest rather than a liberty interest. *See, e.g., City of Cuyahoga Falls v. Buckeye Community Hope Foundation*, 123 S.Ct. 1396 (2003). Occasionally, however, a substantive due process claim does succeed in the lower courts even though no fundamental right is at stake and the standard of review is rational basis. In *Seal v. Morgan*, 229 F. 3d 567 (6th Cir. 2000), for instance, a student used substantive due process to challenge a school board's decision to expel him, under a "zero tolerance" weapons policy, for having a knife in his car that he did not put there and did not know was there. Rejecting the school board's motion for summary judgment, the court ruled that "expelling a student for weapons possession...even if the student did not knowingly possess any weapon, would not be rationally related to any legitimate state interest" (229 F. 3d at 575).

In 1997, in *Washington v. Glucksberg* (above), the Court reaffirmed the "two-tier" system for standards of review (strict scrutiny or minimum rational basis) and emphasized that the fundamental rights approach is the "established method of substantive-due-process analysis" through which the "liberty" protected by the Fourteenth Amendment has "been carefully refined by concrete examples involving fundamental rights found to be deeply rooted in our legal tradition" (521 U.S. at 720-722). Nevertheless, in other newer-era substantive due process cases, the Justices have utilized analyses that do not focus on fundamental rights, and have applied standards of review other than strict scrutiny or rational basis. For example, in the *Cruzan* case (Sec. C.3 above), when considering whether there is a constitutional right to refuse life-sustaining medical treatment, the Court used an ad hoc "balancing" of the individual's "liberty interests against the relevant state interests" (497 U.S. at 279, quoting *Youngberg v. Romeo*, 457 U.S. 307 (1982)). In *Planned Parenthood of Southeastern Pennsylvania v. Casey*, 505 U.S. 833 (1992) (Sec. C.2 above), a plurality of the Court utilized an "undue burden" standard in lieu of conventional strict scrutiny review. And in 2003, in *Lawrence v. Texas*, 123 S.Ct. 2472 (2003) (Sec. C.3 above), the Court majority engaged in a rigorous review of a Texas same-sex sodomy statute without using fundamental rights analysis or a strict scrutiny standard of review, and without discussing or citing *Glucksberg*. Instead, the *Lawrence* majority spoke of "constitutional liberty interests" and the "right to liberty;" and for a standard of review, the majority asked whether the Texas statute "furthers [a] legitimate state interest which can justify [the state's] intrusion into the personal and private life of the individual" (123 S.Ct. at 2484).

The *Lawrence* approach to judicial review may be seen as a type of ad hoc "balancing" similar to that in *Cruzan* (above) or, perhaps more likely, a type of "rational-basis-with-bite" scrutiny similar to that used in some equal protection cases (see Chap. 10, Sec. C.3). The *Lawrence* majority relied heavily on one such equal protection case — *Romer v. Evans*, 517 U.S. 620 (1996) (Chap. 10, Sec. D.5) — using it as support for overruling *Bowers* (Sec. C.3 above). *Romer*, like *Lawrence*, concerned the rights of homosexuals; and the *Romer* majority opinion, like the *Lawrence* majority opinion, was written by Justice Kennedy.[7] Whether *Lawrence* does establish a type of rational-basis-with-bite scrutiny (or ad-hoc balancing) for certain substantive due process cases, and the extent to which such a regime would supplement or replace the fundamental rights/strict scrutiny regime that the Court reaffirmed in 1997 in *Glucksberg*, are matters that the Court will need to clarify in subsequent substantive due process cases.

Sec. D. Procedural Due Process: A Conceptual Overview

D.1. The Contours of Modern Procedural Due Process

Procedural due process comprises half of the non-incorporated content of the due process clause (see Sec. A.1 above). Procedural due process focuses on whether particular governmental decisions are made with the kind of procedural regularity and fairness that renders these decisions procedurally valid in terms of due process. Only governmental decisions that deprive a particular individual of an interest in life, liberty, or property raise such concerns. A government agency or official must have made an individualized determination about a particular individual, and the individualized determination must have imposed a burden on or denied a benefit to the individual that infringes the individual's liberty or property (or life) interests. Thus the kind of decision that a legislature makes when it passes a law or that an administrative agency makes when it promulgates a regulation is usually not the kind of decision that would require procedural due process protections; it is not an individualized decision about a particular individual but a generalized decision affecting a large group of people. *United States v. Florida East Coast R. Co.*, 410 U.S. 224, 244–245 (1973). If, for example, a state worker's compensation board promulgates a general rule concerning eligibility for worker's compensation, the procedures for adopting the rule will not be subject to a procedural due process challenge. But if the board applies its eligibility rule to a particular individual and terminates that individual's compensation, the procedures for making the individualized determination will be subject to procedural due process analysis.

Goldberg v. Kelly, 397 U.S. 254 (1970), establishes a foundation for exploring procedural due process questions and also illustrates the profound impact that the absence of procedural protections may have on the lives of individuals. In March 1968, a New York State welfare agency had cut off further welfare payments to Angela Velez. Erroneously, the agency believed that she was cohabitating with her estranged husband.

---

7. In his *Lawrence* opinion, Justice Kennedy called *Romer v. Evans* a "post-*Bowers* case [that] cast...doubt" on the *Bowers* reasoning (*Id.* at 2841, 2842). But the majority did not expressly overrule or contradict the assertion in *Bowers* that there is no *fundamental* right to engage in homosexual sodomy—a point Justice Scalia took pains to emphasize in his *Lawrence* dissent (*Id.* at 2488, 2491–2493). Since the *Lawrence* majority declined to engage in fundamental rights analysis, but nevertheless conducted a probing review relying in part on *Romer*, rational-basis-with-bite scrutiny seems an appropriate way to describe the majority's standard of review.

Velez immediately requested a hearing, which was granted in June. On July 10, the State Commissioner of Social Services ruled in favor of Velez and reinstated her welfare benefits. In the four months between termination and reinstatement, however, Velez found herself in a desperate situation, unable to provide for her children's subsistence and her own. She and her four children were evicted from her apartment for nonpayment of rent and went to live with her sister, who also subsisted on welfare with her nine children. The district court summarized Mrs. Velez's plight:

> Mrs. Velez and three children have been sleeping in two single beds in a small room, and the youngest sleeps in a crib in the same room. Thirteen children and two adults have been living in one apartment, and Mrs. Velez states that she has been unable to feed her children adequately, so that they have lost weight and have been ill. [*Kelly v. Wyman*, 294 F. Supp. 893, 899 (1968).]

Mrs. Velez and other New York welfare recipients challenged the adequacy of the state's termination proceedings. They argued that the existing procedures, which provided only a *post*-termination hearing, failed to safeguard the property interests of recipients such as Velez, and that procedural due process required a *pre*-termination hearing. In opposition, the State argued that countervailing governmental interests justified the delayed evidentiary hearing. Post-termination hearings conserved fiscal and administrative resources, noted the state, by promptly stopping payments to ineligible individuals and by reducing the number of evidentiary hearings actually held.

The U.S. Supreme Court first considered whether welfare benefits constituted a property interest, such that their termination would be a deprivation of property. If the recipient did not have a property interest in the benefits, then no due process procedures would be required. But in a landmark ruling, the Court recognized the receipt of such benefits to be a property interest. "Such benefits are a matter of statutory entitlement for persons qualified to receive them. Their termination involves state action that adjudicates important rights. The constitutional challenge cannot be answered by an argument that public assistance benefits are 'a privilege' and not a 'right'" (397 U.S. at 262). The Court explained:

> It may be realistic today to regard welfare entitlements as more like 'property' than a 'gratuity.' Much of the existing wealth in this country takes the form of rights that do not fall within traditional common-law concepts of property. It has been aptly noted that:
>
>> society today is built around entitlement. The automobile dealer has his franchise, the doctor and lawyer their professional licenses, the worker his union membership, contract, and pension rights, the executive his contract and stock options; all are devices to aid security and independence. Many of the most important of these entitlements now flow from government: subsidies to farmers and businessmen, routes for airlines and channels for television stations; long term contracts for defense, space, and education; social security pensions for individuals. Such sources of security, whether private or public, are no longer regarded as luxuries or gratuities; to the recipients they are essentials, fully deserved, and in no sense

a form of charity. It is only the poor whose entitlements, although recognized by public policy, have not been effectively enforced.

[397 U.S. at 263, fn. 8, quoting Charles Reich, "Individual Rights and Social Welfare: The Emerging Legal Issues," 74 YALE L.J. 1245, 1255 (1965).]

Having concluded that government entitlements are property interests triggering due process protections, the Court turned to the adequacy of the state's procedures for terminating welfare benefits. The Court reasoned that "[t]he fundamental requisite of due process of law is the opportunity to be heard...at a meaningful time and in a meaningful manner" and that this "opportunity to be heard must be tailored to the capacities and circumstances of those who are to be heard" (397 U.S. at 267, 268–269). Because of the unique situation of welfare recipients, the Court required the state to build additional procedural safeguards into its termination process. In particular, the Court agreed with the recipients that the state must grant a *pre*-termination, rather than merely a *post*-termination, evidentiary hearing:

> It is true, of course, that some governmental benefits may be administratively terminated without affording the recipient a pre-termination evidentiary hearing. But we agree with the District Court that when welfare is discontinued, only a pre-termination evidentiary hearing provides the recipient with procedural due process. For qualified recipients, welfare provides the means to obtain essential food, clothing, housing, and medical care. Thus the crucial factor in this context—a factor not present in the case of the blacklisted government contractor, the discharged government employee, the taxpayer denied a tax exemption, or virtually anyone else whose governmental entitlements are ended—is that termination of aid pending resolution of a controversy over eligibility may deprive an eligible recipient of the very means by which to live while he waits. Since he lacks independent resources, his situation becomes immediately desperate. His need to concentrate upon finding the means for daily subsistence, in turn, adversely affects his ability to seek redress from the welfare bureaucracy. [397 U.S. at 263–264 (citations omitted).]

The great importance of welfare benefits to the recipients, and the unique harm that befalls a recipient whose benefits are terminated, outweighed any countervailing governmental interests in conserving fiscal and administrative resources. "[T]he stakes are simply too high for the welfare recipient, and the possibility for honest error or irritable misjudgment too great, to allow termination of aid without giving the recipient a chance, if he so desires, to be fully informed of the case against him..."(397 U.S. at 266, quoting district court opinion, 294 F. Supp. at 904–905).

The Court in *Goldberg* also required that the pre-termination hearing be accompanied by several additional procedural safeguards. Prior to the hearing, due process requires "adequate notice detailing the reasons for a proposed termination...." The hearing itself must include the opportunity to present arguments *orally*. Most recipients "lack the educational attainment necessary to write effectively....Moreover, written submissions do not afford the flexibility of oral presentations; they do not permit the recipient to mold his argument to the issues the decision maker appears to regard as important. Particularly where credibility and veracity are at issue, as they must be in many termination proceedings, written submissions are a wholly unsatisfactory basis for decision." Furthermore, because welfare termination proceedings hinge on questions of fact, "due process requires an opportunity to confront and cross-examine adverse witnesses." The recipient must also be able to retain counsel if she so desires; "[c]ounsel can help delineate the issues, present the factual contentions in an orderly manner, conduct cross-examination, and generally safeguard the interests of the recipient." Finally, there must be an impartial decisionmaker, and the decision "as to a recipient's eligibility must rest solely on the legal rules and evidence adduced at the hearing." (See 397 U.S. at 267–271.)

D.2.   Identifying "Liberty" and "Property" Interests

The search for liberty and property interests constitutes the first stage of a two-stage due process methodology that the U.S. Supreme Court has developed. This methodology applies to all procedural due process issues concerning individualized government decisions. The first inquiry is whether the government's decision constitutes a deprivation of liberty or property, that is, whether it deprives a particular individual of an interest that qualifies as a "liberty interest" or a "property interest" under the due process clause. If the answer to that question is yes, then the second inquiry is: What procedural protections must be accorded the individual who is deprived of the liberty or property interest? In substantive due process cases, courts seldom tarry over the question whether a liberty (or property) interest has been infringed; usually such an interest is obviously involved or the courts assume arguendo that it is. In procedural due process cases, in contrast, there is a great emphasis on the first inquiry, and courts frequently reject claims by concluding that no liberty or property interest has been infringed. The first-stage inquiry thus can often be dispositive.

A case two years after Goldberg, *Board of Regents v. Roth*, 408 U.S. 564 (1972), is instructive. David Roth was hired in 1968 for his first teaching job as an untenured assistant professor at Wisconsin State University-Oshkosh. He received a contract appointing him to this position for a period of one year. Subsequently, the university declined to renew his employment for a second year, giving no reasons for its decision. Of the 442 non-tenured teachers at the university, only four teachers, including Roth, were denied contract renewals for the next year (*Roth v. Board of Regents*, 310 F. Supp. 972, 974.) Roth believed that his contract was not renewed because of certain statements he had made that were critical of the university's administration. In his lawsuit, Roth charged that the university had violated his procedural due process rights by failing to provide notice of the reasons for non-retention and a hearing on the issues. Dismissing Roth's claim, the U.S. Supreme Court held that he could not challenge the adequacy of the university's procedures because the non-renewal had not deprived him of any interest in liberty or property. Thus *Roth*, like *Goldberg*, focused on the presence or absence of a property or liberty interest, but in *Roth*, unlike *Goldberg*, the Court did not find any infringement of such an interest.

The Court noted that "'[l]iberty' and 'property' are broad and majestic terms. They are among the '[g]reat [constitutional] concepts... purposely left to gather meaning from experience....'" Although the Court "eschewed rigid or formalistic limitations" of these terms, it nevertheless recognized the need to set boundaries that would give meaning to the terms.

Liberty, the Court explained:

> "denotes not merely freedom from bodily restraint but also the right of the individual to contract, to engage in any of the common occupations of life, to acquire useful knowledge, to marry, establish a home and bring up children, to worship God according to the dictates of his own conscience, and generally to enjoy those privileges long recognized... as essential to the orderly pursuit of happiness by free men." [408 U.S. at 572, quoting *Meyer v. Nebraska*, 262 U.S. 390, 399 (1923).] [8]

Additionally, the Court recognized that liberty interests may be at stake when government impugns one's "good name, reputation, honor, or integrity" in the context of denying employment or some other benefit; and when government imposes "a stigma or other disability that foreclose[s]... freedom to take advantage of other employment opportunities" (408 U.S. at 573). "In a Constitution for a free people, there can be no doubt that the meaning of 'liberty' must be broad indeed" (408 U.S. at 572).

Despite the breadth of the concept, the Court quickly dismissed Roth's argument that his non-renewal infringed a liberty interest. "The State, in declining to rehire [Roth], did not make any charge against him that might seriously damage his standing and associations in his community. It did not base the nonrenewal of his contract on a charge, for example, that he had been guilty of dishonesty or immorality." Furthermore, "there is no suggestion that the State, in declining to re-employ [Roth], imposed on him a stigma or other disability that foreclosed his freedom to take advantage of other employment opportunities." The Court concluded that "it stretches the concept too far to suggest that a person is deprived of 'liberty' when he simply is not rehired in one job but remains as free as before to seek another" (408 U.S. at 573–575).

The Court in *Roth* then addressed property interests and their distinction from liberty interests. Property interests represent "the security of interests that a person has already acquired in specific benefits" (408 U.S. at 576). These interests "may take many forms," including intangible interests such as statutory entitlements (*Goldberg* is a key example here) as well as ownership of tangibles such as personal property, real estate, or money:

> "To have a property interest in a benefit, a person clearly must have more than an abstract need or desire for it. He must have more than a unilateral expectation of it. He must, instead, have a legitimate claim of entitlement to it.... Property interests, of course, are not created by the Constitution. Rather, they are created and their dimensions are defined by existing rules or understand-

---

8. This is the same definition as set out in Section C.5 above with respect to substantive due process.

ings that stem from an independent source such as state law—rules or understandings that secure certain benefits and that support claims of entitlement to those benefits. [408 U.S. at 577.]

Since Roth had been hired for a fixed one-year term under a contract that did not provide for renewal, and since no university rule or state statute provided for renewal, Roth had no "legitimate claim of entitlement" to re-employment after his term expired. He thus had neither a property interest nor a liberty interest that the state had infringed, and the due process clause afforded him no procedural protection in these circumstances.

D.3. The "Process" That is "Due"

At the second stage of procedural due process analysis, which applies only if there is a deprivation of liberty or property, one identifies the particular procedures that the government has utilized to effect the deprivation and asks whether they are constitutionally adequate. The analysis typically emphasizes the need to assure accuracy in decision-making and the need to assess the costs and benefits of requiring additional procedures to lessen the risks of error. As the Court explained in *Mathews v. Eldridge*, 424 U.S. 319, 348 (1976): "[M]ore is implicated in cases of this type than ad hoc weighing of fiscal and administrative burdens against the interests of a particular category of claimants. The ultimate balance involves a determination as to when, under our constitutional system, judicial-type procedures must be imposed upon administrative action to assure fairness...." The focus is typically on the provision of notice and opportunity for some kind of adjudicatory hearing: "the fundamental requirement of due process is the opportunity to be heard 'at a meaningful time and in a meaningful manner'" (*Mathews*, 424 U.S. at 333, quoting *Armstrong v. Manzo*, 380 U.S. 545, 552 (1965)).

Mathews, like *Goldberg*, involved a termination of governmental benefits, but the benefits at issue were Social Security disability benefits rather than welfare benefits. As in *Goldberg*, the recipient in *Mathews* was found to have a property interest in the benefits, and the analysis moved to stage two. The Court used this occasion for further elucidation of the "what process is due" analysis that it had developed in *Goldberg*.

The issue in *Mathews* was whether the due process clause required that the federal government afford the recipient a *pre-termination* (before-the-fact) hearing in which to challenge the termination of disability benefits.[9] Eldridge, the recipient, had been afforded only a *post*-termination (after-the-fact) hearing in which to challenge the government's decision. As a result, "[T]here was a foreclosure...and the family's furniture was repossessed, forcing Eldridge, his wife, and their children to sleep in one bed." (424 U.S. at 350 (Brennan, J., dissenting)). The lower courts, relying heavily on *Goldberg*,

---

9. Since the recipient was challenging a federal government decision, the Fifth Amendment due process clause applied rather than the Fourteenth Amendment due process clause.

found the government's existing procedures to be inadequate and held that due process required a pre-termination evidentiary hearing. The U.S. Supreme Court reversed the lower courts and upheld the existing procedural scheme. In justifying its decision, the Court announced and applied a three-factor test for determining the constitutional sufficiency of the procedures that government uses when it deprives an individual of a liberty or property interest:

> [O]ur prior decisions indicate that identification of the specific dictates of due process generally requires consideration of three distinct factors: (1) the private interest that will be affected by the official action; (2)(a) the risk of an erroneous deprivation of such interest through the procedures used, and (2)(b) the probable value, if any, of additional or substitute procedural safeguards; and (3) the Government's interest, including the function involved and the fiscal and administrative burdens that the additional or substitute procedural requirement would entail. [424 U.S. at 334–335 (numbering and lettering added).]

Applying these factors, the Court distinguished *Goldberg* and held that due process did not require a pre-termination hearing before termination of disability benefits.

The Court conceded that Eldridge's private interest (factor 1 above), as affected by the termination of benefits, was significant. The delay between the cut-off of benefits and a final decision after a post-termination hearing typically exceeded one year. "In view of the torpidity of this administrative review process and the typically modest resources of the family unit of the physically disabled worker, the hardship imposed upon the erroneously terminated disability recipient may be significant." Nevertheless, the Court determined that "the disabled worker's need is likely to be less than that of a welfare recipient." Unlike welfare benefits, eligibility for Social Security disability benefits was not based upon financial need. The disabled worker whose benefits were terminated could seek other temporary sources of income, making his plight less desperate than the welfare recipient's. "[A]ccess to private resources" was one possibility for a disabled worker; another was welfare benefits, should the family income and resources fall below the subsistence level. "In view of these potential sources of temporary income, there is less reason here than in *Goldberg* to depart from the ordinary principle, established by our decisions, that something less than an evidentiary hearing is sufficient prior to adverse administrative action" (424 U.S. at 343).

In assessing factor 2 (especially 2(b)), the additional value of a pre-termination hearing), the Court again distinguished *Goldberg*. In *Goldberg*, the Court had deemed an oral hearing prior to the termination of welfare benefits to be essential, since most recipients lacked the "educational attainment necessary to write effectively" and the resources to obtain professional assistance. Furthermore, because welfare termination often hinged on the testimony of others, an oral hearing provided the necessary opportunity to confront and cross-examine adverse witnesses. In contrast, the termination of disability benefits turned upon "routine, standard, and unbiased medical reports by physician specialists." Easily documented, the physician's conclusions were "more amenable to written than to oral presentation." Thus, "[t]he potential value of an evidentiary hearing, or even oral presentation to the decisionmaker, is substantially less in this context than in *Goldberg*" (424 U.S. at 344–345).

Factor 3—the government's programmatic, fiscal, and administrative interests— also weighed against the requirement of a pre-termination hearing. "The most visible burden would be the incremental cost resulting from the increased number of hearings and the expense of providing benefits to ineligible recipients pending decision. No one can predict the extent of the increase, but the fact that full benefits would continue until after such hearings would assure the exhaustion in most cases of this attractive option" (424 U.S. at 347). As the Court explained:

> Financial cost alone is not a controlling weight in determining whether due process requires a particular procedural safeguard prior to some administrative decision. But the Government's interest, and hence that of the public, in conserving scarce fiscal and administrative resources is a factor that must be weighed. At some point the benefit of an additional safeguard to the individual affected by the administrative action and to society in terms of increased assurance that the action is just, may be outweighed by the cost. [424 U.S. at 348.]

Balancing all these factors, the Court concluded that the Social Security system's existing procedures satisfied the constitutional demands of due process, and that therefore no pre-termination hearing was required.

The three *Mathews* factors, or the "*Mathews* balancing test," applies to a broad range of issues concerning the constitutionality of particular governmental procedures. But the Court has cautioned that "[a]lthough we have…invoked *Mathews* to evaluate due process claims in [many] contexts,…we have never viewed *Mathews* as announcing an all-embracing test for deciding due process claims" (*Dusenbery v. United States*, 534 U.S. 161, 167–168 (2002)). The major exception is apparently the cases concerning the adequacy of the notice of a pending disposition of property that government gives to individuals who may have a legal claim to the property. The test that the Court applies in such cases is whether the notice was "reasonably calculated, under all the circumstances, to apprise [the potential claimant] of the pendency of the action" (*Mullane v. Central Hanover Bank & Trust Co.*, 339 U.S. 306, 314 (1950). In *Dusenbery*, above, for instance, the Court applied this test—calling it the "reasonableness under the circumstances test" (122 S.Ct. at 699)—in upholding a certified mail procedure that the FBI had used to notify a prisoner of a pending forfeiture of property seized during a search of his residence on the day he was arrested.

The epitome of a full-blown due process hearing is the judicial trial in state and federal courts, especially the criminal trial. But due process does not usually require that type of hearing. As the Court remarked in *Mathews*, above, "[t]he judicial model of an evidentiary hearing is neither a required, nor even the most effective, method of decisionmaking in all circumstances." The general question at the second stage of analysis, then, is *how much* of the procedural protection available in accorded by a judicial trial must be accorded the individual being deprived of a liberty or property interest in the case at hand? Or, in other words, how closely

must the procedures provided the individual in the case at hand parallel the procedures for a judicial trial? The familiar components of the judicial trial that could
thus become issues in second-stage due process analysis would therefore include:
advance notice of the charges, advance notice of the hearing date, opportunity to
"discover" evidence in advance, opportunity to tell one's "side of the story" to an
impartial decisionmaker, opportunity to present the oral testimony of witnesses,
opportunity to submit documentary evidence, opportunity to receive or hear all
evidence to be presented by the opposing party, opportunity to cross-examine adverse witnesses, the right to counsel or other representation, a transcription or
recording of the hearing, the maintenance of an official record of the proceedings,
and right to a decision on the record (that is, a decision based solely on the evidence in the record of the proceedings). *Goldberg v. Kelly* addresses most of these
procedures (*see* 397 U.S. at 254). Issues may also arise concerning the timing of a
hearing: Must it occur before any decision to deprive an individual of a protected
interest, or only before such a decision becomes final? (Besides *Goldberg* and *Mathews*, which present this issue, see also *Cleveland Board of Education v. Loudermill*,
470 U.S. 532 (1985).) In addition, issues may sometimes arise concerning creative
alternative procedures that government may seek to use in lieu of those associated
with judicial trials.

D.4. The Vagueness Doctrine

Procedural due process principles also give rise to a requirement that regulations under which individuals may be penalized must be sufficiently clear to provide such individuals fair warning or notice of what conduct is prohibited. This
requirement is embodied in the "vagueness" (or "void for vagueness") doctrine. As
the U.S. Supreme Court explained the doctrine in *Connally v. General Construction
Co.*, 269 U.S. 385, 391 (1926): "a statute which either forbids or requires the doing
of an act in terms so vague that [persons] of common intelligence must necessarily guess at its meaning and differ as to its application violates the first essential of
due process of law." The vagueness doctrine also helps prevent arbitrariness in decision-making by assuring that those who apply the regulation will have reasonably clear standards to guide them. *See generally Grayned v. City of Rockford*, 408
U.S. 104, 108–109 (1972).

Lanzetta v. New Jersey, 306 U.S. 451 (1939), provides a classic example of the vagueness doctrine's application. In 1934, New Jersey enacted a statute making it a crime to
be a "gangster." The statute defined gangster as a person who is "not engaged in a lawful occupation," is "known to be a member of any gang," and "has been convicted of
any crime." Applying the test from *Connally*, above, the Court focused on the word
"gang" and the phrase "known to be a member." Regarding "gang," the Court reasoned
that "[t]he meanings of that word indicated in dictionaries and in historical and sociological writings are numerous and varied. Nor is the meaning derivable from the common law, for neither in that field nor anywhere in the language of the law is there definition of the word" (306 U.S. at 455). Regarding the "known to be" requirement, the

Court reasoned that "[i]t is ambiguous" because it could mean "actual membership" or "reputed membership," and the statute does not reveal which meaning is intended (306 U.S. at 458). The Court therefore concluded that "the terms [the statute] employs to indicate what it purports to denounce are so vague, indefinite and uncertain that it must be condemned as repugnant to the due process clause of the Fourteenth Amendment" (306 U.S. at 458).

The void-for-vagueness doctrine is usually reserved for the review of criminal statutes, since the potential penalties are so great for persons charged with violations. But the courts occasionally apply the doctrine to other types of regulations that entail substantial penalties. In *Jordan v. De George*, 341 U.S. 223 (1951), for example, the Court applied the doctrine to a provision in a federal immigration statute that required deportation of aliens who have been convicted at least twice of "any crime involving moral turpitude."

The Court has also declared that the vagueness doctrine will be applied more strictly when the statute's vagueness may inhibit individuals from exercising certain federal constitutional rights due to fear of being charged with violating the statute. In *Colautti v. Franklin*, 439 U.S. 379 (1979), for example, the Court used the vagueness doctrine to invalidate a Pennsylvania abortion statute that required doctors to make certain determinations about fetal viability before performing an abortion, and imposing criminal and civil penalties on doctors who failed to do so. The vagueness of the viability provisions could affect women's rights to obtain abortions, and the Court therefore applied the vagueness doctrine with special force because "the uncertainty induced by the statute threatens to inhibit the exercise of constitutionally protected rights" (439 U.S. at 391). In other cases, and more commonly, the courts have applied the vagueness doctrine more strictly to regulations applicable to expressive activities, since vagueness in such a regulation could inhibit or "chill" speakers' willingness to express themselves; this problem is discussed in Chapter 12, Section C.3(2).

Sec. E. Exercise No. 8: Differentiating Substantive Due Process, Procedural Due Process, and Equal Protection Claims (*Skinner v. Oklahoma*)

This exercise, based upon a classic U.S. Supreme Court case, will help develop your capacity to distinguish the concepts of equal protection, substantive due process, and procedural due process from one another. Before beginning this exercise, study (or review) Chapter 10, Section E ("A Comparison of Equal Protection and Due Process") and Section B above in this Chapter ("The Distinction Between Substantive Due Process and Procedural Due Process"). Then read *Skinner v. Oklahoma*, which is reprinted immediately below, and answer the questions set out after the case. Suggested answers to the questions are set out after the case for you to consult once you have considered the questions.

SKINNER V. OKLAHOMA
Supreme Court of the United States
316 U.S. 535 (1942)*

MR. JUSTICE DOUGLAS delivered the opinion of the Court.

This case touches a sensitive and important area of human rights. Oklahoma deprives certain individuals of a right which is basic to the perpetuation of a race—the right to have offspring. Oklahoma has decreed the enforcement of its law against petitioner, overruling his claim that it violated the Fourteenth Amendment. Because that decision raised grave and substantial constitutional questions, we granted the petition for certiorari.

The statute involved is Oklahoma's Habitual Criminal Sterilization Act. That Act defines an "habitual criminal" as a person who, having been convicted two or more times for crimes "amounting to felonies involving moral turpitude," either in an Oklahoma court or in a court of any other State, is thereafter convicted of such a felony in Oklahoma and is sentenced to a term of imprisonment in an Oklahoma penal institution. Machinery is provided for the institution by the Attorney General of a proceeding against such a person in the Oklahoma courts for a judgment that such person shall be rendered sexually sterile. Notice, an opportunity to be heard, and the right to a jury trial are provided. The issues triable in such a proceeding are narrow and confined. If the court or jury finds that the defendant is an "habitual criminal" and that he "may be rendered sexually sterile without detriment to his or her general health," then the court "shall render judgment to the effect that said defendant be rendered sexually sterile" by the operation of vasectomy in case of a male, and of salpingectomy in case of a female. Only one other provision of the Act is material here, and that is § 195, which provides that "offenses arising out of the violation of the prohibitory laws, revenue acts, embezzlement, or political offenses, shall not come or be considered within the terms of this Act."

Petitioner was convicted in 1926 of the crime of stealing chickens, and was sentenced to the Oklahoma State Reformatory. In 1929 he was convicted of the crime of robbery with firearms, and was sentenced to the reformatory. In 1934 he was convicted again of robbery with firearms, and was sentenced to the penitentiary. He was confined there in 1935 when the Act was passed. In 1936 the Attorney General instituted proceedings against him. Petitioner in his answer challenged the Act as unconstitutional by reason of the Fourteenth Amendment. A jury trial was had. The court instructed the jury that the crimes of which petitioner had been convicted were felonies involving moral turpitude, and that the only question for the jury was whether the operation of vasectomy

---

* Some of the Justices' citations and footnotes are omitted. The remaining footnotes retain original numbering, and the name of the Justice writing the opinion is included in parenthesis in the footnote for clarification.

could be performed on petitioner without detriment to his general health. The jury found that it could be. A judgment directing that the operation of vasectomy be performed on petitioner was affirmed by the Supreme Court of Oklahoma by a five to four decision. 189 Okla. 235, 115 P. 2d 123.

Several objections to the constitutionality of the Act have been pressed upon us. It is urged that the Act cannot be sustained as an exercise of the police power, in view of the state of scientific authorities respecting inheritability of criminal traits.[1] It is argued that due process is lacking because, under this Act, unlike the Act upheld in *Buck v. Bell*, 274 U.S. 200 [1927],* the defendant is given no opportunity to be heard on the issue as to whether he is the probable potential parent of socially undesirable offspring. It is also suggested that the Act is penal in character and that the sterilization provided for is cruel and unusual punishment and violative of the Fourteenth Amendment. We pass those points without intimating an opinion on them, for there is a feature of the Act which clearly condemns it. That is, its failure to meet the requirements of the equal protection clause of the Fourteenth Amendment.

We do not stop to point out all of the inequalities in this Act. A few examples will suffice. In Oklahoma, grand larceny is a felony. Larceny is grand larceny when the property taken exceeds $ 20 in value. Embezzlement is punishable "in the manner prescribed for feloniously stealing property of the value of that embezzled." Hence, he who embezzles property worth more than $20 is guilty of a felony. A clerk who appropriates over $ 20 from his employer's till and a stranger who steals the same amount are thus both guilty of felonies. If the latter repeats his act and is convicted three times, he may be sterilized. But the clerk is not subject to the pains and penalties of the Act no matter how large his embezzlements nor how frequent his convictions. A person who enters a chicken coop and steals chickens commits a felony; and he may be sterilized if he is thrice convicted. If, however, he is a bailee of the property and fraudulently appropriates it, he is an embezzler. Hence, no matter how habitual his proclivities for embezzlement are and no matter how often his conviction, he may not be sterilized. Thus, the nature of the two crimes is intrinsically the same and they are punishable in the

---

1. (Douglas fn.) Healy, The Individual Delinquent (1915), pp. 188–200; Sutherland, Criminology (1924), pp. 112–118, 621–622; Gillin, Criminology and Penology (1926), c. IX; Popenoe, Sterilization and Criminality, 53 Rep. Am. Bar. Assoc. 575; Myerson et al., Eugenical Sterilization (1936), c. VIII; Landman, Human Sterilization (1932), c. IX; Summary of the Report of the American Neurological Association Committee for the Investigation of Sterilization, 1 Am. Journ. Med. Jur. 253 (1938).

* (Author's footnote.) In this case, the Court upheld the compulsory sterilization of Carrie Buck, then a young woman confined — erroneously, as it later appeared — in a Virginia state institution for the "feeble-minded." Justice Oliver Wendell Holmes, for the majority, rejected both substantive due process and equal protection challenges, concluding that "[t]hree generations of imbeciles are enough" (274 U.S. at 207), a reference to Carrie Buck, her mother, and her daughter. *See generally* Stephen Jay Gould, "Carrie Buck's Daughter," 2 Const. Comm. 331 (1985).

same manner. Furthermore, the line between them follows close distinctions—distinctions comparable to those highly technical ones which shaped the common law as to "trespass" or "taking"....

* * * *

It was stated in *Buck v. Bell*, supra, that the claim that state legislation violates the equal protection clause of the Fourteenth Amendment is 'the usual last resort of constitutional arguments.' 274 U.S. page 208. Under our constitutional system the States in determining the reach and scope of particular legislation need not provide 'abstract symmetry.' *Patsone v. Pennsylvania*, 232 U.S. 138, 144. They may mark and set apart the classes and types of problems according to the needs and as dictated or suggested by experience....Thus, if we had here only a question as to a State's classification of crimes, such as embezzlement or larceny, no substantial federal question would be raised. For a State is not constrained in the exercise of its police power to ignore experience which marks a class of offenders or a family of offenses for special treatment. Nor is it prevented by the equal protection clause from confining "its restrictions to those classes of cases where the need is deemed to be clearest." *Miller v. Wilson*, 236 U.S. 373, 384....

But the instant legislation runs afoul of the equal protection clause, though we give Oklahoma that large deference which the rule of the foregoing cases requires. We are dealing here with legislation which involves one of the basic civil rights of man. Marriage and procreation are fundamental to the very existence and survival of the race. The power to sterilize, if exercised, may have subtle, far-reaching and devastating effects. In evil or reckless hands it can cause races or types which are inimical to the dominant group to wither and disappear. There is no redemption for the individual whom the law touches. Any experiment which the State conducts is to his irreparable injury. He is forever deprived of a basic liberty. We mention these matters not to reexamine the scope of the police power of the States. We advert to them merely in emphasis of our view that strict scrutiny of the classification which a State makes in a sterilization law is essential, lest unwittingly, or otherwise, invidious discriminations are made against groups or types of individuals in violation of the constitutional guaranty of just and equal laws.... When the law lays an unequal hand on those who have committed intrinsically the same quality of offense and sterilizes one and not the other, it has made as invidious a discrimination as if it had selected a particular race or nationality for oppressive treatment. *Yick Wo v. Hopkins*, 118 U.S. 356. Sterilization of those who have thrice committed grand larceny, with immunity for those who are embezzlers, is a clear, pointed, unmistakable discrimination. Oklahoma makes no attempt to say that he who commits larceny by trespass or trick or fraud has biologically inheritable traits which he who commits embezzlement lacks. Oklahoma's line between larceny by fraud and embezzlement is determined..."with reference to the time when the fraudulent intent to convert the property to the taker's own use" arises. *Riley v. State*, 64 Okla. Cr. 183, 189, 78 P. 2d 712, 715. We have not the slightest basis for inferring that line has any significance in eugenics, nor that the inheritability of criminal traits follows the neat legal distinctions which the law has marked between those two offenses. In terms of fines and imprisonment, the crimes of larceny and embezzlement rate the same under the Oklahoma code. Only when it comes to sterilization are the pains and penalties of the law different. The equal protection clause would indeed be a formula of empty words if such conspicuously artificial lines could be drawn. In *Buck v. Bell*, supra, the Virginia statute was upheld though it applied only to feeble-minded persons in institutions of the State. But it was pointed out that "so far as the operations enable those who otherwise must be kept confined to be returned to the world, and thus open the asylum to others, the equality aimed at will be more nearly reached." 274 U.S. p. 208. Here there is no such saving feature. Embezzlers are forever free. Those who steal or take in other ways are not. If such a classification were permitted, the technical common law concept of a "trespass" based on distinctions which are "very largely dependent upon history for explanation" (Holmes, The Common Law, p. 73) could readily become a rule of human genetics.

* * * *

Reversed.

MR. CHIEF JUSTICE STONE, concurring:

I concur in the result, but I am not persuaded that we are aided in reaching it by recourse to the equal protection clause.

If Oklahoma may resort generally to the sterilization of criminals on the assumption that their propensities are transmissible to future generations by inheritance, I seriously doubt that the equal protection clause requires it to apply the measure to all criminals in the first instance, or to none.

Moreover, if we must presume that the legislature knows—what science has been unable to ascertain—that the criminal tendencies of any class of habitual offenders are transmissible regardless of the varying mental characteristics of its individuals, I should suppose that we must likewise presume that the legislature, in its wisdom, knows that the criminal tendencies of some classes of offenders are more likely to be transmitted than those of others. And so I think the real question we have to consider is not one of equal protection, but whether the wholesale condemnation of a class to such an invasion of personal liberty, without opportunity to any individual to show that his is not the type of case which would justify resort to it, satisfies the demands of due process.

* * * *

Although petitioner here was given a hearing to ascertain whether sterilization would be detrimental to his health, he was given none to discover whether his criminal tendencies are of an inheritable type. Undoubtedly a state may, after appropriate inquiry, constitutionally interfere with the personal liberty of the individual to prevent the transmission by inheritance of his socially injurious tendencies. *Buck v. Bell*, 274 U.S. 200. But until now we have not been called upon to say that it may do so without giving him a hearing and opportunity to challenge the existence as to him of the only facts which could justify so drastic a measure.

Science has found and the law has recognized that there are certain types of mental deficiency associated with delinquency which are inheritable. But the State does not contend—nor can there be any pretense—that either common knowledge or experience, or scientific investigation,[1] has given assurance that the criminal tendencies of any class of habitual offenders are universally or even generally inheritable. In such circumstances, inquiry whether such is the fact in the case of any particular individual cannot rightly be dispensed with. Whether the procedure by which a statute carries its mandate into execution satisfies due process is a matter of judicial cognizance. A law which condemns, without hearing, all the individuals of a class to so harsh a measure as the present because some or even many merit condemnation, is lacking in the first principles of due process. And so, while the state may protect itself from the demonstrably inheritable tendencies of the individual which are injurious to society, the most elementary notions of due process would seem to require it to take appropriate steps to safeguard the liberty of the individual by affording him, before he is condemned to an irreparable injury in his person, some opportunity to show that he is without such inheritable tendencies. The state is called on to sacrifice no permissible end when it is required to reach its objective by a reasonable and just procedure adequate to safeguard rights of the individual which concededly the Constitution protects.

Mr. Justice Jackson concurring:

I join the Chief Justice in holding that the hearings provided are too limited in the context of the present Act to afford due process of law. I also agree with the opinion of Mr. Justice Douglas that the scheme of classification set forth in the Act denies equal protection of the law. I disagree with the opinion of each in so far as it rejects or minimizes the grounds taken by the other.

Perhaps to employ a broad and loose scheme of classification would be permissible if accompanied by the individual hearings indicated by the Chief Justice. On the other hand, narrow classification with reference to the end to be accomplished by the Act might justify limiting individual hearings to the issue whether the individual belonged to a class so defined. Since this Act does not present these questions, I reserve judgment on them.

I also think the present plan to sterilize the individual in pursuit of a eugenic plan to eliminate from the race characteristics that are only vaguely identified and which in our present state of knowledge are uncertain as to transmissibility presents other constitutional questions of gravity. This Court has sustained such an experiment with respect to an imbecile, a person with definite and observable characteristics, where the condition had persisted through three generations and afforded grounds for the belief that it was transmissible and would continue to manifest itself in generations to come. *Buck v. Bell*, 274 U.S. 200.

There are limits to the extent to which a legislatively represented majority may conduct biological experiments at the expense of the dignity and personality and natural powers of a minority—even those who have been guilty of what the majority define

---

1. (Stone fn.) See Eugenical Sterilization, A Report of the Committee of the American Neurological Association (1936), pp. 150–52; Myerson, Summary of the Report, 1 American Journal of Medical Jurisprudence 253; Popenoe, Sterilization and Criminality, 53 American Bar Assn. Reports 575; Jennings, Eugenics, 5 Encyclopedia of the Social Sciences 617, 620–21; Montagu, The Biologist Looks at Crime, 217 Annals of American Academy of Political and Social Science 46.

as crimes. But this Act falls down before reaching this problem, which I mention only to avoid the implication that such a question may not exist because not discussed. On it I would also reserve judgment.

Questions

QUES. 1. What kind of analysis is undertaken by the majority opinion: substantive due process, procedural due process, or equal protection? By the Stone concurrence? By the Jackson concurrence? What are the essential characteristics of the analysis in each opinion that determine the category into which the analysis fits and distinguishes it from analysis in the other categories?

QUES. 2. Suppose Skinner's attorneys developed scientific evidence demonstrating that criminal traits and tendencies are not to any significant degree inheritable. Would this evidence be most appropriately used to support an equal protection argument, a substantive due process argument, or a procedural due process argument? How would you articulate this argument?

QUES. 3. If Skinner were to prevail on an equal protection argument, what should be the court-imposed remedy, and what options would the state legislature have if it sought to "fix" its law on sterilization of habitual criminals? How would the judicial remedy and the legislative options differ if Skinner were to prevail on a substantive due process argument? A procedural due process argument?

Answers

ANS. to QUES. 1: The majority opinion is based on equal protection analysis, in particular the fundamental interest strand of strict scrutiny analysis (see generally Chap. 10, Sec. D.8). Justice Stone's concurrence is based on procedural due process analysis (see generally this Chap., Sec. D, above). Justice Jackson's concurrence accepts the validity of both the equal protection and the procedural due process analysis, but then goes on to raise other issues that apparently are grounded in substantive due process analysis regarding invasions of personal liberty. There are important conceptual distinctions among the three types of analysis (see generally Chap. 10, Sec. E, and this Chap., Sec. B, above). The analytical steps or analytical pathways for the three types of analysis also differ from one another (see generally Chap. 10, Sec. E, and this Chap., Secs. C and D).

ANS. to QUES. 2: Such new evidence would provide clear support for a substantive due process argument, and could apparently be used to sharpen and strengthen the type of analysis suggested by Justice Jackson's concurrence. The minimalist argument, using this new evidence, would be that the state's sterilization law is arbitrary and capricious and would not meet the minimal scrutiny, or rational basis, standard of review for substantive due process (see this Chap., Sec. C.4). The more far-reaching argument would be that the state's law deprives individuals of a fundamental liberty interest in reproductive autonomy; that the law is not necessary to, or narrowly tailored to, any compelling governmental interest, and that the law therefore fails the strict scrutiny standard of review.

ANS. to. QUES. 3: If the state loses on equal protection grounds, it would have to cease using the particular classification that it had used in determining who gets sterilized. If it wanted to continue applying such a law, it would have to draw the classification more broadly or more narrowly than it had done in the invalidated law. Presumably, for instance, it could decide to sterilize *all* criminals. If the state loses on substantive due process grounds, however, it presumably would not have this choice; it could not sterilize *any* criminal. If the state loses on procedural due process grounds, it would have to provide additional procedural protections to criminals before making any final decision about sterilization, but could presumably still sterilize a particular criminal if the requisite procedures are provided and the evidence in the record supports a decision to sterilize.

Sec. F. Study Suggestions

Making and understanding conceptual distinctions is the key to any successful study of due process. Such distinctions frame the entire subject matter and provide the foundation for all problem-solving. First, one must understand the distinction between the function of the due process clause and that of its next door neighbor in the Fourteenth Amendment, the equal protection clause (see especially Chap. 10, Sec. E). Second, one must understand the distinction between the "incorporated" and the "nonincorporated" sectors of Fourteenth Amendment due process, and in particular the differences in the content of these two sectors (see especially Sec. B above). Third, one must understand the distinction between substantive and procedural due process that underlies the nonincorporated sector of Fourteenth Amendment due process as well as the Fifth Amendment's due process clause (see Sec. A above). Finally, one must understand the differences between the "old" and the "new" substantive due process. You should also seek to understand, as a matter of theory, why and how the Court has drawn these conceptual distinctions; seek also to understand, as a matter of practice, how the analysis of problems differs from one side to the other side of each of these distinctions.

The greatest challenge in these materials is likely to be substantive due process. As you read the cases, consider these questions: How do courts distinguish fundamental from non-fundamental rights? What standard of review do courts apply to laws infringing fundamental rights? What standard of review do courts apply to laws impinging on personal liberty interests that do not rise to the level of fundamental rights? How would the courts now deal with laws that impinge only on economic or business interests?

More broadly, consider whether the "new" substantive due process arising from *Griswold v. Connecticut* (Sec. C.2 above) is itself experiencing serious growing pains or undergoing transformation. Consider for example, the contrast between *Roe v. Wade*'s fundamental rights analysis and the "undue burden" analysis of *Planned Parenthood of Southeastern Pennsylvania v. Casey* (Sec. C.2 above); and the contrast between *Bowers v. Hardwick* and *Lawrence v. Texas* (Sec C.3 above), with the latter case expressly overruling the former seventeen years after it was decided. And especially consider the contrast between *Washington v. Glucksberg*, where the Court in 1997 affirmed its fundamental rights approach to substantive due process and its two-tiered (strict scrutiny/ minimal scrutiny) system of review; and *Lawrence v. Texas*, where the Court six years later applied substantive due process analysis without using the fundamental rights approach or either of the two tiers of review (Sec. C.7 above). Do these cases suggest a pruning back of substantive due process? New growth of substantive due process in new directions? Or just conflicting views among the Justices that have resulted in some confusion or instability of substantive due process doctrine?

Not every government decision adverse to an individual will infringe a liberty or property (or life) interest of that individual. Since only such deprivations are subject to the due process clause, careful attention must be given to the concepts of "liberty interest" and "property interest" that emerge from the Supreme Court case law (Sec. D.2, above). To understand these concepts, it is necessary to distinguish an "interest," as the Court uses the term, from a right or vested right. It is then necessary to consider the sources from which liberty interests derive, and those from which property interests derive. Are they created by the Constitution itself? By federal and state statutes? By the common law? By contractual arrangements? It is also necessary to consider the extent of these interests. For instance, are property interests limited to traditional notions of real and personal property? Do liberty interests cover anything more than the freedom from physical restraint?

FOR FURTHER READING: (1) Erwin Chemerinsky, "Procedural Due Process Claims," 16 Touro L. Rev. 871 (2000). (2) David Crump, "How Do Courts Really Discover Unenumerated Fundamental Rights? Cataloguing the Methods of Judicial Alchemy," 19 Harv. J. of Law & Pub. Policy 795 (1996). (3) John Hart Ely, "The Wages of Crying Wolf: A Comment on *Roe v. Wade*," 82 Yale L. J. 920 (1973). (4) Russell Galloway, "Basic Substantive Due Process Analysis," 26 U. San Francisco L. Rev. 625 (1992). (5) Jerold Israel, "Selective Incorporation Revisited," 71 Geo. L. J. 253 (1982). (6) Paul Kauper, "Penumbras, Peripheries, Emanations, Things Fundamental and Things Forgotten: The Griswold Case," 64 Mich. L. Rev. 235 (1965). (7) Jerry Mashaw, "Administrative Due Process: The Quest for a Dignitary Theory," 61 Boston U. L. Rev. 885 (1981). (8) Jerry Mashaw, "The Supreme Court's Due Process Calculus for Administrative Adjudication in *Mathews v. Eldridge*," 44 U. Chi. L. Rev. 28 (1976). (9) Henry Monaghan, "Of 'Liberty' and 'Property,'" 62 Cornell L. Rev. 401 (1977).

Chapter 12

Freedom of Expression

Sec. A. Introduction to the First Amendment

A study of freedom of expression should begin with a careful reading and textual analysis of the entire First Amendment. Ratified in 1791 as part of the Bill of Rights, the First Amendment is only 45 words in length. But in those 45 words are six rights clauses, each with its own distinct importance: the establishment clause, the free exercise clause, the free speech clause, the free press clause, the assembly clause, and the petition clause.

For study purposes, these six clauses can be sorted into three sets of two clauses each. The establishment and free exercise clauses combine to protect freedom of religion; these clauses are addressed in Chapter 13. The freedom of speech and freedom of press clauses combine to protect freedom of expression; these clauses are addressed in this chapter. The assembly and petition clauses provide additional protections for speech-related activities in certain special circumstances. Although the latter two clauses protect essential political rights, they have played a lesser role in constitutional litigation than the other four and are usually given little independent attention in constitutional law courses.[1] In addition to the express protections in these six clauses, the First Amendment also protects the implied right of freedom of association, which is discussed in Section F below.

A key threshold term is associated with each of the four primary First Amendment clauses. For the first two clauses, the term is "religion"; for the third clause it is "speech"; and for the fourth clause it is "press." Each clause applies only to situations where gov-

---

1. The leading U.S. Supreme Court case on the right of assembly is *Hague v. Committee for Industrial Organization*, 307 U.S. 496 (1939); see pp. 516-518 (opinion of Roberts, J.) and pp. 521-527 (opinion of Stone, J.). The leading U.S. Supreme Court case on the right to petition is *McDonald v. Smith*, 472 U.S. 479 (1985).

ernment has intruded into the realm defined by that clause's key threshold term. Thus important definitional problems arise, with which courts and commentators have frequently struggled.

Yet another threshold textual problem arises at the very beginning of the First Amendment, with the language "Congress shall make no law...." Taken literally, the language suggests that the Amendment applies only to Congress and limits only the lawmaking functions of government. But the courts have not applied this language literally; indeed the U.S. Supreme Court has never directly addressed and interpreted this language. *See* Mark Denbeaux, "The First Word of the First Amendment," 80 NORTH-WESTERN U. L. REV. 1156 (1986). In modern times the courts have applied the First Amendment to the executive and judicial branches of the federal government as well as to Congress, and—pursuant to the incorporation doctrine (Chap. 11, Sec. A.2, above)—to the states as well as to the federal government. In short, the First Amendment now applies to all types of governmental actions that intrude into the realms of religion, expression, assembly, or petition.

Sec. B. A Conceptual Overview of Freedom of Expression

B.1. Predominant Themes

The law of free speech and press is a voluminous body of law with many categories and branches. It is a body of law filled with values clashes, interpretive difficulties, and theoretical questions concerning the role or function of free expression in American society. It is a body of law spawning numerous analytical techniques which together create a complex maze of pathways to follow in problem-solving. And it is a body of law that frequently tells us less than we would wish to know about the particular values the courts are upholding in particular cases (see generally Chap. 9, Sec. B), and about whether there is or could be some general, unifying theory of free expression to guide the work of courts.

It will be helpful to begin with basic questions about the roles or functions of free expression and the values that the free speech and press clauses protect. Over time, judges and commentators from many disciplines have provided eloquent rationales for protecting freedom of expression. The rationales generally fall into two categories. Rationales in the first category stress the importance of free expression to robust public debate on public issues, and the importance of such robust debate to the operation of our democratic system of government. Rationales in the second category stress the role that free expression plays in facilitating the self-actualization of each individual—which includes development of all the individual's faculties, and individual self-expression in both the cognitive and the emotive domains. *See generally* Thomas Emerson, THE SYSTEM OF FREEDOM OF EXPRESSION, pp. 6–14 (Random House, 1970). Each set of rationales takes account of both the speaker's right to speak and the listener's or viewer's right to receive information and ideas; the "right to receive" gets more emphasis under the first set of rationales, however, since it is a necessary component of public debate.

For the first set of rationales, it is "political speech" or "public concern speech" that is the most valued and protected. For the second set of rationales, other types of expression—such as artistic expression, scientific expression, and religious expression—are highly valued and protected. Even commercial expression—advertising—is valued and protected for reasons drawing on both sets of rationales (*see Virginia State Board of Pharmacy v. Virginia Citizens Consumer Council*, 425 U.S. 748, 761–765 (1976)).

Two early-twentieth century statements, one by Justice Oliver Wendell Holmes and one by Justice Louis Brandeis, provide good explanations of the role and importance of free speech in American society. In *Abrams v. United States*, 250 U.S. 616 (1919), a case upholding convictions for statements that violated a federal espionage law, Justice Holmes dissented and remarked:

> But when men have realized that time has upset many fighting faiths, they may come to believe even more than they believe the very foundations of their own conduct that [the ultimate good desired is better reached by free trade in ideas—that the best test of truth is the power of the thought to get itself accepted in the competition of the market, and that truth is the only ground upon which their wishes safely can be carried out. That at any rate is the theory of our Constitution. It is an experiment, as all life is an experiment. Every year if not every day we have to wager our salvation upon some prophecy based upon imperfect knowledge. While that experiment is part of our system, I think that we should be eternally vigilant against attempts to check the expression of opinions that we loathe and believe to be fraught with death, unless they so imminently threaten immediate interference with the lawful and pressing purposes of the law that an immediate check is required to save the country. [250 U.S. at 630, Holmes, J., dissenting.]

In *Whitney v. California*, 274 U.S. 357 (1927), a case upholding a conviction under state law for helping organize a communist political party, Justice Brandeis concurred and remarked:

> Those who won our independence believed that the final end of the state was to make men free to develop their faculties, and that in its government the deliberative forces should prevail over the arbitrary. They valued liberty both as an end and as a means. They believed liberty to be the secret of happiness and courage to be the secret of liberty. They believed that freedom to think as you will and to speak as you think are means indispensable to the discovery and spread of political truth; that without free speech and assembly discussion would be futile; that with them, discussion affords ordinarily adequate protection against the dissemination of noxious doctrine; that the greatest menace to freedom is an inert people; that public discussion is a political duty; and that this should be a fundamental principle of the American government. They recognized the risks to which all human institutions are subject. But they knew

that order cannot be secured merely through fear of punishment for its infraction; that it is hazardous to discourage thought, hope and imagination;
that fear breeds repression; that repression breeds hate; that hate menaces stable government; that the path of safety lies in the opportunity to discuss freely
supposed grievances and proposed remedies; and that the fitting remedy for
evil counsels is good ones. [274 U.S. at 375–375, Brandeis, J., concurring.]

In later years, other Justices have added to the theoretical base laid down by Holmes
and Brandeis. Two of the best examples are Justice Robert Jackson's majority opinion
in *West Virginia State Board of Education v. Barnette*, 319 U.S. 624 (1943), and Justice
John Harlan's majority opinion in *Cohen v. California*, 403 U.S. 15 (1971). In *Barnette*,
in invalidating a regulation that required all public school students to salute the American flag at the beginning of the school day, Justice Jackson spoke of "the sphere of in-
tellect and spirit which it is the purpose of the First Amendment…to reserve from all
official control" (*Id.* at 642). Regarding this sphere of freedom, Justice Jackson explained:

Those who begin coercive elimination of dissent soon find themselves ex-
terminating dissenters. Compulsory unification of opinion achieves only the
unanimity of the graveyard.

It seems trite, but necessary to say that the First Amendment to our Constitution was designed to avoid these ends by avoiding these beginnings.…

[W]e apply the limitations of the Constitution with no fear that freedom
to be intellectually and spiritually diverse or even contrary will disintegrate
the social organization.…

We can have intellectual individualism and the rich cultural diversities that
we owe to exceptional minds only at the price of occasional eccentricity and
abnormal attitudes.…

[F]reedom to differ is not limited to things that do not matter much. That
would be a mere shadow of freedom. The test of its substance is the right to
differ as to things that touch the heart of the existing order.

If there is any fixed star in our constitutional constellation, it is that no official, high or petty, can prescribe what shall be orthodox in politics, nationalism, religion, or other matters of opinion. [319 U.S. at 641–642.]

Subsequently, in *Cohen*, in reversing the conviction of a man who had entered a municipal court building wearing a jacket with profanity printed on the back, Justice Harlan declared:

[The] constitutional right of free expression is powerful medicine in a society
as diverse and populous as ours. It is designed and intended to remove governmental restraints from the arena of public discussion, putting the decision as to
what views shall be voiced largely into the hands of each of us, in the hope that
use of such freedom will ultimately produce a more capable citizenry and more
perfect polity and in the belief that no other approach would comport with the
premise of individual dignity and choice upon which our political system rests.

To many, the immediate consequence of this freedom may often appear to
be only verbal tumult, discord, and even offensive utterance. These are, however, within established limits, in truth necessary side effects of the broader

enduring values which the process of open debate permits us to achieve. That the air may at times seem filled with verbal cacophony is, in this sense not a sign of weakness but of strength.…

[I]t is…often true that one man's vulgarity is another's lyric. Indeed, we think it is largely because governmental officials cannot make principled distinctions in this area that the Constitution leaves matters of taste and style so largely to the individual.

[M]uch linguistic expression serves a dual communicative function: it conveys not only ideas capable of relatively precise, detached explication, but otherwise inexpressible emotions as well. In fact, words are often chosen as much for their emotive as their cognitive force. We cannot sanction the view that the Constitution, while solicitous of the cognitive content of the individual speech, has little or no regard for that emotive function which, practically speaking, may often be the more important element of the overall message sought to be communicated.…[403 U.S. at 24–26].

B.2. The Distinction Between Free Speech and Free Press

Freedom of expression encompasses both free speech and free press. Since the First Amendment uses both terms, the presumption is that each has some meaning or application different from the other. What is the conceptual distinction? What does the free press clause add to the protections already available under the free speech clause? It is tempting to answer, as a layperson might, that the free speech clause protects oral communications and the free press clause protects written communications. That answer, however, does not draw an appropriate relationship between the two clauses. A person who communicates by personal letter, or poster, or tee-shirt imprint is not employing the spoken word, but courts and commentators are nevertheless likely to consider this activity as speech rather than press. On the other hand, radio announcers and station owners are engaged in oral communication, yet courts and commentators are likely to consider this activity as press rather than speech. Thus, whatever the distinction may be between speech and press, it is more subtle than a distinction between oral and written communications. The nature of the distinction is a theoretical and debatable subject (*see, e.g.*, Melville Nimmer, "Is Freedom of Press a Redundancy: What Does It Add to Freedom of Speech?" 26 HASTINGS L. J. 639 (1975)), and the U.S. Supreme Court has not yet provided a full explanation of the distinction.

In thinking about this problem, one helpful perspective to consider is whether the free press clause's purpose is to indicate that the gathering, editing, and dissemination of information and ideas is also part of the expression protected by the First Amendment. Under this view, these activities — typically carried on by what we call the mass media or the "institutional press" — are directly protected by the First Amendment; and mass media entities (*e.g.*, a newspaper, a cable TV station, a TV network) are the particular focus of the free press clause. The institutional press, in turn, acts as a surrogate or trustee for the general public, to which the press disseminates the material it gathers and edits. It does not necessarily follow that the institutional press has special status or privileges under the press clause beyond those which speakers themselves would have under the speech clause. That is a separate question. But it is at least clear, under the institutional press perspective, that a broader range of activities and interests are protected by the speech and press clauses together than what might be comprehended under the speech clause alone, and that it is therefore important to sort out the two clauses and give attention to each.

B.3. The Mass Media and Free Press

Once press cases are distinguished from speech cases, as suggested in Sec. B.2 above, it becomes necessary to distinguish further between press cases involving the print media and press cases involving the broadcast media. The courts treat the two types of media differently, according the broadcast media less protection from government regulation than the print media receives. This difference is well illustrated by two U.S. Supreme Court cases decided five years apart: the *Red Lion* case and the *Miami Herald* case.

In *Red Lion Broadcasting Co. v. FCC*, 395 U.S. 367 (1969), a broadcast media case, the Court considered the validity of FCC regulations that, *inter alia*, required broadcasters to grant a right of reply to any person whose character is attacked during the broadcast of views on a matter of public controversy. Even though this regulation would intrude upon the broadcaster's editorial control over the content of broadcasts, the Court nevertheless unanimously upheld the regulation. The Court's reasoning relied heavily on the "technological scarcity" of broadcast frequencies:

> Where there are substantially more individuals who want to broadcast than there are frequencies to allocate, it is idle to posit an unabridgeable First Amendment right to broadcast comparable to the right of every individual to speak, write, or publish. . . .
>
> There is nothing in the First Amendment which prevents the Government from requiring a licensee to share his frequency with others and to conduct himself as a proxy or fiduciary with obligations to present those views and voices which are representative of his community. . . .
>
> The people as a whole retain their interest in free speech by radio and their collective right to have the medium function consistently with the ends and purposes of the First Amendment. It is the right of the viewers and listeners, not the right of the broadcasters, which is paramount. [395 U.S. at 389–390.]

In *Miami Herald Publishing Co. v. Tornillo*, 418 U.S. 241 (1974), a print media case, the Court considered the validity of a Florida statute that required newspapers to grant a right of reply to any candidate for public office whose character is attacked in any material published by the newspaper. Despite the similarity of the regulation to that in the *Red Lion* case, the Court did not cite *Red Lion* and unanimously invalidated the Florida statute. The Court's reasoning, in stark contrast to *Red Lion*, focused on the importance of editorial control to the operation of newspapers:

It is correct...that a newspaper is not subject to the finite technological limitations of time that confront a broadcaster but it is not correct to say that, as an economic reality, a newspaper can proceed to infinite expansion of its column space to accommodate the replies that a...statute commands the readers should have available.

Even if a newspaper would face no additional costs to comply with a compulsory access law and would not be forced to forego publication of news or opinion by the inclusion of a reply, the Florida statute fails to clear the barriers of the First Amendment because of its intrusion into the functions of editors. A newspaper is more than a passive receptacle or conduit for news, comment, and advertising. The choice of material to go into a newspaper, and the decisions made as to limitations on the size of the paper, and content, and treatment of public issues and public figures—whether fair or unfair— constitutes the exercise of editorial control and judgment. [418 U.S. at 256–258.]

In subsequent years, beginning with *FCC v. Pacifica Foundation*, 438 U.S. 726 (1978), the Court has used two other rationales, quite different from the technological scarcity rationale, for according less protection to broadcast media than to print media. The *Pacifica* case concerned federal government regulation of "indecent" speech on radio (see 18 U.S.C. § 1464). A five-Justice majority, speaking through Justice Stevens, affirmed that "of all forms of communication, it is broadcasting that has received the most limited First Amendment protection" (*Id.* at 748). The Court then identified two reasons "relevan[t] to the present case" for according broadcast media less protection. First:

[T]he broadcast media have established a uniquely pervasive presence in the lives of all Americans. Patently offensive, indecent material presented over the airwaves confronts the citizen, not only in public, but also in the privacy of the home, where the individual's right to be alone plainly outweighs the First Amendment rights of an intruder. *Rowan v. Post Office Dept.*, 397 U.S. 728 [1970]. Because the broadcast audience is constantly tuning in and out, prior warnings cannot completely protect the listener or viewer from unexpected program content. To say that one may avoid further offense by turning off the radio when he hears indecent language is like saying that the remedy for an assault is to run away after the first blow.... [438 U.S. at 748-749.]

Second:

[B]roadcasting is uniquely accessible to children, even those too young to read.... Pacifica's broadcast could have enlarged a child's vocabulary in an instant.... We held in *Ginsberg v. New York*, 390 U.S. 629 [1968], that the government's interest in the "well being of its youth" and in supporting "parents' claim to authority in their own household" justified the regulation of otherwise protected expression.... The ease with which children may obtain access to broadcast material, coupled with the concerns recognized in *Ginsberg*, amply justify special treatment of indecent broadcasting. [438 U.S. at 749-750.]

These rationales (technological scarcity, privacy of the home, protection of children) for the dichotomy between broadcast and print media continue to be topics of debate. Regarding the scarcity rationale from *Red Lion*, there are questions of whether it should continue to apply at a time when technological advances have greatly expanded the number of licensees that may access the airwaves. Regarding the *Pacifica* rationales, there are questions of whether they should apply only to television and not to radio; whether they should be inapplicable to broadcasting during weekday school hours and late night hours when few young children are in the TV audience; and whether they should continue to apply if there is technology, readily accessible to families, for blocking, scrambling, and otherwise controlling or monitoring television usage. For all three rationales, there are also questions concerning their applicability to newer technologies such as cable TV, satellite TV, and the Internet.

Thus far, the Court has found little cause to apply the regulatory rationales for broadcast to other technologies. In *Sable Communications v. FCC*, 492 U.S. 115 (1989), for example, the Court refused to apply the *Pacifica* rationales to telephone 900 no. messages generally called "dial-a-porn." And in a key 1997 case, *Reno v. American Civil Liberties Union*, 521 U.S. 844 (1997), the Court declined to apply the *Red Lion* or *Pacifica* rationales to the Internet.

At issue in *Reno* were two provisions of the federal Communications Decency Act of 1996 (§§ 223 (a)(1)(b) and 223 (a)(2)) which prohibited transmission of certain "indecent" or "patently offensive" communications to children over the Internet. Applying principles much the same as it had developed for the print media, the Court invalidated both provisions: "Notwithstanding the legitimacy and importance of the Congressional goal of protecting children from harmful materials, we agree.... that the statute' abridges 'the freedom of the press' protected by the First Amendment" (521 U.S. at 849). The Court reasoned that the challenged provisions were content-based restrictions on speech (see Sec. D below) that created "an unacceptably heavy burden on protected speech." "In order to deny minors access to potentially harmful speech, the CDA effectively suppresses a large amount of speech that adults have a constitutional right to receive and to address to one another" (521 U.S. at 874). The Court invalidated the indecency provision (§223 (a)(1)(b)) only as it applied to indecent speech; its applications to obscenity were not challenged and remain valid because, as the Court noted, "obscene speech...can be banned totally because it enjoys no First Amendment protection" (521 U.S. at 883; see generally Sec. C.2(1) below).

The Court in *Reno* left no doubt about its view of the capacities and importance of cyberspace as a communication medium. It described the Internet as a "new marketplace of ideas" and a "unique and wholly new medium of worldwide human communication" (521 U.S. at 885, 850). The World Wide Web itself, according to the Court, is "comparable, from the readers' viewpoint, to...a vast library, including millions of readily available and indexed publications,...and "from the publishers' point of view, it constitutes a vast platform from which to address and hear from a world-wide audience of millions of readers, viewers, researchers, and buyers." Moreover, using the Internet, "any person with a phone line can become a town crier with a voice that resonates farther than it could from any soap box..., and the same individual can become a pamphleteer" (521 U.S. at 870).

Since the challenged provisions burdened the content of speech, the Court in *Reno* applied strict judicial scrutiny—a standard of review requiring the government to demonstrate that its regulation is supported by a "compelling" government interest and that there are no "less restrictive alternatives" by which the government could effectuate its interest (521 U.S. at 874). The Court refused to craft any exception to these standards for the new medium of cyberspace, and emphatically subjected the statute to "the most stringent review" (521 U.S. at 868). According to the Court, the medium of cyberspace could not be analogized to the broadcast media and treated more leniently under the law, nor is there any other "basis for qualifying the level of First Amendment scrutiny that should be applied to this medium" (521 U.S. at 870).[2]

In another case, involving cable television, *Turner Broadcasting System v. FCC*, 512 U.S. 622 (1994), after remand, 520 U.S. 180 (1997), the Court again applied standards of review more like those for print media than for broadcast media. As in *Reno*, the Court again attempted to take account of the unique aspects of the medium. The standards of review it applied, again as in *Reno*, paralleled existing standards for free speech cases and print media (vs. broadcast media) cases. The Justices in *Turner*, however, divided on the question whether the Congressional statute at issue, requiring cable operators to carry a portion of local broadcast programming on their cable channels, was a content-based or a content-neutral restriction on speech. The five-Justice majority that ultimately prevailed characterized the requirement as content-neutral and, applying an intermediate scrutiny standard drawn primarily from the *O'Brien* case (see Secs. C.2 and E.2 below), upheld the regulations. The four dissenters characterized the restrictions as content-based and would therefore have invoked strict scrutiny. In another cable television case, however, *Denver Area Educational Telecommunications Consortium v. FCC*, 518 U.S. 727, 743-747 (1996), a plurality (not a majority) of the Court did invoke the *Pacifica* rationales in order to uphold one of three statutory provisions regulating "patently offensive" material on cable TV (Cable Television Consumer Protection and Competition Act of 1992, 47 U.S.C. § 10(a), (b), and (c)).

Sec. C. Analytical Techniques for Resolving Free Expression Problems

C.1. Overview

A key concern in studying freedom of expression is the identification and understanding of the various analytical techniques that courts have developed for analyzing

---

2. As this book went to press, the U.S. Supreme Court granted certiorari (124 S. Ct. 399 (2003)) in *Ashcroft v. American Civil Liberties Union*, a case challenging the Child Online Protection Act (COPA), 47 U.S.C. § 231, which is a successor to the Communications Decency Act provisions struck down in *Reno v. American Civil Liberties Union*.

the issues. The discussion below focuses primarily on the free speech clause—the clause for which the variety and complexity of analytical techniques is most apparent. In general, however, the techniques utilized in free speech analysis will also apply to the free press clause.

Three types of analytical techniques have been developed for use in free speech cases:

> First, the Court has sometimes defined "free speech" so as to exclude certain types of expression and thereby permit abridgement that would otherwise be prohibited by the First Amendment. Second, it has developed procedural techniques that focus not on whether a given activity is constitutionally protected but on whether the regulatory devices utilized by the government meet rigorous standards of procedural sufficiency. Finally, when the Court has faced up to the substantive content of alleged infringements of the First Amendment, it has applied a variety of self-created "tests" to determine the result. [Dorsen, Bender, & Neuborne, 1 EMERSON, HABER, & DORSEN'S POLITICAL AND CIVIL RIGHTS IN THE UNITED STATES, v. I, pp. 51–52 (4th ed. (lawyer's ed.), 1976).]

Analytical techniques of the first type may be termed "non-speech" techniques; those of the second type may be termed simply "procedural" techniques; and those of the third type may be termed "substantive" or "standard-setting" techniques.

C.2. Non-Speech Techniques

Non-speech techniques focus on the threshold question of whether "speech" has been abridged. Activity that appears or is claimed to be "speech" may sometimes be determined to be "non-speech" and thus outside the scope of the free speech clause. This may occur in either of two circumstances: (1) if the activity has no *communicative value* (Sec C.2(1) below) or (2) if the activity has no *communicative capacity* (Sec. C.2(2) below).

C.2(1). *Communicative Value*

The first of the non-speech circumstances arises from the famous, and partially outmoded, dictum from *Chaplinsky v. New Hampshire*, 315 U.S. 568 (1942):

> There are certain well-defined and narrowly limited classes of speech, the prevention and punishment of which has never been thought to raise any Constitutional problem. These include *the lewd and obscene, the profane, the libelous, and the insulting or "fighting" words....* [S]uch utterances are no essential part of any exposition of ideas and are of such slight social value as a step to truth that any benefit that may be derived from them is clearly outweighed by the social interest in order and morality. [315 U.S. at 571–572, emphasis added.]

Under this approach to free expression issues, the U.S. Supreme Court has created constitutional definitions for certain narrow categories of speech that are excluded from the First Amendment's protection. The approach is thus often called the "categorization" approach to free speech analysis. The Court creates the category, and excludes the speech falling within it, by doing a kind of global, once for all, balancing of the speech's communicative value against the societal interests that the speech intrudes upon. When the speech's value or benefit is "slight" and "clearly outweighed" by the societal interests, the speech is and remains unprotected. The balance need not be struck again in each successive case. The primary question in later cases is whether the speech falls within the definition that the Court has crafted to describe the category (for example, the definition of "obscenity" or the definition of "fighting words"); if it does, then the speech is unprotected.

Since *Chaplinsky*, the Court has brought "profane" speech within the protection of the speech and press clauses (*Cohen v. California*, 403 U.S. 15 (1971)). It has also brought "libelous" speech within their protection (*New York Times v. Sullivan*, 376 U.S. 254 (1964); *Gertz v. Robert Welch*, 418 U.S. 323 (1974) (see Sec. D.2 below)).[3]

"Fighting words" remain unprotected, but the Court has utilized the category stringently (*see, e.g., Lewis v. New Orleans*, 415 U.S. 130 (1974)). In *Chaplinsky*, the Court had defined fighting words as "those [words] which (1) by their very utterance inflict injury or (2) tend to incite an immediate breach of the peace" (315 U.S. at 572; numbering added). Chaplinsky's words were of the second type, said the Court; they were "epithets likely to provoke the average person to retaliation" (*Id.* at 574). In later cases, the Court has used only this second definition of fighting words and has never again affirmed or applied the first ("words which by their very utterance inflict injury") definition. In addition, later cases have confined the fighting words category to words that "are, as a matter of common knowledge, inherently likely to provoke violent reaction" (*Cohen v. California*, 403 U.S. 15, 20 (1971)), that are "directed to the person of the hearer" (*Id.*), and that are "a direct personal insult or an invitation to exchange fistcuffs" (*Texas v. Johnson*, 491 U.S. 397, 409 (1989)).

"Obscene" speech also remains unprotected. In *Miller v. California*, 413 U.S. 15 (1973), while reviewing Miller's conviction for mailing allegedly obscene pictures in advertising brochures, the Court crafted the current constitutional definition of obscenity. The category of obscenity includes only "works (1) which, taken as a whole, appeal to the prurient interest in sex, (2) which portray sexual conduct in a patently offensive way, and (3) which, taken as a whole, do not have serious literary, artistic, political, or scientific value" (*Id.* at 24; numbering added). Statutes regulating obscenity must therefore be limited to works falling within this three-part definition; and whether a particular work does fall within the definition is generally a question for the jury (*Id.* at 26), which must apply "contemporary community standards" in making its determination (*Id.* at 26). In cases after *Miller*, however, the Court made clear that juries were not to use community standards in applying the third, "serious . . . value," part of the *Miller* obscenity definition. Since "the value of

---

3. At the time of *Chaplinsky*, commercial speech was also outside the scope of the free speech and press clauses (*see Valentine v. Chrestensen*, 316 U.S. 52 (1942)), but it has since been brought within their scope (*Virginia Pharmacy Board v. Virginia Citizens Consumer Council*, 425 U.S. 748 (1976)). See Section D.5(1) below.

[a] work [does not] vary from community to community based on the degree of local acceptance it has won," juries must apply a "reasonable person" standard in determining whether the work has serious value (*Pope v. Illinois*, 481 U.S. 497, 500–501 (1987)).

The *Miller* ruling, moreover, does not apply to consenting adults reading or viewing obscene materials in the privacy of their own homes. In *Stanley v. Georgia*, 394 U.S. 557 (1969), the Court granted constitutional protection in this circumstance, asserting that this protection was based on a First Amendment right to be free from governmental "control [of] the moral content of a person's thoughts," as well as on a "fundamental…right to be free, except in very limited circumstances, from unwanted governmental intrusions into one's privacy" (*Id.* at 565, 564). In subsequent cases, however, the Court strictly limited *Stanley* to its facts. In *Paris Adult Theatre I v. Slaton*, 413 U.S. 49 (1973), for example, the Court held that the *Stanley* reasoning did not apply (but *Miller* did apply) to the viewing of obscene movies by consenting adults in an adult movie theatre. See also Chapter 14, Section E, footnote 8.

Besides fighting words and obscenity, other types of speech that the Court has deemed to have little or no communicative value and to be unprotected include: non-obscene child pornography (*New York v. Ferber*, 458 U.S. 747 (1982)); commercial speech that proposes unlawful activities or that is false or deceptive (*Central Hudson Gas and Electric Corp. v. Public Service Comm'n*, 447 U.S. 557, 563–564 (1980), and Sec. D.5(1) below); "true threats" (see the *Black* case immediately below); other expression that involves a crime or constitutes an element of a crime, for example bribery (*see State v. Blyth*, 226 N.W. 2d 250 (Iowa, 1975), and *see generally* Kent Greenawalt "Speech and Crime," 1980 Am. B. Found. Res. J. 645, 742–747); certain private speech of public employees that addresses only matters of purely "private concern" (see Sec. F.4 below); and, possibly, purely private defamation involving only private individuals and private concerns (see Sec. D.2 below).

A 2003 U.S. Supreme Court case, *Virginia v. Black*, 123 S.Ct. 1536 (2003), provides the Court's most extensive statement to date on the First Amendment status of "true threats," a concept arising from the earlier case of *Watts v. United States*, 394 U.S. 705 (1969) and further developed in *R.A.V. v. City of St. Paul*, 505 U.S. 377, 388 (1992). It now appears that the reasoning of the *Chaplinsky* dictum is applicable to "true threats," defined as "statements where the speaker means to communicate a serious expression of an intent to commit an act of unlawful violence to a particular individual or group of individuals" (*Virginia v. Black*, 123 S.Ct. at 1548). It also now appears that intimidation is included within the category of true threats. The Court in *Black* defined intimidation as statements in which "a speaker directs a threat to a person or group of persons with the intent of placing the victim in fear of bodily harm or death" (*Id.* at 1548). Such intentional statements, whether termed threats or intimidation, "are outside the First Amendment…." (*Id.* at 1549, quoting *R.A.V. v. City of St. Paul, supra*, at 388).

Thus, using the *Chaplinsky* categorization approach, the U.S. Supreme Court has defined various categories of speech that have no communicative value and are therefore considered to be "non-speech" outside the bounds of the free speech and press clauses. This approach might better be called "categorical exclusion" or "extreme categorization" to distinguish it from other areas where the Court has created categories of speech in order to specify the level and type of protection the speech receives rather than to exclude the speech entirely from the First Amendment. Examples of such other speech categories include incitement (Sec. D.1 below); defamation (Sec. D.2 below); offensive speech (see, *e.g.*, *Cohen v. California*, 403 U.S. 15 (1971), and *Texas v. Johnson*, 491 U.S. 397 (1989), discussed in Section D.3 below); commercial speech (Sec. D.5(1) below); and sexually explicit speech (Sec. D.5(2) below).

C.2(2).   *Communicative Capacity*

The second circumstance in which speech may be determined to be "non-speech" emerges from the Court's dictum in the draft-card burning case, *United States v. O'Brien*, 391 U.S. 367 (1968). The government had prosecuted the defendant, O'Brien, for burning his draft registration card. O'Brien claimed that he burned his card to protest the Vietnam War, and the burning was therefore protected "symbolic speech." In the course of rejecting his claim, the Court asserted that "[w]e cannot accept the view that an apparently limitless variety of conduct can be labeled 'speech' whenever the person engaging in the conduct intends thereby to express an idea" (*Id.* at 376). The most the Court would do in *O'Brien* was to assume, without deciding, "that the alleged communicative element in O'Brien's conduct is sufficient to bring into play the First Amendment" (*Id.*at 376). Similarly, in *Clark v. Community for Creative Non-Violence*, 468 U.S. 288 (1984), the majority and dissenters debated whether sleeping overnight in tents, as part of a demonstration on behalf of homeless persons, was expressive conduct (*Id.* at 293–294(White, J., for the majority) & 304–308 (Marshall, J., dissenting)). The majority was willing to "assume" for purposes of the litigation that the sleeping was speech, but would go no further; it was the dissenters who strongly characterized the sleeping as expressive political speech central to the demonstration's message. (For more on the *Clark* case, see Sec. E below.)

In other cases both before and after *O'Brien*, however, the Court has acknowledged that "[s]ymbolism is [an] effective way of communicating ideas. The use of [a symbol to represent] some system, idea, institution, or personality, is a short cut from mind to mind" (*West Virginia State Board of Education v. Barnette*, 319 U.S. 624, 632 (1943), quoted in *Texas v. Johnson*, 491 U.S. 397, 405 (1989)). In cases after *O'Brien*, the Court has also indicated that the free speech clause will extend to activity that, in context, would reasonably be understood by its viewers or listeners to be communicative. In *Ward v. Rock Against Racism*, 491 U.S. 781 (1989), for example—a case concerning a city's regulation of the volume of concert music in a public park—the threshold question was whether music is speech for First Amendment purposes. The Court answered in the affirmative:

> Music is one of the oldest forms of human expression. From Plato's discourse in the Republic to the totalitarian state in our own times, rulers have known its capacity to appeal to the intellect and to the emotions, and have censored musical compositions to serve the needs of the state. The Constitution pro-

hibits any like attempts in our own legal order. Music, as a form of expression and communication, is protected under the First Amendment. [491 U.S. at 790.]

And in *Virginia v. Black*, 123 S.Ct. 1536 (2003), as the Court considered the constitutionality of a conviction for cross-burning, it addressed the question whether cross-burning is speech under the First Amendment. "The burning of a cross is symbolic expression," said the Court, which "carries a message in an effective and dramatic manner" (*Id.* at 1548).

In two cases about flag burning, *Texas v. Johnson*, 491 U.S. 397 (1989), and the earlier case of *Spence v. Washington*, 418 U.S. 405 (1974), the Court established the test to use in determining whether conduct has communicative capacity. In *Texas v. Johnson*, the Court overturned Johnson's conviction for burning the American flag as part of a protest. Johnson argued that the burning, in context, was expressive conduct. The Court explained that, to decide "whether particular conduct possesses sufficient communicative elements to bring the First Amendment into play," courts must determine "whether '[a]n intent to convey a particularized message was present, and (whether) the likelihood was great that the message would be understood by those who viewed it'" (491 U.S. at 404, quoting *Spence v. Washington*, 418 U.S. at 410–411). Applying this test, the Court agreed that the flag burning, in context, was speech within the scope of the free speech clause.

C.3. Procedural Techniques

Procedural techniques, the second of the three types of techniques, focus on the particular procedure, device, or other means by which government has limited freedom of expression. The question is whether the particular means employed is an unconstitutional means. If a court rules that it is, the government may still be able to regulate the same expression using a different (constitutional) means. Thus, the use of procedural techniques may "often offer the judiciary an escape valve, permitting a decision that insulates a party against government action without requiring the enunciation of substantive doctrine which the court is unprepared to announce." Dorsen, Bender, & Neuborne, *supra*, at 53. The most frequently invoked procedural techniques arguments are: (1) "overbreadth" arguments (*see, e.g., Broadrick v. Oklahoma*, 413 U.S. 601 (1973)); (2) "vagueness" arguments (*see, e.g., Smith v. Goguen*, 415 U.S. 566 (1974)); and (3) "prior restraint" arguments (*see, e.g., Near v. Minnesota*, 283 U.S. 697 (1931)).

C.3(1).   Overbreadth

The first type of procedural argument is based on the overbreadth doctrine, which provides that government may not implement "overbroad" regulations that would exert a "chilling effect" on individuals wishing to engage in expressive activity prohibited by the regulation at issue. "The doctrine is predicated on the sensitive nature of protected expression: persons whose expression is constitutionally protected may well refrain from exercising their rights for fear of criminal sanctions by a statute susceptible of application to protected expression." The "mere existence" of such a "sweeping statute . . . has the potential to repeatedly chill the exercise of expressive activity by many individuals. . . ." (*New York v. Ferber*, 458 U.S. 747, 772 (1982)).

A government regulation of speech or press is overbroad, and thus unconstitutional on its face, if it sweeps within its coverage a substantial amount of expressive activity that is protected by the First Amendment. The test is one of "substantial overbreadth": "the overbreadth of a statute must not only be real, but substantial as well, judged in relation to the statute's plainly legitimate sweep" (*Broadrick v. Oklahoma*, 413 U.S. 601, 615 (1973)). When a substantial number of the regulation's potential applications would be invalid under the First Amendment, a court may invalidate the entire regulation, in all its applications, so that the regulation will no longer exert a chilling effect on free speech.

Moreover, a person whose expression is limited by such an overbroad regulation may invoke the overbreadth doctrine in court even if the regulation's application to that person would not be invalid under the First Amendment. So understood, the overbreadth doctrine is, in effect, a special rule of standing (see generally Chap. 5, Sec. D.3) allowing a party to challenge a regulation *on its face* even when that regulation would be constitutional *as applied* to that party's specific conduct (see Chap. 2, Sec. C, regarding facial and as applied challenges). As the U.S. Supreme Court has declared, "[i]t is well-established that in the area of freedom of expression an overbroad regulation may be subject to facial review and invalidation, even though its application in the case under consideration is unobjectionable" (*Forsyth County v. The Nationalist Movement*, 505 U.S. 123, 129 (1992)). The affected party, in other words, may challenge the regulation's potential applications to hypothetical circumstances and hypothetical third parties, whose expressive rights may be "chilled" by the continued existence of the overbroad statute. *See Gooding v. Wilson*, 405 U.S. 518, 520–521 (1972). Overbreadth, therefore, should be distinguished from the general type of facial challenge to a regulation that is unconstitutional in all its applications, including its application to the party before the court. *See generally* Richard Fallon, "Making Sense of Overbreadth," 100 YALE L. J. 853 (1991).

C.3(2). *Vagueness*

The second type of procedural argument is based on the vagueness doctrine, which provides that government may not implement "vague" regulations that (somewhat like overbreadth) would exert a "chilling effect" on individuals who cannot discern whether the expressive activity they wish to undertake is prohibited by the regulation at issue. The vagueness doctrine actually has two variants, the more general one based upon Fourteenth Amendment procedural due process (see Chap. 11, Sec. D.4), and the more particular one arising from the First Amendment's speech and press clauses. The basic requirement is the same under each variant: the regulation must provide an intelligible standard (a) to guide the conduct of persons subject to it, and (b) to guide the discretion of decisionmakers who apply the regulation. But courts will apply the requirement more strictly, and require a greater degree of regulatory clarity, when the regulation at issue could apply to and restrict expressive activities (*see, e.g., Smith v. Goguen*, 415 U.S. 566, 573 (1974)). This is because a vague regulation that may apply to expressive activities will not only violate notice requirements of procedural due process but will also inhibit potential speakers from expressing their ideas, thus "chilling" the free speech or press rights of those arguably subject to the regulation. In *Keyishian v. Board of Regents of the University of the State of New York*, 385 U.S. 589 (1967), for example, the Court invalidated provisions in state statutes and administrative regulations that prohibited seditious words or acts by professors and teachers, and made sedition grounds for termination of employment. The Court held that New York's "regulatory maze" had "the quality of 'extraordinary ambiguity,'" such that persons "must necessarily guess at its meaning and differ as to its application....'" (385 U.S. at 604, quoting *Baggett v. Bullitt*, 377 U.S. 360, 367 (1964)). Because the New York provisions could trench upon the freedoms of speech and press, they were subject to especially strict standards of vagueness:

> We emphasize once again that '[p]recision of regulation must be the touchstone in an area so closely touching our most precious freedoms,' *N.A.A.C.P. v. Button*, 371 U.S. 415, 438, '[f]or standards of permissible statutory vagueness are strict in the area of free expression .... Because First Amendment freedoms need breathing space to survive, government may regulate in the area only with narrow specificity.' Id., at 432–433. New York's complicated and intricate scheme plainly violates that standard. When one must guess what conduct or utterance may lose him his position, one necessarily will 'steer far wider of the unlawful zone .... *Speiser v. Randall*, 357 U.S. 513, 526. For [t]he threat of sanctions may deter ... almost as potently as the actual application of sanctions.' *N.A.A.C.P. v. Button*, supra, 371 U.S., at 433. The danger of that chilling effect upon the exercise of vital First Amendment rights must be guarded against by sensitive tools which clearly inform teachers what is being proscribed. [385 U.S. at 603–604.]

C.3(3). *Prior Restraints*

The third type of procedural argument is based on the prior restraint doctrine. This doctrine prohibits government from using certain regulatory devices—in particular, licensing or permit systems and court injunctions—that restrain expression in advance of its occurrence in ways that create dangers of censorship. As the U.S. Supreme Court has emphasized:

> [P]rior restraints on speech and publication are the most serious and the least tolerable infringement on First Amendment rights. A criminal penalty or a judgment in a [civil] case is subject to the whole panoply of protections afforded by deferring the impact of the judgment until all avenues of appellate review have been exhausted.... [But] a prior restraint...has an immediate and irreversible sanction. If it can be said that a threat of criminal or civil sanc-

tions after publication 'chills' speech, prior restraint 'freezes' it at least for the time. [*Nebraska Press Ass'n v. Stuart*, 427 U.S. 539, 559 (1976).]

The opposite of a *prior* restraint is a *subsequent* restraint, an example of which (as suggested by the quote above) is the imposition of a criminal penalty on the speaker after the expression has occurred. Governments may sometimes be able to use a subsequent restraint to regulate speech or press that they could not regulate using a prior restraint.

The famous case of *New York Times v. United States*, 403 U.S. 713 (1971), set out and discussed in Chapter 3, Section D, provides a classic example of a prior restraint: an injunction against publishing certain material based on its content. In its brief *per curiam* opinion invalidating the injunction, the Court confirmed that "'[a]ny system of prior restraints of expression [bears] a heavy presumption against its constitutional validity,'" and that the government "'thus carries a heavy burden of showing justification for the enforcement of such a restraint'" (403 U.S. at 714, quoting *Bantam Books, Inc. v. Sullivan*, 372 U.S. 58, 70 (1963) and *Organization for a Better Austin v. Keefe*, 402 U.S. 415, 419 (1971)). In their concurring opinions, Justices Brennan and Stewart developed the substantive standard applicable to prior restraints (403 U.S. at 726-727, 727-730). Even when the government can meet this stringent substantive standard, a prior restraint is still subject to a rigorous set of procedural safeguards to assure prompt and accurate decisionmaking regarding the justifications for imposing the restraint (*see, e.g., Southeastern Promotions, Ltd. v. Conrad*, 420 U.S. 546 (1975)).

These stringent rules for prior restraints do not apply, however, when the denial of a license or permit, or the injunction, is not based on the content of the speech and therefore does not raise concerns of censorship. In *Thomas v. Chicago Park District*, 534 U.S. 316 (2002), for example, the Court upheld a requirement that groups of 50 or more persons, and persons using sound amplification equipment, must obtain a permit before using the public parks. This "licensing scheme ... is not subject-matter censorship, but content-neutral time, place, and manner regulation...," said the Court. "The Park District's ordinance does not authorize a licensor to pass judgment on the content of speech: None of the [thirteen] grounds for denying a permit has anything to do with what a speaker might say" (534 U.S. at 322). (See Section C.4 below regarding content-based versus content-neutral restrictions on speech and Section E below regarding content-neutral regulations.)

Similarly, in *Schenck v. Pro-Choice Network of Western New York*, 519 U.S. 357 (1997), the Court determined that content-neutral injunctions were not subject to the strict scrutiny applicable to content-based injunctions. The Court then established this test for ascertaining the validity of content-neutral injunctions: "Whether the challenged provisions of the injunction burden no more speech than necessary to serve a significant government interest" (*Id.* at 371, quoting *Madsen v. Women's Health Center*, 512 U.S. 753, 756 (1994)). Applying this standard in *Schenck*, the Court upheld some, but not all, provisions of a multifaceted injunction limiting protest activities in the vicinity of abortion clinics.

C.4. Substantive Techniques

Substantive or standard-setting techniques focus on the development and application of standards for the resolution of free speech issues that are not disposed of using non-speech techniques or procedural techniques. Of the three types of analytical techniques, the substantive techniques are the most frequently invoked. They require the court to directly address the competing free speech and governmental interests at stake in the case. A classic example is the "clear and present danger" standard that originated in *Schenck v. United States*, 249 U.S. 47, 52 (1919); this standard is discussed in Section D.1 below. Over time, the courts have developed a variety of standards, each applicable to a particular circumstance or a particular type of speech. The courts have also developed a critical distinction between standards that apply to "content-based" restrictions on speech and standards that apply to "content-neutral" restrictions. The former type of standard embodies a stricter scrutiny of the restriction than does the latter type of standard.

A restriction on speech is content based if government's concern is with the content, that is, the information disseminated or the ideas or opinions expressed, and if government imposes the restriction in order to alleviate its concern about content. There are a variety of content-based standards that the courts have created to guide strict scrutiny review of particular types of content-based restrictions. (See generally Sec. D below.)

A content-neutral restriction on speech, in contrast, is a restriction that is unrelated to the content of the speech being restricted; government does not regulate because of the content, but because it has some other "neutral" concern about the expressive activity at issue. As the U.S. Supreme Court explained in *Ward v. Rock Against Racism*, 491 U.S. 781 (1989):

> The principal inquiry in determining content neutrality, in speech cases generally..., is whether the government has adopted a regulation of speech because of disagreement with the message it conveys....The government's purpose is the controlling consideration. A regulation that serves purposes unrelated to the content of expression is deemed neutral .... [*Id.* at 791.]

Content-neutral restrictions are generally subject to an intermediate scrutiny standard of review. Rather than a variety of standards, as with content-based restrictions, there are basically two standards by which to measure the validity of content-neutral restrictions on speech: the "time, place, and manner" standard, and the *O'Brien* "symbolic speech" standard. Both are discussed in Section E.2 below.

Sec. D. Content-Based Restrictions on Expression

D.1. Subversive Speech: Advocacy of Unlawful Action

As indicated in Section C.4 above, a restriction on speech is "content-based" when government has regulated the speech because of its concern for the content of the message itself—that is, the information conveyed, or the ideas or opinions expressed, by the speaker. The case of *Schenck v. United States*, 249 U.S. 47 (1919), reviewing a federal prosecution for advocating illegal action, provides a classic and early example of judicial review of a content-based restriction on speech. (Prior to *Schenck*, American courts had paid little attention to freedom of expression. For an overview of the original history of the speech and press clauses, and developments up to World War I, *see* Zechariah Chafee, Jr., FREE SPEECH IN THE UNITED STATES, ch. 1 (Harv. U. Press/Atheneum, 1941 and 1969).)

Schenck was the general secretary of the Socialist Party. He and the other defendants were opposed to the U.S. involvement in World War I and, in particular, to the military draft. They devised a circular urging opposition to conscription, printed 15,000 copies, and began mailing them to draft registrants and draftees. Arguing that the draft was unconstitutional, the circulars quoted the Thirteenth Amendment and compared conscription to slavery or involuntary servitude. "Do not submit to intimidation," the circulars asserted. "If you do not assert and support your rights, you are helping to deny or disparage rights which it is the solemn duty of all citizens and residents of the United States to retain" (249 U.S. at 51). The circulars further declared that conscription is the worst sort of despotism supported by Wall Street and cunning politicians. For mailing these circulars, the defendants were charged and convicted under the Espionage Act of 1917, 40 Stat. 217, for conspiring to cause insubordination in the United States military, to obstruct military recruitment and enlistment, and to use the U.S. mail for transmission of material declared non-mailable by the Act.

In an opinion by Justice Oliver Wendell Holmes, the Court upheld Schenck's conviction. Justice Holmes emphasized that freedom of speech hinges on the circumstances in which the speech is uttered:

> We admit that in many places and in ordinary times the defendants in saying all that was said in the circular would have been within their constitutional rights. But the character of every act depends upon the circumstances in which it is done. The most stringent protection of free speech would not protect a man in falsely shouting fire in a theatre and causing a panic. [249 U.S. at 52.]

He then announced a test for determining what circumstances will justify a restraint on freedom of speech:

> [The] question in every case is whether the words are used in such circumstances and are of such a nature as to create *a clear and present danger that they will bring about the substantive evils that Congress has a right to prevent.* It is a question of proximity and degree. When a nation is at war many things that might be said in time of peace are such a hindrance to its effort that their utterance will not be endured so long as men fight, and that no Court could regard them as protected by any constitutional right. [249 U.S. at 52 (emphasis added).]

This test became known as the "clear and present danger" standard. Applying this test to the defendants' publication and dissemination activities, Justice Holmes determined that the message conveyed did constitute a clear and present danger of obstructing the federal government's recruitment and enlistment for the armed services. The Court therefore rejected the defendants' First Amendment argument and upheld the convictions.

As applied in *Schenck*, the "clear and present danger" standard was not as protective of free expression (that is, not as "speech protective") as one might at first surmise. It was not a genuine strict scrutiny standard. It did not require any proof, for instance, of the quantum or gravity of the danger, the imminency of the danger, or the likelihood that the speech would be successful in accomplishing a "substantive evil." Justice Holmes himself sought to strengthen the standard later that year in *Abrams v. United States*, 250 U.S. 616 (1919). Arguing that the defendants' Espionage Act convictions should be overturned, Holmes asserted that: "[T]he United States constitutionally may punish speech that produces or is intended to produce a clear and imminent danger that it will bring about forthwith certain substantive evils.... [I]t is only the present danger of immediate evil or an intent to bring it about that warrants Congress in setting a limit to the expression of opinion where private rights are not concerned. Congress certainly cannot forbid all effort to change the mind of the country" (250 U.S. at 628). But Justice Holmes was speaking in dissent in this case, with Justice Brandeis concurring. (For a longer quote from the Holmes dissent in *Abrams*, see Section B.1 above.) Some years later, Justice Brandeis could still assert that "[t]his court has not yet fixed the standard by which to determine when a danger shall be deemed clear; how remote the danger may be and yet be deemed present; and what degree of evil shall be deemed sufficiently substantial to justify resort to abridgement of free speech and assembly as the means of protection" (*Whitney v. California*, 274 U.S. 357, 374 (1927)).

The clear and present danger standard was finally strengthened, bit by bit, in a series of cases in the 1950s and 1960s, culminating with *Brandenburg v. Ohio*, 395 U.S. 444 (1969). In the process, it became evident that the clear and present danger standard was not and never had been a generic First Amendment test for all content-based restrictions on speech. Instead, it is a test to apply when government has regulated the content of speech due to a concern that the ideas expressed or information conveyed are dangerous to the safety and security of the citizenry. In *Brandenburg*, for instance, the Court reviewed an Ohio statute making it a crime to "advocate the...propriety of crime, sabotage, violence, or unlawful methods of terrorism as a means of accomplishing industrial or political reform." Rather than applying the clear and present danger standard as such, the Court articulated what commentators have called a "restatement" or "synthesis" of the clear and present danger cases. *See, e.g.*, Gerald Gunther, "Learned Hand and the Origins of Modern First Amendment Doctrine: Some Fragments of History," 27 STANFORD L. REV. 719, 745–755 (1975). According to the Court in *Brandenburg*:

> [T]he constitutional guarantees of free speech and free press do not permit a state to forbid or proscribe advocacy of the use of force or of law violation except where such advocacy (1) is directed to inciting or producing imminent lawless action and (2) is likely to incite or produce such action. [395 U.S. at 447 (numbering added).]

This new "incitement" standard, applicable to cases concerning the advocacy of allegedly dangerous ideas, is generally considered to be the most speech-protective of all the variations on clear and present danger articulated from *Schenck* up to the *Brandenburg* case itself (*see*, *e.g.*, Gunther, *supra*, at 754–755).

The clear-and-present-danger standard itself, rather than *Brandenburg* variation, may still apply to certain types of cases that do not involve advocacy of ideas—the situation to which the *Brandenburg* standard is adapted. If the problem concerns the revelation of allegedly dangerous *facts* (factual information) rather than the advocacy of allegedly dangerous *ideas*, for example, the clear-and-present-danger standard apparently still applies. See *New York Times v. United States*, 403 U.S. 713 (1971), at 726–727 (Brennan, J., concurring), 727–730 (Stewart, J., concurring), and 732–733 (White, J., concurring). (These opinions are set out in Chapter 3, Section D of this book.) Similarly, for problems concerning contempt of court or other expression that interferes with the operation of the courts—for example, the mass media's release of confidential information from a judicial proceeding—the clear-and-present-danger standard may still have some application. See *Landmark Communications v. Virginia*, 435 U.S. 829, 842–845 (1978).

Moreover, it appears that courts may still use the clear-and-present-danger test for problems concerning hostile audience reaction to the offensive words of a speaker (rather than the speaker's incitement of the audience, to which *Brandenberg* itself would apply). In *Terminiello v. Chicago*, 337 U.S. 1 (1949), for instance, the Court reviewed a speaker's breach of peace conviction for having "stir[red] the public to anger, invit[ed] dispute," or created "unrest." In reversing the conviction, the Court, per Justice Douglas, held that "freedom of speech…is …protected against censorship or punishment, unless shown likely to produce a clear and present danger of a serious substantive evil that rises far above public inconvenience, annoyance, or unrest" (*Id.* at 4). And in *Feiner v. New York*, 340 U.S. 315 (1951), while upholding a disorderly conduct conviction of a speaker whose words had created unrest in the audience, the Court emphasized that the state may punish a speaker whose speech produces a "clear and present danger of riot, disorder, interference with traffic upon the public street or other immediate threat to public safety, peace, or order" (*Id.* at 320, quoting *Cantwell v. Connecticut*, 310 U.S. 296, 308 (1940)).

D.2. Defamation

Another, and quite different, example of a content-based restriction on speech comes from the famous case of *New York Times v. Sullivan*, 376 U.S. 254 (1964). In March 1960 the *New York Times* published a full-page fund-raising advertisement by the Committee to Defend Martin Luther King and the Struggle for Freedom in the South. Titled "Heed Their Rising Voices," the advertisement alleged the existence of "an unprecedented wave of terror" against blacks engaged in nonviolent protests in the South. Sullivan, the Montgomery, Alabama police commissioner, sued the *Times* and the ad's sponsors for libel. Sullivan objected to the claim that Dr. King had been assaulted and arrested seven times (in fact, Dr. King had been arrested four times). Sullivan also took offense to the claim that "truckloads of police armed with shotguns and tear gas ringed the Alabama State College Campus" in Montgomery (376 U.S. at 257). Sullivan sued the Times in an Alabama state court, claiming that the statements in the ad had libeled him in violation of Alabama libel law. Although he offered no proof of a pecuniary loss, Sullivan was awarded $500,000 in damages.

The New York Times argued before the U.S. Supreme Court that the ad was protected by the First Amendment and that the Alabama libel judgment was therefore unconstitutional. Sullivan argued that the First Amendment does not protect libelous publications. The Court majority, in an opinion by Justice Brennan, summarily rejected Sullivan's argument: "Like insurrection, contempt, advocacy of unlawful acts, breach of the peace, obscenity, solicitation of legal business, and the various other formulae for the repression of expression that have been challenged in this Court, libel can claim no talismanic immunity from constitutional limitations" (376 U.S. at 269). Freedom of speech cases must not be judged in a vacuum; rather, said the Court, they must be considered "against the background of a profound national commitment to the principle that debate on public issues should be uninhibited, robust, and wide-open, and that it may well include vehement, caustic, and sometimes unpleasantly sharp attacks on government and public officials" (376 U.S. at 270).

In robust democratic debate, "erroneous statement is inevitable...and [must] be protected if the freedoms of expression are to have the 'breathing space' that they 'need [to] survive....'" (376 U.S. at 271–272). Moreover, "[i]njury to official reputation affords no more warrant for repressing speech that would otherwise be free than does factual error....If judges are to be treated as 'men of fortitude, able to thrive in a hardy climate,' surely the same must be true of other government officials, such as elected city commissioners. Criticism of their official conduct does not lose its constitutional protection merely because it is effective criticism and hence diminishes their official reputations" (376 U.S. at 272–273).

Thus, the Court concluded, even false statements must sometimes be protected by the First Amendment. Refusing all protection for false statements would create a chilling effect on free speech:

> A rule compelling the critic of official conduct to guarantee the truth of all his factual assertions—and to do so on pain of libel judgments virtually unlimited in amount —leads to a comparable "self-censorship"....[Under] such a rule, would-be critics of official conduct may be deterred from voicing their criticism, even though it is believed to be true and even though it is in fact true, because of doubt whether it can be proved in court or fear of the expense of having to do so. They tend to make only statements which "steer far wider of the unlawful zone." The rule thus dampens the vigor and limits the variety of public debate. It is thus inconsistent with the First [Amendment]. [376 U.S. at 279.]

The Court then articulated the constitutional standard for determining when false speech will be protected, and when it will not, in cases concerning alleged libels of public officials. The public official may prevail, and recover damages, only by showing that the speaker acted with "actual malice":

> The constitutional guarantees require...a federal rule that prohibits a public official from recovering damages for a defamatory falsehood relating to his official conduct unless he proves that the statement was made with "actual malice"—that is, with knowledge that it was false or with reckless disregard of whether it was false or not. [376 U.S. at 279–280].

The public official's proof of actual malice, moreover, must meet the stringent standard of "convincing clarity" (*Id.* at 285–286).

The *Sullivan* standard—the "actual malice" standard—gave broad protection to freedom of expression in the context of libel laws. Originally, this protective standard applied only to cases where the defendant had allegedly defamed a public official in regard to his official conduct. Subsequent cases, however, extended the actual malice standard to public official cases even when the defamation did not concern the official's conduct in office (*Garrison v. Louisiana*, 379 U.S. 64 (1964)); and to cases concerning "public figures" who are not public officials (*Curtis Publishing Co. v. Butts*, 388 U.S. 130 (1967)).

In a later case, *Gertz v. Robert Welch, Inc.*, 418 U.S. 323 (1974), the Court crafted a lesser standard of scrutiny for cases involving the defamation of private individuals who are neither public officials nor public figures. Once the Court had decided *Gertz*, it had almost completely whittled away that part of the earlier *Chaplinsky* dictum (Sec. C.2 above) that included libel within the classes of speech receiving no constitutional protection. The only type of case in which libel arguably still receives no constitutional protection is the case of purely private libel. A case apparently would fall within this category if the plaintiff is a private figure, the defendant is a non-media defendant, and/or the defendant's statements are on matters of private concern (that is, matters that are not of any public interest and with which the public is not concerned). *See Philadelphia Newspapers, Inc. v. Hepps*, 475 U.S. 767, 775 (1986); *see also Dun and Bradstreet, Inc. v. Greenmoss Builders, Inc.*, 472 U.S. 749, 757 (1985) (plurality opinion by Powell, J.).

D.3. Strict Scrutiny Review

Content-based restrictions on speech, as in *Brandenburg, New York Times v. Sullivan*, and many other cases, are subjected to strict judicial scrutiny because they present the greatest threats to the values that are furthered by the free speech and press clauses (see Sec. B.1 above). When Justice Holmes and Justice Brandeis issued their eloquent justifications of free speech in *Abrams* and *Whitney* (Sec. B.1 above), they were explaining why courts should be suspicious of content-based restraints on speech. Justice Brandeis was addressing the question "why a state is, ordinarily, denied the power to prohibit dissemination of social, economic, and political doctrine [that] a vast majority of its citizens believes to be false and fraught with evil consequence" (274 U.S. at

374); Justice Holmes was explaining why "we should be eternally vigilant against attempts to check the expression of opinions that we loathe...." (250 U.S. at 628–630).

In *Brandenburg* and in *New York Times v. Sullivan*, the Court crafted special strict scrutiny standards to use in reviewing particular types of content-based restrictions on speech. The *Brandenburg* standard applies to cases where government regulates speech because it believes that the ideas conveyed are dangerous. The *Sullivan* standard applies to defamation cases in which a public official or public figure is the plaintiff. In many other situations where the Court has confronted content-based restrictions, it has applied a general or generic strict scrutiny standard of review. This standard looks very much like the strict scrutiny standard that is used for certain equal protection cases (see Chap. 10, Sec. C.4) and certain substantive due process cases (see Chap. 11, Sec. C.7). In *Burson v. Freeman*, 504 U.S. 191 (1992), for instance, the Court stated that content-based restrictions on speech will be upheld only if the government can prove that the restriction is "necessary to serve a compelling state interest and...narrowly drawn to achieve that end" (504 U.S. at 198, quoting *Perry Education Ass'n v. Perry Local Educators' Ass'n*, 460 U.S. 37, 45 (1983); *see also* 504 U.S. at 217 (Stevens, J., dissenting)). Sometimes the Court has used the phrase "least restrictive means" as an alternative to the "narrowly drawn" test (*see, e.g., Sable Communications v. FCC*, 492 U.S. 115, 126 (1989)).

As in the areas of equal protection (Chap. 10) and substantive due process (Chap. 11), the Court has "never set forth a general test to determine what constitutes a compelling state interest" (*Waters v. Churchill*, 511 U.S. 661, 671 (1994)). But the Court has acknowledged that "it is the rare case" in which it will hold that a content-based restriction survives strict scrutiny (*Burson*, 504 U.S. at 211). Occasionally, the Court has also provided examples of interests that will permit governmental use of a content-based restriction on speech. In *Burson* (above), for instance, the Court held that preventing voter intimidation and election fraud is a compelling government interest sufficient to support some content-based restrictions on the display and distribution of campaign material. In *Sable Communications v. FCC* (above), the Court agreed that government has "a compelling interest in protecting the physical and psychological well-being of minors" (492 U.S. at 126). In *Snepp v. United States*, 444 U.S. 507 (1980), the Court determined that the federal government "has a compelling interest in protecting both the secrecy of information important to our national security and the appearance of confidentiality so essential to the effective operation of our foreign intelligence service" (*Id.* at 509 fn. 3). And in *Carey v. Brown*, 447 U.S. 455 (1980), the Court affirmed that the "State's interest in protecting the well-being, tranquility and privacy of the home is certainly of the highest order in a free and civilized society" (*Id.* at 471).

More often, however, the Court has educated us about freedom of expression by telling us what is *not* a compelling government interest, rather than what is. In *Tinker v. Des Moines School District*, 393 U.S. 503 (1969), for example, while invalidating the school district's suspension of several students for wearing black armbands to protest the Vietnam War, the Court emphasized that alleviating "undifferentiated fear or apprehension" is not a compelling governmental interest:

In our system, undifferentiated fear or apprehension of disturbance is not enough to overcome the right to freedom of expression. Any departure from absolute regimentation may cause trouble. Any variation from the majority's opinion may inspire fear.... But our Constitution says we must take this risk, and our history says that it is this sort of hazardous freedom—this kind of openness—that is the basis of our national strength and of the independence and vigor of Americans who grow up and live in this relatively permissive, often disputatious society. [393 U.S. at 508–509.]

Similarly, in *Texas v. Johnson*, 491 U.S. 397 (1989), the Court made clear that protecting individuals or society from the offensiveness of speech is not a compelling governmental interest: "If there is a bedrock principle underlying the First Amendment, it is that the Government may not prohibit the expression of an idea simply because society finds the idea itself offensive or disagreeable" (491 U.S. at 414).

D.4. Viewpoint Discrimination and "Strictest" Scrutiny

In free expression cases, the strictest scrutiny of all is reserved for content-based restrictions on speech that constitute "viewpoint discrimination." Viewpoint-based restrictions on speech are a special type of, or subset of, content-based restrictions. A viewpoint-based restriction does not merely prohibit a certain topic or subject matter from being addressed; rather, it prohibits or disfavors certain points of view or perspectives on a particular topic while permitting or favoring others. If a village were to prohibit any presentation on abortion in the village square, that would be a content-based restriction but not a viewpoint-based restriction. If the village were to prohibit only presentations on the pro-choice position, that would be a viewpoint-based restriction and would constitute viewpoint discrimination. *Cf. Planned Parenthood of South Carolina v. Rose*, 236 F.Supp. 2d 564 (D.S.C. 2002). As the U.S. Supreme Court explained in *Rosenberger v. Rector and Visitors of the University of Virginia*, 515 U.S. 819, 828 (1995):

When the government targets not subject matter, but particular views taken by speakers on a subject, the violation of the First Amendment is all the more blatant... Viewpoint discrimination is thus an egregious form of content discrimination. The government must abstain from regulating speech when the specific motivating ideology or the opinion or perspective of the speaker is the rationale for the restriction.

The distinction drawn by the Court in *Rosenberger*, and in other recent cases, is between the subject or topic that the speaker addresses, and the "premise," "perspective," or "standpoint" from which the speaker addresses that subject or topic (*Rosenberger*, 515 U.S. at 831). Speech restrictions falling on the latter side of the dichotomy are considered to be "viewpoint-based" (vs. "viewpoint neutral") restrictions, thus constituting viewpoint discrimination. It will sometimes be difficult to determine on which side of this line a particular restriction should be placed. In *Rosenberger*, for instance, the Court majority and the dissenters differed on whether the university had engaged in viewpoint discrimination by refusing to provide student activity fee funds to pay the printing costs of a Christian student publication. Justice Kennedy, for the majority, held that it was viewpoint discrimination:

> [T]he University does not exclude religion as a subject matter, but selects for disfavored treatment those student journalistic efforts with religious editorial viewpoints. Religion may be a vast area of inquiry, but it also provides, as it did here, a specific premise, a perspective, a standpoint from which a variety of subjects may be discussed and considered. The prohibited perspective, not the subject matter, resulted in the refusal to make [payments for printing costs]....[515 U.S. at 831.]

Justice Souter, for the dissenters, disagreed:

> If the [university's funding] Guidelines were written or applied so as to limit only...Christian advocacy and no other evangelical efforts that might compete with it, the discrimination would be based on viewpoint. But that is not what the regulation authorizes; it applies to Muslim and Jewish and Buddhist advocacy as well as to Christian. And since it limits funding to activities promoting or manifesting a particular belief not only "in" but "about" a deity or ultimate reality, it applies to agnostics and atheists as well as it does to deists and theists. The Guidelines [thus] do not skew debate by funding one position but not its competitors. [T]hey simply deny funding for hortatory speech that 'primarily promotes or manifests' any view on the merits of religion; they deny funding for the entire subject matter of religious apologetics. [515 U.S. at 895–896, Souter, J., dissenting.]

Once a speech restriction is determined to be viewpoint based, it will virtually always be unconstitutional (as it was in *Rosenberger*), no matter what justification the government may assert. This is because a government regulation permitting viewpoint discrimination "raises the specter that the Government may effectively drive certain ideas or viewpoints from the marketplace" (*R.A.V. v. City of St. Paul*, 505 U.S. 377, 387 (1992), quoting *Simon v. Schuster, Inc. v. N.Y. State Crime Victims Board*, 502 U.S. 105, 116 (1991)), thus undercutting a central purpose of the free speech and press clauses.

Even the justification of avoiding establishment clause violations (see Chap. 13, Sec. B) generally does not work for viewpoint-based restrictions. In *Lamb's Chapel v. Center Moriches Union Free School District*, 508 U.S. 384 (1993), for example, the Court invalidated the school district's refusal to allow a religious organization to use school facilities after school hours to show a film series on parenting from a Christian perspective. Pursuant to state statute, the school district allowed a variety of other civic, social, and recreational groups to meet after hours on school premises. The Court held first that "it discriminates on the basis of viewpoint to permit school property to be used for the presentation of all views about family issues and child rearing except those dealing with the subject matter from a religious standpoint" (508 U.S. at 393); and, second, that it would not violate the establishment clause to permit the religious group to meet on school premises, so long as the school district permitted other, secular groups to meet for their own expressive activities. Similarly, in *Good News Club v. Milford Central School*,

533 U.S. 98 (2001), the Court held, first, that it is viewpoint discrimination to refuse after-school use of public school classrooms to a group addressing moral development of children through religious worship and instruction but permit such use by groups addressing moral development in secular ways; and, second, that it would not violate the establishment clause to permit use by the former group so long as the classrooms were available for use by other groups on an evenhanded basis.

D.5. Lesser Scrutiny Standards: Commercial Speech and Sexually Explicit Speech

The Court does not apply strict scrutiny to every content-based restraint on expression. Some content-based regulations will fall into a "non-speech" (no communicative value) category and therefore escape First Amendment scrutiny because the speech's content is "constitutionally proscribable" (*R.A.V. v. City of St. Paul*, 505 U.S. 377 (1992); see also Sec. C.2(1) above).[4] Other content-based restraints, although applying to speech that is within the First Amendment, will nevertheless be subjected to a standard of review that is less than strict scrutiny. The three primary types of governmental regulations that currently receive this treatment are: (1) regulations of "commercial speech"; (2) regulations of sexually explicit, non-obscene speech; and (3) regulations of certain private defamation. Commercial speech and sexually explicit speech are discussed in Sections D.5(1) and D.5(2) below. Private defamation is discussed at the end of Section D.2 above.

The U.S. Supreme Court has developed competing theories or justifications for applying a lower scrutiny to some speech and thus according it less protection than other speech typically receives. The most common justification is that a particular type of speech is of lower value than other types and is thus less worthy of protection. The Court has used this justification for both sexually explicit speech and commercial speech, as discussed below.

The Court's articulated justification for according private or "private figure" defamation less protection than public or "public figure" defamation is very different from the justifications that pertain to sexually explicit speech and commercial speech, and does not depend on any lower value speech theory. In the leading case, *Gertz v. Robert Welch, Inc.*, 418 U.S. 323 (1974), the Court asserted that private figures are "not only more vulnerable to injury than public officials and public figures; they are also more deserving of recovery" (*Id.* at 345). Private figures are more vulnerable because they usually have far less "access to the channels of effective communication" than public figures do and therefore have less opportunity "to contradict the lie or correct the error

---

4. In *R.A.V.*, however, the Court emphasized that government may not discriminate on the basis of viewpoint when it regulates speech that falls within a "non-speech" category. On this basis, the Court struck down a city "fighting words" ordinance even though fighting words are "nonspeech" and generally not protected by the First Amendment. The flaw in the city's ordinance was that it prohibited fighting words used to express racial hatred and bias, but did not prohibit fighting words used to express racial tolerance or support for equality.

and thereby minimize its adverse impact on reputation" (*Id.* at 344). Private figures are more deserving because, in general, "public figures have voluntarily exposed themselves to increased risk of injury from defamatory falsehood..." (*Id.* at 345), while private figures have not. Private figures therefore have "a more compelling call on the courts for redress of injury inflicted by defamatory falsehood" (*Id.*).

D.5(1). Commercial Speech

"Commercial speech" is speech that "propose[s] a commercial transaction" (*Virginia State Board of Pharmacy v. Virginia Citizens Consumer Council*, 425 U.S. 748, 762 (1976)) and that "relate[s] solely to the economic interests of the speaker and its audience" (*Central Hudson Gas v. Public Service Commission*, 447 U.S. 557, 561 (1980)). This definition may be difficult to apply in particular cases because not all commercial promotions propose a transaction as such, and commercial speakers may have public service or public education interests as well as economic interests. Moreover, even when a particular statement is admittedly commercial within the Court's definitions, it may be intertwined with other, noncommercial statements on matters of public interest, thus raising the question of whether to characterize the communication as commercial or noncommercial. *See generally* Alex Kozinski & Stuart Banner, "Who's Afraid of Commercial Speech?", 76 VA. L. REV. 627 (1990).

In *Virginia State Board of Pharmacy*, the case that brought commercial speech within the First Amendment, the Court (per Justice Blackmun) noted the "commonsense differences between [commercial] speech...and other varieties" that support "a different degree of protection" for commercial speech (425 U.S. at 772 fn. 24). Primarily, "commercial speech may be more durable [or "hardy"] than other kinds. Since advertising is the sine qua non of commercial profits, there is little likelihood of its being chilled by proper regulation and foregone entirely" (*Id.*). In *Ohralik v. Ohio State Bar Ass'n*, 436 U.S. 447 (1978), however, the Court (per Justice Powell) provided a quite different justification for according commercial speech less protection—a justification relying expressly on lower-value speech theory: "[W]e...have afforded commercial speech a limited measure of protection, commensurate with its subordinate position in the scale of First Amendment values" (*Id.* at 456). This lesser protection for lower-value speech, said the Court, was necessary to avoid a "devitalization" of the First Amendment: "To require a parity of constitutional protection for commercial and noncommercial speech alike could invite dilution, simply by a leveling process, of the force of the Amendment's guarantee with respect to the latter kind of speech" (*Id.*).

The standard of review for commercial speech comes from the *Central Hudson* case. Under *Central Hudson*, commercial speech: (1) "must concern lawful activity and not be misleading" in order to receive First Amendment protection. When commercial speech meets that threshold requirement, the Court then applies this test to determine the validity of a regulation of the speech: (2) "the asserted governmental interest" must be "substantial"; (3) the government's regulation must "directly advance[ ]" the government interest asserted; and (4) the regulation must not be "more extensive than is necessary to serve that interest" (447 U.S. at 566). This four-part test, parts 2–4 of which are generally considered to create an intermediate scrutiny standard, has been the subject of continuing debate within the Court and among commentators. Various Justices have argued that at least some commercial speech regulations should be subject to strict scrutiny. Justice Stevens, for example, extensively developed this position for a plurality of the Court in *44 Liquormart, Inc. v. Rhode Island*, 517 U.S. 484, 489–495, 514–516 (1996). *See generally* Kathleen M. Sullivan, "Cheap Spirits, Cigarettes, and Free Speech: The Implications of *44 Liquormart*," 1996 SUP. CT. REV. 123. In several cases since *44 Liquormart*, however, the Court has consistently applied the *Central Hudson* standard, with only Justices Thomas, Scalia, and Kennedy expressing doubts about all or part of the *Central Hudson* standard. *See, e.g., Lorillard Tobacco Co. v. Reilly*, 533 U.S. 525 (2001).

D.5(2). *Sexually Explicit Speech*

The sexually explicit speech cases are a melange of split decisions and contending opinions that employ various analyses of governmental restrictions on sexual expression. Sexually explicit speech is not the same as obscene speech and does not fall within the definition of obscenity set out in *Miller v. California,* nor does it fall within the definition of child pronography set out in *New York v. Ferber* (see Sec. C.2 above). The Court has not provided a specific definition for this category of speech. In general, however, it can be said to be speech that is communicated through the depiction or performance of adults engaged in explicit, erotic (but not obscene) sexual activity. The leading cases concern adult movies (*Young v. American Mini Theatres*, 427 U.S. 50 (1976); *City of Renton v. Playtime Theatres*, 475 U.S. 41 (1986)) and live, nude dancing performances (*Barnes v. Glen Theatre*, 501 U.S. 560 (1991); *City of Erie v. Pap's A.M.*, 529 U.S. 277 (2000)).

The Justices have struggled to identify the appropriate analytical approach and appropriate standard of review for sexually explicit speech cases. For the Justices advocating lesser protection for sexually explicit speech, the rationale (or at least part of the rationale) is usually that such speech is of less value than other types of speech. In the *Young* case, for example, in which the Court upheld a Detroit zoning ordinance requiring the dispersal of adult movie theatres, Justice Stevens asserted: "[I]t is manifest that society's interest in protecting [erotic materials] is of a wholly different, and lesser, magnitude than the interest in untrammeled political debate.... [F]ew of us would march ours sons and daughters off to war to preserve the citizen's right to see 'Specified Sexual Activities' exhibited in the theatres of our choice" (427 U.S. at 70 (plurality opinion)). And in the later *City of Erie* case, upholding an ordinance requiring live nude dancers to wear a "G-string" and "pasties," Justice O'Connor emphasized that, although "nude dancing of the type at issue here is expressive conduct,...it falls only within the outer ambit of the First Amendment's protection" (529 U.S. at 289 (plurality opinion), citing *Barnes*, 501 U.S. at 565-566 (plurality opinion)). In support of this statement, Justice O'Connor quoted the passage set out above from Justice Stevens' *Young* opinion.

In addition to the asserted lower value of the speech, other factors have influenced the Justices who have upheld restrictions on sexually explicit speech. The most important of these other factors have been: whether the restriction totally prohibited the speech or only regulated the form (as in the nude dancing cases) or the place (as in the adult theatre cases) of the speech; whether the restriction was based on the viewpoint expressed or only on the subject matter (see Sec. D.4 above); whether the government had regulated the speech because of its effect on the audience or only because of its harmful "secondary effects" on the surrounding community (*e.g.*, causing an increase in crime or the diminution of property values); and whether important governmental interests were threatened by the secondary effects of the speech. *See, e.g., City of Erie*, 529 U.S. at 293-297 (plurality opinion).

When the government is only regulating (and not totally prohibiting) sexually explicit speech, the regulation is based on the subject matter and not the viewpoint expressed, and the regulation is supported by the government's interest in the "secondary effects" of the speech, the Court has been willing to treat the regulation as a content-neutral rather than a content-based regulation (see Sec. C.4 above). In the *City of Renton* case, for example, the majority applied a "time, place, and manner" standard derived from *Clark v. Community for Creative Non-Violence* (see Sec. E.1 below). And in the *City of Erie* case, the majority applied the standard from *United States v. O'Brien* (see Sec. E.2 below): "[G]overnment restrictions on public nudity such as the ordinance at issue here should be evaluated under the framework set forth in *O'Brien* for content-neutral restrictions on symbolic speech" (*City of Erie*, 529 U.S. at 289). As the Court has applied each of these standards in the sexually explicit speech cases, it has accorded considerable deference to the government's own judgments about the interests it is protecting (the "secondary effects"), the extent to which the regulated speech threatens these interests, and the extent to which the regulation diminishes the threat by alleviating the harmful "secondary effects" that the government's regulation addresses. *See, e.g., Erie*, 529 U.S. at 296–300 (plurality opinion), and *compare* 529 U.S. at 311–316 (Souter, J., concurring in part and dissenting in part).

Sec. E. Content-Neutral Restrictions on Speech

E.1. Overview

If a governmental restriction on speech is not content-based (see Sec. C.4 above) or viewpoint-based (Sec. D.4 above), it will generally be classified as a content-neutral restriction. The problem of content-neutral restrictions on speech is well illustrated by the case of *Clark v. Community for Creative Non-Violence*, 468 U.S. 288 (1984). The Community for Creative Non-Violence (CCNV) was an organization that advocated with and on behalf of the homeless and poor and provided food, shelter, clothing, and medical care to meet their subsistence needs. In the winter of 1981, CCNV had held a round-the-clock demonstration in Washington, D.C. to dramatize the plight of homeless persons. CCNV erected nine tents in Lafayette Park, across from the White House, in which homeless persons slept during the demonstration. CCNV had been permitted to engage in the demonstration, which it dubbed "Reaganville," after the U.S. Court of Appeals for the District of Columbia Circuit found that U.S. Park Service regulations in force at the time did not prohibit the sleeping activities that were part of the demonstration (*Community for Creative Non-Violence v. Watt,* 670 F.2d 1213 (D.C. Cir. 1982)).

In light of the first event's success, CCNV planned a larger demonstration to commence on the first day of winter the following year: a 20-unit "tent city" housing 50 persons, to be called "Reaganville II," in Lafayette Park; and a 40-unit "tent city" housing 100 persons, to be called "Congressional Village," on the "Mall"—a strip of land running from the U.S. Capitol to the Lincoln Memorial.

Meanwhile, in response to the U.S. Court of Appeals' decision, the Park Service issued revised "anti-camping" regulations (47 Fed. Reg. 24,299–24,306 (1982)) that defined camping to include symbolic sleeping, such as CCNV had used in its 1981 demonstration, and prohibited such "camping." When CCNV applied for a permit for the new planned demonstration, the Park Service issued a permit authorizing the construction of tents in both locations but, citing the revised anti-camping regulations, it specifically denied permission for participants in the demonstration to sleep in the tents. CCNV then sued to prevent the Park Service from applying the revised regulations to the new planned demonstration. The U.S. District Court granted summary judgment for the Park Service but was reversed by the U.S. Court of Appeals, sitting *en banc,* in a 6 to 5 decision (*Community for Creative Non-Violence v. Watt,* 703 F.2d 586 (D.C. Cir. 1983)).

The *en banc* court noted that, under the Park Service's new regulations, "one's participation in a demonstration as a sleeper becomes impermissible 'camping' when it is done within any temporary structure erected as part of the demonstration" (703 F.2d at 589). This prohibition "will clearly affect expression [because] the sleeping proposed by CCNV is carefully designed to, and in fact will, express the demonstrators' message that homeless persons have nowhere else to go" (*Id.* at 592). Acknowledging that "sleeping will serve both an expressive and functional purpose" during the vigil (*Id.*, fn. 16), the court highlighted the demonstrators who "propose to sleep within the conspicuous context of two organized sites that create a backdrop—by the combined use of structures, explanatory signs, and verbal discourse—to ensure that the message sought to be sent will . . . be received" (*Id.* at 593).

Taking up the case on *certiorari,* the U.S. Supreme Court reversed the en banc appellate court, upholding the Park Service regulations "as applied to prohibit demonstrators from sleeping in Lafayette Park and the Mall in connection with a demonstration intended to call attention to the plight of the homeless" (*Clark v. Community for Creative Non-Violence, supra,* 468 U.S. at 289). In an opinion by Justice White, the Court majority assumed without deciding that the "overnight sleeping in conjunction with the demonstration is expressive conduct," as the Court of Appeals had held. The Park Service's ban on the overnight sleeping, or "camping," however, was a content-neutral rather than a content-based restriction (see Sec. C.4 above) on CCNV's expressive conduct: "The courts below accepted [this] view, and it is not disputed here that the prohibition on camping, and on sleeping specifically, is content-neutral and is not being applied because of disagreement with the message presented" (*Id.* at 295). The Court then used two different tests for determining the validity of the Park Service's content-neutral restriction on CCNV's speech: the "time, place, and manner" test (the Park Service regulation being "a limitation on the manner of demonstrating"); and the "*O'Brien* symbolic speech" test from *United States v. O'Brien,* 391 U.S. 367 (1968). (Both tests are further discussed in Section E.2 below.) Under both tests, the government had a "substantial interest in maintaining the parks in the heart of our Capital in an attractive and intact condition, readily available to the millions of people who wish to see and enjoy them by their presence" (*Id.* at 296). This government interest is a "neutral" interest, unrelated to the content of the regulated speech, under each of the tests. In applying each test, the Court accorded considerable deference to the judgment of the Park Service. Neither of these tests, the Court emphasized, "assign[s] to the judiciary the authority to replace the Park Service as the manager of the Nation's parks or endow[s] the judiciary with the competence to judge how much protection of park lands is wise and how that level of conservation is to be attained" (*Id.* at 299).

Justice Marshall, joined by Justice Brennan, vigorously dissented from the majority's opinion. The dissenters criticized the majority for avoiding any close examination of "the reality of [CCNV's] planned expression," thereby "denatur[ing] [CCNV's] asserted right and . . . mak[ing] all too easy [the] identification of a Government interest sufficient to warrant its abridgement" (*Id.* at 302, Marshall, J., dissenting).

Justice Marshall took a much more sympathetic view than the majority of the context, methods, and purposes of the planned demonstration, and a much less sympathetic view of the government's regulatory interests:

> Missing from the majority's description is any inkling that Lafayette Park and the Mall have served as the sites for some of the most rousing political demonstrations in the Nation's history . . . . [T]hese areas constitute, in the Government's words, "a fitting and powerful forum for political expression and political protest." Brief for Petitioners 11.
>
> The primary purpose for making sleep an integral part of the demonstration was "to re-enact the central reality of homelessness," Brief for Respondents 2, and to impress upon public consciousness, in as dramatic a way as possible, that homelessness is a widespread problem, often ignored, that confronts its victims with life-threatening deprivations. As one of the homeless men seeking to demonstrate explained: "Sleeping in Lafayette Park or on the Mall, for me, is to show people that conditions are so poor for the homeless and poor in this city that we would actually sleep outside in the winter to get the point across." *Id.* at 3.
>
> . . . . Here respondents clearly intended to protest the reality of homelessness by sleeping outdoors in the winter in the near vicinity of the magisterial residence of the President of the United States.

* * * *

According to the majority, the significant Government interest advanced by denying respondents' request to engage in sleep-speech is the interest in "maintaining the parks in the heart of our capital in an attractive and intact condition, readily available to the millions of people who wish to see and enjoy them by their presence." That interest is indeed significant. However, neither the Government nor the majority adequately explains how prohibiting respondents' planned activity will substantially further that interest.

* * * *

The majority cites no evidence indicating that sleeping engaged in as symbolic speech will cause substantial wear and tear on park property.... In short, there are no substantial Government interests advanced by the Government's regulations as applied to respondents. All that the Court's decision advances are the prerogatives of a bureaucracy that over the years has shown an implacable hostility toward citizens' exercise of First Amendment rights. [468 U.S. at 303–305, 308, 312 (footnotes omitted).]

Justice Marshall also joined issue with the majority regarding the level or degree of scrutiny that courts should apply to content-neutral restrictions on speech. This is a key concern in free speech law that has subsequently arisen in various court cases and scholarly commentaries. According to Justice Marshall, the majority applied the time, place, and manner test and the *O'Brien* test with so much deference to the government that its regulation in effect received only "a minimal level of scrutiny" rather than genuine intermediate scrutiny. This is problematic for free speech law because:

[C]ontent-neutral restrictions are also capable of unnecessarily restricting protected expressive activity.... The consistent imposition of silence upon all may fulfill the dictates of an evenhanded content-neutrality. But it offends our "profound national commitment to the principle that debate on public issues should be uninhibited, robust, and wide-open." [*Id.* at 313–314, Marshall, J., dissenting and quoting *New York Times v. Sullivan*, 376 U.S. 254, 270 (1964).]

Moreover, said Justice Marshall, the majority did not sufficiently take account of the dynamics of governmental regulations affecting freedom of expression, and thus accorded unjustifiable deference to the regulators:

[T]he disposition of this case reveals a mistaken assumption regarding the motives and behavior of government officials who create and administer content-neutral regulations. The Court's salutary skepticism of Governmental decisionmaking in First Amendment matters suddenly dissipates once it determines that a restriction is not content-based. The Court evidently assumes that the balance struck by officials is deserving of deference so long as it does not appear to be tainted by content discrimination. What the Court fails to recognize is that public officials have strong incentives to overregulate even in the absence of an intent to censor particular views. This incentive stems from the fact that of the two groups whose interests officials must accommodate — on the one hand, the interests of the general public and, on the other, the interests of those who seek to use a particular forum for First Amendment activity—the political power of the former is likely to be far greater than that of the latter. [468 U.S. at 314–315 (footnotes omitted).]

E.2. The Two Types of Standards for Content-Neutral Restrictions

There are two basic types of standards applicable to content-neutral restrictions on speech. Both are generally considered to provide a kind of intermediate scrutiny review, but there is continuing controversy over how strong this review actually turns out to be in particular cases (see, e.g., Justice Marshall's dissent in *Clark v. Community for Creative Non-Violence*, Sec. E.1 above).

The first type of standard is usually called the "time, place, and manner" standard, which is the standard that applies to government regulations of the time at which, place in which, or manner in which the speech is expressed. A leading case on content-neutral standards, subsequent to *Clark v. Community for Creative Non-Violence*, is *Ward v. Rock Against Racism*, 491 U.S. 781 (1989). At issue was a New York City regulation of the volume or noise level of music performed at a Bandshell in Central Park. After acknowledging that "[m]usic [is] a form of expression and communication…protected under the First Amendment" (491 U.S. at 790), the Court determined that New York's regulation of the music was a content-neutral restriction on the place and manner of speech. The Court then applied this standard of review to New York City's regulation:

> Our cases make clear…that even in a public forum, the government may impose reasonable restrictions on the time, place, or manner of protected speech, provided (1) that the restrictions "are justified without reference to the content of the regulated speech, (2) that they are (a) narrowly tailored to serve (b) a significant governmental interest, and (3) that they leave open ample alternative channels for communication of the information." [491 U.S. at 791 (numbering and lettering added), quoting *Clark v. Community for Creative Non-Violence*, 468 U.S. 288, 293 (1984).]

Holding that the New York City regulation met all three prongs of this test, the Court upheld the regulation's constitutionality. In so doing, it reversed the decision of the U.S. Court of Appeals, which had held that the noise regulation failed the narrow tailoring part of the second prong because "there were several alternative methods of achieving the desired end that would have been less restrictive of" the concert sponsor's "First Amendment rights" (*Id.* at 797). The U.S. Supreme Court rejected that interpretation of the second prong's narrow tailoring requirement:

> [W]e reaffirm today that a regulation of the time, place, or manner of protected speech must be narrowly tailored to serve the government's legitimate content-neutral interests but that it need not be the least restrictive or least intrusive means of doing so. Rather, the requirement of narrow tailoring is satisfied "so long as the…regulation promotes a substantial government interest that would be achieved less effectively absent the regulation." To be sure, this standard does not mean that a time, place, or manner regulation may burden substantially more speech than is necessary to further the government's legitimate interests.

Government may not regulate expression in such a manner that a substantial portion of the burden on speech does not serve to advance its goals. [491 U.S. at 799, quoting *United States v. Albertini*, 472 U.S. 675, 689 (1985).]

As they did in *Clark v. Community for Creative Non-Violence*, (Sec. E.1 above), Justices Marshall and Brennan dissented in *Ward*, this time joined by Justice Stevens (who had voted with the majority in *Clark*). Justice Marshall's dissenting opinion stated a view of the three-prong standard that was closer to the Court of Appeals' than the Supreme Court majority's, and developed themes about the Court's insufficiently rigorous review similar to those in his *Clark* dissent.

The second type of standard for content-neutral restrictions on speech is generally called the "*O'Brien* standard," after the case in which the standard was first articulated. In *United States v. O'Brien*, 391 U.S. 367 (1968), the Court upheld a provision of the Federal Draft Registration law that prohibited the burning of draft cards. The Court determined that this provision was content-neutral on its face. Then, in analyzing the provision's constitutionality under the free speech clause, the Court used this standard:

> [A] government regulation is sufficiently justified (1) if it is within the constitutional power of the Government; (2) if it furthers an important or substantial governmental interest; (3) if the governmental interest is unrelated to the suppression of free expression; and (4) if the incidental restriction on alleged First Amendment freedoms is no greater than is essential to the furtherance of that interest. [391 U.S. at 377 (numbering added).]

For both the *Clark/Ward* standard and the *O'Brien* standard, the question of the regulation's neutrality becomes a part of the standard itself. In *Ward*, the restriction must be "justified without reference to the content of the regulated speech." In *O'Brien*, the regulation must be "unrelated to the suppression of free expression." If a restriction on speech does not meet this neutrality part of the standard, a court should normally conclude that the restriction is content-based rather than content-neutral, and thus apply a strict scrutiny standard appropriate for the particular restriction at issue.

The Court has also confirmed that the *Clark/Ward* standard and *O'Brien* standard are similar in other respects beyond the neutrality requirement. Indeed, in *Clark v. Community for Creative Non-Violence* (Sec. E.1 above), the Court majority asserted that "the four-factor standard of *O'Brien*…in the last analysis is little, if any, different from the standard applied to time, place, or manner restrictions" (468 U.S. at 298). Even the dissenters agreed with this assessment (468 U.S. at 308 (Marshall, J., dissenting)). The Court in *Ward* subsequently re-affirmed this parallelism between the two standards (491 U.S. at 798). The similarity between the two standards does mean, however, that they are both equally applicable to all cases concerning content-neutral restraints. The Court's use of these standards over time in a range of cases suggests that the time, place, and manner standard is usually (but not always) preferred when the restraint on expression appears on the face of the regulation being challenged (as in *Ward*), while the *O'Brien* standard is usually (but not always) preferred when the regulation is neutral on its face and the restraint on expression occurs only with particular applications of the regulation (as in *O'Brien*). (For an example of this dichotomy, see the sexually explicit speech cases in Section D.5(2) above, in which the Court used the time, place, and manner standard for restrictions on adult movies (facial restraint on expression) and the *O'Brien* standard for restrictions on public nudity (neutral regulation) as applied to the expressive activity of nude dancing.)

Sec. F. The Varied Roles of Government Vis-à-Vis Free Expression

F.1. The Roles and Their Significance

In free expression cases, it is important to pay close attention to the role that government is playing with regard to the speech that is at issue. In most cases and problems, the government is acting as a *regulator* of private speech—that is, the speech of non-governmental individuals or entities. In this context, in regulating speech, government acts in its sovereign capacity. The principles set forth in Sections B through E of this Chapter apply primarily to situations where government acts as a *regulator* of private speech. Generally, the same principles that apply to government as a *regulator* of speech also apply when government *taxes* the speech of others. This problem arises most frequently when government imposes a tax on print publications; *see, e.g., Arkansas Writers' Project, Inc. v. Ragland,* 481 U.S. 221 (1987).

The regulator role (or taxation role), however, is not the only one that government may play in situations implicating the freedom of expression. There are examples in the case law of other governmental roles. Primary among them are: government as speaker; government as subsidizer; government as employer; and government as landowner, manager, or proprietor (all discussed in Sections F.2 to F.5 below). These other roles regarding speech involve considerations and principles quite different from those that apply when government is acting only as a *regulator* of private speech.

F.2. Government as Speaker

At the other extreme from government acting as *regulator* is the situation where government acts as a *speaker*. In this role, government has its own message to convey and takes steps to do so. When a government agency prepares and issues its own publication, for example, or a high-level government official issues a press release or holds a press conference on a current public issue, or a public school board approves curriculum for its public schools, the rules and principles that limit government as *regulator* do not apply. There is, for instance, no requirement that the government refrain from favoring or disfavoring a particular of viewpoint (see Sec. D.4 above). When government speaks itself by "transmit[ing] specific information pertaining to its own program...it is entitled to say what it wishes" (*Rosenberger v. Rectors and Visitors of University of Virginia,* 515 U.S. 819, 833 (1995). "[W]hen the State is the speaker, it may make content-based choices.... [W]e have permitted the government to regulate the content of what is or is not expressed when it is the speaker...." (*Id.* at 833).

There are, however, two major exceptions to the rule that government may say whatever it wishes when it is the speaker. First, the government as speaker may not coerce private persons into conveying its message. In *Wooley v. Maynard*, 430 U.S. 705 (1977), for example, the Court invalidated a New Hampshire statute that required motor vehicle owners to have license plates that displayed the state's motto, "Live Free or Die." The Court explained that "New Hampshire's statute in effect requires that [motorists] use their private property as a 'mobile billboard' for the State's ideological message— or suffer a penalty," and that where the State's interest is to communicate an "official view as to the proper appreciation of history, state pride, and individualization" or to disseminate any ideology,...such interest cannot outweigh an individual's First Amendment right to avoid becoming the courier for such a message" (430 U.S. at 715, 717). Second, the establishment clause of the First Amendment (see Chap. 13, Sec. B) prohibits government, as *speaker*, from making statements that support or endorse, or that inhibit or express hostility to, religion. *See, e.g., Santa Fe Independent School District v. Doe*, 530 U.S. 290 (2000).

F.3. Government as Subsidizer of Speech

Government may also act as a *subsidizer* of speech. Sometimes it may subsidize its own speech or message; at other times, it may subsidize the speech or messages of others. When government is subsidizing its own speech, it is still the government that is the *speaker*, and the rules that apply will be the same as in other situations where government *speaks* as government. In *Rust v. Sullivan*, 500 U.S. 173 (1991), for instance, Congress had authorized grants to public and nonprofit organizations for family planning services and required that project staff discourage resort to abortion as a method of family planning. The Court rejected a challenge to this requirement based on viewpoint discrimination because the federal government was subsidizing project staff to convey the government's own message. Thus, in *Rust*, the government had "disburse[d] public funds to private entities to convey a governmental message" and "used private speakers to transmit specific information pertaining to its own program"; it was therefore "entitled to say what it wishes" (*Rosenberger v. Rectors and Visitors of University of Virginia*, 515 U.S. 819, 833 (1995)).

In other situations, however, where government is subsidizing the speech or messages of others, constitutional principles will restrict the choices that government may make when deciding what private speech it will subsidize and what private speech it will not subsidize. In the *Rosenberger* case, for example, the University refused to subsidize religiously-oriented student publications but subsidized other student publications. The Court emphasized that "the University does not itself speak or subsidize transmittal of a message it favors but instead expends funds to encourage a diversity of views from private speakers" (515 U.S. at 834). In this context, the First Amendment limited the University in much the same way that it would if the University were a *regulator* of private speech. Invoking the public forum doctrine (Sec. F.5 below) and the viewpoint neutrality principle (Sec. D.4 above), the Court majority held that the University's refusal to subsidize a religious publication because of its religious viewpoints violated the free speech and press rights of the publication's editors.

In a later subsidy case, *Legal Services Corp. v. Velazquez*, 531 U.S. 533 (2001), the Court struggled to determine whether *Rust* (above) or *Rosenberger* (above) was the appropriate precedent to apply. The case concerned a funding condition imposed by Congress on grants for legal services under the Legal Services Corporation Act (42 U.S.C. § 2996 *et. seq.*), specifically, that grantees could not use LSC funds to amend or challenge the validity of welfare laws. The plaintiffs sought to use *Rosenberger* as the governing precedent that served to invalidate the funding condition; the government sought to use *Rust* to uphold the condition. In a 5 to 4 decision, the Court's majority sided with the plaintiffs. The Court agreed that the program at issue was unlike *Rosenberger* in that "its purpose is not to 'encourage a diversity of views;'" but on "a more salient point" the LSC program was like the *Rosenberger* subsidy program because it "was designed to facilitate private speech, not to promote a governmental message." The private speech was the "advice from the attorney to the client and the advocacy by the attorney to the courts." This speech "cannot be classified as government speech," according to the majority, because "[t]he lawyer is not the government's speaker.... The LSC lawyer...speaks on the behalf of his or her private, indigent client." The free speech clause therefore restricted the government's choices of what speech to subsidize, and Congress was subject to the more stringent requirements akin to those applicable to a *regulator* of private speech. Congress' funding condition regarding welfare laws was invalid because it was inconsistent with the requirement that governmental funding conditions regarding private speech "cannot be aimed at the suppression of ideas thought inimical to the Government's own interest." *Velazquez*, 531 U.S. at 542, 549.

F.4.   Government as Employer

In yet other free speech situations, government will be in the role of *employer*. In this situation, government will sometimes act as a *regulator* of speech, but it is regulating only the speech of its own employees, not the speech of citizens generally. In this arena, government has somewhat more freedom to impose content-based restrictions on speech than would be the case if government were acting in its sovereign capacity to regulate the speech of citizens generally. If the employee speech that government is regulating is speech "on a matter of public concern," the employee may have a substantial level of protection under the First Amendment—depending on the extent to which the speech interferes with the legitimate workplace interests of the government as employer. *See, e.g., Pickering v. Board of Education*, 391 U.S. 563 (1968). If the employee's speech is not on a matter of public concern—that is, the speech is on a matter of only private concern—the employee receives virtually no protection under the free speech and press clauses. *See, e.g., Connick v. Myers*, 461 U.S. 138 (1983). Predictably, the distinction between the two types of speech has been difficult to make. In *Waters v. Churchill*, 511 U.S. 661 (1994), the U.S. Supreme Court indicated that it would give considerable deference to the government-employer's reasonable beliefs concerning the content of the employee's speech and to its reasonable prediction of the disruptiveness of the employee's speech — thus diluting to some extent the protections for employees originally established in *Pickering*.[5]

F.5.   Government As Landowner: The Special Problem of the "Public Forum"

Government may also play the role of *landowner, proprietor,* or *manager* of the property on which speech activity takes place. In this situation, government will sometimes also be a *regulator* of speech (see Sec. F.1 above), since it may decide to regulate private speech that is taking place on its own property. Government may also be a *subsidizer* of speech (see Sec. F.3 above) in this situation, since it may be using its own property to subsidize the private speech of others. Rather than "subsidiz[ing] transmittal of a message it favors," however, government may be using its property "to encourage a diversity of views from private speakers" (*Rosenberger v. Rectors and Visitors of University of Virginia*, 515 U.S. 819, 834 (1995)). To account for this overlapping of roles, the U.S. Supreme Court has created the concept of the "public forum" and a doctrine called "the public forum doctrine."

"Public forum" issues arise (or may arise) when speech activities take place on government property, or, more particularly, when a government regulates speech activities that take place on its own property. The "public forum doctrine" is intended to help resolve these types of issues. The general questions addressed by the public forum doctrine are (1) whether a government's status as *owner, proprietor,* or *manager* affords it additional legal rationales (beyond traditional rationales such as incitement, fighting words, obscenity, or defamation) for regulating speech that occurs on its own property; and (2) whether the free speech rights of the speaker may vary depending on the *character* of the government property on which the speech activity occurs. In other words, can government regulate speech on its own property that it could not regulate elsewhere and, if so, does the constitutionality of such speech regulations depend on the character of the government property at issue? These questions are sometimes framed as *access* questions: to what extent do individuals have a First Amendment *right of access* to government property for purposes of expressive activity?

The first case to recognize a speaker's right of access to government property was *Hague v. Committee for Industrial Organization*, 307 U.S. 496 (1939). There a plurality of the Court characterized "streets and parks" as property that has "been held in trust for the use of the public and, time out of mind, [has] been used for purposes of assembly, communicating thoughts between citizens, and discussing public questions" (307 U.S. at 515). Public streets and parks are therefore "public forums" that must remain available for expressive activities. Since *Hague*, the Court has decided numerous cases that have further developed the "public forum doctrine" and expanded the types of government property that courts will characterize as "public forum" property that

---

5. The same principles, and the same level of protection, apply to governmental regulation of the speech of government contractors; *see Board of County Commissioners v. Umbehr*, 518 U.S. 668 (1996).

is open to speakers for expressive activities. At the same time, the Court has made clear that governments do have additional rationales for regulating speech on their own property, and that the applicability of these rationales will depend on the character and uses of the property at issue.

The basic question is whether the property is "forum" property; some, but not all, government property will fit this characterization. The cases reveal three categories of forum property: (a) the "traditional" public forum; (b) the "designated" public forum; and (c) the "nonpublic" forum. *See generally Perry Education Association v. Perry Local Educators' Association*, 460 U.S. 37, 44–46 (1983); *Cornelius v. NAACP Legal Defense and Education Fund*, 473 U.S. 788, 800–802 (1985); *Arkansas Educational Television Comm'n v. Forbes*, 523 U.S. 666, 677–678 (1998). Government property that does not fall into any of these three categories is considered to be "non-forum" property, that is, "not a forum at all" (*Arkansas Educational Television Comm'n*, 523 U.S. at 678). For such property, the government, in its capacity as owner, proprietor, or manager, may exclude all private speech activities from the property and preserve the property solely for its intended governmental purposes.

Consistent with the *Hague* case, courts consider streets and parks, as well as sidewalks and town squares, to be traditional public forums. A traditional public forum is generally open to all persons to speak on any subjects of their choice. The government may impose restrictions regarding the time, place, or manner of the expressive activity in a public forum, so long as the restrictions are content-neutral and otherwise meet the requirements for such regulations (see Sec. E above). But the government cannot exclude a speaker from the forum based on content or otherwise regulate the content of forum speech unless the exclusion or regulation "is necessary to serve a compelling state interest and…is narrowly drawn to achieve that interest" (*Arkansas Educational Television Comm'n*, 523 U.S. at 677, quoting *Cornelius*, 473 U.S. at 800). The traditional public forum category may also include a sub-category called "new forum" property or (ironically) "nontraditional forum" property that, according to some Justices, encompasses property that is the functional equivalent of, or a modern analogue to, traditional forum property. *See especially International Society for Krishna Consciousness, Inc. v. Lee*, 505 U.S. 672, 697–699 (Kennedy, J., concurring in the judgment).

A designated public forum, in contrast to a traditional public forum, is government property that the government has, by its own intentional action, designated to serve the purposes of a public forum. Designated forum property may be land or buildings that provide physical space for speech activities, but it also may include different forms of property, such as bulletin boards, space in print publications, or (as in *Rosenberger*, above) even a student activities fund that a university uses to subsidize expressive activities of student groups. A designated forum may be just as open as a traditional forum, or access may be limited to certain classes of speakers (*e.g.*, students at a public university) or to certain classes of subject matter (*e.g.*, curriculum-related or course-related subjects). The latter type of designated forum is called a "limited forum" or a "limited designated forum." Thus, unlike traditional public forums, which must remain open to all, governments retain the choice of whether to open or close a designated forum as well as the choice of whether to limit the classes of speakers or classes of topics for the forum. However, for speakers who fall within the classes of speakers and topics for which the forum is designated, the constitutional rules are the same as for a traditional forum. Government may impose content-neutral time, place, and manner requirements on the speaker but may not regulate the content of the speech (beyond the original designation of permissible topics) unless it meets the strict scrutiny standard. In addition, if government does limit the forum by designating permissible classes of speakers and topics, its distinction between the classes must be "reasonable in light of the purpose served by the forum" (*Cornelius*, 473 U.S. at 806) and must also be viewpoint neutral (*Rosenberger*, 515 U.S. at 829-830); *see generally Good News Club v. Milford Central School*, 533 U.S. 98, 106–107 (2001). As the Court further explained in *Rosenberger*: "In determining whether the...exclusion of a class of speech is legitimate, we have observed a distinction between...content discrimination, which may be permissible...and viewpoint discrimination, which is presumed impermissible when directed against speech otherwise within the forum's limitations" (515 U.S. at 829–830). (See Sec. D.4 above regarding viewpoint discrimination.)

A non-public forum, in contrast to a traditional or designated forum, is open neither to persons in general nor to particular classes of speakers. It is open only on a selective basis for individual speakers. In other words, "the government allows selective access for individual speakers rather than general access for a class of speakers" (*Arkansas Educational Television Commission v. Forbes*, 523 U.S. 666 (1998)). Governments have more rationales for prohibiting or regulating speech activities in non-public forums, and governmental authority to exclude or regulate speakers is correspondingly greater, than is the case for traditional and designated forums. In *International Society for Krishna Consciousness v. Lee*, 505 U.S. 672 (1992), for example, the Court held the interior public areas of an airport terminal to be a non-public forum, thus according the airport authority considerable discretion to regulate soliciting in these areas. A reasonableness requirement and the viewpoint neutrality requirement, however, do limit government's discretion in selecting individual speakers and regulating their speech in a nonpublic forum. The constitutional requirements for a nonpublic forum, therefore, are similar to the requirements that apply to the government's designation of classes of speakers and topics for a limited designated forum. The nonpublic forum, however is not subject to the additional strict scrutiny requirements that apply to a limited designated forum when government regulates the speech of persons who fall within classes designated for the forum.

Sec. G. Freedom of Association

Although the First Amendment's text does not explicitly recognize a right to freedom of association, the U.S. Supreme Court has nevertheless found the right "to be implicit in the freedoms of speech, assembly, and petition" (*Healy v. James*, 408 U.S. 169, 181 (1972)). To protect these express rights, individuals must also have a right to associate with others of similar persuasion for the purpose of advancing their beliefs. The Court has recognized, for instance, that "[e]ffective advocacy of both public and private points of view, particularly controversial ones, is undeniably enhanced by group association" (*NAACP v. Alabama*, 357 U.S. 449, 460 (1958)). Applying this principle in *NAACP v. Button*, 371 U.S. 415 (1963), the Court held that the NAACP's practice of assisting in litigation which furthers the objectives of their group is a protected form of political association.

This First Amendment right is now generally called the "freedom of expressive association" to distinguish it from the "freedom of intimate association," a substantive due process concept applicable to certain types of highly intimate human relationships. As the Court explained this distinction in *Roberts v. U.S. Jaycees*, 468 U.S. 609 (1984):

> Our decisions have referred to constitutionally protected "freedom of association" in two distinct senses. In one line of decisions, the Court has concluded that choices to enter into and maintain certain intimate human relationships must be secured against undue intrusion by the State because of the role of such relationships in safeguarding the individual freedom that is central to our constitutional scheme. In this respect, freedom of association receives protection as a fundamental element of personal liberty. In another set of decisions, the Court has recognized a right to associate for the purpose of engaging in those activities protected by the First Amendment — speech, assembly, petition for the redress of grievances, and the exercise of religion. The Constitution guarantees freedom of association of this kind as an indispensable means of preserving other individual liberties. [468 U.S. at 617–618.]

This right of expressive association is an implied right, or a "correlative" right, under the First Amendment:

> An individual's freedom to speak, to worship, and to petition the government for the redress of grievances could not be vigorously protected from interference by the State unless a correlative freedom to engage in group effort toward those ends were not also guaranteed.... According protection to collective effort on behalf of shared goals is especially important in preserving political and cultural diversity and in shielding dissident expression from suppression by the majority.... Consequently, we have long understood as implicit in the right to engage in activities protected by the First Amendment a corresponding right to associate with others in pursuit of a wide variety of political, social, economic, educational, religious, and cultural ends.... Freedom of association therefore plainly presupposes a freedom not to associate. [468 U.S. at 622–23.]

The case of *Boy Scouts of America v. Dale*, 530 U.S. 640 (2000), illustrates the freedom of expressive association and the problems that can arise in determining when this right has been violated. James Dale had joined Monmouth Council's Cub Scouts in 1978 at the age of eight, advancing to Boy Scouts in 1981, and remaining a member until age 18. He was an exemplary scout, earning 25 merit badges, admission to the Order of the Arrow, and the rank of Eagle Scout (achieved by only three percent of all scouts). He applied for adult membership in the organization in 1989 and was appointed as an assistant scoutmaster. He began attending Rutgers University around the same time and, while there, Dale "came out," acknowledging to himself and others that he is gay. He became involved in the Rutgers University Lesbian/Gay Alliance, eventually becoming co-president. While attending a seminar addressing the health needs of gay teens in 1990, Dale was interviewed by a newspaper, which later published the interview along with Dale's photograph and a caption identifying his position in the Lesbian/Gay Alliance. Within the month, Dale received a letter from a Monmouth Council executive revoking his adult membership. When Dale wrote requesting the reason for the revocation, he received a response stating that the Boy Scouts "specifically forbid membership to homosexuals."

Dale sued the Boy Scouts, alleging that the organization had violated New Jersey's public accommodations law when it revoked Dale's membership based solely on his sexual orientation. The public accommodations law (N.J. Stat. Ann. § 10:5–4 (West Supp. 2000)) prohibits discrimination on the basis of several traits, including sexual orientation, with respect to the "privileges of any place of public accommodation." New Jersey's highest Court held that the Boy Scouts was a place of public accommodation subject to the statute, and that the organization had violated the statute's non-discrimination provision when it revoked Dale's membership.

The Boy Scouts had defended in part on grounds that application of the state law violated the organization's constitutional right "to enter into and maintain . . . intimate or private relationships . . . [and] to associate for the purpose of engaging in protected speech" (530 U.S. at 646, quoting *Rotary International v. Rotary Club of Duarte*, 481 U.S. 537, 544 (1987)). The New Jersey Supreme Court rejected this defense, holding that Dale's inclusion would not significantly affect the members' ability to carry out their purposes, and that the state has a compelling interest in eliminating discrimination through its public accommodations law.

The U.S. Supreme Court reversed by a 5 to 4 vote, ruling that Dale's forced inclusion in the organization violated the Boy Scouts' First Amendment freedom of association. Writing for the majority, Chief Justice Rehnquist recognized that the right to associate "is crucial in preventing the majority from imposing its views on groups that would rather express other, perhaps unpopular, ideas" (530 U.S. at 647, quoting *Roberts v. Jaycees*, 468 U.S. 609, 622 (1984)), and that "the forced inclusion of an unwanted person in a group infringes the group's freedom of expressive association if the presence of that person affects in a significant way the group's ability to advocate public or private viewpoints" (530 U.S. at 648). This freedom "is not absolute," however, and may "be overridden 'by regulations adopted to serve compelling state interests, unrelated to suppression of ideas, that cannot be achieved through means significantly less restrictive of associational freedoms'" (530 U.S. at 648, quoting *Roberts*, 468 U.S. at 623)).

To determine whether the Boy Scouts was engaged in expressive association, the Court reviewed the organization's mission statement and the Scout Oath and Law. The former cites the group's purpose as "helping to instill values" in youth and "preparing them to make ethical choices," while the latter includes language on the Scout's obligation to be "morally straight" and "clean." The Court concluded that it was "indisputable that an association that seeks to transmit such a system of values engages in expressive activity" (530 U.S. at 650). The Court also made clear that "the First Amendment...does not require that every member of a group agree on every issue in order for the group's policy to be 'expressive association'" and that it "is sufficient for First Amendment purposes" that the group professes an official position (530 U.S. at 656).

The Court then turned to the question "whether forced inclusion of Dale as an assistant scoutmaster would significantly affect the Boy Scouts' ability to advocate public or private viewpoints" (530 U.S. at 650). Focusing on the Boy Scouts' views on homosexuality, the Court accepted the organization's assertion that "homosexual conduct is inconsistent...particularly with the values represented by the terms 'morally straight' and 'clean'" (*Id.*). In so doing, the Court cautioned that "it is not the role of the courts to reject a group's expressed values because they disagree with those values or find them internally inconsistent" (530 U.S. at 651).

The Court next asked "whether Dale's presence as an assistant scoutmaster would significantly burden the Boy Scouts' choice to avoid 'promot[ing] homosexual conduct as a legitimate form of behavior'" (530 U.S. at 653). Giving deference to the "association's view of what would impair its expression," and noting that "Dale was the co-president of a gay and lesbian organization at college and remains a gay rights activist," the Court determined that "Dale's presence in the Boy Scouts would, at the very least, force the organization to send a message, both to the youth members and to the world, that the Boy Scouts accepts homosexual conduct as a legitimate form of behavior" (530 U.S. at 653). Thus, accepting "Dale as an assistant scoutmaster would...surely interfere with the Boy Scouts' choice not to propound a point of view contrary to its beliefs" (530 U.S. at 654).

Having determined that the BSA engages in expressive association and that Dale's membership "would significantly affect its expression," the Court then inquired whether application of New Jersey's public accommodations law to force Dale's inclusion infringes the organization's freedom of expressive association. The Court distinguished *Roberts* and *Rotary International v. Rotary Club of Duarte*, 481 U.S. 537 (1987), two earlier cases in which a state public accommodation statute had survived freedom of association challenges, arguing that "enforcement of [the statutes in those cases] would not materially interfere with the ideas that the organization sought to express" (530 U.S. at 657).

Then, considering New Jersey's asserted justification for its public accommodations law, the Court brusquely concluded that "the state interests embodied in New Jersey's public accommodations law do not justify such a severe intrusion on the Boy Scouts' right to freedom of expressive association," in particular "the organization's right to oppose or disfavor homosexual conduct" (530 U.S. at 659).

Four Justices strenuously dissented, disagreeing especially with the majority's conclusion that reinstating Dale as a member would seriously burden the Boy Scouts' ability to express its message. Justice Stevens, for instance, argued that the Boy Scouts had never clarified "why the presence of homosexuals would affect its expressive activities..." and had not made its view of "morally straight" and "clean"...a part of the values actually instilled in Scouts through the Handbook, lessons, or otherwise" (530 U.S. at 678). The New Jersey law therefore does not "impose any serious burdens" on the BSA's "collective effort on behalf of [its] shared goals" (530 U.S. at 664, quoting *Roberts v. Jaycees*, 468 U.S. at 622).

Similarly, Justice Souter concluded that:

> BSA has not made out an expressive association claim … because of its failure to make sexual orientation the subject of any unequivocal advocacy, using the channels it customarily employs to state its message. As Justice Stevens explains, no group can claim a right of expressive association without identifying a clear position to be advocated over time in an unequivocal way. To require less, and to allow exemption from a public accommodations statute based on any individual's difference from an alleged group ideal, however expressed and however inconsistently claimed, would convert the right of expressive association into an easy trump of any anti-discrimination law. [530 U.S. at 701–702.][6]

Sec. H. Study Suggestions

The U.S. Supreme Court's opinions on freedom of expression, and the scholarly commentary on the Court's opinions, raise numerous questions on several levels. So much is at work that it becomes a challenge even to organize your thinking or to keep track of what is most important. Here are three suggested targets for your attention — three questions for which you can seek answers in the totality of materials you study as well as in each case you read. First, what are the roles or functions that freedom of expression serves in American society? A general understanding of these functions will help you work more sensitively with the various concepts the courts have constructed in this area of law. Second, how do courts and other decisionmakers interpret the words of the free speech and press clauses? Consideration of the textual, historical, and values approaches (see Chap. 2, Sec. F.4, Chap. 4, Sec. C.2, and Chap. 9, Sec. B.2), as applied to these two clauses, will help you better understand the interpretive process and its difficulties. Third, what analytical techniques have the courts developed for the resolution of concrete speech and press issues? An ability to identify and apply the various techniques outlined in Section C above will help you organize this massive field. These analytical techniques are useful guides both for understanding and evaluating judicial opinions and for analyzing new free expression problems. Thus, for each case

---

6. Because of the position that the Boy Scouts had taken in this litigation, there was a possibility that local public schools, and other places where the scouts held their meetings, would withdraw their permission for the scouts to use their property. Congress sought to guard against this possibility by passing the Boy Scouts of America Equal Access Act, 20 U.S.C. §7905. The Act applies to public elementary and secondary schools that receive federal funds, prohibiting them, under certain circumstances, from denying "equal access or a fair opportunity to meet" to Boy Scout groups and other specified youth groups.

your read, attempt to identify the particular technique(s) used to resolve each issue in the case; and for any free expression problem you work on, attempt to identify which technique(s) can be usefully applied in developing each part of your analysis.

FOR FURTHER READING: (1) Dean Alfange, Jr., "Free Speech and Symbolic Conduct: The Draft-Card Burning Case," 1968 Sup. Ct. Rev. 1. (2) Daniel Farber, The First Amendment, chs. 1–12 (2nd ed. 2003). (3) Marjorie Heins, "Viewpoint Discrimination," 24 Hastings Const. L. Q. 99 (1996). (4) Melville Nimmer, "Is Freedom of Press a Redundancy: What Does it Add to Freedom of Speech?" 26 Hastings L.J. 639 (1975). (5) Robert O'Neil, The First Amendment and Civil Liability (Indiana U. Press, 2001). (6) Geoffrey Stone, "Content-Neutral Restrictions," 54 U. Chi. L. Rev. 46 (1987).

Chapter 13

Freedom of Religion

Sec. A. Protecting Freedom of Religion: An Overview

As noted in Chapter 12, Section A, the First Amendment has two religion clauses, the establishment clause and the free exercise clause. The first clause is discussed in Section B below; the second is discussed in Section C below. Each clause protects certain aspects of religious freedom, as discussed below, and the two clauses are often complementary to one another, as must have been the framers' intention. Sometimes, however, the clauses seem to be in tension with one another, and courts must consider whether to elevate free exercise values over anti-establishment values, or vice versa, in a given case. This problem is discussed in Section D below.

The U.S. Supreme Court has acknowledged that the establishment clause and free exercise clause "may in certain instances overlap," but has also emphasized that the two clauses "forbid two quite different kinds of governmental encroachment upon religious freedom" (*Engel v. Vitale*, 370 U.S. 421, 430 (1962)). One major difference is that:

> The Establishment Clause, unlike the Free Exercise Clause, does not depend upon any showing of direct governmental compulsion and is violated by the enactment of laws which establish an official religion whether those laws operate directly to coerce non-observing individuals or not. [*Engel*, 370 U.S. at 430.]

The common objective of the two clauses is government neutrality toward religion, but they pursue this objective in quite different ways:

> The wholesome "neutrality" of which this Court's cases speak...stems from a recognition of the teaching of history that powerful sects or groups might bring about a fusion of governmental and religious functions or a concert or dependency of one upon the other to the end that official support of the state or federal government would be placed behind the tenets of one or of all orthodoxies. This the establishment clause prohibits. And a further reason for neutrality is found in the free exercise clause, which recognizes the value of religious training, teaching, and observance and, more particularly, the right of every person to freely choose his own course with reference thereto, free of

any compulsion from the state. This the free exercise clause guarantees.... The distinction between the two clauses is apparent—a violation of the free exercise clause is predicated on coercion, whereas the establishment clause violation need not be so attended. [*Abington School District v. Schempp*, 374 U.S. 203, 223–223 (1963).]

The two religion clauses are not the only sources of constitutional protection for freedom of religion. For many years, the U.S. Supreme Court has also used the free speech clause to protect religious freedom. In *Cantwell v. Connecticut*, 310 U.S. 296 (1940), for example, the Court used the free speech clause to protect a Jehovah's Witness who was proselytizing on the streets of a Connecticut city. In *Kunz v. New York*, 340 U.S. 290 (1951), the Court used the free speech clause to protect a Baptist minister who was holding public worship meetings in New York City streets. In *West Virginia State Board of Education v. Barnette*, 319 U.S. 624 (1943), the Court used the free speech clause to protect school children who were Jehovah's Witnesses from being compelled to salute the flag: "[N]o official, high or petty, can prescribe what shall be orthodox in politics, nationalism, *religion*, or other matters of opinion or force citizens to confess by word or act their faith therein" (319 U.S. at 642 (emphasis added)).

In more recent years, the Court has also protected religious adherents under the free speech clause even when government has argued that according them free speech rights would impinge upon anti-establishment values. In *Widmar v. Vincent*, 454 U.S. 263 (1981), for example, the question was whether a student religious group at a large public university could hold their meeting in campus facilities generally open to other student groups. The students claimed that their religious worship was expressive activity and that they had a free speech right of access to the university's facilities to engage in this expressive activity. The university claimed that allowing their facilities to be used for religious worship would constitute government support for religion. The Court sided with the students, holding that exclusion of their group from the facilities violated their free speech rights (see Chap. 12, Sec. F.5) and that the university's provision of the facilities to the religious group—in common with other student groups—would not violate the establishment clause.[1]

In addition to the establishment, free exercise, and free speech clauses, there is an implied right of *religious* association under the First Amendment that protects the freedom of believers to join together in furtherance of their religious beliefs and practices. As the Court remarked in *Roberts v. U.S. Jaycees*, 468 U.S. 609, 622 (1984): "An individual's freedom to...worship...could not be vigorously protected from interference by the State unless a correlative freedom to engage in group effort toward those ends were not also guaranteed.... Consequently, we have long understood as implicit in the

---

1. For later U.S. Supreme Court cases with similar reasoning and the same result, see *Rosenberger v. Rector and Visitors of the University of Virginia*, 515 U.S. 819 (1995), discussed in Chapter 12, Section F.5, and *Good News Club v. Milford Central School*, 533 U.S. 98 (2001), discussed in Chapter 12, Section D.4. For an example of a case that reaches the opposite result, rejecting the free speech claim and upholding the establishment clause claim, *see Lassonde v. Pleasonton Unified School District*, 320 F.3d 979 (9th Cir. 2003).

right to engage in activities protected by the First Amendment a corresponding right to associate with others in pursuit of…religious…ends." Depending on the circumstances, group religious activity could also be protected by the implied freedom of *expressive* association under the First Amendment or the implied right of *intimate* association under the Fourteenth Amendment (see Chap. 12, Sec. G). In addition, the equal protection clause of the Fourteenth Amendment protects against discrimination on grounds of religion. Either religion would be considered a suspect classification or freedom of religion would be considered a fundamental interest for equal protection purposes, thus resulting in strict scrutiny of the classification.

Finally, Article VI, paragraph 3, of the U.S. Constitution protects the religious freedom of persons holding or seeking offices in the federal government by providing that "[N]o religious Test shall ever be required as a Qualification to any Office or public Trust under the United States."

Sec. B. The Establishment Clause: A Conceptual Overview

B.1. In General

The establishment clause is different from the other individual rights clauses in the Constitution. It does not create personal rights in the sense that other clauses do. It does not focus on governmental infringements upon the personal liberties of particular individuals, as does the equal protection clause, or the free speech clause, or even the free exercise clause. In contrast, the establishment clause is a general prohibition on church-state involvement one with the other. The underlying rationale apparently is that such involvement damages our system of government in the long run and thus damages us collectively rather than as particular individuals. Any taxpayer, in fact, can raise an establishment clause claim concerning the expenditure of government funds. *See Flast v. Cohen*, 392 U.S. 83 (1968).

In order for the establishment clause to apply, government must have involved itself with an activity, organization, or viewpoint that is considered "religious." Government, in other words, must be involved in "religion" as that term is used in the First Amendment. *See generally* Lee Stang, "The Meaning of 'Religion' in the First Amendment," 40 Duquesne L. Rev. 181, 200–210 (2002). Most cases concern generally recognized religions that concededly fit within the First Amendment. But occasionally the lower courts have confronted issues concerning the character of an organization or activity with which government has become involved. In *Malnak v. Yogi*, 592 F. 2d 197 (3d Cir. 1979), for example, five public high schools offered an elective course in transcendental meditation. The court determined that transcendental meditation is a religion within the meaning of the First Amendment and that the schools' offering of the courses violated the establishment clause. Similarly, in *Warner v. Orange County Department of Probation*, 115 F. 3d 1068 (2nd Cir. 1997), *reaffirmed after remand*, 173 F. 3d 120 (2nd Cir. 1999), the court determined that Alcoholics Anonymous is a religion for purposes of the First Amendment because the A.A. program has "a substantial religious component" and A.A. meetings included religious activities. The county's requirement that the plaintiff attend A.A. meetings as a condition of his probation therefore violated the establishment clause. On the other hand, in *Smith v. Board of School Commissioners*, 827 F. 2d 684 (11th Cir. 1987), the court reversed a district court decision that "secular humanism" was a religion for First Amendment purposes; without directly ruling on this question, the appellate court rejected an establishment clause challenge to the textbooks used in the public schools of Mobile County, Alabama.

As its text reveals, the establishment clause is not simply concerned with laws that establish a religion but with any law "respecting an establishment of religion." In effect, this has come to mean any law that tends in some significant way toward the establishment of a religion. In an early case, *Everson v. Board of Education*, 330 U.S. 1 (1947), the U.S. Supreme Court explained the non-establishment concept as follows:

> The "establishment of religion" clause of the First Amendment means at least this: Neither a state nor the Federal Government can set up a church. Neither can pass laws which aid one religion, aid all religions, or prefer one religion over another.... No tax in any amount, large or small, can be levied to support any religious activities or institutions, whatever they may be called, or whatever form they may adopt to teach or practice religion. Neither a state nor the Federal Government can, openly or secretly, participate in the affairs of any religious organizations or groups and *vice versa*. [330 U.S. at 15–16.]

Typically, the metaphor of a "wall of separation" has been used to portray the establishment clause's prohibition on state involvement with religion. The phrase was penned by Thomas Jefferson and appears in his letter of January 1, 1802, to the Danbury Baptist Association in which Jefferson extols the virtues of the establishment clause (*see Reynolds v. United States*, 98 U.S. 145, 164 (1878)). In *Everson*, the Court used Jefferson's metaphor to support its view of church-state separation: "In the words of Jefferson, the clause against establishment of religion by law was intended to erect 'a wall of separation between church and State'" (330 U.S. at 16, quoting *Reynolds* at 164).

Over the years, the Supreme Court has often confirmed the existence of this separation principle. But persistent questions remain concerning the strictness of the church/state separation that the establishment clause demands. Is there flexibility in the separation principle that would allow some interactions between government and religion? If so, in what circumstances and to what extent would such accommodations to religion be permissible? How clear, and how workable, is the "line" that divides permissible from impermissible interaction with or accommodation to religion?

Establishment clause issues — issues concerning the application of the separation principle — may arise whenever government has allegedly supported or sponsored religious activity. There are two primary situations in which this problem of government support or sponsorship has been brought to court: (1) situations involving religious exercises, symbols, and displays; and (2) situations involving government aid for private religious activities or organizations. Almost all of the Supreme Court's establishment clause cases can be divided into two categories of cases encompassing these two situations. The first category is discussed in Section B.2 below, and the second category is discussed in Section B.3.

B.2. Religious Exercises, Symbols, and Displays

The first category of establishment clause cases includes the cases on religious symbols or displays that are placed on government property and religious exercises that are part of a government program. This type of problem is exemplified by the school prayer cases (*e.g., Wallace v. Jaffree*, 472 U.S. 38 (1985)) and the cases about Nativity scenes or other religious holiday displays on public property (*e.g., Allegheny County v. Greater Pittsburgh ACLU*, 492 U.S. 573 (1989)). The general question in such cases is whether there is government sponsorship of the religious viewpoint or religious practice that is suggested by the exercise, display, or symbol. *Engel v. Vitale*, 370 U.S. 421 (1962), the first of the U.S. Supreme Court's cases on prayer in public schools, provides a classic example.

In *Engel*, the New York State Board of Regents (the head of the state's education system) had composed a prayer and had recommended to local school districts that their students recite the prayer at the beginning of the school day. The Regents Prayer was as follows: "Almighty God, we acknowledge our dependence upon Thee, and we beg Thy blessings upon us, our parents, our teachers, and our Country" (as quoted by the Court at 370 U.S. at 422). The local school board of a school district in New Hyde Park, New York, adopting the Board of Regents' recommendation, directed that the prayer be recited in each classroom at the start of each school day. The parents of ten students then sued the school district in state court, challenging the constitutionality of both the state laws authorizing the Regents Prayer and the school district's regulation directing the recitation of the prayer. The New York courts upheld the validity of the Regents Prayer, largely because they deemed it consistent with our "spiritual heritage." The U.S. Supreme Court reversed and ruled that the Regents Prayer violated the establishment clause.

The Supreme Court emphasized the religious nature of the Regents Prayer and its recitation: "There can, of course, be no doubt that New York's program of daily classroom invocation of God's blessings as prescribed in the Regent's Prayer is a religious activity. It is a solemn avowal of divine faith and supplication for the blessings of the Almighty" (370 U.S. at 424). The Court then reasoned that government sponsorship of such a religious activity violated the establishment clause:

> [P]etitioners argue [that] the State's use of the Regents' prayer in its public school system breaches the constitutional wall of separation between Church and State. We agree with that contention since we think that the constitutional prohibition against laws respecting an establishment of religion must at least mean that in this country it is no part of the business of government to compose official prayers for any group of the American people to recite as a part of a religious program carried on by government. [370 U.S. at 425.]

It did not matter that the prayer was nondenominational, or that recitation was voluntary:

> Neither the fact that the prayer may be denominationally neutral nor the fact that its observance on the part of the students is voluntary can serve to free it from the limitations of the Establishment Clause, as it might from the Free Exercise Clause, of the First Amendment. [370 U.S. at 430.]

The Court did, however, seek to limit the scope of its ruling by stating that it would not apply to "patriotic or ceremonial occasions" in the schools that include reference to the Deity or to religious faith:

> There is of course nothing in the decision reached here that is inconsistent with the fact that school children and others are officially encouraged to express love for our country by reciting historical documents such as the Declaration of Independence which contain references to the Deity or by singing officially espoused anthems which include the composer's professions of faith in a Supreme Being, or with the fact that there are many manifestations in our public life of belief in God. [370 U.S. at 435 fn. 21.]

Similar cautionary words have continued to appear over the years in dicta, and in concurring and dissenting opinions, in Supreme Court establishment clause cases. This matter is discussed in Section B.4(6) below.

In cases after *Engel v. Vitale*, the Court applied and extended its ruling to invalidate other prayer and prayer-related activities in public schools. In *Abington School District v. Schempp*, 374 U.S. 203 (1963), for instance, the Court invalidated a Bible-reading exercise; in *Wallace v. Jaffree*, 472 U.S. 38 (1985), it invalidated a state "moment of silence" designed to encourage voluntary student prayer; in *Lee v. Weisman*, 505 U.S. 577 (1992), it invalidated a policy under which local religious leaders delivered prayers during graduation exercises; and in *Santa Fe Independent School District v. Doe*, 530 U.S. 290 (2000), the Court invalidated a policy of student-led prayer at football games.

B.3. Government Aid for Private Religious Organizations or Activities

The second category of establishment clause cases concerns government aid, monetary or otherwise, for private religious organizations or activities. The long and meandering line of cases on aid for sectarian education programs provides the primary example.

Everson v. Board of Education of Ewing Township, 330 U.S. 1 (1947), the first of the U.S. Supreme Court's government aid cases, provides a classic illustration. Acting pursuant to state statute, the local school board had adopted a resolution authorizing reimbursement of parents for the costs of transporting their children to school on the buses operated by the local public transportation system. Some of these reimbursements went to parents whose children attended local Catholic parochial schools. A taxpayer objected to the payments of public funds to these parents and contended that such payments violated the establishment clause.

In a 5 to 4 decision, the Court held that the New Jersey law did not establish religion; rather, it applied generally to all parents and helped them transport their children to schools, public schools and private secular schools as well as religious schools.

> [W]e cannot say that the First Amendment prohibits New Jersey from spending taxraised funds to pay the bus fares of parochial school pupils as a part of a general program under which it pays the fares of pupils attending public and other schools.... The State contributes no money to the schools. It does not support them. Its legislation, as applied, does no more than provide a general program to help parents get their children, regardless of their religion, safely and expeditiously to and from accredited schools. [330 U.S. at 17, 18.]

The New Jersey program of transportation cost reimbursement, thus construed, satisfied the establishment clause's requirement of neutrality respecting religion. The First Amendment, said the Court, "requires the state to be a neutral in its relations with groups of religious believers and non-believers; it does not require the state to be their adversary. State power is no more to be used so as to handicap religions than it is to favor them" (330 U.S. at 18). Similarly, the New Jersey program, as construed by the Court, was consistent with the Jeffersonian wall of separation between Church and State: "The First Amendment has erected a wall between church and state. That wall must be kept high and impregnable. We could not approve the slightest breach. New Jersey has not breached it here" (330 U.S. at 18).

There have been many U.S. Supreme Court cases since *Everson* on government aid to sectarian schools. By the Justices' own admissions, underscored by commentators, this line of cases has not been a model of clarity. The "wall of separation," as developed in these cases, evolved from the "high and impregnable" partition envisioned in *Everson* (above) to a "'line of separation' [that], far from being a 'wall,' is a blurred, indistinct, and variable barrier depending on all the circumstances of a particular relationship" (*Lemon v. Kurtzman*, 403 U.S. 602, 614 (1971)). The Justices generally drew fine distinctions between types of aid programs, and the distinctions drawn in one case did not always appear consistent with those drawn in another. In *Board of Education v. Allen*, 392 U.S. 236 (1968), for instance, the Court approved a state program for lending textbooks to students in private (including sectarian) schools; while in *Wolman v. Walter*, 433 U.S. 229, 248–251 (1977), the Court invalidated a state program for lending other instructional materials — such as maps, globes, and weather charts — to students in private (including sectarian) schools.

On occasion, in this line of cases, the Court has also overruled a prior decision. *Aguilar v. Felton*, 473 U.S. 402 (1985), for example, involved the provision of services to educationally deprived children in private religious schools under Title I of the Elementary and Secondary Education Act of 1965 (20 U.S.C. § 3801 *et seq*). The federal government permitted local school districts to send public school teachers into private religious schools to provide special educational services. By a 5 to 4 vote, the Court held that this practice entangled the government with religion and thus violated the establishment clause. But in *Agostini v. Felton*, 521 U.S. 203 (1997), by a 5 to 4 vote, the Court overruled its earlier decision in *Aguilar* and permitted public teachers to provide Title I services to private religious school children on the premises of the private school. Similarly, in *Mitchell v. Helms*, 530 U.S. 793 (2000), a splintered Court over-ruled *Wolman v. Walter*, above, as well as an earlier similar case, *Meek v. Pittinger*, 421 U.S. 349 (1975), and upheld the loan of educational materials and equipment, includ-ing computers and computer software, to religiously affiliated private schools under Chapter 2 of the Educational Consolidation and Improvement Act of 1981 (20 U.S.C. §7301 *et. seq.*).

Beginning in the early 1980s, the Court has developed a "distinction between gov-ernment programs that provide aid directly to religious schools…, and programs of true private choice, in which government aid reaches religious schools only as a result of the genuine and independent choices of private individuals.…" *Zelman v. Simmons-Harris*, 536 U.S. 639, 649 (2002). *Aguilar, Agostini*, and *Mitchell v. Helms*, above, are all examples of the former type of aid program. The latter type of aid program—the "true choice" program—is illustrated by the *Mueller, Witters*, and *Zobrest* cases, discussed below, all of which were relied on in the *Zelman* case in 2002, also discussed below.

In *Mueller v. Allen*, 463 U.S. 388 (1983), the Court upheld a Minnesota program providing small tax deductions to parents for specified education expenses including tuition payments to private religious schools. In *Witters v. Washington Department of Services for the Blind*, 474 U.S. 481 (1986), the Court upheld a Washington program of vocational scholarships that students could use at any higher educational institution in the state, including religious institutions. And in *Zobrest v. Catalina Foothills School District*, 509 U.S. 1 (1993), the Court upheld a provision of the federal Individuals With Disabilities Education Act (IDEA), 20 U.S.C. § 1400 *et seq.*, that provided for sign lan-guage interpreters who would provide services to hearing-impaired children in what-ever school the parents chose for the child.

This line of cases was capped in 2002 by "the Cleveland voucher case," *Zelman v. Simmons-Harris*, 536 U.S. 639 (2002), in which the Court rejected an establishment clause challenge to the Ohio legislature's school voucher program for the Cleveland City School District. Under the program, low-income parents could receive vouchers of up to $2250 that they could use to pay the tuition at any participating private school within the district. Parents could choose tutorial aid in lieu of a voucher and magnet schools and community schools provided other options for parents. Most of the par-ticipating schools in the voucher program were in fact religious schools, however, and the vast majority (96% at the time of the litigation) of the students selecting vouchers used them to attend a private religious school. The Court nevertheless upheld the pro-gram because it "is a program of true private choice, consistent with *Mueller, Witters*, and *Zobrest*.…" (536 U.S. at 653). "[T]he Ohio program is entirely neutral with respect to religion. It provides benefits directly to a wide spectrum of individuals, defined only by financial need and residence in a particular school district. It permits such individ-uals to exercise genuine choice among options public and private, secular and religious. The program is therefore a program of true private choice" (536 U.S. at 662).

For both types of school aid cases—the direct aid cases and the indirect aid, or true choice, cases—the recent trend has been toward a less strict application of the estab-lishment clause. The *Agostini* case clearly marks that trend for the direct aid cases, and *Zelman* does so for the true choice cases. The types and amounts of aid that are considered constitutional today go far beyond, very far beyond, anything the narrow majority of five Justices authorized is *Everson*, and the "wall of separation" now seems not nearly as "high" or "impregnable" as the *Everson* court said it must be.

B.4. The Establishment Clause "Tests"

When establishment issues arise, courts and other decisionmakers must have some means of distinguishing government interactions with religion that violate the separation principle from those that do not. The U.S. Supreme Court has developed various tests or approaches to serve this purpose: the *Lemon* test (Sec. B.4(1) below), the endorsement test (Sec. B.4(2) below), the coercion test (Sec. B.4(3) below), the denominational preference test (Sec. B.4(4) below), the original history approach (Sec. B.4(5) below), and the ceremonial deism approach (Sec. B.4(6) below). The first two tests (*Lemon* and endorsement) are essentially generic tests, designed for and used in a broad array of establishment clause cases. The third test, coercion, is for use in a particular type of establishment clause case where there is evidence of governmental coercion (direct or indirect, formal or informal) of religious belief or practice. The fourth, fifth, and sixth approaches (denominational preference, original history, and ceremonial deism) are narrower alternatives to the first three tests, designed for the specific limited circumstances described below.

B.4(1). The Lemon Test

Since 1971, the courts have typically used the three-pronged "*Lemon* test" in establishment clause cases. Courts have applied this test to cases in both the religious exercises category (Sec. B.2 above) and the government aid category (Sec. B.3 above). An amalgam of earlier tests, the *Lemon* test provides that, to survive an establishment challenge, a government action must meet each of three requirements: "First, the statute must have a secular legislative purpose; second, its principal or primary effect must be one that neither advances nor inhibits religion; finally, the statute must not foster 'an excessive government entanglement with religion'" (*Lemon v. Kurtzman*, 403 U.S. 602, 612–613 (1971), citing *Walz v. Tax Commission*, 397 U.S. 664, 674 (1970)). Each requirement, or prong, triggers a different inquiry, and each inquiry leads the courts into difficult tasks requiring them to distinguish secular from non-secular activity, primary from secondary effects, and excessive from non-excessive involvements.

For many years, the *Lemon* test has been the target of substantial critique and criticism by academic commentators and judges alike. Eventually, the U.S. Supreme Court took steps to refine the test. In *Agostini v. Felton*, 521 U.S. 203 (1997), for instance, the Court determined that the second prong (primary effect) and third prong (entanglement) are both, in essence, part of a single broad inquiry into the effect of government action at issue (521 U.S. at 218, 232–233). As the Court explained:

> The factors we use to assess whether an entanglement is "excessive" are similar to the factors we use to examine "effect." That is, to assess entanglement,

we have looked to "the character and purposes of the institutions that are benefitted, the nature of the aid that the State provides, and the resulting relationship between the government and religious authority." [*Lemon*, 403 U.S.
at 615.] Similarly, we have assessed a law's "effect" by examining the character
of the institutions benefitted (*e.g.*, whether the religious institutions were "predominantly religious"), and the nature of the aid that the State provided (*e.g.*,
whether it was neutral and non-ideological)....Indeed, in *Lemon* itself, the entanglement that the Court found "independently" to necessitate the program's
invalidation also was found to have the effect of inhibiting religion. *See, e.g.*,
403 U.S., at 620 ("[W]e cannot ignore here the danger that pervasive modern
governmental power will ultimately intrude on religion..."). Thus, it is sim-
plest to recognize why entanglement is significant and treat it...as an aspect
of the inquiry into a statute's effect. [*Agostini*, 521 U.S. at 233–234.]

B.4(2).   The Endorsement Test

Beginning in 1984, the Court has developed a modification of, or substitute for,
Lemon known as the "endorsement" test or the "endorsement or disapproval" test.
This test was first articulated by Justice O'Connor in her concurrence in *Lynch v.
Donnelly*, 465 U.S. 668, 687–695 (1984), a case in which the majority upheld the inclusion of a creche (or manger scene) in a city's Christmas display. Justice O'Connor
argued that a "government endorsement or disapproval of religion" is a "direct infringement" of the establishment clause. This is so because "[e]ndorsement sends a
message to non-adherents that they are outsiders, not full members of the political
community, and an accompanying message to adherents that they are insiders, fa-
vored members of the political community;" while "[d]isapproval sends the opposite message" (465 U.S. at 688 (O'Connor, J., concurring)). Under the endorsement
test, the question to be addressed is whether, in its purpose or effect, the government's action "conveys a message of endorsement or disapproval" (*Id.* at 690). This
test thus parallels the purpose, and especially the effect, prongs of the *Lemon* test (*Id.*;
see also Agostini v. Felton, 521 U.S. 203, 222 (1997)), in that an "endorsement" is similar to an advancement of religion under *Lemon* and a "disapproval" is similar to an
inhibition of religion.

In *Allegheny County v. Greater Pittsburgh ACLU*, 492 U.S. 573 (1989), another creche
case, Justice Blackmun and Justice Stevens accepted Justice O'Connor's endorsement
test as "a sound analytical framework for evaluating government use of religious symbols" (492 U.S. at 595; *see generally* 594–597 and 616–621). Justices Brennan and
Stevens also joined Justice O'Connor in applying the endorsement test (492 U.S. at
627–629; *see generally* 624–632). A majority of the Court in *Allegheny* thus accepted
and used the endorsement test. These Justices also accepted and applied the "reasonable observer" standard, suggested by Justice O'Connor, under which courts ask
whether a "reasonable observer" would perceive the government's action as an endorsement or disapproval of religion. The effect of the government's action, in other
words, "must...be judged according to the standard of a reasonable observer" (492

U.S. at 620 (Blackmun, J.); 492 U.S. at 632, 635–636 (O'Connor, J.); 492 U.S. at 642–643 (Brennan, J.); *but see* 492 U.S. at 668, 677 (Kennedy, J.)).

In cases after *Allegheny*, various Justices and lower courts have continued to use the endorsement test. Given these developments, this test has become a strong competitor of the *Lemon* test and has the potential to match or overtake it in terms of importance or frequency of use. Since there is already considerable overlap between the *Lemon* test and the endorsement test, it is also possible that the U.S. Supreme Court will eventually merge the two tests into one.

B.4(3). The Coercion Test

The modern version of the coercion test was articulated in *Lee v. Weisman*, 505 U.S. 577 (1992). In that case, a 5 to 4 majority held that a middle school principal violated the establishment clause by including prayers by a member of the clergy in the school's graduation ceremony in such a way that "attendance and participation in the state sponsored religious activity are in a fair and real sense obligatory" (*Id.* at 586). The Court's concern was "that in the hands of government what might begin as a tolerant expression of religious views may end in a policy to indoctrinate and coerce" (*Id.* at 591–592), thus creating a need for courts to "protect[] freedom of conscience from subtle coercive pressure...." (*Id.* at 592).

The majority in *Lee v. Weisman* provided this statement of its coercion test: "It is beyond dispute that, at a minimum, the Constitution guarantees that government may not coerce anyone to support or participate in religion or its exercise...." (*Id.* at 587). The majority also made clear that psychological as well as physical coercion are covered by this test, and that psychological coercion includes "subtle and indirect" coercion such as peer pressure. In concurring opinions, four of the five Justices in the majority emphasized that coercion is a "sufficient" but not a "necessary" element of establishment clause analysis (*Id.* at 604 (Blackmun, J., concurring) and 618–619 (Souter, J., concurring)), and that the clause protects "more than freedom from coercion" (*Id.* at 606 (Blackmun, J., concurring)). In addition, these Justices emphasized that coercion is also an element — a necessary element — of free exercise clause analysis (see Sec. C below), and that the Court has addressed problems of coercion more frequently under that clause than the establishment clause. Given these considerations, it does not appear that the coercion test will be applied to as broad a range of establishment clause cases as the *Lemon* and endorsement tests.

B.4(4). The Denominational Preference Test

The denominational preference test might also be called the strict scrutiny discrimination test, since it works very much like strict scrutiny under the equal protection clause (see Chap. 10, Sec. C.4). The denominational preference test is used as an alternative to the *Lemon* and endorsement tests in one particular kind of case — the case where government has created what is called a "denominational preference" by passing a law that favors one or more particular religions at the expense of others. The

best example of this type of case is *Larson v. Valente*, 456 U.S. 228 (1982). There a state
had passed legislation regulating the solicitation of funds by religious organizations.
It was apparent from the legislative history that the state was attempting to limit solicitation activities of certain nontraditional religions whose members solicited on the
public streets, but not the activities of other religions. The Court thus considered the
legislation to have created a denominational preference that was subject to a strict
scrutiny standard similar to the equal protection standard. Declaring that "[t]he clearest command of the Establishment Clause is that one religious denomination cannot
be officially preferred over another" (*Id.* at 244), the Court invalidated the legislation.

B.4(5).   The Original History Test

The original history test may be used when there is a record of original historical
practices concerning the governmental activity at issue. The courts look at these original historical practices and ask whether the government practice now being challenged
was well accepted at the time of the First Amendment's adoption. If so, according to
this approach, the framers must have accepted this practice and must therefore have
considered it consistent with the establishment clause. (See Chap. 4, Sec. D.2 on using
original history.) The best example of this kind of reasoning is *Marsh v. Chambers*, 463
U.S. 783 (1983). The question was whether a state legislature could have a state-em-
ployed chaplain lead prayers to open the legislative session. The Court upheld that
practice because similar practices were well established, at and immediately after the
adoption of the First Amendment, in Congress as well as state legislatures.

B.4(6).   Ceremonial Deism

The last approach to establishment clause analysis, often called "ceremonial deism"
(*see Allegheny*, 492 U.S. at 595 n. 46, 603), has appeared thus far in U.S. Supreme Court
cases only in occasional dicta in majority opinions, and in concurrences and dissents.
For example, Justice Brennan argued in *Lynch v. Donnelly*:

> [W]e have noted that government cannot be completely prohibited from rec-
> ognizing in its public actions the religious beliefs and practices of the American
> people as an aspect of our national history and culture. See *Engel v. Vitale, supra*,
> 370 U.S., at 435, n. 21, *Schempp, supra*, 374 U.S., at 300–304, (BRENNAN, J.,
> concurring). While I remain uncertain about these questions, I would suggest
> that such practices as the designation of "In God We Trust" as our national
> motto, or the references to God contained in the Pledge of Allegiance can best
> be understood…as a form of "ceremonial deism," protected from Establishment
> Clause scrutiny chiefly because they have lost through rote repetition any sig-
> nificant religious content. See *Marsh v. Chambers, supra*, 463 U.S. at 811, 103
> S.Ct., at 3346 (BRENNAN, J., dissenting). Moreover, these references are
> uniquely suited to serve such wholly secular purposes as solemnizing public oc-
> casions, or inspiring commitment to meet some national challenge in a manner
> that simply could not be fully served in our culture if government were limited
> to purely non-religious phrases. Cf. *Schempp, supra*, 374 U.S., at 265, 83 S.Ct., at

1594 (BRENNAN, J., concurring). The practices by which the government has long acknowledged religion are therefore probably necessary to serve certain secular functions, and that necessity, coupled with their long history, gives those practices an essentially secular meaning. [465 U.S. at 716–717 (Brennan, J., dissenting; *see also* 465 U.S. at 693 (O'Connor, J., concurring).] [2]

The ceremonial deism approach is apparently grounded in the statement, from *Zorach v. Clauson*, 343 U.S. 306, 313 (1952), that: "We are a religious people whose institutions presuppose a Supreme Being;" and in a footnote in *Engel v. Vitale*, 370 U.S. 421, 435 n. 21 (1962), that addresses "patriotic or ceremonial occasions" (see Chap. 13, Sec. B.2). From this basis, it has been argued "that a vast portion of our people believe in and worship God[;] that many of our legal, political and personal values derive historically from religious teachings"; and that such government acknowledgments, on certain "patriotic or ceremonial occasions," do not violate the establishment clause (*School District of Abington Township v. Schempp*, 374 U.S. 203, 306, 308, (1963) (Goldberg, J., concurring)). The ceremonial deism approach is also sometimes combined with what is usually called a "de minimus" argument. In his concurrence in the *Schempp* case, for instance, Justice Goldberg argued that the establishment clause "does not prohibit practices which by any realistic measure create none of the dangers which it is designed to prevent and which do not so directly or substantially involve the state in religious exercises or in the favoring of religion as to have meaningful and practical impact" (374 U.S. at 307 (Goldberg. J., concurring)).

Thus, under a ceremonial deism approach, a reading of the Declaration of Independence at a government-sponsored Fourth of July celebration, or a reading of the Gettysburg Address in a public school ceremony for Lincoln's birthday, would not violate the establishment clause even though both documents contain references to the Deity. Such exercises, it is argued, "no longer have a religious purpose or meaning" (*Id.* at 304 (Brennan, J., concurring)). Similar arguments are used to justify governmental use of the motto "In God We Trust," on coins and elsewhere, because the motto has been "interwoven so deeply into the fabric of our civil polity" (*Id.* at 303; *see also Allegheny* at 669–674 (Kennedy, J., dissenting); and *see generally* Louis Fisher and Nada Mourtada-Sabbah, "Adopting 'In God We Trust' As the U.S. National Motto," 44 JOURNAL OF CHURCH AND STATE 671 (2002)). Ceremonial deism, and the "de minimus" argument, also were involved in a controversial Pledge of Allegiance case, *Newdow v. U.S. Congress*, 328 F.3d 466 (9th Cir. 2003). The plaintiff, a father of a public elementary school student in California, challenged the inclusion of the phrase "under God" in the Pledge of Allegiance, as specified by Congress in 1954 (68 Stat. 249, 4 U.S.C. § 4), and as recited by California school children pursuant to state law (Cal. Educ. Code § 52720). In a 2 to 1 decision, the majority in *Newdow*, using the coercion test, held that "the school district's policy…of teacher led recitation of the Pledge, with the inclusion of the added words, 'under God,' violates the Establishment Clause" because it "impermissibly co-

---

2. According to Justice Brennan, the phrase "ceremonial deism" originates from a public lecture by Eugene Rostow, former Dean of the Yale Law School, which was subsequently quoted in Arthur Sutherland, Book Review, 40 IND. L. J. 83, 86 (1964). *See Lynch* at 716 (Brennan, J., dissenting).

erces" school children to perform "a religious act...." (328 F.3d at 490, 487). A dissenting judge, however, gave short shrift to the majority's reasoning and instead relied on a de-minimus and ceremonial deism argument to conclude that "such phrases as 'In God We Trust' or 'under God' have no tendency to establish a religion in this country or to suppress anyone's exercise, or non-exercise, of religion...." (328 F.3d at 492).[3]

Since the ceremonial deism approach relies upon American history and tradition, it has some parallels to the original history approach (Sec. B.4(5) above). Ceremonial deism arguments, however, are not limited to original history and may consider subsequent history and the evolution of our traditions to the present time. Ceremonial deism is also related to the endorsement test (Sec. B.4(2) above), insofar as the former considers whether particular government references to God serve to endorse religion rather than merely to acknowledge it. The ceremonial deism approach often seems, however, to be used as an *exception* to the endorsement test, as well as the *Lemon* test itself, rather than as an expansion or refinement of these tests. *See, e.g., Allegheny*, 492 U.S. at 669–674 (Kennedy, J., dissenting).[4]

B.4(7). Application of the Tests

Not infrequently, more than one of the six establishment clause tests or approaches may apply to the same problem, or there may be disagreement on which test applies. If a particular governmental action *fails* any one of the first four tests—*Lemon*, endorsement, coercion, or denominational preference (Secs. B.4(1) to B.4(4) above)—that action violates the establishment clause. But if a particular governmental action *passes* one of the first four establishment clause tests, it is not necessarily constitutional; one or more of the other three tests may apply and may result in the practice being invalidated. Thus these four tests, although they have many similarities among them (especially the first two), are not identical; the same result is not necessarily reached under each one.

The other two establishment clause tests (or approaches) work differently. If a particular governmental action *fails to meet*, or is incompatible with, the requirements for these approaches, the analysis moves to one or more of the other tests before constitutionality under the establishment clause may be ascertained. Conversely, if a particular governmental action *meets* or is compatible with the requirements of the original history approach, the action is apparently constitutional under the establishment clause

---

3. When the judges of the Ninth Circuit voted to deny rehearing and rehearing *en banc* in this case, one of them issued a lengthy opinion that also reads as a dissent to the majority's opinion; see 328 F.3d at 471–482 (O'Scannlain, dissenting from denial of rehearing en banc). Subsequently, the U.S. Supreme Court agreed to review this case (*cert. granted, Elk Grove Unified School District v. Newdow*, 124 S.Ct. 384 (2003)), but it had not issued any decision as of press time for this book

4. Justice Kennedy was arguing against use of the endorsement test but in favor of protecting governmental discretion to engage in activities that fall within the rubric of ceremonial deism. For an extended canvassing of the cases and issues regarding ceremonial deism, and argument against judicial recognition of ceremonial deism, *see* Steven Epstein, "Rethinking the Constitutionality of Ceremonial Deism," 96 Columbia L. Rev. 2083 (1996).

and no other test is consulted. The ceremonial deism approach may work in the same way, especially if the approach is considered an exception to the *Lemon* and endorsement tests (see Sec. B.4(6) above). But since the case law is still confined to dicta, concurrences, and dissents, it is too early to tell with certainty that characterizing a practice as ceremonial deism would insulate it from analysis under the other tests.

Sec. C. The Free Exercise Clause: A Conceptual Overview

C.1. Identifying Burdens On Religious Belief or Practice

Unlike the establishment clause, the free exercise clause protects personal rights of particular individuals in the same sense as other rights clauses such as the free speech or equal protection clauses. Although the free exercise and establishment clauses "may in certain instances overlap, they forbid two quite different kinds of governmental encroachment upon religious freedom" (*Engel v. Vitale*, 370 U.S. 421, 430 (1962); see Sec. A above). The focus of the free exercise clause is upon governmental interference with an individual's own religious beliefs or religious practices. The key to identifying the type of interference that may offend the clause is the element of compulsion or coercion. In general, if government places a burden (or penalty) upon a religious belief or practice, the burden will constitute compulsion or coercion sufficient to raise a free exercise issue.[5] Governmental imposition of a burden on religious *belief*—that is, penalizing a person solely because he/she holds a particular religious belief, or testing the truth or falsity of an individual's religious belief, or requiring a person to profess a belief or disbelief in some religious creed—is virtually always unconstitutional. *See, e.g., Torcaso v. Watkins,* 367 U.S. 488 (1961); *United States v. Ballard*, 322 U.S. 78 (1944). But whether a burden on religious *practice* is unconstitutional will depend on the application of the particular standard of review to which the governmental action is subjected.

The belief or practice that is burdened must be one that can be characterized as *religious*. In most of the cases to date the beliefs or practices involved have been associated with a generally recognized religious denomination or faith and thus have been easily accepted by the courts as religious. But in other cases troublesome questions of what is "religious," or what is "religion," have arisen. (Compare Sec. B.1 above, and *see generally* Lee Stang, "The Meaning of 'Religion' in the First Amendment," 40 Duquesne L. Rev. 181, 200–210 (2002)). The courts have yet to provide much guidance on how to answer such questions outside the realm of traditional or conventional religion. It is clear, however, that ethical or philosophical beliefs do not themselves count as religious; something more is required. *See generally Wisconsin v. Yoder*, 406 U.S. 205, 215–216 (1972); *see also United States v. Seeger*, 380 U.S. 163 (1965). On the other hand, it is also

---

5. A case that was awaiting decision by the U.S. Supreme Court as this book went to press raises important issues concerning the identification of burdens on religion. See *Locke v. Davey*, 299 F.3d (9th Cir. 2002), *cert. granted*, 123 S. Ct. 2075 (2003), also discussed briefly in footnote 7 of Chapter 14 below.

clear that a belief may be considered religious even though it does not arise from a tenet or command of some particular religious denomination in which the believer claims membership. *Frazee v. Employment Security Department*, 489 U.S. 829 (1989).

C.2. The Problem of Religiously Neutral Laws that Burden Religion

Unlike the establishment clause, most of the leading free exercise cases have not concerned schools and colleges. Myriads of situations besides education have spawned free exercise problems, especially during the 1980s when the free exercise clause was a major growth area of constitutional law. One of the most widespread and frequently debated problems concerns religiously-neutral laws of general applicability. The question is whether and when such a law may constitutionally be applied to religious adherents even though it would burden their religious practice. Or, put differently, the question is whether and when the free exercise clause will require government to exempt the religious adherent from a neutral law of general applicability. May a state, for instance, apply a compulsory school attendance law to Amish students and parents who have religious objections to attending school beyond eighth grade (*Wisconsin v. Yoder*, 406 U.S. 205 (1972))? As the discussion in Section D below indicates, such exemption questions may also implicate the establishment clause (Sec. B above) because exemptions favoring religious adherents may appear to constitute support or sponsorship of religion.

Issues concerning exemption from general legislation may arise under civil or criminal regulatory laws (as in *Yoder*), under government benefits laws (as in *Sherbert v. Verner*, discussed below), and occasionally under tax laws (as in *United States v. Lee*, 455 U.S. 252 (1982), where the Court rejected an Amish employer's claim that payment of Social Security taxes violated his free exercise rights).

For many years, the leading precedent on such matters was *Sherbert v. Verner*, 374 U.S. 398 (1963), in which the Court utilized a strict scrutiny standard of review to exempt a Seventh Day Adventist from an unemployment benefits requirement that she be available to work on Saturdays, her Sabbath day. The *Sherbert* standard of strict scrutiny required the government to show (1) that "some compelling state interest [justifies] the substantial infringement of...First Amendment right[s]" (*Id.* at 406); and "that no alternative forms of regulation would combat [the threat to its interests] without infringing First Amendment rights" (*Id.* at 407). Beginning in the mid 1980s, however, various Supreme Court opinions created exceptions to or suggested other limits on the *Sherbert* analysis. The most important of these cases, *Employment Division v. Smith*, 494 U.S. 872 (1990), apparently undercuts much of the ground upon which *Sherbert* stood and raises critical questions concerning the future sweep of the free exercise clause.

The *Smith* case concerned Alfred Smith and Galen Black, who both worked as counselors in a county drug prevention and treatment program. They were fired from their jobs for ingesting peyote during a Native American Church religious ceremony. Both Smith and Black were members of the Native American Church, which considers peyote use a sacrament of the church. After their firing, Smith and Black applied for unemployment benefits from the State of Oregon. The state's Employment Appeals Board denied their claims, asserting that the two were ineligible for unemployment benefits because they had been discharged for work-related misconduct. This misconduct was defined by the criminal law of the state of Oregon, which prohibited the use of peyote. Smith and Black brought suit charging that the denial of benefits violated the free exercise clause. The Oregon Supreme Court determined that the state's ban on the sacramental use of peyote violated the First Amendment's free exercise clause, and that the state therefore could not deny Smith and Black unemployment benefits. The sole issue before the U.S. Supreme Court, then, was whether Oregon could constitutionally prohibit the religious use of peyote.

It was clear that the Oregon law criminalizing peyote use, as applied to Smith and Black, substantially burdened their free exercise of religion. But neither the existence nor the extent of this burden played a significant role in the Court's analysis. Writing for the Court, Justice Scalia asserted that "the right of free exercise does not relieve an individual of the obligation to comply with a 'valid and neutral law of general applicability on the ground that the law proscribes (or prescribes) conduct that his religion prescribes (or proscribes)'" (494 U.S. at 879). The Oregon law criminalizing peyote use applied generally to all peyote users and did not target Native American religious uses of the drug. Consequently, the law was both general and neutral, and therefore did not violate the free exercise clause. "Respondents urge us to hold, quite simply, that when otherwise prohibitable conduct is accompanied by religious convictions, not only the convictions but the conduct itself must be free from governmental regulation. We have never held that, and decline to do so now" (*Id.* at 882).

Justice Scalia declined to apply *Sherbert v. Verner*, 374 U.S. 398 (1963), to his analysis in the *Smith* case. *Sherbert* sets forth a strict scrutiny standard of review to be used whenever government has substantially burdened the free exercise of religion. Such strict scrutiny would apply, according to Justice Scalia, only when the law being challenged was *not* generally applicable and neutral. When the law *is* general and neutral, the government's authority to enforce the law "cannot depend on measuring the effects of a governmental action on a religious objector's spiritual development." To excuse an individual from obeying a law when it impinges upon his religious beliefs, unless the State can show that its "interest is 'compelling'—permitting him, by virtue of his beliefs, 'to become a law unto himself,'—contradicts both constitutional tradition and common sense" (494 U.S. at 885).

The *Smith* case's juxtaposition with the *Sherbert* case thus deserves close and careful attention. It appears that *Smith* has created a dichotomy between "religiously based" and "religiously neutral" restrictions on free exercise that parallels the "content-based" vs. "content-neutral" dichotomy that arises in free speech cases challenging regulations that do not purport to regulate speech at all (*i.e.*, are "speech-neutral"). But different standards and results attach to application of this dichotomy under the free exercise clause than is the case under the free speech clause. Courts apply an intermediate scrutiny standard of review to content-neutral or speech-neutral regulations that burden speech (Chap. 12, Sec. E). Under *Smith*, however, it appears that courts are to apply, at most, a minimal rational basis standard of scrutiny to religiously-neutral regulations that burden religion.[6]It is not clear why there should be such a difference when one switches from the free speech clause to the free exercise clause.[7]

C.3. Basic Free Exercise Analysis

Both before and after *Employment Division v. Smith* (Sec. C.2 above), the first question to consider in applying the free exercise clause is whether a government regulation has burdened an individual's religious belief or practice. This part of the analysis is explained in Section C.1 above. If the answer to the first question is affirmative, the next question, as developed in *Smith*, is whether the government regulation is "generally applicable" and "neutral." "Generally applicable" seems to mean that the regulation does not apply only to religious activities but applies to a range of secular activities as well. "Neutral" seems to mean that the regulation does not display or reflect hostility or favoritism toward religion. If the government regulation *is* generally applicable and neutral, then a court would apply only a minimal scrutiny standard of review, and would virtually never find the regulation invalid under the free exercise clause. If the government regulation *is not* generally applicable or *is not* neutral, then a court would apply the strict scrutiny standard of review derived from *Sherbert v. Verner* (above).

An important post-Smith case, *Church of the Lukumi Babalu Aye v. City of Hialeah*, 508 U.S. 520 (1993), provides needed guidance on how to determine whether a regulation is *not* generally applicable and neutral. The Hialeah City Council had enacted a series of resolutions and ordinances that prohibited the slaughtering of animals. The city's enactments were challenged by adherents of the Santeria religion—a religion imported to this country from Cuba and claiming about 50,000 adherents in South Florida at the time of the litigation. The Santeria religion practices ritual animal sacrifice as a "central element" of worship services. The plaintiff church asserted that the ordinances unconstitutionally targeted and burdened these practices in violation of the free exercise clause. The Court (per Justice Kennedy) agreed. Looking at the text of the ordinances, their interrelation with one another and with the resolutions, the history of the city's passage of the ordinances, and the "real operation" of the ordinances, the Court concluded that they were neither generally applicable nor religiously neutral. To the contrary, the ordinances "improper[ly] target[ed] . . . the Santaria religion" (508 U.S. at 534). The Court therefore applied strict scrutiny to the ordinances and, finding that the City could not meet this heavy burden of justification, invalidated the ordinances.

---

6 In *Barnes v. Glen Theatre*, 501 U.S. 560, 572, 576–579 (1991) (Scalia, J. concurring in judgment), and in *City of Erie v. Pap's*, 529 U.S. 277, 307–310 (2000) (Scalia, J. concurring in judgment), Justice Scalia sought to create a similar analysis and similar result for generally applicable and speech-neutral regulations that burden speech. But no other Justice joined Scalia in his *Barnes* concurrence, and only Justice Thomas joined him in his *City of Erie* concurrence.

7. For instance, the Court treated the "expression neutral" law in *Boy Scouts of America v. Dale*, 530 U.S. 640 (2000) (Chap. 12, Sec. G) and the "expression neutral" law in *United States v. O'Brien*, 391 U.S. 367 (1968) (Chap. 12, Sec. E.2) with substantially greater scrutiny than the "religion-neutral" law in *Smith*.

Thus, in light of *Hialeah*, courts faced with an issue concerning the general applicability or neutrality of a regulation burdening religious practice must first look to the face of the regulation. If the text of the regulation is not determinative of the issue, the court must look beyond the regulation to discern its purpose, or "object," from the background and context of its passage and from its operation. If this investigation reveals that the regulation "targets religious conduct for distinctive treatment" or otherwise reflects "animosity" toward religion or a particular religious practice, the court will not apply *Smith* but instead will subject the regulation to strict scrutiny. As articulated in *Hialeah*, the strict scrutiny standard requires that the challenged regulation be "justified by a compelling interest and narrowly tailored to advance that interest" (508 U.S. at 533). In applying the narrow tailoring test, courts are to consider the "underinclusiveness" and "overinclusiveness" of the regulation much like courts do in equal protection analysis (see Chap, 10, Sec. C.5).

Sec. D. The Tension Between the Establishment and Free Exercise Clauses

Unlike the free speech and press clauses, which appear naturally to supplement and reinforce one another using similar methodology, the establishment and free exercise clauses often appear to exist in tension with each other and even to be in conflict. It is not just that the methodology for applying each religion clause is different; rather, it is that the anti-establishment objective of the one clause may appear in particular circumstances to be inconsistent with the free exercise objective of the other. Both clauses may apply to the very same case, in other words, and may appear to point in opposite directions.

Take, for example, the question of whether a state may provide and pay for chapels and chaplains to serve the inmates in its state prison system. What is the constitutional problem if the state does so, and what is the constitutional problem if the state does not do so? At first blush, there appears to be a problem either way: if the state provides the chapels and chaplains, it would seem to be supporting religion in violation of the establishment clause; if the state does not provide the chapels and chaplains, it would seem to be infringing upon the prisoners' capacity to practice their religion, in violation of the free exercise clause. Similarly, consider the problem of conscientious objector status under federal military draft laws. If Congress decides to have a conscientious objector status for persons with religious objections to war, such status may constitute a kind of exemption that gives preference to religious adherents over non-adherents, thus creating an establishment problem. But if Congress decides not to have any such exemptions, everyone is susceptible to being drafted and ordered to fight a war—a result that would be a gross intrusion into the religious value systems of persons religiously opposed to war. *See generally Welsh v. United States*, 398 U.S. 333 (1970); *Gillette v. United States*, 401 U.S. 437 (1971). Or consider the problem of state and local taxation of church property. If a state or local government taxes churches, the tax may constitute a governmentally imposed burden on the practice of religion by the church corporation and its members, thus creating an apparent free exercise problem. But if the state or local government exempts the church property from taxation, the exemption may constitute an indirect financial subsidy for and a preference for religion, thus creating an apparent establishment problem. See *Walz v. Tax Commission*, 397 U.S. 664 (1970).

These types of tensions frequently lurk just beneath the surface of freedom of religion issues. Sometimes Congress or a state legislature may seek to resolve these tensions by creating a legislative exemption from a particular law whose requirements would burden religion. (*See* Louis Fisher, "Statutory Exemptions for Religious Freedom," 44 JOURNAL OF CHURCH AND STATE 291 (2002), for a collection of the various types of exemption.) The constitutional issue that then arises is whether the establishment clause permits a legislature to bestow this particular benefit on the specified religious organizations or their members. At other times there is not any religious exemption from a particular law even though application of that law to certain religious adherents does burden their religious freedom. The problem is then left to the courts. The constitutional issue would be whether the free exercise clause requires that the affected religious adherents be exempted from the statute's requirements even though the legislature has not so provided.

When the constitutional issue is of the first type—the legislatively created religious exemption—*Employment Division v. Smith* (Sec. C.2 above) suggests that courts may uphold "nondiscriminatory religious-practice exemption[s]." While acknowledging that the states have created such exemptions, including exemptions from drug laws prohibiting use of peyote (the problem in *Smith*), the Court majority in *Smith* also recognized a problem that arises from "leaving [such] accommodations to the political process." It would "place at a relative disadvantage those religious practices that are not widely engaged in." The Court majority accepts this result, however, as an "unavoidable consequence of democratic government [that] must be preferred to a system in which each conscience is a law unto itself or in which judges weigh the social importance of all laws against the centrality of all religious beliefs" (494 U.S. at 890).

When the constitutional issue is of the second type—the absence of any legislative exemption—*Employment Division v. Smith* (Sec. C.2 above) has clear application when the law at issue is a generally applicable, religiously neutral law. In such a circumstance, the *Smith* Court ruled, the free exercise clause does not allow courts to create a judicial exemption to protect religious observers. On the other hand, when the law is not generally applicable or religiously neutral, the free exercise clause may require courts to create a judicial exemption—depending on whether the government can justify the law under the strict scrutiny standard of review (*see generally Church of the Lukumi Babalu Aye v. City of Hialeah*, Sec. C.3 above). In other cases, the issues will not concern legislative or judicial exemptions as such, but rather other governmental actions benefitting or declining to benefit religious adherents or religious organizations. This type of problem is illustrated by the example above concerning chaplains for prisoners. Does government have *discretion* to provide or not provide chaplains; or is it *obligated* to provide chaplains; or is it *prohibited* from doing so? The case of *Wallace v. Jaffree*, 472 U.S. 38 (1985), suggests how courts might resolve these issues. In *Wallace*, the Alabama legislature had passed two statutes authorizing a daily "moment of silence"in the public schools of the state. The first statute stipulated that the moment of silence was for "meditation;" the second statute, passed three years later, stipulated that the moment of silence was for "meditation or voluntary prayer." The plaintiff argued that the second statute, because of its express authorization of prayer, violated the establishment clause. In their opinions, the Justices debated whether such a statute would be saved from an establishment clause attack if it was passed to protect the free exercise of religion by resolving confusion about whether students could pray during the moment of silence. (*See Id.* at 57 n. 45 (Stevens, J., for the majority); *Id.* at 81-84 (O'Connor, J., concurring); *Id.* at 87-88 (Burger, Ch. J., dissenting).) Justice O'Connor provided the most helpful analysis of how to resolve such tension between the establishment and free exercise clauses. Her guideline is that, if government has acted in order to remove "a governmentally imposed burden on the free exercise of religion," its action does not violate the establishment clause. In such a circumstance, in other words, the "free exercise clause values" that government is pursuing take precedence over establishment clause values. (*Id.* at 83.) Although the Alabama statute did not fit within this guideline, in Justice O'Connor's view, she concluded that other governmental actions benefitting religion could do so in certain narrow circumstances. Governmental provision of chaplains for prisoners to alleviate the burden on religious exercise occasioned by their imprisonment would seem to be a classic example of an action that fits within the O'Connor guideline.

If a particular case does not fit within the *Smith* and *Hialeah* guidelines for judicial exemptions or the O'Connor guideline for governmental actions protecting free exercise values, then one must resort to general principles to resolve establishment/free exercise tensions. The starting point should be the premise that the establishment and free exercise clauses are designed to work in tandem to achieve some common underlying goal or objective. This much is clear from their placement together in the First Amendment. It is often said that the common goal is neutrality—government neutrality in matters of religion (see Sec. A above). It is also often said that the two clauses share a common underlying value—the value of religious liberty for individuals and for society. Thus, even though the U.S. Supreme Court has not provided specific guidelines for resolving all tensions between the clauses, interpreters are at least guided generally by the common goal and underlying value that the two clauses share.

Sec. E. Exercise No. 9: Differentiating Free Speech, Non-Establishment, and Free Exercise (Student Prayer Activities on Public School Grounds)

Each of the six situations below describes a public junior high school principal's action or inaction regarding particular student prayer activities on school grounds.

1.   The principal requires that the school day begin with a group prayer in each homeroom. Every student must participate.

2. The principal initiates a program of group prayer in each homeroom *before* the official school day begins. Participation is voluntary. Students may attend only with the written consent of a parent or guardian, and must be at school ten minutes early in order to participate.

3. A group of students organizes a student prayer club. Club members ask the principal if they can meet for group prayer before school begins, for ten minutes each day, in one of the school's activity rooms. (Activity rooms are open before school and are used by various student organizations). The principal grants the request.

4. Under the same circumstances as in situation 3 above, students organize a student prayer club and ask this principal if they can meet before school. But the principal denies the students' request.

5. A number of individual students undertake to pray individually during the school day—in particular before eating lunch and before tests. The principal is aware of this activity and permits it to continue.

6. Under the same circumstances as in situation 5 above, students pray individually during the school day. When the principal becomes aware of this activity, she prohibits the individual students from praying.

For each of these six situations, consider the following questions.

Questions

QUES. 1. Might the principal's action violate the establishment clause? The free exercise clause? Both? Neither? Support your analysis with reference to the essential elements of an establishment or free exercise cause of action and with reference to the relevant tests or standards of judicial review.

QUES. 2. Would any of the alternative constitutional means for protecting religious freedom (see Sec. A above) be available to protect the students in any of these situations?

Answers

ANS. to QUES. 1. The analytical methods discussed in Sections B and C above, and the suggestions on accommodation of religion in Section D, will all be helpful in answering this question. In general, situations 1, 2, 3, and 5 would raise establishment issues involving possible government support or sponsorship of religion. Situations 1 and 2 would apparently violate the establishment clause (*see Engel v. Vitale* (Sec. B.2 above) regarding situation 2 and *Lee v. Weisman* (Sec. B.4 above) regarding situation 1), but it is unlikely that situations 3 and 5 would do so. As to situation 3, see *Board of Education of Westside Community Schools v. Mergens*, 496 U.S. 226, 247–253 (1990).

In general, situations 1, 4, and 6 would raise free exercise issues due to possible burdens on or coercion of religious practice. A critical question would be whether these situations would be analyzed under the standards of review in *Employment Division v. Smith* (Sec. C.2 above) or under those in *Sherbert v. Verner* and *Wisconsin v. Yoder* (Sec. C.1 and C.3 above).

Situation 1 would apparently violate the free exercise clause. Situations 4 and 6 may also do so. For situation 4, there would be a question whether the inability to engage in *group* prayer, on *public school premises* would substantially burden the students' religious practice, since they could still have group prayer at another location before or after school and could still pray individually (without a club) on school premises before and after school and during the school day. For situation 6, there could be a question whether a particular individual's prayer activity was so vocal or animated that it distracted other students' attention from the education process; if so, this could provide justification for limiting that prayer activity.

Situations 4 and 6 may also raise establishment clause issues involving possible government hostility to or inhibition of religion. Note that under the *Lemon* test (Sec. B.4 above), the establishment clause is violated either by governmental support for, or hostility toward, religion.

ANS. to QUES. 2. In situation 4, the students could apparently assert a free speech claim based on an alleged infringement of their "religious speech" (*see Widmar v. Vincent*, 454 U.S. 263, 269–270 (1981)(Sec. A above). In such a case, the school might *defend* itself against the students' speech claims by arguing that the establishment clause prohibits it from granting the request (*see Widmar* at 270–275, and *Mergens* in answer 1 above, at 247–253), but this argument is not likely to prevail when the school permits other student groups to meet before school.

In situation 4, it is also feasible that the students could assert a violation of their freedom of religious association or expressive association (see Sec. A above). Moreover, since the principal permits secular clubs to meet before school, the students could feasibly assert that they have been discriminated against on grounds of religion in violation of the equal protection clause (see Sec. A above).

In situation 6, the students could feasibly assert a free speech claim if their manner of praying had "communicative capacity" (see Chap. 12, Sec. C.2), as in the case of spoken words meant for others to hear or religious gestures meant for others to see. In such a circumstance, however, questions would arise whether the prayer activity disrupted the educational process and was therefore not protected by the free speech clause (*see Tinker v. Des Moines School District*, 393 U.S. 503 (1969)).

Sec. F. Study Suggestions

For each establishment clause case you read, consider whether the Court was applying the *Lemon* test, a modification or derivation of the *Lemon* test, or one of the alternative tests. If it was applying *Lemon*, determine which prong or prongs of the test the Court relied on, and consider whether any of the Justices proposed a modification of the *Lemon* test. Consider the relative strictness with which the Court applies the separation principle in the particular case, as well as in the range of modern cases. Also consider what the essential elements of establishment clause problems are that distinguish them from, or interrelate them with, free exercise problems.

When you read free exercise cases, focus on the threshold requirement that there must be a *burden* on *religious practice* before the free exercise clause will apply. Seek to discern how courts identify such burdens. Once a burden on religious practice has been identified, it then is critical to distinguish between statutes (or administrative regulations) that are generally applicable and religiously neutral within the meaning of *Employment Division v. Smith*, and those that are not. Seek to discern how courts determine whether a particular law is or is not generally applicable and religiously neutral. For laws that are not, look for strict scrutiny review; check to see whether the court follows the strict scrutiny standards set out in *Sherbert v. Verner*.

In addition, as you read either establishment cases or free exercise cases, be attentive to situations in which establishment-free exercise tension arises. Seek to distinguish the question of whether government *may* accommodate religion, by creating exemptions for religious adherents or otherwise, from the question of whether government *must* accommodate religion. Look for suggestions for conceptually resolving such accommodation issues and for harmonizing the two religion clauses.

FOR FURTHER READING: (1) Daniel Farber, THE FIRST AMENDMENT, chs. 13–14 (Foundation Press, 2nd ed. 2003). (2) Douglas Laycock "The Remnants of Free Exercise," 1990 SUP. CT. REV. 1. (3) Suzanna Sherry, "*Lee v. Weisman*: Paradox Redux," 1993 SUP. CT. REV. 123.

Chapter 14

Alternative Sources of Individual Rights

Sec. A. An Overview of Other Rights That Supplement Federal Constitutional Rights

This Chapter considers: (a) the various sources of rights, beyond the U.S. Constitution, that supplement federal constitutional rights; and (b) the federal constitutional issues that arise concerning these alternative sources of rights. The basic premise is that the U.S. Constitution is not the only legal source of individual rights to liberty, equality, and personal dignity. While the Constitution creates a fundamental fabric of national rights which cannot be contradicted by any other legal source, other sources of legal rights may and do supplement the constitutional base. Individuals frequently receive greater protection from these other sources of rights than they do from the U.S. Constitution.

The two most important sources of individual rights, in addition to the U.S. Constitution, are federal statutes and state constitutions. These two sources are reviewed in Sections B and E below. Furthermore, state statutes and state common law, as well as the local legislation of counties, cities, towns, and villages, may all be important sources of individual rights. A state statute or a local ordinance, for instance, may provide protection against private race or sex discrimination that is not subject to the federal equal protection clause due to the lack of state action (see Chap. 9, Sec. D); or may prohibit discrimination on the basis of characteristics, such as sexual orientation, that are not subject to heightened scrutiny under the federal equal protection clause (see Chap. 10, Sec. C.4). In *Rotary Club of Duarte v. Board of Directors of Rotary International*, 178 Cal. App. 3d 1035, 224 Cal. Rptr. 213 (1986), *affirmed*, 481 U.S. 537 (1987), for example, a California appellate court applied the state's Unruh Civil Rights Act to a private organization not engaged in state action, holding that the Act prohibited the organization from restricting its membership to men. Or state common law may provide protection against certain acts of private corporations or associations that intrude upon individual rights but are not covered by the federal Constitution due to a lack of state action.

In *Novosel v. Nationwide Ins. Co.*, 721 F.2d 894 (3rd Cir. 1983), for example, the court considered whether Pennsylvania law permitted a former employee to bring a wrongful discharge claim against a private employer where the employer terminated the employment because the employee had refused to participate in the company's effort to lobby the state legislature regarding a no-fault insurance bill. Applying Pennsylvania tort law, the court held that a termination on these grounds would interfere with the employee's freedom of political expression and association, would therefore be against public policy, and would thus support a tort claim for wrongful discharge. *Id.* at 898–901.

Just as it is important to understand the relationship between federal constitutional rights and federal statutory rights (see Sec. B.2 below), and between federal constitutional rights and state constitutional rights (see Sec. E below), it is also important to understand the relationship between federal constitutional rights and state or local statutory rights. The state legislatures have ample powers with which to enact and enforce individual rights legislation, and they may delegate some of this authority to local governments (see Chap. 4, Sec. A.2). Such enactments must not conflict with the U.S. Constitution. In the aftermath of *Roe v. Wade*, 410 U.S. 113 (1973), for example, some states passed laws creating "fetal rights" (rights of the unborn), rights for the husbands of pregnant women, or rights for the parents of pregnant minors; the courts invalidated many of these laws as being in conflict with the constitutional rights of the woman articulated in *Roe. See, e.g., Planned Parenthood of Central Missouri v. Danforth*, 428 U.S. 52 (1976).

Similarly, many states and local governments have passed non-discrimination legislation that covers private sector discrimination more broadly than federal legislation does. Some of this legislation has been subject to constitutional challenge for intruding upon expressive rights or associational rights of the alleged discriminators. In *Hurley v. Irish-American Gay, Lesbian, & Bisexual Group*, 515 U.S. 557 (1995), for example, Massachusetts had a public accommodations law that prohibited "any distinction, discrimination or restriction on account of... sexual orientation... relative to the admission of any person to, or treatment in any place of public accommodation, resort or amusement" (Mass. Gen. Laws, § 272.98). This law was invoked by the Irish-American Gay, Lesbian, and Bisexual Group of Boston when it was excluded from marching in a St. Patrick's Day parade organized by a war veterans organization. The Massachusetts courts held that the war veterans organization had discriminated against the Gay, Lesbian, and Bisexual group and thus violated the Massachusetts public accommodations law. The U.S. Supreme Court, however, reversed the state courts. The Court acknowledged that the Massachusetts law is "well within the State's usual power to enact when a legislature has reason to believe that a given group is the target of discrimination...." (*Id.* at 572). But as applied to this case, the law intruded upon the free speech right of the war veterans organization to exclude the Gay, Lesbian, and Bisexual Group's message from the parade, which was an "expressive" activity. "This use of the State's power violates the fundamental rule of protection under the First Amendment that a speaker has the autonomy to choose the content of his own message" (*Id.* at 573).[1]

---

1. For another example of a federal First Amendment right overcoming a state public accommodations law, see *Boy Scouts of America v. Dale*, a case regarding the freedom of expres-

Besides avoiding conflict with the federal constitution, state and local rights laws must also avoid conflict with federal individual rights laws. If there is a conflict, the federal law will preempt the state or local law. The federal rights law will also preempt the state or local law if the federal statute expressly provides for preemption or if the federal government has occupied the field covered by the state or local law (see Chap. 7, Sec. C). In *California Federal Savings and Loan v. Guerra*, 479 U.S. 272 (1987) for example, various plaintiffs challenged a state statute granting female employees pregnancy leave rights, arguing that the law was preempted by the federal employment discrimination statute (Title VII of the Civil Rights Act of 1964, 42 U.S.C. §2000e *et seq.*). The U.S. Supreme Court considered the various bases for preemption, and determined that the federal law did not preempt the state law.

Sec. B. Federal Statutory Rights and Congress' Powers to Create Them

B.1. Overview

Two general questions underlie any consideration of federal legislation as a source of individual rights: (1) What are the existing statutes that protect individual rights, and the specific rights that each of these statutes protects? (2) What are the sources of Congressional power that support enactment of the existing federal statutes protecting individual rights or would support new individual rights legislation in the future? The first of these questions is discussed in Section B.2 below using federal non-discrimination legislation for illustration. The second question raises constitutional power issues that are already addressed generally in Chapter 6 above (see especially Secs. C, D, and E). The relevant power sources are applied specifically to federal non-discrimination legislation in Sec. B.3 below. The most pertinent (and complex) of these Congressional powers, the enforcement powers, are then given additional attention in Sec. C below.

B.2. Federal Individual Rights Statutes

Federal individual rights statutes may either create new rights beyond those defined by the Constitution's individual rights guarantees, or create new remedies for those rights already defined by the Constitution. In either case, the federal statute will usu-

---

sive association that is discussed in Chapter 12, Section G. For examples of cases where an asserted constitutional right does *not* prevail over a state non-discrimination statute, see *Roberts v. United States Jaycees*, 468 U.S. 609 (1984) (Minnesota Human Rights Act prohibiting sex discrimination prevails over Jaycee's claim of a freedom of association right to restrict its membership to men); *Board of Directors of Rotary International v. Rotary Club of Duarte*, 481 U.S. 537 (1987) (California's Unruh Civil Rights Act prevails over Rotary International's claim of a freedom of association right to restrict club membership to men).

ally be one of two basic types: (1) a regulatory statute, which compels government, or private individuals and corporations, or both, to recognize and protect certain rights of individuals; or (2) a spending statute, which conditions the receipt of federal grants and contracts upon the recipient's compliance with requirements for protection of certain individual rights. There is also an occasional third type, a tax statute, which conditions the receipt of a tax exemption or deduction upon the taxpayer's compliance with requirements for protection of certain individual rights.

The early federal rights statutes, the Reconstruction-era civil rights laws, were regulatory statutes. The most important of these, now codified in 42 U.S.C. § 1983 and known as "Section 1983," provides civil judicial remedies for deprivations of federal constitutional rights (and some statutory rights) when the perpetrator has acted "under color of" state law—a requirement that parallels the state action doctrine (Chap. 9, Sec. D).

The more modern statutes, whose numbers have grown substantially since the early 1960s, are a mix of regulatory and spending types. The bulk of these statutes deal with discrimination. Title VI of the Civil Rights Act of 1964 (42 U.S.C. § 2000d), for example, is a spending statute covering race or national origin discrimination by recipients of federal funding. Title II of the same Act (42 U.S.C. sec. 2000a *et seq.*, in contrast, is a regulatory statute prohibiting race, national origin, and religious discrimination in places of public accommodation; while Title VII (42 U.S.C. sec. 2000e *et seq.*) is a regulatory statute prohibiting race, national origin, sex, and religious discrimination in employment. Other modern statutes also cover disability discrimination and age discrimination. Section 504 of the Rehabilitation Act of 1975, 29 U.S.C. § 794 ("Section 504"), for example, is a spending statute covering disability discrimination by federal funding recipients, while the Americans With Disabilities Act, 42 U.S.C. § 12101 *et seq.* (ADA) is a regulatory statute prohibiting disability discrimination in various contexts.

B.3. Congressional Powers to Create Individual Rights and Remedies: In General

Congress has express power to "enforce" the various rights guaranteed by the Thirteenth, Fourteenth, and Fifteenth Amendments. These "enforcement powers" (Chap. 6, Sec. E and Sec. C below) were the source for the Reconstruction-era civil rights statutes (Sec. B.2 above). But the enforcement powers are only one of several bases for modern exertions of Congressional power regarding individual rights. The commerce power (Chap. 6, Sec. C), the spending power (Chap. 6, Sec. D), and to a lesser degree the tax power (Chap. 6, Sec. D) are also important sources of modern rights legislation. The commerce power, for example, is the basis for Title II of the Civil Rights Act of 1964 (Sec. B.2 above) whose constitutionality the U.S. Supreme Court upheld in *Katzenbach v. McClung*, 379 U.S. 294 (1964) (Chap. 6, Sec. C.1) and *Heart of Atlanta Motel v. United States*, 379 U.S. 241 (1964). The spending power is the basis for Congress' conditional spending statutes such as Title VI of the Civil Rights Act of 1964 and Section 504 of the Rehabilitation Act of 1975 (Sec. B.2 above). And the tax power is the basis for the Internal Revenue Service's authority to deny tax-exempt status to racially segregated private schools. In *Bob Jones University v. United States*, 461 U.S. 574 (1983), the U.S. Supreme Court upheld this authority as a valid exercise of the tax power that Congress had delegated to the IRS.

Under some of its powers, Congress may protect individuals from both governmental and private, non-governmental actions that intrude upon individual equality or liberty, while under other powers Congress may protect individuals only from the actions of government. The commerce, spending, and tax powers are of the former type; using these powers, Congress clearly may create legislation applicable to the private sector. A good example is *Katzenbach v. McClung*, above, which upholds Congress' use of the commerce power to prohibit race discrimination by private restaurants. In contrast, Congress' Fourteenth Amendment enforcement power is the latter type of power; Congress may use this power only to regulate "state action," that is, governmental action of the states or local governments. *United States v. Morrison*, 529 U.S. 598 (2000) (Sec. C below).

The Fifteenth Amendment enforcement power would presumably be subject to a similar limitation, since that Amendment applies only to actions "by the United States or by any state." But the Thirteenth Amendment enforcement power is different; it applies directly to private as well as governmental activity, and Congress therefore may use this power to regulate the private sector. In *Jones v. Alfred H. Mayer Co.*, 392 U.S. 409 (1968), for example, the Court upheld the application, to a private real estate developer, of a Reconstruction-era statute (Section 1982) that prohibited race discrimination in housing.

The enforcement powers are further discussed in the next section.

Sec. C. Congress' Enforcement Powers

Of the various Congressional powers over individual rights, the enforcement powers present the greatest constitutional complexities. An understanding of both constitutional powers and constitutional rights (especially equal protection rights) must be brought to the consideration of these issues, since they present one of the clearest examples in constitutional law of the inter-mixing of powers and rights concerns. An understanding of the state action concept (Chap. 9, Sec. D) is also important to a study of the enforcement powers, since Congress may use its enforcement powers only to regulate the actions of state and local governments. In addition, an understanding of federalism and separation-of-powers values are important to an understanding of the enforcement powers, since such values are sharply implicated in many enforcement power cases (see, e.g., the discussion of *Katzenbach* v. *Morgan* in Chap. 4, Sec. B). Finally, one must consider the relationship between enforcement power issues and issues concerning the states' immunity from suit on federal law claims, since both sets of issues are intertwined in many enforcement power cases, including most of the cases discussed in this section. The state sovereign immunity aspect of these cases is addressed in Section D below.

To begin, it is of prime importance, in applying Congress' enforcement powers, to distinguish between federal statutes that create *new remedies* for rights guaranteed by the Thirteenth, Fourteenth, or Fifteenth Amendments, and federal statutes that create *new rights* beyond those defined by these amendments (see Sec. B.1 above). Statutes of the former type will generally fit within the "remedial power" that the enforcement clauses bestow upon Congress. *See, e.g., Rome v. United States*, 446 U.S. 156 (1980). Statutes of the latter type, however, are unlikely to be justifiable under the enforcement powers. *See, e.g., City of Boerne v. Flores*, 521 U.S. 507 (1997) (Chap. 6, Sec. E).

There is also a middle ground, however, in which a federal statute creates new rights, beyond those protected by the Constitution, but the exercise of those statutory rights may, in turn, provide a *remedy* for *existing* violations of constitutional rights or *deter future* violations of constitutional rights. Statutes of this type may be upheld under broad constructions of the remedial power. In *Katzenbach v. Morgan*, 384 U.S. 641 (1966), for example, the U.S. Supreme Court upheld a Voting Rights Act provision that prohibited the use of English literacy tests to deny voting rights to certain Spanish-speaking Puerto Ricans (see Chap. 6, Sec. E). Even though the equal protection clause did not itself create a right to be free from voting discrimination based on literacy tests, the new statutory right nevertheless could be used by the Puerto Rican community, in the political process, to remedy governmental discrimination in the provision of public services — discrimination that did violate the equal protection clause (*Id.* at 652–653).

Since the Court narrowed the scope of the section 5 power in the *City of Boerne* case (above) in 1997, Congress' use of its enforcement powers has been subject to numerous challenges. Most of the challenges have focused on Congress' exercise of its Fourteenth Amendment enforcement power (the section 5 power).

In *City of Boerne*, the key case, the Court not only affirmed the remedial rationale and rejected the substantive rationale for the Fourteenth Amendment enforcement powers (see Chap. 6, Sec. E); it also began a process of refining and narrowing the scope of this power. The narrowing trend for the enforcement powers parallels the similar trend for the commerce clause that began in 1995 with *United States v. Lopez* (Chap. 6, Sec. C.2). The effect of this narrowing trend on federal civil rights statutes is illustrated by *Kimel v. Florida Board of Regents*, 528 U.S. 62 (2000). The Court applied the remedial rationale as narrowed in *City of Boerne* to hold that Congress' application of the Age Discrimination in Employment Act (29 U.S.C. § 621 *et seq.*) to the states was beyond the scope of Congress' Fourteenth Amendment enforcement power. After noting that age discrimination is not a "suspect" classification under the Fourteenth Amendment's equal protection clause and receives only "rational basis" review (see Chap. 10, Sec. C.3), the Court determined that:

> Judged against the backdrop of our equal protection jurisprudence, it is clear that the ADEA is "so out of proportion to a supposed remedial or preventive object that it cannot be understood as responsive to, or designed to prevent, unconstitutional behavior." *City of Boerne*, 521 U.S. at 532, 117 S.Ct. 2157. The Act, through its broad restriction on the use of age as a discriminating factor, prohibits substantially more state employment decisions and practices than

would likely be held unconstitutional under the applicable equal protection, rational basis standard. [528 U.S. at 86.]

The four dissenters in *Kimel* used quite different reasoning to dispute the majority's position:

> [T]he burdens the statute imposes on the sovereignty of the several States were taken into account [by Congress] during the deliberative process leading to the enactment of the measure.... [O]nce Congress has made its policy choice, the sovereignty concerns of the several States are satisfied.... The importance of respecting the Framers' decision to assign the business of lawmaking to the Congress dictates firm resistance to the present majority's repeated substitution of its own views of federalism for those expressed in statutes enacted by the Congress and signed by the President. [528 U.S. at 96 (Stevens, J., dissenting).]

This reasoning of the dissenters, emphasizing political limits on federalism rather than judicial limits (see Chap. 6, Sec. B.4), and advocating deference to Congress' judgments, is reminiscent of the majority's reasoning is *Garcia v. San Antonio Metro Transit Authority* (Chap. 6, Sec. C.4).

In another 5 to 4 decision in *Board of Trustees of the University of Alabama v. Garrett*, 531 U.S. 356 (2001), the Court relied on *Kimel* to hold that Congress' application of Title I of the Americans With Disabilities Act (42 U.S.C. §§ 12111–12117) to the states was also beyond the scope of the enforcement power.[2] Disability discrimination, like age discrimination, receives only a "rational basis" review under the equal protection clause (see Chap. 10, Secs. C.3 and C.5). Thus, "to uphold the Act's application to the States would allow Congress to rewrite the Fourteenth Amendment law laid down by this Court.... Section 5 does not so broadly enlarge congressional authority" (531 U.S. at 374). In other words, according to the majority, upholding Congress' action would have accorded Congress a substantive (rather than a remedial) power under Section 5 — a result that the line of cases subsequent to *Katzenbach v. Morgan* had rejected.[3]

---

2. Another case on the Americans With Disabilities Act and Congress' enforcement power was pending before the U.S. Supreme Court as this book went to press. *Lane v. Tennessee*, 315 F.3d 680 (6th Cir. 2003), *cert. granted, Tennessee v. Lane*, 123 S. Ct. 2622 (2003), presents issues concerning Title II (42 U.S.C. §§ 12131–12165) of the Americans With Disabilities Act, rather than Title I as in *Garrett*. Moreover, *Lane* originated as a case concerning Congress' authority to implement the Fourteenth Amendment's due process clause, rather than the equal protection clause as in *Garrett*.

3. After *Garrett*, Congress could still use its *commerce power* to apply the Americans With Disabilities Act to the states; under *Garcia v. San Antonio Metro Transit Authority*, 469 U.S. 528 (1985) (see Chap. 6, Sec. C.4), the states would have no immunity from such Congressional regulation. The same would be true for Congress' authority, after *Kimel* (above), to use the commerce clause to apply the Age Discrimination in Employment Act to the states. HOWEVER, Congress could not enforce these statutes against the states by allowing the victims of discrimination to bring private suits against the states that allegedly violated their rights. This is because the states could assert a sovereign immunity defense to any such private action (see Chap. 5, Sec. E), and Congress could not use the commerce power to abrogate this state immunity (see Chap. 6, Sec. C.4). This problem is explored below in Section D of this Chapter.

In *Nevada Dep't. of Human Resources v. Hibbs*, 123 S.Ct. 1972 (2003), however, the Court reached a different result, upholding Congress' use of its enforcement power to apply the Family and Medical Leave Act (FMLA) (29 U.S.C. § 2611 *et seq.*) to the states. The six-Justice majority, in an opinion by Chief Justice Rehnquist, noted that the "FMLA aims to protect the right to be free from gender-based discrimination" in the administration of employers' medical leave policies, and that "[w]hen it enacted the FMLA, Congress had before it significant evidence of a long and extensive history of sex discrimination with respect to the administration of leave benefits by the States" (*Id.* at 1979). The Court then distinguished *Kimel* and *Garrett* on two grounds. First, age discrimination (as in *Kimel*) and disability discrimination (as in *Garrett*) are subject only to rational basis scrutiny under the equal protection clause (Chap. 10, Sec. C.4), while gender discrimination (as in this case) is subject to heightened judicial scrutiny (Chap. 10, Sec. D.4). Second, the statues at issue in *Kimel* and *Garrett* "applied broadly to every aspect of state employers' operations," while "the FMLA is narrowly targeted at the fault line between work and family — precisely where sex-based overgeneralization has been and remains strongest — and affects only one aspect of the employment relationship" (*Id.* at 1983). Since the heightened scrutiny makes it more difficult for the states to justify gender classifications, compared to age and disability classifications that are subject only to rational basis scrutiny, "it was easier for Congress" to demonstrate the "pattern of state constitutional violations" that section 5 requires (*Id.* at 1974–1975). In this context, Congress' evidence of the causes, manifestations, and extent of gender discrimination by states in their leave policies was "weighty enough to justify enactment of [the FMLA as] prophylactic §5 legislation." Moreover, the "narrowly targeted" provisions of the FMLA are "congruent and proportional to [their] remedial object," as required by *City of Boerne* (*Id.* at 1984). The FMLA was thus a constitutional exercise of Congress' section 5 power and could be enforced against the states.

In addition to all these developments, the Supreme Court has recently imposed another type of restriction on Congress' Fourteenth Amendment enforcement power. In *United States v. Morrison*, 529 U.S. 598 (2000), the Court narrowly interpreted the section 5 power to preclude its application to the private sector. The plaintiff, a female, had sued two males whom she alleged had raped her. The statute under which the plaintiff sued, the Violence Against Women Act, 42 U.S.C. § 13981, provided a civil remedy against private individuals who had engaged in gender-motivated violence. The Fourteenth Amendment, however, is directed only to "state action" (see Chap. 9, Sec. D). Since the civil remedy imposed by the statute was directed to private action, and not to states or state officials who may have discriminated by gender in administering state laws, the Court determined that the statute could not be considered to be congruent or proportional to any state violations of the Fourteenth Amendment.

The Court's recent enforcement power cases emphasize and clarify that Congress' Fourteenth Amendment enforcement power may be used only to *remedy actual* violations, or to *deter potential* violations, of the Fourteenth Amendment's equal protection and due process clauses. The violations must be ones committed by the states and their local governments (as in *Morrison*). In other words, enforcement power legislation must be either remedial or "reasonably prophylactic" to fit within the scope of section 5. There must be an evidentiary basis in the legislative record to support Congress' belief that the legislation was needed to remedy or deter a pattern of equal protection or due process violations by state and local governments. Such violations are more likely to exist, and the courts are more likely to find Congress' evidence to be weighty, when the discrimination or other allegedly unconstitutional action is subject to heightened scrutiny (as in *Nevada v. Hibbs*). Moreover, "Congress may…do more than simply proscribe conduct that [the Court has] held unconstitutional." Its "'authority both to remedy and to deter violation of rights'" allows it to prohibit "'a somewhat broader swath of conduct, including that which is not itself forbidden by the [Fourteenth] Amendment's text'" (123 S.Ct at 1977, quoting *Garrett*, 531 U.S. at 365), so long as "proscrib[ing] [the] facially constitutional conduct" serves "to prevent and deter unconstitutional conduct" (*Id.*). Congress' legislation must also display "congruence and proportionality," that is, "the remedy imposed by Congress must be congruent and proportional to the targeted violation" of the Fourteenth Amendment that Congress has identified (*Garrett*, 531 U.S. at 372, 374). Parallel restrictions would likely also apply to Congress' exercise of its enforcement powers under the Thirteenth and Fifteenth Amendments.

Sec. D. Enforcing Federal Individual Rights Statutes Against the States: The Sovereign Immunity Problem

When Congress seeks to apply its individual rights statutes to the states, and to enforce these rights by allowing private individuals to sue the states for violations of their rights, special problems arise. Typically, the states will assert that sovereign immunity protects them from being sued by private individuals (see Chap. 5, Sec. E). Congress typically will take legislative steps to "abrogate" or cancel the states' immunity. After *Seminole Tribe v. Florida*, 517 U.S. 44 (1996) (Chap. 6, Sec. G.2), however, Congress may abrogate the states' sovereign immunity and authorize federal court suits against the states only if: (1) Congress has clearly indicated its intention to abrogate state immunity (*see Atascadero State Hospital v. Scanlon*, 473 U.S. 234, 242 (1985)); and (2) the statute authorizing the particular suit is within the scope of Congress' Fourteenth Amendment enforcement power. In U.S. Supreme Court cases after *Seminole Tribe*, these two considerations have framed the analysis. In *Kimel v. Florida Board of Regents*, 528 U.S. 62, 73 (2000), for instance, the Court stated that "[t]o determine whether [immunity has been abrogated], we must resolve two predicate questions: first, whether Congress unequivocally expressed its intent to abrogate that immunity; and second, if it did, whether Congress acted pursuant to a valid grant of constitutional authority." Analysis of the second of these questions requires consideration not only of *Seminole Tribe* but also other recent Court decisions that restrict the scope of Congress' enforcement authority under section 5 of the Fourteenth Amendment (see Sec. C above, discussing *City of Boerne v. Flores*, *Kimel v. Florida Board of Regents*, *Garrett v. Board of Trustees*, *Nevada v. Hibbs*, and *United States v. Morrison*).

In these recent cases, the Court has strikingly strengthened state immunity from suit. It did so in several interrelated steps. First, in *Seminole Tribe*, the Court prohibited Congress from using the commerce clause, or any other source of power except the Fourteenth Amendment (and presumably the Thirteenth and Fifteenth Amendment) enforcement power, to abrogate state immunity. The Court then further strengthened state immunity in the *City of Boerne* line of cases by narrowing the scope of Congress' section 5 enforcement power so as to limit the occasions on which it may serve as a tool of abrogation. This combination of events makes it very difficult for private plaintiffs to enforce federal individual rights statutes directly against the states in federal court.

Finally, at the same time that the Court was taking these steps to strengthen the states' sovereign immunity from *federal court* suits, it used other constitutional principles to strengthen state sovereign immunity from private suits to enforce federal law claims in *state* court and in federal *administrative agencies*. The key case on state courts is *Alden v. Maine*, 527 U.S. 706 (1999) (see Chap. 5, Sec. E). The state asserted a constitutional immunity from federal Fair Labor Standards Act (FLSA) claims brought in state court. The *Alden* plaintiffs (state employees) argued that the FLSA contained provisions permitting suits against states, and that these provisions constituted a clear Congressional abrogation of state sovereign immunity. Echoing *Seminole Tribe*, however, the Court ruled that Congress had no authority under the commerce clause, or its other powers under Article I of the Constitution, to abrogate state sovereign immunity in state courts. The Court therefore affirmed the state courts' dismissal of the case because Maine could successfully assert a sovereign immunity defense against its employees' attempts to enforce federally created FLSA rights.

Similarly, in *Federal Maritime Commission v. South Carolina Ports Authority*, 535 U.S. 743 (2002) (Chap. 6, Sec. G.2.)—the key case on federal administrative agencies—the state asserted sovereign immunity from federal claims brought against it in an adjudicative proceeding before the Federal Maritime Commission. The plaintiff, who sought to enforce rights under a federal shipping act, argued (along with the FMC) that sovereign immunity did not extend to private claims in federal administrative forums. The Court rejected this argument and upheld the state Ports Authority's assertion of sovereign immunity.

Taken together, *Seminole Tribe*, the *City of Borne* line of cases, *Alden*, and *South Carolina Ports Authority* close off most of the existing avenues by which private parties had enforced federal statutory rights against the states. These cases thus place in bold relief the question of what options are now available to Congress for enforcing federal statutory rights against the states. There are still some circumstances—though greatly narrowed—in which Congress can successfully abrogate state immunity; *Nevada Dept. of Human Resources v. Hibbs*, above, makes this point well.[4] In addition, Congress may still provide for enforcement by private individuals through prospective injunctive re-

---

4. As this book went to press, another possibility for Congressional abrogation was before the U.S. Supreme Court in *Tennessee v. Lane*, discussed in footnote 2 above. This case presents two interrelated possibilities: (1) whether some federal statutory provisions that cannot be upheld under Congress' power to enforce the Fourteenth Amendment's *equal protection clause* could nevertheless be upheld under Congress' power to enforce the *due process clause*; and (2) whether selected *applications* of a federal statute could be upheld under Congress' enforcement power even though other applications of the same statute would not be upheld.

lief against state officers who violate federal rights; as the Court recognized in *Garrett*, such suits would fall into the *Ex Parte Young* exception to state sovereign immunity (531 U.S. at 374, fn. 9; and see generally Chap. 5, Sec. E of this book). Beyond these two limited options, there are apparently two other plausible alternatives for enforcing federal statutory rights against the states.

First, under its spending power (Chap. 6, Sec. D), Congress apparently may require that state institutions waive their immunity from certain private suits as a condition of their participation in federal grant programs. In the *Alden* case the Supreme Court supports this approach by remarking that, under the spending power, "the Federal Government lack[s] [neither] the authority [n]or means to seek the States' voluntary consent to private suits" (527 U.S. at 755).

Second, the federal government itself may sue the states, on behalf of aggrieved private parties, for damages for federal law violations. The Court in *Seminole Tribe* distinguished its holding from such situations where the federal government is the plaintiff: "[T]he Federal Government can bring suit in federal court against a State, *see, e.g., United States v. Texas*, 143 U.S. 621, 644–645 (1892)..." (517 U.S. at 71 n. 14). Similarly, in *Alden*, the Court emphasized that "[i]n ratifying the Constitution, the States consented to suits brought by...the Federal Government" (527 U.S. at 755). And in the *Garrett* case, the Court noted that the Americans With Disabilities Act "can be enforced by the United States in actions for money damages" (531 U.S. at 374 n. 9). *See generally* Evan Caminker, "State Immunity Waivers for Suits by the United States," 98 Mich. L. Rev. 92 (1999).

It is also important to recall that state sovereign immunity does not protect the state's local governments from suit—at least not from suit in federal court (see Chap. 5, Sec. E). Thus Congress may continue to provide for private parties' suits against a state's local governments as a means of enforcing federal statutory rights.

Sec. E. State Constitutional Rights

In recent times there has been a rebirth and expansion of interest in state constitutions. *See, e.g.,* Shirley Abramson, "Divided We Stand: State Constitutions in a More Perfect Union," 18 Hastings Const. L.Q. 723 (1991); Yvonne Kauger, "Reflections on Federalism: State Constitutions' Role as Nurturers of Individual Rights," 4 Emerging Issues in State Constitutional Law 105 (1991). State constitutions, of course, establish the structure of the state government and provide for the creation of local governments within the state. But state constitutions also contain individual rights guarantees (as well as mandates and other provisions) that limit the exercise of power by the state government and local governments.

A recent series of three cases overturning state statutory prohibitions on same-sex marriage vividly illustrates the modern importance of state constitutional rights. In the first of these cases, *Baehr v. Lewin*, 852 P. 2d 44 (Hawaii, 1993), a plurality of the Hawaii Supreme Court determined that the state's marriage laws created a sex classification by making eligibility for marriage dependent on the sex of one's partner. The plurality then determined that this sex classification was subject to strict scrutiny under a provision of the Hawaii Constitution (Art. I, sec. 5) that expressly prohibits discrimination on grounds of sex. On remand, the trial court held that the state's justifications for its classification did not meet strict scrutiny requirements (*Baehr v. Miike*, 1996 WL 694235 (1996)). Then, while the case was on appeal for the second time to the Hawaii Supreme Court, the voters of Hawaii approved an amendment to the Hawaii Constitution that authorizes the state legislature "to reserve marriage to opposite-sex couples" (Hawaii Const., Art. I, sec. 23). The Hawaii Supreme Court thereupon vacated the trial court's judgment in favor of the plaintiff same-sex couples and ordered entry of judgment for the state (*Baehr v. Miike*, 994 P. 2d 566 (Hawaii 1999)).

The second and third of the cases on same-sex marriage are from Vermont and Massachusetts. In the Vermont case, *Baker v. State of Vermont*, 744 A. 2d 864 (Vt., 1999), the state's Supreme Court held that the state could not deny same-sex couples the benefits of civil marriage that opposite-sex couples enjoyed. This court relied on the "common benefits clause" in the Vermont Constitution (Chap. 1, Art. 7), which provides that "government is...instituted for the common benefit...of the people...." In the Massachusetts case, *Goodridge v. Department of Public Health*, 798 N.E. 2d 941 (Mass., 2003)—a 4 to 3 decision attracting instant attention in the media, in national and state political circles, and among the bench and bar —the Massachusetts Supreme Judicial Court also ruled in favor of the plaintiff same-sex couples. The court held that it is unconstitutional for the state to refuse to provide same-sex couples with "the protections, benefits, and obligations conferred by civil marriage." Basing the decision on the state constitution's equal protection clause, the court applied rational basis review (compare Chap. 10, Sec. C.3) and determined that the state's limitation of marriage benefits to opposite-sex couples could not meet even this low-level review. Subsequently, in *In Re Opinions of the Justices to the Senate*, 440 Mass. 1201 (2004), the same court ruled that the state legislature must extend the status of marriage as such to same-sex couples, rather than an alternative "civil union" status.

All state constitutions have a bill of rights, declaration of rights, or other detailed listing of rights.[5] These rights may be similar to those in the federal constitution; the language of some state individual rights provisions, in fact, may be virtually identical to that of the parallel federal provision. But state courts sometimes construe state rights clauses more broadly than similar federal clauses are construed—which, in the U.S. Constitution's system of federalism, state courts are entitled to do (*see* Paul Kahn, "Interpretation and Authority in State Constitutionalism," 106 HARV. L. REV. 1147 (1993)). Some state courts have intricate reasoning processes for determining whether to interpret a rights clause the same as the parallel federal clause, thus permitting use of

---

5. Many state constitutions also have clauses protecting unenumerated rights, somewhat similar to the Ninth Amendment to the U.S. Constitution. State courts apparently utilize these clauses more frequently than the federal courts utilize the Ninth Amendment. See Louis Karl Bonham, Note, "Unenumerated Rights Clauses in State Constitutions," 63 TEX. L REV. 1321 (1985).

federal constitutional precedents in construing the state constitution's clause; or whether to interpret the state clause independently of the parallel federal provision. *See, e.g., Seeley v. State of Washington*, 940 P.2d 604, 609–611 & 620–621 (Wash. 1997).[6]

State constitutions also contain rights clauses that have no parallel in the federal Constitution's text. For instance, some state constitutions contain an express right to privacy. Federal constitutional privacy rights, in contrast, arise by implication and are a matter of controversy (see Chap. 11, Secs. C.2 and C.3). The Alaska Constitution, for example, includes an express right to privacy in Article I, section 22, which the Alaska Supreme Court applied in *Ravin v. State*, 537 P. 2d 494 (Alaska 1975), to protect the right to smoke marijuana in the privacy of one's home; *see generally* Erwin Chemerinsky, "Privacy and the Alaska Constitution: Failing to Fulfill the Promise," 20 ALASKA L. REV. 29 (2003). Another example of an express right to privacy is Article I, section 6 of the Hawaii Constitution. In *State of Hawaii v. Kam*, 748 P. 2d 372 (Hawaii, 1988), the Hawaii Supreme Court relied on this provision to uphold the right of adult persons to purchase obscene materials for use in their own homes. In *State of Hawaii v. Mallan*, 950 P. 2d 178 (Hawaii, 1998), however, the same court declined to interpret the right-to-privacy clause to create a right to possess marijuana in one's own home—a result contrary to that of the Alaska Supreme Court in *Ravin* (above).

Similarly, some state constitutions have equal rights amendments (ERA's) that expressly cover gender discrimination (*e.g.*, Pa. Const., Art. I, sec. 28), while under the federal Constitution gender discrimination is dealt with under the generic terms of the equal protection clause).[7] Many state constitutions have right-to-education provisions that guarantee a certain level or quality of education or educational opportunity (*e.g.*, N.J. Const. Art. VIII, sec. 4, ¶ 1), while the federal equal protection clause does not protect such rights *(see San Antonio Indep. School Dist. v. Rodriguez*, below, and in Chap. 10, Sec. D.8). The California Constitution even includes an express "right to fish," which guarantees access to public waters of the state without restriction other than for matters such as seasons and catch limits (Cal. Const., Art. I, sec. 25). And the Montana Constitution, and several others, contain an "armed body of men" clause that accords citizens the right to be free from law enforcement imposed by persons imported from out-of-state. *See* Robert Natelson, "'No Armed Bodies of Men'—Montanans' Forgotten Constitutional Right," 63 MONTANA L. REV. 1 (2002).

In addition, some rights clauses in state constitutions may apply to private activity that would not be covered by federal constitutional rights because of the federal state action doctrine (Chap. 9, Sec. D). A provision of the Illinois Constitution, for example, prohibits discrimination on the basis of disability in employment and real property transactions (Ill. Const., Art. I, sec. 19). The New Jersey Supreme Court has inter-

---

6 Regarding the approaches to interpretation of state constitutions and interpretive problems encountered with state constitutions, *see* G. Alan Tarr, UNDERSTANDING STATE CONSTITUTIONS, ch. 6 (Princeton U. Press, 1998).

7. In 1972, Congress did submit a proposed federal ERA to the states for ratification pursuant to Article V of the U.S. Constitution. The proposed amendment fell several states short of the three-fourths needed for ratification. See Chap.9, Sec. E, under 1972.

preted the free speech provisions of the New Jersey Constitution (Art. I, ¶'s 6 and 18) apply to some private action, thus according individuals some rights to speak on private college campuses (*State v. Schmid*, 423 A.2d 615 (N.J. 1980)) and at regional shopping centers (*New Jersey Coalition Against War in the Middle East v. J.M.B. Realty Corp.*, 650 A.2d 757 (N.J. 1994)). State courts in several other states have reached similar conclusions under their own constitutions; see, for example, the *Prune Yard Shopping Center* case, below in this Section.

To understand state constitutional rights developments such as these, it is important to consider the conceptual relationship, in the American system of federalism, between state constitutions and the federal Constitution. Federalism principles concerning the role of the states (Chap. 6, Sec. A), especially supremacy principles (Chap. 6, Sec. B.1), provide a necessary background. The following case illustrates the relationship between state and federal constitutional rights.

In *Prune Yard Shopping Center v. Robins*, 592 P.2d 341 (Cal. 1979), *affirmed*, 447 U.S. 74 (1980), a private shopping center had ejected a group of high school students who were distributing political material and soliciting petition signatures on the premises. The students sued the shopping center in state court, claiming that the shopping center had violated their rights under the "liberty of speech clause" (Art. 1, sec. 2) and the petition clause (Art. I, sec. 3) of the California Constitution. The California Supreme Court sided with the students, construing the state constitutional clauses more broadly than the first amendment's speech clause and holding that, so construed, the state constitution protected the students' expressive activities on private property such as the shopping center. When the U.S. Supreme Court reviewed the case, the shopping center argued that the California court's ruling was inconsistent with the Supreme Court's decision in *Lloyd v. Tanner*, 407 U.S. 551 (1972), which held that the first amendment of the federal Constitution does not guarantee individuals a right to free expression on the premises of a private shopping center. The Court rejected the shopping center's argument, emphasizing that the state had a "sovereign right to adopt in its own constitution individual liberties more expansive than those conferred by the federal Constitution" (447 U.S. at 81). The Court also rejected the argument that the California court's interpretation of the state constitution violated the shopping center's property rights and freedom of speech under the federal Constitution; although state constitutional rights of the students could not be construed in such a way as to violate the federal constitutional rights of the shopping center, no such violation was evident in this case.

Pruneyard thus makes clear that state courts may interpret state constitutions to grant individuals more extensive rights than those granted under the federal Constitution—so long as the state does not apply and enforce these state rights in a way that interferes with other individuals' federal constitutional rights. Numerous cases in the state courts have upheld specific state constitutional rights that are more protective than their counterparts in the federal Constitution. The following cases are illustrative.

In *State of Oregon v. Henry*, 732 P. 2d 9 (Ore. 1987), the Oregon Supreme Court considered the validity of a state statute prohibiting the distribution of obscene material. Under federal constitutional law, obscenity receives no protection under the First

Amendment (see Chap. 12, Sec. D; but see footnote 8 below). The Oregon court expressly rejected this approach, holding that: "In this state any person can write, print, read, say, show, or sell anything to a consenting adult even though that expression may be generally or universally considered 'obscene'" (*Id.* at 18). The court therefore held that the Oregon obscenity statute violated the free speech clause in The Oregon Constitution. The Hawaii Supreme Court reached a similar result in *State of Hawaii v. Kam* (above), relying on the state constitution's right-to-privacy clause rather than its free speech clause.[8]

In *Edgewood Indep. School District v. Kirby*, 777 S.W. 2d 391 (Tex. 1989), the Texas Supreme Court considered the constitutionality of the state's system for financing its public schools—a system that resulted in substantial disparities among local school districts in the per pupil financial resources available for education. This same system had earlier been challenged in federal court as a violation of the federal equal protection clause; and in *San Antonio Indep. School Dist. v. Rodriguez*, 411 U.S. 1 (1973), the U.S. Supreme Court had rejected the challenge and upheld the system's constitutionality (see Chap. 10, Secs. D.3 and D.8). But the Texas court in *Kirby* came to a different conclusion, relying exclusively on a state constitutional provision mandating an "efficient" public school system "for the general diffusion of knowledge":

> [T]he state's school financing system is neither financially efficient nor efficient in the sense of providing for a "general diffusion knowledge" statewide, and therefore that it violates Article VII, Section 1 of the Texas constitution.... [D]istricts must have substantially equal access to similar revenues per pupil at similar levels of tax effort. Children who live in poor districts and children who live in rich districts must be afforded a substantially equal opportunity to have access to educational funds. [777 S.W.2d at 397.]

In *Moe v. Secretary of Administration*, 417 N.E.2d 387 (Mass. 1981), the Supreme Court of Massachusetts considered whether a state statute providing funds for childbirth costs but denying funds for abortion costs violated the due process clause of the state constitution. The Massachusetts court noted that, in *Harris v. McRae*, 448 U.S. 297 (1980), "the Supreme Court of the United States upheld enactments substantially identical to those challenged here against claims that they violated the due process and equal protection components of the Fifth and Fourteenth Amendments to the United States Constitution" (417 N.E.2d at 399). But *Harris* did not stand in the way of a contrary ruling by the state court because the state constitution's "Declaration of Rights affords a greater degree of protection to the right asserted here than does the Federal Constitution as interpreted by *Harris v. McRae*" (417 N.E.2d at 400). The Massachusetts court thus held the state statute unconstitutional under the state constitution.

---

8. The federal Constitution actually does protect a part of the privacy interest addressed in *State of Hawaii v. Kam*. In *Stanley v. Georgia*, 394 U.S. 557 (1969), the U.S. Supreme Court recognized a constitutional right to read and view obscene materials in the privacy of one's own home. But in later cases, the Court refused to recognize a "correlative" constitutional right to purchase obscene materials and transport them to one's home for use there. *United States v. 12 200 Ft. Reels*, 413 U.S. 123 (1973); *United States v. Orito*, 413 U.S. 139 (1973).

In *Witters v. State Comm'n for the Blind*, 771 P.2d 1119 (Wash. 1989), the Supreme Court of Washington considered whether a state constitutional prohibition against using public moneys to pay for religious instruction (Art. I, Sec. 11) prevented the state from granting funds to a disabled student who would attend a private Bible college to become a pastor, missionary, or church youth director. The case was on remand from the United States Supreme Court, which had rejected the state's argument that granting the funds would violate the federal Constitution's establishment clause (*Witters v. Washington Dep't of Services for the Blind*, 474 U.S. 481 (1986); see Chap. 13, Sec. B.3). The Washington court held that the state constitution's anti-establishment protection is more comprehensive than the protection afforded by the federal establishment clause. According to the court, "the 'sweeping and comprehensive' language of Const. Art. 1, Sec. 11…prohibits not only the *appropriation* of public money for religious instruction, but also the *application* of public funds to religious instruction," and this is "a major difference between our state constitution and the establishment clause of the first amendment to the United States Constitution" (771 P.2d at 1122). So construed, the state constitution prohibited the state from expending funds for purposes that would be permissible under the federal Constitution's establishment clause. (The Washington court went on to find that the state's denial of the funds, pursuant to the state constitution, would not violate the student's right to free exercise of religion under the federal Constitution's First Amendment or his equal protection rights under the Fourteenth Amendment.)[9]

Occasionally, the U.S. Supreme Court may take note of the expansive state constitutional rights recognized by state courts and interpret federal constitutional rights more broadly to accord with the state interpretations. *Lawrence v. Texas*, 123 S.Ct. 2472 (2003) (Chap. 11, Sec. C.3), in which the Court overruled *Bowers v. Hardwick*, 478 U.S. 186 (1986), provides a striking recent example. In *Bowers*, the Court rejected a substantive due process challenge to a Georgia statute making sodomy a crime and upheld the statute as applied to homosexual sodomy (Chap. 11, Sec. C.3). Subsequently, in *Powell v. State of Georgia*, 510 S.E.2d 18 (Ga. 1998), the Supreme Court of Georgia invalidated the Georgia sodomy statute upheld in *Bowers* because it infringed the defendant's "liberty of privacy" under the state constitution's due process clause (Ga. Const., Art. I, §1, par. 1). The Georgia court described this liberty as "a fundamental constitutional right" under Georgia's Constitution (510 S.E.2d at 22) and found the protection of "unforced, private, adult sexual activity" to be "at the heart of" Georgia's constitutional protection of privacy (*Id.* at 24). The state could not limit this liberty unless "the limitation is shown to serve a compelling state interest and to be narrowly tailored to effectuate only that compelling interest" (*Id.*)—a standard that the state could not meet. Thus, while *Bowers* had upheld the Georgia statute's constitutionality

---

9. A subsequent case involving the State of Washington, and presenting similar state and federal constitutional issues, was awaiting decision by the U.S. Supreme Court as this book went to press. *Locke v. Davey*, 299 F.3d 748 (9th Cir. 2002), *cert. granted*, 123 S. Ct. 2075 (2003). The particular issue in this case is whether the state's denial of a scholarship, in reliance on Article I, section 11 of the state Constitution, violates the First Amendment free exercise clause (see Chap. 13, Sec. C) of the federal Constitution.

under the federal Constitution's due process clause, *Powell* held the statute unconstitutional under the state Constitution's due process clause, declaring that "the right of privacy…guaranteed by the Georgia Constitution is far more extensive than the right of privacy protected by the U.S. Constitution" (*Id.* at 22).

In the wake of *Powell*, other state courts reached results similar to *Powell* and different from *Bowers* in cases specifically involving same-sex sexual activity. In *Commonwealth v. Wasson*, 842 S.W. 2d 487 (Ky. 1992), for example, the Kentucky Supreme Court used the right-to-liberty clause and an equal rights clause of the Kentucky Constitution to invalidate a Kentucky statute that criminalized sexual activity between persons of the same sex. Similarly, the Arkansas Supreme Court, relying on liberty and equality clauses in the Arkansas constitution, determined "that a fundamental right to privacy is implicit in the Arkansas Constitution" and that the state's same-sex sodomy law violated this fundamental right (*Jegley v. Picado*, 80 S.W. 3d 332, 350 (Ark. 2002)). Then, in *Lawrence*, the U.S. Supreme Court cited *Powell*, *Wasson*, and *Jegley*, as well as similar decisions in Montana and Tennessee, specifically noting that "[t]he courts of five different states have declined to follow [*Bowers*] in interpreting provisions in their own state constitutions parallel to the Due Process Clause of the Fourteenth Amendment" (123 S.Ct. at 2483). The Court used these state constitutional rights interpretations as part of the basis for overruling *Bowers* and revising the interpretation of the federal due process clause to provide protections similar to those provided by these state constitutions.

In modern times, and especially since the early 1980s, state courts have decided many hundreds of state constitutional rights cases such as those discussed in this Section. (*See* Ronald Collins & David Skover, "The Future of Liberal Legal Scholarship," 87 MICH. L. REV. 189, 216–218 (1988).) Frequently, the state courts have interpreted state constitutional rights to be more expansive than those in the federal Constitution. Moreover, as the U.S. Supreme Court has indicated in its decision in *Lawrence v. Texas* (above), the federal courts may be influenced by state constitutional developments as they interpret the federal Constitution. Given such developments, it is critically important that both state and federal constitutional rights, and the conceptual relationship between them, be understood by students and practitioners alike.

Sec. F. Exercise No. 10: Alternative Sources of Law Applicable to National Origin Discrimination (The Exclusion of an Iraqi Guest from a Private Club)

Sometimes a particular course of action will invade an individual's equality or liberty interests, but federal constitutional rights will not protect the individual. Either the action is not state action, and federal constitutional rights therefore do not apply (see Chap. 9, Sec. D), or no federal rights clause is construed broadly enough to cover the challenged action. Creative lawyering, using alternative sources of law, is therefore required to protect the individual's rights. The challenge is to discover and tap some other, non-constitutional "right" that would protect the liberty or equality interest that is being invaded. With this challenge in mind, and against the backdrop of possibilities outlined in sections A, B, and E above, consider the following scenario and then address the questions that follow. (Suggested answers to the questions are set out immediately after the questions.)

Each of the following hypothetical situations deals with a problem of national origin. For each situation, assume that the entity involved is *not* engaged in state action and that the challenged action is not violative of *federal constitutional* rights.

Assume that you are dealing with a private club called the "Order of the Walleye Pike." The club is located in a medium-sized city. It is incorporated under state law as a non-profit corporation. Being a membership club, it is not open to the general public, although club members may bring guests to the facilities. To join the club, an applicant must be accepted by a vote of the existing members. According to the club's by-laws, as recently amended, persons of Middle-Eastern or Arabic descent are not eligible for membership.

The club owns its own building and the land on which the building is located. In its building, the club has a cocktail lounge and a dining room in which alcoholic beverages are served. The club holds a liquor license issued by the state which allows it to serve drinks in its facilities. Many other private clubs, restaurants, and bars in the city also hold liquor licenses issued by the state.

A white member of the club decides to invite a native of Iraq to the club facilities for dinner and drinks. The club's sergeant-at-arms determines that the club's "no Middle Eastern or Arabic members" policy also applies to guests, and he therefore excludes the Iraqi guest from the premises.

When the Iraqi guest is excluded from the private club, the member takes the guest to a local restaurant for dinner and drinks. The restaurant also holds a liquor license from the state and serves alcoholic beverages. It also has a recently instituted policy of refusing service to persons of Middle Eastern or Arabic descent.

Questions

QUES. 1. On the federal level, are there any statutes that Congress has passed that would apply to national origin discrimination in private clubs? In restaurants? What Congressional power(s) might support such a statute?

QUES 2. On the state level, what source(s) of law might apply to national origin discrimination in private clubs? In restaurants? Regarding state statutes, what types of statutory provisions would you search for, and what types of arguments could you make, in seeking to protect the Iraqi guest?

QUES. 3. If Congress or the states did prohibit national origin discrimination in private clubs or restaurants, might either the clubs or the restaurants have a plausible argument that application of this requirement to them would violate their federal constitutional rights, or those of their members or customers? Suppose, for example, that the state's constitution creates a state constitutional right to be free from national origin discrimination by private clubs. Would this *state* constitutional right be trumped by the *federal* constitutional rights of club members? What principle would apply to the resolution of the situation if state and federal constitutional rights are in conflict?

Answers

ANS. to QUES. 1. The closest federal statute is Title II of the Civil Rights Act of 1964, the public accommodations title (42 U.S.C. § 2000a *et seq.*). Application of the law to restaurants and motels was upheld as an appropriate exercise of Congress' commerce power in *Katzenbach v. McClung* (the *Ollie's Barbecue case*), 379 U.S. 294 (1964), and *Heart of Atlanta Motel v. United States*, 379 U.S. 241 (1964) (Sec. B.3 above). Title II would likely prohibit the restaurant from discriminating by national origin, assuming a substantial portion of the food it serves has moved in interstate commerce (42 U.S.C. § 2000a (c)(2)). Title II would not likely apply to the private club (42 U.S.C. § 2000a(e)).

ANS. to QUES. 2. One possibility is a state constitutional provision regarding equality or non-discrimination, construed more broadly than the federal equal protection clause. Another possibility is a state statute or a local government ordinance (such as a human relations or human rights ordinance), either standing alone or as implemented by administrative regulations. There are two likely types of such statutes or ordinances that could apply to this problem. The first is a liquor license law that makes non-discrimination a condition for receipt of a license (*see B.P.O.E. Lodge No. 2043 v. Ingraham*, 297 A.2d 607 (Me. 1972)(race discrimination); *Coalition for Open Doors v. Annapolis Lodge No. 622*, B.P.O.E., 635 A.2d 412 (Md. 1994) (gender discrimination). The second is a public accommodations law that prohibits places of public accommodation from discriminating in the selection of customers or members (*see Commonwealth Human Relations Comm'n v. Loyal Order of Moose*, 294 A.2d 594 (Pa. 1972) (race discrimination); *Benyon v. St. George-Dixie Lodge No. 1743, Benevolent and Protective Order of Elks*, 854 P. 2d 513 (Utah, 1993) (gender discrimination). The first type of law would apply both to the private club and the restaurant; the second type would apply to the restaurant and may or may not apply to the club, depending on how expansively the term "public accommodation" is defined in the law.

ANS. to QUES. 3. The most likely argument would be that such prohibitions on national origin discrimination by a private entity violate the entity's, member's, or customer's freedom of association under the First Amendment or Fourteenth Amendment (see Chap. 12, Sec. G). Restaurants are unlikely to prevail on such an argument, since they could not show they were organized for expressive purposes or that their relationships with customers were characterized by intimacy and personal privacy. The argument would also be a difficult one for many private clubs, especially clubs with large memberships or rapid turnover of members. *See New York State Club Ass'n v. New York*, 487 U.S. 1 (1988). But if the club were engaged in expressive activities regarding Iraq or the Middle East, an expressive association claim might be feasible. *See Boy Scouts of America v. Dale*, 530 U.S. 640 (2000) (Chap. 12, Sec. G).

Were the private club to argue that a state non-discrimination requirement violated its federal constitutional freedom of association, the questions would be: (1) whether the club could substantiate such a violation of federal constitutional rights under either the First Amendment or the Fourteenth Amendment; and (2) whether these rights, if substantiated, would prevail over the member's or guest's state constitutional or statutory right to non-discrimination. If the answer to the first question were yes, as for instance in *Boy Scouts of America v. Dale*, then — under federal supremacy princi- ples — the answer to the second question must be yes also (see Sec. E above). For pur- poses of the supremacy clause, it would not matter whether the member's or guest's right were a state statutory or a state constitutional right.

Sec. G. Study Suggestions

The materials in this chapter provide a reminder that, in some cases, rights claims may be asserted under a federal statute, a state constitution, or state or local legislation as well as — or instead of — the federal Constitution. Be on the lookout for such cases and for the potential conflicts they may present between one source of rights and an- other. Look also for situations in which a federal constitutional right preempts or in- validates a right created under state law, and situations in which state courts go their own way, implementing state constitutional rights that are stronger than comparable federal constitutional rights or different in kind from any federal constitutional right. The most basic lesson to be derived from such cases is that, for any one studying or working in the field of individual rights, federal constitutional rights by no means stand alone; there are *multiple* sources of rights to consult, many of which will provide more protections for individuals than the federal constitution does.

Section C above on Congress' enforcement powers focuses on some fundamental questions concerning Congress' authority to create federal statutory rights for indi- viduals. You should associate this power with Congress' other domestic powers in Chapter 6. As you read the cases on the enforcement powers, seek to identify the role that the necessary and proper clause, and means/ends analysis, play in the Court's rea- soning. Also, for each part of each opinion, determine whether the Court is address- ing the remedial rationale or the substantive rationale for the enforcement powers. Note how the Court has narrowed the enforcement powers over time since the broad interpretation in *Katzenbach v. Morgan*; and consider *why* the Court has engaged in this narrowing process.

FOR FURTHER READING: (1) William Brennan, State Constitutions and the Pro- tection of Individual Rights," 90 HARV. L. REV. 489 (1977). (2) Lawrence Friedman, "The Constitutional Value of Dialogue and the New Judicial Federalism," 28 HASTINGS CONST. L. Q. 93 (2000). (3) Roger Hartley, "Enforcing Federal Civil Rights Against Pub- lic Entities After *Garrett*: Only Creative Lawyers Need Apply," 28 J. OF COLLEGE AND UNIV. LAW 41 (2001).

Chapter 15

Concluding Perspectives: The Integration of Constitutional Law

Sec. A. Introduction

This book has provided an extended commentary on the U.S. Constitution and American Constitutional Law. The powers of all three branches of the federal government have been explored, from the perspectives of both federalism and separation of powers. The federalistic limits on state powers have been addressed. The various individual rights guarantees constraining the exercise of government power have also been explored. In the process, the conceptual bases of these powers and rights have been examined; key conceptual distinctions have been made; foundational U.S. Supreme Court cases have been presented and analyzed; the analytical methods by which constitutional principles are developed and applied have been set out and explained; and the process by which the courts and others interpret the Constitution has been explored.[1]

It may be helpful — indeed may be critically important — to reflect at the end of this study on all that has been encountered along the way. To maximize the benefits of the study and their retention over time, it may also be critically important, upon reflection, to *synthesize* the materials that have been studied and to *integrate* the learning experiences that have occurred. This book has provided assistance with these tasks all along the way. This final chapter provides additional materials to facilitate synthesis and integration. The goal is for the reader to confirm, and put the finishing touches

---

1. For students studying constitutional law in a formal course, or as independent learners, this book has also provided numerous study aids. Some are in the text proper — such as the ten "Exercises" to sharpen understanding that appear in various chapters and the "Study Suggestions" sections at the end of Chapters 5 through 8 and 10 through 14. Other study suggestions are in Appendix B at the end of this book.

on, an understanding of constitutional law that is based on the constitutional law forest and not merely on its trees.

Sec. B. The Litigation Process for Constitutional Issues

The first view of the "constitutional law forest" focuses on the litigation process. Although the courts are not the only constitutional decisionmakers (see Chap. 5, Sec. C), constitutional issues are typically resolved in the courts, state as well as federal. The litigation of constitutional issues is a complex process that extends from the trial court to the U.S. Supreme Court. Various views of this process have been presented throughout this book, especially in Chapter 5. This Section presents a more integrated picture of the litigation process. Besides enhancing understanding of the judicial power and the work of the federal courts, this integrated view of the litigation process will help readers discern when and how constitutional issues arise in litigation, and how the various subjects addressed in this book relate to the various steps of the litigation process.

The steps in litigation will differ somewhat depending on whether the initial forum is a federal court or a state court, and on whether the constitutional issues are raised in civil or criminal litigation. The litigation process will also unfold differently from the perspective of the plaintiff (or the prosecution, in criminal cases) than from the perspective of the defendant. The following listing focuses primarily on federal civil litigation from the plaintiff's perspective. The entire process, of course, takes place within the context of judicial supremacy principles (see Chap. 5, Secs. A & B).

1. *Choice of forum.* The plaintiff must decide whether to file the case in federal court or in state court. The choice involves many factors, tactical as well as legal. One of the most important legal considerations may be whether the plaintiff can meet the requirements for access to federal court (steps 2 and 3 below), which tend to be stricter than state court access requirements.

2. *Federal court subject matter jurisdiction.* The plaintiff must determine and plead the basis for federal court jurisdiction over the subject matter of the claims alleged. This is usually an easy matter in cases presenting constitutional issues because they are cases "arising under the Constitution" within the meaning of Article III, section 2, paragraph 1, and thus will fall within the statutory "federal question" jurisdiction (28 U.S.C. sec. 1331) (see Chap. 5, Sec. A). On rare occasions, however, there may be a case that (1) falls within the "arising under" category of federal jurisdiction, or perhaps another of Article III's nine subject matter categories, but also (2) falls within the scope of a statute that Congress has passed in order to preclude or withdraw jurisdiction over that particular type of case. In this narrow circumstance, constitutional issues concerning Congress' power to regulate federal court jurisdiction may arise (see Chap. 5, Sec. F.3) and may need to be resolved as the court's first order of business.

3. *Other prerequisites to suit.* Even if the case falls within the court's subject matter jurisdiction, the plaintiff must still be prepared to establish that the litigation presents

a "case or controversy" within the meaning of Article III and also meets the prudential requirements of justiciability (see Chap. 5, Sec. D). The defendant may argue, for instance, that the plaintiff does not have "standing" to assert the claim or that the claim is not "ripe" for consideration. When the federal government, a state government, or officials of either are defendants in the lawsuit, the plaintiff may also have to confront "sovereign immunity" issues that the defendants may raise to keep the case out of court or to limit the damage remedies available to the plaintiff (see Chap. 5, Sec. E).

4. *Private cause of action.* The plaintiff must also establish that he/she may bring a "private cause of action" against the defendant to enforce the particular rights that provide the basis for the plaintiff's claim on the merits (see point 5 below). When the case is against a state or local government, or its officers or employees, the federal statute called Section 1983 (42 U.S.C. § 1983) provides an express private cause of action to enforce constitutional rights (see Chap. 14, Sec. B.2). When the case is against the federal government or its officials or employees, Section 1983 does not apply; but the U.S. Supreme Court does recognize an implied private cause of action to enforce constitutional rights against federal employees and some federal officials. *See, e.g., Bivens v. Six Unknown Named Agents of Federal Bureau of Narcotics,* 403 U.S. 388 (1971). This implied cause of action does not extend to suits against the federal government itself or against federal agencies. *See Federal Deposit Insurance Corporation v. Meyer,* 510 U.S. 471 (1994).

Section 1983 also provides a private cause of action to enforce some federal statutory rights against state and local governments. *See, e.g., State of Maine v. Thiboutot,* 448 U.S. 1 (1980); *Middlesex County Sewerage Authority v. National Sea Clammers Association,* 453 U.S. 1 (1981). When Section 1983 does not apply, other federal statutes may create a private cause of action, either expressly or by implication, to enforce the rights established in that statute. In *Cannon v. University of Chicago,* 441 U.S. 677 (1979), for instance, the U.S. Supreme court recognized an "implied private cause of action" to enforce "Title IX" (20 U.S.C. § 1681 *et. seq.*), a federal statute prohibiting sex discrimination by recipients of federal funds.

5. *Theory of the case.* Once the plaintiff has dealt with the preliminary considerations in steps 1–4, attention shifts to the "merits" of the case, that is, to the legal claims that the plaintiff raises in the complaint. The emphasis at this stage is on developing the "theory of the case" and the facts necessary to support the theory. As an initial matter, it is important for the plaintiff to distinguish between power issues and rights issues (Chap. 2, Sec. C) in developing the theory of the case, and to carefully assign each claim alleged, and each issue the claims will raise, to either the power category or the rights category. Whenever a claim challenges the constitutionality of a statute or other written regulation, the plaintiff must also determine whether the challenge is a *facial* or an *as-applied* challenge (see Chap. 2, Sec. C). Once the claims on the merits have been carefully crafted, the plaintiff must establish the elements of each claim (the "prima facie case") and determine the pleading and the proof necessary to support each element (see generally Secs. C.2 and C.3 below). The plaintiff must also identify the issues raised by the prima facie case and develop the arguments necessary to prevail on each issue, as against whatever arguments and defenses on the merits the defendant may assert.

6. *The remedy.* Should the plaintiff successfully plead and prove a prima facie case of a constitutional violation (*e.g.*, a violation of due process rights), and should the plaintiff surmount all defenses the defendant asserts, the plaintiff will prevail in the "violation phase" of the case. The plaintiff, in other words, will have demonstrated that the defendant's actions violated the Constitution. The litigation then will enter the "remedy phase." The distinction between violation and remedy is basic to most fields of law. For constitutional law, the distinction is nicely illustrated by the *Brown* desegregation litigation (see Chap. 3, Sec. E, Exercise No. 4). In *Brown v. Board of Education*, 347 U.S. 483 (1954), a case that has come to be called "*Brown I*," the U.S. Supreme Court determined that the defendant school boards had violated the Constitution (specifically the Fourteenth Amendment's equal protection clause) by operating school systems racially segregated by law. The Court did not determine what the defendants must do to remedy the constitutional violation, however, and instead scheduled further argument on these issues. The following year, in a case known as "*Brown II*," the U.S. Supreme Court established guidelines on the constitutional duty of school districts to remedy the racial segregation that they had maintained in their schools, and assigned authority to the federal district courts to implement these guidelines in remedial orders (*Brown v. Board of Education*, 349 U.S. 294 (1955)).

In the remedy phase of a case, the plaintiff may request compensatory damages, punitive damages, declaratory relief, injunctive relief, or some combination of these. Injunctive relief may be either prohibitory (prohibiting the defendant from taking future actions of the type that the court has held to violate the Constitution) or mandatory (ordering the defendant to take affirmative steps to undo or ameliorate the continuing effects of the constitutional violation). While non-constitutional sources of law govern most aspects of judicial remedies, constitutional law also has an important — and sometimes very direct — bearing. This is true both for suits claiming money damages and for suits claiming injunctive relief, especially mandatory injunctive relief.

Regarding money damages, the issues are different for compensatory damage claims than for punitive damage claims. For the former, the constitutional issue usually concerns whether a jury may base a damages award in part on the "intrinsic" or "abstract" value of the constitutional right that the defendant has infringed. The U.S. Supreme Court generally has said no and has required other proof of measurable damages from injury, pain, or economic loss flowing from the violation of the constitutional right. Absent such proof, the only damages the plaintiff may receive are nominal damages (*e.g.*, $1.00). *See Memphis Community School District v. Stachura*, 477 U.S. 299 (1986) (free speech violation); *Carey v. Piphus*, 435 U.S. 247 (1978) (procedural due process violation). For suits for punitive damages, on the other hand, the constitutional issue usually concerns whether and how substantive due process limits the amount of a punitive damages award. In *BMW of North America v. Gore*, 517 U.S. 559 (1996), for example, the U.S. Supreme Court invalidated a $2 million punitive damages award. In its opinion, the majority held that "grossly excessive" punitive damage awards violate the due process clause and listed three factors for courts to consider when determining whether a particular award is excessive.

Regarding injunctive relief, the school segregation cases provide an excellent example of constitutional requirements applicable to remedies. There is a large body of constitutional law, derived from the equal protection clause and developed in the wake of *Brown II,* to govern the extent of the defendant's affirmative remedial obligations. In *Swann v. Charlotte-Mecklenburg,* 402 U.S. 1 (1971), for instance, the Court articulated the extent of school districts' obligations to use student bussing as a means of desegregation. Procedural due process cases provide another example. Once a court has determined that the defendant's action violated the due process clause, it may then consider what procedures it should order the defendant to provide to the plaintiff before depriving the plaintiff of liberty or property. Constitutional principles of due process will guide this remedial inquiry (see Chap. 11, Sec. D).

7. *The appeal.* Appeals may be taken from a court's judgment concerning the constitutional violation as well as from its order concerning the remedy. The appellate jurisdiction of the federal appellate courts, like the jurisdiction of the federal district courts, is prescribed by federal statute (see step 2 above). The parties in federal district court litigation have a right to appeal adverse judgments to the federal courts of appeals. Further review by the U.S. Supreme Court—which also reviews decisions of the highest courts of the states—is discretionary, by writ of certiorari, in almost all cases. If in a rare circumstance the Congress were to withdraw, or decline to provide for, the U.S. Supreme Court's appellate jurisdiction over a particular type of case, issues concerning Congress' power over the Court's jurisdiction would arise (see Chap. 5, Sec. F.3). In order for an appellate court to review a case decided by a lower court, the litigation must continue to present a case or controversy and to meet the other requisites of justiciability (see step 3 above).

Sec. C. Constitutional Analysis and Its Components

C.1. Overview

Various aspects of constitutional analysis have been discussed throughout this book. This section synthesizes what has been said and adds some further dimensions to the task of analysis. As presented here, there are four major components to constitutional analysis:

I.   The Use of Precedents.

II. The Use of Facts.

III. The Use of the Approaches to Interpretation.

IV. The Use of Institutional and Legal Policy Considerations.

These components and the norms implicit in them serve to establish a general methodology for analyzing constitutional issues and problems in the context of particular fact circumstances.

C.2. The Use of Precedents (Component I)

Precedents are a "secondary" source for constitutional interpretation and analysis. They derive from, and their legitimacy for the most part depends upon, the primary sources of interpretation (see Chap. 2, Sec. F.2). Precedents are the most practical of the legal sources used in constitutional analysis and are usually the first place to turn for legal guidance concerning the issue or problem at hand (see Chap. 3, Sec. A). U.S. Supreme Court precedents, the highest order of precedent, bind all other courts, state as well as federal. The Court usually pays high regard to the principle of *stare decisis* ("to stand by things decided" or "let the decision stand") and is therefore most reluctant to overrule its own prior precedents, even when subsequently appointed Justices may doubt that the precedent was correctly decided. (See also Sec. C.5 below, and *see generally* Henry Monaghan, "Stare Decisis and Constitutional Adjudication," 88 COLUM. L. REV. 723 (1988).)

The key to working with precedents is to understand that they may serve numerous and varied purposes in constitutional analysis. These are the primary purposes:

- Precedents are a source of prior interpretations on the current issue that one is addressing. Such precedents may be *controlling precedents* meaning that they would dictate a resolution of the current issue that is the same as the resolution in the prior precedents. When there are no controlling precedents resolving issues that are the same as the current issue, precedents on related issues may exist, and these precedents may be applied to the current issue by analogy (that is, by arguing that the issues and underlying rationale in the precedents are analogous to the current issue and, therefore, these precedents should apply to the current issue).
- Precedents are a source of standards and tests to use in resolving future problems. In a gender discrimination case, for instance, prior precedents would provide the intermediate standard of review that is to be applied; in a commerce power case, prior precedents would provide the "affects" test and the aggregation test to apply to Congress' regulations of intrastate commerce; and in a free speech case about advocacy of unlawful acts, precedents would provide the two-part incitement test to apply to the speech at issue.
- Precedents are a source of information on which interpretive approach or approaches (see Chap. 2, Sec. F) to use for particular types of issues. Similarly, precedents are a source of information on how to read the text of particular constitutional clauses; on the sources of original constitutional history and the explication of original history; on the identification of inferences to be drawn from the Constitution's structure; and on the identification and the development of particular values rooted in the Constitution.
- Precedents are a source of information on what institutional or legal policy considerations (Component IV below) are relevant to the interpretation of particular clauses or the analysis of particular problems.
- Precedents are a source of information on what constitutional or legislative facts and what adjudicative facts (see Component II) are relevant to the application of particular constitutional clauses or the analysis of particular problems.

See Henry Monaghan, "Taking Supreme Court Opinions Seriously," 39 MD. L. REV. 1 (1979); Frederick Schauer, "Precedent," 39 STANFORD L. REV. 571 (1987).

In addition to grasping the multiple purposes served by precedents, it is important to understand that the legal principles and standards that emerge from precedent, "however well conceived, cannot, in and of themselves, assure freedom and justice. They must be particularized to the circumstances of individual human beings" (Walter Oberer, "On Law Lawyering, and Law Professing: *The Golden Sand*," 39 J. LEGAL EDUC. 203, 205 (1989)). This particularizing must be done with respect to the relevant facts, as discussed in the next section (Component II).

C.3. The Use of Facts (Component II)

In constitutional analysis there is a necessary dynamic between facts and law (precedent). Careful analysis requires a fluid back-and-forth movement between potentially relevant facts and potentially applicable precedents (see Sec. C.2 above). The process should continue until the analyst ascertains with some assurance what the relevant facts really are, and why; what the most pertinent precedents are, and why; and what the precise relationship is between facts and precedents in the context of that particular case.

There are two types of facts that are pertinent to constitutional analysis: "adjudicative facts" and "constitutional facts" (sometimes also called "legislative facts"). Adjudicative facts are a source of information on the immediate parties to the case: who they are; what they did; and where, when, how, and why they did it. Adjudicative facts play much the same role in constitutional cases as they do in other fields of law.

Constitutional facts may not and need not relate to the immediate parties to the case. Instead, these are facts that broadly inform the court or other decision-maker about societal conditions, or about governmental judgments of the legislative or executive branches, that provide the context for the dispute. *See* Kenneth Karst, "Legislative Facts in Constitutional Litigation," 1960 SUPREME COURT REV. 75; and Rachael Pine, "Speculation and Reality: The Role of Facts in Judicial Protection of Fundamental Rights," 136 U. PA. L. REV. 655 (1988). In *Katzenbach v. McClung*, 379 U.S. 294 (1964) (Chap. 6, Sec. C.1), for example, the facts concerning Ollie's Barbecue Restaurant and the amount of food the restaurant purchased in interstate commerce were adjudicative facts; the facts (from Congressional hearings) about race discrimination in the South generally, and the resultant effects on interstate commerce (*Id.* at 299–300, 303–304) were constitutional facts. And in *Brown v. Board of Education*, 347 U.S. 483 (1954) (Chap. 3, Sec. E), the facts concerning segregated conditions in the defendant school districts were adjudicative facts, while the social science data concerning the stigmatizing effects of racial segregation upon racial minorities (see *Brown's* footnote 11) were constitutional facts. Those particular constitutional facts, and the supporting social science, were not central to later school desegregation cases, but other types of constitutional facts and other bodies of social science data have continued to play an important role. *See, e.g.,* William Taylor, "The Role of Social Science in School Desegregation Efforts," 66 J. OF NEGRO EDUCATION 196 (1997).

C.4. The Use of the Approaches to Interpretation (Component III)

There are four basic approaches to constitutional interpretation that emerge from the primary sources of interpretation (see Chap. 2, Sec. F). The textual approach focuses on the words of the particular constitutional clause at issue, read in context. The goal is to ascertain the express meaning and the clear implications of the language. This approach is discussed in Chapter 2, Section F.4. The historical approach focuses on "original" historical practices, prior to or contemporaneous with adoption of the Constitution or a particular amendment, and the "framers intent" concerning such practices. This approach is discussed in Chapter 4, Section C.2. Original history arguments should be distinguished from arguments relying on historical practices developed *subsequent* to the adoption of the Constitution or a particular amendment, which do not have the same interpretive force as original history arguments.

The structural approach focuses on the overall structure of the Constitution, the political principles undergirding the structure, and the inferences to be drawn therefrom. This approach is set out in Chapter 4, Section C.3. The values approach focuses on "fundamental" social or moral values that may or may not be identified in the constitutional text itself but may nevertheless be developed from history and traditions pre-dating the Constitution or a particular amendment or inferred from the Constitution's text and structure. This approach—the most controversial of the four—is discussed in Chapter 9, Sections B.2–B.4.

The four interpretive approaches should work together in constitutional analysis. With this goal in mind, Section D below sorts out and interrelates the four approaches.

C.5. The Use of Institutional and Legal Policy Considerations (Component IV)

The institutional and legal policy considerations comprising this component supplement the other considerations embodied in the first three components. Institutional and legal policy considerations focus on the institutional role and competency of the courts under the Constitution, in comparison with the roles and competencies of Congress, the Executive, and the states; as well as on broader factors concerning the role and effectiveness of the legal system as a whole. Such considerations may be used, in analysis and argument, to influence particular constitutional decisionmakers, such as courts, to change or refuse to change the law; to interpret the Constitution differently from some other constitutional decisionmakers to reach a unique resolution in a case of first impression; or to defer to the judgment or authority of some other constitutional decision-maker. A central premise of many of these uses of institutional and legal policy considerations is that the courts are not the only authoritative constitutional interpreters and thus not the only constitutional decisionmakers whose judgments must be taken into account (see Chap. 5, Sec. C).

Examples of institutional and legal policy considerations may include: the need to recognize and respect the policy judgment of some other decisionmaker; the need to recognize and respect the superior fact-finding competence of some other decision-maker; and the need to adhere to the prior decision of, or support the general authority of, some other decisionmaker. *See generally* Paul Brest, PROCESSES OF CONSTITUTIONAL DECISIONMAKING 9–10, 44–46, 87–101, 979–986, 1099–1118, 1156–1166 (Little, Brown, 1st ed. 1975). In *Eldred v. Ashcroft*, 123 S.Ct. 769 (2003), for example, the U.S. Supreme Court considered whether the 1998 Copyright Term Extension Act (112 Stat. 2827–2828) was a valid exercise of Congress' power under the copyright and patent clause (U.S. Const., Art. I, sec. 8, clause 8). In rejecting the plaintiffs' challenges and upholding the Act, the Court emphasized that it would "defer substantially to Congress" because the Act embodies judgments more appropriate for Congress to make than the courts (*Id.* at 781). "[W]e are not at liberty to second-guess congressional determinations and policy judgments of this order, however debatable or arguably unwise they may be" (*Id.* at 782–783). "'[I]t is not our role to alter the delicate balance Congress has labored to achieve'" (*Id.* at 785, quoting *Stewart v. Abend*, 495 U.S. 207, 230 (1984)).

As *Eldred* illustrates, institutional considerations like those listed above are often folded into the concept of "deference" or "judicial deference," under which the courts determine when they should "defer substantially" to some other decision-maker such as Congress, the President, a state legislature, or a local board of education. The classical scholarly foundation for such deference is James Bradley Thayer's 1893 article in the Harvard Law Review (James B. Thayer, "The Origin and Scope of the American Doctrine of Constitutional Law," 7 HARV. L. REV. 129 (1893)). But the concept of deference had been a part of constitutional law long before the Thayer article, indeed from the very beginning. In *Marbury v. Madison*, 5 U.S. (1 Cranch) 137 (1803), for instance, the Court gave extensive attention to whether it should defer to the President's and Secretary of State's decision to withhold Marbury's judicial commission—and more generally when it should defer to decisions of the President and Executive branch (see Chap. 8, Sec. E). And in *McCulloch v. Maryland*, 17 U.S. (4 Wheat.) 316 (1819), the Court addressed the extent to which it should defer to Congress' judgment that the Bank of the United States was a "necessary and proper" means of executing Congressional powers (see Chap. 6, Sec. A).

There are also many modern examples of the Court's application of deference principles. The *Eldred* case above provides an example of how deference may work in the context of power issues. The *Rostker* case and the *Grutter* case, discussed below, provide other modern examples in the context of rights issues. (For a contemporary scholarly critique of judicial deference, *see* Michael Perry, "Protecting Human Rights in a Democracy: What Role for the Courts?" 38 WAKE FOREST L. REV. 635, 679-687 (2003).)

In *Rostker v. Goldberg*, 453 U.S. 57 (1981), the Court considered whether an all-male military draft registration violated principles of equal protection. The issue was thus a rights issue, in contrast to the power issue in *Eldred* (above), and the Court acknowledged that heightened scrutiny would apply to the gender classification at issue (see Chap. 10, Sec. D). Nevertheless, the Court's 6 to 3 majority emphasized that:

> The case arises in the context of Congress' authority over national defense and
> military affairs, and perhaps in no other area has the Court accorded Congress

greater deference.... In deciding the question before us we must be particularly careful not to substitute our judgment of what is desirable for that of Congress, or our own evaluation of evidence for a reasonable evaluation by the Legislative Branch. [453 U.S. at 64–65.]

Maintaining this deferential posture — and apparently largely because of this deferential posture — the Court rejected the equal protection challenge to the all-male draft system.

A later case, *Grutter v. Bollinger*, 123 S.Ct. 2325 (2003) (see Chap. 10, Sec. D.7), illustrates comparable deference to a quite different governmental actor — a state university. *Grutter* was an equal protection challenge to a law school's race-conscious admissions policy designed to increase the diversity of the student body. The Court applied strict scrutiny review, requiring the university to show that maintaining the diversity of its student body is a compelling state interest. In concluding that it is, the Court emphasized that:

> The Law School's educational judgment that such diversity is essential to its educational mission is one to which we defer.... Our scrutiny of the interest asserted by the Law School is no less strict for taking into account complex educational judgments in an area that lies primarily within the expertise of the university. Our holding today is in keeping with our tradition of giving a degree of deference to a university's academic decisions, within constitutionally prescribed limits. [123 S.Ct. at 2339.]

This deference was a critical aspect of the Court's reasoning that led it, in a landmark decision, to uphold the law school's affirmative action plan.

Other examples of institutional and legal policy considerations include: the stability of legal principles and legal institutions; the coherency, consistency, and workability of legal principles; the manageability and workability of remedial measures (that is, measures for remedying constitutional violations); and *stare decisis*. In *Planned Parenthood of Southeastern Pennsylvania v. Casey*, 505 U.S. 833 (1992) (Chap. 11, Sec. C.2), for example, the Court majority began its lengthy opinion with a reminder of the need for coherency and consistency: "Liberty finds no refuge in a jurisprudence of doubt" (*Id.* at 844). Then the Court asserted that it would consider not only "the fundamental constitutional questions" presented but also "principles of institutional integrity" as well as "the rule of *stare decisis*" (505 U.S. at 845–846). In analyzing Pennsylvania's abortion statute and addressing the question whether *Roe v. Wade*, 410 U.S. 113 (1973) (Chap. 11, Sec. C.2), should be overruled, the Court explained that, when it re-examines a prior holding, "its judgment is customarily informed by a series of prudential and pragmatic considerations designed to test the consistency of overruling a prior decision with the ideal of the rule of law, and to gauge the respective costs of reaffirming and overruling a decision" (*Id.* at 854). Two of these considerations are whether the rule of the prior case "has been found unworkable," and whether removal of the rule would do "significant damage to the stability of the society governed by it...." (*Id.* at 855). Relying on these considerations and others, the Court concluded that "the essential holding of *Roe v. Wade* should be retained and once again reaffirmed" (*Id.* at 846).[2]

Another example of judicial reliance on such considerations—particularly the consideration of workability—comes from *Garcia v. San Antonio Metropolitan Transit Authority*, 469 U.S. 528 (1985), the state immunity case that overruled *National League of Cities v. Usery*, 426 U.S. 833 (1976). (*Garcia* and *National League* are both discussed in Chapter 6, Section G.) In *National League* the Court had held that states are immune from Congressional regulation of their "traditional governmental functions." In *Garcia*, the Court reconsidered this distinction between traditional and nontraditional governmental functions and found it to be "unworkable." Moreover, said the Court, "[none] of the alternative standards that might be employed to distinguish between protected and unprotected governmental functions appear *manageable*" (*Id.* at 543; emphasis added). The Court therefore rejected the *National League of Cities* rule for determining state immunity because it was not only "unsound in principle" but also "unworkable in practice" (*Id.* at 546). In its opinion, the Court emphasized that "constitutional distinction(s)" must have some coherent "organizing principle" as their basis; that "constitutional standards" must be "workable" and "manageable;" and that, in its case-by-case application, a constitutional standard or rule must not "lead[] to inconsistent results" or "breed inconsistency" (*Id.* at 539–548).

Adarand Constructors v. Pena, 515 U.S. 200 (1995), a case on race-conscious affirmative action plans for government contracting, provides yet another example of institutional considerations. In that case, the Court relied on a principle of "consistency" as well as a related principle of "congruence" (*Id.* at 224). The consistency principle required that the Court apply the same strict scrutiny review to all racial classifications, rather than having two different standards of review—one for classifications burdening a racial minority and the other for classifications burdening the majority. The congruency principle required that the Courts apply the same strict scrutiny review to federal government racial classifications as it does to state and local government racial classifications. Both of these principles seem to be crafted to enhance the coherence and workability of the Court's equal protection jurisprudence.

---

2. For contrasting examples, where the Court did overrule prior decisions, see *Mitchell v. Helms*, 530 U.S. 793, 835–836 (2000), where the Court overruled two prior decisions that were 23 and 25 years old respectively (see Chap. 13, Sec. B.3); and *Lawrence v. Texas*, 123 S.Ct. 2472, 2483–2484 (2003), where the Court overruled a prior decision that was 17 years old (see Chap. 11, Sec. C.3).

C.6. Assembling the Components

The four components discussed in Sections C.2 to C.5 above can be assembled into a working model for constitutional analysis. To begin, components I and II above capture the basic law-fact dynamic common to most fields of law. "[T]he search for relevant facts energizes, expands the search for, the relevant law, and vice versa. Law and fact are yin and yang, each meaningless except in union. Creative expansion in the scope of one expands, reciprocally, the scope of the other" (Walter Oberer, "On Law, Lawyering, and Law Professing: *The Golden Sand*," 39 J. LEGAL EDUC. 203, 208 (1989)). Some of the uses of legal precedent in constitutional law (Component I), however, may be different from the uses of precedent in other fields. In addition, the types of facts utilized in constitutional law (Component II), in particular "constitutional" or "legislative" facts, may be broader than in most other fields.

Components III and IV above present the broader backdrop against which the law-fact dynamic plays out in constitutional law. These two components encompass more subtle and elusive influences on legal analysis. Although most fields of law are affected by such considerations, the particular uses of these considerations in constitutional law are in some ways unique.

In areas where constitutional law is well developed, components III and IV will play a diminished role because much of the relevant learning regarding applicable interpretive approaches (Component III) and key institutional or legal policy considerations (Component IV) will already have been incorporated into precedent (Component I). Therefore the precedents or "secondary sources" (Chap. 2, Sec. F.2), applied in light of the relevant facts (Component II), will be the focus of concern. Where constitutional law is not well developed, however, Components III and IV will play the leading role, as the "primary" interpretive sources (Component III) and the relevant institutional and legal policy considerations (Component IV) must be studied directly to uncover the learning and insight that will guide analysis.

An understanding of these four components and their interrelationships will enhance the ability of practitioners and students to *apply* and to *integrate* their knowledge of constitutional law. These components, for instance, can facilitate one's ability to critique judicial opinions, particularly with respect to whether the opinion "justifies" the result reached (see Chap. 3, Sec. B). The further an opinion strays from the interpretive norms embodied in the four components, or the more an opinion lacks support for its application of a particular norm to the case, the more likely it is that the opinion does not justify the result. An understanding of these components can also guide problem-solving efforts, especially for large-scale problems, and help assure that the problem-solver will not miss essential ingredients of the problem-solving mix. Thirdly, an understanding of these components can enhance one's ability to sort out and interrelate various types of constitutional arguments, thereby enhancing the power and coherency of these arguments and sharpening critiques of others' arguments.

Sec. D. The Process of Constitutional Interpretation: A Final Look

D.1. A Critique of the Four Approaches to Interpretation

In various sections above, this book considers four primary approaches to interpreting the Constitution: the textual approach, the historical approach, the structural approach, and the values approach. This Section critiques the four approaches, focusing on the relationships among them and on their respective roles and limitations. This Section also reconciles the four approaches, showing how they can work together in the interpretive process and thus contribute to an integrated understanding of constitutional law.

Of the four approaches, the textual approach has the most secure claim to legitimacy. The text is the only interpretive source that was presented to the state ratifying bodies for approval and the only source that was adopted. Most constitutional issues implicate one or more specific clauses of the text; thus the text usually provides the authoritative starting point, and continuing reference point, for interpretation (see Chap. 2, Sec. F.4). The text is also a controlling source for interpretation; no other source may be used to contradict it. But the enlightenment gained from the text will vary from clause to clause and problem to problem, and in most situations the text itself will not resolve the issue being addressed. In the cases that really count, therefore, the text must be used in conjunction with one or more other interpretive sources.

The historical approach is fraught with theoretical and practical problems that challenge its legitimacy (see Chap. 4, Sec. C.2). Yet the courts, and many commentators, continue to ascribe some interpretive role to this approach. When refined and limited in response to the useful critiques that have been made, the historical approach retains a plausible claim to legitimacy within a narrowed range of operation and expectation.

For instance, many of the historical approach's difficulties can be ameliorated by adopting more modest and less dispositive objectives for it. Occasionally a search of original history, in conjunction with text, may provide an answer to a specific constitutional question concerning a practice steeped in history. But in most circumstances, if history speaks at all to an issue, it is in a different way. History may be searched, in conjunction with other sources, not for specific answers but for a reflection of principles that may have undergirded the framers' deliberations—principles of enduring vitality that provide guidelines for later interpreters but do not bind them to the framers' specific reactions to the particular issues of the times. It would therefore be inappropriate, in most circumstances, to argue that the framers prejudged for all time the particular result to be reached for particular problems whose latter-day ramifications they could not have perceived. Instead, the better argument, in most circumstances, is that the framers' deliberations rested on various broad judgments and presuppositions that provide touchstones for latter-day constitutional decision-making.

Structural interpretation is probably better established, and more often used by courts, than is commonly recognized (see Chap. 4, Sec. C.3). Its long history dates at least from 1803 in *Marbury v. Madison*, 5 U.S. (1 Cranch) 137 (1803), and its modern resurgence can be seen in separation-of-powers cases (*e.g.*, *INS v. Chadha*, 462 U.S. 919 (1983); *United States v. Nixon*, 418 U.S. 683 (1974)), in state autonomy cases (*e.g.*, *New York v. United States*, 505 U.S. 144 (1992), *Garcia v. San Antonio Metropolitan Transit Authority*, 469 U.S. 528 (1985)); and in state sovereign immunity cases (*e.g.*, *Seminole Tribe of Florida v. Florida*, 517 U.S. 44 (1996)); *Alden v. Maine* 527 U.S. 706 (1999)). Nevertheless, the theoretical base and the methodological problems of structural interpretation have not been studied as often or as comprehensively as the other interpretive approaches. Nor has the particular methodology for applying the structural approach been fully refined and articulated. Not enough is known about techniques for drawing inferences from constitutional structure, about the process of reasoning from inferences once they are drawn, about the levels of abstraction at which inferences may appropriately be drawn, or about the role of structural inference in individual rights cases. Consequently, the full potential of structural interpretation is yet to be tapped.

The values approach holds promise of playing a leading role in the future development of constitutional law. It has become and should remain the predominant approach for individual rights questions, and also has potential applications to power questions. This approach brings to center stage what should be in the spotlight: the critical questions of values that are at the core of most constitutional issues. Applying the values approach, the interpreter can focus forthrightly on these questions, rather than clouding them with speculations about specific framers' intent or technical parsing of less-than-enlightening reasoning from prior precedents. Such a direct focus on value questions will also obligate the interpreter to justify the result reached in terms of competing values, thus encouraging a more precise identification of these values and a clearer demonstration of how the value being upheld is derived from the Constitution. To realize the potential of the values approach, an enhanced understanding of constitutional values is needed. The emphasis should be on clearer identification of the values that are served by the Constitution and its structures and processes, a better account of how such values derive from the Constitution, and better comprehension of how they have developed over time and may be further refined in the future. It is one thing, for example, to assert that "personal privacy" is a constitutional value; it is quite another thing to identify the particular aspects or zones of privacy that implicate constitutional values, demonstrate their emanation from the Constitution, and critique their evolution over time.

The development of the values approach is being facilitated by the rejection of the dichotomy that commentators had developed between "interpretive" and "non-interpretive" approaches to value questions, and between constitutional and "extra-constitutional" values. Most commentators now agree that the key question is *how* one is to interpret the Constitution, not *whether* one can or should do so. *See*, *e.g.*, John Valauri, "We Are All Interpretivists Now," 46 WAYNE L. REV. 1499 (2000). Interpreters thus should affirm that the values used in constitutional interpretation must be derived from the Constitution; extra-constitutional values do not count. Any contrary conclusion could free interpretation from its anchor in the Constitution and allow interpreters to drift in the currents of time and circumstance, thus diminishing constitutional law's stability and authoritativeness. At the same time, interpreters should recognize that constitutional values are not fixed for all time according to the dimensions they may have had at the creation of the Constitution or its amendments. Thus constitutional values may be developed and refined over time, as interpreters encounter new circumstances and new knowledge not extant at the Constitution's framing. Through the experience of such successive new encounters, interpreters may better understand the ramifications of constitutional values and discover their previously unexplored dimensions.

In addition, an enhanced understanding is needed of the levels of abstraction at which values may be stated. As with the historical and structural approaches, attention to this problem of abstraction or generalization is a key to effective use (see Chap. 9, Sec. B, and Chap. 11, Sec. C.6). By their very nature, values must be stated with some degree of abstraction. Values capture fundamentals, not details, and translate into general principles, not specific and narrow rules. The fundamentals captured by, and the principles derived from, values should be sufficiently general or abstract to maintain a timeless quality, providing guidance over the long range of varying and yet-to-be-perceived conditions. On the other hand, constitutional values must be capable of concrete application to specific cases. Values thus cannot be stated so abstractly that they lose their capacity to meaningfully guide interpreters and constrain interpretive judgments. Using privacy as an illustration, to state the constitutional value simply as "personal privacy" would be overly abstract; to state the value as "privacy of procreative choice" (*e.g.*, *Carey v. Population Services Int'l.*, 431 U.S. 678, 684–85 (1977)), or "privacy of intimate personal associations" (*Roberts v. United States Jaycees*, 468 U.S. 609, 617–22 (1984)), or "privacy of the home" (*Stanley v. Georgia*, 394 U.S. 557, 568 (1969), as *construed in Paris Adult Theatre I v. Slaton*, 413 U.S. 49, 66–67 (1973)), though still abstract, is much more meaningful.

D.2. Interrelating the Four Approaches to Interpretation

Although the textual approach controls the other three approaches, no one of these three—history, structure, values—necessarily controls or has priority over the other two. In practice, these approaches are often used in combination with each other and with the textual approach. Depending upon the particular constitutional clause being interpreted and the particular problem at issue, some of the four approaches will be more pertinent than the others. The historical approach will be more pertinent in cases where the current practices or conditions at issue are analogous to original historical practices or conditions, and in cases where there is an available historical record of original practices or conditions. The structural approach will be more pertinent in cases where the particular problem at issue implicates the interrelationship between two or more components of the constitutional structure (*e.g.*, Congress and the states). The values approach will be more pertinent in cases where the clause to be interpreted contains open-ended language embodying a broad value judgment.

The Constitution's numerical clauses illustrate the predominance of the textual approach, *e.g.*, the clause setting the minimum age of 35 years for the Presidency (Art.

II, sec. 1, ¶ 4); the clause establishing a six-year term of office for Senators (Art. I, sec. 3, ¶ 1), and the clause specifying a two-thirds vote for conviction on impeachment (Art. I, sec. 3, ¶ 6). Because of the specificity of their language, these clauses leave little room for other interpretive approaches. Other clauses, such as the bill of attainder and ex post facto clauses (Art. I, sec. 9, ¶ 3; Art. I, sec. 10, ¶ 1), the habeas corpus clause (Art. I, sec. 9, ¶ 2), and the self-incrimination clause (Amend. 5), whose language suggests technical meanings known to the framers, may be interpreted with considerable reliance on history. For most power clauses, such as the commerce clause, (Art. I, sec. 8, cl. 3), structural considerations are particularly important due to the federalism or separation-of-powers contexts in which federal power issues must be considered. And for rights clauses such as the free speech, due process, and equal protection clauses, the values approach may be predominant because the clause's language suggests but does not explicate a value whose protection is the clause's mission. In general, then, the applicability and force of particular interpretive approaches will vary with the clause at issue and the problem to be addressed. The interpreter's task is to make use of whatever approaches would best illuminate the problem at hand.

Just as there is no predetermined pecking order among the historical, structural, and values approaches, there are no crisp boundary lines separating these three approaches from one another or from the textual approach. The intent of the framers, for instance, may be gleaned not only from historical sources but also from the clear implications of the text itself. Inferences to be drawn from the Constitution's structure may be discoverable in part from an exploration of original history or from the political values that underlie the structure. Values may be identified in large part through evidence gleaned from text, history, and structure. Thus, although one approach may prove more useful than the others in a particular situation, interpreters should not apply the historical, structural, or values approaches in isolation from one another, any more than they should be applied in isolation from the text. As one commentator has remarked, "[N]o sane judge or law professor can be committed solely to one approach. Because there are many facets to a single constitutional problem and...many functions performed by a single opinion, the jurist or commentator uses different approaches as a carpenter uses different tools, and often many tools, in a single project" (Philip Bobbitt, "Constitutional Fate," 58 TEX. L. REV. 695, 726 (1980)).

D.3. The Exercise of Judgment

There are no bright-line guides for applying any of the four interpretive approaches (Sec. D.1 above) that would shield interpreters from exercising discretion or making value judgments. Despite the claims of some originalists, there is no approach capable of deciding a range of real-life issues that can lay claim to complete objectivity or value neutrality. Thus, the lure of achieving this goal provides no basis for rejecting some approaches or embracing others. All four approaches, given their limits, are subject to some charge of subjectivity or indeterminacy; all will therefore engender some controversy because all allow some room for judgment that, in an imperfect world, may be subject to abuse.

We should not be surprised or uncomfortable that constitutional interpretation inevitably involves continuous judgment, not only judgment concerning the interpretive approaches to apply to particular issues and the institutional considerations to take into account (Sec. C.5 above), but also judgment concerning the competing values at stake in particular cases. As lawyers know from experience, and as legal philosophers have argued, our law is characterized by degrees of uncertainty and malleability. They have been prominent characteristics of the common law. They have been characteristics of constitutional law from the very beginning, as illustrated by *Marbury v. Madison* itself, which recognized judicial review of congressional acts even though the constitutional text establishing the courts' powers does not mention judicial review (5 U.S. (1 Cranch) 137 (1803); see Chap. 5, Sec. A). In the real world of constitutional practice, as in Chief Justice Marshall's world, interpreters search within the range of plausible meanings for the one meaning that best responds to the totality of insights gained from the interpretive sources and other relevant considerations.[3]

The exercise of good judgment, then, is a key facet of constitutional interpretation and of judicial review. And a key to good judgment on the part of a judge is good character—not personal character, but judicial character or judicial temperament. *See* Suzanna Sherry, "Judges of Character," 38 WAKE FOREST L. REV. 793 (2003). Good judgment entails "honesty, impartiality, and integrity;" "humility and courage;" and "empathy, imagination, candor, and self-awareness, among other traits" (*Id.* at 797–798).[4] Judicial character, defined by traits such as these, does not substitute for "the necessity of making—and evaluating—hard decisions about value choices," but it does "facilitate[ ]" the exercise of wise judgment in such decisionmaking (*Id.* at 798). Nor does character stand alone as a facilitator of good judgment; it must be combined, for example, with capacities for both concrete and abstract reasoning, and with sound understanding of the process of constitutional analysis (see Sec. C above) and the process of constitutional interpretation (see Secs. D.1 and D.2 above).

Although it is clear that the interpretive process leaves considerable room for the exercise of judgment, it does not follow that interpreters—in particular judges—are free to interpret clauses and decide cases in whatever way seems just and right to them. The U.S. Supreme Court has frequently emphasized that "we may not draw on our

---

3. For suggestions on improving the process of constitutional interpretation, see William Kaplin, "The Process of Constitutional Interpretation: A Synthesis of the Present and a Guide to the Future," 42 RUTGERS L. REV. 983, 1015–1021 (1990). Much of the discussion in this Section (Sec. D) of this book is adapted from other sections of this article.

4. Professor Sherry's article focuses primarily on the traits of humility and courage. For discussion of honesty, impartiality, and integrity, Professor Sherry cites, among other sources, Anthony Kronman, "Practical Wisdom and Professional Character," in Jules Coleman & Ellen Frankel Paul (eds.), PHILOSOPHY AND LAW, pp. 220–221 (Blackwell, 1987). For discussion of the third group of traits, Professor Sherry cites John C.P. Goldberg, "The Life of the Law," 51 STANFORD L. REV. 1419, 1456–1461 (1999).

merely personal and private notions and disregard the limits that bind judges in their judicial function" (*Rochin v. California*, 342 U.S. 165, 170 (1952)). "[T]hese limits are derived from considerations that are fused in the whole nature of [the] judicial process," considerations that are "deeply rooted in reason and in the compelling traditions of the legal profession" (*Id.* at 170). Thus the fine art of "reason" and the "traditions" of the law are both constraints on judges and other interpreters. Moreover, according to Justice Frankfurter, writing for the Court in *Rochin*:

> To practice the requisite detachment and to achieve sufficient objectivity no doubt demands of judges the habit of self-discipline and self-criticism, incertitude that one's own views are incontestable and alert tolerance toward views not shared. But these are precisely the presuppositions of our judicial process. They are precisely the qualities society has a right to expect from those entrusted with ultimate judicial power. [342 U.S. at 171–172.]

One part of the legal tradition that has particular importance in constraining legal decisionmaking is the common law tradition. This tradition emphasizes case-by-case decisionmaking, the "justification" of decisions in written opinions (see Chap. 3, Sec. B), and cautious incremental change. The common law tradition has important applications to constitutional law. *See generally* David A. Strauss, "Common Law Constitutional Interpretation," 63 U. CHICAGO L. REV. 877 (1996). In addition, the interpretive norms in this Section (the four interpretive approaches), and the analytical norms in Section C above (the four analytical components)—all of which are consistent with and complementary to the common law tradition—also serve to limit the discretion of interpreters and channel their exercise of judgment. And good judicial character, as described above, can itself provide an important constraint on constitutional decisionmaking (*see* Sherry, *supra*, at 798).

Sec. E. The Integration of Constitutional Law

Constitutional law cannot be compressed into one neat and trim package. That is neither a realistic nor a worthy goal. It is not the goal of this book. For scholars, practitioners, and students of constitutional law alike, there will always be loose ends. There will always be important pieces that are under-developed or are undergoing change. There will always be clashes of values and philosophical differences.[5] In short, there will always be uncertainty and controversy in the field of constitutional law. That is the nature of the subject matter. Professor and Supreme Court Justice Joseph Story underscored this point in the conclusion to his COMMENTARIES:

---

5. For an example, see the account of the contrasting "federalist" and "republican" visions of government that have existed since the drafting of the Constitution, set out in John Arthur, THE UNFINISHED CONSTITUTION, pp. 295–299 (Wadsworth, 1989). See also Daniel Farber & Suzanna Sherry, A HISTORY OF THE AMERICAN CONSTITUTION, pp. 5–21 (West, 1990), for an overview of the various values and philosophies competing with one another in the critical years 1787–1791.

[I]t cannot escape our notice, how exceedingly difficult it is to settle the foundations of any government upon principles which do not admit of controversy or question. The very elements out of which it is to be built are susceptible of infinite modifications; and theory too often deludes us by the attractive simplicity of its plans, and imagination by the visionary perfection of its speculations. [Joseph Story, COMMENTARIES ON THE CONSTITUTION OF THE UNITED STATES, §1912 (5th ed., Melville Bigelow (ed.), 1994).]

But all is not mystery and puzzlement. Far from it. Undergirding the complexities and dynamics of constitutional law are a long and enlightening evolutionary history, an established constitutional structure, and established processes that operate within this structure. There are well-developed concepts to guide understanding of most powers and rights. There are generally accepted frameworks for analysis of most issues (*see* William Kaplin, THE CONCEPTS AND METHODS OF CONSTITUTIONAL LAW (Carolina Academic Press, 1992), Chap. 5, Sec. F; Chap. 6, Sec. C; Chap. 7, Sec. D; and Chap 8, Sec. C). The history, the structure, the processes, the concepts, the analytical methods: all combine to support an integrated understanding of constitutional law. That should be a primary goal of any study of constitutional law — to see the bigger picture, to view the constitutional forest and not just the constitutional trees. With an integrated understanding of constitutional law, one can deal more effectively with its loose ends; its evolutionary (and sometimes discordant) developments; and its uncertainties, controversies and value clashes. One can better apply the law in practice. And one can nurture an in-depth and long-range perspective on the Constitution, serviceable over a lifetime in the law.

Perhaps, with an integrated, big-picture understanding of constitutional law, one may even glimpse the elusive goal of *justice* that appears prominently in the Constitution's Preamble and is at the core of American constitutionalism. "Justice is the end of government," declared Madison during the debates on ratification of the Constitution. "[Justice] is the end of civil society. It ever has been, and ever will be, pursued, until it be obtained, or until liberty be lost in the pursuit." James Madison, *Federalist No. 51*, in THE FEDERALIST, THE GIDEON EDITION, p. 271 (Carey & McClellan (eds.), 2001).

Appendix A

Constitution of the United States of America

(with editorial enhancements)[*]

Preamble

We the People of the United States, in Order to form a more perfect Union, establish Justice, insure domestic Tranquility, provide for the common defence, promote the general Welfare, and secure the Blessings of Liberty to ourselves and our Posterity, do ordain and establish this CONSTITUTION for the United States of America.

Article I

Section 1. **All legislative Powers herein granted shall be vested in a Congress of the United States, which shall consist of a Senate and House of Representatives.**

Section 2. The House of Representatives shall be composed of Members chosen every second Year by the People of the several States, and the Electors in each State shall have the Qualifications requisite for Electors of the most numerous Branch of the State Legislature.

No Person shall be a Representative who shall not have attained to the Age of twenty five Years, and been seven Years a Citizen of the United States, and who shall not, when elected, be an Inhabitant of that State in which he shall be chosen.

Representatives and direct Taxes shall be apportioned among the several States which may be included within this Union, according to their respective Numbers, which shall be determined by adding to the whole Number of free Persons, including those bound to Service for a Term of Years, and excluding Indians not taxed, three fifths

---

[*] Boldface type denotes the provisions that have most frequently been at issue in cases before the U.S. Supreme Court, or that otherwise have been the most important or the most debated in modern constitutional law. Some headings and numbering, not contained in the original copies of the Constitution, have also been added, as well as several explanatory footnotes and text notes.

of all other Persons. The actual Enumeration shall be made within three Years after the first Meeting of the Congress of the United States, and within every subsequent Term of ten Years, in such Manner as they shall by Law direct. The Number of Representatives shall not exceed one for every thirty Thousand, but each State shall have at Least one Representative; and until such enumeration shall be made, the State of New Hampshire shall be entitled to chose three, Massachusetts eight, Rhode-Island and Providence Plantations one, Connecticut five, New-York six, New Jersey four, Pennsylvania eight, Delaware one, Maryland six, Virginia ten, North Carolina five, South Carolina five, and Georgia three.

When vacancies happen in the Representation from any State, the Executive Authority thereof shall issue Writs of Election to fill such Vacancies.

The House of Representatives shall choose their Speaker and other Officers; and **shall have the sole Power of Impeachment.**

Section 3. The Senate of the United States shall be composed of two Senators from each State, chosen by the Legislature thereof, for six Years; and each Senator shall have one Vote.

Immediately after they shall be assembled in Consequence of the first Election, they shall be divided as equally as may be into three Classes. The Seats of the Senators of the first Class shall be vacated at the Expiration of the second Year, of the second Class at the Expiration of the fourth Year, and of the third Class at the Expiration of the sixth Year, so that one third may be chosen every second Year; and if Vacancies happen by Resignation, or otherwise, during the Recess of the Legislature of any State, the Executive thereof may make temporary Appointments until the next Meeting of the Legislature, which shall then fill such Vacancies.

No Person shall be a Senator who shall not have attained to the Age of thirty Years, and been nine Years a Citizen of the United States, and who shall not, when elected, be an Inhabitant of that State for which he shall be chosen.

The Vice President of the United States shall be President of the Senate, but shall have no Vote, unless they be equally divided.

The Senate shall choose their other Officers, and also a President pro tempore, in the Absence of the Vice President, or when he shall exercise the Office of President of the United States.

The Senate shall have the sole Power to try all Impeachments. When sitting for that Purpose, they shall be on Oath or Affirmation. When the President of the United States is tried, the Chief Justice shall preside: And no Person shall be convicted without the Concurrence of two thirds of the Members present.

Judgment in Cases of Impeachment shall not extend further than to removal from Office, and disqualification to hold and enjoy any Office of honor, Trust or Profit under the United States: but the Party convicted shall nevertheless be liable and subject to Indictment, Trial, Judgment and Punishment, according to Law.

Section 4. The Times, Places and Manner of holding Elections for Senators and Representatives, shall be prescribed in each State by the Legislature thereof; but the Congress may at any time by Law make or alter such Regulations, except as to the Places of choosing Senators.

The Congress shall assemble at least once in every Year, and such Meeting shall be on the first Monday in December, unless they shall by Law appoint a different Day.

Section 5. **Each House shall be the Judge of the Elections, Returns and Qualifications of its own Members,** and a Majority of each shall constitute a Quorum to do Business; but a smaller Number may adjourn from day to day, and may be authorized to compel the Attendance of absent Members, in such Manner, and under such Penalties as each House may provide.

Each House may determine the Rules of its Proceedings, punish its Members for disorderly Behaviour, and, with the Concurrence of two thirds, expel a Member.

Each House shall keep a Journal of its Proceedings, and from time to time publish the same, excepting such Parts as may in their Judgment require Secrecy; and the Yeas and Nays of the Members of either House on any question shall, at the Desire of one fifth of those Present, be entered on the Journal.

Neither House, during the Session of Congress, shall, without the Consent of the other, adjourn for more than three days, nor to any other Place than that in which the two Houses shall be sitting.

Section 6. The Senators and Representatives shall receive a Compensation for their Services, to be ascertained by Law, and paid out of the Treasury of the United States. **They shall in all Cases, except Treason, Felony and Breach of the Peace, be privileged from Arrest during their Attendance at the Session of their respective Houses, and in going to and returning from the same; and for any Speech or Debate in either House, they shall not be questioned in any other Place.**

No Senator or Representative shall, during the Time for which he was elected, be appointed to any civil Office under the Authority of the United States, which shall have been created, or the Emoluments whereof shall have been increased during such time; and no Person holding any Office under the United States, shall be a Member of either House during his Continuance in Office.

Section 7. All Bills for raising Revenue shall originate in the House of Representatives; but the Senate may propose or concur with Amendments as on other Bills.

Every Bill which shall have passed the House of Representatives and the Senate, shall, before it become a Law, be presented to the President of the United States; If he approve he shall sign it, but if not he shall return it, with his Objections to that House in which it shall have originated, who shall enter the Objections at large on their Journal, and proceed to reconsider it. If after such Reconsideration two thirds of that House shall agree to pass the Bill, it shall be sent, together with the Objections, to the other House, by which it shall likewise be reconsidered, and if approved by two thirds of that House, it shall become a Law. But in all such Cases the Votes of both Houses shall be determined by yeas and Nays, and the Names of the Persons voting for and against the Bill shall be entered on the Journal of each House respectively. If any Bill shall not be returned by the President within ten Days (Sundays excepted) after it shall have been presented to him, the Same shall be a Law, in like Manner as if he had signed it, unless the Congress by their Adjournment prevent its Return, in which Case it shall not be a Law.

Every Order, Resolution, or Vote to which the Concurrence of the Senate and House of Representatives may be necessary (except on a question of Adjournment) shall be presented to the President of the United States; and before the Same shall take Effect, shall be approved by him, or being disapproved by him, shall be repassed by two thirds of the Senate and House of Representatives, according to the Rules and Limitations prescribed in the Case of a Bill.

Section 8. The Congress shall have Power:

(1) To lay and collect Taxes, Duties, Imposts and Excises, to pay the Debts and provide for the common Defence and general Welfare of the United States; but all Duties, Imposts and Excises shall be uniform throughout the United States;

(2) To borrow Money on the credit of the United States;

(3) To regulate Commerce with foreign Nations, and among the several States, and with the Indian Tribes;

(4) To establish an uniform Rule of Naturalization, and uniform Laws on the subject of Bankruptcies throughout the United States;

(5) To coin Money, regulate the Value thereof, and of foreign Coin, and fix the Standard of Weights and Measures;

(6) To provide for the Punishment of counterfeiting the Securities and current Coin of the United States;

(7) To establish Post Offices and post Roads;

(8) To promote the Progress of Science and useful Arts, by securing for limited Times to Authors and Inventors the exclusive Right to their respective Writings and Discoveries;

(9) To constitute Tribunals inferior to the Supreme Court;

(10) To define and punish Piracies and Felonies committed on the high Seas, and Offenses against the Law of Nations;

(11) To declare War, grant Letters of Marque and Reprisal, and make Rules concerning Captures on Land and Water;

(12) To raise and support Armies, but no Appropriation of Money to that Use shall be for a longer Term than two Years;

(13) To provide and maintain a Navy;

(14) To make Rules for the Government and Regulation of the land and Naval Forces;

(15) To provide for calling forth the Militia to execute the Laws of the Union, suppress Insurrections and repel Invasions;

(16) To provide for organizing, arming, and disciplining, the Militia, and for governing such Part of them as may be employed in the Service of the United States, reserving to the States respectively, the Appointment of the Officers, and the Authority of training the Militia according to the discipline prescribed by Congress;

(17)   To exercise exclusive Legislation in all Cases whatsoever, over such District (not exceeding ten Miles square) as may, by Cession of particular States, and the Acceptance of Congress, become the Seat of the Government of the United States, and to exercise like Authority over all Places purchased by the Consent of the Legislature of the State in which the Same shall be, for the Erection of Forts, Magazines, Arsenals, dock-Yards, and other needful Buildings;—And

(18)   To make all Laws which shall be necessary and proper for carrying into Execution the foregoing Powers, and all other Powers vested by this Constitution in the Government of the United States, or in any Department or Officer thereof.

Section 9. The Migration or Importation of such Persons as any of the States now existing shall think proper to admit, shall not be prohibited by the Congress prior to the Year one thousand eight hundred and eight, but a Tax or duty may be imposed on such Importation, not exceeding ten dollars for each Person.

The Privilege of the Writ of Habeas Corpus shall not be suspended, unless when in Cases of Rebellion or Invasion the public Safety may require it.

No Bill of Attainder or ex post facto Law shall be passed.

No Capitation, or other direct, Tax shall be laid, unless in Proportion to the Census or Enumeration herein before directed to be taken.

No Tax or Duty shall be laid on Articles exported from any State.

No Preference shall be given by any Regulation of Commerce or Revenue to the Ports of one State over those of another: nor shall Vessels bound to, or from, one State, be obliged to enter, clear, or pay Duties in another.

No Money shall be drawn from the Treasury, but in Consequence of Appropriations made by Law; and a regular Statement and Account of the Receipts and Expenditures of all public Money shall be published from time to time.

No Title of Nobility shall be granted by the United States: And no Person holding any Office of Profit or Trust under them, shall, without the Consent of the Congress, accept of any present, Emolument, Office, or Title, of any kind whatever, from any King, Prince, or foreign State.

Section 10. **No State shall enter into any Treaty, Alliance, or Confederation;** grant Letters of Marque and Reprisal; **coin Money;** emit Bills of Credit; make any Thing but gold and silver Coin a Tender in Payment of Debts; **pass any Bill of Attainder, ex post facto Law, or Law impairing the Obligation of Contracts,** or grant any Title of Nobility.

No State shall, without the Consent of the Congress, lay any Imposts or Duties on Imports or Exports, except what may be absolutely necessary for executing its inspection Laws: and the net Produce of all Duties and Imposts, laid by any State on Imports or Exports, shall be for the Use of the Treasury of the United States; and all such Laws shall be subject to the Revision and Control of the Congress.

No State shall, without the Consent of Congress, lay any Duty of Tonnage, keep Troops, or Ships of War in time of Peace, **enter into any Agreement or Compact with another State, or with a foreign Power,** or engage in War, unless actually invaded, or in such imminent Danger as will not admit of delay.

Article II

Section 1. (1) **The executive Power shall be vested in a President of the United States of America.** He shall hold his Office during the Term of four Years, and, together with the Vice President, chosen for the same Term, be elected, as follows:

(2) Each State shall appoint, in such Manner as the Legislature thereof may direct, a Number of Electors, equal to the whole Number of Senators and Representatives to which the State may be entitled in the Congress: but no Senator or Representative, or Person holding an Office of Trust or Profit under the United States, shall be appointed an Elector.

(3) ***[Paragraph 3 is omitted; it has been replaced by the Twelfth Amendment, ratified in 1804.]**

(4) The Congress may determine the Time of choosing the Electors, and the Day on which they shall give their Votes; which Day shall be the same throughout the United States.

(5) No Person except a natural born Citizen, or a Citizen of the United States, at the time of the Adoption of this Constitution, shall be eligible to the Office of President; neither shall any Person be eligible to that Office who shall not have attained to the Age of thirty five Years, and been fourteen Years a Resident within the United States.

(6) In Case of the Removal of the President from Office, or of his Death, Resignation, or Inability to discharge the Powers and Duties of the said Office, the Same shall devolve on the Vice President, and the Congress may by Law provide for the Case of Removal, Death, Resignation or Inability, both of the President and Vice President, declaring what Officer shall then act as President, and such Officer shall act accordingly, until the Disability be removed, or a President shall be elected.

(7) The President shall, at stated Times, receive for his Services, a Compensation, which shall neither be increased nor diminished during the Period for which he shall have been elected, and he shall not receive within that Period any other Emolument from the United States, or any of them.

(8) Before he enter on the Execution of his Office, he shall take the following Oath or Affirmation:—"I do solemnly swear (or affirm) that I will faithfully execute the Office of President of the United States, and will to the best of my Ability, preserve, protect and defend the Constitution of the United States."

Section 2. **The President shall be Commander in Chief of the Army and Navy of the United States, and of the Militia of the several States, when called into the actual Service of the United States;** he may require the Opinion, in writing, of the principal Officer in each of the executive Departments, upon any Subject relating to the Duties of their respective Offices, and **he shall have Power to grant Reprieves and Pardons for Offenses against the United States, except in Cases of Impeachment.**

He shall have Power, by and with the Advice and Consent of the Senate, to make Treaties, provided two thirds of the Senators present concur; and he shall nominate, and by and with the Advice and Consent of the Senate, shall appoint Ambassadors, other public Ministers and Consuls, Judges of the supreme Court, and all other Officers of the United States, whose Appointments are not herein otherwise provided for, and which shall be established by Law: but the Congress may by Law vest the Appointment of such inferior Officers, as they think proper, in the President alone, in the Courts of Law, or in the Heads of Departments.

The President shall have Power to fill up all Vacancies that may happen during the Recess of the Senate, by granting Commissions which shall expire at the End of their next Session.

Section 3. He shall from time to time give to the Congress Information of the State of the Union, and recommend to their Consideration such Measures as he shall judge necessary and expedient; he may, on extraordinary Occasions, convene both Houses, or either of them, and in Case of Disagreement between them, with Respect to the Time of Adjournment, he may adjourn them to such Time as he shall think proper; **he shall receive Ambassadors and other public Ministers; he shall take Care that the Laws be faithfully executed,** and shall Commission all the Officers of the United States.

Section 4. **The President, Vice President and all civil Officers of the United States, shall be removed from Office on Impeachment for, and Conviction of, Treason, Bribery, or other high Crimes and Misdemeanors.**

Article III

Section 1. **The judicial Power of the United States, shall be vested in one supreme Court, and in such inferior Courts as the Congress may from time to time ordain and establish.** The Judges, both of the supreme and inferior Courts, shall hold their Offices during good Behavior, and shall, at stated Times, receive for their Services, a Compensation, which shall not be diminished during their Continuance in Office.

Section 2. **The judicial Power shall extend to all Cases, in Law and Equity, arising under this Constitution, the Laws of the United States, and Treaties made, or which shall be made, under their Authority;**—to all Cases affecting Ambassadors, other public Ministers and Consuls;—to all Cases of admiralty and maritime Jurisdiction;—to Controversies to which the United States shall be a Party;—**to Controversies** between two or more States;—between a State and Citizens of another State;—**between Citizens of different States;**—between Citizens of the same State claiming Lands under Grants of different States, and between a State, or the Citizens thereof, and foreign States, Citizens or Subjects.

In all Cases affecting Ambassadors, other public Ministers and Consuls, and those in which a State shall be Party, the supreme Court shall have original Jurisdiction. In all the other Cases before mentioned, the supreme Court shall have appellate Jurisdiction, both as to Law and Fact, with such Exceptions, and under such Regulations as the Congress shall make.

The Trial of all Crimes, except in Cases of Impeachment, shall be by Jury; and such Trial shall be held in the State where the said Crimes shall have been committed; but when not committed within any State, the Trial shall be at such Place or Places as the Congress may by Law have directed.

Section 3. Treason against the United States, shall consist only in levying War against them, or in adhering to their Enemies, giving them Aid and Comfort. No Person shall be convicted of Treason unless on the Testimony of two Witnesses to the same overt Act, or on Confession in open Court.

The Congress shall have Power to declare the Punishment of Treason, but no Attainder of Treason shall work Corruption of Blood, or Forfeiture except during the Life of the Person attainted.

Article IV

Section 1. **Full Faith and Credit shall be given in each State to the public Acts, Records, and judicial Proceedings of every other State. And the Congress may by general Laws prescribe the Manner in which such Acts, Records and Proceedings shall be proved, and the Effect thereof.**

Section 2. The Citizens of each State shall be entitled to all Privileges and Immunities of Citizens in the several States.

A person charged in any State with Treason, Felony, or other Crime, who shall flee from Justice, and be found in another State, shall on Demand of the executive Authority of the State from which he fled, be delivered up, to be removed to the State having Jurisdiction of the Crime.

No Person held to Service or Labour in one State, under the Laws thereof, escaping into another, shall, in Consequence of any Law or Regulation therein, be discharged from such Service or Labour, but shall be delivered up on Claim of the Party to whom such Service or Labour may be due.

Section 3. New States may be admitted by the Congress into this Union; but no new State shall be formed or erected within the Jurisdiction of any other State; nor any State be formed by the Junction of two or more States, or Parts of States, without the Consent of the Legislatures of the States concerned as well as of the Congress.

The Congress shall have Power to dispose of and make all needful Rules and Regulations respecting the Territory or other Property belonging to the United States; and nothing in this Constitution shall be so construed as to Prejudice any Claims of the United States, or of any particular State.

Section 4. The United States shall guarantee to every State in this Union a Republican Form of Government, and shall protect each of them against Invasion; and on Application of the Legislature, or of the Executive (when the Legislature cannot be convened) against domestic Violence.

Article V

The Congress, whenever two thirds of both Houses shall deem it necessary, shall propose Amendments to this Constitution, or on the Application of the Legislatures of two thirds of the several States, shall call a Convention for proposing Amendments, which, in either Case, shall be valid to all Intents and Purposes, as Part of this Constitution, when ratified by the Legislatures of three fourths of the several States, or by Conventions in three fourths thereof, as the one or the other Mode of Ratification may be proposed by the Congress; Provided that no Amendment which may be made prior to the Year One thousand eight hundred and eight shall in any Manner affect the first and fourth Clauses in the Ninth Section of the first Article; and that no State, without its Consent, shall be deprived of its equal Suffrage in the Senate.

Article VI

All Debts contracted and Engagements entered into, before the Adoption of this Constitution, shall be as valid against the United States under this Constitution, as under the Confederation.

This Constitution, and the Laws of the United States which shall be made in Pursuance thereof; and all Treaties made, or which shall be made, under the Authority of the United States, shall be the supreme Law of the Land; and the Judges in every State shall be bound thereby, any Thing in the Constitution or Laws of any State to the Contrary notwithstanding.

The Senators and Representatives before mentioned, and the Members of the several State Legislatures, and all executive and judicial Officers, both of the United States and of the several States, shall be bound by Oath or Affirmation, to support this Constitution; but **no religious Test shall ever be required as a Qualification to any Office or public Trust under the United States.**

Article VII

The Ratification of the Conventions of nine States, shall be sufficient for the Establishment of this Constitution between the States so ratifying the Same.

Amendment I (1791)*

Congress shall make no law respecting an establishment of religion, or prohibiting the free exercise thereof; or abridging the freedom of speech, or of the press; or the right of the people peaceably to assemble, and to petition the Government for a redress of grievances.

---

* The first ten amendments, all proposed by Congress in 1789 and ratified by the requisite number of states in 1791, are generally called the Bill of Rights. Article V of the Constitution sets out the process by which these amendments, and all subsequent amendments, were adopted.

Amendment II (1791)

A well regulated Militia, being necessary to the security of a free State, the right of the people to keep and bear Arms, shall not be infringed.

Amendment III (1791)

No Soldier shall, in time of peace be quartered in any house, without the consent of the Owner, nor in time of war, but in a manner to be prescribed by law.

Amendment IV (1791)

The right of the people to be secure in their persons, houses, papers, and effects, against unreasonable searches and seizures, shall not be violated, and no Warrants shall issue, but upon probable cause, supported by Oath or affirmation, and particularly describing the place to be searched, and the persons or things to be seized.

Amendment V (1791)

No person shall be held to answer for a capital, or otherwise infamous crime, unless on a presentment or indictment of a Grand Jury, except in cases arising in the land or naval forces, or in the Militia, when in actual service in time of War or public danger; nor shall any person be subject for the same offence to be twice put in jeopardy of life or limb; nor shall be compelled in any criminal case to be a witness against himself, nor be deprived of life, liberty, or property, without due process of law; nor shall private property be taken for public use, without just compensation.

Amendment VI (1791)

In all criminal prosecutions, the accused shall enjoy the right to a speedy and public trial, by an impartial jury of the State and district wherein the crime shall have been committed, which district shall have been previously ascertained by law, and to be informed of the nature and cause of the accusation; to be confronted with the witnesses against him; to have compulsory process for obtaining witnesses in his favor, and to have the Assistance of Counsel for his defence.

Amendment VII (1791)

In Suits at common law, where the value in controversy shall exceed twenty dollars, the right of trial by jury shall be preserved, and no fact tried by a jury, shall be otherwise reexamined in any Court of the United States, than according to the rules of the common law.

Amendment VIII (1791)

Excessive bail shall not be required, nor excessive fines imposed, nor cruel and unusual punishments inflicted.

Amendment IX (1791)

The enumeration in the Constitution, of certain rights, shall not be construed to deny or disparage others retained by the people.

Amendment X (1791)

The powers not delegated to the United States by the Constitution, nor prohibited by it to the States, are reserved to the States respectively, or to the people.

Amendment XI (1798)

The Judicial power of the United States shall not be construed to extend to any suit in law or equity, commenced or prosecuted against one of the United States by Citizens of another State, or by Citizens or Subjects of any Foreign State.

Amendment XII (1804)

The Electors shall meet in their respective states and vote by ballot for President and Vice-President, one of whom, at least, shall not be an inhabitant of the same state with themselves; they shall name in their ballots the person voted for as President, and in distinct ballots the person voted for as Vice-President, and they shall make distinct lists of all persons voted for as President, and of all persons voted for as Vice-President, and of the number of votes for each, which lists they shall sign and certify, and transmit sealed to the seat of the government of the United States, directed to the President of the Senate;—The President of the Senate shall, in the presence of the Senate and House of Representatives, open all the certificates and the votes shall then be counted;—The person having the greatest number of votes for President, shall be the President, if such number be a majority of the whole number of Electors appointed; and if no person have such majority, then from the persons having the highest numbers not exceeding three on the list of those voted for as President, the House of Representatives shall choose immediately, by ballot, the President. But in choosing the President, the votes shall be taken by states, the representation from each state having one vote; a quorum for this purpose shall consist of a member or members from two-thirds of the states, and a majority of all the states shall be necessary to a choice. And if the House of Representatives shall not choose a President whenever the right of choice shall devolve upon them, before the fourth day of March next following, then the Vice-President shall act as President, as in the case of the death or other constitutional disability of the President.—The person having the greatest number of votes as Vice-President, shall be the Vice-President, if such number be a majority of the whole number of Electors appointed, and if no person have a majority, then from the two highest numbers on the list, the Senate shall choose the Vice-President; a quorum for the purpose shall consist of two-thirds of the whole number of Senators, and a majority of the whole number shall be necessary to a choice. But no person constitutionally ineligible to the office of President shall be eligible to that of Vice-President of the United States.

Amendment XIII (1865)

Section 1. Neither slavery nor involuntary servitude, except as a punishment for crime whereof the party shall have been duly convicted, shall exist within the United States, or any place subject to their jurisdiction.

Section 2. Congress shall have power to enforce this article by appropriate legislation.

Amendment XIV (1868)

Section 1. All persons born or naturalized in the United States, and subject to the jurisdiction thereof, are citizens of the United States and of the State wherein they reside. No State shall make or enforce any law which shall abridge the privileges or immunities of citizens of the United States; nor shall any State deprive any person of life, liberty, or property, without due process of law; nor deny to any person within its jurisdiction the equal protection of the laws.

Section 2. Representatives shall be apportioned among the several States according to their respective numbers, counting the whole number of persons in each State, excluding Indians not taxed. But when the right to vote at any election for the choice of electors for President and Vice President of the United States, Representatives in Congress, the Executive and Judicial officers of a State, or the members of the Legislature thereof, is denied to any of the male inhabitants of such State, being twenty-one years of age, and citizens of the United States, or in any way abridged, except for participation in rebellion, or other crime, the basis of representation therein shall be reduced in the proportion which the number of such male citizens shall bear to the whole number of male citizens twenty-one years of age in such State.

Section 3. No person shall be a Senator or Representative in Congress, or elector of President and Vice President, or hold any office, civil or military, under the United States, or under any State, who, having previously taken an oath, as a member of Congress, or as an officer of the United States, or as a member of any State legislature, or as an executive or judicial officer of any State, to support the Constitution of the United States, shall have engaged in insurrection or rebellion against the same, or given aid or comfort to the enemies thereof. But Congress may by a vote of two-thirds of each House, remove such disability.

Section 4. The validity of the public debt of the United States, authorized by law, including debts incurred for payment of pensions and bounties for services in suppressing insurrection or rebellion, shall not be questioned. But neither the United States nor any State shall assume or pay any debt or obligation incurred in aid of insurrection or rebellion against the United States, or any claim for the loss or emancipation of any slave; but all such debts, obligations and claims shall be held illegal and void.

Section 5. The Congress shall have power to enforce, by appropriate legislation, the provisions of this article.

Amendment XV (1870)

Section 1. The right of citizens of the United States to vote shall not be denied or abridged by the United States or by any State on account of race, color, or previous condition of servitude.

Section 2. The Congress shall have power to enforce this article by appropriate legislation.

Amendment XVI (1913)

The Congress shall have power to lay and collect taxes on incomes, from whatever source derived, without apportionment among the several States, and without regard to any census or enumeration.

Amendment XVII (1913)

The Senate of the United States shall be composed of two Senators from each State, elected by the people thereof, for six years; and each Senator shall have one vote. The electors in each State shall have the qualifications requisite for electors of the most numerous branch of the State legislatures.

When vacancies happen in the representation of any State in the Senate, the executive authority of such State shall issue writs of election to fill such vacancies: Provided, That the legislature of any State may empower the executive thereof to make temporary appointments until the people fill the vacancies by election as the legislature may direct.

This amendment shall not be so construed as to affect the election or term of any Senator chosen before it becomes valid as part of the Constitution.

Amendment XVIII (1919)

[Repealed by Amendment XXI]

Section 1. After one year from the ratification of this article the manufacture, sale, or transportation of intoxicating liquors within, the importation thereof into, or the exportation thereof from the United States and all territory subject to the jurisdiction thereof for beverage purposes is hereby prohibited.

Section 2. The Congress and the several States shall have concurrent power to enforce this article by appropriate legislation.

Section 3. This article shall be inoperative unless it shall have been ratified as an amendment to the Constitution by the legislatures of the several States, as provided in the Constitution, within seven years from the date of the submission hereof to the States by the Congress.

Amendment XIX (1920)

The right of citizens of the United States to vote shall not be denied or abridged by the United States or by any State on account of sex.

Congress shall have power to enforce this article by appropriate legislation.

Amendment XX (1933)

Section 1. The terms of the President and Vice President shall end at noon on the 20th day of January, and the terms of Senators and Representatives at noon on the 3rd day of January, of the years in which such terms would have ended if this article had not been ratified; and the terms of their successors shall then begin.

Section 2. The Congress shall assemble at least once in every year, and such meeting shall begin at noon on the 3rd day of January, unless they shall by law appoint a different day.

Section 3. If, at the time fixed for the beginning of the term of the President, the President elect shall have died, the Vice President elect shall become President. If a President shall not have been chosen before the time fixed for the beginning of his term, or if the President elect shall have failed to qualify, then the Vice President elect shall act as President until a President shall have qualified; and the Congress may by law provide for the case wherein neither a President elect nor a Vice President elect shall have qualified, declaring who shall then act as President, or the manner in which one who is to act shall be selected, and such person shall act accordingly until a President or Vice President shall have qualified.

Section 4. The Congress may by law provide for the case of the death of any of the persons from whom the House of Representatives may choose a President whenever the right of choice shall have devolved upon them, and for the case of the death of any of the persons from whom the Senate may choose a Vice President whenever the right of choice shall have devolved upon them.

Section 5. Sections 1 and 2 shall take effect on the 15th day of October following the ratification of this article.

Section 6. This article shall be inoperative unless it shall have been ratified as an amendment to the Constitution by the legislatures of three-fourths of the several States within seven years from the date of its submission.

Amendment XXI (1933)

Section 1. The eighteenth article of amendment to the Constitution of the United States is hereby repealed.

Section 2. The transportation or importation into any State, Territory, or possession of the United States for delivery or use therein of intoxicating liquors, in violation of the laws thereof, is hereby prohibited.

Section 3. This article shall be inoperative unless it shall have been ratified as an amendment to the Constitution by conventions in the several States, as provided in the Constitution, within seven years from the date of the submission hereof to the States by the Congress.

Amendment XXII (1951)

Section 1. No person shall be elected to the office of the President more than twice, and no person who has held the office of President, or acted as President, for more than two years of a term to which some other person was elected President shall be elected to the office of the President more than once. But this Article shall not apply to any person holding the office of President when this Article was proposed by the Congress, and shall not prevent any person who may be holding the office of President, or acting as President, during the term within which this Article becomes operative from holding the office of President or acting as President during the remainder of such term.

Section 2. This article shall be inoperative unless it shall have been ratified as an amendment to the Constitution by the legislatures of three-fourths of the several States within seven years from the date of its submission to the States by the Congress.

Amendment XXIII (1961)

Section 1. The District constituting the seat of Government of the United States shall appoint in such manner as the Congress may direct:

A number of electors of President and Vice President equal to the whole number of Senators and Representatives in Congress to which the District would be entitled if it were a State, but in no event more than the least populous State; they shall be in addition to those appointed by the States, but they shall be considered, for the purposes of the election of President and Vice President, to be electors appointed by a State; and they shall meet in the District and perform such duties as provided by the twelfth article of amendment.

Section 2. The Congress shall have power to enforce this article by appropriate legislation.

Amendment XXIV (1964)

Section 1. The right of citizens of the United States to vote in any primary or other election for President or Vice President, for electors for President or Vice President, or for Senator or Representative in Congress, shall not be denied or abridged by the United States or any State by reason of failure to pay any poll tax or other tax.

Section 2. The Congress shall have power to enforce this article by appropriate legislation.

Amendment XXV (1967)

Section 1. In case of the removal of the President from office or of his death or resignation, the Vice President shall become President.

Section 2. Whenever there is a vacancy in the office of the Vice President, the President shall nominate a Vice President who shall take office upon confirmation by a majority vote of both Houses of Congress.

Section 3. Whenever the President transmits to the President pro tempore of the Senate and the Speaker of the House of Representatives his written declaration that he is unable to discharge the powers and duties of his office, and until he transmits to them a written declaration to the contrary, such powers and duties shall be discharged by the Vice President as Acting President.

Section 4. Whenever the Vice President and a majority of either the principal officers of the executive departments or of such other body as Congress may by law provide, transmit to the President pro tempore of the Senate and the Speaker of the House of Representatives their written declaration that the President is unable to discharge the powers and duties of his office, the Vice President shall immediately assume the powers and duties of the office as Acting President.

Thereafter, when the President transmits to the President pro tempore of the Senate and the Speaker of the House of Representatives his written declaration that no inability exists, he shall resume the powers and duties of his office unless the Vice President and a majority of either the principal officers of the executive department or of such other body as Congress may by law provide, transmit within four days to the President pro tempore of the Senate and the Speaker of the House of Representatives their written declaration that the President is unable to discharge the powers and duties of his office. Thereupon Congress shall decide the issue, assembling within forty-eight hours for that purpose if not in session. If the Congress, within twenty-one days after receipt of the latter written declaration, or, if Congress is not in session, within twenty-one days after Congress is required to assemble, determines by two-thirds vote of both Houses that the President is unable to discharge the powers and duties of his office, the Vice President shall continue to discharge the same as Acting President; otherwise, the President shall resume the powers and duties of his office.

Amendment XXVI (1971)

Section 1. The right of citizens of the United States, who are eighteen years of age or older, to vote shall not be denied or abridged by the United States or by any State on account of age.

Section 2. The Congress shall have power to enforce this article by appropriate legislation.

Amendment XXVII (1992)*

No law, varying the compensation for the services of the Senators and Representatives, shall take effect, until an election of Representatives shall have intervened.

---

* This amendment was originally proposed by Congress in 1789 as part of the package of amendments that became the Bill of Rights. At that time the amendment was not ratified by three-fourths of the states as required by Article V of the Constitution. But Congress had not specified any time limit on the ratification process, as it subsequently did for some other amendments (see, *e.g.*, Amend. XX, sec. 6). The proposed amendment lay dormant until the late 1970's. Between then and 1992 — a period of rising concern about federal budget deficits — enough additional states ratified the amendment to meet the three-fourths requirement of Article V.

Appendix B

*Study and Learning Suggestions for Students in Constitutional Law Courses**

(with cross-references to particular sections of this book)

Study techniques and approaches to learning vary from person to person and from course to course. Just as you give attention to **what** you learn, you should also be attentive to **how** you learn. Thus it is important to give continuing consideration to what study techniques and approaches, and what auxiliary study materials, are best for you in constitutional law. This Appendix sets out twelve suggestions for study and learning. References are included to particular sections of AMERICAN CONSTITUTIONAL LAW that will help you implement particular suggestions. (Your instructor, of course, may have other helpful suggestions.)

1. Before the course starts, or at the very beginning of the course, do some reading that will introduce you to the character and functions of constitutional law – thus giving you a foundation and a guide for your studies. The first three chapters of this book are designed specifically for this purpose. Read them all right away, or read selected sections as time permits. But be sure not to miss Chapter 1, Section B, on "Initial Perspectives on Constitutional Law." Your instructor may also have other introductory readings to assign.

2. At the beginning of the course, become familiar with the course goals as the instructor states them or as they are stated in your required text(s). Seek to adopt study techniques that will best facilitate your progress toward achievement of the course goals. Consider how you can use the materials in this book to help you achieve the course goals. At least for introductory or survey courses, examples of goals to accomplish include: (a) developing an overview

---

* These suggestions are especially directed to students in law school courses and graduate school courses that utilize U.S. Supreme Court cases as assigned readings and that employ some version of the case method or a problem-based method of instruction.

of the constitutional structure of American government, the power relationships upon which the structure is based, and the various forums for constitutional decisionmaking within the structure; (b) developing an overview of the process of constitutional interpretation, including the major sources of interpretation and the interpretive approaches that emerge from these sources; (c) developing an overview of the process of constitutional adjudication, particularly with regard to the role of the federal courts; (d) developing an appreciation for the social, political, and historical values that are reflected in the development of constitutional law and how such values are utilized in constitutional analysis and argument; and (e) developing a facility for clear, precise, and creative communication of constitutional analysis and argument. Chapter 2, Sections B, C, and D of this book will help you with goal (a). Chapter 2, Sections E, F, and G; Chapter 4, Section C; Chapter 5, Section C; Chapter 9, Section B; and Chapter 15, Section D will help you with goal (b). Chapter 5, Sections B, D, E, and F, and Chapter 15, Section B will help you with goal (c). And the entire book, in various ways, will help you achieve goals (d) and (e).

3. As you begin to read assigned cases, take the opportunity to work on your reading comprehension and your ability to analyze constitutional law cases. Chapter 3 of this book ("Judicial Opinions on Constitutional Law Issues") is designed to help you with this task.

4. Study consistently for each class, **before** class, rather than studying for an entire week at once or studying assigned materials only in spurts or bunches. As you study for each class, seek to identify specifically the problem and issues that are presented by each case or chain of cases you read, and to ascertain how the Court resolves or fails to resolve each problem and issue. Seek to identify the **standards** that the Court has established for deciding issues in each problem area. (Chapter 3, Section A, and Chapter 5, Section F.7 of this book discuss standards of judicial review.) Seek also to identify the "analytical frameworks" that the Court utilizes to guide analysis of particular types of constitutional law issues. You may think of an analytical framework as an analytical pathway, or a step-by-step reasoning process, that takes you from the beginning point to the end point of the analysis for a particular problem or issue. For illustrations of such analytical frameworks, see William Kaplin, THE CONCEPTS AND METHODS OF CONSTITUTIONAL LAW, chap. 5, sec. F; chap. 6, sec. C; chap. 7, sec. D; and chap. 8, sec. C (Carolina Academic Press, 1992).

5. Spend time reviewing your notes—and your unrecorded thoughts—from the previous class session before preparing for the next class. Try to fill in any substantial gaps in your notes and to clarify confusing points so that they do not interfere with your future learning. Pay particular attention to questions raised but not fully answered in the previous class, and try to make progress in answering them before or during your study of the next class's materials. Chapters 4 through 8 of AMERICAN CONSTITUTIONAL LAW will often be a place to look for clarification of points and answers to questions concerning constitutional powers. Chapters 9 through 13 will serve the same purpose for constitutional rights.

6. Do not depend on outside reading (including this book) as a **substitute** for extensive study of the materials assigned by your instructor. You should wrestle with the assigned readings and your class notes before looking elsewhere for "answers" or other assistance with the gaps in understanding that you need to fill. When you do need to consult outside sources beyond this book, Chapter 1, Section D provides a listing and description of selected general references, and the "Study Suggestions" sections at the end of Chapters 5–8 and 10–14 provide selected references on particular substantive law topics. In addition, various citations for further reading on particular points of constitutional law are included in the text and footnotes in these and other Chapters of this book. These references should provide the help you need, in conjunction with other readings that your instructor may suggest or your course text(s) may cite.

7. Be an active participant in class discussions rather than a spectator. Participation will allow you to test your understanding of constitutional law and will afford you practice in oral communication. Even when you are not participating directly, engage your mind in the discussion by listening carefully, anticipating the responses you would make to the instructor's questions and the contributions you could make to the discussion. Make reasoned judgments about what belongs in your class notes and what needs follow-up after class.

8. Work on problem-solving. If your instructor assigns a hypothetical or a problem for discussion in class or for your own independent learning, invest considerable time in working it out. If your instructor does not assign such problems, seek appropriate problems from other sources. (For a series of 14 large-scale problems, with review guidelines, see William Kaplin, THE CONCEPTS AND METHODS OF CONSTITUTIONAL LAW (Carolina Academic Press,1992).) Problems will illuminate your study of assigned materials and test your understanding of them, and will help you develop techniques for problem solving that will be critical to your successful study and practice of law.

9. When you are practicing constitutional problem solving, also practice writing answers to problems. To maximize the utility of constitutional analysis, it must often be committed to writing for dissemination to others — to colleagues, to a legislative committee or government agency, to a court, to a client, to opposing counsel, or to scholars in the field. The document may be a report, a memorandum, an opinion letter, a brief, an article, or other variant. But whatever the form, the discipline of converting thinking to writing can itself test and strengthen the analysis. Good writing will also enhance the accessibility and persuasiveness of the analysis to its readers.

10. Give continuing consideration to the various roles in which practicing lawyers and government officials may use constitutional law in the course of their work. Consider also the various forums (besides courts) in which constitutional arguments may be made. Chapter 1, Section B (point 3) and Chapter 5, Section C provide brief overviews of these roles and forums. Such "lawyer-

ing process" considerations will help you maintain perspective on the concrete and practical side of constitutional law.

11. Never underestimate the value of intellectual curiosity and the importance of **questions** to your study of constitutional law. Let your class notes, study notes, and your head be full of questions. The questions — not only yours, but also your instructor's, your classmates', or those of courts and commentators — are as important as the answers. It is especially important to understand the questions for which the courts have not yet provided clear answers. There are many such questions in constitutional law; that is what makes the course so engaging as well as potentially frustrating. Do your best to honor intellectual curiosity by making the abundance of questions a trigger for engagement rather than frustration. By understanding the questions, you focus your thinking so that you can discover ways to analyze an unanswered question, or to argue one side of it persuasively; so that in due time you may discern a satisfactory answer.

12. Periodically during the course, and especially at the end, step back from the specifics (the cases, the holdings, the doctrines, and so forth) and seek to grasp the overall system of constitutional decision making. In other words, seek to focus on the "forest" and not merely the "trees" – to see the "big picture" into which you can integrate all your learning in the course. Chapter 15 of this book ("Concluding Perspectives: The Integration of Constitutional Law") is designed specifically for this purpose and should be especially helpful at or near the end of the course. In addition, Chapter 1, Section B ("Initial Perspectives on Constitutional Law"), Chapter 2, Section B ("The Constitutional System of Government"), and Chapter 2, Section F ("A First Look at the Process of Constitutional Interpretation") provide introductory glimpses of the big picture for use earlier in the course. Taken together, these readings provide an analytical and process-oriented picture of constitutional law. Supplementing these readings, Chapter 2, Section A ("The Concept of a Constitution"), Chapter 4, Section D ("Historical Timeline for the Development of Federal Constitutional Powers"), Chapter 6, Section A ("The American Concept of Federalism"), Chapter 8, Section A ("The American Separation-of-Powers Concept"), and Chapter 9, Section E ("Historical Timeline for the Development of Federal Constitutional Rights") provide historical, evolutionary views of constitutional law that can be used as an alternative big picture.

Table of Cases

U.S. Supreme Court Cases

Lower Federal Court Cases

State Cases

Table of Authorities

-A-

Abramson, Shirley, "Divided We Stand: State Constitutions in a More Perfect Union," 18 *Hastings Const. L. Q.* 723 (1991), 421

Adler, Matthew, "What States Owe Outsiders," 20 *Hastings Const. L. Q.* 391 (1993), 193

Advisory Commission on Intergovernmental Relations, Reflections on Garcia and Its Implications for Federalism (Rpt. M-147, 1986), 173

Alexander, Larry, ed., *Constitutionalism: Philosophical Foundations* (Cambridge Univ. Press, 1998), 23

Alfange, Jr., Dean, "Free Speech and Symbolic Conduct: The Draft-Card Burning Case," 1968 *Sup. Ct. Rev.* 1, 386

Aristotle, *Politics* (Benjamin Jowett, tr.) (Random House, 1943), 23–24

-B-

Baker, Lynn, "Constitutional Federal Spending After Lopez," 95 *Colum. L. Rev.* 1911 (1995), 174

Barnette, Randy, "An Originalism for Nonoriginalists," 45 *Loyola L. Rev.* 611 (1999), 49

Basler, Roy, ed., *The Collected Works of Abraham Lincoln*, vol. IV (Rutgers Univ. Press, 1953), 114

Bell, Derrick, *Race, Racism, and American Law*, (4th ed., 2000), 261

Berring, Robert C. & Elizabeth A. Edinger, *Finding the Law* (11th ed., West Group, 1999), 17

Bickel, Alexander, "The Original Understanding and the Segregation Decision," 69 *Harv. L. Rev.* 1 (1955), 81

Bickel, Alexander, *The Least Dangerous Branch* (Yale Univ. Press, 2nd ed. 1986), 15, 40, 109, 129, 302

Bickel, Alexander, *The Morality of Consent* (Yale Univ. Press, 1975), 64

Binion, Gayle, "Intent and Equal Protection: A Reconsideration," 1983 *Sup. Ct. Rev.* 397, 284

Bittker, Boris & Brannon Denning, *Bittker on the Regulation of Interstate and Foreign Commerce* (Aspen Publishing, 1999), 20

Black, Charles, "Due Process for Death: Jurek v. Texas and Companion Cases," 26 *Catholic Univ. L. Rev.* (1976), 221

Black, Charles, "The Lawfulness of the Segregation Decisions," 69 *Yale L.J.* 421 (1960), 81

Black, Charles, *Structure and Relationships in Constitutional Law* (Louisiana State Univ. Press, 1969), 97

Blackstone, William, *Commentaries on the Laws of England*, (Wayne Morrison, ed., Cavendish Publishing Limited, 2001)), 25

Bloomfield, Maxwell, "Constitutional Values and the Literature of the Early Republic," 4 *J. Am. Culture* 53 (1988), 96

Bobbitt, Philip, "Constitutional Fate," 58 *Tex. L. Rev.* 695 (1980), 446

Bolingbroke, "A Dissertation Upon Parties" (1733–1734), in *The Works of Lord Bolingbroke*, (Henry G. Bohn, 1844; reprinted by Frank Cass and Co., 1967), 24

Bonham, Louis Karl, Note, "Unenumerated Rights Clauses in State Constitutions," 63 *Tex. L. Rev.* 1321 (1985), 422

Bork, Robert, *The Tempting of America: The Political Seduction of the Law* (The Free Press, 1990), 244

Botluk, Diana, *The Legal List: Research on the Internet* (West Group, 2002), 18, 19

Boyd, Julian (ed.), *The Papers of Thomas Jefferson* (Princeton Univ. Press, 1974), 142

Breger, Marshall & Gary Edlees, "Established by Practice: The Theory and Operation of Independent Agencies," 52 *Admin. L. Rev.* 1111 (2000), 214

Brennan, William, "State Constitutions and the Protection of Individual Rights," 90 *Harv. L. Rev.* 489 (1977), 430

Brest, Paul, "Foreword: In Defense of the Anti-Discrimination Principle," 90 *Harv. L. Rev.* 1 (1976), 297

Brest, Paul, *Processes of Constitutional Decision-making*, (Little, Brown, 1st ed., 1975), 41, 54, 58–59, 109, 439

Brown, Barbara, Thomas Emerson, Gail Falk, and Ann Freedman, "The Equal Rights Amendment: A Constitutional Basis for Equal Rights for Women," 80 *Yale L.J.* 871 (1971) 258

Buchanan, G. Sidney, "Women in Combat: An Essay on Ultimate Rights and Responsibilities," 28 *Houston L. Rev.* 503 (1991), 270

Butts and Cremin, *A History of Education in American Culture* (1953), 239

-C-

Calabresi, Steven & Saikrishna Prakash, "The President's Power to Execute the Laws," 104 *Yale L.J.* 541 (1994), 206

Caminker, Evan, "State Immunity Waivers for Suits by the United States," 98 *Mich. L. Rev.* 92 (1999), 421

Cardozo, Benjamin, *The Nature of the Judicial Process* (Yale Univ. Press, 1921), 13, 314

Carey & McClellan, eds., 2001, *The Federalist, The Gideon Edition* (Liberty Fund, 2001), 8, 32, 85, 89, 96, 196, 449

Chafee, Jr., Zechariah, *Free Speech in the United States* (Harvard Univ. Press, 1964), 359

Chemerinsky, Erwin, *Constitutional Law: Principles and Policies*, (Aspen Publishing, 2nd ed. 2002), 20

Chemerinsky, Erwin, "Procedural Due Process Claims," 16 *Touro L. Rev.* 871 (2000), 339

Choper, Jesse and John Yoo, "The Scope of the Commerce Clause After Morrison," 25 *Oklahoma City U. L. Rev.* 843 (2000), 174

Cogan, Neil, *Contexts of the Constitution: A Documentary Collection on Principles of American Constitutional Law* (Foundation Press, 1999), 21

Collins, Ronald & David Skover, "The Future of Liberal Legal Scholarship," 87 *Mich. L. Rev.* 189 (1988), 427

Congressional Research Service, Library of Congress, *The Constitution of the United States of America: Analysis and Interpretation*, 20

Cox, Archibald, "Foreword to the Supreme Court 1965 Term: Constitutional Adjudication and the Promotion of Human Rights," 80 *Harv. L. Rev.* 91 (1966), 60

Crump, David, "How Do Courts Really Discover Unenumerated Fundamental Rights? Cataloguing the Methods of Judicial Alchemy," 19 *Harv. J. of Law & Pub. Policy* 795 (1996), 320

Cubberley, *Public Education in the United States* (1934), 239

Curtis, Charles, "A Better Theory of Legal Interpretation," 3 *Vanderbilt L. Rev.* 407, (1950), 57

Curtis, Charles, *Lions Under the Throne* (Houghton Mifflin Co. 1947), 232

-D-

de Tocqueville, A., *Democracy in America* 181 (H. Reeve trans. 1961), 140

Deutscher & Chein, "The Psychological Effect of Enforced Segregation: A Survey of Social Science Opinion," 26 *J. Psychol.* 259 (1948), 241–242

Dodd, Walter F., "The Foundation of a State Constitution," 30 *Pol. Sci. Q.* 201, (1915), 85

Dorf, Michael (ed.), *Constitutional Law Stories* (Foundation Press, 2004), 20

Dorsen, Bender, & Neuborne, *Emerson, Haber & Dorsen's Political and Civil Rights in the United States*, 350, 354

Douglas, Davison, "The Rhetorical Uses of Marbury v. Madison: The Emergence of a Great Case," 38 *Wake Forest L. Rev.* 375 (2003), 102, 135

Dworkin, Ronald, "The Forum of Principle," 56 *N.Y.U. L. Rev.*, 469 (1981)

-E-

Elliott, Jonathan, ed., *The Debates in the Several State Conventions on the Adoption of*

Nimmer, Melville, "Is Freedom of Press a Redundancy: What Does It Add to Freedom of Speech?" 26 *Hastings L. J.* 639 (1975), 345, 386

Nimmer, Melville, "National Security Secrets v. Free Speech: The Issues Left Undecided in the Ellsberg Case," 26 *Stanford L. Rev.* 311 (1974), 64

Norgren, Jill, "Before It Was Merely Difficult: Belva Lockwood's Life in Law and Politics," 23 *J. of Sup. Ct. History* 16 (1999), 272

Novak, Linda, Note, "The Precedential Value of Supreme Court Plurality Decisions," 80 *Colum. L. Rev.* 756 (1980), 62

Nowak, John & Ronald Rotunda, *Constitutional Law* (West Group, 6th ed. 2000), 20

-O-

O'Neil, Robert, *The First Amendment and Civil Liability* (Indiana U. Press, 2001), 386

-P-

Paine, Thomas, *Rights of Man*, in *The Complete Political Works of Thomas Paine*, vol. II (The Freethought Press Ass'n, 1954), 26

Patterson, James, *Brown v. Board of Education: A Civil Rights Milestone and Its Troubled Legacy* (Oxford U. Press, 2001), 79

Perry, Michael, *The Constitution in the Courts* (Oxford U. Press, 1994), 15, 17

Perry, Michael, *The Constitution, the Courts, and Human Rights* (1982), 303

Perry, Michael, "Protecting Human Rights in a Democracy: What Role for the Courts?" 38 *Wake Forest L. Rev.* 635, 679–687 (2003), 439

Perry, Michael, *We The People: The Fourteenth Amendment and the Supreme Court* (Oxford Univ. Press, 1999), 244

Pine, Rachael, "Speculation and Reality: The Role of Facts in Judicial Protection of Fundamental Rights," 136 *U. Pa. L. Rev.* 655 (1988), 437

Popenoe, *Sterilization and Criminality*, 53 American Bar Assn. Reports 575, 333

Powell, H. Jefferson, "The Oldest Question of Constitutional Law," 79 *Va. L. Rev.* 633 (1993), 174

Powell, H. Jefferson, "The Original Understanding of Original Intent," 98 *Harv. L. Rev.* 885 (1985), 94

Powell, H. Jefferson, *The President's Authority Over Foreign Affairs: An Essay in Constitutional Interpretation* (Carolina Academic Press, 2002), 218

Pratt, Robert, "Crossing the Color Line: A Historical Assessment and Personal Narrative of Loving v. Virginia," 41 *Howard L. J.* 229 (1998), 274

-R-

Rakove, Jack, ed., *The Unfinished Election of 2000* (Basic Books, 2001), 14

Ratner, Leonard, "Majoritarian Constraints on Judicial Review: Congressional Control of Supreme Court Jurisdiction," 27 *Villanova L. Rev.* 929 (1981–1982), 131

Redish, Martin, *Freedom of Expression: A Critical Analysis* (Michie Co., 1984), 20

Reich, "Individual Rights and Social Welfare: The Emerging Legal Issues," 74 *Yale L. J.* 1245 (1965), 324

Regan, Donald, "The Supreme Court and State Protectionism: Making Sense of the Dormant Commerce Clause," 84 *Mich. L. Rev.* 1091 (1986), 193

Rubenfeld, Jeb, "The New Unwritten Constitution," 51 *Duke L.J.* 289 (2001), 269

Rubenfeld, Jeb, "The Moment and the Millennium," 66 *Geo. Wash. L. Rev.* 1085 (1998), 95

Rudenstine, David, *The Day the Presses Stopped* (U. Calif. Press, 1996), 64

-S-

Sandalow, Terrance, "Constitutional Interpretation," 79 *Mich. L. Rev.* 1033 (1981), 230

Saphire, Richard B., "Originalism and the Importance of Constitutional Aspirations," 24 *Hastings Const. L. Q.* 599 (1997), 97

Schauer, Frederick, "Precedent," 39 *Stanford L. Rev.* 571 (1987), 57, 437

Schroeder, Tom, "Out of the Mud," in *The Washington Post Magazine* (Dec. 8, 2002), 272

Sherry, Suzanna, "Judges of Character," 38 *Wake Forest L. Rev.* 793 (2003), 14, 447

Sherry, Suzanna, "Lee v. Weisman: Paradox Redux," 1993 *Sup. Ct. Rev.* 123, 410

Sky, Theodore, *To Provide for the General Welfare: A History of the Federal Spending Power* (U. Del. Press, 2003), 163

Smolla, Rodney, *Smolla & Nimmer on Freedom of Speech: A Treatise on the Theory of the First Amendment* (Clark Boardman Callaghan, 3rd ed. 1996), 20

and Responses," 80 *N. Carolina L. Rev.* 773 (2002), 116

Williams, Robert, "The State Constitutions of the Founding Decade: Pennsylvania's Radical 1776 Constitution and its Influence on American Constitutionalism," 62 *Temple L. Rev.* 541 (1989), 27

Wilkinson, J. Harvey, *Serving Justice: A Supreme Court Clerk's View* (1974), 15

Woo, John, "War and the Constitutional Text," 69 *U. Chi. L. Rev.* 1639 (2002), 200

Wright, Charles Alan & Mary Kay Kane, *Law of Federal Courts*, (West, 6th ed. 2002), 108, 118, 124

Subject Matter Index

This index does not include entries for broad topics such as judicial review, justiciability , commerce power, separation of powers, due process, or freedom of expression. To locate such topics, the reader should use the Table of Contents at the front of this book. In contrast, this index focuses on narrower and more specific topics that arise within the broader topics listed in the Table of Contents, as well as generic topics that cut across the various topics in the Table of Contents.